Advocates for the Oppressed

Other Books by Malcolm Ebright

Four Square Leagues: Pueblo Indian Land in New Mexico
   (with Rick Hendricks and Richard W. Hughes)
The Witches of Abiquiu: The Governor, the Priest, the Genízaro Indians, and
   the Devil (with Rick Hendricks)
Land Grants and Lawsuits in Northern New Mexico
Spanish and Mexican Land Grants and the Law (edited by Malcolm Ebright)
The Tierra Amarilla Grant: A History of Chicanery

Advocates *for the* Oppressed

Hispanos, Indians, Genízaros, and
Their Land in New Mexico

MALCOLM EBRIGHT

UNIVERSITY OF NEW MEXICO PRESS ❧ ALBUQUERQUE

20 19 18 17 16 15   1 2 3 4 5 6

LIBRARY OF CONGRESS CATALOGING-IN-PUBLICATION DATA
Ebright, Malcolm.
 Advocates for the oppressed : Hispanos, Indians, Genízaros, and their land in New Mexico /
Malcolm Ebright.
   pages cm
 Includes bibliographical references and index.
 ISBN 978-0-8263-5505-8 (cloth : alk. paper) — ISBN 978-0-8263-5506-5 (electronic)
 1. Land tenure—New Mexico—History—18th century. 2. Land grants—New Mexico—History—
18th century. 3. Legal assistance to Indians—New Mexico—History—18th century. 4. Indians of
North America—Land tenure—New Mexico—History—18th century. 5. Pueblo Indians—Land
tenure—History—18th century. I. Title.
 HD211.N6E37 2014
 333.309789'09033—dc23
                    2014001547

CHAPTER 1 is a revised version of an essay that appeared as "Advocates for the Oppressed: Indians, Genízaros, and Their Spanish Advocates in New Mexico, 1700–1786," in *New Mexico Historical Review* 71, no. 4 (October 1996): 375–408. Copyright © 2010 by the University of New Mexico
Board of Regents; reprinted by permission with all rights reserved.

CHAPTER 2 is a revised version of an essay that appeared as "A City Different Than We Thought,
Land Grants in Early Santa Fe, 1598–1900," in *All Trails Lead to Santa Fe: An Anthology Commemorating the 400th Anniversary of the Founding of Santa Fe* (Santa Fe, NM: Sunstone Press, 2010),
65–95, and it is reprinted by permission.

CHAPTER 9 is a revised version of an essay that appeared as "Breaking New Ground: A Reappraisal
of Governor Vélez Cachupín and Mendinueta and Their Land Grant Policies," in *Colonial Latin
American Historical Review* 5, no. 2 (1996): 195–223, and it is reprinted by permission.

CHAPTER 10 is a revised version of an essay that appeared as "Frontier Land Litigation in Colonial
New Mexico: A Determinant of Spanish Custom and Law," in *Western Legal History* 8, no. 2 (Summer/
Fall 1995): 199–226, and it is reprinted by permission.

Partial Funds for the research and writing of earlier versions of chapters 4, 6, 7, and 8 were provided
by the New Mexico Historical Records Advisory Board.

CHAPTER AND COVER ILLUSTRATIONS BY Glen Strock
MAPS BY Molly O'Halloran; maps are based on research by Roberto Valdez
   (except for the Pueblo Grazing Grants map)
DESIGNED BY Lila Sanchez
COMPOSED IN Minion Pro 10/14; Display type is Fairfield

Dedicated to the memory of Carisa Williams Joseph
for her dedication, courage, and research excellence.

CONTENTS

INTRODUCTION AND
ACKNOWLEDGMENTS

In the historical struggle for precious land and water in New Mexico, the outcome of a dispute often depended on which party had the strongest advocate arguing their case before a local tribunal or on appeal. This book is about the advocates who represented the parties to these disputes and about the Hispanos, Indians, and Genízaros (Hispanicized nomadic Indians) themselves and the land they lived on and fought for. Often the best advocates were not lawyers at all but government officials such as alcaldes and the governors themselves, governors like Tomás Vélez Cachupín.[1]

The Spanish office of *Protector de Indios*, highlighted in chapter 1, was the most effective Spanish institution for providing legal protection to some of the least empowered members of colonial society: the Pueblo Indians. The Protector of Indians provided legal representation in court to Indians in New Mexico from the mid-1600s to 1717 and then from 1810 to 1821, mostly in disputes involving land. Pueblo Indians achieved basic rights to the 17,350-acre Pueblo league largely because of the efforts of early Protectors of Indians. This official was the most impartial of the advocates discussed in this book, especially the early eighteenth-century protectors like Alfonso Rael de Aguilar.[2] When the office was vacant in the latter half of the eighteenth century, Governor Tomás Vélez Cachupín and the alcaldes serving under him continued the advocacy for Pueblo Indians, refining the methods of measuring Pueblo lands and assisting Pueblo peoples in buying lands from Spaniards at fair prices, thus protecting Pueblo land rights. Litigation between Spaniards and Pueblo Indians over boundary disputes was sometimes appealed to the highest courts in Durango, Chihuahua, and Mexico City. Not all the officials who held the office of Protector de Indios were as effective as Rael de Aguilar, and some were corrupt, but the concept of a paid official of the Spanish government whose job it was to uphold the rights of the Pueblo Indians was revolutionary.[3]

Chapter 2 tells the story of two mostly mythical land grants in early Santa Fe that were created by nineteenth-century lawyers who stood to gain if the claims were confirmed by the courts. This chapter illustrates how easily history was distorted in a way that impedes any effort to find the real truth about early Santa Fe and early New Mexico. Although the four hundredth anniversary of the founding of Santa Fe in 1610 was recently observed, scholarly debate continues about basic questions, such as the exact date and circumstances of Santa Fe's founding, why the present location was chosen, and whether there was a settlement of Mexican Indians in the Analco region at the time of the villa's founding. Unfortunately, the lawyers involved in the claims for the Santa Fe grant and the Cristóbal Nieto grant did more to obfuscate than to illuminate historical truth. The Santa Fe grant was claimed initially by land speculators on the theory that the Villa of Santa Fe was given a formal grant of four square leagues (the same amount of land to which an Indian pueblo was entitled), either by a written grant or by virtue of royal law. This idea turned out to be a myth, which the courts rejected, leaving land titles in Santa Fe in chaos for a few years in the early twentieth century.

The other myth covered in chapter 2 has to do with the Cristóbal Nieto grant made by Governor Rodríguez Cubero in 1697 and revalidated in 1700. Although a land grant was clearly made, its boundaries were greatly expanded by lawyer James Purdy in a fashion similar to other Santa Fe grants he represented. By creating an imaginary land grant, Purdy obscured the truth-is-stranger-than-fiction story of the Cristóbal Nieto grant. An examination of the realities behind the grant reveals that the wife of Cristóbal Nieto was abducted by Pueblo Indians from San Juan (Ohkay Owingeh) Pueblo at the beginning of the Pueblo Revolt in 1680. By 1692, when Petrona Pacheco Nieto was "rescued" from captivity, she had borne three children fathered by an Indian man; these children would be heirs, along with her other children, to the lands of the Cristóbal Nieto land grant, whatever its size. Present-day accounts of the Cristóbal Nieto grant, however, make no mention of the abduction of Petrona Pacheco or of her three mestizo children born in captivity, even though this hidden history of the Nieto grant is much more important in piecing together the true story of early Santa Fe than is the bogus history created by late nineteenth-century land grant advocates like James Purdy. Chapter 2 also goes beyond these two mythical grants to paint a picture of the people and the land of early Santa Fe that reveals a city different than we thought.

Chapter 3 recounts the story of the Ojo Caliente grant, whose origin and early history involved both Spaniards and mixed-blood Genízaros and whose later history was dominated by Santa Fe Ring participant Antonio Joseph. In its early history Ojo Caliente's settlements were made up primarily of Genízaros who were better able to defend their communities against raids by members of nomadic tribes such as the Utes and Comanches. Later, Hispanos predominated and told church authorities, "We are not a community of Indians," in an attempt to assert their Hispano character and obtain preferential treatment over Abiquiu, which at that time was a Genízaro community. Antonio Joseph ended up owning the entire Ojo Caliente grant when he allegedly purchased the interests of the fifty-three Hispano Ojo Caliente grantees who supplanted the Genízaros. Joseph also took over the hot springs and started to convert them into the resort and spa of today. Land grant members, however, still exercise their rights to use their traditional hot springs.[4]

Many people are unaware that New Mexico pueblos received their own grazing grants to protect their traditional grazing lands from encroachment and to provide pasture for their own animals. Chapter 4 covers the Zia, Santa Ana, and Jemez grazing grant, also known as the Ojo del Espíritu Santo grant, and the Cochiti Pueblo pasture grant. Governor Tomás Vélez Cachupín made both these grazing grants in 1766 as he was nearing the end of his second term. He considered them a key part of his plan to provide grazing lands for both Indian pueblos and Hispano communities. New Mexico's Pueblo Indians were just beginning to establish their right to four square leagues surrounding their villages, and the acquisition of additional common grazing land was important. Governor Vélez Cachupín tried to protect the traditional grazing lands of these pueblos but in both cases, the pressure from adjoining or overlapping Hispano land grants was too great: the grazing grants were overrun by later grants that were confirmed by the courts while the pueblo grazing grants were rejected. I also discuss briefly two Hispano grazing grants in the area because of their connection with the two Indian grazing grants. At their inception they were similar in use and legal form to the Cochiti Pueblo pasture grant and the Ojo del Espíritu Santo grazing grant. These four grants, two to Indian pueblos and two to Hispano elites, received different treatment by the U.S. courts, as the grants to the pueblos were rejected and the Cañada de Cochití and the San Isidro grants were confirmed by the Court of Private Land Claims and the U.S. Supreme Court.[5]

La Ciénega and Cieneguilla Pueblos, discussed in chapter 5, were important pre-revolt pueblos whose lands, after they were abandoned, were coveted and fought over by some of the wealthiest Hispano families in New Mexico. Some, such as José Riaño and Juan Páez Hurtado, also had houses in the Villa of Santa Fe. Both La Ciénega and Cieneguilla Pueblos took part in the Pueblo Revolt, but by the time Diego de Vargas passed through on his way to Santa Fe during the reconquest of New Mexico, they had been abandoned. Vargas offered La Ciénega Pueblo five hundred varas of land in each direction if the Indians would return and claim it, but they did not reclaim their land, thus leaving a substantial amount of prime irrigated farmland available for enterprising Spaniards in the area.

The history of La Ciénega and Cieneguilla Pueblos and their lands illustrates how Hispano elites were able to take over former Pueblo lands and expand their holdings. They claimed property within these pueblos with vague or nonexistent boundaries and then conveyed it to family members, providing more definite (and expanded) boundaries in the new deed. The Hispanos who acquired this land, some of whose ancestors were encomenderos with the right to collect tribute from La Ciénega Pueblo, battled for control of these valuable tracts of irrigable land for the next three centuries, often attempting to keep the land within their families by avoiding sales to outsiders. When such sales did take place, traditional methods of farming and village culture were often disrupted. Now, a major portion of the wealth of La Ciénega is in its water rights, among the oldest and most expensive in New Mexico.

Currently, most of La Ciénega and Cieneguilla's residents are trying to preserve their culture and limit water rights transfers and large outside developments that had their genesis in these ancient, complicated, and fiercely fought property disputes. One way of limiting large-scale property development has been to protect the petroglyphs on the mesas surrounding these communities, evidence of earlier indigenous cultures still remembered by present-day pueblo people surrounding La Ciénega and Cieneguilla.

The San Cristóbal Pueblo grant, discussed in chapter 6, has a history similar to the two other Galisteo Basin Pueblo grants of San Marcos and Galisteo covered in following chapters. Each includes three totally different historical narratives enacted on the same tract of land: the story of the ancient pueblos that were there first; the story of the early land grants made to Hispanos in the late eighteenth and early nineteenth centuries; and finally, the story of the acquisition of those grants by Anglo speculators or Hispano elites. In all three cases the three stories are almost independent of each other, slices of history with little transition from one to the other, unified only by the land. In the case of San Cristóbal, little is known about the ancient pueblo, though petroglyphs in the area provide evidence of irrigation through ponds and canals, the ruins of which were still present in 1822 when Domingo Fernández requested a land grant there. Fernández was a member of the ayuntamiento of Santa Fe that made the grant, and he vacillated between asking for a private land grant for himself (which he preferred) or a community grant involving others (which the ayuntamiento encouraged). When he was forced to accept about fourteen others as co-grantees, he tried to foreclose their interests before selling the grant to Ethan Eaton. The grant was confirmed by the courts and partitioned, changing hands many times before becoming the San Cristóbal Ranch, where cattle are now raised and archaeological digs still take place on occasion, searching for clues about San Cristóbal's ancient past.[6]

The San Marcos grant covered in chapter 7 surrounded another ancient pueblo, the largest in the Southwest, whose occupants were mining turquoise, lead, and perhaps copper in the mid-1200s to the early 1300s. The pueblo's prosperity waned and its population dwindled somewhat, but these Pueblo people were still a major force behind the Pueblo Revolt. Then they left their land after 1680 and most moved to Cochiti and Santo Domingo Pueblos. In the early 1700s the presidio of Santa Fe used San Marcos's lush grazing land for its horse herd, as it did the lands of San Cristóbal and Galisteo Pueblos. Then San Marcos became a private speculative grazing grant made to José Urbán Montaño in the mid-1700s, which was eventually acquired by Santa Fe Ring participant Lehman Spiegelberg of the powerful and influential Spiegelberg family. The Spiegelbergs' political and military contacts helped them speed the grant through the confirmation process, but by the time the San Marcos grant was confirmed all the Spiegelbergs had moved to New York. As with the other Galisteo Basin grants, descendants of the original indige-nous inhabitants still visit shrines in the area for ceremonial purposes.[7]

The story of the Galisteo Pueblo grant discussed in chapter 8 is similar to that of San Marcos in that much of the grant land ended up in the hands of a few elite families, but instead of selling the land and leaving New Mexico as did the Spiegelbergs, these families remained. Galisteo was the second largest pueblo in the Galisteo Basin after San Marcos and was occupied from around

1400 until the Pueblo Revolt. Galisteo Pueblo people played an important part in the revolt, then left the area after the reconquest, returning in 1706 when Governor Cuervo y Valdés resettled some of them at their ancient pueblo site. Galisteo suffered a gradual population decline throughout the eighteenth century due to disease and Comanche raids, culminating in 1782 when smallpox reduced the population to only fifty-two. In that year these remnants of the once-thriving pueblo moved to Santo Domingo. The abandoned Pueblo land was then used for grazing by the presidial horse herd and by Santa Fe cattlemen until 1814 when a community grant was made to a group of Santa Fe settlers. The adjudication of the Galisteo grant by the Court of Private Land Claims resulted in the rejection of the common lands and the confirmation of only about 260 acres. While the loss of the common lands was a blow to the community, two powerful families helped maintain the integrity of the village, continuing the tradition of stock raising and helping maintain the rural character of this important community. The ruins of the ancient Galisteo Pueblo lie on Las Madres Ranch and are covered by a protective easement from the Archaeological Conservancy.[8]

When Vélez Cachupín took office in 1749, communities like Ojo Caliente, Abiquiu, and Embudo had been abandoned because of Indian raids. In chapter 9, I discuss the land grant policy of Vélez Cachupín, which encouraged the resettlement of those communities and involved new ways of looking at land grants. Vélez Cachupín established the first true community grants, many of which have survived today: Abiquiu, Truchas, and Las Trampas, among others. Vélez Cachupín's vision included land grants to Hispanos (both private and community grants), land grants to Genízaros (the Abiquiu land grant), and land grants to Indian pueblos (the Cochiti and Ojo del Espíritu Santo grants). All three groups were given common lands, either as part of a community land grant or as a separate land grant. Vélez Cachupín also made grants such as the San Gabriel de las Nutrias grant, which included over 50 percent Genízaros, as shown on the census taken by Vélez Cachupín himself in 1765 (appendix 4). When neighboring landowners sometimes challenged the exclusive use of these land grants by their indigenous and mestizo owners, Vélez Cachupín came to their rescue, matching his overall vision of Hispanos, Indians, and Genízaros sharing the land and water of New Mexico with a practical legal understanding of how to resolve the inevitable conflicts.

Chapter 10 examines the lawsuits adjudicated by Governor Vélez Cachupín and the rules of law the governor followed in the decisions he made in land-related litigation. He attempted to protect marginalized Hispanos, Indians, and Genízaros when their land and water were threatened, often taking the side of the underdog. He adjudicated lawsuits with a thorough understanding of the law and made decisions that followed it to the letter. In the lawsuit between the Suma Indians and the residents of El Paso over the Indians' common lands, the governor protected those lands in accordance with principles laid down in Las Siete Partidas; he had promised that he would protect the Suma Indians when he induced them to settle there. In other cases, he ordered Atrisco not to encroach on the lands of the San Fernando grant and helped protect Pueblo Indian land by allowing Indians to purchase land and making sure they were not overcharged. The governor was able to view land and water conflicts from a broad perspective that included Indian, Hispano, and Genízaro points of view because he was committed to unifying New Mexico to withstand the wide-ranging attacks on the populace by Comanche, Ute, and Navajo raiders. Vélez Cachupín could not control what happened after he left office, however, so in some cases the careful plans he laid were undone by later governors.[9]

Chapter 11 examines the periods in the early history of New Mexico when there was an accommodation between the dominant and indigenous narratives; times when, with the help of advocates for both sides, Hispanos, Genízaros, and Native Americans were able to coexist in relative peace. As Diego de Vargas put it, somewhat optimistically, being "separated both may live quietly being reconciled among themselves with friendship."[10] For Vargas these words were more rhetoric than reality, but for Governor Vélez Cachupín fifty years later, this idyllic-sounding situation came true for a short time in the late 1760s. Vélez Cachupín was not trained in the academy but rather on the job with the viceroy of New Spain. When faced with petitions or lawsuits, Vélez Cachupín often visited the community in question, taking censuses, measuring the land, and providing a hands-on analysis of the situation. He became one of the greatest advocates for the oppressed in New Mexico.

Chapter 12 uses the successful struggle of Zuni Pueblo to recover its sacred lands and artifacts to illustrate a new form of advocacy in which Pueblo leaders took center stage with lawyers in the wings. They used their religious leaders, as well as historians, archaeologists, and anthropologists, as their first line of attack, resorting to lawyers and legal theories only when persuasion was

unsuccessful. Like Taos Pueblo, which undertook a long, arduous, and ultimately successful battle for the return of their sacred Blue Lake watershed,
Zuni used multiple forms of advocacy and persuasion to get back their Zuni
Salt Lake, Zuni Heaven and its 110-mile access route, as well as the Zuni war
gods. Zuni Pueblo's fight for the return of sacred lands illustrates how contemporary advocates for the oppressed have achieved justice through patience,
prayer, and a modern form of advocacy.

The epilogue assesses the types of advocacy illustrated in this book, from
the early Protectors of Indians in eighteenth-century New Mexico to the
Zunis in the twentieth century. Early *Protectores de Indios* were relatively
effective because they participated in the creation of the legal rules under
which they were operating. They helped establish the Pueblo league concept
and used it to protect Pueblo Indian land, while avoiding the conflicts of
interest that would later plague nineteenth-century advocates. Like the
Protectores de Indios, Governor Vélez Cachupín also had some control over
the land grant system he was administering. He could decide which land
grants to make and could adjudicate disputes about boundaries and encroachments after he made the grants. A century later, during the adjudication of
land grants by the surveyor general and the Court of Private Land Claims,
however, lawyers, politicians, and judges presided over a system that was seriously flawed. Advocates often did a disservice to their clients, so Pueblo peoples and Hispanos began to speak for themselves. They acted as their own
advocates, sometimes traveling to Washington, D.C., to make their claims,
sometimes filing memorials in Congress, and employing persuasion, prayer,
and direct action when the traditional forms of advocacy did not work. Recent
successes of both Pueblo Indian and Hispanic communities have shown that
a united community coupled with strong advocacy can bring about both a
restoration of lost lands and the rights to use such lands in traditional ways.

The author wishes to thank the following people who helped bring this book
into being. Denise Holladay Damico, Rick Hendricks, Tom Kowal, Kay
Matthews, Carroll Riley, Richard Salazar, and Cordelia Thomas Snow read
portions of the manuscript and provided helpful comments; any mistakes or
misinterpretations are my responsibility. Particular thanks go to Faith Yoman
and Virginia Lopez, librarians, Southwest Room of the New Mexico State
Library; Alison Colburne, librarian, Laboratory of Anthropology Library;

Melissa Salazar, director of the New Mexico State Records Center and Archives, and staff; and Mark Adams, Peggy Trujillo, and Bruce Mergele of the New Mexico State Library.

Some of my colleagues in addition to those listed previously who provided ideas, encouragement, and support include Anselmo Arellano, Henrietta Martínez Christmas, Robin Collier, José Antonio Esquibel, Jeff Goldstein, Emlen Hall, Steve Hardin, Sandra Jaramillo, Sandra K. Mathews, Lolly Martin, Dawn Nieto, José Rivera, Linda Tigges, Roberto Valdez, and Julián Josue Vigil. My gratitude also to the New Mexico Historical Records Advisory Board for partial funding for the research and writing of chapters 2, 3, 5, 9, 10, and 11, and to the University of New Mexico Press team of W. Clark Whitehorn, editor-in-chief; Lila Sanchez, book designer; Sarah Soliz, copyeditor; and Maya Allen-Gallegos, managing editor and production manager.

Thanks to Glen Strock for the drawings, Molly O'Halloran and Roberto Valdez for the maps, Margaret Moore Booker for the index, Kristi Dranginis for research in the Myra Ellen Jenkins Collection, and Margaret McGee for typing and research assistance. Finally, my deep gratitude goes to Scott Deily, Joe Lehm, Martín Prechtel, Collin Ruiz, Danté Ruiz, Greta Ruiz, Mesa Ruiz, and Molly Ruiz for their support, deep understanding, and love of what this book is about: the land.

CHAPTER ONE

THE *PROTECTOR DE INDIOS*

Spanish Advocates for the Pueblo Indians

Protection of the rights of indigenous people and the less powerful members of society has been a recurring theme in Spanish jurisprudence since the time of Fray Bartolomé de Las Casas, the first successful advocate for the Indians in the New World. Ever since the famous debate between Las Casas and Juan Ginés de Sepúlveda over whether the Indians of the Americas possessed souls and whether the conquest was legally justified, two opposing views have affected litigation between Spaniards and Indians. Las Casas condemned the conquest as having no legal basis and argued that peaceful and voluntary conversion of the Indians was the only justification for Spanish presence in the Americas. Since the Indians were rational beings, equal to and in some respects superior to Spaniards, they should not be required to work for Spaniards and pay tribute, nor should they be deprived of their lands. Sepúlveda argued, on the other hand, that the conquest was the most efficient way to spread the faith, that the Indians were naturally inferior to the Spaniards, and that since some of their customs were sins, the conquest was justified in order to convert the Indians to more enlightened religious practices.[1] At the time of the debate in 1550, Spaniards had little direct knowledge of the New World Indians whose souls were being contested. Sepúlveda had never seen one, and though Las Casas had studied them extensively, the ethnographic studies he published were not read widely, if at all. Hernán Cortés had brought two Indians adept at juggling and presented them to Pope Clement VII in 1529, and in 1550 a group of fifty Brazilian natives performed

I

mock warfare on the banks of the Seine for Catherine de Medici and her court. These rather incongruous events provided little basis for European understanding of New World natives.[2]

On the other hand, in central Mexico judges like Alonso de Zorita, who started his career as *abogado de pobres* (lawyer for the poor) in Granada, Spain, continued to study and work with Indians firsthand. Zorita believed, as did Las Casas and later Governor Vélez Cachupín, that in some character traits the Indians were the equals of if not superior to the Spaniards.[3] Their views about Indians as either wild and unmanageable or rational and civilized moved out of this Aristotelian dichotomy into a more pragmatic viewpoint based on direct contact. They came to see Indians as did Viceroy Mendoza, who said simply that they were "like any other people."[4] It seems that Sepúlveda won the 1550 debate as the practices he supported continued, though no formal declaration was made. But the moral force of Las Casas's argument found its way into numerous laws and practices adopted by Spain to protect and preserve Indian rights. The observance of these laws depended in large part, however, on whether the Spanish system of justice provided for effective advocates to assert Indian rights in Spanish courts.[5] In the Valley of Mexico, where Spanish rule was first imposed on the Aztecs (also called Nahuas), justice was first dispensed by the audiencia (highest court of appeal) established in Mexico City in 1528. Indian litigants there could rely on a small cadre of officials whose job it was to advocate on their behalf. A scribe versed in Nahuatl would take down the facts of a claim, then a translator would render the text of the plea into Spanish, and if the matter were not immediately resolved the case would be handled by a lawyer. Because many cases were disposed of in these early stages, and because translations often distorted the meaning of the original Nahuatl, scribes and translators wielded considerable power in early Indian lawsuits before the Mexico City audiencia.

In the next stage of the proceedings lawyers would craft legal arguments to persuade the *oidores* (judges) of the justice of the Indians' claims under Spanish or Aztec law and custom. *Procuradores* (lawyers with less legal training than abogados) handled this stage of the case by filing documents and petitions with the court. These lawyers, together with scribes and translators, acted as intermediaries for the Aztecs, sometimes abusing their positions.[6] In 1591 as a result of recommendations by Viceroy Luis de Velasco II, the Juzgado General de Indios (General Indian Court) was established to hear only Indian claims.

Key among the viceroy's recommendations was the appointment of a *protector* or *defensor de los Indios* who would be the sole attorney for indigenous claimants and be paid a salary raised by an annual per capita tax on the Indians. Establishing the office of Protector de Indios helped end the abuses of the earlier system, in which translators, scribes, and procuradores were able to parlay their status as intermediaries between Indians and the Spanish courts into excessive fees and undue influence.[7]

Bartolomé de Las Casas's appointment as the first Protector de Indios established the precedent for having members of the clergy protect native rights, but the extent of the protector's powers remained open to debate. The primary question was whether these officials could investigate complaints of mistreatment of Indians or whether they were limited to representing the natives in court after complaints had been filed. In 1575 Viceroy Francisco de Toledo issued a set of ordinances regulating those representing Indian claimants that was later codified into legislation under which the first Protector de Indios was appointed. By setting up a bureaucracy dedicated to the protection of Indian rights, the Spanish government allowed the Indians to limit Spanish dominance to some extent, but the capacity of the Indians to challenge colonial rule at its root was weakened when they became part of the system.[8]

Nevertheless, the Incas, Aztecs, and Mayas all became skilled at using the Spanish legal system to limit encroachment on their land. In Peru in the 1590s, when a powerful landowner named Cristóbal de Serpa claimed vast areas owned by the village of Tiquihua, the villagers themselves traveled to Lima and obtained a decree from the viceroy keeping Serpa off village lands.[9] In Guatemala, the highland Maya learned to compel recognition of their claims by using documents they prepared in Spanish and by retaining Spanish lawyers to make use of Spanish laws adopted for the Indians' protection.[10]

In New Mexico, as in other parts of the New World, the Indians' effectiveness depended to a large extent on whether they had adequate legal representation, whether local alcaldes were sympathetic to their cause, and most importantly, whether the governor was fair and impartial in making his judgments.[11] It is difficult to find a case prior to the Pueblo Revolt in which a Pueblo Indian was treated fairly in litigation against the Spanish. The pueblos were caught between a church-state rivalry for power in seventeenth-century New Mexico, and Indian labor and land were the most valuable resources in the ensuing battle for control of the province. Besides the power struggle on a political level, the clash of native and Spanish worldviews involved a spiritual struggle that was often played out in the courts.[12] Intolerance of Pueblo religious practices and the ferocious attempts at eradicating the sacred ceremonies of the Indians was one of the causes of what John Kessell has called the Pueblo-Spanish War. After the Pueblo Revolt, Indians and Spaniards reached an accommodation whereby the Indians bought and sold land and competed for scarce land and water resources in the courts. If they were not always equals in this process, Indians and other oppressed groups, like Genízaros and poor Spanish settlers on community grants, still achieved major victories in court often as a result of the assistance of advocates for their cause and sympathetic government officials.[13]

The first trial in New Mexico in which a Protector of Indians appeared was the 1659 trial of a twenty-seven-year-old Hopi named Juan Zuni, charged with stealing supplies from the storeroom of the convento (priest's residence) in Santa Fe and selling them in the *villa*. The protector assigned to represent Zuni was Diego Romero, a comanchero who had experience dealing with Plains Indian tribes and who was later himself brought before the Inquisition. Romero defended Zuni by claiming that as an Indian his acts should be excused or pardoned because of "lack of judgment and incompetence." This was essentially a plea for mercy, not a zealous defense aimed at Zuni's acquittal.[14] In contrast, early eighteenth-century Protectors of Indians in New Mexico such as Alfonso Rael de Aguilar were highly effective in protecting Pueblo Indian property rights.

A Protector de Indios operated in New Mexico from the mid-1600s until 1717 but did not appear again as a Spanish official until 1810. During the interim, several self-appointed advocates like Felipe Tafoya and Carlos Fernández appeared in litigation as representatives of various pueblos.[15] The first Spaniard to hold the position of Protector de Indios on a permanent basis in New Mexico was Alfonso Rael de Aguilar, one of Diego de Vargas's most trusted lieutenants. Besides taking part in the reconquest entradas of 1692 and 1693, Rael de Aguilar held the position of secretary of government and war under three governors, was *teniente general* of the province, and was alcalde of Santa Fe as well as protector.[16] Rael de Aguilar's résumé also included appointments as alcalde of Real de los Cerrillos, the silver-mining camp founded by Governor Vargas in 1695, and alcalde of Santo Domingo Pueblo. A native of Lorca in the Spanish province of Murcia, Rael de Aguilar had six children by

Josefa García de Noriega, whom he married in El Paso in 1683, and is often confused with his son, Alfonso Rael de Aguilar II, who was somewhat less of an upstanding citizen than his father.[17] He is sometimes called Alonso instead of Alfonso because official documents may refer to him as Alonso but he signed his name Alfonso or Alphonso.[18]

In 1704 Rael de Aguilar argued before the governor two important cases involving the property rights of San Felipe and San Ildefonso Pueblos, respectively. In both cases the need to determine the land owned by Pueblo Indians arose because Spaniards wanted land adjacent to Pueblo lands and the extent of lands owned by the pueblos had never been clearly defined. Eventually it was determined through a series of cases that an area of land measured from the center of the pueblo, a league (five thousand varas) in each cardinal direction, was the recognized amount to which each pueblo was entitled. The San Felipe case was the first to measure on the ground this so-called Pueblo league, although a similar concept, the *fundo legal*, had existed in central Mexico since the mid-sixteenth century, and the Pueblo league concept was first mentioned in New Mexico by Lázaro de Mizquía in 1696–1697.[19] A full discussion of cases involving the Pueblo league is found in Ebright, Hendricks, and Hughes, *Four Square Leagues*, chapter 1.

The San Felipe case began when Cristóbal and Juan Barela Jaramillo asked that the lands of San Felipe Pueblo at Angostura be measured because they thought the Indians "had more [land] than the law allows and they wanted a land grant adjacent to the pueblo."[20] Governor Vargas ordered Rael de Aguilar ("the defender and protector I have named for the Indians"), Fernando Durán y Chávez, and Diego Montoya to go to the land to determine what lands were in fact owned by the pueblo. Rael de Aguilar argued on behalf of the pueblo that the lands sought by the Jaramillos had been possessed by the Indians "since they were founded" and that the Indians had planted grain and cotton there.[21] The pueblo did not want the Jaramillos to receive a grant adjacent to Pueblo lands for fear that the Spaniards would damage Indian crops with their cattle and sheep. The Protector de Indios referred to the Pueblo league as "granted by royal law to the Pueblo Indians."[22] Here the document ends with no response by Governor Vargas, who died six weeks later. Alfonso Rael de Aguilar should get credit for being the first advocate to make use of the Pueblo league concept in New Mexico, which would eventually become the standard for land ownership by New Mexico's pueblos. It is curious that the San Felipe

document is entirely in Rael de Aguilar's handwriting, except for the Jaramillos'
petition and the governor's signature. Rael de Aguilar wrote the governor's
order, though he was not serving as the governor's secretary at the time, and
drafted the response for Alcalde Diego Montoya, putting Montoya's statements
in the first person and his own in the third person. He then signed the response
himself. This gave Rael de Aguilar an opportunity to put words about the
Pueblo league in the mouths of Governor Vargas, Alcalde Montoya, and the
Jaramillo petitioners, leading to the possibility that the Pueblo league was
the creation of Alfonso Rael de Aguilar.[23]

Rael de Aguilar's involvement later in the same year in another lawsuit
between a Spaniard and a pueblo shows why he was such a skillful advocate
for New Mexico pueblos. In September 1704 Rael de Aguilar represented San
Ildefonso Pueblo in a dispute with the powerful Spaniard Ignacio Roybal over
land opposite San Ildefonso Pueblo. Roybal had received a grazing grant from
Governor Vargas in March 1704 and claimed ownership of some San Ildefonso
land under this document. But the local alcalde had failed to notify the
pueblo and other adjoining landowners when the grant was made, depriving
them of the opportunity to object to the grant.[24] If notified, the pueblo would
have objected to the grant because it encroached on land planted in squash
and watermelons that was irrigated by an acequia dug by the San Ildefonso
Indians.[25] In petitions presented to Lieutenant Governor Juan Páez Hurtado,
who had temporarily succeeded Governor Vargas, Protector Rael de Aguilar
argued that the 1704 Ignacio Roybal grant was void because of the failure to
notify the pueblo "by the nine publications within the period of nine days."
The protector had personal knowledge that the pueblo had not been notified
since at the time the Roybal grant was made Rael de Aguilar was serving as
secretary of government to Vargas and the grant was in his handwriting.[26]
Rael de Aguilar noted that San Ildefonso Pueblo had been given the land
claimed by Roybal before the Pueblo Revolt and that Spanish officials had set
out landmarks showing the boundary of San Ildefonso land. Under the
Recopilación de Leyes de los Reynos de las Indias, Indian lands were protected
from Spanish encroachment, particularly lands that were farmed and irrigated by the Indians, but these laws were vague and inconsistent and were not
strictly enforced.[27] Most irrigable farmland along the Río Grande had been
in Pueblo hands, and Spaniards often encroached on the pueblos prior to the
revolt. Vargas was caught between his duty to protect Indian lands and his

promise to reward those who had helped him reconquer the province.[28] In his most important point Alfonso Rael de Aguilar asserted that San Ildefonso Pueblo was entitled by royal law to four square leagues of land (a league in each direction from the center of the pueblo) whether or not the Indians had planted the land or received a prior grant.[29] Acting governor Juan Páez Hurtado directed Alcalde Cristóbal Arellano to measure a league in each direction from the center of the pueblo,[30] but on the ground the measurements were different: a league to the north, one-half league to the south, one-half league to the east, and one-half league to the west because "there was no farming land on which to mark out the league in every direction."[31] Rael de Aguilar was still adamant, as he said in his initial petition: "The Indians, my clients, shall be informed of the four leagues one to each point of the compass, according to the will of his majesty. The said pueblo of San Ildefonso shall mark out its boundaries and thereby disputes and litigations will cease." But for San Ildefonso litigation did not cease: the pueblo was involved in three more disputes over its league in the eighteenth century.[32]

In 1707 Rael de Aguilar also appeared as Protector de Indios in Santa Fe at a general council of all the pueblos, but Rael's report on the proceedings sounded too good to be true. According to Rael, the meeting came about at the behest of the elected leaders of all New Mexico pueblos who wanted to be confirmed in their offices and to present any concerns they might have to Spanish officials. After four members of the Santa Fe cabildo had assembled with the pueblo leaders at Rael de Aguilar's house, each leader made a statement, either in Spanish or in their own language through an interpreter.[33] Surprisingly, no one had any complaints; instead, the Pueblo leaders took turns praising Governor Francisco Cuervo y Valdés in flowery and exaggerated terms. In what sounded like a scripted response, they said that Cuervo had stopped raids on the pueblos by launching retaliatory expeditions whenever an attack was made so that the "pueblos and frontiers had become quiet and pacified, and the Indian inhabitants had been avenged and satisfied with the useful spoils of war."[34] It seems that the real purpose of the meeting was to promote the candidacy of interim governor Cuervo for permanent appointment as governor of New Mexico by the viceroy, the Duke of Alburquerque. As Cuervo y Valdés himself had been adept at varnishing the truth regarding the founding of Albuquerque, so also Rael de Aguilar was not shy in helping him lobby the viceroy with exaggerated statements of Cuervo's merits.[35]

Rael de Aguilar was an effective advocate for the pueblos, but he did not always take their side. Since he held many important official posts in postrevolt New Mexico, he was sometimes required to take action detrimental to the pueblos. While serving on the cabildo of Santa Fe, Rael de Aguilar also served as alcalde and militia captain for Pecos Pueblo, in which capacity he was ordered by Governor Flores Mogollón to destroy the kivas at Pecos. This Rael did with ruthless efficiency, reporting back to the governor that the largest kiva was demolished so that "there remained not a sign or a trace that there had been on that site . . . any kiva at all."[36]

Rael de Aguilar did not serve in an official capacity as Protector de Indios after 1707, but he appears in lawsuits several times in a similar capacity. In 1722 Rael de Aguilar was appointed *juez receptor* (commissioned judge) by Governor Juan Domingo de Bustamante to mediate a dispute between Santo Domingo and Cochiti Pueblos brought about by a suit filed by Santo Domingo Pueblo over a sale of land from Juana Baca to Cochiti.[37] On the issue of the location of the boundary between the pueblos, Rael de Aguilar was apparently trusted by both pueblos to make a fair decision that would be binding on everyone. The erstwhile Protector de Indios had the authority to call the two pueblos together, conduct a hearing during which he took evidence, and then issue an *auto declarato* (explanatory decree). Rael de Aguilar summoned Miguel Baca of San Juan to testify as to the location of the land his mother had sold to Santo Domingo. Baca told Rael that the deeds in question described the land as being on the west side of the Río Grande. After examining a grant to Juana Baca from Governor Rodríguez Cubero made in 1703, Rael de Aguilar determined that the Baca purchase was indeed on the opposite side of the river from where the boundary dispute was. As he had done in the San Ildefonso suit in 1704, Rael measured with a *cordel* five thousand varas from the cemetery of the Santo Domingo church toward Cochiti and then did the same from Cochiti toward Santo Domingo. When this measurement left a gap of some sixteen hundred varas between the two Pueblo leagues, Rael de Aguilar split the difference and awarded each pueblo an additional eight hundred varas. He then set landmarks and gave each pueblo a certified copy of the results.[38] As he had done in the San Felipe and San Ildefonso cases, Rael de Aguilar recognized the Pueblo league as the norm for the amount of land Pueblo Indians could claim as their own, and established the principle that pueblos were sometimes entitled to additional land as well.[39]

Rael de Aguilar was the most effective advocate for the pueblos in the early part of the eighteenth century. His legal arguments set high standards that were seldom matched by other advocates who appeared off and on during that period. Several other individuals appeared as advocates for pueblos or Genízaros in lawsuits filed during the first half of the eighteenth century, but with little success. One of these was Juan de Atienza, who acted in two cases as Protector de Indios. The first in 1713 required him to defend the ex-governor of Picuris Pueblo against several charges including witchcraft. Jerónimo Dirucaca denied charges of idolatry, cohabitation, and witchcraft, but even with Atienza as his advocate he must have felt his chances of acquittal were slim. Dirucaca worked out a deal with the governor—like a modern plea bargain—whereby he agreed to reveal the location of a hidden silver mine in return for a promise of pardon. Escorted in handcuffs by four Spanish officials, Dirucaca took them to the Cañón de Picurís, where they found four veins of silver ore. The Spaniards were elated with the promise that a major silver mine would finally "provide complete relief for this wretched kingdom." This promise did not pan out, but Dirucaca was released to a Tewa pueblo of his choice anyway with his only penalty the payment of court costs. It seems that Juan de Atienza had little effect on the outcome of this case; it was the quick thinking of Dirucaca that swung the balance in his favor.[40]

Juan de Atienza again acted as Protector de Indios in 1715 on behalf of Pojoaque Pueblo in its lawsuit against several Spaniards who were trespassing on Pojoaque land. This was the only land-related case that Atienza argued in his capacity as Protector de Indios, and it was never brought to a satisfactory conclusion. Atienza did not perform well and was criticized by one of the litigants for his handling of the case. In fact, it appears that Atienza's heart was not in it. The pueblo claimed that in spite of the fact that Pojoaque had purchased land from Spaniards that had once belonged to the pueblo, some of that land was still being occupied by the same Spaniards, in particular Baltasar Trujillo. Pojoaque Pueblo was abandoned in 1700, and grants of former pueblo land were made in 1701 to José de Quirós and Antonio Durán de Armijo by Governor Pedro Rodríguez Cubero (1697–1703).[41] When the pueblo was resettled in 1707 the Indians repurchased both these tracts from Miguel Tenorio de Alba, who appears again in chapter 5, for a large quantity of corn, some tanned buckskins, woolen blankets, and chickens. But now in 1715 part of that land was being occupied by Baltasar Trujillo. Atienza argued that the land in question was irrigated farmland (*tierras laboriegas*) belonging to the pueblo.[42] The case was filed with Governor Juan Ignacio Flores Mogollón, who appointed Alfonso Rael de Aguilar as juez receptor (receiving judge) to assemble the necessary documents and written statements and forward them to the governor for a decision. Unfortunately for the Indians, the purchase from Miguel Tenorio de Alba by the pueblo was not based on a written document, although Tenorio's purchase from José de Quirós for 130 pesos was documented, as was the grant to Quirós by Governor Rodríguez Cubero. But without a written transfer to the Indians, the amount of the purchase price or whether it had been paid in full were matters for debate and extensive testimony.[43]

Tenorio said that the price was a fanega of corn and a blanket from each household in the pueblo—the typical amounts paid to encomenderos—and that only one Indian had given him a blanket. The Indians countered with an itemization of what had been paid in lieu of the missing blankets: thirteen chickens, as many as five buckskins, and the loan of two horses. In minute detail the Indians testified as to who paid what, and they said that Tenorio had been satisfied. But since nothing was in writing, it was Tenorio's word against the pueblo's, and Tenorio had an ace up his sleeve. He produced a decree from Governor Peñuela (Joseph Chacón Medina Salasar y Villaseñor, the Marqués of Peñuela, 1707–1712) compelling the pueblo to pay Tenorio the full purchase price.[44] The difficulty with the Peñuela decree was that Pojoaque Pueblo had not been notified of that lawsuit and given an opportunity to present its side of the story. Instead, Governor Peñuela had taken Tenorio de Alba's word that the purchase price was 130 pesos and that the pueblo had paid only seven fanegas of corn and one blanket. As later testimony indicated, this was only part of the truth. The pueblo claimed that Tenorio had been satisfied with the additional goods he had received, had agreed that the pueblo had paid in full, and had even given the pueblo a written deed but later took it back.[45]

Without witnesses to the transaction or written documents, Pojoaque Pueblo was at a distinct disadvantage, subject to Tenorio de Alba's every whim. Even given its weak position, the pueblo was not particularly well served by the advocacy of Juan de Atienza. He never made the kind of creative arguments Rael de Aguilar did, such as the pueblo's possible claim to four square leagues or the invalidity of the Peñuela decree because of the failure to notify Pojoaque Pueblo. Instead, Atienza's petitions simply stated the claims of the pueblo (that it purchased the land it had owned prior to the 1680 revolt and had paid Tenorio de Alba in full) and asked the governor to do whatever he deemed to be just. Rather than vigorously asserting the position of the pueblo, Atienza blamed the Indians for the delay in the proceedings and even failed to defend himself when he was attacked by Tenorio de Alba for his lack of ability.[46] To be sure, Atienza was hampered by the fact that neither Governor Flores Mogollón nor Governor Felix Martínez were particularly interested in the case. By May of 1716, when the lawsuit had dragged on for over a year, Alfonso Rael de Aguilar was the only official still on the case, though his authority had lapsed. Juez receptor Rael de Aguilar reported to Governor Martínez that Atienza had left Santa Fe, "not having been able to come to attend to [the case] even as he should," and Rael sent the papers back to Governor Martínez.[47] Juan de Atienza seems to have left New Mexico after December 1716, for his father received a license to depart New Mexico "with his family and sons," and no further mention of Juan de Atienza is found in the documents.[48]

This was the last appearance of an official Protector de Indios in New Mexico for almost a century, until 1810. In the interim, advocates were commissioned on a case-by-case basis to defend the rights of specific Pueblo Indians or Genízaros. Some of them performed as well as had official Protectors of Indians like Rael de Aguilar. In 1733, for example, Diego Padilla and Isleta Pueblo joined issue over whether Padilla's animals were encroaching on the planted fields and common lands of Isleta and whether the Indians owed Padilla for certain poles taken from his corrals at San Clemente. When the matter was referred to Isleta Pueblo, they executed a formal power of attorney appointing Ventura de Esquibel as their defense attorney.[49] Esquibel had appeared as a witness in the 1722 suit between Santo Domingo and Cochiti that Rael de Aguilar had mediated and may have learned something from Rael at that time about effective advocacy.[50] In the Isleta case, Esquibel filed a forceful petition stating that Padilla's livestock had damaged the Indians' acequia, which the Spaniard had promised to repair but did not. Esquibel asserted that Padilla's livestock should be withdrawn from Isleta's lands both in the summer and winter, for even in the winter the animals ate the cornstalks and trampled the tilled fields, making them difficult to plow in the spring.[51] In response to Esquibel's answer, Diego Padilla capitulated without a fight, stating that he would keep his livestock out of Isleta's agricultural lands and give up any claim to payment for his corral poles.[52] Esquibel said the pueblo was agreeable as long as Padilla actually kept his livestock away from Isleta's cultivated lands, but he wanted to be sure that the agreement was strictly observed. He told the governor that it was important that the pueblo's horse herd have sufficient fodder since they were used for scouting in the mountains and in other forms of service to the Spaniards in their defense of the province.[53] The governor's final decree in this litigation adopted the agreed settlement, set the fines for violation of its terms, and set the fees to be charged. If any of Diego Padilla's livestock entered the cultivated fields of Isleta Pueblo the pueblo could seize them, and Padilla would have to pay two pesos a head to get them back. The expenses of the lawsuit came to twelve pesos, including two pesos for Esquibel's power of attorney, which was apparently in line with the fees customarily charged in other cases in New Mexico.[54]

Because governors in the first half of the eighteenth century were generally unsympathetic to the pleas of the various advocates for pueblos and Genízaros, not many advocates appear in the documents during this period.[55] Governor Cruzat y Góngora in the 1730s and Governor Joaquín Codallos y Rabal in the 1740s were so preoccupied with Apache, Ute, and Comanche raids that they had little time or inclination to hear complaints from Genízaro or Pueblo litigants. When individuals or their advocates mustered up the courage to file a petition, they were often summarily rejected, as with the 1733 petition by one hundred Genízaro Indians seeking their own land grant at Sandia. The petition was filed before Governor Cruzat y Góngora by an anonymous advocate representing a group of Genízaros who wanted to form a new settlement at the pueblo of Sandia, abandoned since the Pueblo Revolt. These Genízaros were scattered throughout New Mexico, some living in Spanish settlements, some in pueblos. They did not otherwise identify themselves, saying only that they did not include any servants of Spaniards and signing their petition, "los Genízaros."[56]

Genízaro Indians comprised various Plains Indian tribes (the Sandia group included Apache, Kiowa, Pawnee, Ute, and Jumano), whose social status in Spanish society ranked at the lowest level.[57] Normally, Genízaros were purchased (or ransomed, as the euphemism goes) from one Plains Indian tribe that had captured them from another in intertribal warfare and then sold them to the Spanish. But during the term of Cruzat y Góngora, a new practice was instituted whereby the Spanish began to capture Plains Indians and then sell them to friendly tribes who would later sell the Genízaros back to the Spaniards. This practice was prohibited by Cruzat in 1732, but was difficult to stop. The purchase of Genízaros generally was condoned by the government since Spaniards were required to Christianize them during the time they were servants and then emancipate them when they had worked off the amount paid for them. Nevertheless, many considered the practice tantamount to slavery.[58]

It was not until Tomás Vélez Cachupín became governor that land grants were made to Genízaros and Genízaro property rights began to be respected on Spanish grants (see chapters 9 and 10).[59] A request for land from "los Genízaros" in 1733, however, was certain to be met with skepticism by Governor Cruzat y Góngora. In order to overcome the governor's resistance, these Genízaro Indians seeking a land grant needed an advocate. Why the advocate they picked chose to remain anonymous is uncertain, but he seemed to realize that convincing the governor would not be easy. This mysterious advocate covered all the reasons why these Genízaros deserved a land grant, including a theology lesson to convince the governor that they had become good Christians. He began by expressing the gratitude of the Genízaros for the many spiritual blessings they had received through their baptism into the church. He then moved into the temporal world, citing the need to satisfy physical needs for food and clothing as the necessary underpinnings of a spiritual life and used the biblical Adam and Eve story to demonstrate his point: in the garden of Eden, where everything necessary for subsistence was provided, "our first parents, forgetful of so much good and benefit, gave free rein to their disordered desire . . . were expelled from Eden, and forced to work the land for their livelihood, irrigating it with the sweat of their brow."[60] Thus, the Genízaros cautioned the governor that if their petition was not granted, some among them might fall prey to the temptations of the Devil and revert to heathenism because of their hardships. The advocate suggested that the Genízaros' problems could not be solved simply by having them live among the Pueblo Indians, for the pueblos were reluctant to take them in.[61] Then the advocate skillfully repeated the same arguments used almost two centuries earlier in Valladolid, Spain, by Bartolomé de Las Casas and Sepúlveda regarding conversion of the indigenous people of the Americas.[62] Conversion should be voluntary, according to Las Casas, whereas Sepúlveda had argued it could be brought about forcefully by enslaving the Indians. The status of the Genízaro in New Mexico was a compromise between these two views. Purchased as slaves, they were taught Christian doctrine, eventually given their freedom, integrated into Spanish society, and given the opportunity to own land. It involved a bargain similar to that made between Spaniards and Pueblo peoples: the Indians would receive economic benefits in return for accepting Spanish spiritual beliefs. Here the Genízaros were saying, in effect, we have converted to Christianity, now is the time for you to keep your part of the bargain and help provide for our material welfare. The advocate attempted to depict "los Genízaros" as stronger in their beliefs than the Pueblo Indians by alluding to a scandalous witchcraft trial that had concluded a couple of months earlier at Isleta Pueblo.[63] But whether the references to witchcraft by the Genízaros and their advocate was a good tactic can only judged by the outcome of the case.[64]

On receipt of the petition signed by "los Genízaros," Governor Cruzat y Góngora demanded that these Indians identify themselves in alphabetical order, citing their names and tribes.[65] The anonymous advocate for the Genízaros dutifully responded with a list of twenty-five petitioners (seventeen families and eight single males), far fewer than the one hundred settlers mentioned in the petition. From this list Governor Cruzat y Góngora learned the names and tribes of each of the individuals: six Pawnees, six Jumanos, four Apaches, three Kiowas, two from the A tribe, one Tano, one Ute, and two unidentified.[66] Once the governor had the information he wanted, he wasted no time in denying the petition without giving any reason whatsoever. Cruzat simply ordered the petitioners to apply to him individually if they wanted to be assigned to various pueblos.[67] Since the Genízaros had already indicated that the pueblos did not want them, this proposed solution was probably not satisfactory. Genízaro Indians did not receive their own grant until Governor Vélez Cachupín made the Abiquiu Genízaro grant in 1754, though certain Genízaros from Belén claimed to have received a grant there in the early 1740s.[68]

Governor Cruzat y Góngora was also quite strict when it came to petitions from the pueblos. In 1734 Santa Ana Pueblo attempted to purchase from Baltasar Romero lands that the Indians claimed as their traditional lands. Even though the pueblo was willing to pay for lands that once were theirs,

Governor Cruzat y Góngora stepped in to nullify the sale as being "against the dispositions of the royal laws of his majesty."[69] How the matter was brought to the governor's attention is not clear since we have no petition seeking cancellation of the sale. The governor apparently acted on his own, without a specific law prohibiting the sale and in spite of a series of purchases by Santa Ana Pueblo from Spaniards beginning as early as 1709. If Santa Ana had had an advocate, the laws protecting Indian property rights might have been invoked to justify the sale, as they had been invoked three decades earlier by Alfonso Rael de Aguilar.[70]

The judicial climate during the administration of Governor Codallos y Rabal in the 1740s did not improve with regard to Pueblo Indians or Genízaros; in fact, it worsened. Codallos y Rabal seems to have been more concerned with keeping the pueblos and Genízaros under control than with granting them new rights to land and water. By the late 1720s the Comanches had driven the Apaches from the eastern plains, and Spanish settlements were subject to unremitting Comanche attack. The governor had his hands full trying to keep the Pueblo Indian auxiliaries loyal to the Spanish in their defense of the province. In 1746 Governor Codallos y Rabal ordered Taos Pueblo to cease all trade or other dealings with the Comanches on pain of death. Travel of more than a league from the pueblo without a license, even for so innocent a purpose as searching for stray livestock, was still punishable by death. During the term of Governor Codallos y Rabal, criminal charges were brought against Indians from Cochiti, Tesuque, and San Juan for conspiring with the Ute and other Plains Indians to incite an uprising.[71]

Throughout the term of Governor Codallos, few claims seeking recognition of land and water rights were brought by pueblos or Genízaros on their own behalf.[72] Amateur advocates, like Isidro Sánchez, did try to help poor people obtain redress and were told to stop. In 1744 Sánchez was ordered to cease his petition-writing activities or suffer the penalty of a fifty-peso fine and fifteen days in the stocks. He was labeled "a quarrelsome and restless man who incites the poor citizens to file lawsuits by preparing petitions and conspiring with them" by Governor Codallos y Rabal.[73] Apparently, Sánchez kept filing petitions anyway though he did not sign his name.[74] Whether or not Isidro Sánchez encouraged litigation, the governor, by cracking down on him, was restricting the right to petition for redress of grievances, a right protected in New Spain from the first few decades of Spanish rule.[75]

To see how far such rights were further restricted under Governor Codallos y Rabal, one needs to examine the lengthy lawsuit brought by Antonio Casados, a Genízaro from Belén, against Governor Codallos y Rabal himself. Antonio Casados was a Kiowa Indian who had been purchased by another Genízaro named Miguelillo, a servant of Sebastian Martín. When Miguelillo died, Antonio Casados was sold to Alfonso Rael de Aguilar II, the son of the early Protector de Indios. Rael then sold Antonio to Francisco Casados, from whom Antonio took the Casados name. Francisco Casados put Antonio to work in a mine in Chihuahua, but Antonio soon ran away after a disagreement with Francisco. Eventually, Antonio Casados ended up at Belén along with other Genízaros, on the land grant of Diego Torres at the order of Governor Gaspar Domingo de Mendoza. At this point there is a divergence between the Casados story and the story of Diego Torres. Torres claimed to be the first settler at Belén when he was given a land grant there by Governor Mendoza in 1740. Casados, on the other hand, said that prior to the Diego Torres grant, there existed a pueblo of Genízaros at Belén and that he, Antonio Casados, had been elected their captain.[76]

Antonio Casados made the long journey to Mexico City by himself and petitioned the viceroy of New Spain to recognize the rights of this Genízaro pueblo and to eject all Spaniards from their lands. The ostensible purpose of this lawsuit was to find out which story was true. Even with an advocate representing the less powerful party, learning the truth from conflicting stories was often difficult, and in this case it was next to impossible because Casados did not have such an advocate. Casados had angered Governor Codallos y Rabal by traveling to Mexico City without a license and presenting his petition directly to the viceroy, who assumed for the purpose of making his decision, that a Genízaro pueblo did in fact exist at Belén and that Antonio Casados was its captain. Worst of all from the governor's standpoint, Casados had passed himself off as a Pueblo Indian subject to all the protections afforded by royal law, when in fact he was a Genízaro with fewer rights under the law. The viceroy ordered Governor Codallos y Rabal to investigate and if the allegations were true to comply with the petition of Antonio Casados or pay a one-thousand-peso fine.[77]

As further affront, on the day set for the hearing Casados appeared in Santa Fe escorted by seventy Pueblo Indians. Codallos y Rabal lost no time in moving to regain the advantage Casados had achieved by taking the initiative when he filed his petition in Mexico City. Fearing he might have a revolution on his hands because of the "scandal that has been experienced, from clustering Indians with noise and trouble from the pueblos," the governor put Casados in jail. There he stayed for the entire proceedings, except when he was brought before the court convened by the governor. His confinement would have affected how Casados's testimony was received, for he must have been kept in chains and under guard during the proceedings. Added to this indignity was the fact that Casados was not allowed to testify in his own words, although he was fluent in Spanish. Codallos y Rabal ordered Francisco Rendón to act as an interpreter for Casados, partly as punishment for his leaving New Mexico without a license. Thus, the testimony of Antonio Casados would be filtered through the interpreter without his being able to object if the translation distorted his meaning. Held in jail during the trial, and during an indefinite post-trial period, and not able to testify in his own words, Casados never had a chance. He lacked the assistance of an advocate to help him frame his case as he had when he went to Mexico City to appeal to the viceroy; there he had a lawyer named Francisco Córdova prepare his petition. But in New Mexico he had no one to help him, and his testimony was challenged by several elite members of Spanish society. Casados was not even able to complete his statement to the court before he was interrupted by a vigorous cross-examination by the governor himself, who, as presiding judge, was supposed to be neutral.[78]

When the proceedings were concluded, the written record was sent to the viceroy for a decision while Antonio Casados remained in jail. No record of the viceroy's decision has been found and nothing more was heard of Antonio Casados. The Belén grant to Diego Torres remained in effect, although several settlements of Genízaros remained on the grant. Not until the administration of Governor Tomás Vélez Cachupín were Genízaro rights to land recognized on the Belén grant.[79]

Governor Codallos y Rabal was probably no worse then many of his predecessors when it came to deciding cases involving Indians and Genízaros, since recognition of the rights of these marginalized members of society did not occur until Tomás Vélez Cachupín became governor. In his favor it should be said that Codallos did perform a regular *visita general*, when he set aside approximately a month and visited all the pueblos from Taos to Isleta, listening to complaints of individual Indians and ordering restitution where appropriate.

Prior to Vélez Cachupín's arrival in New Mexico in 1749 a small group of corrupt alcaldes and other officials sometimes abused their positions by exploiting Pueblo Indians with impunity. Though charges were brought against them and punishment meted out, the abuses continued. For example, Alcalde Manuel Baca, his son Antonio Baca, and Antonio's son-in-law Francisco Trebol Navarro were all charged with official misconduct over a fifty-year period beginning in 1718.[80] This family network of local officials who abused their office was temporarily checked by Governor Vélez Cachupín, when he relieved Antonio Baca of his duties and appointed Miguel Lucero in his place. In addition, when forced to deal with alcaldes like Antonio Baca, he kept a close watch on their activities and made sure his orders were followed to the letter. For example, in February of 1763, just a few months before he was ousted, Alcalde Baca was sharply rebuked by Vélez Cachupín for deviating from the governor's explicit instructions.[81] Even Vélez Cachupín's allies like Felipe Tafoya sometimes came in for criticism. Felipe Tafoya suffered a similar rebuke when he applied to Vélez Cachupín for a land grant for grazing sheep on the Río Puerco in 1766. The governor rejected his request, telling Tafoya that he should join one of the existing settlements on the Río Puerco if he wanted to graze his sheep in the area. Tafoya had been representing litigants seeking relief from Vélez Cachupín for a decade and a half, with some success, but the governor did not give him any special privileges (the Felipe Tafoya grant is discussed in greater detail in chapter 11).[82]

By the middle of his first term Governor Vélez Cachupín gathered around him a group of local officials who had a similar outlook, including Felipe Tafoya, Bartolomé Fernández, and Bernardo Miera y Pacheco (Carlos Fernández would represent Indian pueblos during Governor Anza's administration). Vélez Cachupín held a measurably different view of the administration of justice than did his predecessors, but it often took some time to impart these concepts to his subordinates. Once the governor got his message across, however, alcaldes and advocates serving under him became part of a team the governor could trust, but also who were part of a system that functioned more effectively than in the past in the administration of justice.[83]

Felipe Tafoya tried numerous lawsuits over a long career beginning in the 1730s; by the 1750s and 1760s he had achieved substantial prestige and competence, particularly during the two terms of Governor Vélez Cachupín. Felipe Tafoya was something of a jack-of-all-trades, like the Renaissance man

Bernardo Miera y Pacheco. Tafoya was active politically, serving as alcalde of Santa Fe; religiously, serving as a charter member of the confraternity of Nuestra Señora de la Luz; and professionally, practicing both law and medicine, though lacking formal training and certification in either profession.[84] Tafoya had five children by his first wife, Margarita González de la Rosa, whom he married in 1728, and six more by his second wife, Teresa Fernández, whom he married in 1750.[85] Tafoya first appeared as a witness in several civil and criminal proceedings beginning in the 1730s and by 1755 was serving as a notary (*notario*) in the ecclesiastical court of the vicar Santiago Roybal.[86]

To see how these local officials were able to act together to advocate and implement better policies for the Pueblo Indians and other marginalized members of society, one must examine cases like the 1763 lawsuit between San Ildefonso Pueblo, represented by Felipe Tafoya, and the Pueblos' Spanish neighbors. Tafoya instigated the lawsuit with a lengthy petition citing encroachments on Pueblo lands by Juana Luján, Pedro Sánchez, his son-in-law Antonio Mestas, and by Marcos Lucero. In spite of the measurement of San Ildefonso's Pueblo league in 1704, encroachments had occurred almost continuously ever since. In the name of the governor of the pueblo Francisco Cata, the elders, and the common people, Felipe Tafoya cataloged these problems, many of which had gone unresolved for over a half century. Tafoya identified himself as attorney (*procurador*) for the Villa de Santa Fe but later in the litigation was called the defender of the Indians. San Ildefonso asked that their four square leagues be measured and that Spaniards found to be within Pueblo land be ejected. San Ildefonso (or an Indian acting alone) had sold one tract of land to Marcos Lucero, but that sale had been annulled so none of the Spaniards within San Ildefonso land had valid titles.[87]

Governor Vélez Cachupín ejected Marcos Lucero immediately because he knew that Lucero had received his purchase money back from the pueblo and been told to leave by Governor Marín del Valle (1754–1760). As to the other Spaniards, several claimed to have received their land through grants, so Vélez Cachupín ordered the Pueblo league measured and Spaniards found to be encroaching given an opportunity to present their titles. Two of the Spaniards claimed to have received grants, and two did not. Felipe Tafoya argued that the grants were invalid because the pueblo had not been notified when the grants were made. Some Spaniards had the temerity to argue that the fact they had remained in possession when ordered to leave gave them rights under Spanish law, and some said that the fact that they had conquered New Mexico and served in the militia gave them rights over the Indians.[88]

Governor Vélez Cachupín had an impossible choice because strictly upholding the Pueblo league would mean evicting Spaniards with arguably valid grants. So the governor referred the question to Licenciado Fernándo de Torija y Leri, a Chihuahua lawyer, for an opinion, and a year later the lawyer replied with a compromise that took the pressure off of Vélez Cachupín. Torija thought that the rights of the Indians and of the Spaniards were equally balanced. The royal laws protected the pueblos from encroachment, but the rights of Spaniards who had legitimate titles (like Juana Luján), had to be respected since they were the ones most motivated to defend the province because they were also defending their own lands. The compromise suggested by Torija was to recognize the theoretical right of the pueblo to four square leagues while allowing Juana Luján to remain on the peublo's land while measuring additional land to the north and west to make up for what the pueblo lost. Since the rights of the Indians were about equal to those of the Spaniards in Torija's view, this compromise would be fair to both parties "without opening the door to many cases which will arise for other pueblos under similar conditions." Vélez Cachupín adopted the opinion in his decision since it was the kind of compromise he favored, allowing him to give something to both sides.[89]

In spite of Vélez Cachupín's ejectment order, Marcos Lucero was still there twenty years later in 1786 when former alcalde Carlos Fernández filed a petition on behalf of San Ildefonso and Santa Clara asking that the leagues of both pueblos (Santa Clara on the north, San Ildefonso on the south) be measured. The claim of Marcos Lucero was between the two pueblos, and if their four square leagues overlapped, that would dispose of his claim. Carlos Fernández appeared as advocate for both pueblos, much like Alfonso Rael de Aguilar had acted as both judge and advocate in the 1722 dispute between Santo Domingo and Cochiti over the measurement of their leagues. But in the intervening years procedures had developed to protect Pueblo lands, such as more precise measurements and better boundary markers.

Born in Spain, Carlos Fernández served in several important positions in local government in northern New Mexico. From 1762 to 1763 he was both alcalde of Santa Cruz and *teniente* of the Santa Fe presidio. In the 1780s he became alcalde of Santa Fe, one of the most prestigious political jobs in New

Mexico, and was also named *primer soldado distinguido* (most outstanding soldier) at the Santa Fe presidio. In his petition Fernández noted the long history of Pueblo grievances that had given rise to the petition he was filing for both pueblos. Santa Clara Pueblo had not been involved in as many lawsuits as had San Ildefonso, so its need was greater, according to Fernández. Santa Clara's four square leagues, which by the 1780s were well recognized as "the league which the king our lord . . . grants to each pueblo," had never been measured, and Fernández wanted them measured properly.[90]

Governor Anza ordered that a "waxed cordel containing one hundred varas" be used to measure the Pueblo leagues and that boundaries be marked with lime and rocks, or if lime was not available, then cedar stakes were to be firmly driven in the ground to form a circle or square two varas around to be filled with four or five cartloads of stone.[91] Alcalde José Campo Redondo performed the measurement proceedings. In the presence of Carlos Fernández and Marcos Lucero and his family, the cordel was soaked in water because no one could find any wax to follow the governor's instructions. Then Alcalde Campo Redondo appointed officials to hold each end of the cordel and make the measurement and another official to count the fifty *cordeles* it would take to reach five thousand varas. The first measurement started from the cross in the cemetery of the Santa Clara church and headed in a direct southerly line; a landmark was placed where it reached five thousand varas. Then the same procedure was followed from south to north starting at the San Ildefonso church. The cordel reached the Santa Clara boundary landmark and then overshot it by thirty-nine and three-quarters varas before reaching the end of the five-thousand-vara San Ildefonso league. Alcalde Campo Redondo then returned the proceedings to Governor Anza, who referred them to Carlos Fernández.[92]

Carlos Fernández made the most of the overlap by arguing passionately how incredible it was that any former New Mexico governor could make a grant of land between the pueblos when there was no excess land to be granted. Any grant that was made had to be based on misinformation, he argued, and in any case, these grants to Spaniards were void, and no period of possession could change that. Even though no one was living in the house that had been built on the Marcos Lucero ranch, the Indians of Santa Clara continued to suffer damages from the Spanish presence because Spanish livestock was damaging the acequias and planted fields of the pueblo. Therefore, concluded Carlos Fernández, Marcos Lucero and his relatives should be expelled.[93]

Marcos Lucero was grasping for straws when he argued that a landmark from the 1763 litigation showed that he was outside the San Ildefonso Pueblo league. In fact, the measurement of the San Ildefonso Pueblo league in 1763 placed Marcos Lucero 628 varas *inside* the pueblo boundary. Finally, Lucero challenged the just-completed measurement by Alcalde José Campo Redondo. He said that the measurement was not commenced at the proper spot, that the measurement was made with an old cordel that was not waxed but was spliced together with straps, and that the Indians were trying so hard to stretch the cordel by pulling it that they broke it twice.[94]

Governor Anza ordered that the Santa Clara and San Ildefonso leagues be remeasured in conformity with his prior order, using a waxed cordel that was to be measured in full view of all the interested parties, a step that had been omitted during the earlier measurement.[95] When the second measurement was made with the waxed cordel (apparently the parties had found some wax), a gap of 236 varas, instead of a 40-vara overlap, was found between the boundaries of the two pueblos. Alcalde Campo Redondo measured the Santa Clara league twice and came up with the same result. Then he measured the cordel used in the first measurement against the one used in the second and found the first one to be longer "because the waxed cordel does not stretch and the unwaxed stretches very much."[96]

Fernández then had his chance to comment on the latest measurement. He had agreed with the first one, it being the most favorable to the pueblos, and was still satisfied with the second, though he believed that it was not customary to use a waxed cordel in New Mexico. He did acknowledge that the cordel used to measure the league in 1763 may have been flawed as it was "made of lariats, ropes, and leather straps," but both the 1763 and the two 1786 measurements showed that Marcos Lucero's grant lay inside the San Ildefonso Pueblo league.[97] Fernández touched on all the points previously mentioned and concluded his three-page statement by referring to a law (presumably in the *Recopilación*) stating that land farmed by the Indians in excess of their four square leagues was also protected from Spanish encroachment. Since the land between the San Ildefonso and Santa Clara Pueblo leagues was farmed by means of an Indian-dug acequia, Carlos Fernández asked that this land be given to the two pueblos, a similar result as had occurred in the 1722 lawsuit between Santo Domingo and Cochiti Pueblos.[98] Lucero then charged Fernández with altering the second measurement by incorrectly measuring the cordel so that it was three-quarters of a vara longer than one hundred varas, resulting in about thirty varas over the five-thousand-vara league. He said that the witnesses who were present during the second measurement would corroborate his charges. But when Juan Ignacio Mestas and Cristóbal Maese were questioned about Lucero's latest charge, they both testified that Fernández had measured the cordel after they measured it and all agreed that the measurement was accurate.[99]

Now Governor Anza had all the information he needed to make a decision, and he approved the proceedings leading to the second measurement, which showed a gap of 236 varas between San Ildefonso and Santa Clara. Anza ordered that the pueblos each receive the land encompassed by these measurements and that Marcos Lucero must limit himself to the 236 varas between the pueblos. If Lucero should decide to sell, he must offer the land first to San Ildefonso Pueblo.[100] Governor Anza was careful, as Vélez Cachupín had been, to set forth all the reasons for his decision. Vélez Cachupín's decree, which was mentioned by Anza, had been based on the Chihuahua lawyer's opinion, whereas Anza cited the law in the *Recopilación*,[101] giving a league of commons to each pueblo and another providing protection to all the lands farmed by the Indians.[102]

Carlos Fernández was not able to participate in the final step of this litigation due to sickness. Instead, Juan Ignacio Mestas appeared on behalf of the pueblos to oversee the placement of permanent landmarks. A circle of cedar stakes was driven into the ground, as Governor Anza had ordered, and three (not five) cartloads of stones were dumped into the circle. But the Indians had seen too many so-called permanent boundary markers moved or disappeared, so they built a wall of stone and mud one vara in height as an additional landmark.[103]

Fernández was instrumental in helping the pueblos achieve a favorable result in this protracted and sometimes dramatic litigation, so it was unfortunate that he could not be present for the last act. His major accomplishment was the clear establishment of the Pueblo league as the amount of land to which a pueblo was entitled. Whereas the Pueblo league had been mentioned by Rael de Aguilar as early as 1704, it had generally been more honored in the breach than in the observance. Even in 1763, the Chihuahua lawyer had said that the rights of the Indians to the Pueblo league were no greater that the rights of the Spaniards living within Pueblo boundaries. By 1786, however,

Anza was willing to tip the balance in favor of the pueblos. They owned the land within their league by virtue of royal law. The laws in the *Recopilación* that defined and protected Pueblo Indian property had been cited by Rael de Aguilar, Felipe Tafoya, and Carlos Fernández, but encroachers like Lucero had ignored them. Lucero could do so because he was never penalized. Following Anza's ruling, however, Lucero was subject to a one-hundred-peso fine if he failed to obey any part of the decree or attempted to move the landmarks that had been established.[104]

Another issue that Fernández laid to rest was whether the pueblos needed to show grant documents in order to establish their property rights. Lucero had made this argument in May 1786, but Fernández answered that "it is use-less to ask that the Indians established in pueblos present the grants to the lands which they justly possess, because the same appear in the laws of our sovereigns."[105] This response impressed even Marcos Lucero, who agreed that the pueblos did not need grant documents. Lucero said that he would accept the pueblos' leagues as long as they were measured properly.[106]

Litigation between the pueblos and their Spanish neighbors continued through the end of Spanish rule in New Mexico and throughout the Mexican period. An official Protector de Indios was again appointed in 1810 at the request of Cochiti Pueblo, whose representative, Juan José Quintana, journeyed all the way to Chihuahua to get action. Quintana recommended Felipe Sandoval for the job and the audiencia accepted his recommendation. Sandoval was the stepson of Felipe Tafoya and must have gained considerable knowledge from his stepfather about how to represent Indian pueblos and about the judicial system in New Mexico.[107]

Unfortunately for the pueblos he represented, Felipe Sandoval was not as effective in advocating for the pueblos as were some of his predecessors like Alfonso Rael de Aguilar. In the ten-year period that the office of Protector of Indians was revived in the early 1800s, the protectors were more influenced by politics and self-interest than the desire to advocate impartially for the various pueblos. If the protectors had been more vigorous, the pueblos may not have suffered the loss of land they did starting in about 1815. In that year Felipe Sandoval represented Pecos Pueblo in the face of a concerted attack on the Pecos Pueblo league by several prominent Santa Fe residents who petitioned for land on both sides of the Pecos River. When asked by Governor Manrique whether the proposed grant would encroach on the Pecos Pueblo league,

Sandoval notified the governor that the requested land was "independent of the league and farmland of the Natives." Sandoval distorted the measurement of the league by starting well to the south of the pueblo complex at the cross in the cemetery. Normally, the cemetery was at the church in the pueblo complex, and the Pecos Indians protested the measurement. Nevertheless, in reliance on Felipe Sandoval's assurances, Governor Manrique made the first grant to encroach on the Pecos Pueblo league on 29 March 1815, which later became known as the Alexander Valle grant.[108]

Felipe Sandoval was less than aggressive in protecting the Pecos Pueblo league, as he was charged with doing, and his connection with the elites of Santa Fe, including those who petitioned for the land, may explain his performance. In addition, he was a member of the ayuntamiento of Santa Fe, which during his tenure approved the Alexander Valle grant and the Los Trigos grant, both of which encroached on the Pecos Pueblo league.[109] In other cases in which he represented the pueblos he mainly went through the motions. In 1812 Sandoval filed a petition on behalf of Jemez Pueblo protesting an unauthorized sale of land by a member of the pueblo to the local alcalde. The governor sent the case to Chihuahua, and nothing more was heard of it.[110] At Taos, Governor Máynez ruled strongly in favor of Taos Pueblo and its Pueblo league and asked the local alcalde and Felipe Sandoval to work out a compromise with the numerous Spaniards encroaching on the league. Sandoval suggested a renter's agreement between the encroaching Spaniards and Taos Pueblo, while noting that "the vecinos who may have purchased within the tract [Pueblo league] do not have a right to the land that belongs to the cited pueblo." A compromise was never reached in that case.[111]

Perhaps Sandoval's most important case was on behalf of Cochiti Pueblo in their claim against Luis María Cabeza de Baca, who was encroaching on the southeast portion of the Cochiti League. In April of 1815 Sandoval argued on behalf of the pueblo that Cabeza de Baca had removed boundary markers and threatened harm to Indians who might oppose him. Cabeza de Baca claimed land within the Cochiti league based on a sale from a Cochiti Indian that the pueblo disavowed as null and void because it was the result of intimidation and fraud.[112] This dispute had been building for some time and may well have been the reason that the Cochiti leader Juan José Quintana traveled to Chihuahua in 1810 to get Felipe Sandoval appointed as Protector of Indians. For some reason, Sandoval was no longer involved with the case after filing the petition. In April 1815 Governor Máynez ordered Cabeza de Baca to depart, leaving his house and farmland to the pueblo. But he did not leave. So several Cochiti Indians, along with Juan José Quintana, traveled to Durango seeking redress from the *asesor* (legal adviser) of the *comandante general*. There the Protector de Indios argued for the pueblo raising the same charges against Cabeza de Baca, but the asesor did not rule. Instead, he sent the case to the next judicial level, which should have been the audiencia of Guadalajara, but it ended up in the Juzgado General de Indios in Mexico City. Antonio Quintana (perhaps related to Juan José) traveled to Mexico City where he received a favorable hearing and an award of court costs. The ultimate decision was rendered by the Guadalajara audiencia, which ordered Cabeza de Baca to leave the disputed tract and pay court costs. That judgment was in 1819, but Baca was still there in 1833 when he died at Peña Blanca.[113]

The Cochiti case illustrates how ineffective advocates for the pueblos had become by 1815 and beyond. The legislation of the 1812 Cortes de Cádiz seemed to authorize the making of grants to Spaniards within the Pueblo leagues. Encroachment on Indian lands was becoming commonplace as Taos and Cochiti, among other pueblos, obtained favorable decrees against encroaching Spaniards that could not be enforced. Even the Pueblo Indians themselves, though successful in Mexico City when they made the long trip to the viceregal capitol, could not, when acting as their own advocates, get local authorities in New Mexico to back them up. Felipe Sandoval was a somewhat lackluster advocate for the Pueblo Indians, but at least, with the exception of the Pecos encroachment in 1815, he did not personally acquire Pueblo land or advocate against the pueblos. The same cannot be said for his successor as Protector de Indios, Ignacio María Sánchez Vergara. When Felipe Sandoval died in December 1816, Sánchez Vergara replaced him in June of 1817.[114]

Ignacio María Sánchez Vergara was an unpredictable figure who, more often than not, was attacking Pueblo land rather than protecting it. When he was alcalde of Jemez in 1808 and later alcalde of Sandia, allegations against him ranged from extortion to tampering with land titles; he was also said to have "made a career out of taking advantage of his position as alcalde."[115] Unfortunately, even after his appointment as Protector de Indios, and more so after that appointment expired, Sánchez Vergara embarked on a course of trying to acquire Indian land for himself and his Hispanic friends. For example, in 1821 Sánchez Vergara wrote to Governor Facundo Melgares asking whether he could petition the ayuntamiento for a grant *for himself* within the Sandia Pueblo league. Melgares answered that it would not be proper for Sánchez Vergara to submit such a petition.[116] In 1823 Sánchez Vergara argued in Durango on behalf of Eusebio Rael de Aguilar, who was claiming land within the boundaries of Sandia Pueblo.[117] Even though he was no longer Protector de Indios, he still cloaked himself in that authority; he should have at least remained neutral rather than attacking the Sandia Pueblo league. Sánchez Vergara was even accused of fraud in regard to the Sandia grant when one witness testified that he saw Sánchez Vergara and Eusebio Rael altering the Sandia grant documents by "pinching out" some lines. Those alterations can still be seen in the papers on file in the Archives in Santa Fe.[118]

In another case, this time involving Santa Ana and San Felipe Pueblos, Sánchez Vergara engaged in several kinds of fraud, misleading conduct, and attempted exercise of authority he did not possess, outdoing his conduct in the Sandia case. In a boundary dispute between the two pueblos, Sánchez Vergara first appeared for Santa Ana when he approved on their behalf an adjudication by the local alcalde that established a boundary line between the pueblos. When that adjudication was appealed to the audiencia of Guadalajara and affirmed, Sánchez Vergara switched sides in order to protect a local landowner who was encroaching on Santa Ana land. Pablo Montoya was to Santa Ana Pueblo what Luis María Cabeza de Baca had been to Cochiti.[119]

When San Felipe Pueblo agreed to provide other land that it owned to the last Spaniards on Santa Ana land, most of the encroaching Spaniards moved. All, that is, except Pablo Montoya. Montoya claimed to have documents showing a sale by Santa Ana Pueblo to him, but he never produced them. By early 1821, just after the position of Protector de Indios had been abolished, Sánchez Vergara began a complicated campaign to protect Pablo Montoya and his land from the effect of the 1819 audiencia decree requiring encroaching Spaniards to move. After having told Santa Ana that he agreed with the audiencia's decision in 1819, in 1821 Sánchez Vergara reversed himself, saying that upon reexamining the audiencia's decree he now believed that it was not intended to affect certain lands sold by Santa Ana, specifically the lands of Pablo Montoya. When this unilateral action was ineffective because Pablo Montoya had no documents showing a land sale from Santa Ana, Sánchez Vergara took another tack, claiming that the audiencia's decision had been reversed.[120] Without any authority at all, Sánchez Vergara was acting like a judge with the power to interpret decrees from an appellate court.

It appears that Pablo Montoya must have made an under-the-table arrangement with Sánchez Vergara, for in May of 1822, undaunted by his lack of authority, the erstwhile Protector of Indians ordered the two pueblos to appear at the disputed land along with the local alcalde. When the leading Indians of both pueblos had gathered, Sánchez Vergara announced that the audiencia's decision had been reversed. In a grand gesture that reached the height of audacity, Sánchez Vergara purported to deliver the disputed land back to San Felipe Pueblo, all the while waving a "document" in his hand that he said justified this action—a document that he did not show to anyone. Outraged by Sánchez Vergara's antics, the governor of Santa Ana Pueblo notified Governor Melgares that the pueblo strongly disagreed with Sánchez Vergara's actions and asked that the decision of the audiencia in Santa Ana's favor be enforced. Governor Melgares seemed surprised at all Sánchez Vergara had done without the his knowledge. He ordered the local alcalde "to have Don Ignacio Sánchez Vergara appear before me with all that he has done and with the decree" he had been waving about. There is no record that Sánchez Vergara ever appeared before the governor or produced the document that he claimed reversed the audiencia's decision.[121]

In spite of Sánchez Vergara's extralegal activities, he was never disciplined, though several pueblos filed complaints against him. Although his activities seemed to benefit San Felipe Pueblo, even that pueblo charged that he had filed misleading information with the audiencia in May of 1819.[122] San Juan Pueblo also complained that Sánchez Vergara did not adequately protect them and asked for a new protector, noting that since Felipe Sandoval died they had been "as orphans" because they did not understand Spanish well, nor did they comprehend legal matters as completely as did the Spaniards. Even Felipe Sandoval, tepid as he was in protecting native land rights, was preferable in Pueblo eyes to chameleon-like Sánchez Vergara.[123]

In the wake of the liberal ideals sweeping Europe, the office of Protector of Indians was abolished by royal decree in January 1821, with the declaration that "all free men born and residing in Spanish territory are Spaniards . . . [so] the Indians have emerged from their state of minority . . . and for this same reason the office of *Protector de Indios* should not exist." Thus, according to royal decree, the Indians no longer needed special protection in theory, but in fact nothing could be further from the truth. As the Indians of San Juan protested, not only did they still need protection, they needed protection from Sánchez Vergara. They would soon need protection from a cadre of elite Spaniards casting longing glances at Pueblo Indian lands—including the governor himself, Bartolomé Baca. Without official protectors the Pueblo Indians had to learn to be their own advocates. And their familiarity with the Hispanic justice system carried over into the Mexican period, when "pueblos appear to have been even more confident of their ability to further their ends by pursuing Spanish justice."[124]

They needed to be wary and vigilant, however, especially as their former protector, Sánchez Vergara, continued to be active throughout the 1820s, often cloaking himself in authority he did not have. In 1824 he asked Governor Bartolomé Baca for a grant of land between Santo Domingo and San Felipe Pueblos, knowing full well it was owned by the Indians; it had been granted to those pueblos by Governor Mendinueta in 1770. Others had also been requesting the same land, in 1823 for instance, when six members of the presidial troops asked for a grant of the land between the two pueblos.[125] Instead of granting the land to a Spaniard, over the objections of both Santo Domingo and San Felipe Pueblos, the Mexican government privatized the grant to individual Indians who then had the power to sell the land to Spaniards.[126]

The sale of Pueblo land by individual Pueblo Indians over the objections of the rest of the members of the pueblo was perhaps the most important issue facing Pueblo Indians and their advocates because Spaniards encroaching on Pueblo land usually claimed to have purchased from a Pueblo Indian. Sometimes pueblos—like Abiquiu Pueblo, the owner of the Abiquiu Genízaro grant—brought suit against Spaniards for restoration of lands sold by individual Indians without the authorization of the pueblo. In 1824 three Abiquiu Pueblo members brought suit seeking restoration of lands lost due to unauthorized sales by Pueblo members. The pueblo was successful in the first round, after which they were assigned an advocate to present their case before the governor: none other than Ignacio María Sánchez Vergara. Though he was no longer Protector de Indios, he argued quite convincingly that the land sold to one Teresa Cortés should be returned to the pueblo and she should be refunded the purchase price. Sánchez Vergara's credibility is somewhat tarnished, however, when one remembers that this was the same year that he sought to acquire the previously granted land between Santo Domingo and

San Felipe Pueblos. Not only was he involved in the acquisition of lands of other pueblos, Sánchez Vergara had earlier issued a decree *approving* another sale of Abiquiu land, this time to María Manuela Perea. It seems that doña María was a member of the elite who, along with the priest Teodoro Alcina and Alcalde García de la Mora, had all purchased land from Abiquiu Pueblo; those sales were never set aside.[127]

Abiquiu continued to resist the sale of its lands by Pueblo members to outsiders and retained its identity as a pueblo throughout the nineteenth century. In 1885 Surveyor General George Washington Julian, in an uncharacteristically generous and liberal ruling, held that while the Abiquiu Genízaro grant contained numerous technical defects, in his view it was entitled to confirmation because it was made to Indians and "the Spanish government was very lenient towards Indians." Whether this was true historically, the fact that the Abiquiu Genízaro grant retained its relationship with an Indian pueblo was beneficial in the confirmation process despite the efforts of the erstwhile Protector de Indios, Ignacio María Sánchez Vergara, to split the pueblo fifty years earlier.[128]

The work performed by Spanish advocates on behalf of Pueblo Indians and Genízaros in the early part of the eighteenth century was moderately effective in protecting native rights. The post–Pueblo Revolt accommodation between Spaniards and Pueblo peoples proceeded erratically, depending on how the sitting governor viewed the notion of property rights for pueblos. By 1749, Governor Vélez Cachupín and his cadre of local officials began to show more concern for protecting Pueblo land and water. Procedures for measuring the Pueblo league and for appraising and accounting for land sold to the pueblos by Spaniards were refined and expanded. The methods of measuring land and marking boundaries became more specific and included the use of the waxed cordel. The Indians became adept at preserving evidence, realizing that landmarks were likely to be moved. They sometimes placed a hidden landmark underground so that a boundary could be relocated even if the aboveground marker was relocated.[129] This practice anticipated one followed today in northern New Mexico whereby state-funded brass-cap survey monuments, used as a starting point in many modern surveys, are protected from removal by having their location tied to a buried monument or reference point.[130]

The battles won by the eighteenth-century advocates and chronicled herein were built upon by nineteenth-century advocates like Felipe Sandoval. The

Pueblo league was measured, landmarks were moved and reestablished, and advocates for the pueblos presented increasingly sophisticated arguments. The effectiveness of Alfonso Rael de Aguilar, Bartolomé Fernández, Felipe Tafoya, Carlos Fernández, and the other advocates for Pueblo Indians in eighteenth-century New Mexico is attested to by the fact that the accommodation between Spaniards, Indians, and Genízaros that began in the early 1700s is still going on, with contemporary lawyers representing the pueblos and using arguments similar to those carefully developed by those early Spanish advocates for the oppressed, along with many new ones.[131]

CHAPTER TWO

A City Different
than We Thought

Land Grants in Early Santa Fe

S ANTA FE—ESTABLISHED AS THE CAPITAL OF NEW MEXICO IN 1610— is still a mystery to many archaeologists and historians. Because the archives of New Mexico were burned at the time of the 1680 Pueblo Revolt, the records generated by the Spanish authorities within New Mexico are no longer available for study, except for a few copies found in the archives in Mexico City, Seville, and smaller cities. These records would have provided a great deal of information about early Santa Fe, but they would necessarily give us only the perspective of the Spanish conqueror. Myths and fictions have grown up around the history of early Santa Fe and early New Mexico, myths that have been punctured only to be replaced by new myths. Basic historical questions are still debated by scholars: when was the Villa of Santa Fe founded; why did Governor Pedro de Peralta pick the present location as the site for the Villa of Santa Fe when later governors tried to move the villa;[1] and did a settlement of Mexican Indians exist at the site of the Barrio of Analco prior to the founding of the Villa of Santa Fe?[2]

To begin to answer some of these thorny questions it is necessary to strip away several false ideas about early Santa Fe that have been imposed by nineteenth-century lawyers, civic boosters, and historians. The following case studies deal respectively with the Santa Fe League, which never existed, and with the Cristóbal Nieto grant, which was greatly stretched and expanded in size by the lawyer for the Nietos. Both claims were asserted before the Court of Private Land Claims in the 1880s and 1890s in an effort to establish title to land based on an imaginative history of early Santa Fe that was created to suit the needs of those late nineteenth-century claimants who were trying to stake a claim to what had become valuable property in territorial period Santa Fe. After these fictions are exposed, we will be able to draw a more realistic map of early Santa Fe that more closely represents the true story of this place.[3]

The year 1610 was also a year of important literary happenings all over the world, which provide us with a sense of the European mindset at this moment in history. In England, William Shakespeare was working on his last major work, *The Tempest*, in part an examination of the great encounter between the European powers and the natives of the New World.[4] Ironically, Shakespeare's inspiration for *The Tempest* came partly from accounts of a 1609 shipwreck near Bermuda of one of a fleet of ships headed for Jamestown with new colonists to save the struggling English colony.[5] The shipwreck in a great storm, the wonders of strange lands, and the great gulf of understanding that existed between the Europeans and the natives were common elements in *The Tempest* and in historical events of the time. In Spain, the country whose conquistadores conquered the province of New Mexico, Miguel Cervantes was working on the second part of *Don Quixote*, which was published in 1615 (part one was published in 1605). It is appropriate that this great work encompassing the world of knights errant, heroic adventures, and the problem of fiction's relationship to reality was carried by some New Mexico governors in their baggage and was found in some early New Mexican libraries. We might consult this work today as we try to separate fiction, myth, and reality in the landscape of early Santa Fe.[6]

The "Santa Fe Grant"

Like many ideas connected with early Santa Fe, the notion that the king of Spain made a formal municipal grant to the Villa of Santa Fe is a myth. Like the "oldest house" in Santa Fe, which is not that old and more a tourist attraction than a historical building, the Santa Fe grant never existed,[7] though surveyor general and Court of Private Land Claims records include three long case files, litigated by numerous lawyers, all designated as "the Santa Fe Grant."[8] The idea of a municipal grant to the Villa of Santa Fe first saw the light of day in 1874 and again in 1892, when petitions were filed with the

surveyor general of New Mexico and the Court of Private Land Claims, respectively, for confirmation of four square leagues of land (about 17,350 acres)
to the municipality of Santa Fe, in spite of the fact that the area was already
covered with almost twenty smaller grants (a list of those grants is attached as
appendix B). Some of these small grants were confirmed prior to the Santa Fe
grant case, some were joined as parties to that litigation, and some were what
J. J. Bowden calls "ghost grants." To piece together this complicated story of
myths and reality, we should start at the time when Spaniards first arrived in
New Mexico.[9]

After the sixteenth-century explorations of Coronado, Espejo, Chamuscado-
Rodríguez, and Castaño de Sosa revealed the existence of a large native population in New Mexico and the possibility of mineral wealth,[10] Juan de Oñate
(1598–1608) established the first permanent settlement in New Mexico in 1598
at San Juan Pueblo on the east bank of the Río Grande. A few months later the
capital was moved across the river to San Gabriel del Yunge Owingeh (today's
Ohkay Owingeh),[11] which remained the capital of New Mexico until Santa Fe
was established by Juan de Oñate's successor, Governor Pedro de Peralta. Early
explorers such as Castaño de Sosa[12] and Oñate were aware of the location that
became Santa Fe, and as early as 1607 a military camp (*real*) was established at
the site that became Santa Fe.[13] In the spring of 1605, when he crossed the Santa
Fe River on his way to the Great Plains, Oñate noted that the locale had many
of the requirements for a new capital: an adequate water supply, fertile soil, an
abundance of timber, and a strategic position for dealing with hostile nomadic
Indians.[14]

In 1609 Pedro de Peralta (1609–1614) was appointed governor of New Mexico
and was ordered to establish a new capital to be designated as a villa.[15] Peralta
arrived in New Mexico late that year and by early 1610 had moved the capital
of New Mexico from San Gabriel to the site of present-day Santa Fe, on the
ruins of the prehistoric pueblo of Kuapoge (Bead Water Place).[16] By May of
1610, if not before, the move had probably been completed, the two main acequias dug, and the fields of the villa planted.[17] Viceroy Luis de Velasco II had
given precise instructions as to how the villa should be laid out, but it is unlikely
that this work was accomplished exactly as called for by the viceroy. As was
true of the other later villas of Santa Cruz de la Cañada (1695) and Albuquerque
(1706), Santa Fe was primarily an agricultural settlement with ranches scattered along the Santa Fe River, rather than a compact urban municipality.[18]

The core of the villa was built around 1610, with later additions forming "a large government-military compound containing arsenals, offices, a jail, a chapel, and the governor's residence and offices." The outer walls of these structures served as defensive walls of the compound, which enclosed two interior plazas. The fortified villa had four watchtowers (*torreones*), two on the south wall and two on the north side, and only one gate. Outside of this enclosure were the homes and fields of the settlers. In 1610, or soon thereafter, a temporary church was constructed, but it collapsed after a few years.[19] A settlement of Mexican Indians who were servants to the Spaniards, presidial soldiers, and those who performed various other occupations formed the Barrio of Analco. It may have been settled by 1607 or before, centered around the chapel of San Miguel south of the Santa Fe River. It seems that the lands of Analco were the best lands in the area, which would explain why Santa Fe was established north of the river where it was swampy and where the lands were inferior, since the lands south of the river were already occupied.[20]

Although Santa Fe was designated as a villa when it was founded, no formal charter specifying the villa's ownership of the land within its boundaries had been discovered at the time of the litigation of the Santa Fe grant in the 1880s and 1890s.[21] This missing document was crucial to the later claim by the municipality of Santa Fe that it owned four square leagues of land, measured from the center of the plaza, in a corporate capacity to be held in trust for the inhabitants of the villa. We cannot know exactly how the Villa of Santa Fe acted in regard to the property it encompassed prior to the Pueblo Revolt of 1680. When the Pueblo Indians and their Apache allies occupied Santa Fe after expelling all the Spaniards from the province and destroying the archives, it is likely that many important documents concerning early Santa Fe went up in smoke. So historians are mostly left with archives outside of New Mexico from which to piece together the pre-revolt history of the Villa of Santa Fe.[22]

In 1693, when Diego de Vargas was in El Paso gathering the soldiers and colonists needed for the reconquest of New Mexico, he told prospective members of his expedition that he would "give them the lands, homesites, and haciendas they had left at the time of the uprising." However, he could not find sufficient land to meet this promise, as he followed a resettlement plan that seemed to differ from the pre-revolt settlement pattern, although we do not know exactly what that settlement looked like. The Vargas plan involved an area of common pasture southwest of Santa Fe and another area of common

woodlands north and east of the villa, similar to the common lands of a community land grant. Individual tracts, corn-planting plots of one to two fanegas
each (nine to eighteen acres), were granted to pre-revolt families and to new
settlers together with pastureland. The resulting tracts were probably substantially smaller than what returning colonists claimed they owned before the
revolt. The only public land in Santa Fe at this time was the land where the
governor's palace, the Santa Fe plaza, the churches, and other public buildings
were situated.[23]

Another kind of municipal property called *propios* was the subject of a lawsuit between the cabildo or town council of Santa Fe and Diego Arias de
Quirós in 1715. Propios were lands owned by a municipality as private property,
rented by the municipal council with the rent applied toward public works.
This situation was the ideal, but it did not always work this way. Propios were
often confused with common property owned by the community, as was the
case with the Ciénega property being litigated between Arias de Quirós and
the cabildo of Santa Fe. The case of *Arias de Quirós v. Santa Fe* illustrates how
the municipality of Santa Fe viewed the property it owned in 1715 and provides
a glimpse of what Santa Fe looked like at that time.

The Ciénega of Santa Fe, a tract of spring-fed marshy land east of the plaza
and the governor's palace, was initially used by Santa Fe residents to graze
their animals in common. Arias de Quirós owned land surrounding the
Ciénega, and prior to 1715 he built a pond (*tanque*) on the Ciénega to collect
water from one of the springs that kept the area wet and green. In July of 1715
the Santa Fe cabildo ordered Arias to remove his pond, claiming that the
Ciénega was municipal property. Arias de Quirós responded by appealing
directly to Governor Flores Mogollón (1712–1715), claiming that the Ciénega
was unappropriated royal lands (*realengas*), not owned by the Villa of Santa Fe.
The governor ordered the cabildo to produce any documents it might have
showing that the Ciénega had been granted to the villa. After admitting it had
no such document, the cabildo asked Governor Flores Mogollón to make a
grant of the Ciénega to the Villa of Santa Fe as its propios. Flores Mogollón
responded favorably to this request, giving the Villa of Santa Fe the first written document granting it the Ciénega as its municipal property. This document, covering a relatively small area, would work against the later claim by
the municipality of Santa Fe that it was entitled to four square leagues, either
by express grant or by virtue of Spanish law.[24]

The first claim of a municipal four-square-league grant to the Villa of Santa Fe was made in 1874 by land speculator Gaspar Ortiz y Alarid as probate judge for Santa Fe County.[25] Ortiz y Alarid petitioned Surveyor General James K. Proudfit for a four-square-league tract of land to be measured from the stone monument in the center of the plaza, based on the possible existence of a written grant from the king of Spain and on book 4, title 5, law 6 of the *Recopilación de Leyes de los Reynos de las Indias.* Ortiz y Alarid claimed that this statute provided for a grant by operation of law to a community of at least thirty families as long as the settlement was at least five leagues from any other settlement and did not prejudice the interests of any Indian pueblo or private party. If confirmed, the grant would be held in trust for the inhabitants of Santa Fe until the city became incorporated and could become the rightful custodian of the patent.[26] With unaccustomed alacrity and little or no investigation of possible conflicting grants, Surveyor General Proudfit recommended confirmation of the claim based primarily on the law cited in the petition, which supposedly provided four square leagues of land to a community of at least thirty families meeting the other requirements of the statute in the *Recopilación.* Unfortunately, Proudfit's staff did not thoroughly research the Spanish law, as we shall see.[27] In September 1877, Deputy Surveyors Griffin and McMullin surveyed the Santa Fe grant and found it to contain 17,261 acres.[28] As was the case with almost all land grant claims submitted to Congress in the 1870s, no action was taken on the Santa Fe grant claim, which was still pending when the Court of Private Land Claims was established on 2 December 1891.[29]

The precarious foundation upon which the claim for the Santa Fe grant was built was not evident until its examination by the Court of Private Land Claims. Ironically, Gaspar Ortiz y Alarid, the petitioner on behalf of Santa Fe County, had engaged in two massive land grant frauds just prior to his 1874 petition for the Santa Fe grant. In 1871 he succeeded in getting Surveyor General T. Rush Spencer to approve the fraudulent Roque Lovato grant, which was stretched from a plot of about 15 acres to a tract of 6 square miles or about 3,840 acres. He was able to sell the Roque Lovato grant, whose ownership was based on a forged deed, before the forgery was detected by Will Tipton, handwriting expert for the Court of Private Land Claims. Then in 1873, don Gaspar, as he was called, claimed the forged Sierra Mosca grant. In this case the forgery was detected and the grant claim rejected. Don Gaspar Ortiz y Alarid's reputation did not suffer because of his involvement with boundary stretching, fraud, and forgery, however. In fact, his name is permanently affixed to the current landscape of Santa Fe: both Ortiz Street and Don Gaspar Avenue are named after him.[30]

Because of its importance, the Santa Fe grant claim was one of the first submitted to the Court of Private Land Claims. On 14 July 1892 the Board of County Commissioners of Santa Fe County filed its claim as successor to the ancient Villa of Santa Fe for confirmation of a four-square-league (approximately 17,350 acres) tract of land. The petition alleged that the king of Spain had made such a grant to the villa, but the document could not be produced because of the destruction of the Spanish archives during the Pueblo Revolt of 1680. The complaint also alleged that the municipality was entitled to four square leagues by operation of book 4, chapter 5, law 6 of the *Recopilación*, since the Villa of Santa Fe contained at least thirty families when it was reestablished in 1693 after the revolt and met all the other requirements of the law.[31] However, U.S. Attorney Matthew Reynolds and his staff of experts, including Will Tipton and Henry Flipper, again failed to research and challenge the Spanish law cited by the city. Instead, the government challenged the petition on the grounds that the plaintiff had no authority to prosecute the claim on behalf of the Villa of Santa Fe.[32] The Court of Private Land Claims agreed and dismissed the petition without prejudice to the rights of the City of Santa Fe.[33]

About this time the City of Santa Fe was incorporated for the first time, and in its new corporate capacity it filed another petition similar in most respects to the earlier July 1892 petition filed by the Board of County Commissioners. Again, the city claimed a four-square-league grant both by means of a written grant from the king of Spain and by operation of *Recopilación* 4.5.6. The population of Santa Fe had grown from about six thousand to seven thousand since the 1892 petition was filed, but in most other respects the two petitions were the same.[34] Again, the United States objected to the petition both on the ground that it failed to state a cause of action and because it failed to disclose the adverse claims by numerous claimants whose ancestors had received grants in Santa Fe.[35]

Finally, after three tries the City of Santa Fe filed an amended petition naming the adverse claimants and basing its claim solely on the provisions of *Recopilación* 4.5.6, which it claimed provided for a four-square-league grant to the villa by operation of law. No longer did the City of Santa Fe claim the existence of a written grant from the king, but claimed instead that if such a written grant had existed it was destroyed when the archives were burned during the Pueblo Revolt.[36] The amended petition was a bit more flowery than the earlier ones and was signed by no fewer than six lawyers. Instead of referring simply to the Villa of Santa Fe, the lawyers who drafted the amended petition said that the predecessor to the City of Santa Fe was called La Villa Real de San Francisco de Santa Fe, San Francisco de Assisi de la Santa Fe, or La Villa Real de Santa Fe. However, most documents, including Governor Flores Mogollón's grant of the Ciénega to the villa, refer to Santa Fe simply as the Villa of Santa Fe. With its amended petition, the city had raised the issues that would decide the outcome of the City of Santa Fe grant: was the Villa of Santa Fe and its successor municipality entitled to a four-square-league grant by operation of law?[37]

The U.S. attorney denied the grant by operation of law theory in his answer and alleged that the Villa of Santa Fe never claimed ownership of any land within the four square leagues except for the Ciénega, which had been granted to the villa in 1715 by Governor Flores Mogollón.[38] The adverse claims that were supposed to have been litigated during the main litigation between the City of Santa Fe and the United States were almost all represented by attorney James Purdy.[39] With all the legal talent involved in this case, including the ever-present Thomas B. Catron, one would have expected a more vigorous legal discussion about Spanish law relating to municipalities. Instead, it was Justice Murray of the Court of Private Land Claims who would provide the most incisive analysis of *Recopilación* 4.5.6 and the grant by operation of law theory in his dissenting opinion.[40]

The claim for the Santa Fe grant finally came to trial starting 21 April 1894. The parties introduced transcriptions and translations of numerous Spanish documents into evidence, many of which came from the territorial library. Included among these documents were copies of the 1790 census for both New Mexico and Santa Fe, descriptions of Diego de Vargas's entry into Santa Fe on 16 December 1693, and many miscellaneous documents included simply because they mentioned the Villa of Santa Fe. The plaintiff was attempting to show the existence of the Villa of Santa Fe, a historical fact of which no one had any doubt. Also introduced was a translation of *Recopilación* 4.5.6 that was the basis for the municipality of Santa Fe's claim.[41]

Less than a week after the commencement of the trial, the case was submitted to the Court of Private Land Claims and decided by a majority opinion rendered by Chief Justice Reed and Justice Thomas C. Fuller. The justices found in favor of the claimants, agreeing with their contention that the municipality of Santa Fe was entitled to four square leagues by operation of law.[42] The majority opinion recognized that Santa Fe's claim was analogous to the claims of San Francisco, California, and Brownsville, Texas, both of which had been upheld by the U.S. Supreme Court.[43] But this victory for the City of Santa Fe was not the end of the story. Justice W. W. Murray wrote an incisive dissent that examined *Recopilación* 4.5.6 carefully for the first time in the litigation. First Murray pointed out that the law was mistranslated, and he provided another translation. More importantly, he noted that the law applied solely to empresario grants, which existed only in Texas and not in New Mexico.[44]

An empresario grant was made to a contractor who, in return for bringing settlers onto a grant, would receive one-fourth of the grant himself. Thus, *Recopilación* 4.5.6 did not provide for four square leagues to be given to a municipality as the majority opinion had held. Rather, it provided for four square leagues to be allocated as follows: three-fourths to the inhabitants and one-fourth to the contractor after sufficient lands for a town site and for common lands were set aside, as long as the empresario met the terms of his agreement. The primary conditions of the contract were that the empresario provide thirty families who would each build a house and have a specified number of livestock.[45] If the empresario failed to meet the terms of his agreement, the four square leagues would revert to the crown, and he would be fined one thousand ounces of gold. This law did not even come close to providing for four square leagues of land to a villa or other municipality.[46]

Encouraged by the analysis in Justice Murray's dissent, the U.S. government appealed the decision of the Court of Private Land Claims to the U.S. Supreme Court, which reversed the decision of the lower court. The Supreme Court's forty-three-page opinion written by Justice Edward D. White went beyond Murray's dissent on two major points. It cited additional historical evidence (mostly mythical and incorrect) about the early history of Santa Fe, and it discussed the Brownsville and San Francisco cases, claiming an analogy with the Santa Fe claim.[47]

Arguing the Supreme Court case for the plaintiff were Thomas B. Catron and William H. Pope. Catron was probably the lead attorney, and though he was hated by many Santa Feans for his aggressive acquisition and sale of large land grants and had narrowly escaped an assassination attempt a few years earlier,[48] he probably knew more about the history of the Villa of Santa Fe than anyone in the august chambers of the U.S. Supreme Court on the seventh and eighth of January 1896, when the case was argued. It is thus unaccountable that Justice Edward White could write in his opinion that Santa Fe was settled "in the midst of the native Indians . . . as early as 1543 . . . by deserters from the Spanish military force under Coronado who refused to accompany their commander on his return to Mexico."[49] This wildly inaccurate statement indicates how far removed (both physically and in understanding) Justice White was from New Mexico, the Southwest, and the laws of Spain. Justice White's selection of citations for the opinion also reveals a snobbishness regarding, and even prejudice toward, the laws he was charged with interpreting and, indeed, on which the decision would turn. He cited Gustavus Schmidt's characterization of the *Recopilación* as "derived from the orders, decrees and regulations of different sovereigns and often temporary in their character [which] are often dignified with the title of laws," revealing a deep-seated prejudice that was all too common among lawyers and judges in the late nineteenth century.[50]

Appointed to the Supreme Court in February of 1894, Edward D. White was a U.S. senator who had developed into a corpulent, thick-maned legislator whose position on virtually every public policy issue was "what is good for Louisiana sugar is good for America." Justice White famously interpreted the language of the Sherman Antitrust Act prohibiting *all* business combinations in restraint of trade to prohibit only *unreasonable* restraints on trade, thus ushering in the concept of judicial subjectivity in both statutory and constitutional interpretation.[51]

In *U.S. v. Santa Fe*, Justice White held that *Recopilación* 4.5.6 could not be construed as providing a four-square-league grant to the Villa of Santa Fe and that the laws involved in the Brownsville, and especially the San Francisco, case applied only to settlements established after 1789. The 1789 Plan of Pitic (the settlement plan for the town of Pitic, now Hermasillo, Sonora) may have expanded the provisions of the *Recopilación* to provide for a four-square-league entitlement even when no grant had been made, but simply an agreement to found a municipality. Even if the history of the founding of Santa Fe could provide a basis for such an agreement, the villa's founding in 1610 meant that the 1789 provisions of the Plan of Pitic would not apply. Thus, the claim of the City of Santa Fe was rejected by the U.S. Supreme Court, reversing the decision of the Court of Private Land Claims. While Justice White's decision may have been technically correct, it left the ownership of the municipality of Santa Fe up in the air.[52]

Since the Land Claims Court had rejected most of the small private land grants that overlapped the Santa Fe League, and since James Purdy, the lawyer for those claims, had not appealed that decision, the inhabitants of Santa Fe in 1900 were left in a rather absurd position: they were living in a no-man's-land where no one knew for sure who owned the land upon which Santa Fe had been established almost three hundred years earlier. Luckily, the San Francisco case had established a precedent for seeking relief from Congress, to which the city now turned for help.[53] On 9 April 1900 Congress passed an act releasing and quitclaiming to the City of Santa Fe all the lands within the four square leagues that the municipality had fought so hard for. Thus, with the stroke of a pen the Santa Fe League was created where none had existed before. The city then issued deeds to occupants of land within the Santa Fe League—those who owned land under valid deeds—which served as quitclaims from the United States to the property described. The city retained "all parks, streets, alleys, vacant unoccupied lands or other public places," and the United States reserved its federal title to land and buildings located within the league, such as the federal courthouse and Fort Marcy.[54]

Thus ended the saga of the Santa Fe League. It never existed under Spain or Mexico but was, in effect, granted to the inhabitants of Santa Fe by the Congress of the United States in 1900. Decades of litigation of the Santa Fe grant might seem like a waste of time and legal talent, but this work was probably necessary to build the record of the historical existence of Santa Fe before Congress could grant the Santa Fe League. It is unfortunate that the numerous documents introduced into evidence were not organized and indexed in some fashion, for study of those documents without the motive of acquiring land might shed light on questions about the early history of Santa Fe that we are still struggling with.[55] It is supremely ironic that the most important document, the one that could have convinced the Supreme Court and all the judges of the Court of Private Land Claims of some official authorization for the founding of the Villa of Santa Fe, was not discovered until the 1920s. Lansing B. Bloom discovered the instructions for the founding of Santa Fe in the General Archive of the Indies in Seville, Spain, "which directed Governor

Peralta to inform himself of the condition of said settlements endeavoring before any thing else the foundation and settlement of the Villa they claim. . . . Until the above mentioned Villa shall have been founded and inhabited nothing else shall be attended to."[56] After Governor Peralta had chosen a site for the villa he was to mark out an area in its center for propios (like the Ciénega), streets, and public buildings. Whether that was done in 1610 is not clear, but this document establishes how important it was to Viceroy Velasco that the Villa of Santa Fe be established. The introduction into evidence of the instructions of Viceroy Velasco could have changed the outcome of the litigation about the Santa Fe grant, though it was not the grant from the king that the plaintiffs had been searching for.[57]

The disciplines of history, anthropology, and archaeology were still in their infancy at that time. Many of the early historians of New Mexico, such as Ralph Emerson Twitchell and L. Bradford Prince, were lawyers who probably became interested in the field as they learned about New Mexico in their legal cases.[58] Adolph Bandelier was at the height of his career just about the time the Santa Fe case was tried. Other eminent archaeologists, anthropologists, and historians were just beginning their careers in the first decades of the twentieth century, studying Pueblo ruins and searching for documents in the archives of Spain and Mexico. The important work of scholars such as Lansing B. Bloom and of the next generation of scholars, such as Herbert E. Bolton, France V. Scholes, George P. Hammond, Charles W. Hackett, Edgar L. Hewett, Frederick W. Hodge, Alfred V. Kidder, and Paul A. F. Walter, would provide answers to many of the questions raised by this land grant litigation.[59]

The Cristóbal Nieto Grant

Another mythical Santa Fe land grant is the Cristóbal Nieto grant, whose fascinating history in the seventeenth and eighteenth centuries bore little re-lationship to the claim submitted to the Court of Private Land Claims in the late nineteenth century by lawyer James Purdy. Purdy's attempt to construct a bogus history whereby he stretched the boundaries of a fifteen-acre grant into a twelve-hundred-acre one, changed the name from the Nieto to the Pino grant, and jiggered the genealogy to tie the claimant to the grantee was remi-niscent of the shenanigans of Gaspar Ortiz y Alarid, the first petitioner for the Santa Fe grant. Hidden behind the made-up story was a fascinating real tale of abduction, captivity, and the mixed-blood children of Nieto's wife, Petrona Pacheco, that contained the makings of an episode of *Don Quixote* or *The Tempest*. The most exciting parts of the story of the Cristóbal Nieto grant occurred before the grant was made and at the time of confirmation of the grant in the late 1800s. What happened before the Cristóbal Nieto grant was made concerned Nieto's wife more then Cristóbal Nieto himself.

When Cristóbal Nieto's father, Alcalde José Nieto, heard the news of the Pueblo Indian uprising at Galisteo on 10 August 1680, he rounded up his family at his nearby estancia and tried to escape. Tragically, José Nieto, his wife (Lucía), and his daughters (María and Juana) were killed by Galisteo Indians, but fortunately for him, Cristóbal Nieto was away from home, either in Sonora or El Paso, and survived. Nieto's wife, Petrona Pacheco Nieto, and two of their children were taken captive by Pueblo Indians during the confusion and taken to San Juan Pueblo (now Ohkay Owingeh Pueblo), where they lived for twelve years. By 10 May 1700, when Cristóbal Nieto returned to Santa Fe and received a revalidation of a small land grant on the south side of the Santa Fe River, his wife, Petrona, had been through a saga of loss and captivity at San Juan Pueblo that has the makings of a good historical adventure movie. At the time of the reconquest of New Mexico in 1692, Petrona Pacheco Nieto was "rescued" from San Juan Pueblo by Roque Madrid, by which time Petrona had given birth to three more daughters (these numbers vary) in captivity. Little is known about the conditions under which Petrona Pacheco Nieto was held captive by the Pueblo Indians, but apparently she was treated well and became part of a San Juan Pueblo family.[60]

It was not uncommon for captive Spaniards to be adopted into Pueblo families and clans, to marry and have children, and sometimes to be so well treated that they preferred to stay among their captors. This was the case throughout early America and was described by John Demos in a book about the 1704 capture of the John Williams family by Mohawk Indians in Deerfield, Massachusetts.[61] In Texas, the abduction by Comanches of Cynthia Ann Parker was front-page news in 1836, but even more sensational was her refusal to return to her white family after she became the wife of a prominent war chief and bore three children. One of those children was Quanah Parker, who later became the last and most powerful Comanche leader. Cynthia Ann was "rescued" in 1861 and restored to her relatives but was never reconciled to the loss of her Comanche family.[62] Closer to New Mexico is the case of

Juana "la Galvana" Hurtado, who lived on a rancho near Zia Pueblo and who was also abducted at the outbreak of the Pueblo Revolt in 1680. Juana Hurtado lived with the Navajos for the next twelve years during which time she bore two children and may have been adopted into a Navajo clan. In 1692 Juana la Galvana was ransomed by her half brother and returned to Spanish society. Surprisingly, as James Brooks notes, "instead of being stigmatized by her experience, Juana used her connections with Spanish, Pueblo, and Navajo society to make trading contacts that allowed her to acquire a substantial amount of property."[63]

Unlike Juana Hurtado, who was only seven at the time she was captured, Petrona Pacheco Nieto was married with three children when she was abducted. However, like Juana, whose mother was a Zia Indian, Petrona's grandfather was a mestizo with some connection to San Juan. In 1628 Gerónimo Pacheco, a soldier at the Santa Fe presidio, was accused of "having taken part in certain pagan games at San Juan Pueblo. He denied the charges." Petrona's grandfather's connection to San Juan Pueblo may help explain her abduction to that pueblo.[64] From the pueblo's point of view, the incorporation of an outsider with some connection to the Pueblo people could provide the pueblo with a mediator as well as a translator. Petrona Pacheco and her three children fathered by a Pueblo Indian man may well have provided a link that continued between the family and San Juan Pueblo. Petrona had no choice but to leave the pueblo when she was "rescued" by Vargas, but if given a choice she may have preferred her life there.[65]

When Diego de Vargas entered San Juan Pueblo on 2 October 1692, three Spanish captives (and their children) were released to him, including Petrona Pacheco Nieto. Nieto's relatives recognized Petrona, who was released with "three sons and daughters, all of whom she had at this time,"[66] although accounts varied sharply as to the actual number of children Petrona had with her when she was released from captivity. It was common knowledge among the New Mexico settlers at El Paso that "three or four mestizas" were being held captive by the various pueblos, and rescuing them was one of the first priorities of the reconquest of New Mexico.[67] Petrona was taken to El Paso with a larger group of captives who had been held during the revolt in various pueblos. One of four Spaniards on the list of freed captives, Petrona Nieto is first on the list "with five daughters and two sons" (again, the numbers are different in every account) and escorted by Captain Roque Madrid. It is not clear which of Petrona Nieto's six surviving children were born in captivity, but the most likely are Josefa Pacheco (who married Jacinto Perea), Sebastiana, and another Petrona.[68]

In 1697 Cristóbal Nieto, now reunited with Petrona, was living in Santa Fe with their son Simón and four daughters: Sebastiána, María, Lucía, and Josefa (the young Petrona Pacheco does not appear until 1712). In 1697, as part of a general distribution of livestock and supplies by the Spanish government, they received 10.5 varas of wool, 8.75 fanegas of maize, twenty-two mantas, and animals consisting of twenty-five sheep, three cows, and a bull. Cristóbal and Petrona (who is listed as "Petronila" in the livestock distribution) must have been farming land in Santa Fe at the time; in August of 1697 they apparently received a grant of land from Governor Pedro Rodríguez Cubero (1697–1703).[69] Somehow, the title papers to the 1697 land grant were destroyed before possession of the land could be delivered, so in 1700 Cristóbal Nieto asked Governor Cubero (serving his second term) to revalidate the earlier grant. Apparently, Alcalde Antonio de Aguilera Isasi (who was then serving on the cabildo [town council] of Santa Fe) did not investigate whether the grant would prejudice Nieto's neighbors, and he placed Nieto in possession of a tract of land along the Santa Fe River.[70] The boundaries included the Camino Real and the house of Domingo de la Barreda, the armorer at the Santa Fe presidio. The armorer was an important military official responsible for the repair and maintenance of the weapons and equipment of the presidio soldiers. He was one of the few military officials, besides the governor and perhaps the captain of the presidio, who received a salary from the royal treasury. Barreda had land at La Ciénega, and his presence next to Cristóbal Nieto shows that this area was where important settlers lived, though not the elite who lived north of the river near the plaza.[71] On 1 August 1700 Aguilera met Nieto at his home and performed a rudimentary survey "starting . . . from a small cedar standing behind the house, and some piles of stones, running in a straight line to the main road, and from a small acequia to a pile of small stones separating the lands of Domingo de la Barreda, and from said pile of stones running in a straight line to the ruins of an old house behind said house of Domingo de la Barreda, to the river and running along the same to the first cedar." From later records it appears that the grant covered a small tract of land south of the Santa Fe River in the Analco barrio.[72]

By early 1712 Cristóbal Nieto had died, but the composition of his family was clarified by records from a distribution of tools to Santa Fe settlers later in

1712. According to the list, five members of the Nieto family were living in separate households as heads of families probably on the Cristóbal Nieto grant. In household 143 was Simón Nieto, who was buying and selling land in the area before and after the tool distribution. In household 144 was the widow Petrona Pacheco, who was living alone. Next to her was Jacinto Perea, married to Josefa Pacheco, a daughter of Petrona by a Pueblo Indian man. Next to her in household 146 was Lucía Nieto, who was married to Salvador Olguín, a soldier at the Santa Fe presidio who was absent at the time of the tool distribution. Finally, next to Lucía in household 147 was Petrona Nieto the younger, another daughter of Petrona Pacheco by a Pueblo Indian man.[73] Thus, at least two of those listed in the record of the distribution of tools were probably children of Petrona by a Pueblo Indian man from San Juan Pueblo: Petrona Pacheco the younger and Josefa Pacheco. These were the settlers living on the real (not the fabricated) Cristóbal Nieto grant. Other Nietos living in Santa Fe included Simon's nephew, Francisco Nieto, the son of Simón's sister Lucía and the soldier Salvador Olguín.[74]

By 1750, when a census was taken for the Villa of Santa Fe, Francisco was the only Nieto head of household left in Santa Fe. Francisco Nieto was living with his wife, Isabel Gutiérrez; his aunt María (Magdalena) Nieto, daughter of Cristóbal; his mother, Lucía Nieto; and his aunt Petrona Pacheco, daughter of the San Juan Pueblo man. Francisco's grandmother Petrona Nieto the elder died in 1750, so the reference to Petrona Pacheco must have been to Francisco's aunt, his mother's (Lucía's) half sister, who was mentioned in the 1712 tool distribution.[75]

The Pino Grant

The Pino grant was not really a grant at all but was tied to the Cristóbal Nieto grant in the 1890s because of the family name and because it was convenient for lawyer James Purdy to make a larger claim by consolidating the Pino grant with the real Cristóbal Nieto grant. In 1765 Francisco Nieto, who was serving as a soldier in the Santa Fe presidio, partitioned land south of Agua Fría that he had purchased from Andrés Montoya of Cieneguilla. This land was several miles south of the Nieto grant but would become associated with it. The partition document is the first to connect a Nieto with the place called El Pino. The land was described as being "in the locality of El Pueblo Quemado [Agua Fría], towards El Pino, Rio Abajo," and bounded on the north by the hills, on the south by the Camino Real, on the east by an arroyo that divided the lands of Pueblo Quemado, and on the west by some tall oak trees marking the boundary of the lands of Lázaro García at El Pino. Francisco Nieto had purchased the land from Montoya partly with funds provided by Jacinto Perea, husband to Francisco's aunt Josefa Pacheco. Josefa was one of the children fathered by a Pueblo Indian man during the time her mother, Petrona Nieto, was a captive at San Juan Pueblo. When Jacinto Perea married Josefa Pacheco, she was described in the *diligencia matrimonial* (prenuptial investigation) as "a daughter of the church" or of unknown parentage.[76] Jacinto Perea was also a soldier at the Santa Fe presidio, where he must have met Francisco Nieto. Jacinto was one of the few survivors who escaped after the 1720 surprise attack on the Villasur Expedition by Plains Indians (Pawnees), when thirty-two Spaniards and twelve Pueblo Indians were killed.[77] In the partition with Francisco Nieto, the property south of Agua Fría was divided in half, giving Jacinto Perea 4,463 Castilian varas from east to west. Jacinto Perea seemed to have accumulated sufficient funds to purchase this and other property in Santa Fe.[78]

After this point the documentation on the Nieto family in Santa Fe and the rancho at El Pino is sparse. The only other available document is from 1788, when the ranch at El Pino was the subject of a partition suit by Rita Padilla, the daughter-in-law of Juan García, who died owning an interest in "a Rancho of cultivable lands at the place of El Pino." This land was not part of the 1765 partition between Jacinto Perea and Francisco Nieto, nor was it part of the Cristóbal Nieto grant. Nevertheless, when the Cristóbal Nieto grant was submitted to the Court of Private Land Claims as El Pino grant in 1893, this document was filed with the court. It seems to have been used by attorney James Purdy to expand the boundaries of the Nieto grant to twelve hundred acres, much more than the probable fifteen-acre size of the original Cristóbal Nieto grant.[79]

Based on all the evidence from the descriptions of the land in these and other deeds, the following picture emerges of the early history of Santa Fe. Records of owners of encomiendas (encomenderos) that did survive the Pueblo Revolt refer to spheres of influence exercised around the pre-revolt pueblos by Spaniards who later received land grants from Governors Diego de Vargas and Pedro Rodríguez Cubero. The encomenderos for Cieneguilla Pueblo were Cristóbal and Francisco de Anaya Almazán, names that show up in the Francisco de Anaya Almazán grant west of the so-called El Pino grant (see chapter 5, "La Ciénega and Cieneguilla Pueblos").[80] The location of the Francisco de Anaya Almazán grant a little southwest of El Pino, toward Cieneguilla, suggests that this tract was quite a distance from and quite a bit larger than the Cristóbal Nieto grant in the Analco barrio. In fact, the two tracts were not connected in any way, except that Francisco Nieto and Jacinto Perea were both members of the Nieto/Pacheco family. Francisco Nieto was a grandson (not a son) of Cristóbal Nieto through his daughter Lucía, while Jacinto Perea was married to Josefa Pacheco, the daughter of Petrona Pacheco. The first use of the name El Pino is in the 1765 transaction whereby Francisco Nieto and Jacinto Perea partitioned the large tract of land the two purchased near El Pino, partly with Jacinto Perea's money. By the 1890s, largely through the efforts of attorney James Purdy, this land had morphed into the new Cristóbal Nieto grant.[81]

On 11 February 1893 a Juan Nieto who claimed to be a direct descendant of Cristóbal Nieto filed a claim with the Court of Private Land Claims for confirmation of the Cristóbal Nieto grant. The land claimed was also said to be known as El Pino or El Pino Ranch and was described as containing twelve hundred acres. This land was not the Cristóbal Nieto grant made by Governor Rodríguez Cubero in 1700. The boundaries of the claimed tract were a combination of boundaries from the 1700 Cristóbal Nieto grant and the 1765 Francisco Nieto/Jacinto Perea purchase and partition: the Santa Fe River on the north, the Camino de los Carros on the south, the land of Domingo de la Barreda (armorer of the Santa Fe presidio) on the west, and the house of Domingo de la Barreda on the east. Attorney James Purdy combined boundaries from the Cristóbal Nieto grant with boundaries from the much larger 1765 El Pino purchase/partition to make it seem like this area was one large grant made to Cristóbal Nieto. Attorney Purdy, who prosecuted most of the claims for land within the Santa Fe area, took the south boundary of the Nieto/Perea El Pino tract, the Camino de los Carros (today's Cerrillos Road), which does not appear in the Cristóbal Nieto grant description, and combined it with the house and lands of Domingo de la Barreda on the east and west, boundaries that do appear in the original Cristóbal Nieto grant but not in the 1765 Nieto/Perea El Pino purchase and partition.[82] Given this fictitious legal description, the land claimed by Juan Nieto could not be located on the ground. But no one realized this fact at the time because the land claims case never came to trial.[83]

Lawyer James Purdy had combined the legal descriptions of the two tracts (the Cristóbal Nieto grant in the Analco region of the Villa of Santa Fe and the much larger El Pino Ranch purchase south of Agua Fría) to make a nonexistent tract of land. Juan Nieto, the plaintiff before the Court of Private Land Claims, could tie himself to Cristóbal Nieto and his grant, but since that grant was relatively small, lawyer Purdy tried to tie Juan Nieto to other members of the Nieto family who owned land in the Santa Fe area. Purdy did not worry about competing claims since he represented most of the small Santa Fe grants with claims before the Court of Private Land Claims; he simply drew the map of Santa Fe land grants to suit his purpose. Grants like the Sebastián de Vargas grant, south of El Pino, were simply expanded without regard for the original boundaries.[84] Adjoining land grants represented by the same lawyer represent a potential conflict of interest: lawyer James Purdy had nothing to gain by having the boundary around his client's property correctly determined since he received a portion of all the confirmed grants no matter where the boundaries were located.[85]

In addition to the creative construction of a new legal description to increase the size of the Cristóbal Nieto grant, Purdy submitted a genealogy for Juan Nieto that was mostly false. While it seemed to connect Juan Nieto with Cristóbal Nieto, several other Nieto family lines that might have had a claim to the Cristóbal Nieto grant were unaccounted for. The Nieto genealogy submitted to the Court of Private Land Claims showed the plaintiff Juan Nieto to be a direct descendant of Cristóbal Nieto through his only son, Francisco Nieto. As we have seen, Cristóbal Nieto had *three* children who survived the Pueblo Revolt and Petrona Pacheco's captivity at San Juan Pueblo: Simón, María, and Lucía, but no Francisco. All three show up in Santa Fe censuses and other records, and their heirs were the descendants of Cristóbal Nieto. Lucía Nieto and Salvador Olguín had a son named Francisco who used the name Nieto though his father was Olguín and was probably the one involved in the 1765 El Pino partition with Jacinto Perea. It was convenient to link Juan Nieto, the petitioner, with Francisco Nieto since attorney Purdy needed to connect the 1765 El Pino tract with the Cristóbal Nieto grant to increase the size of the claim. But they were not connected since, as mentioned, El Pino was not a land grant and was located south of Agua Fría toward La Ciénega and Cieneguilla, several miles from the Cristóbal Nieto grant. The only justification for inclusion of the El Pino tract in the Cristóbal Nieto claim would have been if it had been acquired by the Nieto family as an addition to the Nieto grant and was adjacent to that grant. This was clearly not the case.[86]

Even if El Pino had been adjacent to and connected with the Cristóbal Nieto grant, other heirs besides the descendants of Francisco Nieto would have been entitled to the grant. Also entitled were the heirs of Cristóbal Nieto's other children through Petrona Pacheco (Simón and María Magdalena) *and* one of Petrona Pacheco's mestizo children: Josefa Pacheco. Josefa was married to Jacinto Perea, who put up at least half of the purchase price for the Pino tract. Even if the Nieto grant and El Pino had been connected, Juan Nieto, the claimant before the Court of Private Land Claims, would have had to share the land if his claim was approved by the court, not only with the descendants of Simón Nieto and María Magdalena Nieto, but also with those of Josefa Pacheco, the daughter of a Pueblo Indian man and not Cristóbal Nieto.

The Court of Private Land Claims did not unravel this mystery because no trial was held. When the case came up for hearing on 11 June 1898, Attorney James Purdy announced that the plaintiff no longer wished to prosecute the suit, so the court rejected the claim. Attorney Purdy had been successful in obtaining confirmations of a few Santa Fe grants, such as the large Sebastián de Vargas grant (also based on sketchy evidence), and he knew it was unlikely that the Court of Private Land Claims would confirm the Cristóbal Nieto grant.[87] As we have seen, the City of Santa Fe had been successful in April 1894 in establishing its right to the so-called Santa Fe League, which partially conflicted with the Nieto/El Pino grant—another reason that Purdy dropped the Nieto claim. As mentioned earlier, the opinion of the Court of Private Land Claims confirming the Santa Fe League was overturned by the U.S. Supreme Court in 1897, leaving the ownership of all the land in Santa Fe in limbo for a few years, until the U.S. Congress "passed an act releasing and quitclaiming to the City of Santa Fe all the lands within the four square leagues" on 9 April 1900.[88]

When the house of cards that was the Cristóbal Nieto grant collapsed and the bubble that was the Santa Fe League burst, what is left? First, we have learned a great deal about the Nieto family and their place in the early history of Santa Fe, replacing some myths of Santa Fe with a more nuanced history. Working with living members of the Nieto family like Dawn Nieto, who has investigated her DNA in order to find her place in the Nieto family story, we begin to see that many of the first generation Nietos were actually Pachecos, with ties to San Juan Pueblo (today's Ohkay Owingeh) and possibly other

Nieto Genealogy

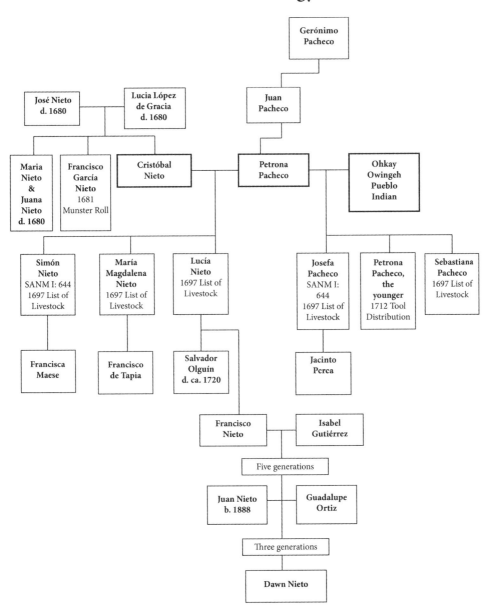

FIGURE 1. Nieto Genealogy, by Malcolm Ebright.

pueblos. Like Juana la Galvana, who used her captivity by Navajos during the Pueblo Revolt to her advantage, Josefa Pacheco was likely able to use her mestiza status, along with her mestizo husband, Jacinto Perea, to their mutual advantage. Hers could be an example of James Brooks's theory about the special status of women captives and their children during the Pueblo Revolt: "Children born in captivity seemed to be implicitly accepted as attached dependents, [and there was] an undercurrent of affinity between former captors [Pueblo Indians] and redeemed women and children."[89]

In other words, children like Josefa Pacheco, born in captivity, married to mestizos like Jacinto Perea, probably retained "an undercurrent of affinity" with their former captors that may have benefited them economically. This benefit can be inferred from the fact that Jacinto Perea became a landowner at El Pino since he was the one who put up a portion of the purchase price for the tract in 1765. As mestizos living in the barrio of Analco, Jacinto Perea and Josefa Pacheco must have been able to negotiate between two worlds: the world of the Spanish *vecino*/landowner and the world of the Pueblo Indian.[90] The story of the Nieto/Pacheco family helps us to piece together a more complete picture of early Santa Fe and the settlement south of the Santa Fe River known as Analco, where mostly Mexican Indians lived. This is a hidden history not found in most land grant records.[91]

As the myths and fictions about early Santa Fe are being discussed and debunked, new myths are springing up that are just as hard to lay to rest. One such myth—that the Villa of Santa Fe was founded not in 1610 but in 1607, 1608, or 1609—is not only damaging to the true and complete history of early Santa Fe, but it tends to emphasize the Spanish viewpoint almost exclusively with little regard for the Indian presence in and around Santa Fe. A disproportionate amount of scholarship and energy is thus focused on the Spanish presence, and our understanding of events is based solely on Spanish documents. This new myth is based primarily on one document: a certificate of services of rejected interim governor Juan Martínez de Montoya that was first discussed by France V. Scholes in 1944.[92] As a result of the 1944 article by Scholes, the Museum of New Mexico Foundation tracked down the document Scholes had studied, purchased it, and deposited it in the Fray Angélico Chávez History Library in Santa Fe in 1994. In the same year, an unannotated, anonymous article in *El Palacio* suggested that Santa Fe was founded as early as 1607,[93] and James Ivey has suggested that Santa Fe was founded in 1607 by Juan Martínez de Montoya "and may have been officially established in 1605."[94] Recently, some other eminent scholars have lent credibility to this earlier founding of Santa Fe in an apparent race to place Santa Fe on a par with Jamestown as the earliest settlement in America.[95]

Before rushing to judgment regarding a 1607 founding of Santa Fe, we should examine the Martínez y Montoya document more closely, as José Antonio Esquibel has done. Esquibel takes the phrase, "el haber hecho Plaza en Santa Fe," upon which much of the scholarly debate is based, and provides the translation "he made a [military] post [or camp] at Santa Fe," rather than "he established the Plaza of Santa Fe." Based on an understanding of the totality of the situation at Santa Fe in the first decade of the 1600s, Esquibel's translation and other evidence show that Santa Fe probably existed as a settlement and military post by 1607 or before, but the founding of the villa did not take place until 1610. If Santa Fe was a military post by 1607 or earlier, it is likely that the Analco settlement was in existence south of the Santa Fe River at that time, since many of the presidio soldiers and most of the Indian auxiliaries were Mexican Indians. The Analco settlement was made up of people like the ancestors of Cristóbal Nieto and the Tlascalan Indian Juan de León Brito, both of whom received grants confirming their pre-revolt holdings in the Analco area.[96]

The actual pre-revolt settlement pattern around Santa Fe can be inferred from the early grants made by Governor Vargas. In a formal order promulgated before he left El Paso, Vargas promised the members of his expedition that he would "give them the lands, home-sites, and haciendas they had left at the time of the uprising."[97] Despite Governor Vargas's efforts to achieve a balanced land use pattern in Santa Fe, with most landowners having sufficient land to plant from one to two fanegas of corn (about nine to eighteen acres), prime farming lands were concentrated in the hands of a few elites, similar to the probable pre-revolt land distribution pattern. Making this possible were various forms of common lands in the villa, which provided resources to all members of the community, and particularly those who acted in a public capacity like the governor and resident priests. These common lands in and around Santa Fe included the Ciénega, lands attached to the convento (the residence of the priests), lands set aside for the governor's exclusive use, common lands farmed by the Analco Indians (*tierras de San Miguel* or *tierras de los Mexicanos*), common grazing lands for the presidio's horse herd, and common wood-gathering land.[98] Most important for the average citizen of early Santa Fe were the

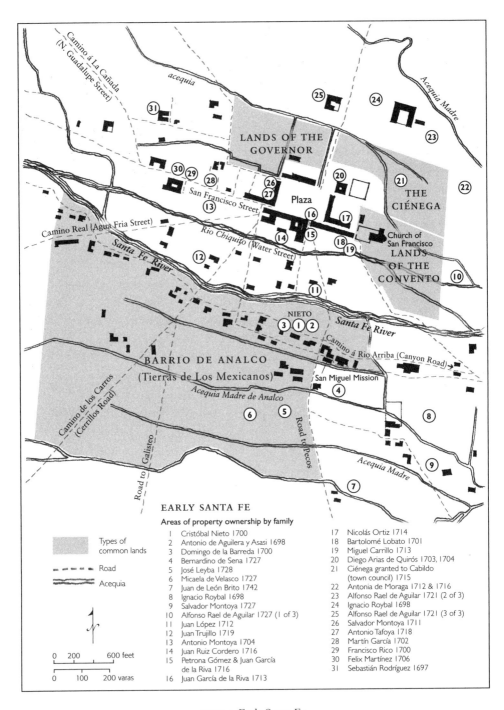

MAP I. Early Santa Fe.

EARLY SANTA FE

Areas of property ownership by family

Types of common lands

- - - Road

Acequia

0   200   600 feet

0   100   200 varas

1 Cristóbal Nieto 1700
2 Antonio de Aguilera y Asasi 1698
3 Domingo de la Barreda 1700
4 Bernardino de Sena 1727
5 José Leyba 1728
6 Micaela de Velasco 1727
7 Juan de León Brito 1742
8 Ignacio Roybal 1698
9 Salvador Montoya 1727
10 Alfonso Rael de Aguilar 1727 (1 of 3)
11 Juan López 1712
12 Juan Trujillo 1719
13 Antonio Montoya 1704
14 Juan Ruiz Cordero 1716
15 Petrona Gómez & Juan García de la Riva 1716
16 Juan García de la Riva 1713

17 Nicolás Ortiz 1714
18 Bartolomé Lobato 1701
19 Miguel Carrillo 1713
20 Diego Arias de Quirós 1703, 1704
21 Ciénega granted to Cabildo (town council) 1715
22 Antonia de Moraga 1712 & 1716
23 Alfonso Rael de Aguilar 1721 (2 of 3)
24 Ignacio Roybal 1698
25 Alfonso Rael de Aguilar 1721 (3 of 3)
26 Salvador Montoya 1711
27 Antonio Tafoya 1718
28 Martín García 1702
29 Francisco Rico 1700
30 Felix Martínez 1706
31 Sebastián Rodríguez 1697

common woodlands located primarily to the northeast of Santa Fe, known as *el monte*. A public road east of the road to Tesuque led to this area, and it was important to the people of Santa Fe that this road be kept open. A settlement or outpost (*puesto*) called Río Arriba was developing upriver and outside the jurisdiction of the Villa of Santa Fe by the 1690s, and whatever farmlands there were in the vicinity of the Puesto de Río Arriba (located at Upper Canyon Road) were probably unirrigated and dependent on rainfall (*de temporal*). Most of the lands surrounding the Puesto de Río Arriba were common woodlands available to the residents of Santa Fe for firewood, vigas, and other building materials.[99]

Just as the landscape and land ownership pattern of early Santa Fe may have been different than what has traditionally been pictured, so were the early settlers a different lot than was formerly imagined. The language of the U.S. Supreme Court in *U.S. v. Santa Fe* conjures a picture of early settlement "in the midst of Native Indians," while others painted a picture of a deserted place picked by the Spanish authorities because no Indians were there. The truth is probably somewhere in the middle. While no Pueblo Indians were settled there, a group of Mexican Indians and mestizos may have lived in the Analco barrio even before Martínez y Montoya's arrival around 1607.[100] The Analco settlement grew in size as it was situated on the best lands south of the Santa Fe River, the tierras de San Miguel or tierras de los Mexicanos.[101] Analco's inhabitants were people like Domingo de la Barreda, the presidial armorer whose land bordered the Cristóbal Nieto grant in 1697, and Petrona Pacheco's grandfather Gerónimo Pacheco. Gerónimo Pacheco, who was a mestizo, probably the reason Petrona Pacheco was referred to as a mestiza, also had some connection with San Juan Pueblo that might explain why Petrona was taken captive there in 1680. As mentioned earlier, Gerónimo was charged by the Inquisition with taking part in a ceremony at the pueblo in 1628. Although he was a mestizo with ties to the Pueblo people, his granddaughter was married to Roque Madrid, a distinguished elite who played a part in the events narrated earlier in this chapter. Roque Madrid had escorted Petrona Pacheco to El Paso in 1692, along with other former captives. The fact that Petrona and Roque Madrid were related explains why he recognized her at San Juan Pueblo and why he was the one to escort her to El Paso.[102]

An understanding of the pre-1610 settlement of Mexican Indians in Analco helps to answer the questions posed at the beginning of this chapter: why did Governor Pedro de Peralta pick the present location as the site for the villa when later governors tried to move it, when was the Villa of Santa Fe founded, and was there an existing settlement at the site of the barrio of Analco?[103] Governor Peralta picked the location of the Villa of Santa Fe and its plaza because the more preferable site south of the river in the Analco barrio was already occupied. While the site north of the river had plenty of water from springs around the Ciénega, there may have been too much water, which made much of the area swampy. The earlier Pueblo people picked the hills north of town, above the swampy areas in what became Fort Marcy, to build their villages, the ruins of which would still have been visible to Juan de Oñate, Juan Martínez de Montoya, and Pedro Peralta. But the area south of the Santa Fe River, irrigated today by the *acequia madre*, was considered the most desirable area.[104]

Early Santa Fe was not a vacant area where the Spaniards settled, imposing their grid-pattern villa on the landscape. Instead, early Santa Fe and vicinity appear to have been a series of isolated settlements, from south to north: La Ciénega, Cieneguilla, El Álamo, El Pino, Agua Fría, Analco, the fortified and walled Villa of Santa Fe, and the puesto of Río Arriba, all surrounded by common lands, such as the common woodlands around the outpost of Río Arriba and the common agricultural lands farmed by the Analco Indians (tierras de San Miguel).

What the early deeds and land grant documents tell us about early Santa Fe is different from the map drawn by lawyer James Purdy or the mythical Santa Fe League—it is a city different than we thought.[105]

CHAPTER THREE

THE OJO CALIENTE GRANT

T HE OJO CALIENTE AREA WAS THE SITE OF SEVERAL PREHISTORIC
   pueblos that were located there because of the hot springs from which the
name Ojo Caliente derives. These springs were sacred to the ancient Pueblo
people, who are said to have left the area in the early 1500s. The prehistoric
pueblo closest to and most connected with the hot springs was Posi-Ouinge,
said to be the pueblo where the mythical culture hero Poseyemu lived when he
was its cacique during a time of great prosperity. According to tradition, when
Poseyemu left the pueblo of Posi-Ouinge it fell into decline and was eventually
abandoned. In one account, the occupants of Posi-Ouinge are said to have
possessed "many green stones, [and] many shell beads . . . for they controlled
the boiling waters." Presumably the green stones were turquoise and they,
along with the shell beads, were left as offerings by those who used the springs
with the permission of Posi-Ouinge Pueblo.[1]

The main hot spring, known to the Tewa as Posipopi, or the Green Springs/
Greenness Pool because of the emerald algae that grew on the surrounding
rocks, was revered by the Tewa and other Pueblo peoples in the region. According
to Tewa myths, Poseyemu "used to enter this pool [the main hot springs]."
Poseyemu's grandmother was said to live in this spring, and he came to visit her
regularly. This sacred green-edged pool was changed and obscured when a bath-
house, owned and operated by land speculator Antonio Joseph in conjunction
with his hotel, was built over the pool.[2] A manuscript by ethnohistorian Adolph
Bandelier that was acquired by Joseph attributes the abandonment of

Posi-Ouinge to magic and witchcraft. It is fitting that Joseph, who not only acquired the hot springs but the entire Ojo Caliente grant as well, also acquired the Bandelier manuscript about Poseyemu and the hot springs. Hot springs were sacred to the Pueblo Indians and other indigenous people because they were dwelling places of native deities and openings through which spirits could pass between this world and the spirit world. By altering the natural features of the hot springs, Joseph altered the sacred nature of Posipopi, the Greenness Pool. While the sacred power of the hot springs could not be destroyed, Joseph's attempt to control the hot springs was a prelude to his acquisition of much of the land in the Ojo Caliente region.[3] Like the priest Bernardino de Sahagún, who studied and wrote about the religion of the Nahuas (Aztecs) in order to eradicate it and supplant it with Christianity, Joseph studied the sacred, historic background of the hot springs in order to acquire them and the land around them for commercial purposes.[4]

Evidence of farm plots "irrigated through stone-lined channels by water taken from an intermittent drainage" reveals the nature of Pueblo agriculture at Ojo Caliente before the arrival of the Spaniards.[5] Spanish settlement at Ojo Caliente began in the early 1700s, although its remote location made it difficult for the Spanish government to hold on to this area because of raids by the Utes and Comanches. Though little direct evidence has been found of early land grants to Spaniards, a lawsuit of 1735 reveals that Antonio Martín received a grant at Ojo Caliente around 1730. The details of this lawsuit help paint a picture of early farming at Ojo Caliente.

The litigation between Lázaro de Atienza and Antonio Martín turned on Martín's promise to give Atienza a deed to some land at Ojo Caliente if he would live there and improve it. Atienza complained to Alcalde Juan Esteban García de Noriega in 1735 that his brother-in-law, Antonio Martín, had promised to give him a tract of land within the grant Martín had received from Governor Juan Domingo Bustamante and was now reneging on his promise. The conditions of the gift were that Atienza would move to Ojo Caliente, live on the land, improve it, and help defend it against the raiding nomadic Indians. According to Atienza, the property was so thickly covered with trees that it was impossible to pass through either on foot or on horseback. Atienza cleared, plowed, and planted the land in 1733 when the donation was made, but Antonio Martín refused to give him a deed. In 1735 Atienza asked Alcalde García de Noriega to order Martín to either pay him for the work he had done improving the land over the past two years or give him the promised deed.[6]

Antonio Martín responded with his defense, which contains some useful information about irrigated agriculture in Ojo Caliente. He said that he had settled the land four or five years earlier (1730 or 1731) and that the land he had agreed to transfer to Atienza was "watered by my acequia and not uncultivated as he says, but broken because I had planted it two [or three years] before." As to the deed, Martín said he would give it, but only in the name of his sister, because were it not for the fact that Atienza was married to Martín's sister, he would not have invited him to the Ojo Caliente land at all.[7] As the charges and countercharges were hurled back and forth, Atienza claimed that the evidence of the work he had done could still be seen, and he urged Governor Cruzat y Góngora to appoint someone to inspect the land where "they will clearly see that many roots of trees will be found . . . which, because I was short of oxen, I cut and burned. Likewise the ashes can be seen even though they are mixed up with the good soil."[8] Governor Cruzat took testimony from witnesses who verified that Atienza had cleared the land and that Martín had planted it two years before Atienza received it (1731).[9] Finally, Governor Cruzat y Góngora ruled that Martín and not Atienza owned the contested land because even if Martín had promised it to Atienza, that promise was not made with the consent of his wife. Governor Cruzat y Góngora was clearly partial to Antonio Martín, for a wife's lack of consent was seldom used as the basis for setting aside a deed or a promise to give a deed, though it was required.[10] The governor was apparently unconvinced by all the testimony of the work done by Atienza on Martín's land; however, Cruzat y Góngora did provide Atienza some solace by awarding him the appraised value of his improvements, which came to thirty-seven pesos.[11] Atienza was somewhat vindicated by this award, but his suit to force Martín to live up to his promise had ultimately fallen on deaf ears.[12]

In August of 1747 the few Spanish settlers who had gradually settled on farms and ranches at Ojo Caliente were suddenly dislodged and forced to temporarily abandon their holdings by a devastating Ute/Comanche raid on Abiquiu and surrounding settlements. The raiders took twenty-three women and children captive, most of whom were never returned. Governor Codallos y Rabal's troops were not able to catch the Indians, though the settlers' militia did pick up their trail and pursue them, finding not the raiding party but only

the dead bodies of three women and a newborn baby. This horrific scene—
together with other similar Spanish casualties—was enough to convince the
settlers in the Abiquiu communities to temporarily leave their homes and
landholdings. They sought permission from Alcalde Juan de Abeyta to withdraw "to other places more secure and convenient because of the imminent
danger of losing their lives" because "they [were] few and unarmed." Indian
raids are certain, said the alcalde on behalf of the settlers, especially at Abiquiu,
"where they are almost within view of the pagan Indian enemies, Utes,
Comanches." Governor Codallos y Rabal granted the request to withdraw
temporarily on the condition that the settlers not lose their lands or houses.[13]

In 1749 a new governor succeeded Codallos y Rabal, bringing with him a
new approach to the difficult task of creating and protecting settlements in
northern New Mexico on the Ute, Comanche, and Jicarilla Apache frontier. As
mentioned earlier, Tomás Vélez Cachupín took quite seriously the Indian
threat and its chilling effect on peripheral Spanish settlements. Vélez Cachupín
had spent three years prior to his appointment in the household of Viceroy
Revillagigedo, learning about colonial administration in general and the views
of the viceroy on Indian policy in particular.[14] Viceroy Revillagigedo maintained a rather harsh position regarding indigenous nomadic people, a position that reached Vélez Cachupín in a formal way in April of 1750 through a
legal opinion by the viceroy's counselor general of war, the Marqués de
Altamira. Altamira set forth the policy to be followed regarding the Indian
threat, which he believed came primarily from the Comanche. Make peace
and encourage trade with the Comanche if possible, he advised, but "if not
they should be treated as enemies and attacked in their own lands until they
are exterminated, obliterated, and entirely destroyed." In particular, the governor of New Mexico was ordered to resettle the communities of Abiquiu,
Embudo, and Ojo Caliente. Six months before signing off on Altamira's order
from the viceroy, Vélez Cachupín issued his own order specifying in detail how
these communities were to be resettled.[15]

In March 1751 Vélez Cachupín's lieutenant governor, Bernardo Antonio
Bustamante y Tagle, who had recently completed the resettlement of Sandia
Pueblo, ordered the Ojo Caliente settlers to "reoccupy their homes and culti-
vate their lands within the term of two months" or lose title to their land.
Lieutenant Governor Bustamante y Tagle ordered the alcalde to ask each of the
settlers if they would return to Ojo Caliente and record their answers. The

answers given by the settlers provide valuable information about the beginnings of the Spanish settlement at Ojo Caliente and about its church.[16] Pablo Francisco Villalpando answered that he could not attend the meeting of the settlers because he was sick but that he would "resettle his lands in Ojo Caliente, just as soon as the other settlers reoccupy the settlement."[17] Five of the remaining settlers were not ready, however, and asked for an additional two months to make the resettlement because their houses and the church were in a tumbledown condition, they lacked oxen to plow the ground, "and for other reasons of no less weight."[18] Bustamante granted their request, giving them until October to make the resettlement,[19] but when Vélez Cachupín asked for a report on his return to the capital at the end of the year, Alcalde Juan José Lovato told him the settlers had not returned and he did not know why.[20] Governor Vélez Cachupín was not interested in reasons at this point. Since they had already promised to go, the governor ordered the settlers to return by "this next spring [1752] and resettle and occupy their homes as they promised and cultivate the land belonging to them." If they did not, they would lose their lands and he would fine them each twenty-five pesos.[21] Alcalde Lovato again notified the settlers of the governor's order, and this time they promised to "go and occupy their homes and cultivate their lands."[22]

Some settlers were more eager to return to Ojo Caliente than others. Most had houses there in differing states of repair, as well as fields that had been cultivated and irrigated, but the danger of Ute and Comanche raids was a huge deterrent. Francisco Durán was so eager to return that he moved to Ojo Caliente with his family as soon as he learned of Vélez Cachupín's order, even before notification by Alcalde Lovato. But when no one else had returned by late February of 1752, Durán asked Vélez Cachupín to assign an escort of soldiers to protect the Durán family.[23] Instead, Vélez Cachupín told Alcalde Lovato to proceed with the resettlement, and Lovato notified the remaining settlers to meet him at Ojo Caliente on 30 March 1752.[24] On that day Lovato reported that nine heads of family had resettled. Antonio Sandoval relinquished the land he had acquired from Antonio Martín (after Martín won the suit against Atienza) because Sandoval was too old to defend it. Alcalde Lovato signed a formal decree of resettlement in which he certified that Ojo Caliente had been reoccupied.[25] Resettlement was now complete, and Vélez Cachupín had complied with the viceroy's order. This resettlement of Ojo Caliente lasted for fourteen years until near the end of Vélez Cachupín's second term, when most of the settlers moved out again. New attempts needed to be made in the late 1760s to bring them back.[26]

In 1766 Alcalde Manuel García Pareja notified Vélez Cachupín that some settlers had "gone to settle some other places out of their fear of the enemies [the Utes and Comanches] . . . and have left their tracts of land to the care and protection of the few vecinos who are at said site."[27] The governor asked the Ojo Caliente settlers who had left the settlement their reasons for leaving; most said they had sold their land or had left tenants there. Vélez Cachupín then asked Francisco Durán, the first settler to return in 1752, and the remaining residents for their opinions.[28] The settlers responded that they would like the governor to order the resettlement of Ojo Caliente "with families who have firearms and gear for riding horseback." They did not want the resettlement to be made by those who would use the land only for grazing because then only unarmed livestock herders would be living at Ojo Caliente, and they would be more trouble than they were worth as potential defenders of the community.[29] Vélez Cachupín accordingly ordered that the land of settlers who would not return be considered public land available to other settlers who might apply for it, as long as they had adequate firearms to defend the community.[30]

Governor Vélez Cachupín was nearing the end of his second term as governor of New Mexico in mid-1766 and was not able to follow up on the repopulation of Ojo Caliente.[31] Without his scrutiny, little changed on the ground over the next two years. Accordingly, Vélez Cachupín's successor, Governor Pedro Fermín de Mendinueta, found that the same situation prevailed in December of 1767: vacant houses and abandoned land. Mendinueta referred to the Vélez Cachupín order of resettlement of February 1766 and gave the affected parties fifteen days to reclaim their lands.[32] When no Spaniards appeared during that period, Mendinueta ordered that the Genízaros who had stayed at Ojo Caliente as well as the Spanish *vecinos* who had stayed should be assigned the lands declared public domain by Vélez Cachupín. Over a dozen Genízaros (hispanicized Plains Indians) had stayed at Ojo Caliente, but they had been completely overlooked by the authorities. As in other settlements, the Genízaros were typically not given title to the land they were living on, so Mendinueta's actions, following in the footsteps of Vélez Cachupín, were revolutionary. He ordered that both the Spanish vecinos and the Genízaros be given deeds to the lands they were farming or to abandoned irrigable lands if they were without farmlands.[33] Vecinos Gregorio Sandoval, Andrés Muñiz, and Gregorio Apodaca were assigned from forty to sixty varas of irrigated lands.[34]

Since Governor Mendinueta had ordered that "those without land be given farmland that is broken and under cultivation," Alcalde Ortiz assembled the remaining Genízaros who lacked lands and took them to the lands that had belonged to Juana de Herrera, allotting them thirteen tracts of forty to sixty varas in width above the Herrera land.[35] This group of Genízaro Indians seems to have been organized like a pueblo, for the first individual listed was Juan Antonio, the war captain, an important office in each pueblo.[36] The other Genízaros to whom allotments were made were Antonio Martín (probably a different Antonio Martín than the one in the 1735 lawsuit), Pasqual Mora, Juan Martín, Francisco Riaño, Joaquín Jaramillo, Juan Archuleta, Juan Diego Martín, Antonio Padilla, Juan de Sena, Francisco Sierra, Andrés Esquibel, and José Sánchez. Now the settlers who had remained at Ojo Caliente had a greater reason to defend their community from attack since they owned more and better land. But the problem of encouraging other settlers to return to their lands at Ojo Caliente still remained.[37]

A year after the allotment of new lands to the Ojo Caliente Genízaros in 1768, the Spanish settlers who owned land there still had not returned as ordered by Governor Vélez Cachupín in 1766. Governor Mendinueta's frustration at not being able to accomplish the resettlement as ordered by the viceroy in 1751 boiled over in late March 1769, when he ordered the Spaniards who had left their homes "filled with a fearful panic caused by the Comanches because of past battles with said nation" to return within four days of being notified of his decree.[38] Those who failed to obey would be fined two hundred pesos and brought to Santa Fe as prisoners to be jailed until they agreed to resettle Ojo Caliente.[39] This severe penalty was meant to enforce compliance. Some of the settlers initially responded that they would resettle,[40] but upon reflection most answered with some defiance that they had held a meeting and found they lacked the supplies necessary to make the resettlement; they therefore would not be able to return within the short span of four days. "If this is a crime," they told the governor, "we completely submit ourselves to the said penalties until we lose our lives in jail in shackles."[41]

The petulant tone of this reply caused an angry response from Governor Mendinueta in which he accused the former Ojo Caliente settlers of cowardice:

"It is inferred that the signers of this document are filled with fear [and are] pusillanimous cowards, though they have those who will defend them." Governor Mendinueta noted that a large squadron of soldiers had been assigned to Ojo Caliente and would be augmented, sufficient not only for defense but also to mount retaliatory expeditions after Comanche raids. Mendinueta tried to shame the Spaniards by comparing their community to other frontier communities in northern New Mexico that had not been abandoned though they had no military guard at all, communities such as Taos, Las Trampas, Picuris, Santa Barbara, Piedra Lumbre, and Abiquiu. The governor ordered Alcalde Ortiz to gather the Spanish settlers together and ask them one more time if they would resettle. If they refused, Alcalde Ortiz was to apply the penalties previously ordered.[42]

Yet again the settlers told stories of their trials and tribulations on the frontier at Ojo Caliente. José Martín would return with his family and his livestock when the others did; until then, "the squadron that is there is unable to prevent the loss of said stock," so he would return alone.[43] Likewise, Gregorio Sandoval would return alone, without his wife and four daughters, who continually told him that "they would rather be torn to pieces than go with him." Sandoval understood how they felt, because the Comanches had stolen his horses, killed fourteen of his cattle, killed one of his servants, and taken the scalp of another. He would return to Ojo Caliente alone and plant by himself with only a hoe because he had no oxen.[44] Miguel Abeyta would go although he was afraid to go with his family and plant because of what had happened to the servants of José Baca: one was killed by Comanches near the Baca house, and the other was killed in the hills where he went to look for their oxen. Therefore, Abeyta would go by himself with his livestock.[45] Juan Luján would also go by himself without his family because Comanches had taken all his horses.[46] Similarly, Andrés Mora said that he would obey and return alone to "plant as much as his poverty will allow." He would not take his immediate family because his parents and other relatives had all been killed by Comanches.[47] Diego Gómez had planted some corn but would not take his family to Ojo Caliente because "five of his relatives [had] been killed in his presence and he was not able to prevent it."[48] Ignacio Alarid said he could not go to Ojo Caliente because fourteen of his horses were stolen in Indian raids, eleven by Comanches and four by Utes, as well as seven mules and a *cabo de serasos* (bolt of chintz).[49] Gabriel Quintana said he could not return because all of those who were his neighbors had either left their lands to live in more secure settlements or had been killed. He would rather forfeit his lands than return.[50] Most of the settlers were saying indirectly what Francisco Márquez said directly and succinctly, that "he [would] take his family up when all the families go up." [51]

When Governor Mendinueta received the declarations of the reluctant settlers, he decided to go to Ojo Caliente and see for himself why it was so difficult to defend the community from attacking Ute and Comanche raiding parties. He discovered that the main plaza was "dominated . . . on the east by a ridge of hills, the arroyos of which allow the enemies to get near it [the plaza] without being seen and attack it [the settlement] from said hills." The plaza was near the Cañada de los Comanches, aptly named because it was the location of many Comanche raids. A similar ridge of hills rose toward the south and west, which in the governor's view made the entire settlement difficult to defend. Later, Mendinueta would suggest that the resettlement take place at a new location, but for now he decided to suspend the execution of his previous order to resettle Ojo Caliente. The settlers were told to wall up their houses and the church and wait until measures were "taken to provide greater protection for the Ojo Caliente settlement."[52]

However, Governor Mendinueta did not allow all the reluctant settlers to escape the punishment outlined in his earlier order. He singled out Miguel Abeyta and Ignacio Alarid for saying that it was not possible to retaliate against the Ute and Comanche raiding parties. The governor characterized these statements as not only false but also "frivolous, denigrating, insolent, and full of malice." The truth, according to Mendinueta, was that the community had always been provided with an adequate militia to guard it, and on one occasion a retaliatory force had killed twenty-two Comanches. Mendinueta sentenced Abeyta and Alarid to serve "one whole month with the militia detachment personally besides . . . they are obliged to serve like the others." Perhaps Governor Mendinueta felt that such a sentence would stifle similar complaints from other Hispano settlers in the future. Whether it improved the frontier defense at Ojo Caliente is questionable.[53]

What did bolster the stability of the community at Ojo Caliente were the few Genízaros who were willing to live there full time. Having accompanied Governor Mendinueta on his inspection, Alcalde Antonio José Ortiz decided to stay a little longer at Ojo Caliente and inquire as to what the Genízaros and the Spaniards had planted and whether they had occupied their houses. First, he asked the war captain of the Genízaros "to show me who lived here with their families and planted." Of the twenty-one Genízaros he questioned, only three had planted and only two had their families with them. The war captain of the Genízaros, José Sánchez, had his family with him and had planted corn, chile, onions, and pumpkins; Juan Domingo Martín also had his family and had planted but did not say what crops; and Juan Domingo Trebol, a bachelor, had planted only one-half almud of corn. The remaining Genízaros had the following notations written after their names: "does not have his family here nor had he anything planted" or "neither he nor his family are here."[54]

When Alcalde Ortiz inspected the Spaniards, he found them in two groups, one in the upper plaza and one in the lower one. In the lower plaza, only two settlers had planted, and none had occupied their houses. Antonio Martín had planted one cornfield, and José Baca and his father-in-law, Paulin Abeyta, had planted two fields of corn, beans, and peas. The two Spaniards who had been singled out for punishment for the defiant tone of their declarations, José Ignacio Alarid and Miguel Abeyta, lived in this lower plaza. They, like the remaining settlers, had the notation "neither planted nor inhabited" written after their names. In the upper plaza nine individuals were listed, and five of them had planted. Four of these had planted only corn, but Andrés Muñiz was listed as having planted corn, peas, chile, and onions. Muñiz was the only settler who lived in his house with his family; all the other houses were found to be deserted and uninhabited.[55]

Andrés Muñiz had been listed as a mulatto in the church records, and his wife, María Chávez, was listed as a *coyota*. Later, both were denoted as Spaniards, though they were probably Genízaros who had achieved vecino status. On the 1775–1776 Domínguez-Escalante expedition to Utah, Andrés Muñiz was hired as the Ute interpreter, and his brother Lucrecio, who was also a landowner at Ojo Caliente, came along uninvited. Fathers Domínguez and Escalante described the Muñiz brothers as Genízaros and wrote disparagingly of them in the journal of the expedition. Father Escalante noted that Andrés and Lucrecio had joined the expedition solely to trade with the Ute, not, as the priests had, "for the Glory of God and the salvation of souls."[56] Normally, it was illegal to trade with the Ute without a license, so the Muñiz brothers must have believed they were immune from prosecution as long as they were traveling with the good fathers. The members of the expedition were told not to bring any merchandise to trade with the Indians, but the

Muñiz brothers apparently disobeyed, and, as facetiously reported by Escalante, they "showed themselves to be so obedient, loyal and Christian that they traded what they had kept hidden, and with great eagerness solicited arms from the heathen."[57]

This episode helps explain why Andrés Muñiz was able to stay in Ojo Caliente in the face of the Ute and Comanche attacks that forced other settlers to retreat to the better-protected settlements around Abiquiu. Muñiz was a Genízaro of Plains Indian or Ute ancestry. Having assimilated into Spanish society, he was able to act as an intermediary between the Utes and the Spaniards who wanted to trade with them. As such, he was not targeted by the Utes or other tribes, who found it more in their interest to trade than to fight, especially when one of the primary items of trade were Indian slaves to be used as servants in Spanish homes.[58]

Governor Mendinueta and Alcalde Antonio José Ortiz did not give up on their mission of getting the Spaniards who had been given land at Ojo Caliente to resettle there and join the hardy and independent frontiersman Muñiz and the other Genízaros. In July 1769 Alcalde Ortiz called together a group of Spaniards who had previously settled at Ojo Caliente to offer them new lands as an inducement to resettle. Ortiz suggested that three new plazas be established at more defensible locations than the previous sites. As an added inducement, Alcalde Ortiz promised the community "a squad of soldiers and some Indians . . . for the length of time that may be considered necessary for their defense." Each former settler was asked whether he would resettle under these terms, and all but two said they would not. Gregorio Sandoval, Diego Gómez, Juan Luján, Santiago Lucero, Ignacio Alarid, Paulín Abeyta, José Baca, and Miguel Abeyta all said that Ojo Caliente was too dangerous, and most agreed to forfeit their lands. Only Blas Durán, on behalf of his mother, and Antonio Martín, who was building a house there, agreed to resettle. Santiago Lucero stated on behalf of his mother, Ana María Martín, that they would not resettle, nor would they forfeit their lands.[59]

Again Governor Mendinueta was faced with a stubborn group of settlers, each of whom would resettle only if all resettled. That did not happen, however, so Ojo Caliente remained unoccupied for two more decades during the 1770s and 1780s. During the administration of Governor Juan Bautista de Anza (1778–1788), peace was achieved with the Comanche and the Ute tribes after the famous defeat in 1779 of the fierce Comanche leader Cuerno Verde. But it was seven years before a formal peace treaty was signed in 1786 with both tribes.[60] We know that Ojo Caliente was unoccupied at this time because Governor Anza passed through the area and camped there with the expedition that would defeat the Comanche band. Anza described Ojo Caliente as "abandoned on account of the hostilities of the enemy," after inspecting the place because of a proposal to establish a presidio there. Anza "found it lacking all the conditions and advantages required for such an establishment [a presidio]." Altogether, he said, "they are twenty-five or thirty families scattered over more than four leagues [10½ miles], their houses unfortified. For this reason, it is not strange that there were such attacks, as this disorder [in the settlement pattern] brought upon them the loss of their poor fields."[61]

As in other New Mexico communities, Ojo Caliente settlers preferred living apart from each other in ranchos scattered along the source of irrigation water rather than in centralized, fortified communities. Governor Vélez Cachupín was the first to establish compact communities in places such as Truchas, Las Trampas, and Abiquiu, ordering settlers to build their houses contiguously around a fortified plaza, in accordance with viceregal policy. Many settlements, like Ojo Caliente, resisted the governor's directions to consolidate into compact communities, however.[62] Governor Mendinueta expressed his frustration at this tendency in a report to Viceroy Bucareli in which he described "churlish types of settlers accustomed to live apart from each other, as neither fathers or sons associate with each other." He went on to ask the viceroy to mandate the consolidation of settlements and to establish a presidio at Taos. It sounded as if Governor Mendinueta had Ojo Caliente in mind when he told Viceroy Bucareli that in his experience, "force not intervening, persuasion does not serve for them, and [if] he wished to force them to congregate, he would make an enemy . . . of each individual."[63] No matter how often they were ordered to settle in a central location, most settlers built their homes close to their fields because they placed a higher priority on practical considerations, such as protecting their crops from bears, raccoons, and raiding Ute and Comanche Indians.[64]

By September 1790, peace with the Comanche and Ute tribes evidently made settlement at Ojo Caliente feasible for the first time in decades, so José Manuel Velarde and eighteen petitioners asked Governor Fernando de la Concha (1778–1794) for permission to resettle the area.[65] Velarde must have been familiar with the governmental policy favoring compact, defensible communities, for he told Governor Concha that he wanted to take possession of his lands at Ojo Caliente and establish a walled settlement.[66] Governor Concha knew the history of the attempts to settle Ojo Caliente, and he notified Velarde that he would only approve the petition if the settlers agreed to "form a well-aligned and regular settlement at the place where there was one years ago, which today is called the [Pueblo] Viejo at the outskirts of the Cañada de los Comanches." Governor Concha believed that this site was the most suitable "as much as for the ease of digging an acequia [to irrigate] their fields, which can run along the foot of said settlement for their subsistence and for raising livestock in all the surrounding area." Concha told Alcalde Manuel García de la Mora to gather the settlers together, determine if they agreed to the governor's condition, and if so, take them to Ojo Caliente and explain the method they should follow in the formation of the settlement.[67]

When notified of the governor's decree, the settlers (who now numbered thirty-two) replied that they would not settle Pueblo Viejo at the Cañada de los Comanches because "the old pueblo is a long way from the water when the acequia is not running in the winter." The settlers wanted to settle at the old plaza near the chapel, where they had settled before.[68] Thus, practical considerations dealing with both irrigation water and drinking water loomed large in the 1790 petition to resettle Ojo Caliente. When Governor Concha received this report he told the settlers, "In no way do I agree to the formation of a settlement in the place proposed by the founders, since experience has proven that nobody can last there in time of war on account of its unfortunate location."[69] Governor Concha must have been aware of the previous report by Governor Mendinueta to the effect that Ojo Caliente was indefensible because the settlers were "scattered over more than four leagues [10½ miles], their houses unfortified."[70] When notified of Governor Concha's uncompromising stance, the settlers (who now numbered thirty-seven) responded equivocally that the governor "may decide whatever [is] the most proper for the royal service and to the best advantage to the interested parties." This was a bureaucratic way of saying that the settlers still wanted to resettle Ojo Caliente but not at the location mandated by Governor Concha.[71]

Three years after the standoff between Governor Concha and the hopeful settlers, a new group of settlers, some of whom were already in possession of land at Ojo Caliente, petitioned Governor Concha for a formal grant. The fifty-three petitioners indicated that Concha had already given his approval for their resettlement, but now they wanted to be placed in possession under a "legal grant." This new attempt to settle Ojo Caliente was finally successful.[72]

After all the earlier forays into Ojo Caliente under Governors Vélez Cachupín and Mendinueta and all the reports of loss of property and deaths of livestock and family members, this routine request for a land grant at Ojo Caliente seemed anticlimactic. On 11 September 1793 Governor Concha granted the land to the community and its fifty-three heads of families. Since the petition by Antonio José Espinosa, Juan Zamora, and Salvador Maese did not specify the boundaries, Governor Concha left it to the alcalde to delineate them. As was often the case with vague boundaries, the situation led to great confusion when the U.S. government later tried to adjudicate who owned the Ojo Caliente grant. Governor Concha provided that "the watering places on the Ojo Caliente River [would be] common between [the grantees] and the balance of the vicinity of Río Arriba," with the condition that the neighboring stockmen cause no damage to the fields of the Ojo Caliente settlers as their cattle approached the Ojo Caliente River to slake their thirst.[73]

When Alcalde Manuel García de la Mora placed the grantees in possession of the land at Ojo Caliente, he specified the boundaries for the first time: to the north, the Cañada de los Comanches; south, a landmark "of stone and mortar with a holy cross made of cedar placed in the center"; east, the foothills; and west, the foothills on the other side of the river. The southern landmark containing a cross of cedar was undoubtedly connected to the official name for the mission of Ojo Caliente: Santa Cruz de Ojo Caliente. It is not clear which foothills García de la Mora intended, however, but it seems likely that the valley or *cañada* containing the agricultural tracts was the primary focus of the grant, not the much larger area later claimed by land speculator Antonio Joseph. Regarding the river-access provision, Alcalde García de la Mora reversed that provision either accidentally or by design so that the Ojo Caliente settlers were obligated not to damage the livestock of their neighbors, instead of the neighboring stockmen being obligated not to damage the fields of the Ojo Caliente settlers. This absurd reversal of the condition designed to protect the Ojo Caliente settlers may have been by design since García de la Mora seems to have been one of the neighboring stockmen.[74]

Alcalde García de la Mora placed the fifty-three grantees (many of whom were already living on and farming the land) in possession of tracts of land each 150 varas wide along the Río del Ojo Caliente from the Cañada de los

Comanches to the *torreón* of the deceased José Baca. At the conclusion of the act of possession, García de la Mora conducted the traditional symbolic ritual the Spanish always performed when they acquired new land: they destroyed a bit of it to prove it was theirs. They also celebrated their good fortune at being given this productive land grant near the sacred hot springs as "each individual walked over the land assigned to him, and they jumped and leaped about and plucked up weeds with their hands, and expressed their thanks to the king and to the colonel [Governor Concha], who made them the grant in the name of His Majesty, manifesting many evidences of satisfaction."[75]

The Ojo Caliente grantees might have jumped with less enthusiasm had they known that within a century Antonio Joseph would own the hot springs and would acquire most of the Ojo Caliente grant from their descendants.[76] The names of "the new settlers of Ojo Caliente" were attached to the act of possession and are listed as follows:

Aguilar, José	Maes, Antonio
Archuleta, Antonio	Maes, Cristóbal
Ávila, Juan de Jesús	Maes, José Manuel
Bachicha, Salvador	Maes, Salvador
Chávez, Luis	Martín, Antonio
Córdova, Ines	Martín, Gregorio, District Lieutenant
Durán Luis, Sergeant	Martín, José
Durán, Gabriel	Martín, Manuel
Espinosa, Antonio José	Martín, Merejildo
Espinosa, José Antonio	Mascareñas, Juan Bautista
Gallego, Francisco	Mestas, José Joaquín
Gálvez, Blas	Mestas, Pascual
Gálvez, Clemente	Naranjo, José María
Gálvez, Juan Bautista	Olguín, José
Gálvez, Salvador	Olguín, Juan
Gonzales, Juan Cristóbal	Rodríquez, Manuel
Léon, José Antonio de	Romero, Lorenzo
Lucero, Cristóbal	Romero, Pedro
Lucero, Pablo	Salas, Ramón
Lucero, Pedro	Sandoval, Juan Domingo
Madrid, José Antonio	Sena, Miguel

Sisneros, Pedro	Ulibarrí, Juan Crisóstomo de
Trujillo, Gabriel	Valverde, Francisco
Trujillo, Ignacio	Vigil, Juan
Trujillo, Manuel	Zamora, Jacinto
Trujillo, Miguel	Zamora, Juan[77]

The fact that many of the names on the list represented new settlers must have helped smooth the way for the first permanent settlement at Ojo Caliente. Governor Mendinueta had lost his patience with the likes of Miguel Abeyta, Ignacio Alarid, and José Baca, whom he referred to generally as "churlish types of settlers."[78] Their family names do not appear among the new settlers of Ojo Caliente, and it seems that allotments were made anew without regard to old property lines. Some children of the older settlers may have been among this new group of settlers, but if so, they were receiving new allotments rather than claiming lands once belonging to their parents.[79] Missing from the group were family names like that of Andrés Muñiz, who had stayed on his land at Ojo Caliente when all the other settlers refused to return.[80] Even José Manuel Velarde, who just three years earlier had asked Governor Concha for permission to settle Ojo Caliente, was absent from the list. It is likely, however, that the thirty-seven unnamed prospective settlers that Velarde had recruited were on the list of settlers given allotments in 1793. Those allotments started at the Cañada de los Comanches near the place that Governor Concha wanted the group to settle in 1790, but it does not appear that the 1793 settlement was exactly where Concha wanted it to be: "at the [Pueblo] Viejo at the outskirts of the Cañada de los Comanches."[81] Rather, it seems that the settlers were able to live where they had always wanted to, near the old plaza and the chapel, as shown by a remeasurement of the Ojo Caliente lands in 1824.[82]

The 1793 settlement of Ojo Caliente was on tracts of land that had been cultivated, planted, and irrigated by the settlers who had repeatedly tried to establish a permanent settlement there starting with the first attempt more than six decades earlier of Lázaro Atienza, who had argued with Antonio Martín about the amount of land each had cleared, planted, and irrigated in the 1730s. Martín's promise to give Atienza a deed to land the latter had farmed and irrigated resulted in litigation that reveals what the first settlement attempts at Ojo Caliente looked like. While many of the family names of earlier Ojo Caliente Hispano settlers were missing from the 1793 list, so, too, were the names of many of the loyal Genízaros who had stayed at Ojo Caliente when all the Spaniards had left. The vagueness of the boundaries of the Ojo Caliente grant, the lack of clarity about the location of the common lands, and the failure to name all the potential owners of the grant sowed the seeds of future problems when the grant was acquired by Antonio Joseph and adjudicated by the Court of Private Land Claims.

A church or chapel was built at Ojo Caliente prior to 1776, for in that year Father Francisco Atanasio Domínguez reported during his inspection of the Abiquiu mission that Antonio Martín (who had won the 1735 lawsuit against Lázaro Atienza) was the patron and owner of the Ojo Caliente chapel and had loaned some of the church ornaments to the Abiquiu mission while Ojo Caliente was abandoned. These included "an old white satin chasuble with accessories and also a chalice with paten and spoon and an old missal." These items were to become a bone of contention in the early 1820s when the controversial priest Father Teodoro Alcina was assigned to serve the spiritual needs of the Ojo Caliente mission.[83]

Father Alcina came to New Mexico around 1793, when he was assigned to Sandia Pueblo. Between 1807 and 1823 he served as the resident priest at Abiquiu, where he was supposed to travel to the *visita* (a church regularly visited by a nearby priest but lacking its own) of Ojo Caliente and minister to that community's spiritual needs.[84] At Abiquiu and Ojo Caliente, Father Alcina not only neglected his duties on a regular basis, but instead of blessing his flock, he publicly chastised the entire pueblo of Abiquiu. In a lawsuit brought by his Abiquiu and Ojo Caliente parishioners, the plaintiffs accused Alcina of getting so angry at his Abiquiu flock that he yelled at them, swearing "to bury them all and finish them off, cursing and damning all of them." The same afternoon a hailstorm of biblical proportions wiped out most of the crops in the Abiquiu area, and later a plague of locusts destroyed what little was left. This incident precipitated the litigation against the Abiquiu priest, but many others had complaints against Father Teodora Alcina.[85] Residents of Ojo Caliente testified that Alcina had refused to celebrate Mass at Ojo Caliente's feast day for two years in a row, had refused to go to Ojo Caliente to perform the last rites for seven dying individuals, and had refused to teach the divine word or explain the Christian doctrine. Father Alcina told his Ojo Caliente parishioners that he would only come to that community to celebrate the annual Mass if they would pay him sixty pesos, provide a corral for his horses and a cover

(*tapeste*) for the hay, fix the rooms where he stayed, and get the church ornaments back to the Ojo Caliente chapel. In their petition, the Ojo Caliente residents said they had delivered the sixty pesos of in-kind products to Father
Alcina at Abiquiu for two years in a row and still the priest refused to come to
Ojo Caliente on their feast day to celebrate Mass. To bring their point home,
the Ojo Caliente petitioners told the Abiquiu ayuntamiento (town council)
that they had not defaulted on their obligation to build a horse corral and
should be listened to because "we are not a community of Indians" but citizens
who paid tithes imposed by the Bishops Pedro Tamerón and Benito Crespo.[86]

This statement by the Abiquiu petitioners—"we are not a community of
Indians"—seems designed to distinguish Ojo Caliente from Abiquiu, a community that retained its Indian identity until the early twentieth century and
still celebrates its Genízaro ancestry. The implication of the statement was that
Ojo Caliente should get preferential treatment over Abiquiu because unlike
Abiquiu, Ojo Caliente was a community of tithe-paying Spaniards. In fact, the
racial makeup of Ojo Caliente in the early 1800s was similar to that of Abiquiu:
primarily Indians and mestizos with some Spaniards. Major Zebulon M. Pike
noted this fact in his journal when he passed through Ojo Caliente in 1807 as
he was being escorted to Santa Fe after his arrest by Spanish authorities in Taos.
Pike wrote that the village of Ojo Caliente "presents to the eye a square enclosure of mud walls, the houses forming the wall. . . . Inside of the enclosure were
the different streets of houses of the same fashion, all of one story; the doors
were narrow, the windows small. . . . The population consists of civilized
Indians, but much mixed blood. . . . This village may contain 500 souls."[87]

It is not clear whether an overt choice was made by the community of Ojo
Caliente to present itself as a Hispano settlement rather than an Indian pueblo,
but the future of Ojo Caliente's land grant turned on that fateful phrase: "we
are not Indians." Unlike Abiquiu, whose land grant was confirmed at about
16,500 acres (almost the full extent of an Indian pueblo) because the surveyor
general and Court of Private Land Claims wanted to show leniency toward
Indians, Ojo Caliente's grant was whittled down from a claimed 38,490 acres
to about 2,200 acres. The Ojo Caliente grant's fate was also tied to the fact that
it was owned by the land speculator Antonio Joseph rather than by an Indian
pueblo.[88]

In 1873, almost twenty years after the Office of the Surveyor General of New
Mexico was created to confirm land grants under the Treaty of Guadalupe

Hidalgo, Felix Gálvez filed a petition for confirmation of the Ojo Caliente grant as a community land grant. After taking testimony from witnesses such as Dionisio Vargas, the surveyor general recommended confirmation of the Ojo Caliente grant to the heirs and legal representatives of the fifty-three grantees under the 1793 grant. The grant was surveyed in 1877 but was not confirmed because by the late 1870s Congress was wary of confirming grants of which it had little knowledge after the unfair confirmation of the Maxwell (1.7 million acres) and Sangre de Cristo (approximately 1 million acres) grants. Meanwhile, as Felix Gálvez was trying to get the Ojo Caliente grant confirmed, land speculator and merchant Antonio Joseph began buying up the interests of the heirs of the original fifty-three grantees.[89]

Antonio Joseph was born in Taos on 25 August 1846, the son of the merchant Pedro Joseph de Tevis and his wife, Mariana Willie. Antonio Joseph's father was Portuguese from the village of San Miguel on one of the Azores, over one thousand miles west of Portugal. Pedro Joseph de Tevis sailed for America in the 1820s, but, like the earlier Spanish explorer Álvar Núñez Cabeza de Vaca, he was shipwrecked in the Gulf of Mexico. He then made his way to New Orleans, where he met and married Mariana Willie, allegedly an African American woman whom Joseph purchased and then freed from bondage. The couple moved to Saint Louis in the late 1830s and then to Taos, where Pedro Joseph opened a general store. Antonio Joseph was born in the Joseph mansion, a two-story structure of eight to ten rooms with the store occupying the first floor. Antonio Joseph was baptized by Padre Antonio José Martínez, after whom he was named.[90]

In 1848 the Joseph house and store were burned to the ground when Indian raiders came into the store while the senior Joseph was in Santa Fe on business. The Indians demanded money from Mariana, and when she told them the cashbox was almost empty, they took two-year-old Antonio outside, tied ropes to his feet, and hung him upside down from a tree to induce his mother to tell them where the money was hidden. When still no money was to be found, the Indians looted and burned the store, taking Antonio and his mother captive for several months. They were rescued by troops under Colonel Sterling Price at the request of Pedro Joseph.[91]

By 1878 Antonio Joseph claimed to have purchased the interests of most of the grantees of the Ojo Caliente grant, and on that basis he objected to the survey of the grant in 1877, claiming that the west boundary was about six miles

too far east. In December 1878 he submitted a supplemental petition claiming the entire common lands of the Ojo Caliente grant; he also claimed that the grant contained forty-four thousand acres instead of the approximately thirty-eight thousand acres surveyed by Deputy Surveyors Griffin and McMullen in 1877.[92]

Sometime in the late 1870s, Joseph started planning the resort and hotel he was to build at the hot springs, but it was not until the early 1880s that he began his development of the hot springs as a health resort. A store had been built at Ojo Caliente shortly after the Civil War by another merchant who was eventually supplied from Joseph's store in Taos. When the proprietor of the Ojo Caliente store was unable to pay Joseph for goods delivered to the store, Joseph took it and the hot springs in payment of the debt. He built a hotel and piped the waters from the springs into pools and tubs. Joseph advertised the hot springs as a health resort, claiming that the healing mineral waters would cure almost any ailment known to science.[93]

Even more outlandish than the health claims, which may actually have had some merit, were the historical claims Joseph made regarding the first Spaniard to visit Ojo Caliente. He noted in one of the early brochures that Álvar Núñez Cabeza de Vaca was the first European to pass through Ojo Caliente. He claimed to know this because he had consulted in depth about Ojo Caliente's history with his friend Adolph Bandelier, who with his wife, Fanny, had studied Cabeza de Vaca and even published a translation of his journal. Fanny Bandelier translated the Cabeza de Vaca narrative, and Adolph wrote the introduction in which he states, however, that Cabeza de Vaca was not the discoverer of New Mexico, nor did he see any of the pueblos. A map of the route of Cabeza de Vaca's travels in the front of the book shows that his only contact with New Mexico was a visit to Zuni Pueblo in the eastern part of the state.[94] Cabeza de Vaca's journey across the Southwest, after he was shipwrecked in the Gulf of Mexico, took him across present-day Florida, Louisiana, Texas, and southern New Mexico, but he never traveled as far north as Ojo Caliente. Joseph's penchant for exaggeration led him to concoct this spurious entry, purportedly from Cabeza de Vaca's journal, in the resort's brochure: "The greatest treasure that I found these strange people to possess are some hot springs which burst out at the foot of a mountain. . . . So powerful are the chemicals contained in this water that the inhabitants have a belief that they were given them by the gods. These springs I have named, OJO CALIENTE."[95]

Joseph was probably fond of the Cabeza de Vaca story because of the similarities between the account of Cabeza de Vaca's shipwreck and that of his father, both of whom survived the hardships they encountered and learned something from the experience. The fact that Joseph could concoct something from whole cloth that was not in the historical record, however, tells us much about the character of this man who was elected to five consecutive terms as New Mexico's delegate to Congress (more than any other New Mexican) and who somehow convinced the heirs of the fifty-three grantees of the Ojo Caliente grant to sign their rights to the common lands over to him.[96]

After earlier forays into the area where he acquired these deeds and while allegedly fathering numerous children, Joseph moved to Ojo Caliente in 1880. At that time he was the acknowledged patrón, entrepreneur, and owner of Ojo Caliente. The account of the many children fathered by Joseph comes from

Maude McFie Bloom, who told the story of Joseph's arrival in Ojo Caliente in 1880 with his new bride, Elizabeth Foree of Washington, D.C., who would live with him at the hot springs:

> As the couple neared the Springs, a group of small children ran out, shouting and waving to Antonio. His wife remarked, "what sweet children these are!" He replied, "My dear, some of these are mine. I didn't have the heart to tell you before, but they will never embarrass you. I have sent word ahead that they are never to cross the bridge to come over to the Springs. You will never see them."[97]

Joseph began his political career as a probate judge in Taos County from 1875 to 1881, and by the fall of 1884 he was making his first campaign to be New Mexico's delegate to Congress. Joseph's record as a land speculator was used against him by his political opponents, often without much specific evidence because little was known about his methods. A *Santa Fe New Mexican Review* article from 6 October 1884 suggests generally that Joseph had purchased interests in the Maxwell grant, the San Joaquín del Río de Chama grant, as well as the Ojo Caliente grant. The article was more specific about Joseph's acquisition of the Cieneguilla grant, in Taos County, however:

> The heirs of the grantors, over 100 in number, were . . . induced by various representations, all of which prove false, to sign deeds to their interest for the miserable pittance of $1.00 each. Some say they signed because they thought the deed was only for a right of way for a road, others that they expected to receive their proper proportion afterwards. But none ever received a cent after that time and the deeds were drawn so as to cover all the right, title, and interest of the settlers, only reserving their little garden patches. Thus over 40,000 acres were obtained for only $113.00.[98]

The methods used by Joseph in buying the Cieneguilla grant seem to have applied to the Ojo Caliente grant as well. Having acquired the Ojo Caliente grant, Joseph needed to get it confirmed by the U.S. government to secure his title. Almost single-handedly, he set about creating the mechanism that would validate what he now considered his land grant, as well as other New Mexico land grants. As territorial delegate to Congress, Joseph—then considered a

member of the Santa Fe Ring—was not only instrumental in passing the legislation that established the Court of Private Land Claims, he also helped secure
an appropriation for the completion of the federal building (still in existence)
where the Land Claims Court held its sessions.[99]

In the March term of 1893, Joseph filed a petition with the Court of Private
Land Claims seeking confirmation of what was then called the Antonio Joseph
grant. Represented by attorney Napoleon Bonapart Laughlin, Joseph set forth
the history of the 1793 grant to the fifty-three grantees, including the boundaries called for in the act of possession. Joseph apparently submitted copies of
deeds through which he claimed to have purchased the interests of those
fifty-three grantees, though they are no longer in the court files. What does
remain in the files is an elaborate chart in Joseph's meticulous handwriting
listing the dates and other information about all the deeds.[100]

The Joseph chart, which he called an abstract of title, shows that between
1873 and 1878 Antonio Joseph obtained deeds from the heirs or assigns of each
of the fifty-three grantees or from the grantees themselves. Whether Joseph
used the methods alleged to have been applied in the Cieneguilla grant is not
clear, but several suspicious circumstances are connected with the list. First,
the consideration for each deed, that is, the amount paid by Joseph, is not
listed, though many other important facts about each transaction are. Second,
in at least fourteen cases the deeds from the initial heirs, if there were any, were
unrecorded, so we have no way to trace whether these initial grantees sold
their interests. And third, more than twenty of the grantees are said to have
sold their interests to Antonio Maes, who eventually sold to Salvador Lucero,
who then sold all his interests in the grant to Antonio Joseph in 1873. The
Lucero deed covered acquisitions that took place as early as 1799, 1812, and 1821,
which then related to the 1873 deed to Joseph. We cannot, however, check the
validity of these deeds from the Court of Private Land Claims records. These
convoluted transactions seem to have followed the pattern of acquisitions of
community land grants by land speculators such as Thomas B. Catron, who
acquired the common lands of the Mora and Tierra Amarilla grants in a similar manner. By 1878, a year after the Griffen and McMullen survey showed the
Ojo Caliente grant to contain 38,490 acres, Antonio Joseph had purchased the
interests of each of the fifty-three grantees, whose names were conveniently
listed on the survey plat.[101]

By 1893, when Joseph filed his petition for confirmation of the grant, most people either did not know he was claiming the entire grant or conceded that he was in fact the owner. As mentioned earlier, the grant was often called the Antonio Joseph grant, and the U.S. government admitted that it was a valid grant based on genuine title papers and a long history of possession of the land. The only dissenting voice came from the heirs of one of the fifty-three grantees who also claimed an ownership interest in the Ojo Caliente grant: Jesús María Olguín, descendant of Antonio Olguín.[102]

The Antonio Olguín claim was consolidated with the Ojo Caliente claim and was apparently dropped when it appeared from Antonio Joseph's abstract of title that he had obtained deeds for Olguín's interest in the grant from his heirs. While Olguín's heirs were the only ones to object to Antonio Joseph's claim to the entire Ojo Caliente grant, it is unlikely that the other heirs were even notified of the proceedings. The Court of Private Land Claims was not required to notify any of these grantees or their heirs, even though they had a potential interest in the property just as the heirs of Antonio Olguín did. In any case, on 28 April 1894 Chief Justice Joseph R. Reed signed a decree confirming the Ojo Caliente grant to the heirs of the fifty-three grantees. Since Antonio Joseph had purchased—or so he said—the interests of those fifty-three grantees, he now owned the Ojo Caliente grant.[103]

After he acquired the Ojo Caliente grant, Joseph continued to operate the hot springs. In the 1915 business directory, Joseph is listed as Anthony F. Joseph, manager of the Hot Springs Hotel, notary public, merchant, and mineral water bottler. By 1919, when the population of the Ojo Caliente area had grown to five hundred inhabitants, Anthony Joseph was also listed as postmaster. In 1915 Ojo Caliente had two blacksmiths (one of whom was also a stonecutter, the other the justice of the peace) and three grocery and general merchandise stores (one of which was also a saloon and the other a billiards parlor). Other businesses included a feed and farm tools store, notary, rooming house, post office, and even the law office of D. A. Vargas. In 1919 the priest, Rev. Joseph Pajot, was still there, but the community listed only one general merchandise store and no lawyer.

Ojo Caliente remained a relatively small community throughout the 1900s with small businesses surrounding the hot springs resort and ranches scattered up and down the Ojo Caliente River. Mary Ann Mauro, who owned the mineral springs in the 1980s, remembers coming to the hot springs in the 1930s when the cook "was well-known throughout the area for his fresh steaks and wonderful food. That's part of what made a trip to the springs so healing—the food really was garden fresh." Over the years the hot springs remained the largest business in Ojo Caliente and eventually developed into a destination resort quite different from the rustic health resort it was in the early 1900s. The famous round dairy barn at the resort is a symbol of this change. Built in 1924 for a dairy operation that supplied milk products to the hotel, it was modeled on a round stone barn built by the Shaker community in Hancock, Massachusetts, in the 1820s. The barn was considered the most efficient design and was surrounded by extensive gardens and orchards that also provided food for the hotel. Other businesses gradually grew up in the area, and today, numerous motels, gift shops, and bed-and-breakfasts surround the hot springs resort.[104]

After the Court of Private Land Claims rejected the common lands of the Ojo Caliente grant, approximately thirty-eight thousand acres of these lands came under the management of the Bureau of Land Management (BLM), and many local ranchers entered into private grazing leases with the federal agency. In 1989 a controversy developed when these cattle owners sued private land-owners along the river (including the owner of the Ojo Caliente Mineral Springs) for blocking their cattle from access to the Ojo Caliente River. The cattle owners claimed that six traditional access routes to the river (*abrevaderos*) had been used by livestock since time immemorial and certainly before these landowners and their predecessors had received title from Antonio Joseph. These access routes are known locally as the Cañada de Tío Pula, Arroyo de los Mules, Jeep trail along the Cañada Anchor Arroyo, Arroyo Cerro Negro, Arroyo Rancho, and Cañada Pueblo. Although the suit does not mention the Ojo Caliente grant, it is interesting that the traditional access to the Ojo Caliente River for livestock specified in the 1793 grant continued to be honored more than two centuries later.[105]

In the late 1970s the Ojo Caliente grant established a board of commissioners and requested help from Senator Harrison Schmitt, Congressman Manuel Luján, Congressman Harold Runnels, and President Jimmy Carter. The land grant board contested the confirmation of the grant on two grounds: (1) the grant should have been confirmed to the descendants of the fifty-three heirs, not to Antonio Joseph; and (2) the grant should contain 38,590 acres instead of 2,244 acres. As a result of the board's petitions, Filiberto García, the director of the Ojo Caliente grant, received letters from the U.S. Forest Service and the Bureau of Land Management through Senator Schmitt. Both letters were noncommittal, however, and suggested that the patent for 2,244 acres issued to Antonio Joseph in 1895 was conclusive and any further claims would have to be pursued in the courts.[106] In further response to the claim, the Congressional Research Service of the Library of Congress wrote a short report on the Ojo Caliente grant at the request of Congressman Luján. The research service offered little encouragement to the current claimants, suggesting that the system for land grant confirmation was at fault. The report noted that the reduction in size of the Ojo Caliente grant from the acreage surveyed in 1877 and 1878 could have been due to "the segregation of the surplus area from valid grants located within exterior boundaries of [a] much larger area." In other words, the reason for the reduction in area was the rejection of the common lands of the community land grant.[107]

A comparison of the Genízaro pueblo of Abiquiu with the Ojo Caliente grant is illuminating. Since the Abiquiu grant kept its identity as an Indian pueblo, the government was more lenient in approving the entire grant. In addition, Abiquiu was fortunate because as an Indian pueblo community grant, no individual owners were listed who could be induced to sell the grant to a land speculator like Antonio Joseph. When the grantees at Ojo Caliente insisted in the 1820s litigation with Father Alcina that "we are not Indians," when the majority of the population at Ojo Caliente was in fact made up of Genízaro Indians, Ojo Caliente cut itself off from the benefits that allowed Abiquiu to hold on to its lands.

The history of Ojo Caliente and the Ojo Caliente grant has elements common to other land grant histories: an indigenous presence and prehistory stretching back over thousands of years; the arrival of the Spanish and their attempts to settle the area over many decades in the 1700s; the making of the land grant, which formalized the possession of land and named its owners; and the acquisition of the grant by a land grant speculator and member of the Santa Fe Ring. Unlike most other grants, however, the Ojo Caliente grant was the site of a traditional hot springs, sacred to and shared by all the Indian pueblos in the area and by the members of the land grant. Some land grant members still have keys to one of the private springs, the last vestige of the original untouched hot springs, known as Posipopi, the Greenness Pool.

CHAPTER FOUR

THE COCHITI PUEBLO
PASTURE GRANT AND THE
OJO DEL ESPÍRITU SANTO GRANT

H ISTORIANS STUDYING NEW MEXICO LAND GRANTS AND LAND HIS-
tory often create artificial divisions that place Indian pueblos in one
category and Hispanic land grants in another. As is usually the case, however,
the historical facts are more nuanced. To be sure, the courts treated most of
these land grants separately, with the surveyor general confirming most four-
square-league Pueblo grants and the surveyor general and the Court of Private
Land Claims confirming some but not all Hispanic land grants. But in addition to Hispanic land grants and Pueblo grants, grants were made to Genízaro
Indians (Abiquiu), to Spanish communities that included a large proportion
of Genízaro Indians (San Miguel del Bado, Manzano, and Belén), and to
Indian pueblos, of the grazing lands traditionally used by those pueblos. This
chapter is about two such grazing grants made to Indian pueblos: the Cochiti
pasture grant and the Zia, Santa Ana, and Jemez grant, also known as the 1766
Ojo del Espíritu Santo grant. Also discussed are two of the grants that overlapped them—the Cañada de Cochití grant and the San Isidro grant.[1] With
the rejection by the courts of both Pueblo grazing grants, knowledge of their
existence has almost been lost to history. Only Bowden mentions them, and
he omits the Cochiti pasture grant from his map, as does Herbert Brayer with
the Zia, Santa Ana, and Jemez grant.[2] This chapter is an attempt to resurrect
these lost histories.

During the early 1700s many Indian pueblos began accumulating substantial
herds of cattle and horses and flocks of sheep as they adopted the horse and cattle

culture inherited from the Spanish. At the time of their retreat to the El Paso area during the Pueblo Revolt, many Spaniards left behind large numbers of sheep, cattle, and horses, which the Pueblo Indians acquired. Upon the return of the Spaniards, pueblos such as Santa Ana used cattle and horses as currency when they bought back from Spaniards land they had lost as a result of the reconquest. Tomás Vélez Cachupín was the first governor to recognize the pueblos' need for their own common grazing lands for these herds and flocks, just as the Spaniards had grazing grants in addition to the common lands of their own community grants. While the courts willingly confirmed grazing grants to Spaniards (Bartolomé Fernández, Felipe Tafoya, the Cañada de Cochití), the Pueblo Indian grazing grants discussed here were uniformly rejected by the courts. This rejection was partly the result of poor legal representation of the pueblos: most advocates for the Pueblo Indians were poorly prepared, and a special attorney for the pueblos was not appointed until 1898. A similar categorization seems to have happened in the late nineteenth century, when Hispanic land grants were confirmed, on the one hand, and Pueblo Indian land grants rejected, on the other. Courts seldom stated the real reasons for these rejections but often used the technical explanation that Pueblo grazing grants were considered temporary licenses rather than outright grants. As mentioned, similar grazing grants made to Hispano elites were confirmed, however.

Although pueblos were entitled to additional land beyond their four square leagues (about 17,350 acres), and governors like Vélez Cachupín made grants of such additional lands, by the 1890s Pueblo Indian land was under assault from all quarters. U.S. government attorneys, who were attempting to have as many claims rejected as possible, were able to convince the courts to reject Indian grazing grants. This chapter will discuss the rise and fall of two Indian grazing grants, the 1766 Ojo del Espíritu Santo grant and the 1766 Cochiti pasture grant, and two grants that overlapped them, the Cañada de Cochití grant and the San Isidro grant. In this chapter I will compare the Pueblo Indian grazing grants with similar Hispano grants and examine their treatment by the courts.[3]

The Cochiti Pasture Grant

In 1766 Cochiti Pueblo sought its own pasture grant from the Spanish government as its land was being encroached upon by its Spanish neighbors, people like Miguel and Domingo Romero; Antonio Lucero's Cañada de Cochití grant;

and the Caja del Río and La Majada grants. The first instance of Spanish encroachment on Cochiti grazing lands arose two years earlier in April 1765, when Alcalde Bartolomé Fernández complained to Governor Vélez Cachupín about the brothers Miguel and Domingo Romero. They had settled on lands called "El Capulín" and were trespassing on land adjacent to Cochiti Pueblo that had never been inhabited and was the summer pasture for the pueblo's horse herds and cattle.[4] The governor, relying on Fernández's judgment, immediately ordered the alcalde to eject the Romeros, subject to their producing proof of their ownership of the place called El Capulín. Apparently, Vélez Cachupín had seen too many situations where encroaching Spaniards remained in possession while looking for their documents, thus dragging out the procedure.[5] Within a few days, Miguel Romero of Cieneguilla presented his documents, including a 1739 grant by Governor Mendoza to Andrés Montoya of Cieneguilla for the lands "between the orchards of Cochiti on the south and [the orchards] of San Ildefonso on the north." Andrés Montoya had been placed in possession of the land by Captain Antonio Montoya, probably his son, but neither pueblo was notified at that time.[6] On 18 April 1765, Vélez Cachupín reaffirmed his earlier ejectment "because of the suspicion aroused by the grant" but notified all parties that they would have the opportunity to present their arguments to him. The governor ordered that neither Romero should build a house nor plant a field at El Capulín on pain of a fifty-peso fine to be applied to the construction of a jail in Santa Fe.[7] Both Romeros said they would like the opportunity to respond, as did Andrés Montoya, who provided a copy of the grant mentioned earlier. This response was not filed until 1 October 1766, however, a year and a half after the ejectment order.[8] Alcalde Fernández made the final statement on behalf of Cochiti Pueblo and the adjoining residents, arguing that the 1739 Mendoza grant to Antonio Montoya was fraudulent because (1) adjoining residents had not been summoned, (2) the grant was not properly settled, and (3) the 1740 will of Andrés Montoya showed that the grant encroached on the lands of both San Ildefonso and Cochiti Pueblos. The grant was void according to Fernández because the will stated that it was half a league from the orchards of San Ildefonso on the north and Cochiti on the south, well within the Pueblo league boundaries of each pueblo.[9]

In response to the attempted trespass by the Romeros and in a move similar to that made in relation to the Zia, Jemez, and Santa Ana pasture grant, to be discussed later, Cochiti Pueblo petitioned Governor Vélez Cachupín in

July for a grant surrounding the pueblo to be used as pasture for Cochiti live-stock. Just as with the contemporaneous Zia, Santa Ana, and Jemez grant that Vélez Cachupín made the same day, Felipe Tafoya urged the governor to make the grant to protect a portion of Cochiti pasturelands that were being overrun by grants to neighboring Spaniards "who pretend to acquire a grant [there] ... of great injury to Cochiti who have a great number of stock, cattle and sheep and horses for the royal service."[10] Apparently, Cochiti people were highly valued as Indian auxiliaries and had traditionally kept their animals on this land, "which is surplus of the [Pueblo] League and is used as commons for the horses."[11]

Governor Vélez Cachupín asked the local alcalde to report on the boundaries of the land and whether they would "injure any neighbor."[12] Alcalde Juan María Rivera reported that the land described was good for pasturing the large amounts of sheep and cattle the pueblo owned and would not injure any "neighbor in possession."[13] The description of the land requested was somewhat vague, but it was in an area surrounding and enveloping the pueblo, bounded and apparently within the eastern part of the Cañada de Cochiti grant. When he made the Cochiti pasture grant to the pueblo on 6 August 1766, Governor Vélez Cachupín was restoring to Cochiti Pueblo land that might have been usurped by the Cañada de Cochiti grant.[14]

Governor Vélez Cachupín made the Cochiti pasture grant on 6 August of 1766, and soon thereafter the local alcalde delivered possession of the land to Cochiti Pueblo in the presence of the residents of the community of Cañada de Cochiti. The details of the act of possession are somewhat sketchy because only a fragment of the document has come to light, but the description of the Cochiti Pueblo pasture grant contained in Vélez Cachupín 's granting decree is of a roughly circular tract surrounding the pueblo.[15]

Cochiti's pasture grant, like that of Zia, Santa Ana, and Jemez, was a legitimate grazing land grant that the surveyor general or the Court of Private Land Claims should have confirmed, just as happened with Hispanic grazing grants. Instead, both Pueblo grazing grants were rejected: Cochiti 's because of its size, because it conflicted with two Hispanic land grants that were confirmed (La Majada and Cañada de Cochiti), because the Supreme Court decision on the Ojo del Espíritu Santo grant established a precedent that worked against Cochiti, but most of all, because of the inept handling of the case by Cochiti's lawyer, Napoleon Bonaparte Laughlin.[16]

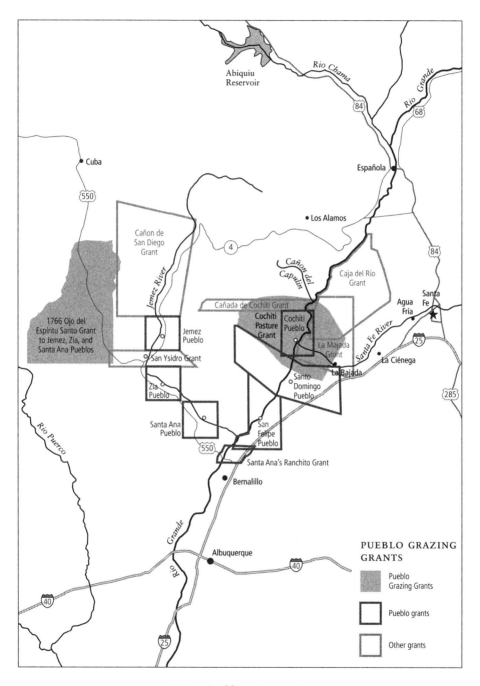

MAP 2. Pueblo grazing grants.

Laughlin, who filed the petition for confirmation of the Cochiti pasture grant together with attorney J. H. Crist, was so disorganized that it was difficult for the judges of the Court of Private Land Claims to determine just what Cochiti Pueblo was requesting. Laughlin had not sought confirmation of the Cochiti pasture grant from the surveyor general, so this petition was the first time the courts had heard of the grant. Instead of focusing on the pasture grant alone, Laughlin included a 1722 Cochiti land purchase from Juana Baca in his petition for confirmation, which completely confused the issue. No maps were included to show where these two tracts were, and the title papers for the tracts were thrown together with little effort to distinguish and explain them. Aside from this procedural confusion, the legal and historical issues involved with the two claims were completely different. The decision to consolidate the two claims confused even the clerks at the Court of Private Land Claims, who listed the claim as the Juana Baca grant without mentioning the more important Cochiti pasture grant. Thus, to find the Cochiti pasture grant in the records of the Court of Private Land Claims, one must look under the totally unrelated Juana Baca grant.[17]

The government's attorney, Matthew Reynolds, pointed out these anomalies and challenged the petition on procedural grounds. In addition, he pointed to the unfavorable decision of the U.S. Supreme Court on the almost identical Ojo del Espíritu Santo grant the previous year in 1897. The lawyers for Cochiti Pueblo failed to amend their petition, and the Court of Private Land Claims rejected the Cochiti pasture grant in October 1898.[18] The unfavorable U.S. Supreme Court decision in the Ojo del Espíritu Santo case and the inept handling of the Cochiti pasture grant by attorney Napoleon B. Laughlin were the primary causes of its rejection. Ironically, the less-deserving Cañada de Cochití grant that encroached on the Cochiti pasture grant and on Cochiti sacred sites was confirmed by the Court of Private Land Claims.

The Cañada de Cochití Grant

One of the private grazing grants made to Hispanos, which impinged on both the Cochiti pasture grant and on Cochiti Pueblo itself, was the Cañada de Cochití grant. In 1728 Antonio Lucero asked Governor Juan Domingo de Bustamante for a tract of land bounded on the north by the "old pueblo of Cochití"; on the south by the Indians of Cochiti; on the east by the Río Grande;

and on the west by the Jemez Mountains. Depending on the surveyor and his instructions, later surveys conducted by the surveyor general and the Court of Private Land Claims indicated that this tract contained anywhere from five thousand to one hundred thousand acres. Surveying the grant should not have been difficult: two of the boundary calls were natural monuments—though identifying where the boundary described as "the Jemez Mountains" might be located would be a problem—and the other two involved Cochiti Pueblo, though the pueblo was never notified of the grant request. Although Lucero asked for wheat- and corn-planting land, it was clear that the primary purpose of the grant was to provide pastureland to graze his livestock.[19]

Governor Bustamante granted the petition for the grant on 2 August 1728, ordering Alcalde Andrés Montoya to notify adjoining landowners and to place Lucero in possession if no one with a better right to the land objected.[20] Montoya placed Antonio Lucero in possession of the land on 6 August 1728, after claiming that no one objected to the grant. It seems clear that Montoya did not notify Cochiti Pueblo, for in other cases when it received notification the pueblo objected, and Montoya did not say that he notified Cochiti Pueblo. Cochiti had numerous sacred shrines within the grant (including one set of stone lions), and this fact, together with its use of the tract for grazing, were ample reasons for the pueblo's objection to the Cañada de Cochití grant.[21] In addition, Alcalde Montoya was not particularly known as an advocate for the pueblos; he was more likely to covet Pueblo land for himself.[22]

Andrés Montoya was the grandson of Pedro Montoya, who in pre-revolt New Mexico was one of the encomenderos entitled to receive tribute from Cochiti Pueblo. Often in the eighteenth century, descendants of the encomenderos of an Indian pueblo considered themselves entitled to special treatment from the Pueblo Indians, even though the institution of the encomienda was abolished after the revolt. When these individuals became alcaldes for the pueblos, they often claimed Pueblo lands for themselves and did not consider the Pueblo Indians to have property rights or boundaries that needed to be respected.[23]

In the mid-eighteenth century, Cochiti Pueblo seems to have shared the Cañada de Cochití with the Lucero family and others for grazing purposes. During the eighteenth century, there was often fierce competition over lands between Spaniards and Pueblo Indians, who had traditionally used the land surrounding their four square leagues for grazing, gathering herbs and firewood, and ceremonial purposes. In addition, certain areas were specifically designated as grazing land for the presidial horse herd. In 1785 Alcalde Antonio Armenta rendered a decision regarding grazing rights on the Cañada de Cochití grant, which implied that others besides the family of Antonio Lucero were also grazing their animals on that land. Lucero's heirs complained to Armenta, who also claimed land in the area, that Antonio Gallego, a resident of Cañada de Cochití, was asking Governor Anza to prevent any grazing on the Cañada de Cochití grant since it was supposedly reserved as pasture for the presidial horse herd. Armenta made a verbal presentation to Governor Anza, and Anza responded with a decision holding that "when a community objects [to grazing by a non-heir] they [the community] should enjoy what is rightfully theirs" over an individual who once received permission to graze a few sheep on the land "but has no title document." In other words, the heirs, Cayetano Montaño and others, should prevail over non-heirs (Antonio Gallego) even though the non-heirs were also living on the grant. This interpretation would also apply to individuals from Cochiti Pueblo who had customarily grazed their animals on their traditional grazing land outside the Pueblo league.[24]

It is not surprising that Armenta came down strongly in favor of the rights of absentee owners of large grazing grants since he was the co-owner of such a grant, the San Isidro grant, to be discussed next. He decided that the Cañada de Cochití grant was not reserved as pasture for the presidial horse herd but was the property of Lucero's heirs and subject to their exclusive use. Armenta gave the Lucero heirs a copy of his decision, "so that before any tribunal . . . they may be heard with the right . . . their grandfathers and fathers . . . acquired by royal grant." As the owner of a large grazing grant himself, Armenta used language about the supremacy of private property under a land grant that he probably hoped would apply to his own grant as well. This trend toward privatization of grazing land in favor of absentee owners was just what Vélez Cachupín was trying to prevent when he refused to make the Felipe Tafoya grant in 1766 and when he made the Cochiti pasture grant, also in 1766.[25]

During the latter part of the eighteenth century, the community of Cañada de Cochití, settled by the large family of Antonio Lucero, grew up on the grant with the same name. The village of Cañada de Cochití, "blessed with rich pasturelands, continued growing for a century in spite of severe winters" and Navajo raids. "After 1800 the town [of Cañada de Cochití] was abandoned at least once [and] several families then moved . . . much further east from the valley, to be among the pioneer settlers of San Miguel County." By the time the surveyor general of New Mexico and the Court of Private Land Claims adjudicated the Cañada de Cochití grant, few people were living there. Most of the heirs of Antonio Lucero had sold their interest to Joel Parker Whitney.[26]

Little is known about the use of the Cañada de Cochití grant during the early nineteenth century, but since it was not fenced, nearby communities undoubtedly used the land for grazing. Pueblo members also visited their holy places there because the grant contained several Cochiti shrines and sacred sites.[27] In April 1867 the heirs of Antonio Lucero filed a petition for confirmation of the Cañada de Cochití grant with the surveyor general of New Mexico, along with the grant documents. The grant documents were copies made in 1817 by the alcalde of Cochiti and were fragmentary: Governor Bustamante's signature had been torn off the granting decree, and the act of possession was missing. In 1882 James G. Whitney, another family member, again petitioned Surveyor General Henry Atkinson for confirmation of the grant in his name. The Whitney family had been systematically purchasing the interests of Lucero's descendants, and on 12 July 1884 they filed an eleven-page "Abstract of Title" showing the names and dates of all the deeds transferring property interests from the Lucero heirs to the Whitneys.[28]

Atkinson received testimony indicating that the boundaries claimed embraced a large area, "something like 500 square miles of territory, extending from the Rio Grande on the east to the top the Jemez Mountains on the west, northwest of the present Pueblo of Jemez, measuring 40 miles from east to west and from 12 to 15 miles in width." On 25 August 1883, Surveyor General Atkinson decided that the grant was valid, although he held that the title papers were not admissible because Governor Bustamante had not executed the mutilated copy of the *testimonio* and because an alcalde lacked authority under Spanish law to make a copy of any document. This specious reason was the same as that given by the court for the rejection of the 1725 Embudo grant.[29] Atkinson did recommend confirmation of the Cañada de Cochití grant, however, based on a presumption that a grant had been made in favor of Lucero for the lands his heirs had occupied for agricultural and grazing purposes. Surveyor General Atkinson drew no conclusions on the extent of the grant, leaving that to his successor.[30]

Deputy Surveyor Jacob Laderer surveyed the Cañada de Cochití grant under the direction of General Land Office commissioner L. Harrison in 1885.

Harrison told Atkinson's successor, Surveyor General Clarence Pullen, to survey the claim "according to the boundary calls in the grant." This was easier said than done, since the northern boundary was the old pueblo of Cochiti and the southern boundary was Cochiti Pueblo, and there had never been any negotiation with Cochiti Pueblo to establish where these boundaries were. The northern and western boundaries also became a bone of contention in the Court of Private Land Claims.[31]

To determine the location of the western boundary, the top of the Jemez Mountains, Deputy Surveyor Laderer took the affidavits of three Cochiti Indians, who stated that the Jemez Mountains were located twenty-five to thirty miles west of the Río Grande. The survey, made during May and June 1885, depicted the grant as measuring about six miles from north to south, twenty-six to thirty-one miles in width, and containing about 104,000 acres. It also showed that the grant conflicted with several other grants as well as with the lands of Cochiti Pueblo.[32]

In 1884 Grover Cleveland was elected president of the United States, and soon after taking office he appointed Lucius Q. C. Lamar as secretary of interior and William A. Sparks as commissioner of the General Land Office, directing them both to institute widespread land reforms. George W. Julian was appointed surveyor general of New Mexico, and the Cañada de Cochiti was one of the many grants he reexamined. In an opinion dated 27 February 1886, Julian agreed with Atkinson that the certified copy of the grant papers were not properly authenticated and were therefore unacceptable as evidence; he recommended that the claim be rejected. Regarding the validity of the survey, Julian noted, in his typical fashion, that its mere size indicated that it was erroneous. He called attention to the fact that Lucero had requested only a piece of land to cultivate ten fanegas of wheat and two of corn and to pasture his herds of small stock and horses. Julian calculated the land requested for agricultural purposes at about thirty-two acres. Julian's opinion essentially terminated any consideration of the grant by the surveyor general's office.[33]

On 2 March 1893, Joel Parker Whitney and several of Lucero's other heirs and assigns filed suit in the Land Claims Court, seeking confirmation of the Cañada de Cochiti grant.[34] Another set of claimants, who also claimed interests as Lucero's heirs, filed a similar suit the following day. Since the two cases covered the same land, the court consolidated them for purposes of trial.[35] The answer of U.S. Attorney Matthew Reynolds addressed the same issues as did

Surveyor General Julian: denying the execution of the grant, denying the authority of Alcalde Armenta to make the adjudication contained in the 1785 proceedings, and denying the authority of an alcalde to issue a certified copy of the testimonio of the grant. The government also alleged that if a valid grant had been made it was limited to a small tract similar in size to the thirty-two acres Julian had estimated.[36]

Once the government's claims of invalidity were met with evidence of the long occupation of the grant, the trial of the Cañada de Cochití grant claim became a contest about boundaries, particularly the northern and western boundaries, but also about sacred sites. The court seemed ready to confirm the grant to some extent, the opposite of its approach to the Pueblo grazing grants. The testimony about the northern boundary, "the old Pueblo of Cochiti," dealt with the historic sites of Cochiti Pueblo, although no Pueblo member testified on this issue. Whitney argued that the northern boundary should be located at the old pueblo of Cochiti on the mesa of Cochiti, where the Indians had retreated during the reconquest of New Mexico in 1692. There was no dispute over the location of the mesa and pueblo, but Whitney's attorney pointed out that an older pueblo known as the "Pueblo Viejo" was also located on the mesa about seven miles farther northwest. The Lucero petition for the Cañada de Cochití grant had located the land requested as "situated upon the mesa of Cochiti to which the Indians who rebelled retreated," apparently pinpointing which "old Pueblo of Cochiti " was being referred to.[37] The search for the truth about which Pueblo ruins were being proposed as a grant boundary was not as important to the plaintiffs as was acquiring a larger tract of land by choosing the location that was the farthest north. This attempted stretching of boundaries was similar to what James Purdy did with the Cristóbal Nieto grant and other Santa Fe grants.[38]

Since the question of which mesa-top ruins were the site of the Pueblo Revolt–era Cochiti occupation was a historical one, the plaintiffs put forth Will Tipton, who usually testified for the government as their historical witness. Tipton was an extremely able translator and paleographer and had picked up a fair amount of historical information, but he was not the best witness, as he was neither historian, archaeologist, nor ethnohistorian. Adolph Bandelier, the Swiss anthropologist who had worked at Cochiti and was a friend of Tipton's, would have been ideal as he wore all these hats and had worked at Cochiti for several months.

Bandelier left New Mexico in 1892, however, just as the Court of Private Land Claims was getting started, but not before he had written an article critical of the court. One of Bandelier's major criticisms of the Court of Private Land Claims centered on the provision excluding citizens of New Mexico, Arizona, and Colorado from serving as its judges. Bandelier believed that an understanding of the history, legal culture, and customs of southwestern people was not only helpful but necessary for a judge on the court. Bandelier's article emphasized, in a deft ironic tone, that judges of the Court of Private Land Claims should have knowledge of the history and geography of the Southwest, where the land grants were made, including the Spanish laws then in force. Although Tipton considered Bandelier a close friend, he felt obliged to publish a rejoinder to Bandelier's article, defending the Court of Private Land Claims. Tipton's response was almost dismissive of Bandelier's cogent reasoning: "The question is one of law and not of sentiment: one requiring a knowledge of legal methods rather than familiarity with the topography of the country in which the claims to be adjudicated are situated, or an acquaintance with the people." However, such a knowledge of the Southwest and particularly the area around Cochiti Pueblo would have been helpful to the Court of Private Land Claims justices as they tried to make sense of the conflicting testimony about the ruins of the old pueblo of Cochiti.[39]

The Cañada de Cochití grant contained sacred sites and shrines that Bandelier had hiked to with his informant, José Hilario Montoya, and these shrines marked the Cañada de Cochití grant as Cochiti 's ancestral land. Bandelier, however, was in Peru and Bolivia at the time and thus could not testify, as Tipton noted. Tipton was familiar with the old pueblo of Cochiti and with Bandelier's publications and was possibly his closest friend. Tipton was able to have one of Bandelier's scholarly works introduced into evidence, and he testified from his own knowledge about the old pueblo of Cochiti, stating that "the ruins nearest the point of the mesa were very much older than the others." He did not testify, however, as to which ruins were the stronghold to which Cochiti had retreated during the Pueblo Revolt. Of course, the best witness on that issue would probably have been Bandelier 's Cochiti informant, José Hilario Montoya, a Cochiti Indian whose ancestors were the ones who retreated to the mesa-top stronghold, but he was never called as a witness.[40]

The Court of Private Land Claims confirmed the Cañada de Cochití grant on 29 September 1884 in the name of Antonio Lucero, along with his heirs and assigns, and fixed the boundaries of the grant as follows: on the north, the old pueblo of Cochiti, which is situated on the mesa of Cochiti on the south side of the Cañada de Cochití and which is located about 8,190 feet in a northerly direction from the northwest corner of the lands of the Indians of Cochiti Pueblo; on the south along the lands of the Indians of Cochiti Pueblo; on the east, along the Río Grande; and on the west, "the crest of the first sierra of Jemez situated to the west of the said Mesa of Cochiti."[41]

The grant as confirmed by the Court of Private Land Claims was closer to five thousand acres than the 1885 survey containing more than one hundred thousand acres, so Whitney and his fellow plaintiffs appealed the decision to the U.S. Supreme Court. They were apparently pleased with the confirmation of the grant but hoped to increase its size. They failed to have the cause filed and docketed properly, however, and the court dismissed the appeal on 4 February 1895. Whitney petitioned the Supreme Court again on 8 March 1895, requesting a new appeal because the clerk of the court had not been able to prepare the transcript of the trial in time for them to perfect their first appeal. He was granted a new appeal on 11 March 1895. The Supreme Court on 24 May 1897 found that although the "Pueblo Viejo" (the ruin that was farther north than the site identified by the Court of Private Land Claims) was undoubtedly the oldest pueblo on the mesa, the old pueblo of Cochiti, to which the Indians retreated in 1693, marked the northern boundary of the grant. The court noted that when the grant was made the old pueblo of Cochiti was not yet an "old" pueblo, having been burned by the Spaniards not much more than thirty years before, but added that it does not take long for ruins to become known as "old."[42] The Cañada de Cochití grant over-lapped Cochiti Pueblo's traditional lands as well as the Cochiti pasture grant. It is noteworthy how much more readily the Cañada de Cochití grant was confirmed with the urging of Joel Parker Whitney than was the ill-fated but equally deserving Cochiti pasture grant.

The Ojo del Espíritu Santo Grant

The other Pueblo grazing grant in contention in the second half of the eighteenth century was the Ojo del Espíritu Santo grant made by Governor Vélez Cachupín to the three pueblos of Zia, Santa Ana, and Jemez. It was made the same day as the Cochiti pasture grant, but it must have taken some time to prepare the groundwork leading up to the making of the grant. Like Cochiti Pueblo, Zia, Santa Ana, and Jemez Pueblos had large herds of cattle and flocks of sheep; they used the land west of Jemez Pueblo for common grazing land and also maintained numerous sacred sites there. By 1766 more and more Spaniards were competing with the pueblos—and with the horse herd of the Santa Fe presidio—for the use of this land. Governor Vélez Cachupín was aware of the problem of Spanish encroachment on Pueblo land, having made some of the adjacent grants to Spanish settlers himself. As noted earlier, Vélez Cachupín was attempting to protect both the Pueblo peoples and their Spanish neighbors by achieving a balanced land utilization regime among them.[43]

The Ojo del Espíritu Santo Valley constituted the approach of raiding Navajos and Apaches, who would enter the valley at a place called La Ventana (the Window), "a rock formation in the shape of a window that marks the northwest boundary of the grant. Just west is the pass that threads through the rock formations. . . . By sealing off the pass the pueblos could better guard the trail leading to their villages along the Jemez River." As the common pasture-lands of the Ojo del Espíritu Santo grant came under increasing pressure from encroaching Spaniards, Vélez Cachupín and his trusted local officials Felipe Tafoya and Bartolomé Fernández began to prepare the way for the ground-breaking Ojo del Espíritu Santo grant as well as the Cochiti pasture grant, discussed earlier.[44]

The first step was the filing by Felipe Tafoya of a petition on behalf of the pueblos of Zia, Jemez, and Santa Ana in June 1766, requesting the Ojo del Espíritu Santo grant and alleging that the land had been used as common pastures (*pastos concejiles*) for grazing sheep, cattle, and horses since "the time of the foundation" of each pueblo. The boundaries requested were La Ventana to the north, where some Navajos resided; the lands of the settlers of the Río Puerco to the south; the pueblos of Zia, Santa Ana, and Jemez to the east; and the bank of the Río Puerco to the west.[45] After receiving the petition, Governor Vélez Cachupín ordered Alcalde Bartolomé Fernández to go to the Espíritu Santo tract, examine the boundaries, determine whether the grant would prejudice the rights of third parties, and find out whether the three pueblos had sufficient livestock to justify the amount of land requested.[46] The tract was not suitable for farming, only for grazing, since very little water, besides the spring of the Espíritu Santo could be found on the land. Alcalde Fernández made his investigation and found that the distance from La

Ventana on the north to the stone ford where the settlers of the Río Puerco were located was about eight leagues (about twenty-one miles) and the distance from Zia Pueblo (the nearest pueblo to the land petitioned for) and the Río Puerco was about six leagues (about fifteen and a half miles). Since the three pueblos had abundant cattle and sheep and no place else to pasture them, and since the proposed grant would not prejudice the rights of any third party, Governor Vélez Cachupín decided to grant the land to the three pueblos.[47] He made the grant to Zia, Santa Ana, and Jemez Pueblos for grazing their livestock on 6 August 1766, but with one condition: that the stallions of the presidial horse herd might also graze there. Otherwise, the land within the boundaries was to be considered the property (*derecho legítimo*) of the three pueblos and not subject to any other grant or use by the Spaniards. To make this fact crystal clear, Vélez Cachupín added that the pueblos "would hold [the land] with legitimate title under this royal grant."[48] However, this prohibition against later grants of the same land would soon be violated.

In September 1766 Zia, Santa Ana, and Jemez Pueblos were placed in possession of the land in the presence of representatives of the settlers of the Río Puerco settlement and the governors, caciques, and war captains of the three pueblos. Alcalde Fernández was fulfilling his mandate regarding conflicting claims by having the Río Puerco settlers present, but it would later turn out that threat of encroachment on the Ojo del Espíritu Santo grant would come from the east, from the San Isidro grant and the Baca heirs who would receive a grant to the same lands, also called the Ojo del Espíritu Santo grant. In the meantime, there being no objection by the Río Puerco settlers, Alcalde Fernández completed the ceremony of delivery of possession of the Espíritu Santo grant by having the grantees throw stones and pull up grass as proof of their possession and ownership. The land described in the act of possession extended, north to south, from La Ventana to the stone ford and, east to west, from the boundary of Zia Pueblo to the bank of the Río Puerco.[49] By making this grant, Governor Vélez Cachupín was placing the capstone in the edifice of his land grant policy that was designed to provide grazing grants to both Indian pueblos and Hispanic settlements, protect the pueblos from encroachment on their lands by neighboring Spaniards, and protect both Spanish and Pueblo villages from attack by Ute, Comanche, and Apache raiders by establishing more communities on the periphery of existing settlements.[50]

Several grants were made adjacent to and overlapping the 1766 Ojo del

Espíritu Santo grant in spite of the protection that the grant was supposed to afford from encroaching Spaniards. Soon after the grant was made, Spanish settlers, mostly from the Baca family, began to settle in the vicinity of the Espíritu Santo Spring in the middle of the grant. In 1815 the Baca heirs received their own grant, also called the Ojo del Espíritu Santo grant, covering roughly the same area as the grant to Zia, Santa Ana, and Jemez Pueblos. Not only did the two land grants with the same name confuse future historians, but the 1815 Ojo del Espíritu Santo grant became one of the reasons the 1766 Ojo del Espíritu Santo grant was rejected. In fact, the 1815 Ojo del Espíritu Santo grant completely erased the 1766 grant from the map; most current maps do not even show the 1766 Zia, Santa Ana, and Jemez (Ojo del Espíritu Santo) grant.[51] The heirs of Luis María Cabeza de Baca were in possession of a large part of the grazing grant to the three pueblos and used this claim to argue that the Indians were not in exclusive possession of the 1766 Ojo del Espíritu Santo grant. Thus, the illegal grant that Vélez Cachupín and Felipe Tafoya were trying to protect the Indians from became a major reason for the rejection of the 1766 grazing grant to the Indians of Zia, Santa Ana, and Jemez.[52]

The San Isidro grant (1786) and the 1815 Ojo del Espíritu Santo grant were the two grants adjacent to or overlapping the 1766 Espíritu Santo grant. Only the San Isidro grant southeast of the grazing grant, which was made by Governor Juan Bautista de Anza, gave notice to the three pueblos who owned the Ojo del Espíritu Santo grant.[53] A discussion of the San Isidro grant follows later in the chapter.

The three pueblos of Zia, Santa Ana, and Jemez submitted a claim for the Ojo del Espíritu Santo grant to the surveyor general of New Mexico in 1856, but for some reason the claim was not acted on until 1874, when the three pueblos hired attorney Samuel Ellison to prosecute their claim.[54] Ellison petitioned Surveyor General James Proudfit for confirmation of the grant, and the claimants submitted the certified copy of the Vélez Cachupín grant proceedings.[55] Proudfit took extensive testimony about the pueblo Indians' use of the land. One witness testified that the three pueblos had used the grant for grazing their livestock and that no one claimed an adverse interest in the grant except "Diego Baca [who] has resided at the spring for the last three or four years and has been cultivating the land and has some livestock there." In February 1874 Surveyor General Proudfit recommended confirmation of the grant by Congress, noting that the three pueblos had proven "an absolute grant and full possession under it." The grant was surveyed in 1877 and found to contain 382,849 acres.[56]

By the late 1870s, however, the entire surveyor general system for land grant confirmation had broken down. Congress was suspicious of each grant that was recommended, and not until the Court of Private Land Claims was established in 1891 were the pueblos of Zia, Santa Ana, and Jemez able to file suit for confirmation of their grant.[57] George Hill Howard, who later became special attorney to the Pueblo Indians, represented the plaintiffs. He claimed that the three pueblos had received "a formal and final grant, in fee absolute, coupled with no conditions," except that the presidial horse herd could also use the land when necessary. Howard noted the several nearby or overlapping grants in the area but claimed that the Ojo del Espíritu Santo grant was senior to all of them.[58] The issue of encroachment of other grants on the Ojo del Espíritu Santo grant had already been brought to the attention of the commissioner of Indian affairs in June 1888 by Indian Agent M. C. Williams, who listed several grants as lying wholly or partially within the 1766 Espíritu Santo grant. Indian Agent Williams was completely frustrated in his attempts to protect the Espíritu Santo grant from encroachment: "No steps have been taken to protect the land from being encroached upon save [for] notices posted. . . . The greater part of the parties who are occupying the said land have been there for many years [and] . . . it is utterly impracticable for me to attempt to remove any of them [even] if I had the power."[59] But he suggested that the Indian Department "prevent the confirmation and patenting of any more [overlapping] grants . . . until the grant to the Indians is confirmed and patented." The Indian Service was not inclined to become involved in the adjudication of Pueblo lands, however, especially since, as noted, the pueblos did not have an attorney appointed to represent them until 1898, when George Hill Howard was appointed special attorney for the Pueblo Indians.[60] The petition for confirmation of the Ojo del Espíritu Santo grant referred to the conflicting grants and alleged that all of them were subsequent to the 1766 Ojo del Espíritu Santo grant, and even if they had been confirmed by the Court of Private Land Claims (as was the case of the 1815 Ojo del Espíritu Santo grant), they had been made without notice to the pueblos of Zia, Santa Ana, and Jemez and were therefore void.[61]

The list of claimants in opposition to the three pueblos read like a Who's Who of New Mexico elites. Mariano Otero had a ranch on the Ojo del Espíritu Santo grant, and he, Pedro Perea, and Charles Gildersleeve were claiming that interest, while Diego Baca claimed under the 1815 Ojo del Espíritu Santo grant along with Thomas B. Catron. The lengthy trial focused primarily on the issue of the use and occupancy of the grant by the three pueblos. Much of the testimony was elicited under cross-examination by Thomas Catron, who sought to minimize the testimony of the pueblos regarding their occupancy and to establish his clients' title to the conflicting 1815 Ojo del Espíritu Santo grant. Very little testimony was provided about the so-called revocable nature of the grant, the issue upon which the Court of Private Land Claims eventually based its decision. Ironically, it was the occupancy of the very land grants that had encroached on the 1766 Ojo del Espíritu Santo land of the three pueblos that was used against them.[62]

Both Pueblo Indians and non-Indians testified about their use of the land. Francisco Archibeque testified under examination by Catron that one Jesús Trujillo had established a sheep ranch on the land and that Mariano Perea had a house and cattle ranch on the land, as did Diego Baca, Jesús Sandoval, and Joaquín Sandoval. Mariano Perea was one of the defendants in the case, and Thomas Catron both represented him and claimed an interest in the encroaching grant, the 1815 Ojo del Espíritu Santo grant. Catron extensively examined Diego Baca, claimant of the 1815 Ojo del Espíritu Santo grant. Baca was the grandson of Luis María Cabeza de Baca, a claimant of the Las Vegas grant after whom the Baca locations were named and a thorn in the side of Cochiti Pueblo for many decades. Diego Baca's father was an Indian agent assigned to the Ojo del Espíritu Santo area to make peace with the Navajos. When his father became sick, Diego Baca's uncle was appointed Indian Agent in his place, and Baca was appointed as his assistant. This testimony established that the Bacas had encroached on the Ojo del Espíritu Santo grant of the three pueblos just as they had encroached on the Cochiti Pueblo grant, but that did not prove the invalidity of the 1766 Espíritu Santo grant.[63] The Baca family had even obtained their own grant to the Ojo del Espíritu Santo tract in 1815, to be discussed later, but had not given notice to the three pueblos or even mentioned the earlier grant when they received a private grant from Governor Alberto Máynez (1808, 1814–1816). Catron dominated the trial with little opposition from lawyers for the Indians. He was trying to establish the existence of competing grants, such as the 1815 Espíritu Santo grant, as a way of showing that the three pueblos did not have exclusive possession of the land and also, incidentally, establish his own claim.[64] Contrary to testimony that none of the pueblos used the grant for grazing because of Navajo hostilities, Francisco Archibeque testified that he had been familiar with the entire grant as a shepherd from the time he was ten or twelve years old and that both Zia and Jemez used the area to pasture their animals. According to Archibeque, the people of Zia would graze their sheep and cattle as far as the Cañada de las Milpas, where they had some farms, and the Jemez Indians kept their cattle and horses at what was known as the Chihuahua Ranch.[65] Another witness, Zia governor Lorenzo Lobato, testified that the Santa Ana Indians had both grazed and planted land at the Cañada de Achavarria.[66]

In spite of this testimony about the use of the land by Zia, Santa Ana, and Jemez Pueblos and of the priority of the 1776 Ojo del Espíritu Santo grant over later grants, the Court of Private Land Claims rejected the grant to the pueblos. The court held, in a highly legalistic decision, that the grant was not an outright grant but a mere license subject to revocation or forfeiture. The three pueblos had not received an absolute grant that vested title in them, according to the court, but rather a "possessory right which could be revoked by the Spanish or Mexican authorities at any time and was liable to be forfeited by abandonment or nonuse, [and] that the re-granting of various portions of the grant . . . evidenced its forfeiture." None of this language about vested rights, possessory rights, or licenses is found in the Spanish law—either in statutory law or court decisions—of the late eighteenth-century period, when the Zia, Santa Ana, and Jemez grant was made. Although numerous reasons could have been found in Spanish law that *would have* justified the rejection of a land grant—failure to settle the grant, failure to notify adjoining owners, and failure to meet a condition of the grant, among others—none of those reasons were present.[67] Thus, in rejecting the grant, the court failed to apply the Spanish law under which the Ojo del Espíritu Santo grant was made.[68]

Clearly, the 1766 Ojo del Espíritu Santo grant was intended to be permanent and irrevocable, not temporary and revocable as the court held. Governor Vélez Cachupín made it clear that the Ojo del Espíritu Santo grant was permanent and the absolute property (derecho legítimo) of the three pueblos and not subject to another grant or even usage by Spaniards. Vélez Cachupín knew how to draft a grant that *was* revocable, and he had done so on several occasions. The claim that the Ojo del Espíritu Santo grant was not a grant but was instead a revocable license was barely discussed in the long trial. Nevertheless, the

Court of Private Land Claims entered its decree rejecting the Zia, Santa Ana, and Jemez grant on 18 August 1893.[69]

The pueblos of Zia, Santa Ana, and Jemez appealed the decision of the Court of Private Land Claims to the U.S. Supreme Court. The case was briefed and argued by some of the same lawyers who had handled the case in the lower court: Henry Earle for the three pueblos (for some reason lawyer George Hill Howard was no longer involved) and Matthew G. Reynolds for the U.S. government. The court included a translation of the grant documents (but not a Spanish transcription), and most of the opinion was an analysis of these documents. Just as it had shown with many other Court of Private Land Claims cases, the Supreme Court had difficulty interpreting this Spanish land grant in accordance with Spanish rather than Anglo-American law. Right at the beginning of the short opinion rendered by Justice Henry Billings Brown, the court opined that the Ojo del Espíritu Santo pasture grant established "a right somewhat akin to the right of common under the English law." [70] As Justice Brown continued his examination of the grant documents, he indicated the direction he was headed when he wrote, "Nor are there any words indicating an intention to pass a fee simple [title]." By using this typically Anglo-American phrase, "fee simple title," which was not found in Spanish land grant documents, Justice Brown ignored the clear language of Governor Vélez Cachupín's granting decree: "*They will hold the same with legitimate title* under this royal grant" (emphasis added).[71]

The rejection of the 1766 Ojo del Espíritu Santo grant by the Court of Private Land Claims and ultimately by the U.S. Supreme Court was highly unfair as mentioned earlier, especially since the Court of Private Land Claims confirmed several grazing grants to Spaniards that were similar to the 1766 Ojo del Espíritu Santo grant. In fact, those confirmed grazing grants were made to some of the same Spanish alcaldes who had officiated at the making of the Zia, Santa Ana, and Jemez grant. It was extremely unjust that three Indian pueblos that had traditionally used the land covered by the 1766 Ojo del Espíritu Santo grant should be denied that land by an American court, while the same court confirmed similar grants made to Spaniards.[72]

While the pueblos did receive some compensation for the lost land, it was the land itself that was important. In addition, the historical record has been skewed by the rejection of the Pueblo Indian grazing grants. As will be discussed further in chapter 11, Governor Vélez Cachupín was attempting to achieve a balance between Pueblo land and Hispanic land so that each group would have land for both farming and grazing their livestock and sheep. In the 131 years since the Vélez Cachupín grant, land had become more valuable for development, and the Supreme Court had become more restrictive in its interpretation of indigenous land rights. Ironically, this restrictive viewpoint was also applied to the common lands of Hispano community grants, which were lost because of similarly incorrect Supreme Court decisions.[73]

Just as the Cochiti pasture grant was rejected, while the encroaching Cañada de Cochití grant was confirmed by the courts, two grants encroaching on the 1766 Ojo del Espíritu Santo grant either in the whole or in part were approved while the 1766 Ojo del Espíritu Santo grant was rejected. The first grant encroaching on the 1766 Ojo del Espíritu Santo grant was also called the Ojo del Espíritu Santo grant (known here as the 1815 Ojo del Espíritu Santo grant) and was made to Luis María Cabeza de Baca and his large family of fifteen children. Baca's family had been encroaching on the Cochiti Pueblo league and had established the community of Peña Blanca on the southern portion of the Cochiti Pueblo league.[74] Now in 1815 Baca claimed that he needed additional land to graze his herds of cattle and horses.[75] Governor Alberto Máynez made the grant with scant investigation on 24 May 1815. Baca mentioned that Antonio Ortiz had received a grant of the same land twenty years earlier (which he had not occupied), but he failed to note the 1766 Vélez Cachupín grant to the pueblos of Zia, Santa Ana, and Jemez about fifty years earlier.[76] Without notifying any of the neighbors or the pueblos of Zia, Santa Ana, or Jemez, the alcalde of Jemez, Ignacio María Sánchez Vergara, placed Luis María Cabeza de Baca and his family in possession of the land.[77] The participation of Sánchez Vergara in the granting process raises serious questions about the legitimacy of the grant because of Sánchez Vergara's acquisition of Pueblo land for himself and his double dealings when he was acting as Protector of Indians.[78]

Besides the questions of notice to neighboring landowners was the question of whether the Baca family had actually settled on the grant. Nevertheless, after the 1846 U.S. occupation of New Mexico and the establishment of the surveyor general of New Mexico in 1854, the heirs of Luis María Cabeza de Baca filed a petition for confirmation of the 1815 Ojo del Espíritu Santo grant through lawyer John L. Watts. (Earlier, because the Las Vegas grant had already been confirmed, Watts was able to obtain the same amount of land in five roughly one-hundred-thousand-acre tracts chosen by the same Baca heirs, known as the Baca Floats, located throughout New Mexico and Arizona.)[79] Watts's petition for confirmation of the 1815 Ojo del Espíritu Santo grant was recommended for confirmation by Surveyor General Alexander Wilbar on 12 December 1860, with little investigation of the historical background of the grant.[80] However, it was not until March 1869 that the 1815 Ojo del Espíritu Santo grant was confirmed by Congress. It was surveyed at 127,000-plus acres in 1876 and modified in April 1885 to about 113,000 acres.[81] By January of 1895 the General Land Office had decided to "carry into patent" the amended survey of the grant upon payment of the cost of survey, $502.65.[82] Over twenty years later the patent was issued based on a formal request received by the Honorable Thomas B. Catron as president of the Ojo del Espíritu Santo Company in early October of 1816. Catron had been threatened with suit by the U.S. attorney in August of 1911, but he must have paid the U.S. government the cost of survey by October 1916, when the patent was transmitted to him by the Department of the Interior." [83]

With the rejection of the Indian grazing grant known as the 1766 Ojo del Espíritu Santo grant and the confirmation of the 1815 Ojo del Espíritu Santo grant, the land that had once been a garden spot in New Mexico was soon heavily overgrazed as Hispano farmers and ranchers, and later Frank Bond, began large-scale grazing activities in the area. They also began farming with extensive irrigation facilities that used water diverted from the Río Puerco. Heavy grazing and a drought led to severe erosion and a lowering of the water table. "In less than twenty years a one time spring became a twenty foot well." The garden spot that was once the Ojo del Espíritu Santo grant had become a wasteland, leaving the local population bereft of their once-abundant grazing land and spring-fed water holes. After rejecting the Ojo del Espíritu Santo grant, a valid subsistence-related grazing grant to Indian stock raisers, the federal government had to make loans to support local farmers and ranchers displaced by large-scale operators like Frank Bond.[84]

The San Isidro Grant

The second grant that encroached on the 1766 Ojo del Espíritu Santo grant was known as the San Isidro grant. The San Isidro grant was a large grazing grant made to Hispano elites that also encroached on Jemez Pueblo land and yet was readily recommended for confirmation by the surveyor general of

New Mexico, while the similar Ojo del Espíritu Santo grazing grant made to Zia, Santa Ana, and Jemez Pueblos was rejected. The San Isidro grant was made in 1786 to Antonio Armenta, alcalde of the Keres pueblos, and Salvador Antonio Sandoval, a presidial soldier. We met Antonio Armenta in our discussion of the Cañada de Cochití grant—he was the alcalde who decided in favor of the absentee owners of the Cañada de Cochití grant versus a grant resident who was not an heir but wanted to graze his animals on the grant. Armenta and Sandoval requested a tract of land southeast of the Ojo del Espíritu Santo grant from Governor Juan Bautista de Anza. The boundaries requested were Jemez Pueblo to the north, Zia Pueblo to the south, the lands of Nerio Antonio Montoya to the east, and the mountains of the Espíritu Santo Spring to the west. Since the proposed grant was bounded by Jemez Pueblo on the north and Zia Pueblo on the south, Governor Anza granted the request of the petitioners on condition that the grant not conflict with the lands of those two pueblos and that the two pueblos not be disturbed in their prior use of the water.[85]

On the day when the grantees of the San Isidro grant were to be placed in possession by Alcalde Nerio Antonio Montoya, representatives of both Zia and Jemez Pueblos appeared to object, claiming that the San Isidro grant did in fact encroach on their lands. Alcalde Montoya, though not exactly a disinterested party, for he owned the land at the east boundary of the grant, nevertheless notified both Jemez and Zia Pueblos and listened to their objections. Jemez Pueblo claimed to have planted some land within the boundaries of the proposed San Isidro grant, so Alcalde Montoya extended the boundaries of the Jemez League south by 262 additional varas to include the planted land. Alcalde Montoya also extended the boundary of the Zia League by one thousand varas to encompass two tracts of land Zia had purchased from Spaniards. Besides encroaching on the Pueblo leagues of both Jemez and Zia, the San Isidro grant encroached on the western part of the Ojo del Espíritu Santo grant to a small extent. Governor Anza made the San Isidro grant with the following boundaries: north, Jemez Pueblo; south, Zia Pueblo; east, the lands of Antonio Nerio Montoya; and west, the Ojo del Espíritu Santo Mountains at the place called Los Bancos. The reference to Los Bancos was added by Alcalde Montoya to the western boundary at the request of the petitioners. Because of the possibility of encroachment by the San Isidro grant on the lands of Zia and Jemez Pueblos and the Ojo del Espíritu Santo grant, Spanish government officials were quite solicitous of the rights of the pueblos. However, neither Jemez nor Zia Pueblos would ever have that additional land confirmed to them.[86]

Sometime after the establishment of the San Isidro grant, a community called San Isidro, south of Jemez Pueblo, developed partly on Jemez Pueblo land. Members of this community had large flocks of sheep that often invaded the fields of Jemez Pueblo as well as the Ojo del Espíritu Santo grant. In 1857 a group of six individuals led by Francisco Sandoval, all of whom claimed to be heirs of the original grantees of the San Isidro grant, petitioned Surveyor General William Pelham for confirmation of the grant—not to the community of San Isidro, but to the individual petitioners as heirs of the original grantees. Thus, even though the surveyor general file refers to the Town of San Isidro grant, it was considered to be a private grant by the petitioners. The six petitioners filed the testimonio of the grant with no other evidence.[87] On 8 June 1859, Pelham held that "the [grant] documents are assumed as genuine unless they are proven to be fraudulent and counterfeit." Pelham thus recommended confirmation of the grant solely on the presumption that the grant document was genuine, a more leniant approach than was taken with the Ojo del Espíritu Santo grant, for instance.[88] Based on Pelham's favorable report, Congress confirmed the grant on 21 June 1860, and the grant was surveyed in March 1877 by Deputy Surveyors Sawyer and McElroy for 11,476.88 acres.[89]

Ten years later on 18 August 1887, Surveyor General George Julian requested permission to resurvey the grant in a letter to G. L. O. commissioner Strother M. Stockslager. Julian believed that the north boundary of the grant should have been located 262 varas south of the southern boundary of the Jemez Pueblo grant, 2,632 varas north of the northern boundary of the Zia Pueblo grant, and along the summit of the Espíritu Santo Mountains instead of the cliffs known as Los Bancos. These new boundaries would have reduced the size of the grant by approximately ninety-four hundred acres.[90] Julian, as was his custom, was arguing for a reduction in the size of the San Isidro grant and not for a corresponding enlargement of either the Jemez Pueblo or Zia Pueblo lands. Nevertheless, in November 1888 Stockslager rejected the request, stating, "If, however, you care to furnish additional and convincing reasons for a resurvey of the grant as proposed, I would have no hesitation in recommending it."[91] On 5 December 1888 Julian again urged that a resurvey of the grant be made on the grounds that the act of possession showed that the Jemez Indians had been given 262 varas in addition to their league of land, that the

Zia Indians had received an additional 2,632 varas, and that the west line should be located along the summit of the mountains, which was about five miles east of Los Bancos.[92] As mentioned, Julian was more interested in reducing the size of the San Isidro grant than he was in providing for a corresponding slight increase in the lands of Zia and Jemez Pueblos.

Since the San Isidro grant had been approved by Congress and surveyed at 11,476 acres, the new owners did not need Julian's approval to start using the grant, mostly for grazing. They did need a patent, but that would be delayed for over four decades, until a sale of the grant was pending.[93]

The confirmation of the San Isidro grant without regard to its overlap with Jemez Pueblo and the 1766 Ojo del Espíritu Santo grant was unjust. Although it did not overlap the 1766 Ojo del Espíritu Santo grant as much as the 1815 Ojo del Espíritu Santo grant did, its proximity to the 1766 Ojo del Espíritu Santo grant meant that livestock from San Isidro wandered onto the Pueblo grazing grant, making it more difficult for the three pueblos to prove exclusive possession of the grant.[94] Like the approval of the Cañada de Cochití grant and the rejection of the Cochiti pasture grant, here again we have the confirmation of two less deserving grants (San Isidro and the 1815 Ojo del Espíritu Santo grants) and the rejection of the legitimate and more deserving 1766 Ojo del Espíritu Santo grant.

It is hoped that this chapter will restore the lost history of these two authentic Pueblo Indian grazing grants: one to Cochiti Pueblo and the other—known as the 1766 Ojo del Espíritu Santo grant—to the pueblos of Zia, Santa Ana, and Jemez.

CHAPTER FIVE

La Ciénega and
Cieneguilla Pueblos

THE ANCIENT PUEBLOS OF LA CIÉNEGA AND CIENEGUILLA ARE THE
least studied of the little-studied Galisteo Basin pueblos. Bandelier barely
mentions them and seems to have made a conscious decision to concentrate on
the ancient pueblos on the Pajarito Plateau where Bandelier National
Monument is now located. Nels Nelson investigated both pueblos in his 1914
and 1915 studies in the most complete excavation to date. Recently, the Galisteo
Basin Archaeological Sites Assessment Project has identified the areas covered
by these two pueblos. La Ciénega Pueblo was found to contain about eighty-
four acres on the mesa top above the confluence of the Santa Fe River and La
Ciénega Creek, including the hill slopes descending from the mesa to those
two watercourses. This area does not include the Pueblo site at the base of the
mesa that is located on private land. It is this site that will be discussed in the
following narrative. The site of Cieneguilla or Tzeguma Pueblo contains about
eleven acres, 40 percent of which are owned by the Bureau of Land Management
and the remainder by private owners who are the heirs of La Cieneguilla Land
grant.[1]

Both La Ciénega and Cieneguilla were occupied at the time of the Pueblo
Revolt but abandoned shortly thereafter. Vargas and earlier Spanish conquistadores sometimes confused the two, calling La Ciénega, Cieneguilla, and vice
versa.[2] The land surrounding and including both pueblos was soon acquired
by Spaniards. La Ciénega Pueblo was apparently granted by Diego de Vargas
to Miguel García de la Riva, but that information is based on a recitation in a

deed to García de la Riva from José Castellanos, rather than a grant from Governor Vargas. As for Cieneguilla Pueblo, Vargas planned in 1693 to resettle Cieneguilla Pueblo with Pueblo captives from the battle of Santa Fe, but that plan fell apart. Vargas later made a grant of Cieneguilla Pueblo land but not to the people of Cieneguilla. Instead, it was a grant to Francisco Anaya Almazán of one fanega of corn-planting and grazing land for two hundred head of sheep, twenty head of cattle, and some oxen, which Anaya Almazán's heirs later expanded to over thirty-two hundred acres. The early history of this area is found in the private deeds and lawsuits over the acquisition and division of this property.[3]

What follows is a complex history of the early settlement of the Cieneguilla/ La Ciénega area, made by a wide range of members of New Mexican society, from Indians, Genízaros, and poor Spaniards to the wealthiest families in the state. The Indians lived in the ancient pueblos of La Ciénega and Cieneguilla, most of the poor Hispanos and Genízaros remain nameless (except on lists of the names of victims of Comanche attacks), and the wealthy Hispanos came from old New Mexico families whose descendants still live in the area. Some of the Hispano family names include Miguel García de la Riva, Miguel Tenorio de Alba, and María de la Vega y Coca for La Ciénega; José Riaño and Antonio Sandoval, Felipe Sandoval y Rojas, and María Roybal for El Álamo and Las Golondrinas; and Francisco Anaya Almazán, Felipe Rico de Rojas, and Andres Montoya for Cieneguilla. Steeped in a history going back to their origins in Spain, these families were often fighting among themselves over the verdant fields beneath the petroglyphs of the ancient pueblos. Yet these communities retained the traditional village life of rural northern New Mexico communities until recently, when several large-scale developments planned for the Ciénega area threatened to split these communities apart.[4]

La Ciénega

The pueblo of La Ciénega, two leagues (five miles) from the pueblo of San Marcos, is often considered a Galisteo Basin pueblo, though it is beyond that area and its inhabitants were mixed Tano and Keres speakers.[5] It was visited by the Castaño de Sosa expedition in February 1591 during which "the natives pledged obedience to his Majesty; a governor, an alcalde, and an *alguacil* were named; and a large cross was raised to the sound of trumpets and *harquebus* shots." A few weeks before their visit to La Ciénega Pueblo, the members of the Castaño de Sosa expedition visited six pueblos north of Santa Fe, probably Nambe, Tesuque, Pojoaque, Cuyamungue, Jacona, and San Ildefonso. The comments in the journal of the expedition would most likely apply to La Ciénega Pueblo as well: "All six of these settlements have canals for irrigation, which would be incredible to anyone who had not seen them with his own eyes. The inhabitants harvest large quantities of corn, beans, and other vegetables." Most farming at La Ciénega Pueblo was done in the area below where the Santa Fe River and La Ciénega Creek meet.[6]

Like other pre-revolt pueblos, La Ciénega was subject to tribute (usually a cotton blanket and a fanega [bushel] of corn per household). Spaniards with the right to collect such tribute were encomenderos who were granted an entire pueblo (or part of one) in encomienda.[7] One of the few references to the pueblo of La Ciénega prior to 1680 comes from the administration of Governor López de Mendizábal, who was continually at odds with the Franciscan priests whose job it was to Christianize the Pueblo Indians. As part of that responsibility the priests sought to stamp out all aspects of Pueblo religion, including ceremonial kachina dances. In 1660, to the shock of the priests, Governor López de Mendizábal decreed that the Pueblo Indians could resume their ceremonial dances. La Ciénega was one of the pueblos that began performing the kachina dances again, which were described by the Spaniards as "some evil and idolatrous dances called kachinas."[8]

The pueblo of La Ciénega must have been engaged in substantial farming activities both to feed its members and to supply maize tribute to its encomendero. La Ciénega Pueblo was a visita of San Marcos Pueblo, as was San Lázaro Pueblo. This meant that the priest resident at San Marcos would travel to San Lázaro and La Ciénega Pueblos to celebrate Mass. All three pueblos were estimated to have a population of 777 in 155 households by 1626. The encomienda tribute required of both pueblos has been estimated at 387 fanegas of maize, part of which would have been grown at the pueblo of La Ciénega.[9] Scattered references to La Ciénega Pueblo testify to its continued existence during the seventeenth century. The pueblo was mentioned in 1664 by Fray Gabriel de Torija, who referred to La Ciénega Pueblo as being halfway between Santo Domingo and Santa Fe,[10] and in 1665 by Diego de Peñalosa.[11] In 1661 Fray Miguel Sacristán reported the burial of a figurine doll "at the pueblo of San Marcos, called La Ciénega." This statement was part of the evidence against Governor López de

Mendizábal during his trial conducted by the Inquisition in Mexico City. Tried
along with López de Mendizábal was Cristóbal Anaya Almazán, the son of
Francisco Anaya Almazán.[12]

La Ciénega Pueblo played a conflicted part in the Pueblo Revolt of 1680, the
first round of the Spanish-Pueblo War of 1680–1696. When the knotted cord
was being passed from pueblo to pueblo to give notice of the planned revolt
and its date, the governors of San Marcos and La Ciénega Pueblos were unwilling to agree to the revolt plans. At the time they received the cord, it contained
two knots indicating that the revolt would take place in two days, on 11 August.
When La Ciénega Pueblo received the cord from the two representatives from
Tesuque, they were notified that any pueblo not taking part in the revolt would
be destroyed by the other pueblos, which may be the reason that San Marcos
and La Ciénega decided to reverse course and join the revolt. Nevertheless, on
9 August 1680 the governors of San Marcos and La Ciénega Pueblos appeared
at the Casas Reales and told Governor Otermín that the revolt would take
place on the thirteenth. The Pueblo Revolt actually began on 10 August 1680,
having been moved forward after its discovery, and when it was over, over
four hundred Spaniards and their allies had been killed and the rest had
retreated to El Paso, where a temporary capital was established. Twelve years
later Governor Diego de Vargas returned to reconquer New Mexico for the
Spanish crown.[13]

When Diego de Vargas arrived at the pueblo of La Ciénega (which he called
Cieneguilla) at the time of his 1692 reconquest, he noted in his journal: "Today,
Friday, 12 September . . . I . . . arrived at this pueblo called Cieneguilla [La
Ciénega], which I reconnoitered and found abandoned."[14] The next year, when
Vargas returned, he again found the pueblo abandoned, but this time he
referred to it correctly as La Ciénega and stated, "Should some Keres Indians
return to settle there, they will be limited to 500 varas from the door of the
church in the four directions and no more. The person who demonstrates his
right to them will also be given the lands of the abandoned hacienda of El
Álamo, with the limitation of not being able to make claims for damage the
horses may do."[15]

This statement by Governor Vargas suggests that the primary pre-revolt
population sites in the area were the hacienda of El Álamo and La Ciénega
Pueblo, and it is reinforced by statements taken from witnesses during the
Pueblo Revolt of 1696. On 13 June 1696 Alonso Guique, a Santo Domingo

Indian who was temporarily living at Jemez Pueblo and who was then serving as governor of Santo Domingo, said that when he heard the news of the 1696 revolt he left Santo Domingo to see what was going on. When he reached Cerrillos and found no one there, "he [went] to spend the night between La Ciénega and El Álamo." When asked why he had spent the night there, Alonso Guique said that "he had gone to sleep between La Ciénega and El Álamo because he found the house [there] had been abandoned." It appears from this statement that the primary settled area, both before the revolt and during the second Pueblo Revolt of 1696, encompassed the Hacienda del Álamo, La Ciénega, and the area in between.[16] During most of the eighteenth century the area around La Ciénega was composed of ranchos at El Álamo and La Ciénega, and at midcentury the entire area was known as El Álamo. Prior to the Pueblo Revolt we know that some Spaniards were living at or near La Ciénega Pueblo at least by 1629. Tree-ring analysis from an archaeological site (LA 20,000) at the present-day village of La Ciénega shows cutting dates of 1629 and 1631 for tree samples taken from the structure known as unit B. The site, near the confluence of the Alamo and La Ciénega Creeks with the Santa Fe River, contained the headquarters of an extensive Spanish rancho or estancia, including a main dwelling with either an enclosed patio or back-to-back rooms and outbuildings such as a torreón and *horno* opening into the interior of the dwelling and corrals. The primary activity of the Spanish families living in LA 20,000 was farming and ranching.[17]

Besides the Indian residents of La Ciénega Pueblo and the Spanish site known as LA 20,000, other pre–Pueblo Revolt Spanish settlers lived at La Ciénega. Dated about the same time as LA 20,000 was the estancia of one of the colonists who came north with Juan de Oñate, Catalina Pérez de Bustillos. She was the widow of Pedro Márquez and in 1631 or 1632 had married Alonso Varela de Losada, who also had an estancia at La Ciénega. Since we do not know the location of either the Pérez de Bustillos or the Varela de Losada estancias, it is quite possible that one of them could have been located at LA 20,000.[18] In addition to the Pérez de Bustillos and Varela de Losada families, a third family with a pre-revolt estancia lived in the area: the family of Ana Baca, who was Antonio Jorge's sister-in-law.[19] Her ranch was called the Estancia del Alamo, which was probably the same land referred to by Vargas when he announced, "He who demonstrates his right to them shall be given the lands of the abandoned hacienda of El Álamo."[20] Other Bacas also lived

around La Ciénega, as evidenced by the northern boundary call of the grant
called Los Cerrillos. On 18 September 1692 Alfonso Rael de Aguilar, one of
Diego de Vargas's most trusted lieutenants, asked Vargas for what became
known as Los Cerrillos grant, bounded "on the north [by] the limits of the
Canada del Guicú and the Baca land."[21] Though it is not clear who the other
pre-revolt Bacas living at La Ciénega were, the name is present in deeds, wills,
and litigation throughout the eighteenth century.

In 1750 the Pecos parish priest, Father Trigo, took a census at El Álamo, which
was included in the jurisdiction of the Villa of Santa Fe. He counted thirty-seven
households with 207 people. The leading citizens of El Álamo were Manuel
Tenorio (de Alba), Ana Baca, and Miguel (Vega y) Coca, who were listed first in
the census and were the given the honorific title "don." María Roybal, the
wealthy widow of José Riaño Tagle, was called "doña."[22] In the 1750 census
three Baca families are listed at La Ciénega (then called El Álamo): Antonio Baca
(married to María Aragón), Nicolas Baca (married to Teodora Fernández), and
Pablo Baca (married to Lorenza Rivera). Although the information is scanty, the
outlines of the landholdings at La Ciénega begin to emerge. After the Vargas
reconquest, Spaniards would expand their holdings to include all of La Ciénega
Pueblo and its environs.[23]

The growth of the community of La Ciénega revolved around the location
of the ancient pueblo of La Ciénega. No one knew the exact boundaries, but
in the early 1700s several Spaniards claimed the land and began expanding
the estimated boundaries of the pueblo proper. The first to claim the land
surrounding the pueblo of La Ciénega was José Castellanos, who deeded the
entire pueblo to Miguel García de la Riva in 1701. It seems that the chain of
title recited in the deed is the only evidence of title to La Ciénega Pueblo that
García de la Riva produced. Not only did García de la Riva create the title in
the 1701 deed, he established (and probably expanded) the boundaries for the
first time when in 1704 he conveyed the pueblo of La Ciénega to his son. Thus,
in two self-serving deeds García de la Riva attempted to establish that he had
received a grant of La Ciénega Pueblo and establish what the boundaries of
the pueblo were. In fact, no grant of La Ciénega Pueblo has ever appeared.
Castellanos recited in the deed that he had acquired the land from Domingo
de la Barreda, whom we met in chapter 2 and who was *alférez* at the presidio
and lived in Santa Fe, where he was also the presidio's armorer.[24]

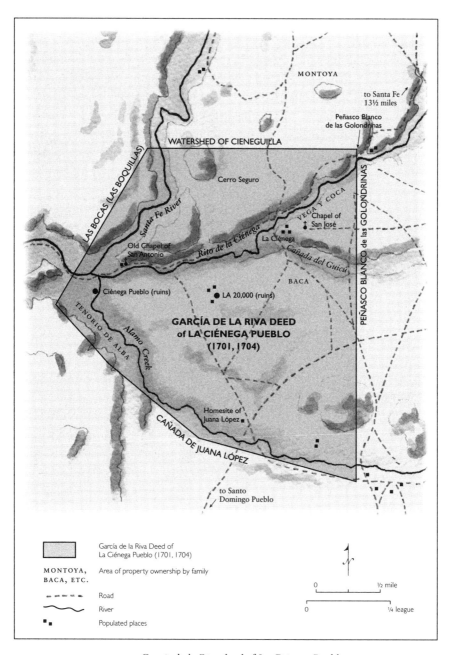

MONTOYA

to Santa Fe
13½ miles

Peñasco Blanco
de las Golondrinas

WATERSHED OF CIENEGUILLA

Cerro Seguro

LAS BOCAS (LAS BOQUILLAS)

Santa Fe River

VEGA Y COCA

Chapel of
San José

PEÑASCO BLANCO de las GOLONDRINAS

Rito de la Ciénega

Old Chapel of
San Antonio

La Ciénega

Cañada del Guicú

Ciénega Pueblo (ruins)

LA 20,000 (ruins)

BACA

TENORIO DE ALBA

Alamo Creek

GARCÍA DE LA RIVA DEED
of LA CIÉNEGA PUEBLO
(1701, 1704)

Homesite of
Juana López

CAÑADA DE JUANA LÓPEZ

to Santo
Domingo Pueblo

García de la Riva Deed of
La Ciénega Pueblo (1701, 1704)

MONTOYA,   Area of property ownership by family
BACA, ETC.

N

Road

River   0   ½ mile

Populated places   0   ¼ league

MAP 3. García de la Riva deed of La Ciénega Pueblo.

In 1704 Miguel García de la Riva sold the site of old La Ciénega Pueblo to his son Juan García de la Riva for one hundred pesos and included specific boundary calls for the first time; apparently, the primary purpose of the transfer was to expand the boundaries beyond what may have been the original boundaries of the pueblo. The boundary calls specified by Miguel were the watershed of Cieneguilla to the north, the Cañada de Juana López to the south; the Peñasco Blanco de las Golondrinas to the east, and Las Boquillas to the west. Another indication that the 1704 deed was designed primarily to expand the boundaries of the "sitio del antigua pueblo de Ciénega" is that this tract was the only one transferred by Miguel García de la Riva to his son during his lifetime, and several other tracts owned by García de la Riva remained in his hands as of 1713. In 1713 Juan García de la Riva listed the property acquired by his father in the Book of the Cabildo, a list of all the documents deposited in the archives of the cabildo of Santa Fe.[25] The property is described as "three *fanegas* of corn-planting land on the other side of the river," which would have been about twenty-five acres, not the much larger tract described in the 1704 deed.[26]

While title to these tracts of land was being passed between largely absentee owners, the García de la Riva genealogical line found its way into La Ciénega. In 1705 Miguel García de la Riva's daughter Teodora married the powerful elite general Juan Páez Hurtado. Though they did not live at La Ciénega, Páez Hurtado may have been responsible for the place-name of Los Palacios at La Ciénega. Cordelia Thomas Snow surmises that "Los Palacios" came from Páez Hurtado's birthplace of Los Palacios y Villafranca in Andalusia, Spain.[27] Someone who *did* put down roots at La Ciénega was José Terrus, who married Antonia Páez Hurtado, daughter of Juan Páez Hurtado and Teodora García de la Riva.[28] José Terrus came to New Mexico from Vique in Catalonia, Spain, and received property from his father-in-law, Juan Páez Hurtado. In his will of 1745, José Terrus referred to "part of the ranch . . . left to me by the general Don Juan Páez [Hurtado]." Though the specific location of the ranch is not mentioned in the will, it was probably located in La Ciénega. In addition to Miguel García de la Riva and Juan Páez Hurtado, who were connected by Páez Hurtado's marriage to García de la Riva's daughter, several other property owners in the Cieneguilla/La Ciénega area also intermarried, establishing "a large extended family clan [that] dominated the politics of Santa Fe as influential leaders and socially prominent members of the community." Most of them owned property in both Santa Fe and the Cieneguilla/La Ciénega area. The

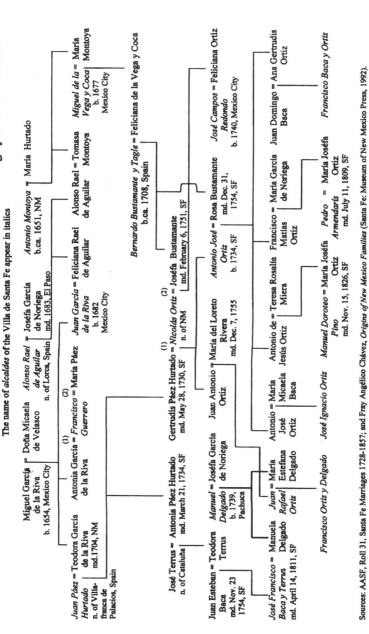

A Dominant Political Clan of Santa Fe: Páez Hurtado–García de la Riva-Ortiz-Vega y Coca-Bustamante

The name of *alcaldes* of the Villa de Santa Fe appear in italics

Sources: AASF, Roll 31, Santa Fe Marriages 1728-1857; and Fray Angélico Chávez, *Origins of New Mexico Families* (Santa Fe: Museum of New Mexico Press, 1992).

FIGURE 2. Páez Hurtado/García de la Riva Genealogy, from *All Trails Lead to Santa Fe*, 407.

genealogical chart shown in figure 2 helps to sort out the intricate network of this extended family.[29]

Another important landowner in La Ciénega was Diego Manuel Baca, the son of Manuel Baca and María Salazar. In his will of 1727 Diego Manuel Baca referred to two tracts of land in La Ciénega. The first, inherited from his father along with his three brothers, was a tract called Codiana, bounded on one side by lands of Josefa Baca and on the side of the Angostura by Ambrosio Sáiz. The other tract owned by Diego Manuel Baca consisted of a house and farmlands next to the lands of his father-in-law, Miguel de la Vega y Coca, which he had given as dowry to his first wife, María de la Vega y Coca. This property contained irrigable land of sufficient size to plant three fanegas of wheat (four and one-half acres) and a half fanega of corn (approximately four acres). Diego Manuel Baca died in 1727, the year he made his will, and was survived by three sons from his marriage to María de la Vega y Coca: Manuel, Nicolas, and Juan Estevan.[30] María de la Vega y Coca died in 1748, and by 1751 Manuel Baca was acting as executor of her estate. In that capacity, Manuel Baca executed a deed to Josefa Montoya of a portion of the ranch listed in Diego Manuel Baca's will of 1727. The sale of the part of the property owned by María de la Vega y Coca was for 140 pesos, and the tract was bounded on the east by Lázaro García, on the west by Antonio Baca. The boundaries on the north and south were listed as those in the deed of sale for the Puesto de la Cieneguilla, but the scribe must have meant Ciénega because the land was at La Ciénega, south of Cieneguilla.[31]

Litigation over partition of the estate of María de la Vega y Coca at La Ciénega further established the property locations at La Ciénega and Cañada de Guicú, and the records reveal several power plays over land. In 1764 Juan Esteban Baca requested partition (division of the land on the ground) of the remaining land in the estate of his mother, María de la Vega y Coca, in accordance with her will. After examining the will, Alcalde Francisco Guerrero divided the land into three parts, one for Juan Esteban, one for his brother Manuel Baca, and a third for the children of their deceased brother, Nicolás Baca. The share of the minor children was measured next to the Arroyo de Agua because that is where the deceased Nicolás Baca had started to build his house. The boundaries of the children's share, received on their behalf by their stepfather, Miguel Tenorio (de Alba), were the Arroyo de Agua on the north and south, the beginning (*principio*) of the Cañada (de Guicú) on the east, and the shoulder of the hill ("el hombro de la loma") on the west. The partition was signed by the two Baca brothers and on behalf of Cristóbal Martín, who could not sign his name. In addition, three Tenorio de Albas signed the partition: Manuel, Alejandro, and Miguel Tenorio de Alba, who had received the share of the minor children.[32]

It was soon to become clear that Miguel Tenorio de Alba was not acting in the best interest of the minor children of Nicolás Baca. Only two years after receiving the share of the children, Tenorio de Alba was the beneficiary of a power of attorney signed by Domingo de Luna on behalf of María Baca, one of the children of Nicolás Baca, authorizing Tenorio de Alba to sell a tract of irrigable land at the Cañada de Guicú in La Ciénega. This document, executed at Santo Domingo Pueblo before Alcalde Bartolomé Fernández, was suspicious because it did not contain the consent of María Baca and would become the source of extensive litigation almost fifty years later.[33] In spite of the questionable nature of the Luna power of attorney, Miguel Tenorio de Alba sold this valuable tract of irrigable land to Miguel Tafoya in 1767 for three hundred pesos. Among the questions raised by this transaction are (1) what happened to the interest of the other minor daughter of Nicolás Baca, and (2) if María Baca had married Domingo de Luna, thus giving him authority to execute the power of attorney, why did they not use this authority to sell the land themselves? Since Miguel Tafoya had only paid 260 of the 300-peso purchase price, Tenorio de Alba gave him a receipt for the 260 pesos and a promise to sign a deed when he received the balance due.[34]

It appears that the questionable nature of Miguel Tenorio de Alba's title was the real reason he did not execute a deed to Miguel Tafoya. It took a petition by Felipe Tafoya, acting as attorney for Miguel Tafoya, to finally get Miguel Tenorio de Alba to sign a deed. In 1767 Governor Pedro Fermín de Mendinueta ordered Miguel Tenorio de Alba to execute a deed with the boundaries listed in the 1764 partition, and for the first time the interest of the other child of Nicolás Baca was mentioned. The deed for this valuable tract of irrigated land stated that the property was for the benefit of María Baca's younger brother, Diego Baca. Now Miguel Tafoya had a deed (albeit one that showed that the young Diego Baca still had an interest in the property), and Miguel Tenorio de Alba had his three hundred *pesos de tierra* (goods valued at three hundred pesos). Tenorio de Alba still had other property in La Ciénega, however, and engaged in several more shady transactions with land he claimed to have inherited from his father, Manuel Tenorio de Alba.[35]

In 1771 Miguel Tenorio de Alba sold two tracts of land in the Cañada de Juana López that he claimed through his father's estate. The first was not irrigated but had been given under Manuel Tenorio de Alba's will to be held in trust with the income "to be applied for masses for the blessed souls [in purgatory]." Ignoring the condition in the deed with a statement that the land was of no benefit to the church, Miguel sold it to Manuel Gallegos for 288 pesos.[36] Whether Miguel Tenorio de Alba applied those funds to the church is questionable in light of his later activities. Miguel also sold a tract of land north of this church tract (called *tierras de ánimas*, or lands of the souls [of the deceased]) to Manuel Gallegos. This second tract was located at the mouth of the Cañada de Juana López and was probably irrigated land. Gallegos then sold the combined tract to Jaime Ortiz for six hundred pesos. The net effect of these transactions was to abrogate the intent of Manuel Tenorio de Alba that the proceeds from the land would be applied for the benefit of the church.[37]

In 1772 Miguel Tenorio de Alba sold another tract of irrigated land north of the tracts he had sold to Manuel Gallegos, a sale that caused further controversy. Tenorio de Alba traded this tract, which he had inherited from his father, to Antonio Ortega for Ortega's house and lands in Santa Fe and for an additional one hundred pesos. One week after signing this deed, Miguel Tenorio de Alba's neighbors filed a suit with Governor Mendinueta in an attempt to block the sale. Antonio José López and Matías Tenorio (brother to Miguel Tenorio de Alba) claimed a right of first refusal whereby they would be offered the right to purchase the property before it was sold to an outsider. López and Tenorio advised Governor Mendinueta that they did not want "to deal with new neighbors" ("experimentar vecinos estraños"), but Tenorio de Alba replied that he was satisfied with the trade he had made with Antonio Ortega and did not want to be forced to accept something different. Miguel added that it served his brother and López right if they suffered damage because they had caused him damage by preventing him from raising a crop on the land in question, though he had "always planted it." López and Matías Tenorio answered that if Miguel had been unable to raise a crop on the land it was not because of anything *they* had done, but because Miguel Tenorio de Alba had neglected his crops. The documents contain the hint of a squabble over water here, as well as evidence that Miguel had been farming the land he sold to Antonio Ortega for some time. In the end, Governor Mendinueta let the sale to Ortega stand, accepting Tenorio de Alba's argument that he should not be required to accept different terms than what he bargained for. Governor Mendinueta also said that he would require some specific evidence of why Ortega would not be a good neighbor before he would set aside the sale.[38]

Although Miguel Tenorio de Alba apparently moved to Santa Fe after his 1772 land swap with Antonio Ortega, he still retained property at La Ciénega. This fact is revealed by the deed from Antonio José López to Alejandro Ortega, son of Antonio Ortega, of a tract of land adjacent to the land Miguel traded to Antonio Ortega. Apparently, Alejandro Ortega was joining his father, Antonio, as a new neighbor in La Ciénega and possibly justifying the fears of the individuals who tried to block the sale by Miguel to the first Ortega in 1772. Ironically, though, one of the petitioners who had tried to block the 1772 sale, Antonio José López, was the one who was selling in 1774. The tract sold to Alejandro Ortega was irrigated land (*tierras de pan llevar*) bounded on the north by the Cañada del Cañón, on the south by Miguel Tenorio (de Alba) and the arroyo that runs through the middle of the land, on the east where the arroyo and the mesa meet next to the old pueblo, and on the west by the entrance to Las Bocas. This deed establishes the character of the Tenorio de Alba lands as irrigated when examined with the 1772 deed since this tract was formerly owned by Miguel Tenorio de Alba. It also helps establish the location of the pre-revolt La Ciénega Pueblo since the eastern boundary places the pueblo next to the point where the arroyo meets the mesa.[39]

By 1791 Alejandro Ortega, who was then living in Río Arriba, jurisdiction of La Cañada, decided to sell to one of the largest landowners in the Cieneguilla area, Pablo Montoya. Alejandro Ortega had made a good investment in 1774, for less than twenty years later he sold the land he had purchased from Antonio José López for six hundred pesos de tierra, twice the price he had paid. The boundaries of this sale were more specific than in the 1774 deed: on the north the mouth of the Cieneguilla Cañón; on the south the place where the lands of Antonio Ortega were divided, looking toward the lands inherited from his father; on the east where the mesa approaches the arroyo and the ruins of the old pueblo adjacent to the Angostura; and on the west the entrance to Las Bocas. Pablo Montoya must have been raising substantial numbers of cattle and sheep at his base of operations at Cieneguilla because he paid the purchase price in cows, oxen, sheep, and wool. The sale to Montoya also included an adjacent tract of land that Alejandro Ortega had inherited from his father, Antonio Ortega. That was the tract that Miguel Tenorio had sold in 1772, when

Matías Tenorio and Antonio Joseph López had tried to block the sale. Now the land was back in the hands of a local, Pablo Montoya. Whether Matías Tenorio considered him to be an acceptable neighbor might be judged by the litigation to be discussed, in which Pablo was involved at Cieneguilla. Based on that lawsuit in the summer of 1831, one may surmise that Pablo Montoya and Miguel Tenorio de Alba were cut from the same cloth.[40]

El Álamo and Las Golondrinas

The Hacienda del Álamo, also called Rancho del Álamo, is one of several inter-related communities (including Las Golondrinas, El Álamo, and La Ciénega). The Hacienda del Álamo was frequently mentioned before the Pueblo Revolt and during the Vargas reconquest, though it is not clear who the pre-revolt occupants of the hacienda were. As mentioned earlier, Governor Vargas found the hacienda abandoned and offered to make a grant of its lands to the original owners. But he did not make a grant of the Hacienda del Álamo because those former owners did not appear, although a grant was claimed in the Court of Private Land Claims in 1893.[41]

The relative locations of these places were described by Fray Juan Agustín de Morfi in his 1782 *Geographical Description of New Mexico*:

> Cieneguilla—La Cieneguilla is a ranch four leagues distant to the west of Santa Fe, situated on the bank of the Río de la Villa and settled with nine families of Spaniards, Alamo—to the south and a quarter of a league from La Cieneguilla is the Alamo, a small ranch with a single family of Spaniards, Golondrinas—Close to the Alamo and the east of it is the ranch of Sandoval, called Las Golondrinas, with only the family of its owner, Ciénega—La Ciénega is another ranch with four families on the banks of the same stream and contiguous to the Alamo on the western side.[42]

Evidence that the Rancho del Álamo land was occupied after the Pueblo Revolt, is found in the will of José Riaño Tagle, which was executed on 15 April 1743, a few days before he died. José Riaño had been living in Santa Fe prior to 1732, for in that year he was involved in litigation with Juan Lucero de Godoy over a road that passed between their houses. Riaño had houses in both the Rancho del Álamo and in Santa Fe, like many of the other elites from the

Cieneguilla/La Ciénega area.[43] Riaño listed in his will a residence with its lands
at Hacienda del Álamo together with a house in Santa Fe on San Francisco
Street, both of which he claimed to have purchased from María Francisca
Fernández de la Pedrera.[44] Little is known about Riaño's predecessor at the
Rancho del Álamo, and although her family was intimately connected with
other La Ciénega area landowners like Miguel Tenorio de Alba, we have no
record of exactly when or how María Francisca Fernández de la Pedrera
acquired the Rancho del Álamo. Church records tell us that María Francisca
may have inherited the land from her father, Juan Fernández de la Pedrera. Her
brother, Juan Fernández de la Pedrera II, had a son named Bartolomé who had
at least seven children with Luisa Tenorio de Alba. Three of these women
(grandnieces of María Francisca) married into important La Ciénega area
families: Teodora married Miguel Tenorio de Alba in 1758, Leonarda married
Manuel Baca, and Teresa married Felipe Sandoval Martínez in 1743.[45]

Although the boundaries of the Rancho del Álamo were supposed to have
been found in a deed in Riaño's possession, that deed has not come to light.
Riaño noted in his will that the Alamo tract in 1743 was "much more improved
than when I purchased it." This language, together with the agricultural tools
listed in the will ("coas, pickaxes, and the rest"), indicates that irrigated agriculture had probably been practiced for some time, even before the Pueblo
Revolt, on the Alamo Ranch, which was west of La Ciénega Creek and is irrigated by the Acequia de la Ciénega.[46] During the pre-revolt period and continuing until the death of José Riaño in 1743, the Alamo Ranch covered a large
area south of Cieneguilla and east of La Ciénega. The Golondrinas tract
(roughly the same land now occupied by the Rancho de las Golondrinas) was
severed from the larger Alamo tract as the result of a provision in the 1743 José
Riaño will and power of attorney regarding his mayordomo.[47]

Antonio Sandoval was the mayordomo or foreman of the Alamo Ranch. In
the inventory of Riaño's property taken after his death, a notation similar to
the following is often found: "declare as his [Riaño's] property, the herds which
may be declared by Antonio de Sandoval, his mayordomo." José Riaño was so
grateful to Antonio Sandoval for the good services he rendered in taking care
of Riaño's property and building up his estate that he bequeathed Sandoval a
tract of land at Las Golondrinas and the funds necessary to build a house
there. If Sandoval did not want the property at Las Golondrinas, Riaño provided that the property should be appraised and that its value, together with

the cost of building a house on the property, should be given to Sandoval in cash. Antonio Sandoval decided to take the land instead of the money.[48]

In April of 1744 little had been done in the administration of the Riaño estate, even though the Vicar Santiago Roybal and Juan José Moreno were named executors, and Riaño's widow, María Roybal, took the blame with the excuse that she found "herself habitually ailing." To remedy the problem, the governor of New Mexico himself took over administration of this large estate. Joaquín Codallos y Rabal had had much of the property in the estate appraised again, while María Roybal gave her power of attorney to Juan Gabaldón to protect her interest in her husband's estate. Since José Riaño was one of the wealthiest men in New Mexico, upon his death his widow became one of the wealthiest women. Ailing or not, whomever she married would also become wealthy.[49]

It appears that the potential for fraud on the part of some fortune hunter was what Governor Codallos y Rabal's participation was designed to prevent—to no avail as it turned out. The governor accepted an appraisal by Juan Gabaldón of the livestock, tools, houses, and grazing land at Rancho del Álamo: he valued the house at 1,200 pesos, a smaller house at 38 pesos, and the house in Santa Fe at 565 pesos. The valuation of the Rancho del Álamo house was higher than the 1743 appraisal and was more detailed. The vigas, crossbeams, and canales were all counted and separately valued, as were the doors and windows. The land at the Alamo Ranch was valued at one thousand pesos, a substantial amount considering the house had already been valued at twelve hundred pesos. The land was described as bounded on the north by the loma of the Cieneguilla, on the south by an arroyo at the end of *los tanques*, on the east by the point of the loma where the two roads fork, and on the west by the ranch of Antonio Sandoval. It thus appears that sometime between the date of Riaño's death in 1743 and the appraisal in May of 1744, the Antonio Sandoval tract at Las Golondrinas had been segregated. It included some of the choicest irrigated fields within the larger Alamo Ranch.[50]

The remains of the thirteen-room house of José Riaño and María Roybal were still evident when John Walker surveyed a small holding claim in the area in 1895. Walker noted that the adobe house was said to be 230 years old, giving a date of 1665 for a Spanish presence on the Alamo Ranch, if Walker's information was correct.[51] Whoever built that house was probably the one Governor Vargas was referring to when he offered to make a grant to whoever demonstrated their right to the lands.[52] The names of the owners of this land prior to the Pueblo Revolt are lost, as are the identities of the people who worked the fields. But the record of land transactions after the probate of the Riaño estate show how soon the estate that José Riaño and his mayordomo, Antonio Sandoval, had so carefully built would be lost by the widow María Roybal.[53]

Sometime prior to 1755, a mysterious stranger also named Sandoval appeared on the scene at the Alamo Ranch: Felipe Rojas de Sandoval, who also signed papers as Felipe de Sandoval y Rojas. He would turn out to be just the opposite of Antonio Sandoval as a steward of the land. Rojas de Sandoval arrived in New Mexico in 1749 or 1750 with some French fur traders. He had left Spain in 1742 but was captured by the British and imprisoned in Jamaica for two years. He finally escaped and made his way to Arkansas, where he became a hunter and learned about New Mexico through members of the Mallet party, the first French traders to reach the province. Sandoval set out for New Mexico in the fall of 1749, following the Arkansas River with six companions. After a series of adventures, including a stay in a Jumano Indian village of farmers and fierce cannibals, where Sandoval "saw them eat two captives," he reached Taos along with three others: a German, a French priest, and a Comanche guide who was going to New Mexico to sell slaves to the Spaniards. Rojas de Sandoval must have had quite a few stories to tell when he arrived in midcentury Santa Fe, and one of the people to whom he told his adventures was the wealthy widow of José Riaño, María Roybal. By this time the Riaño estate had been settled, and María had received the Alamo Ranch and about fourteen thousand pesos in cash, a huge sum for the time.[54]

We do not know the details of Felipe Rojas de Sandoval's courtship of María Roybal, or whether her health had improved by the 1750s, but we do know that on 13 July 1755 Rojas de Sandoval married her. Just four months later this adventurer sold a portion of María Roybal's land for three hundred pesos in silver or, if silver was lacking, six hundred pesos in kind (*efectos de tierra*). The boundaries of this tract of irrigated farmland (*tierras de labor de par llevar*) were the boundary of María Roybal's land on the north, the boundary of Antonio de Sandoval's land at Las Golondrinas on the south, the Cañada de los Tanques on the east, and a large spring on the west. The southern boundary call indicates that the Antonio Sandoval tract at Las Golondrinas had been distributed and was still occupied by Sandoval in 1755. María Roybal had retained some land from the Alamo Ranch on the north. The purchaser under the Sandoval y Rojas deed was the son of the deceased José Riaño, José

Riaño II.[55] The young Riaño's life soon took an unlucky turn that took him away from the land once owned by his father that he purchased in 1755. Sometime around the year 1759, José Riaño II was thrown by his horse and suffered an injury that caused him to lose his mind, as it was put in the documents. He was held in protective custody in the Santa Fe presidio as a result, since Santa Fe lacked an institution to care for the mentally ill. José Riaño II escaped in February 1763 with a cousin, Antonio Matías Ortiz, and four Genízaros, but he soon perished, and most of this group was found dead on the buffalo plains the following July, apparently victims of an attack by Plains Indians.[56] In just twenty years a good part of the José Riaño estate had been sold by Felipe Rojas de Sandoval, and Riaño's son, who had tried to redeem some of that land, was dead after a series of tragic accidents. We do not know how Riaño's widow fared after she inherited the fortune of the richest man in New Mexico. The widow of José Riaño II was apparently able to get the property Riaño II had repurchased from Rojas de Sandoval, but the one who seems to have benefited the most from the unfortunate string of events was María Roybal's opportunistic husband, Felipe Rojas de Sandoval.

Father Domínguez and the Comanche Raid of 1776

A few years after Antonio José López and Miguel Tenorio de Alba started their land speculation in La Ciénega in the early to mid-1770s, Father Francisco Atanasio Domínguez arrived in Santa Fe with instructions to report on the economic and spiritual status of the missions of New Mexico. Father Domínguez arrived in the villa on 22 March 1776 and began his visitation of the missions on 10 April.[57] When Father Domínguez took a census of the Cieneguilla/La Ciénega area, he counted twenty-five families with 185 persons at Cieneguilla and sixteen families with 101 persons at La Ciénega, which the priest called Ciénega Grande.[58] In April Father Domínguez had summoned Father Silvestre Vélez de Escalante to Santa Fe to join him on an expedition searching for a route to Monterey, California. But a tragic event at La Ciénega delayed their departure on this great adventure. Escalante had been in Santa Fe for two weeks when Comanches raided La Ciénega, killing eleven people on 20 June 1776. Father Escalante went with the scouting expedition pursuing the Indians to serve as chaplain while Father Domínguez officiated at the burials, completing and signing the burial entries in the church records.[59] The records of this tragic affair provide information about the people counted in the earlier census and where they lived, as well as about others who were not residents of La Ciénega but just happened to be there planting or herding cattle at the time of the raid. Of the eleven killed, five were local: one from the Puesto de la Cieneguilla, two from the Puesto de las Golondrinas, and two from La Ciénega (one from the Puesto de la Ciénega and one from the Puestas de las Bacas in the Rancho de la Ciénega). The other victims included José Vicente, who was listed as the *coyote* servant of Antonio José Ortiz, and Manuel de Coca and his two sons, all of whom were in the area temporarily. José Vicente was killed by the Comanches while herding his master's cows and mares at the Puesto de la Ciénega.[60] Manuel de Coca was captured with his two sons while planting at the Puesto de la Cieneguilla, and all three were killed. José Antonio Sandoval was taken prisoner by the Comanche raiders at Las Golondrinas and killed near Santo Domingo.[61] It would be another decade before Comanche attacks subsided with the defeat of Cuerno Verde and the 1786 Anza peace treaty.[62]

In 1776, the same year that Father Domínguez made his tour of the missions of New Mexico, Juan Candelaria, a resident of the villa of Albuquerque, recorded his version of the history and settlements of New Mexico. Candelaria listed four settlements with his estimation of the dates they were founded: Cieneguilla (1698), La Ciénega (1715), El Álamo (1730), and Los Palacios (1698). Based on the deed records discussed in this chapter, these dates are relatively accurate except for Los Palacios, which may have been later. Father Domínguez also provided information on Ciénega Pueblo in his visitation of 1776.[63]

Cieneguilla

Before Diego de Vargas left El Paso on his second expedition in the reconquest of New Mexico, he published an edict at the *plaza de armas*, setting forth the rights and responsibilities of the colonists who accompanied him. After promising to feed them "meat, maize, wheat, and other cereals," he notified prospective settlers about what land grants they could request: "I shall give them the lands, homesites, and haciendas they had and left at the time of the uprising."[64] Soon after the recolonizing expedition left El Paso, Sergeant Major Francisco Anaya Almazán, one of Vargas's most trusted lieutenants, took advantage of a stop along the route to Santa Fe to ask Vargas for a tract of land at Cieneguilla, which he represented as his pre-revolt holdings. While Anaya Almazán had probably held Cieneguilla Pueblo in encomienda, it is not clear whether either Cristóbal or Francisco Anaya Almazán were living at the pueblo prior to the Pueblo Revolt. Though it was often the case that the holder of an encomienda would live near or in the pueblo from which he collected tribute, Spanish law prohibited the practice.[65] On 2 September 1693, Anaya Almazán formally petitioned Vargas for the grant, describing the land as being four leagues (approximately ten miles) from Santa Fe and one league (about two and a half miles) from the pueblo of La Ciénega. In the petition Anaya Almazán was vague about his use of the land, saying on the one hand that he was requesting the site in response to Vargas's proclamation offering to grant settlers their pre-revolt holdings and on the other hand admitting that he had sold the tract to Sebastian de Herrera. Herrera was said to live in Nueva Vizcaya, so Anaya Almazán must have thought that he, Anaya Almazán, was the proper person to request the land. In addition, Anaya Almazán pointed out that he had performed loyal service during the reconquest as Vargas's adjutant.[66]

Vargas considered Anaya Almazán to be the most senior of all his officials and had been willing to grant his request for Indian labor a year earlier when they were in the area of El Paso. In July of 1692 Anaya Almazán had asked Vargas to order fifteen Indians from each of the southern pueblos of Ysleta del Sur, Socorro, and Senecú to assist in the repair of the diversion dam that channeled water into his acequia. Vargas granted the request immediately upon receiving this petition, ordering the Indians to work for three days for Anaya Almazán on the dam and donating two beef cattle to feed the Indians during that period. A year later, when they reached New Mexico, Vargas would not be as obliging in his response to Anaya Almazán's request for land.[67]

In New Mexico Vargas was faced with the challenge of fulfilling his promise to make new grants, though he knew that Spaniards' pre-revolt holdings would have to be reduced since many more colonists were planning to live in the same area that the pre-revolt settlers and Pueblo Indians had occupied. Since Anaya Almazán had sold his tract, Vargas may have thought his claim less deserving than others. In any case, the governor seems to have made an example of Anaya Almazán in order to put his limited land grant settlement plan into effect, which was somewhat at variance with the proclamation at El Paso. Diego de Vargas notified Anaya Almazán that the area south of Santa Fe to the Boca of Santo Domingo Pueblo would be reserved as commons for livestock grazing and for the presidial horse herd. Therefore, instead of the tract Anaya Almazán requested, Vargas granted him one fanega of corn-planting land (about nine acres) with additional land sufficient to pasture two hundred sheep, twenty head of cattle, and the oxen used for plowing and pulling Anaya Almazán's cart. This was a substantially smaller tract than Anaya Almazán was expecting.[68]

Francisco Anaya Almazán, "whose protruding eyes gave him a look of perpetual amazement," must have been surprised by this reduction. Since this amount of land was less than Anaya Almazán had requested, he verbally repetitioned Vargas for a larger tract two years later. Vargas showed some irritation in his written response when he told Anaya Almazán that the 1693 grant was to be "complied with to the letter without innovation, but precisely and punctually observed." While Vargas could not have made himself more clear, Francisco Anaya Almazán and his family still would not accept any diminution in the amount of land they thought they owned. It was Anaya Almazán's children who would again attempt to expand the grant.[69]

Francisco Anaya Almazán had two children with his first wife, Gerónima Pérez de Bustillo. Upon Gerónima's death, Anaya Almazán married Francisca Domínguez, daughter of Captain Tomé Domínguez, a leading settler in the Río Abajo, who had an estancia two leagues north of Sandia Pueblo.[70] After the death of his second wife, Anaya Almazán married a third time, this time to Felipa Cedillo Rico de Rojas.[71] By 1714 Francisco had died, so his widow, Felipa Rico de Rojas, and his brother Salvador Anaya Almazán sought to have the Vargas grant revalidated by then governor Juan Ignacio Flores Mogollón. The basis for the request was a novel one: that mice had gnawed holes in the original grant document, which they attached to their petition. However, the land requested exceeded the original grant, which was still apparent on the original. The boundaries requested included La Ciénega (on the south) and Rancho del Álamo (on the east), meaning that the requested grant would include the land north and west of these boundaries. By 1714 some farming and irrigation must have been taking place on the tract because Felipa Rico de Rojas told Governor Flores Mogollón in the revalidation petition that Francisco Anaya Almazán had possessed the grant for over six years without opposition, residing on the land "and gathering the crops he sowed therein."[72] Unfortunately for the Anaya Almazán heirs, enough of the initial grant by Vargas was legible around the mice-chewed holes for Governor Flores Mogollón to see through this ruse.

The governor revalidated the grant for only the fanega of corn-planting land together with the grazing land.

In spite of this rejection of the expanded grant, in 1716 two of the children, Joaquín and Juana Anaya Almazán, deeded the larger Cieneguilla tract (inherited from Francisco Anaya Almazán) to Andrés Montoya. They attached the Vargas grant and the Flores Mogollón revalidation to the deed, but instead of the description specified by Flores Mogollón, the boundaries in the deed were the woods called Debocandos on the north, the mesa on the west, the lands of La Ciénega on the south, and the lands of El Álamo on the east.[73]

By 1740 Andrés Montoya had expanded the planted area on the Cieneguilla tract that he had received in 1716 to twenty fanegas, probably both corn and wheat. Montoya also had another tract between the huertas of San Ildefonso and Cochiti that he had not planted because of his illness (this tract is discussed in chapter 4). This sickness caused Montoya to make a will in which he assigned areas of farmland in the Cieneguilla tract to his sons-in-law and to his married sons who were already farming these irrigated pieces of land. Now that Andrés Montoya was contemplating his death, he notified his executors to assign additional irrigated land to his unmarried children also, equal in size and quality to the land already being farmed by the married sons and sons-in-law.[74]

One of Andrés's sons, Francisco Montoya, jumped the gun, and before his father died he sold the tract of land he had been bequeathed for one hundred pesos, even though the land had not been partitioned on the ground because Andrés was still alive so his will was not in effect. But Andrés Montoya was a forgiving man, and he directed his executors to give Francisco another tract "because he has no [land] in which to plant." This tract was to come out of Francisco's fifth of the estate.[75] While Andrés Montoya showed forgiveness when his son Francisco sold land from the larger Cieneguilla tract, he hoped that the land would remain intact, undivided, and in the family for as long as possible. This landholding pattern in which large undivided tracts remained in one family was similar to that of La Ciénega, where the sale of land from the large Tenorio de Alba tract by Miguel Tenorio caused extensive litigation.[76] Andrés Montoya would get his wish for a while, as the Cieneguilla tract remained substantially intact throughout the eighteenth century. Decades after Andrés Montoya died on 31 August 1740, the Cieneguilla tract was still referred to as the land of Andrés Montoya.[77]

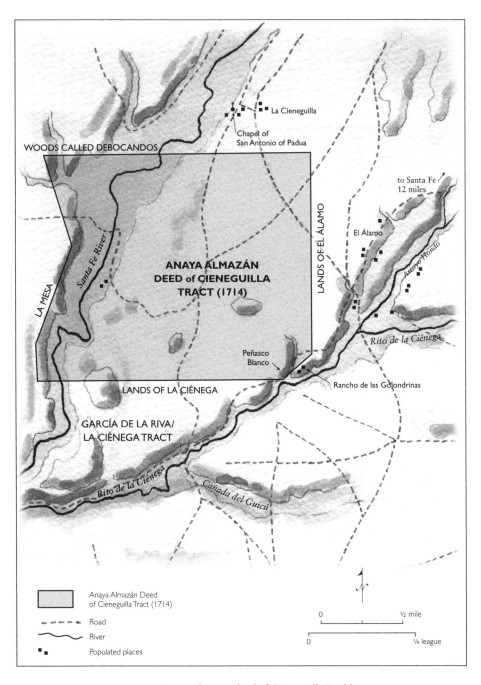

WOODS CALLED DEBOCANDOS

La Cieneguilla

Chapel of
San Antonio of Padua

LANDS OF EL ÁLAMO

to Santa Fe
12 miles

El Álamo

LA MESA

Santa Fe River

ANAYA ALMAZÁN
DEED of CIENEGUILLA
TRACT (1714)

Arroyo Hondo

Rito de la Ciénega

Peñasco
Blanco

Rancho de las Golondrinas

LANDS OF LA CIÉNEGA

GARCÍA DE LA RIVA/
LA CIÉNEGA TRACT

Rito de la Ciénega

Cañada del Guicú

N

Anaya Almazán Deed
of Cieneguilla Tract (1714)

Road

River

Populated places

0   ½ mile

0   ¼ league

MAP 4. Anaya Almazán deed of Cieneguilla Pueblo.

While the Cieneguilla tract remained relatively intact, one of Andrés Montoya's children, Josefa Montoya, was acquiring land south of the Cieneguilla tract at La Ciénega. In 1751 Josefa purchased land between the lands of Antonio Baca and Lázaro García for 140 pesos. With this purchase the Montoya family property included not only the Cieneguilla tract, but some valuable land in La Ciénega. These combined tracts were the subjects of fierce litigation between members of the Montoya family concerning the partition of their land.[78] The litigation began with a *conciliación* procedure brought by Pablo Montoya, one of Andrés Montoya's sons, for damages caused by cows getting into his planted fields; while he was at it, Pablo Montoya also requested that all the lands of Andrés Montoya be physically divided among the owners. Up to that point only the irrigated farmlands had been partitioned in accordance with the wishes of Andrés Montoya. After a family discussion, Pablo Montoya was overruled by the other family members with an interest in the tract who preferred not to partition the lands they were using in common. The parties agreed to leave those lands "free for pastures, with the understanding that the farmlands in the *cañón* be fenced so that those who work the said fields" could no longer claim damages to their fields caused by loose animals.[79] By helping the Montoya family craft this agreement, Alcalde Domingo Fernández (whom we will meet again in the next chapter), was essentially establishing a community grant for the family with common lands shared by family members only. This agreement was signed by Pablo Montoya, Juan Manuel Montoya, Bartolo Montoya, Rafael Romero, Miguel Montoya, Gaspar Romero, Manuel Baltasar Montoya, María Josefa Fernández, José Antonio de Herrera, Francisco Urbano, José Mora, and Miguel Gallego.[80]

In 1831 Pablo Montoya was still not satisfied with the conciliation agreement at Cieneguilla. Montoya was a contentious individual who would later be accused by the alcalde of "add[ing] more affliction to the afflicted" at Cieneguilla (during the 1820s and 1830s he refused to leave land owned by Santa Ana Pueblo even after being ordered to do so by the audiencia, or supreme court, of Guadalajara).[81] In May he filed a complaint with Alcalde Domingo Fernández against Juan Manuel Montoya (who had sold his share of the Cieneguilla tract to Pablo Rael) and Rael's mother. Pablo Montoya tried to prevent the sale, claiming that he should have been given the opportunity to buy the tract under the custom of giving adjoining neighbors the "right of first refusal." Pablo Montoya also claimed that Juan Manuel Montoya was not a legitimate son but had acquired his interest in the Cieneguilla tract as payment for clearing trees from the land.[82] This time the case was handled by Alcalde Francisco Archibeque, who, after more legal maneuvering by the parties, asked them to state their positions.[83] Juan Manuel Montoya stated that while he was not an heir by blood, he had received his share in the Cieneguilla tract by inheritance from Isidro Montoya. Since Isidro had no descendants, he left the property to Juan Manuel Montoya because "he wished to favor him as one of his servants." Juan Manuel Montoya admitted selling to Pablo Rael but claimed that he did not sell the pastures and notified Rael that the pastures were held in common. Juan Manuel closed by stating that Isidro Montoya had died thirteen years before (1818) and that he (Juan Manuel) had been in undisputed possession since that time.[84] When new alcalde, Francisco Rascón, temporarily succeeded Archibeque, the matter was referred to asesor (legal adviser) Antonio Barreiro for his opinion. Barreiro decided that the sale to Rael should be nullified and the land partitioned.[85]

It was two months before the partition of the Cieneguilla tract directed by Barreiro was undertaken, and again it was Francisco Archibeque who attempted the task, probably because of his long familiarity with the case. On 21 September 1831 Archibeque notified the parties to appear on the land with their documents. Although Archibeque again failed to reach an agreement on the partition of the lands, the documents submitted to the alcalde are instructive. The first document was the deed from Joaquín and Juana Anaya Almazán to Andrés Montoya for the entire Cieneguilla tract. Alcalde Archibeque said that the land covered by this deed had been planted for over fifty years, and he declared that cultivation, planting, and, presumably, irrigation had occurred on tracts covered by other documents for periods of twenty-four to over fifty years. But when Archibeque tried to partition the land he was again faced with the conflicting desires of the owners.[86]

Pablo Montoya wanted partition to be made on the farmland first, but all the other owners and family members objected. Apparently most of the agricultural land was still being farmed in common, so by resisting partition the Montoyas were resisting the privatization and sale of the land to individuals outside the family, just what Andrés Montoya had tried to prevent. Alcalde Archibeque finally refused to make the partition since the majority of owners objected and because Pablo Montoya "was agitating him to do it." Archibeque saw Montoya as a troublemaker who wanted to "add more affliction to the afflicted by damaging the small fields in the Cieneguilla *cañón* of the poor unfortunates" who farmed there. Apparently, these were tenant farmers who might be ousted from their fields if the land was privatized and sold.[87]

Even though there was one more attempt made at partition, the case remained in this posture of stalemate indefinitely. Additional legal maneuvering found asesor Antonio Barreiro criticizing Archibeque for not abiding by the conciliación agreement and telling him: "Even if bothered night and day [by Pablo Montoya], do not move to partition without consulting me."[88] In fact, Archibeque defied Barreiro and made one more attempt at partition, hoping "that through this they will quiet down." Juan Manuel Montoya did not attend, probably because Alcalde Archibeque had already decided that he no longer owned land there because his sale to Pablo Rael and Rael's mother was valid, since Juan Manuel *had* offered the land to the other Montoyas, who did not want to purchase it. The agricultural land was measured at 1,250 varas "from below upwards," but the boundaries of each tract still needed to be surveyed. Since none of the Montoyas would assist Alcalde Archibeque with the measurement, he terminated the proceedings, telling the litigants that if they still wanted to pursue the case they would have to bring their documents to Santa Fe.[89]

The litigation between Pablo Montoya and the rest of the Montoya family is emblematic of struggles—often within families—between those who wanted to keep the land together for traditional uses and those who wanted to sell and develop the land. This struggle is still being played out in La Ciénega as some families sell their land to developers like La Ciénega de Santa Fe, and others continue farming and holding on to their land.[90]

Adjudication of the Cieneguilla Grant

The Cieneguilla grant was the only land grant in the Cieneguilla/La Ciénega area that was submitted to and adjudicated by the surveyor general and the Court of Private Land Claims.[91] Pinito Pino submitted a claim for the Hacienda del Álamo grant in 1893, but no grant document was produced. Pino claimed that the grant had been given to José Riaño, and he produced documents citing the Alamo Ranch as a boundary. Pino also referred to the settlement of Riaño's estate as evidence of a grant, but he expanded the boundaries of the Hacienda del Álamo to encompass a tract he estimated to contain fifty thousand acres.

The attorney representing Pino withdrew before the case was tried in the Court of Private Land Claims, and the case was dismissed for failure to prosecute the claim.[92]

When the Cieneguilla grant was submitted to the surveyor general of New Mexico in 1878, Surveyor General Atkinson decided that the grant papers were genuine but that the 1697 grant, its revalidation and especially the 1714 deed, were self-serving and did not reflect the intent of Governor Vargas in making the grant to Anaya Almazán. Surveyor General Atkinson attempted to interpret the governor's intent and held that the land granted was a fanega of planting land and a *criadero de gañado menor*.[93] Testimony of witnesses was taken by affidavit to determine the location of the boundaries of the Cieneguilla grant. Juan Antonio Rodríguez said that he had known the town of Cieneguilla for seventy-four years and that he had lived there his entire life except in 1806. Rodríguez was not familiar with the grant documents, but he testified that the boundaries of the grant were pointed out to him some twenty years before by Juan Manuel Montoya, the son of Isidro Montoya. Rodríguez testified that about ten people lived in the town of Cieneguilla the last time he was there.[94] Tomás Rendón, age seventy-eight, testified that the town of Cieneguilla was within the grant, that a number of people lived in the town of Cieneguilla, and that two families lived in the canyon below.[95] Francisco Gonzales testified that the northern boundary of the grant, the monte called Debocandos, was twelve miles northwest of the town of Cieneguilla.[96] In spite of all the testimony about the boundaries of the Cieneguilla grant, Surveyor General Atkinson recommended confirmation of the grant in accordance with the area of land granted by Governor Vargas in 1697, a fanega of corn-planting land, together with sufficient grazing land for two hundred head of sheep, twenty head of cattle, and the horses and oxen of Francisco Anaya Almazán. Atkinson determined that a tract of land 1,666 2/3 varas square was the proper quantity of land. Atkinson said that the land covered by the deed from Anaya Almazán to Andrés Montoya would cover an area of two by three miles or approximately thirty-eight hundred acres.[97] But when the preliminary survey of the grant was made it far exceeded both these estimates. It could be that the estimates of the area of the grant were influenced by the testimony of P. F. Herlon, who said that in his opinion the amount of grazing land needed for each head of cattle was twenty-five to thirty acres and the amount needed for sheep was three to four acres. This calculation would have resulted in a tract containing about fourteen hundred acres—far less land than was actually surveyed.[98] Following Surveyor General Atkinson's decision, a pre-liminary survey of the Cieneguilla grant was made in August 1879, showing the grant to contain over forty-five thousand acres, substantially in excess of the land Atkinson recommended for confirmation. Atkinson was criticized by his suc-cessor, George W. Julian, for his approval of the Marmon survey when the area Atkinson recommended for confirmation was about five hundred acres. J. J. Bowden believes that criticism was misplaced because Atkinson had told the claimants to select a 491-acre tract from within the larger tract.[99]

When Congress failed to act on Surveyor General Atkinson's recommenda-tion in 1893, the Cieneguilla grant was submitted to the Court of Private Land Claims by Feliciano Montoya, an heir of Andres Montoya. The Court of Private Land Claims was faced with the same indefinite boundaries that had puzzled the surveyor general, though again the court did not doubt that the grant doc-uments—though not necessarily the 1714 deed—were valid and genuine. Faced with conflicting evidence, the court made its own decision concerning the boundaries, resulting in a survey that was over forty thousand acres smaller than the 1879 Marmon survey. The court found that the Ciénega mentioned in the deed to Montoya and the revalidation was located in the Alamo Arroyo and that "grants of land within an arroyo extended to the crest of the hills on each side." So the court fixed the southern boundary at the "crest of the ridge lying between the Santa Fe River and the Arroyo Hondo."[100] The eastern boundary call in the 1714 deed was the Hacienda del Álamo. That land was being occupied by Archbishop John B. Lamy at the time the court rendered its decision, so the western boundary of Lamy's land became the eastern boundary of the Cieneguilla grant. The northern and western boundaries were also established in accordance with the 1714 deed to Andrés Montoya, giving an area much larger than called for by Surveyor General Julian (approximately five hundred acres), but less than surveyed by Deputy Surveyor Marmon. When the Cieneguilla grant was surveyed in 1898 it was found to contain 3,202 acres. While this amount may have been less land than called for in the 1714 deed to Andrés Montoya (because the surveyed northern boundary was somewhat south of the Debocandos woods), it was probably more than was covered by the 1697 Vargas grant, and it covered the occupied area in the southern part of grant where the irrigated lands were. The survey shows the houses in the community of Cieneguilla, which roughly comports with the testimony of Juan Antonio Rodríguez as to the size of the community.[101]

The Cieneguilla grant was treated as a private grant even though several communities, including the community of Cieneguilla, were located on the grant. The Cieneguilla grant is still in existence, is used mainly for housing, and is owned primarily by the descendants of and purchasers from about ten families. The San Antonio de Padua chapel is also located in this area, built in 1814 by the García de la Mora family in gratitude for the cessation of Indian raids.[102]

The communities of La Ciénega, Alamo, and Cieneguilla are among the oldest in New Mexico, settled soon after Santa Fe by some of the same families who lived in Santa Fe. Because of the early dates of settlement, water rights in the area are among the oldest in New Mexico and perhaps the most expensive. Development in the Cieneguilla/La Ciénega area has caused friction between traditional families and those that have sold their land to developers. In addition, activists near the community of Cieneguilla have been attempting to protect petroglyphs associated with the ancient pueblo of Cieneguilla from souvenir hunters—who have chiseled out sections of rock containing images— as well as from developers.[103] A step toward historic preservation occurred when the Pueblo of Cieneguilla was placed on the State Register of Cultural Properties as number 199 on 10 August 1970.[104]

A bright spot in the preservation of the history of the area is the Rancho de las Golondrinas, which preserves and displays examples of traditional Hispanic folkways, including a fully operational gristmill.[105] The entire La Ciénega/Cieneguilla area is emblematic of a traditional Hispanic community attempting to preserve and protect its culture in the face of land development, higher taxes, and increased property values. However, according to former lieutenant governor Roberto Mondragón, it is not inevitable that the land and culture will be lost: "Northern New Mexico has proven it is an unwilling canvas for developers," and "big-time development plans in Pecos, Villanueva, and Chama have been . . . stifled by community opposition." The early history of the Cieneguilla/La Ciénega area shows that conflicts between those who support traditional community values and those who wish to divide and sell their land have existed from the beginning. Presently, it appears that the forces supporting traditional values—farming over land development, acequia agriculture over luxury homes—have prevailed.[106]

CHAPTER SIX

THE SAN CRISTÓBAL
PUEBLO GRANT

S AN CRISTÓBAL PUEBLO WAS ONE OF A NETWORK OF AT LEAST FOUR
major precontact pueblos in the Galisteo Basin; three of these were Tano
(Galisteo, San Lázaro, and San Cristóbal), and the remaining pueblo of San
Marcos was Keresan. San Cristóbal was the principal Tano pueblo with fifteen
hundred warriors there in 1626. Early Spanish expeditions such as
Chamuscado-Rodríguez (1581), Espejo (1582), and Castaño de Sosa (1590) all
visited San Cristóbal, along with the other Galisteo Basin pueblos. At the time
of the Rodríguez-Chamuscado expedition, San Cristóbal Pueblo was reported
to have been built five to six stories high with as many as three hundred house
blocks.[1] Castaño de Sosa visited the pueblo in 1591 and obtained maize, flour,
beans, and turkeys as he did at the other pueblos. While San Cristóbal Pueblo
seems to have been friendly toward the Spaniards during the early exploratory
expeditions, after more than eight decades of Spanish rule under Juan de
Oñate and successive governors the pueblo became more hostile. San Cristóbal
Pueblo was one of the leaders of the successful 1680 Pueblo Revolt, when the
Pueblo Indians drove the Spaniards from New Mexico for twelve years.[2]

Juan de Oñate visited San Cristóbal Pueblo on 22 July 1598 and brought
with him the Indian woman known as doña Inés, whom Castaño de Sosa had
taken from San Cristóbal eight years earlier to be an interpreter for the
Spanish just as Malinche had been for Cortés.[3] Apparently, doña Inés no longer spoke Tano, for Oñate reported: "On the 22nd we went to the pueblo of San
Cristóbal, where Doña Inés was born. She is the Indian woman we brought

from Mexico like a second Malinche, but she does not know that language or any other spoken in New Mexico, nor is she learning them. Her parents and almost all of her relatives were already dead, and there was hardly anyone who remembered how Castaño had taken her away."[4] Soon after Oñate's visit to San Cristóbal, priests were assigned to the Galisteo Basin pueblos, and a church was started at San Cristóbal in the 1620s. It was the ruins of this church about which the petitioner for the San Cristóbal grant in 1824 would express such indignation as he began the process of acquiring the San Cristóbal Pueblo land for himself. We will learn more of Domingo Fernández's acquisition and sale of the land of San Cristóbal Pueblo, but first we will examine an account of how the people of San Cristóbal, so intimately connected with the Pueblo Revolt, were dispossessed of their land after Diego de Vargas's reconquest of New Mexico in 1692.

The Galisteo Basin pueblos were in the vanguard of the initial attack on Santa Fe in the early days of the Pueblo Revolt. Although San Marcos Pueblo is said to have warned Governor Otermín of the impending revolt, all four Galisteo Basin pueblos were reported to be on their way to attack Santa Fe on the morning of 14 August 1680, as reported by Governor Antonio de Otermín (1677–1683): "All the Indians of the pueblos of Los Pecos, San Cristóbal, San Lazaro, San Marcos, Galisteo, and La Ciénega, who numbered more than five hundred, were one league from this villa on the way to attack it and destroy the governor and all the Spaniards." [5]

During the twelve-year abandonment of the province of New Mexico by the Spanish, the pueblos of San Cristóbal and San Lázaro were forced, perhaps by Apache raids, to move to a location near San Juan Pueblo, two miles east of Santa Cruz on the Río Santa Cruz.[6] Then, soon after the return of the Spaniards under Diego de Vargas, San Cristóbal and San Lázaro joined the Tewas in an unsuccessful second revolt against the Spanish. Partly because of their participation in the revolt of 1696, San Cristóbal Pueblo was treated harshly by Governor Vargas and successive governors. San Cristóbal was forced to move by the Spaniards, this time to the valley of Chimayo to make room for new Hispanic settlers from Mexico. Then, in 1706 Governor Cuervo y Valdés reestablished the pueblo of Galisteo by moving the scattered Galisteo Indians, and some from San Cristóbal, back to their original pueblo.[7] The resettled Galisteo Pueblo was short lived, however, and in the early 1700s the remaining San Cristóbal Pueblo people joined other Tanos and some Tewas to take refuge with the Hopi in a new pueblo established there called Hano. Descendants of the San Cristóbal people who helped establish Hano Pueblo are still living there. Moving to Hopi was the only way for a pueblo like San Cristóbal, whose population was dwindling, to survive.[8]

Although the San Cristóbal people moved to Hano Pueblo early in the eighteenth century, the neighboring Galisteo Pueblo, to be discussed in a later chapter, hung on until 1782, when its inhabitants moved to Santo Domingo Pueblo. The Spaniards had wanted Galisteo to remain populated to serve as a buffer against frequent Comanche attacks, but those attacks, along with smallpox epidemics, decimated the pueblo. With the buffer gone, Hispanic troops built a small house near the abandoned Galisteo Pueblo and stayed there until 1814 when the first Hispanic settlers requested the Galisteo grant.

During the interim between the abandonment of San Cristóbal and the first Hispanic land grant in 1824, the San Cristóbal grant was used mainly for grazing, first by the presidial horse herd in the mid-1700s and later by Spanish settlers who began to move into the area in the early 1800s, encouraged by the protection of the military outpost. That post may have been abandoned intermittently as the fierce Comanches continued to raid throughout the area, stealing horses and killing settlers.[9] Meanwhile, Hispanos began to notice the land available at the abandoned pueblo of San Cristóbal and began to request grants of that land during the Mexican period in the 1820s.[10]

The second chapter of San Cristóbal story covers the acquisition of the San Cristóbal grant by Domingo Fernández, a member of the Santa Fe ayuntamiento (town council) and custodian of the Spanish and Mexican archives of New Mexico from 1825 to 1846. Fernández was familiar not only with the archives, but also with the laws governing grants of land in New Mexico, particularly of Indian land. Church records show that he was about seventy-three in 1857, just a few years after he would sell the San Cristóbal grant. Domingo Fernández lived in Santa Fe, where he had a large library, including the library and sacred vessels of the Franciscans, which were left in his care when that order was expelled from New Mexico after Mexico won its independence from Spain. *Venerable* would be the word best describing Domingo Fernández's outward appearance: he wore the Franciscan habit, for at one time he had been a priest. He also had the gravitas of a learned man of the law and was called upon by the local magistrates "to come before them for the purpose of advising [them] on matters of law, in which branch he was well versed, having made a

thorough study of the Legislation of Spain and Mexico." As we shall see from
his relationship with the San Cristóbal grant, Domingo Fernández was part
priest and lawyer on the outside, but on the inside was hidden an astute land
grant speculator. During the time that he was negotiating with the bureaucracy
in Santa Fe to acquire the San Cristóbal grant he was also trying to position
himself to obtain an interest in the not-yet-abandoned Pecos Pueblo lands.[11]

In his petition for the San Cristóbal grant, written in his characteristically
cramped handwriting, Domingo Fernández used his considerable rhetorical
skill to obtain the grant, claiming that he wanted to protect the Catholic mission church and other ruins on the land. At first glance, Domingo Fernández
seemed sincere in his apparent desire to protect the dilapidated church at San
Cristóbal, as well as the relics from the earlier occupation of the land by San
Cristóbal Pueblo. But as he often did, Fernández got carried away with his
rhetoric, "upon seeing that sacred place where upon so many occasions the
sacred and awful sacrifice of the Mass has been offered, and where the most
august sacrament was consecrated; considering that it is more than one hundred years since the natives who inhabited it have abandoned it, . . . this holy
place, which is suffering under the disgrace of being a habitation for beasts,
stable for sheep, and a manger for cows and calves, and in a word, a lodging for
brutes." After requesting the San Cristóbal grant so that he might protect the
dilapidated church, Fernández went on to emphasize the purity of his motives:
"[God] has moved my spirit for so great a purpose, that it may not be possibly
thought [that] I solicit said land through avarice." Fernández may have protested too much, for he did not repair the church; instead, he later proceeded
to manipulate all the interests in the grant in such a way that he was able to sell
it when it was not clear that he in fact owned the entire grant.[12] Fernández
concluded his petition by setting forth the boundaries of the tract he was
requesting and citing the laws he felt governed the request: "on the east, where
the canyon in the direction of the *vaca* spring commences to disappear; on the
west, the Puertecito, which [designates the boundary of] the Galisteo grant; on
the north, the descent of the Pueblito; on the south, the ascent called de Los
Comanches, which are the boundaries which I assign, without embracing
within their limits anything not belonging to it; strictly complying with the
provisions of law, 3d and 11 of title 12, book 4, of the *Recopilación* and sovereign
decrees concerning the matter."[13] Fernández asked for the land for himself, his
son, "and other persons who may desire the repair of that sacred temple."

Fernández did not think that the inhabitants of the adjoining Galisteo grant would object to his grant because they were accustomed to getting wood and water from the San Cristóbal land, and Fernández would not object to their continued use of the land for this purpose. Almost as an afterthought, Domingo Fernández mentioned that although water was scarce on the San Cristóbal grant he planned to engage in farming, since he knew that the encouragement of agriculture was one of the highest priorities of the government of Governor Facundo Melgares. This plan would require a community of farmers, and although the San Cristóbal grant initially appeared to be a community grant, Fernández would later do everything he could to acquire the interests of the other settlers. Like some later land grant petitioners, Fernández wanted to have it both ways: to be part of a community land grant, but to own the entire grant himself.[14]

The development of agriculture soon became a priority with Domingo Fernández and the San Cristóbal grant, eclipsing almost entirely his plan to restore the dilapidated church. This change was due in part to the neighboring Galisteo grant, which was a community grant bounding the San Cristóbal grant on the west. As a member of the Santa Fe ayuntamiento, Domingo Fernández was involved with the making of the Galisteo grant, and his statements in those proceedings demonstrate that he saw himself as the sole owner and proprietor of the San Cristóbal grant. The Galisteo grant was first made by Governor Máynez in 1814, but it was not until 7 April 1822 that the grant was finalized. Just a few days after Domingo Fernández's petition for the San Cristóbal grant, the Galisteo petitioners were put into possession of their land. Domingo Fernández wanted to be on good terms with the Galisteo grantees, but he also wanted to have first use of the stream flowing through the Arroyo San Cristóbal. Fernández tried to accomplish both goals by inserting language into a later Galisteo act of possession in which he admonished the Galisteo grantees to "live ever grateful to Domingo Fernández, who owing to his being the oldest settler and the proprietor of the tract and water of San Cristóbal, is entitled to the same and they are confined only to the surplus portions thereof." This statement in 1843 shows how Fernández felt at that time and sheds light on the veracity of some of Fernández's earlier statements in his petition for the San Cristóbal grant.[15]

On the day following Domingo Fernández's petition, Governor Facundo Melgares referred it to the ayuntamiento of Santa Fe, noting that "the citizen who has no lands to cultivate can only aspire by donation to such an amount as may be necessary and sufficient to support his family." The Santa Fe ayuntamiento referred the petition back to Domingo Fernández over a month later, asking him to state "how much water there is at San Cristóbal, and how much land can be cultivated with it, and who are the petitioners, in order to grant to each one the necessary land for raising wheat for the support of their families." It took Domingo Fernández over a month to respond, but on 25 June 1822 he provided a detailed report about the water and irrigable land at San Cristóbal and for the first time the names of the fourteen settlers who would accompany him.[16]

Domingo Fernández was being forced to focus on the possibility of farming on a community grant owned by many, rather than the preservation of a church on a grant that he owned as sole proprietor. Fernández took José Luis Lovato with him in his investigation and counted twelve springs and eight ponds in the cañón or arroyo of San Cristóbal. The first one, known as El Caballo, was said to be twice as abundant as the one called El Tanque in Santa Fe. Fernández also mentioned two reservoirs, one of which was dry, and noted that "the *lagunita* [the large reservoir], which, at this dry season, is full of water, and which, by closing up the outlet, will aid materially in irrigating; besides another dry lake, its great extent being favorable to the collection of rain water, which will remain by closing the outlet, and will then be in the same condition in which it was used by the natives in former times."[17]

Fernández was aware of how the San Cristóbal Indians had managed the scarce water that was available to them, and he indicated that if similar practices were continued, the settlers of the San Cristóbal grant would have enough irrigation water. In an important passage that is torn in several places, Fernández refers to three types of irrigation water used by the Indians, which he proposed using for the San Cristóbal grant:

> And by this circumstance I consider that I will see the water run in the canyon and increase the water for the purpose of irrigating the land which it is proposed to cultivate, concerning the land which can be cultivated with the running water and the aid of the Lagunita and the rain water which may be collected . . . [torn] and that coming down the canyons during the rainy season, which is an irrigation, . . . [torn] which reason the natives in those times had their fields in the Cañon of La Casita, where the ruins can be seen of the houses in which they watched their fields.

The three sources of water were the runoff flowing in cañón or arroyo of San Cristóbal, the rain that directly watered the fields, and the rainwater collected in the lagunita.[18]

As for the proposed settlers, Fernández provided the following fourteen names, including his son Francisco at the top of the list:

Francisco Fernández	Miguel Lobato
Antonio Sena	Pablo Ortiz
Juan de Jesús Rivera	Florentino Ortiz
Miguel Rivera	José Trujillo
José María Rivera	Mariano Baca
Ignacio Ortega	Miguel Rodríguez
José Ortiz	José de Jesús Chávez

In response to Domingo Fernández's report on water availability on the San Cristóbal grant, the ayuntamiento appointed three people to go to San Cristóbal and investigate. They were Julián Lucero, lieutenant of Galisteo; José Miguel Baca of La Ciénega; and Rafael Sarracino, an alderman of the Santa Fe ayuntamiento. After the three investigators went to San Cristóbal with José Luis Lobato, who had accompanied Fernández on his earlier visit in June, they rendered their report on 8 July 1822, finding the situation on the ground a bit different from that reported by Fernández. According to this committee, the spring called El Caballo was not twice as large as the one in Santa Fe called El Tanque, it was a little less than twice as large. Instead of twelve springs in the Cañón de San Cristóbal, they found only two; according to José Luis Lobato, Fernández had identified about ten ponds as springs. The lagunita and the Laguna Seca were as described by Domingo Fernández, and his statement as to how the San Cristóbal Indians had managed the water was deemed accurate by the committee. They closed their report with a nod toward the wise water management of the San Cristóbal Pueblo Indians and a sort of blessing on Domingo Fernández's enterprise: "If the petitioners' labor with as much perseverance as it is seen those [San Cristóbal Indians] did, they will be rewarded for their labor if they are aided by God our father with water from heaven to fill their tank, as, in truth, from the existing springs they will reap very little benefit." In other words, the primary source of water for irrigation was rain, whether directly on the ground or indirectly by the filling of a tanque.[19]

After this favorable report by the three-man commission, Domingo Fernández's request to obtain a grant of San Cristóbal Pueblo's lands seems to have languished. During the two-year period following the favorable committee report on the San Cristóbal grant petition, Domingo Fernández focused his attention on what he considered the surplus lands of Pecos Pueblo. In September of 1823, Domingo Fernández and thirty-two others asked Governor Bartolomé Baca for lands at Pecos Pueblo, even though a handful of Indians still lived at the pueblo. When his petition was rejected by the ayuntamiento of San Miguel del Bado on the ground that these lands were "already owned," Domingo Fernández turned his attention back to San Cristóbal Pueblo.[20] Having been turned down regarding Pecos, Fernández finally was able to get the ayuntamiento of Santa Fe to rule on his petition for the San Cristóbal grant, which he had filed almost two years earlier. The members of the ayuntamiento reported that they saw no obstacle to making the grant for agricultural purposes to Fernández and his companions as long as it did not interfere with pastures and watering places; in any case, it "should not by any means be recognized as the property of the petitioners." It seems that the ayuntamiento was aware of the possibility that Fernández would try to obtain title to the entire grant in his own name, even though they were recommending in favor of the grant. It would be three years, however, before the San Cristóbal grant was made to Domingo Fernández.[21] In June of 1827 Fernández refiled his petition for the San Cristóbal grant, this time on behalf of thirty others. He noted that part of the delay was because the ayuntamiento claimed to have lost his first petition, but it is also likely that some of the ayuntamiento members saw Fernández more as a land speculator than as a farmer. Fernández added more information about the availability of water and about where "the ornaments and sacred vessels are buried." Domingo Fernández stated that a Pueblo Indian from Pojoaque named Ramón promised to show him where these artifacts were, as well as where there was water that was "covered up." Fernández said that another Indian named Francisco the White-Eyed had provided the same information about the buried artifacts. Fernández was adding everything he could think of to his earlier petition; he ended this new petition with a jab at the ayuntamiento, of which he was still the secretary. After noting that the ayuntamiento had never returned his first petition, "having given several pretexts for not returning it," he asked that this new petition be favorably attended to, "as has been done to several of our countrymen."[22] Fernández may have been referring to the large Pablo Montoya grant, which was made in November of 1824 at the time his San Cristóbal petition had been sidetracked.[23]

Surprisingly, Domingo Fernandez's tactics worked. After the Territorial Deputation ordered the Santa Fe ayuntamiento to make a report, that body noted, in an understated way, that it saw "no inconvenience in granting the aforesaid land on condition that the water and pastures shall be common."[24] Finally, on 9 August 1827 Fernández's quest to obtain the San Cristóbal community grant ended with the grant by Governor Manuel Armijo. Armijo added a more stringent condition than had the ayuntamiento when he stated in the granting decree that "no other use will be made of the land but for cultivation, on condition that if, at any time, they make any other use of it, it shall be considered as abandoned, and the grantees without any right to its possession, and that these have the same right with the rest of the public to pasture their animals in the vicinity thereof."[25] Thus, the grant was subject to a condition of continuous agricultural use, though the condition was never enforced.

While it seemed that Domingo Fernández had finally obtained the lands of San Cristóbal, which he had sought for so long, he still had to contend with the other grantees who were now twenty-one in number. In the act of possession on 21 August 1827, Fernández tried to set the stage for cutting off their rights by including a clause stating that all the grantees bound "themselves to each one erect a house and [participate] in the work of the church, ditch and tank." This condition was imposed not by the governor but by Domingo Fernández, and he would soon attempt to enforce it. Another condition applied to the individual tracts distributed to the twenty-one co-grantees (as well as the tract received by Domingo Fernández) was that if anyone wished to sell their tract, they should first offer it to their co-grantees in possession. This condition was similar to the one imposed by Governor Armijo and was not in Domingo Fernández's interest. It appears that other members of the ayuntamiento and Governor Armijo were all aware of Domingo Fernández's land speculation tendencies.[26]

In fact, some of Fernández's co-grantees were also land speculators, though most of them were farmers. The following is a list of the co-grantees in the order shown in the document, each of whom received one hundred varas of land through the act of possession on that twenty-first day of August 1827:

Miguel Sena	Ignacio Armenta
Domingo Fernández	Vitorino Padilla
Juan José Luján	Jesús Rivera
Gregorio García	Antonio Anaya
Juan Mares	Juan Anaya
Felipe Sena	José Chaves
Luis Lovato	Francisco Chaves
Bartolomé Lovato	José de la Cruz Alire
Joaquin Chaves	Antonio Sena
Ignacio Ortiz	José Antonio Sena
José Ortiz	

Miguel and Felipe Sena were the sons of the gunsmith of the Santa Fe presidio, both of whom were also trying to acquire land at the soon-to-be-abandoned Pecos Pueblo. Miguel Sena, whose name topped the list, would become a famous Santa Fe *rico* and was probably less interested in farming than in acquiring part of the lands of another abandoned Indian pueblo.[27] The lion's share of the allotted private lands of the San Cristóbal grant went to Domingo Fernández, who received the land from the Cañón de la Cueva to the spring of La Baca, the Cañón de la Cueva being divided among the remaining grantees. Upon completion of the allotments, the alcalde pointed out the boundaries of the grant—"on the east, the spring of La Baca; on the west, opposite the middle *cretón*; on the south, the Bajada de los Comanches; on the north, the summit of the cretón"— and performed the traditional ceremony of possession in which he took "Fernández by the hand, he pulled up weeds, scattered handfuls of earth, broke off branches from the trees, and uttered loud exclamations of joy and pleasure, [shouting] 'Long life to our actual president, Don Guadalupe Victoria! Long life to the Mexican nation!'"[28]

Now that Domingo Fernández had possession of the San Cristóbal grant together with his co-grantees, he attempted to terminate their rights by claiming that they had failed to show up for a workday Fernández himself claimed to have called. On 2 September 1829, about two years after the act of possession, Domingo Fernández petitioned Governor Armijo's successor in the governor's palace, José Antonio Chaves (1829–1832), to require Fernández's co-grantees to begin cultivating their land or lose their rights. Fernández claimed that a day had been set for everyone to go to the grant and "aid in the clearing out of springs, construction of ponds, and other works." No mention was made of when this workday had occurred, who had ordered the settlers to go to the grant and perform this work, and to what extent the grantees (including Fernández) had planted and cultivated their land. This omission is important because later purchasers of the San Cristóbal grant from Domingo Fernández would claim that the co-grantees forfeited their rights solely because of this petition. Fernández claimed that a day had been appointed, that he had appeared on that day, both at Galisteo and San Cristóbal, and when no one else showed up, he worked on cleaning and maintaining the springs and other places himself.[29] After receiving the petition, Governor Chaves notified the local alcalde to order the co-grantees to appear before him and proceed to cultivate the land at San Cristóbal; if they failed to, they would forfeit their rights. Neither the governor nor the local alcalde took any further action regarding the farming land at San Cristóbal.[30]

Domingo Fernández's attempt to foreclose the rights of the other grantees lacked a factual foundation, however, for we have no evidence that any official of the Mexican government noted a failure to cultivate the land on the part of any of the grantees. In fact, several of the co-grantees later testified before the surveyor general that when the alcalde notified them that they would forfeit their rights unless they moved onto the grant, they began farming their land, cleaning the springs, and remained on the land until driven off by the Indians around 1841.[31] Although this version of events did not surface until 1879, there must have been early evidence of farming on the San Cristóbal grant, including cultivated fields and houses of owners besides Domingo Fernández.

In spite of this evidence of multiple ownership of the grant, on 20 January 1851 Domingo Fernández sold the entire San Cristóbal grant to Ethan W. Eaton and Alexander Reynolds for five hundred dollars. The land was described as follows: "the lands of the pueblo of San Cristóbal, near the town of Galisteo, commencing at the Lagunita in a direct line to the spring of La Baca; and from thence to the south and west to the Bajada de los Comanches; and then from the Lagunita to a stone rock known as the Creston, on the north; and from said rock to the spring of La Baca, including said spring of La Baca, drawing direct line to the Bajada de los Comanches, to where it intersects a line from north to south on a line with the Lagunita." Domingo Fernández had Donaciano Vigil, another speculator in abandoned Pueblo land, witness the deed for him.[32] Soon after the deed from Fernández to Eaton and Reynolds, Eaton acquired

Reynolds's interest in the land, and Ethan Eaton became the sole owner of what I will still call the San Cristóbal grant, though the surveyor general would name it the Ethan Eaton grant.[33]

The history of San Cristóbal as an Indian pueblo was revived around the 1860s or so when a claim for a four-square-league Pueblo grant for San Cristóbal Pueblo was filed with the surveyor general by an unknown party, most likely Domingo Fernández. The San Cristóbal claim was one of twelve Cruzate grants to Indian pueblos submitted to the surveyor general in the late 1850s. The claim was not submitted to Congress, probably because Surveyor General Pelham was aware that San Cristóbal had not been in existence as a pueblo for over a century and a half.[34] Meanwhile, Ethan Eaton pursued his claim to the Domingo Fernández version of the San Cristóbal grant.

Ethan Eaton was a military man in southern New Mexico, a colonel in the army, and post commander at Fort Wingate in 1864. Eaton helped organize the Socorro vigilantes to bring justice to Socorro after Ethan's friend, Anthony M. Conklin, a publisher, was murdered and the local sheriff refused to prosecute. The suspected members of the Baca family were said to be related to the sheriff. Ethan Eaton was born in New York in 1827, so when he purchased the San Cristóbal grant in 1851 he was only twenty-four years old. We do not know how Ethan Eaton met Domingo Fernández, but they appear to have been from two different worlds. It is ironic that Fernández, who showed some awareness of and sensitivity to the history of San Cristóbal Pueblo, would sell the land to a young military man whose relationship to Indians was similar to that of Kit Carson: at Fort Wingate Eaton "processed" the Navajos; later, he was part of the party that searched for Manuelito, and when that Apache leader was found, Ethan Eaton is said to be the one who executed him.[35]

After Ethan Eaton acquired the San Cristóbal grant (which became known as the Ethan Eaton grant), he petitioned Surveyor General William Pelham for its confirmation, claiming on 11 October 1855 that all of the original grantees had forfeited their rights to Domingo Fernández's grant by failing to comply with its conditions and that he had purchased the land from Fernández.[36] Two years later, on 10 August 1857, Pelham called a hearing to take the testimony of José María Martínez and Francisco Baca, both of whom testified to the authenticity of signatures of the officials on the grant documents.[37] A month later, on 18 September, Pelham rendered a decision in which he found, somewhat ambiguously, that the grant was good and valid and recommended its confirmation "to E. W. Eaton, as the assignee and legal representative of Domingo Fernández, and to the remaining grantees who had not forfeited their right to the land by a noncompliance with the conditions of the grant."[38] The confirmation by Congress of the San Cristóbal/Ethan Eaton grant was also ambiguous because it left it up to the surveyor general and other officials in the U.S. Department of the Interior not only the question of who owned the grant but also how much land was encompassed within its boundaries. In order to locate the boundaries of the grant, a contract to survey the grant was awarded to Deputy Surveyors William Pelham and Reuben Clements in November 1860. The survey showed the grant to be in the shape of an inverted triangle and to contain 27,854 acres.[39] Ethan Eaton protested the approval of the survey, pointing out that the act of possession described a rectangular tract of land.[40]

General Land Office commissioner Willis Drummond investigated the question of what had been confirmed by the act of 21 June 1860 and rendered his decision on 11 November 1875.[41] Drummond's investigation went beyond the question of boundaries and the shape of the grant; he also looked at Domingo Fernández's share of the grant vis-à-vis the other grantees. Drummond noted that the grant documents showed that Fernández had been allotted only the lands lying between "the *mesita* of the Lagunitas upwards as far as the spring of the *Vaca* under the boundaries of the grant" and that while Fernández had informed the governor that his co-grantees had not complied with the conditions of the grant and the alcalde was directed to take action against the co-grantees, there was no evidence showing that the co-grantees had forfeited their interests. Drummond noted further that "even if their title had been forfeited, it would not necessarily follow that Fernández would have gained any additional land, [for] in his complaint Fernández merely asked that the delinquent grantees be either compelled to perform their duties or resign their rights." The alcalde was instructed to notify the co-owners that if "they would not cultivate the land, they would be substituted with other industrious individuals." Drummond was of the opinion that the act had confirmed only the "just claim, which Eaton can now have as his assignee." In effect, Drummond argued that Eaton held only the partial interest that Domingo Fernández had held in the San Cristóbal grant.[42]

Soon after GLO commissioner Drummond's decision, Ethan Eaton, as might be expected, appealed that decision to Secretary of the Interior C. Delano, who held that

the language of this award by the Surveyor General is ambiguous. It
confirms the grant to E. W. Eaton, as the assignee and legal representative
of Fernández *and to the remaining original grantees, who had not forfeited
their rights.* . . . I am of the opinion that the confirmation extends to any
of the original grantees who have not forfeited their rights to the grant.
It does not appear that any such grantees are claiming any portion of the
original grant, [but] I am not disposed, however, to so construe the act of
confirmation as to give to Eaton the entire grant or any portion of it, unless
he shows himself entitled to it by an assignment [emphasis added].[43]

Delano's decision gave Eaton a little more leeway by suggesting that Eaton
could claim the entire grant if he could obtain assignments from the other
co-grantees, which might not be difficult to accomplish since none of them had
filed a claim in the case.

In fact, it was difficult. Although Eaton thought he had purchased the entire
grant free and clear from Domingo Fernández, those outstanding interests in
the grant would dog Eaton in the coming decades. Eventually he would have to
recognize these claims, which were represented by Thomas B. Catron. Catron
began buying up the interests of Domingo Fernández's co-grantees as early as
1869, when Catron went into partnership with Nicolás Pino, a wealthy Galisteo
landowner. Most of the deeds of the co-grantees are to Pino alone, but Catron
had a one-half interest in the purchased shares as a partner of Nicolás Pino.[44]

As Eaton began to realize he had problems with his title to the San
Cristóbal grant, he started selling fractional interests in the grant, even as he
was pressuring the surveyor general to resurvey the grant. In 1874 Ethan
Eaton and his wife, Marcelina, sold about one-third of the grant to Saron and
Hattie Laughlin of San Francisco for about forty-five cents an acre. Eaton also
mortgaged his remaining two-thirds interest in the grant several times, once
to the Seligman brothers of Santa Fe and in 1876 to Thomas B. Catron. Eaton
realized that it was easier to ally with Catron then to fight him, and he agreed
with Catron to use the proceeds of the 1876 mortgage to purchase about
forty-five hundred sheep, raise them, and split the profits with Catron.[45]
Before long, however, Eaton tired of the hassles of operating the grant and
sold his remaining interest to his son-in-law, Charles Gildersleeve, a well-
known Santa Fe judge and former business partner of Catron's.[46]

In 1879 Surveyor General Henry M. Atkinson awarded a new contract for the resurvey of the San Cristóbal grant to Deputy Surveyor John Shaw. Additional testimony was taken as to the location of the natural objects mentioned in the act of possession, and witnesses testified as to the interests held by Fernández's co-grantees in the San Cristóbal grant. One of those witnesses was Ramón Serna y Rivera, who testified that when the alcalde notified the twenty-five co-grantees that they would forfeit their rights unless they performed the conditions of the grant, they moved onto the grant, cultivated their lands, cleaned the springs, and fulfilled all the other conditions necessary to perfect their interests. In what sounded more like a legal brief than an identification of boundaries, Serna y Rivera went on to testify that most of the co-grantees had continued to live on the grant until the Indians drove them off in 1841. He also noted that under the law, land once granted could be forfeited only by a proceeding called a denouncement and that Domingo Fernández had not instituted such a proceeding against the co-grantees. It is not surprising that this testimony seemed to favor the co-grantees because by this time Eaton had sold his interest in the San Cristóbal grant, leaving Catron as one of the remaining owners along with Laughlin and Gildersleeve. Although witnesses such as Serna y Rivera seemed more interested in reducing the amount of land to which Ethan Eaton was entitled than in establishing boundaries, the Shaw survey showed the San Cristóbal grant as a rectangular tract of land containing 81,032 acres, three times larger than the Pelham and Clements survey.[47]

By this time Ethan Eaton had sold his interest in the grant, but the new owners still had not won. First, they would have to deal with a protest from the owners of the Galisteo grant on the west of San Cristóbal and later claims from the co-grantees who still had an interest in the grant. The Galisteo grantees protested the approval of the Shaw survey on the grounds that the Pelham and Clements survey had incorrectly located the west line of the grant. The commissioner of the General Land Office, James Williamson, held in an opinion dated 14 July 1879 that the boundaries of the lands confirmed were correctly located and it was up to the interested parties to identify and adjust their respective claims within the grant by mutual agreement and partition or other proceedings in the proper judicial tribunals.[48] Commissioner Williamson dismissed the protest in part because the inhabitants of Galisteo had failed to show that they had any interest in the lands covered by the survey. The grant was patented on 8 December 1880 for 81,032 acres.[49]

Ironically, by the time the San Cristóbal grant was patented in 1880 Ethan Eaton had sold his interest in the grant and moved to Socorro. At the time the patent to the San Cristóbal grant was signed by President Rutherford B. Hayes, the ownership of the San Cristóbal grant was divided between Saron Laughlin, who owned a one-third interest; Charles Gildersleeve, who owned a large portion; T. B. Catron and Nicolás Pino, who owned a large number of individual plots; and individual Hispanic settlers, who owned about one thousand acres of small tracts. Between 1880 and 1888 Thomas B. Catron began asserting more influence over the San Cristóbal grant by purchasing in his own name more of the small tracts of Domingo Fernández's co-owners. In April of 1890 Charles Gildersleeve sold his portion of the San Cristóbal grant to Saron Laughlin, who now had a majority interest in the grant. When Laughlin started stocking the ranch with a large herd of cattle, Catron filed a partition suit and a quiet title suit to establish everyone's respective interest in the San Cristóbal grant and then divide those portions among the respective owners.[50]

Once again, the two competing histories of the San Cristóbal grant in the time of Domingo Fernández were pitted against one another. Thomas B. Catron's version emphasized the settlement of Fernández's co-grantees on the grant, describing how he (Catron) had talked to many of the co-grantees, who "stated that they had gone upon the property, broken up the land, worked on the springs, increased the supply of water, had made dams to hold the same and had dug ditches and had built small houses, into which they had moved and occupied until they had complied with the terms of the grant to them."[51] Laughlin replied that all the co-grantees had abandoned their allotments soon after they received them, so that the entire grant reverted to Domingo Fernández, who then sold it to Eaton, who sold it to him (Laughlin). After seven years of legal wrangling the district court decided in Laughlin's favor. In 1897 Catron appealed, and six years later the appellate court decided in Catron's favor, stating that none of the co-grantees gave up their rights to the grant even if they did leave the land at some point, and thus Catron was still the owner of the tracts he had purchased.[52]

In August of 1903 Catron and Laughlin agreed to divide the grant in half, with the western half going to Catron and the eastern half to Laughlin, who would buy Catron's half at about $1.25 per acre or about $50,000. Meanwhile, the partition suit was completed, and in November 1903 the final decree was signed by Associate Justice Benjamin S. Baker. Catron was determined to own almost 70 percent (⁹⁄₁₃) of the grant. Saron Laughlin owned about 15 percent (²⁄₁₃), and the balance of 15 percent was owned by the co-grantees with small tracts who had not sold to Catron. Thomas B. Catron had somehow managed to parlay his minority interest in the grant that Domingo Fernández had tried to wipe out completely into a majority interest. Justice Baker painstakingly listed the smaller shares (as small as ¹⁄₁₀₉₂ of the grant) and concluded the decree by appointing three commissioners to go to the grant and determine if and how the grant could be physically divided among all those owners.[53]

As was usually the case in these situations, the three commissioners decided that the San Cristóbal grant could not be equitably divided between its owners. This decision was due to the location of the "watered places and valuable portions" of the grant, which were "so scarce that it was not possible for all tracts to have access to the water," an issue that had been at the forefront from the early days of San Cristóbal Pueblo through the 1820s and 1830s, when Domingo Fernández was the primary owner of the San Cristóbal grant.[54]

In the final part of the partition suit, Justice Benjamin Baker ordered that the San Cristóbal grant be sold to the highest bidder on 30 January 1904 at the front door of the Santa Fe County courthouse. On the appointed day, Thomas B. Catron was the highest bidder, purchasing the entire grant for fifty-two hundred dollars. After conveying the eastern half of the grant to Saron Laughlin in 1904, Catron sold the western half to Laughlin for the prearranged price of fifty thousand dollars, thus making a profit of about fifty times his original investment.[55] Catron had reversed his usual practice of buying an entire grant and then attempting to minimize the interests of the settlers who occupied the grant (as he did with the Tierra Amarilla and Mora grants). In the case of the San Cristóbal grant, Catron was more successful in buying the interests of the settlers and parlaying those into his own majority interest in the grant.

Today, most of the San Cristóbal grant is occupied by the San Cristóbal Ranch, a large cattle operation pictured and described by Christina Singleton Mednick in her book *San Cristóbal: Voices and Visions of the Galisteo Basin*. The ranch owners are "planning to create a conservancy to protect the stunning petroglyphs and ruins of the indigenous inhabitants of San Cristóbal, whose culture has not been studied adequately to this day."[56] Mostly forgotten is the early history of a grant with many names: the San Cristóbal grant, the

Domingo Fernández grant, or the Ethan Eaton grant, not counting the early Tano names for San Cristóbal. Also mostly forgotten is that master of ambiguity Domingo Fernández, whose speculative tendencies prevailed, though the confusion he created was not sorted out for over fifty years. And above all, not to be forgotten are the San Cristóbal Indians, whose descendants still live at Hopi and perhaps at nearby pueblos, and who alone remember the sacred sites where their ancestors once worshipped and left offerings.[57]

CHAPTER SEVEN

THE SAN MARCOS PUEBLO GRANT

S AN MARCOS IS CONSIDERED TO BE A KERES PUEBLO, UNLIKE ALL the other Galisteo Basin pueblos, which are Tano. Oral history at Santo Domingo Pueblo, which is closely related to San Marcos, suggests that San Marcos and other Galisteo Basin pueblos may have split off from some Keres pueblos, giving them a mixed Tano/Keres identity.[1] Prior to the Pueblo Revolt, San Marcos was known as "Turquoise Pueblo Ruin" in Tewa. The members of San Marcos Pueblo mined turquoise, copper, and lead (for making glaze paint) in the nearby Cerrillos Hills before Juan de Oñate arrived in New Mexico in 1598.[2] San Marcos was probably mining substantial amounts of turquoise during precontact times because we have abundant evidence of Cerrillos-area turquoise in Mesoamerica and throughout the Southwest and much of that turquoise came from Mount Chalchihuitl and San Marcos Pueblo after 1300. According to Phil Weigand and Acelia García de Weigand, "The ruin of San Marcos is one of the largest architectural complexes within the southwest. Much of its prosperity must have come from turquoise mining."[3]

San Marcos was much larger during its earlier occupation in the fourteenth century than it was at the time of Spanish contact. Pottery found on the surface of the site indicates occupation in the mid- to late 1200s and early 1300s. This pueblo was called Ya'atze in the Keres language. The presence of reliable springs at the southwest corner of the pueblo and the site's proximity to the turquoise and lead deposits in the Cerrillos Hills were factors in the success of this pueblo, but with a population almost six times that of Pecos, the pueblo

may have had difficulty growing enough corn to feed everyone. Fields surrounding the pueblo show evidence of both irrigated and dry farming, as was
true at San Cristóbal. A reservoir for irrigation, cobble-grid gardens, and
pebble-mulched gardens with associated pottery sherds, chert, obsidian, and
basalt flakes (possibly representing offerings) are some of the agricultural features at the ancient San Marcos Pueblo. Covering approximately sixty acres,
the pueblo had twenty-two room blocks enclosing from eight to ten plazas and
about two thousand ground-floor rooms. At the northwest corner are the
remains of the Spanish Franciscan mission church and convento (priest's residence), built in the seventeenth century. San Marcos is listed in the National
Register of Historic Places and may be the largest prehistoric pueblo in the
United States.[4]

San Marcos is mentioned in almost every explorer's account through the
Southwest from 1582 to 1600 and always in relation to mines, but it is not
mentioned in Coronado's journal. From 1540 to 1542 Francisco Vásquez de
Coronado along with almost three hundred soldiers, many priests, and
one thousand Mexican Indians arrived in New Mexico, but his chronicles
make no mention of San Marcos Pueblo. The Spanish did not return until
the Fray Agustín Rodríguez and Captain Francisco Sánchez Chamuscado
expedition of 1581, when they visited the Galisteo area and the pueblo of
Ya'atze/San Marcos in search of buffalo. Soon after they arrived at what
became known as San Marcos Pueblo and had commandeered food supplies,
one of the priests, Fray Juan de Santa María, decided to depart Ya'atze for
Mexico. Everyone "condemned the decision as inadvisable for he would not
only endanger his own life, but imperil the soldiers and . . . jeopardize further exploration of the land." Nevertheless, Santa María was determined to
leave and departed on 8 September 1518. Sadly, the expedition soon learned
that the Indians had followed the priest for three days, caught him on the
third day, and clubbed him to death. The San Marcos people were worried
that the priest "would bring back more Christians . . . to put them out of
their homes."[5] The expedition gave this pueblo the name "Malpartida" (Evil
Parting). Fray Rodríguez and Fray Francisco López stayed behind in Puaray
and were soon killed as well.[6] "In 1590 Captain Gaspar Castaño de Sosa,
arrived in New Mexico and in January 1591 visited twenty-two pueblos, naming San Lucas (Galisteo), San Marcos ('San Marcos where the mines had
been discovered'), and San Cristóbal. While Castaño went to visit other

pueblos, many in his party remained at San Marcos. They prospected for seventeen days and 'made many tests which showed silver.'"[7] When Juan de Oñate visited San Marcos, he assayed ores from nearby mines that yielded "four ounces of metal."

What form the precontact San Marcos mines might have taken is not known, though recent archaeological investigations have unearthed two features associated with fire-based metallurgy: the base of an adobe furnace or furnaces and a slag dump or clean-out deposit associated with the furnace. Analysis of the slag heap by Ann Ramenofsky indicates that metal processing was occurring at San Marcos prior to the Pueblo Revolt, probably in the early 1600s and possibly before that. However, we have no indication as to what metal was being smelted, though lead and copper are likely. It appears that the furnace was of pre-revolt construction, and the slag heap seems to have been generated by a mining operation run by Spaniards as well as Indians.[8] Other Spanish colonial mining sites where copper was being smelted or mined include the mines of La Plata Verdi, the Tuerto smelting site, and the Spanish Queen smelting site, in addition to Pa'ako Pueblo. It is possible that Indian labor was coerced at the San Marcos mines, which would help explain the ambiguous attitude of the pueblo toward the Pueblo Revolt. San Marcos Indians first informed Governor Otermín of the impending revolt and then killed their own priest and joined the attack on Santa Fe. But whatever the nature and extent of the mines at San Marcos, it represents one of only two mission communities with evidence of seventeenth-century metal production.[9]

Soon after Juan de Oñate settled at San Juan Pueblo (present-day Ohkay Owingeh) in 1598, Father Juan de Rozas was appointed as priest at San Marcos and several other pueblos. He probably started construction of a church and convento at that time, but in 1638, when Fray Agustín de Cuellar was appointed guardian of the pueblo, the convento was still under construction. Eventually, the mission complex at San Marcos was completed with its two *visitas* of San Lázaro and La Ciénega.[10] Like La Ciénega Pueblo, it was a Spanish mission up to the time of the 1680 Pueblo Revolt, when it contained about six hundred inhabitants. San Marcos joined the Tanos and others in the attack on Santa Fe, after destroying its own church. When Diego de Vargas led the reconquest of New Mexico in 1692, he found San Marcos Pueblo abandoned and its people living with the Cochitis on Cieneguilla Mesa.[11]

Vargas found the church and convento at San Marcos still standing when he visited the pueblo on 18 October 1692—at least the walls were considered sound.[12] In 1694 the Cerrillos Hills were known as the Cerros de San Marcos. Vargas referred to the Cerros de San Marcos mine as "Madrid's mine" because the mine was owned by Roque Madrid's father, Francisco Madrid II. The family had their hacienda at the Arroyo de San Marcos, a little less than two leagues from Santa Fe.[13] Diego de Vargas mentions the abandoned Madrid hacienda on 15 December 1693 in his campaign journal: "On 15 of the present month of December of the current year [1693], I, the governor and captain general, arrived at this abandoned hacienda and outpost belonging to the captain and military leader, Roque Madrid."[14] Vargas inspected his troops and their weapons in early February 1694 and found many in need of repair. He also inspected the ammunition and found seven hundred cannon-balls in a sack. In order to replenish their supplies of lead cannonballs on 12 February 1694, Governor Vargas "ordered Capt. Roque Madrid to go to the supposed mines with twelve knowledgeable soldiers, for there were many such in this presidio among those I enlisted and brought from Zacatecas and Sombrerete to attend to this matter."[15]

In his report, Governor Vargas summarized Roque Madrid's examinations of the Cerros de San Marcos mines as follows:

> Supplied with crowbars and hide bags, they went to the hill and mines with the captain [Roque Madrid] who saw that the Indians had worked it as an open cut, going for the lode and lead-colored ore of the vein. Because it had been well covered up, they saw that it was impossible to work it. The captain brought some stones from among those they found around the mine [and] I, and the soldiers with knowledge of mining found them to show signs of containing some lead. An examination of the mine to make an assay of it was postponed until an opportune time in the summer.

After this reference to a possible lead mine at Roque Madrid's Cerros de San Marcos hacienda, the Spaniards made very little further mention of mining at San Marcos, but there are several references to Pueblo Indian use of the turquoise mines.

After the Pueblo Revolt some of the inhabitants of San Marcos moved to Cochiti and some moved to Santo Domingo.[16] The San Marcos area was then used as a grazing *paraje* for the Santa Fe presidio because of its tall grass. In 1737 Alferez Juan José Moreno, who was a sergeant at the presidio, petitioned Governor Enrique de Olavide y Michelena (1736–1739), asking him to designate San Marcos and six other nearby areas as grazing lands for the exclusive use of the presidio's horse herd. Moreno complained that for the three years prior to 1737, the presidio's horses had been losing weight due to lack of good grazing lands near the military headquarters. He pointed out that with almost daily raids by nomadic Plains Indian tribes, presidio horses needed to be in good condition and near the presidio so that soldiers could readily give chase to the raiding Comanche, Apache, Ute, and other tribes. Moreno noted that herds of cattle and flocks of sheep owned by private individuals were often found grazing on these pasturelands, preventing their use by the presidio's horse herd. Governor Olavide y Michelena responded favorably to this petition and designated the grazing areas at Caja del Río, Santa Cruz, La Májada de Domínguez, Las Bocas, Los Cerrillos, Maragua, and San Marcos as ancient pasturelands (*comedores antiguos*) to be used exclusively by the presidio's horse herds. Stockmen with herds of cattle or flocks of sheep that were grazing on these seven ancient pasturelands were notified to remove their animals within fifteen days or be subject to a fine of fifty pesos.[17]

It is not apparent from Governor Olavide y Michelena's 1737 order whether the San Marcos pasturelands were being used by private stockmen at that time, but if they were it is likely that the family of Antonio Urbán Montaño was among those cattle owners.[18] In 1754 José Urbán Montaño asked Governor Tomás Vélez Cachupín (1749–1754 and 1762–1767) for a grant of the land formerly belonging to San Marcos Pueblo as a place on which to graze his animals. Vélez Cachupín was aware that the presidio's horse herd was using San Marcos, but he also wanted to establish a Spanish settler presence in the area. If both private stockmen and the presidio's horse herd would share the same grazing area, there might be greater protection from nomadic Indian raids than if the presidio's horses were grazing the area alone, for Hispanic stockmen would be motivated to protect their herds. Vélez Cachupín was keenly aware of this situation, for he had served his apprenticeship for governor of New Mexico as the viceroy's equerry, the official in charge of all aspects of care of the horses in the viceregal stable.[19] Antonio Urbán Montaño described the tract he was seeking as bounded "on the north by a ridge of rocks which is on the plains; on the south by the ridge which divides the said place from the Vasquez arroyo; on the east by the main road leading to the Pueblo of Galisteo; and on the west by the skirt of the hills between the said place and the arroyo of lo de Vasquez."[20]

Montaño stated that he had a large family and some stock but no land upon which to support them, and he asked that the land be granted to him so he could build a house for his family and establish a ranch to pasture his stock.[21] Montaño was asking for a private grant for himself, so on 15 June 1754 Governor Vélez Cachupín found that although the lands were vacant Montaño had asked for more land than was reasonable. Therefore, he made a grant of a tract measuring thirty-three 50-vara cordels or 1,650 varas (a vara is about thirty-three inches) in each direction from the center, where Montaño would build his house and corrals. The grant was made subject to the condition that Montaño was to prevent his herds from damaging the commons where the horses and livestock of the soldiers stationed at the presidio of Santa Fe were pastured. If he should violate this condition, his grant would automatically terminate, and Montaño and his family would be ejected from the land. Vélez Cachupín directed Alcalde Bartolomé Fernández to place Montaño in possession of the grant and return the *expediente* to him in order that a testimonio of the proceedings could be given the grantee.[22] On 26 July 1754 Fernández went to San Marcos and placed Montaño in possession of a tract of land that he described as being bounded "on the north by some red rocks in the arroyo; on the east by two cedar trees; on the south by a large cottonwood by the road; and on the west, by a small hill called Chachihuitl [*sic*]," a different description than the one found in Vélez Cachupín's granting decree.[23]

For some reason, Alcalde Fernández did not follow Vélez Cachupín's directions to measure a grant 1,650 varas in each direction, which would form a square about one-third the size of a 5,000-vara Pueblo league (5,800 acres instead of 17,350 acres). Instead, Fernández established natural landmarks as the boundaries, three of which were so vague and ill-defined that the later surveyors for the Court of Private Land Claims were unable to locate them. Usually, Governor Vélez Cachupín was able to catch such a mistake and order the alcalde to reestablish the boundaries in accordance with the granting decree, but in this instance the governor was near the end of his second term, and the matter seems to have been overlooked. The measurement of the boundaries of the San Marcos Pueblo grant would remain a thorny issue throughout the adjudication of the grant by the surveyor general and the Court of Private Land Claims 120 years later. The vague boundary calls were "some red rocks in an arroyo, two cedars, and a large cottonwood near the road." It is not surprising that 140 years after Antonio Urbán Montaño was put in possession of the San Marcos Pueblo grant, these trees and red rocks, which at the time everyone knew about, could not be located.[24]

In 1854, six years after the Treaty of Guadalupe Hidalgo ended the U.S. war with Mexico, the United States established the Office of the Surveyor General to adjudicate land grants in New Mexico. On 25 February 1873 the legal representatives of Antonio Urbán Montaño presented a claim to Surveyor General James K. Proudfit for confirmation of the San Marcos Pueblo grant.[25] Manuel Bustamante testified that "many years ago when I desired to purchase this San Marcos spring property, I ascertained that a man residing at Abiquiu, named Juan Antonio Ortega, had the papers in the grant, and understood that he was the owner of the property. . . . The reason I did not purchase the property . . . was that upon examining the tract I found that the supply of water afforded by the spring was small and inadequate."[26] This testimony casts doubt on the continuous occupancy of the grant and shows that from the beginning the San Marcos (Spring) grant may have been a speculative grant. Surveyor General Proudfit found the title papers to be genuine and recommended confirmation of the San Marcos Pueblo grant to the legal representatives of the original grantee according to the boundaries set forth in the act of possession.[27] A preliminary survey of the grant made by Deputy Surveyors Griffin and McMullen in November 1877 found the grant to contain 1,890.62 acres.[28]

Surveyor General George W. Julian reexamined the claim pursuant to instructions from General Land Office commissioner William A. J. Sparks, and in a supplemental report dated 23 January 1888 he raised several objections to confirmation of the grant. Julian pointed out that no documents had been filed connecting the petitioners with Antonio Urbán Montaño and no evidence had been found to suggest that Montaño had ever occupied the grant. These two objections, particularly the first one, had some merit. It was often the case, as was true with the Cristóbal Nieto grant, that the surveyor general and the Court of Private Land Claims were lax in making claimants prove their connection to the grantee of the land grant they were seeking to have confirmed.[29] Surveyor General Julian also maintained that the Griffin and McMullen survey was erroneous because the lines were run east–west and north–south through the specified points to form a square tract instead of the four points being connected to form a diamond-shaped tract. According to Julian, the grant had thus been enlarged to cover an area twice the size originally granted by Governor Vélez Cachupín.[30] There was no basis for this objection, however, since in the Spanish and Mexican periods New Mexico grants measured in the four cardinal directions from a center point were always connected to form a square-shaped—not a diamond-shaped—tract. As was often true, Julian had no historical basis for his objections. In addition, his objections violated instructions from the General Land Office to deal with land grant claims the way the governments of Spain and Mexico would have done.[31]

In addition, Julian presumed that the geometrical figure ordered in the Vélez Cachupín decree would prevail over the boundary description by natural features called for in the Fernández act of possession. Under Spanish and Mexican law, however, the act of possession boundary description prevailed over the boundaries called for in the grant. Measurements and boundary calls often differed between the granting decree and the act of possession because the conditions on the ground were the paramount factor. Nevertheless, when the surveyor general and the Court of Private Land Claims surveyed the San Marcos grant, they surveyed a square measuring 1,650 varas or sixty-eight and a half chains (4,521 feet) in each direction because the natural features like the cedar trees and the red rocks could not be located.[32]

No action was taken on Julian's supplemental opinion during the 1880s, but behind the scenes members of the Spiegelberg family were acquiring deeds from the descendants of Antonio Urbán Montaño. The Spiegelberg family included Lehman and Willi Spiegelberg, two of ten children born to Jacob Spiegelberg, who came to the United States from Prussia and Westphalia, Germany, and established a prosperous retail store in Santa Fe. Lehman came to New Mexico in 1857, thirteen years after his brother Solomon Jacob Spiegelberg had arrived to learn the merchandising trade from Eugene Leitensdorfer.[33] The success of the Spiegelberg firm led Solomon Jacob Spiegelberg to send for his younger brothers to join him. Levi came in 1848, Elias in 1850, Emanuel in 1853, Lehman in 1857, and Willi in 1861. After establishing their mercantile business in Santa Fe, the Spiegelberg brothers engaged in numerous other business enterprises. According to Henry Tobias, "The Spiegelbergs were among the first to move into the reestablished Indian trade and when the Navajos moved to their reservation in August 1868, the first trading license issued at Fort Defiance went to Lehman Spiegelberg. He named his brother Willi as one of his clerks, and they had the right, not later granted to others, to trade at the agency or anywhere on the reservation. Willi Spiegelberg, in turn, was the first trader at Fort Wingate in July 1868." Willi Spiegelberg later became sutler to the Navajo Indian Agency. The success of the Spiegelbergs in obtaining Indian Agency contracts may have been due in part to their close ties to the military and civil leaders of New Mexico.[34] "The Spiegelbergs had a history of interest in mining that dated at least to the 1860s. Lehman Spiegelberg served on the board of directors of the Willison Silver Mining Company in 1872,"[35] and in 1861 the Spiegelbergs joined a group of investors who incorporated the Montezuma Copper Mining Company of Santa Fe, and they were probably familiar with William F. M. Arny's report concerning the presence of copper in the area. Lehman Spiegelberg's interest in copper mining may have been the impetus that impelled him to acquire the San Marcos Pueblo grant.[36]

In July of 1892 the Spiegelberg brothers and a third party named Raunheim filed suit against the United States, seeking the confirmation of the San Marcos Pueblo grant, although their identity as the claimants is not apparent from the petition.[37] Surprisingly, in a rare move by Matthew Reynolds, the U.S. attorney declined to file an answer, putting the plaintiffs to the proof of the allegations in their complaint. When the case came up for trial on 12 December 1892, the Spiegelbergs introduced the grant papers into evidence, as well as an abstract of title connecting them with the original grantee. They also produced oral testimony demonstrating that Montaño and those claiming under him were in possession of the grant since the date possession was delivered to him by Alcalde Fernández. The government did not counter this testimony, so in an opinion dated 16 December 1892 Justice Reed declared that the grant papers were genuine and the plaintiffs' proof of possession was sufficient, and he confirmed the grant to Montaño's heirs and assigns in accordance with the boundaries set forth in the act of possession. Predictably, because of the favoritism shown by the government toward the Spiegelbergs, the government did not appeal the decision.[38]

Deputy Surveyor Sherrard Coleman was awarded a contract to survey the grant in March 1894, and after spending several days trying to find the boundary calls cited in the act of possession, Coleman came to the conclusion that it would be impossible to survey the grant since three of the natural monuments could not be located.[39] On 6 October 1894 the government and claimants stipulated that the description of the boundaries of the grant in the court's final decree were mistaken because "some of said landmarks being of a perishable nature have disappeared, [accordingly,] it is agreed by said claimants that they accept . . . the measurement as given in the original grant, *viz*: 33 cordeles of fifty varas in each direction, measured from the center where he built his house and corrals."[40] The court modified the decree accordingly, and the grant was surveyed by Coleman as a 1,895-acre square tract. The survey commenced at a stone monument at a central point located near the ruins of an old corral. Each of the four boundary lines was located thirty-three cordels or sixty-eight and a half chains in each of the cardinal directions from this central point. On 23 June 1896 a patent for the lands embraced within the survey was issued to the legal successors of Antonio Urbán Montaño.[41]

Even after Surveyor General Julian's critical examination of the San Marcos Pueblo grant, the confirmation process was remarkably easy once the grant was acquired by the Spiegelbergs. This may have been due in part to the Spiegelbergs' connections with those in high places in the military and in the civil government of New Mexico.[42] Willi Spiegelberg was a close friend of Governor Lew Wallace, and "among guests of the Spiegelbergs in Santa Fe were president and Mrs. [Rutherford] Hayes, Generals Grant, Pope, Logan, Miles, Sheridan, and Sherman."[43]

By the time the San Marcos Pueblo grant was confirmed, all the Spiegelbergs had left New Mexico and moved to New York. Unlike other immigrant merchants such as Charles Ilfeld in Las Vegas and Karl Bode in Abiquiu—who remained in their communities and whose stores are still there—the Spiegelbergs were drawn back to the economic networks and family ties of New York City. The San Marcos Pueblo grant was just another investment that, however astute, did not bring with it a sense of the history of the land. Unlike the San Cristóbal Pueblo grant, where Domingo Fernández cited preservation of the church as a reason for acquiring the land, the Spiegelbergs had little appreciation for the history of San Marcos Pueblo.[44]

In spite of the land speculation surrounding San Marcos Pueblo, the people of Santo Domingo Pueblo have always regarded themselves as the heirs of San Marcos and claimed ownership of the San Marcos turquoise mines. Since the

1880s references have been made to Pueblo Indians mining turquoise from Mount Chalchihuitl and neighboring mines in the Cerrillos area. In 1881, for instance, several "young men from Santo Domingo boarded the train to sell specimens of turquoise," which they may have mined at Mount Chalchihuitl. In 1882 an Anglo visitor to the Chalchihuitl Mine encountered some Indians who "seem[ed] to think they [had] a right to this mine," and in 1910 some Santo Domingo Indians who "still claim[ed] the turquoise mines from which their forefathers took turquoise centuries ago" were caught and charged with theft. The newspaper headline read, "Tiffany Turquoise Mine Robbed by Santo Domingo Indians." Later that same year, "four Cochitis were arrested for a similar offense having entered at night the Castillian Mine . . . and were sentenced to the penitentiary."[45] In the mid-1970s Santo Domingo received compensation from the Indian Claims Commission for the U.S. government taking about ten thousand acres of claimed aboriginal lands that included San Marcos and some of the turquoise mines. During the periods of mining booms and busts in the Cerrillos Hills, the pueblos of Cochiti and Santo Domingo, and possibly others, have not only claimed ownership of the mines but have continued to "return to the area for ceremonial purposes." Santo Domingo also claims other ruins of the Galisteo Basin as ancestral villages.[46]

Three stages of the history of the San Marcos Pueblo grant have been recounted here in a story as layered as an archaeological dig: the precontact history of San Marcos Pueblo, one of the few pueblos known to have been involved in smelting metals; the mid-eighteenth-century history of the area as an ancient grassland protected for the use of the presidio's horse herd and shared with the San Marcos land grant of José Urbán Montaño; and the acquisition of the grant by the Spiegelberg family and its adjudication in 1892 by the Court of Private Land Claims. Today, San Marcos Pueblo is still being studied to unlock more secrets of this once magnificent pueblo, probably the largest and least understood in the Southwest. In 1980 the Archaeological Conservancy acquired most of the site of San Marcos Pueblo to preserve and protect it.[47] In addition, the San Marcos Pueblo Historic District was registered on the National Register of Historic Places and the State Register of Cultural Properties.[48] Several important studies have been completed, especially of San Marcos metallurgy, that shed some light on this largest of the Galisteo Basin pueblos. Meanwhile, members of Cochiti and Santo Domingo Pueblos continue to visit shrines in the area for ceremonial purposes.[49]

CHAPTER EIGHT

THE GALISTEO PUEBLO GRANT

T HE GALISTEO PUEBLO GRANT WAS A COMMUNITY GRANT MADE ON the abandoned lands of the ancient Galisteo Pueblo. Like Pecos Pueblo, Galisteo Pueblo suffered from smallpox epidemics, Plains Indian raids, and Hispanic encroachment, and in 1782 the remaining fifty-two Galisteo Indians moved to Santo Domingo, where their descendants live to this day. The privatization of the Galisteo Pueblo land took a somewhat different course than that of the other abandoned pueblos of Ciénega, Cieneguilla, San Cristóbal, and San Marcos, discussed in earlier chapters. Today, the prehistoric remains of the ancient Galisteo Pueblo are being preserved as the communities of the Galisteo Basin attempt to protect these ruins and the information they hold from development, particularly oil and gas drilling.[1]

The Galisteo Pueblo ruins left a large, though subtle, footprint. The ancient pueblo had over fifteen hundred rooms in twenty-six room blocks, six of which are remnants of Pueblo occupation in the historic period. The ancient pueblo was known as Tanu'ge, Las Madres, or "the Tano Place." Occupation of the pueblo probably commenced around 1400, and Galisteo is thought to have been part of an interconnected series of pueblos in the basin. "People walked (and ran) fast and steadily across this harshly beautiful landscape, traveling afar and returning, finding multiple refuges and resources."[2] Nels Nelson wondered why the Galisteo people settled at the place they did because of its distance from timber and lack of a readily accessible water supply. His conclusion: "to enable the inhabitants the better to guard their cornfields."[3] While

Bandelier did not believe the "Tanos of the Galisteo Basin had . . . watercourses to derive channels" to irrigate their crops, Nelson discovered the remains of irrigation ditches.[4] At the time of the Pueblo Revolt in 1680, Galisteo Pueblo had a population of about eight hundred and was the largest of the pre-revolt pueblos still occupied in the Galisteo Basin.[5] Between 1540 and 1598, three early Spanish conquistadores mentioned Galisteo Pueblo in their journals. In 1540 Coronado referred to Galisteo but noted that only one section was occupied. The Chamuscado-Rodríguez Expedition of 1581 noted that Galisteo was comprised of 140 houses with some house blocks three to four stories high. Castaño de Sosa visited Galisteo (which he called San Lucas), on 17 February 1591 after entering San Cristóbal and before visiting San Marcos. The Castaño party was well received at all three pueblos and obtained maize, flour, beans, and turkeys. Finally, in 1598 Oñate visited Galisteo, which he called Santa Ana, among several other names. He had come to stay.[6]

At the time of the Pueblo Revolt on 10 August 1680, the Galisteo Indians killed their priests, Father Juan Domingo de Vera and Juan Bernal, and joined with other Galisteo Basin pueblos in an attack on the Villa of Santa Fe. The Tanos from Galisteo and the other neighboring pueblos attacked the Analco area south of the Santa Fe River "and soon occupied the houses [of the Mexican Indians] on the outskirts of the villa with the intent of besieging the Casas Reales (Palace of the Governors)."[7] Galisteo's leader, simply referred to as Juan, was in the vanguard of this assault, "on horseback, wearing a sash of red taffeta, which was recognized as being from the missal of the convent of Galisteo, and with harquebus, sword, dagger, leather jacket, and all the arms of the Spaniards." The Spaniards under Otermín asked the Galisteo leader to parlay with them, but when Juan appeared at the meeting there was no middle ground to discuss. Juan and his associates brought "two crosses, one red and the other white, so that his lordship Governor Otermín might choose. The red signified war and the white that the Spaniards would abandon the kingdom." Governor Otermín did not realize then that he had little choice and tried to achieve a treaty with the pueblos and with Juan of Galisteo. It soon became clear that there was no room for compromise and that the Spaniards would have to abandon New Mexico. The Pueblo Indians especially resented having had to give up their traditional religious practices.[8]

The pueblos were successful in ejecting the Spaniards from New Mexico for twelve years, and when the Spaniards came back under Diego de Vargas in

1692–1694 they found that most of the members of Galisteo and the other nearby pueblos had moved into the Casas Reales in Santa Fe. The cabildo of Santa Fe convinced Vargas that he should order the Indians of Galisteo to resettle their pueblo and abandon the Palace of the Governors.[9] But in 1696 when Governor Diego de Vargas considered ordering the people of Galisteo to resettle, many of the Tano people from Galisteo had left their homeland to migrate to Hopi and settle there in the Tewa village of Hano, where many of their descendents remain to this day. As noted earlier, others moved north to the Santa Cruz Valley, where they settled with the displaced San Cristóbal Indians, while still others settled among the pueblos, especially other Keres-speaking pueblos like Santo Domingo.[10]

In 1706 Governor Cuervo y Valdés reestablished the pueblo of Galisteo by moving the scattered Galisteo Indians back to their original lands. If we can take Cuervo y Valdés at his word, he resettled "150 families of Christian Indians of the Tano [sic] Nation." As Marc Simmons has pointed out, Cuervo y Valdés was known to gild the lily in his statement of accomplishments in order to curry favor with the viceroy. Cuervo y Valdés noted that the Galisteo Indians were "very happy in their said Pueblo . . . it has been completely rebuilt and also the church and convent [but without minister, church bells or ornaments]; and the fields sowed and cultivated." In fact, neither were the Galisteo Indians that happy nor were all the other things the governor reported true. Nor does it appear that Galisteo Pueblo contained 150 families of Christian Indians, as the baptismal records for the period do not show anywhere near that number.[11]

During the eighteenth century the population of Galisteo Pueblo was gradually diminished through deaths from Plains Indian raids and, by 1780, smallpox. The presence of the Spanish at Galisteo Pueblo seemed to result in an increase in the number and intensity of the raids, as the Comanches seemed to "have a grudge against these two pueblos [Pecos and Galisteo]. Whenever the occasion offers for stealing horses or attacking the pueblos of Pecos and Galisteo, they do not pass it up."[12] Galisteo Pueblo was required to provide a force of warriors to serve as auxiliaries to Spanish forces in their punitive expeditions against Plains Indian tribes, the Navajo, and the Hopi. Five Galisteo Indians "passed muster . . . with bows, arrows, and *macañas* (obsidian-edged clubs) to participate in the Moqui campaign,"[13] and Galisteo Indians were the mainstay of other punitive expeditions. In 1715, after Apaches in the Albuquerque and Isleta areas killed two Tewas and destroyed crops before taking refuge in the Ladrón Mountains, a combined expedition of fifty Spaniards and three hundred Indians, mostly from Galisteo and Pecos, was sent to "punish the Apaches at their rancherías in the Sandia and Ladrón Mountains." The Galisteo Indians were also fierce in defense of their pueblo from Comanche and Apache attack as reported in 1754 by Father Manuel de San Juan Nepomuceno y Trigo: "[Indian boys] of fifteen scaled the walls, the gates being shut, to give the enemy a warm welcome with arrows and slings."[14]

When Father Domínguez visited Galisteo Pueblo in 1776, he "focused on a dying pueblo . . . due to Comanche enemies and great famine." Attempts to fortify the pueblos with scarce presidio troops were unsuccessful because, as Governor Vélez Cachupín put it, "the presidio cannot always keep the garrison there because it has many places to cover." Both the church (which Father Domínguez deprecatingly referred to as "the so-called church") and the convent were about to fall down for lack of maintenance, leading Domínguez to remark facetiously of the convent, "It is so uninhabitable that to live in it is to enter expecting death, and to remain buried there as soon as one sits down." Father Domínguez also commented on the famine, a result of the persistent drought, that compelled the Galisteo Indians to "eat the hides of cows, oxen, horses . . . or strip the vellum from the saddle trees, or toast old shoes." He wrote that this lack of food was probably why "they do not have one cow; [and] there is not a single horse. Thus, famine and Comanche raids were the captains who compel them to drag out their existence in this way." Though the picture was indeed grim, it should be noted that Domínguez had little good to say in general about the Pueblo Indians whose churches he was surveying. In his census of the pueblo he counted 152 people in forty-one families, a number that would be reduced by two-thirds in six years.[15]

The smallpox epidemic of 1780–1781 was the last straw. With only fifty-two individuals left in 1782, the Galisteo Indians left their homeland for good, moving to Santo Domingo Pueblo. Santo Domingo still claims a cultural and spiritual affinity with Galisteo, as do other Keres and Tewa pueblos; members of those pueblos still make pilgrimages to and place offerings at the shrines, springs, and rock art sites located at Galisteo. After 1782, the grasslands of Galisteo, just like the pastures of San Marcos, were used primarily as grazing lands for the presidial horse herd until the early decades of the nineteenth century.[16]

With the abandonment of Galisteo Pueblo, grazing activity in the area increased, both from the presidial horse herd and from cattle owners in Santa Fe and La Ciénega. The presidial horse herd had been grazing on the nearby pastures of San Marcos and Los Cerrillos, but Galisteo had not been designated as an ancient pasture, probably because the Indian pueblo was using the land. Now that the land was vacant and seen by the government as royal domain, the government decided to establish a permanent military garrison manned by presidio soldiers to protect the presidio's horse herd and their grazing lands. On occasion, civilians would follow the presidial horse herd with their own herds "to take advantage of the protection offered by the army." It seems that the grazing of large private herds continued during the Mexican period, even giving rise to claims for grazing grants in the area at the Court of Private Land Claims. The renowned rico Pedro Bautista Pino (of whom more later), New Mexico's delegate to the Cortes at Cádiz in 1812, is said to have grazed his herds in the area, causing his heirs to submit a claim before the Court of Private Land Claims.[17]

In 1893 Nicolas Pino submitted a claim to the court for the Ojito de Galisteo grant that had been made to the retired soldier Juan Cruz Aragón in 1799 by Governor Fernando Chacón. The threat of Plains Indian raids must not have diminished substantially, for the governor included language in the grant requiring Aragón to arm himself with bows and arrows immediately, and after two years "all the arms shall be firearms under penalty of being deprived of the tract."[18] It might well be that Aragón was a member of the small presidio guard stationed at Galisteo and fronted for Pedro Bautista Pino, who was ineligible to receive a grant because of his holdings elsewhere. In any case, the claim by his son Nicolas Pino was rejected by the Court of Private Land Claims when his attorney, Thomas B. Catron of Catron and Coons, announced that he would not prosecute the case any further.[19] Nevertheless, Nicolas Pino "was a highly regarded member of Galisteo village by the 1840s."[20]

Even though the Comanche threat had diminished with the 1786 peace treaty negotiated by Governor Anza after his famous defeat of the Comanche warrior Cuerno Verde, Apaches were still conducting raids, and Galisteo and the surrounding lands were favorite targets. Thus, when Governor Fernando de la Concha decided to establish a detachment of presidio troops at Galisteo in 1795, he had a small barracks built to house the troops. This structure was the first built at Galisteo since the Pueblo Indians had left in 1782 and its construction marks the beginning of the Spanish community of Galisteo. By 1808 three presidio soldiers were stationed at the Galisteo barracks, but they stayed only until 1814, according to the testimony of Donaciano Vigil, who said that he lived at Galisteo in the years 1819 and 1820. It was probably not a coincidence that in 1814 the first in a series of land grant petitions was sent to the governor, citing protection against raids by the nomadic Indians as one of the reasons a grant was needed in the area.[21]

The lands of the abandoned pueblo of Galisteo were so tempting to neighboring Hispanos that in February 1814 five of them—Felipe Sandoval, José Luis Lovato, Julián Lucero, Matías Sandoval, and Pedro Sandoval—asked Governor Alberto Máynez for a grant of the abandoned pueblo of Galisteo for themselves and other associates. The boundaries requested were the Ojito de Galisteo on the north, the Cañada de la Jara on the south, the Loma Parda on the east, and the Arroyo del Infierno (now called the Arroyo de los Angeles) on the west. The petitioners told Governor Máynez that the Galisteo Indians had abandoned their lands, that few of those Indians were left, and that those remaining had scattered among other pueblos with no intention of returning to their old pueblo. This "abandonment" was not verified by any of the remaining Galisteo Indians, however. If consulted, they would likely have said that they were forced from their homeland by the Spaniards and were later weakened by smallpox epidemics and Comanche attacks. The petitioners, on the other hand, told the governor that they needed the land to support their families and that their presence on the grant would provide protection against hostile Ute, Comanche, and Apache Indians, who were accustomed to raiding Santa Fe and its surrounding settlements.[22]

This line of reasoning impressed Governor Alberto Máynez, who was charged with defending New Mexico and its capital, Santa Fe. He therefore made the Galisteo grant on 14 February 1814, reserving grazing rights on the grant for the presidial horse herd and the inhabitants of Santa Fe and surrounding ranches. The grantees did not receive copies of the grant documents initially, though they continually requested them, nor were they put in possession of the land. Finally, on 8 April 1822, over a decade after the making of the Galisteo grant, Governor Facundo Melgares and the Santa Fe town council confirmed the 1814 grant and ordered Santa Fe alcalde Matías Ortiz to give each grantee an *hijuela* evidencing his title subject to the concurrence of the ayuntamiento of Santa Fe.[23]

On 8 April 1822, as a result of numerous requests from the grantees, Alcalde

Matías Ortiz went to Galisteo to put them in possession of their community grant. He met with sixteen original grantees, six substitutes for deceased original grantees, and others. He placed them in possession of their private tracts, giving them *hijuelas* that evidenced their title and access to the common lands. The private tracts all measured 100 varas, except the tracts of Felipe Sandoval and Rafael Luján, which were each 150 varas wide. Each hijuela said that settlers were to keep the reservoir in good repair, fence the individual tracts, build a house, and cultivate the farm plots in order to maintain title to the individual plots. In addition, each settler was limited to grazing no more than one hundred head of cattle on the common lands. If this maximum was utilized by all the settlers, a herd of up to fourteen hundred animals would be sharing the common lands with the presidial horse herd, which would mark the Galisteo grant unmistakably as a community grant.[24] Those who received hijuelas in April of 1822 included María Nieves Mirabal, Matías Sandoval, José Antonio Alarid, José Baca, Rafael Sena, and Felipe Sandoval.[25]

Not all of these individuals took possession of their tracts of land, for in January of 1841 a group of eight individuals requested that they be put in possession of the Galisteo grant and indicated that some of the private land was vacant. However, other tracts were apparently occupied because the act of possession provided that the new settlers, who were located upstream from the earlier settlers, should not damage those below in their water rights. The eight individuals who were put into possession in 1841 were Ignacio Chávez, Francisco Chavez, Miguel Archuleta, María de Jesús Luján, Joaquín Chávez, José Chávez, Nicanor Hidalgo, and José de la Cruz Chávez. Alcalde Anastacio Sandoval gave each of them two hundred varas of land along the Río Galisteo and gave an additional two hundred varas to Tomás Rafael Sais, a latecomer who received his own tract, for a total of fourteen hundred varas. The new settlers were subject to similar conditions as were the 1822 settlers: not to prejudice the water rights of the settlers below them, not to allow their animals to run loose, not to damage planted fields, not to graze more than fifty sheep and goats on the common lands, and to breed them for milk and common use.[26]

Another group of settlers asked the ayuntamiento of Santa Fe for additional allotments in 1843. Those allotments were situated at the place known as the Mesita Blanca, bounded on the north by the drainage of San Cristóbal, on the south by the elevation called La Jara, and on the west by the Gavilan Hill (no boundary was given on the east). The petitioners, who said they were already residing at Galisteo, were Luis Griego, Francisco Provencio, José Silva, Vicente Roybal, Juan Silva, Marcelino Ortiz, Florencio la Garza, and Benito Varela.[27] The next day the ayuntamiento of Santa Fe approved the petition, giving each of the petitioners two hundred varas of land. It was somewhat unusual that Domingo Fernández wrote and signed the ayuntamiento's decree as its secretary, for he had a conflict of interest since his San Cristóbal grant bounded the Galisteo grant on the west. In fact, it seems that Domingo Fernández's influence had much to do with the approval of the 1843 allotments on the Galisteo grant. The ayuntamiento's report noted that the western boundary of the tract was "the tract of Domingo Fernández" and that the new allotments were "without damage to the irrigating water of the said [Domingo Fernández's] rancho, as it has preference by reason of the priority it enjoys."[28] Diego Archuleta, the prefect of the jurisdiction within which the Galisteo grant was located, recommended that the allotments be made as long as they did not result in injury to any third party.[29]

On 15 February 1843 the ayuntamiento of Santa Fe authorized one of its members, Antonio Sena, to place the petitioners in possession of the private tracts of land they had requested. The petitioners appeared at Galisteo on the appointed day of 15 February 1843 at 5:00 a.m. to see if anyone else would appear and claim a better right. When no one else appeared, Alcalde Sena placed the petitioners in possession of the land as they "walked over the tract, plucked up grass, cast stones, and plucked off boughs, and shouted, long live the Mexican nation." The alcalde also allotted one hundred varas for the formation of a plaza and another one hundred varas for the establishment of public gardens. The grantees were admonished that they should fence their private tracts to prevent damages from grazing animals. They were each allowed to keep up to one hundred head of goats and sheep on the common lands, required to erect houses on their private tracts, and encouraged to "make their gardens in unison, preventing thereby dissensions and lawsuits." The ayuntamiento instructed the settlers to fence their farm tracts and maintain a water tank or reservoir large enough to hold all the water necessary for the irrigation of their crops. The Galisteo settlers were advised by the ayuntamiento that if they failed to continuously cultivate their land for any reason other than the "accidents of war," they would forfeit their rights.[30]

Domingo Fernández did not sign the Galisteo act of possession, but the language in the document protecting his rights to his neighboring San Cristóbal grant to the east read as if he had drafted it himself. The document admonished the Galisteo grantees to "live ever grateful to Domingo Fernández, who owing to his being the oldest settler and the proprietor of the tract and water of San Cristóbal, is entitled to the same and they are confined only to the surplus portions thereof."[31] Having attempted to create a preference in his water rights, Domingo Fernández next established that he had given some of his land to make possible the Galisteo act of possession, again urging the grantees to "entertain towards him true friendship and love him as a brother, for he has divided with them what is his own for their own benefit and they should therefore be ever grateful to him." Domingo Fernández was not shy about pointing out his beneficence while establishing his superior water rights.[32]

Galisteo continued as an important community through the Mexican and territorial periods. The settlement was of great assistance in the protection of travelers and shepherds, and the fruitful crops raised at Galisteo helped relieve the chronic food shortages suffered at the Villa of Santa Fe and its environs. With the American invasion of 1846, Galisteo was mapped and surveyed by Lieutenant J. W. Abert and again four years later by Captain R. B. Marcy, who recommended the route from Anton Chico to Galisteo as part of the best wagon road to Santa Fe. Marcy noted that the Galisteo area had been used by Spaniards and Mexicans "for many years as a grazing for the horses of the Santa Fe garrison owing to the fine grasslands in the locality."[33]

By the time the Galisteo grant was submitted to the surveyor general for confirmation, the neighboring San Cristóbal (Domingo Fernández) grant had been purchased by E. W. Eaton (see chapter 6, "The San Cristóbal Pueblo Grant"). When Ignacio Chávez submitted a claim on 20 July 1871 for himself and the other grantees for an estimated nine thousand acres of the Galisteo grant, Eaton objected, claiming that the Galisteo grant conflicted with the Domingo Fernández/San Cristóbal grant. When the case came up for hearing on 2 December 1871, however, Eaton withdrew his objection and filed an agreement with the owners of the Galisteo grant specifying an agreed boundary line that did not overlap the Galisteo grant. Agustín Durán and Donaciano Vigil filed affidavits with the surveyor general providing information about the settlement of the Galisteo grant. Durán testified that he was born in Santa Fe and had lived there all his life except for a five-year period when he lived in

Chihuahua; he also testified to the authenticity of the Galisteo grant. Durán listed most of the early residents of the Galisteo grant beginning in 1814 but testified that he "always understood it [Galisteo] to have been in existence since long before that year [1814]."[34] Donaciano Vigil testified that as custodian of the archives he was familiar with the signatures of Alberto Máynez and Trinidad Barceló and both were genuine and that he knew both Máynez and Barceló personally. Vigil said that he was familiar with Galisteo, it was about eight leagues south of Santa Fe, and he had known about it all of his life. Donaciano Vigil testified further that "from about the year 1790 to 1795 during the administration of Governors de la Concha and Chacón a house was first built there for the use of a detachment of troops stationed there from 1814."[35] Vigil did all he could to support the approval of the Galisteo grant, even providing a translation of the grant, but to no avail. Surveyor General T. Rush Spencer recommended rejection of the Galisteo grant on several technical grounds that had no basis in Spanish and Mexican law. Most of the objections had to do with the adequacy of the documents submitted and the authority of the officials signing those documents.[36]

On 7 December 1892 the Galisteo grantees tried again to get their grant confirmed when Luciano Chávez filed suit in the Court of Private Land Claims for confirmation based on the 1814 grant and subsequent proceedings. This time the claimants were Luciano Chávez and the heirs of his fellow grantees. The boundaries claimed were the brow of the mesa of the Ojito de Galisteo to the north, the Arroyo de Jara to the south, the Loma Parda to the east, and the Arroyo del Infierno to the west.[37] At the trial of the Court of Private Land Claims case, both the initial grant and the subsequent allotments were introduced. The government claimed that the original grant conflicted with the neighboring Domingo Fernández grant and that the claimants had never claimed any land beyond their individual allotments. This was untrue because the boundaries of the grant in the original grant documents covered a substantial amount of land beyond the allotments, and the language in the allotments and hijuelas about the number of cattle permitted each grantee clearly pointed to the use of the lands for grazing.[38] When the case came to trial, the claimants introduced evidence about the boundaries of the grant and showed that the grantees were in possession of and cultivating the private tracts as well as grazing their stock on the common lands. The government introduced the grant papers for the Domingo Fernández grant and patents for several other tracts that conflicted with the Galisteo grant and contended that the documents did not show a grant to the plaintiffs for any more land than was covered by the individual allotments. On 29 September 1894 the Court of Private Land Claims confirmed only the original allotments made by Alcalde Ortiz in the act of possession of 1816 that did not conflict with the neighboring Domingo Fernández grant.

The decision rejecting the title of grantees of the Galisteo grant to the common lands was part of a trend started as early as 1887 by Surveyor General George Washington Julian, who began building a theory that the Spanish government retained title to the common lands when it made community land grants. But this theory had no historical basis and was made up out of whole cloth. In support of the theory, the U.S. attorney would sometimes argue that the claimants did not claim land beyond their allotments (as with the Galisteo grant), and sometimes he would argue that the alcalde did not intend to pass title to the common lands. In spite of its bogus nature, the theory was finally adopted by the U.S. Supreme Court in the Sandoval case.[39] The allotments were surveyed between the first and fourth of May 1897 by Deputy Surveyor Albert F. Easley and found to contain only 335 acres. Both sides objected to this survey, and a new contact was awarded to Deputy Surveyor George H. Pradt to resurvey the grant. In October 1898 Pradt resurveyed the Galisteo grant, which resulted in a survey that further reduced the size of the grant to 260 acres.[40]

The 260-acre Galisteo grant surveyed by Pradt was comprised of seventeen tracts ranging from around six to eighteen acres that extended in strips of land along and perpendicular to the Galisteo Creek. The rest of the initial land grant that had included the common lands was outside the confirmed grant, leaving much of the village of Galisteo in a sort of no-man's-land, including a major portion of the village of Galisteo known as the townsite, the hill or La Loma portion of the village that was the core of the settlement dating from the 1816 grant, and the Nuestra Señora de los Remedios church. The townsite was put in trust for "the general use and benefit of the occupants of the townsite of Galisteo and the hill or La Loma was also held in trust with individual parcels removed through quit-claim deeds." This fractured land-holding pattern was the result of the breakup of a legitimate community land grant, but the integrity of the village was maintained with the help of two of powerful families.[41]

One powerful Galisteo resident was Sylvester Davis, who became Davis y Ortiz when he married Josefita Ortiz, the daughter of early settlers Juan Grande

Ortiz and Concepción Pino. Josefita Ortiz was the great-granddaughter of the famous Pedro Bautista Pino, mentioned earlier, New Mexico's delegate to the Spanish Cortes of 1812 held in Cádiz, Spain. Pino traveled to Spain at his own expense, though with the aid of substantial donations from his fellow New Mexicans. He published a report on the status of New Mexico and petitioned the king for relief from the difficult conditions in the province. When Pino was ignored by the king and was unable to show any concrete results from his trip, his countrymen were disappointed, and some members of his family felt bitter because of the lack of appreciation shown by Hispanos toward don Pedro. Some cynical New Mexican coined the phrase "don Pedro went away, don Pedro came back" ("don Pedro fue, don Pedro vino"), to sum up his trip, and his great-granddaughter was so hurt that she vowed not to marry a Hispanic man but rather a "true-blue American." That true-blue American was Sylvester Davis.[42]

Sylvester Davis y Ortiz received a patent for 164 acres of land, which together with the townsite and the 260 acres comprising the Galisteo grant and the church today make up the village of Galisteo and the Galisteo Historic District.[43] When the daughter of Sylvester and Josefita Davis y Ortiz married rancher and large-scale landowner José Ortiz y Pino (1874–1951), the two families were united into one large extended family with large houses and compounds next to each other. José Ortiz y Pino built his family compound next to his mercantile store, cantina, wool warehouse, and, eventually, gas station. "With the income from his ranching and mercantile operations Ortiz y Pino . . . purchased many parcels of land . . . including lots owned by heirs of the Galisteo grant and lands homesteaded by other villagers."[44] Much of the land that was not confirmed as part of the Galisteo grant became the public domain of the United States and was homesteaded by some of the same families that had been using the land. As José Ortiz y Pino expanded his ranching empire, he became the benevolent patron of the village of Galisteo, giving credit at his store, providing work, and, according to his grandson José Ortiz y Pino III, "giving advice to villagers as well as tending to their general welfare." In this way the community that had coalesced around the Galisteo land grant was held together even after the grant was reduced in size by the Court of Private Land Claims.[45]

As the village and its lands were thinning out in the early 1900s it was seen by some outsiders as a quaint relic of the past. In 1914–1915 Ethelyn Nelson, the wife of archaeologist Nels Nelson, wrote of the picturesque village where they stayed during some of his fieldwork in the Galisteo Basin and recalled how Josefita Davis y Ortiz, "mother-in-law of the only English-speaking resident of the place," had provided them a room in the Davis y Ortiz hacienda. By the mid-1900s many residents had left the area to seek jobs elsewhere. Small farmers were forced from the land as New Mexico entered a period of sustained drought and falling prices for livestock and wool during the Great Depression following World War I.[46]

In the past few decades, however, Galisteo's population has begun to grow again, and many residents have sought to preserve and pass on village traditions through religious societies associated with the Nuestra Señora de los Remedios church, the Galisteo Citizens Association, and a community newsletter *El Puente de Galisteo*. Within the first decade of the new millennium, the threat of oil and gas drilling using the hydraulic fracturing process sparked concerns over potential environmental harm in Galisteo and other Galisteo Basin communities. As a result, the U.S. Congress passed the Galisteo Basin Archaeological Sites Protection Act on 19 March 2004 to document and preserve over twenty archaeological sites in the Galisteo Basin.[47] Currently, oil and gas drilling have been halted in the Galisteo Basin, and the community of Galisteo remains a "small, quiet, rustic community of about 260 residents, with almost no commercial activity" and a diverse population, including artists, traditional families, and cowboys.[48]

The Galisteo grant was originally a community grant that included a substantial amount of common lands later rejected by the Court of Private Land Claims. This major injustice was similar to the rejection of the common lands on the San Joaquín del Río de Chama and the San Miguel del Bado grants. Nevertheless, a greater injustice occurred when the original Native American occupants of Galisteo Pueblo were displaced, then resettled, and finally had to abandon their lands completely.

Galisteo Pueblo and the Galisteo grant illuminate the cycles of conquest in New Mexico in which every victory is tinged with sadness as we remember the cost of each conquest. Hispano Galisteo grant claimants may have been cheated out of their common lands, but they in turn were part of the wave of conquest that deprived many of the indigenous peoples of their homelands.[49] The Galisteo grant is similar to the Abiquiu grant, which changed from an Indian pueblo into a community of Hispanos. But in the case of Abiquiu the

Indians were Genízaros who were not displaced but stayed and simply changed their religious and cultural identity mostly from Indian to Hispano.[50] Galisteo changed from an Indian pueblo to a Hispano community when the land was abandoned, but the Galisteo Indians did not disappear in 1782. They moved to neighboring pueblos like Santo Domingo as well as the Hopi community of Hano. As with other Galisteo Basin pueblos and their shrines and rock art, Pueblo Indians from neighboring communities continue to visit these sites to place offerings and perform other religious ceremonies. The spiritual connection between Galisteo, the other Galisteo Basin pueblos, and the descendants of their former occupants has not been broken.

CHAPTER NINE

TOMÁS VÉLEZ CACHUPÍN AND HIS LAND GRANTS

TOMÁS VÉLEZ CACHUPÍN WAS PERHAPS NEW MEXICO'S MOST IMPOR-
tant, influential, and underappreciated governor in the eighteenth century. He served as New Mexico's Spanish colonial governor off and on for
almost two decades from 1749 to 1767, administering this incomparably remote
province during a crucial period in New Mexico's history.[1] In his land grant
policies he attempted to balance the competing interests of elite stock raisers,
many of whom were absentee owners, with the interests of *pobladores* trying
to establish land grant settlements at the edge of the frontier. At the same time
he was juggling competing claims of Pueblo Indians, Genízaros, and Spanish
settlers while trying to keep a Navajo peace that had lasted since the 1720s.
Affecting each of these issues was the all-consuming problem of Spanish–
Plains Indian warfare. Governor Vélez Cachupín was reasonably successful in
meeting these challenges, as well as the challenge of administering justice in
disputes between Spaniards, Indians, and Genízaros. Taken together, the land
grants made by Governor Vélez Cachupín reveal a much more consistent government policy than had existed previously regarding land and water,[2] and his
combined administrations provided the basis for the successes of later governors like Juan Bautista de Anza and Fernando de la Concha in establishing
peace with the Comanche while expanding Spanish settlements.[3] Together
with his decisions protecting the land-related rights of marginalized members
of society, Vélez Cachupín's land grants show a vision of Hispanos, Genízaros,
and Pueblo Indians living together and protecting themselves from outside

attack. Instead of being subject to divide and conquer tactics, New Mexicans under Vélez Cachupín sought to unite and protect their freedom.

Tomás Vélez Cachupín served two five-year terms as governor of New Mexico after spending thirteen years in the military battalion at Havana, Cuba. When he first came to New Mexico he was only thirty-one years old and served as captain of the cavalry at the Santa Fe presidio. His military experience was put to the test in New Mexico, where he found a province surrounded by the Ute, Apache, and Comanche tribes and also by the Navajo. His response was to expand Spanish settlements onto the periphery of the already settled areas, make peace with friendly Indians when possible, and fight the hostile ones when necessary. The governor's policies bore fruit with the longest period of peace with the Comanche, the Ute, and the Navajo achieved by any eighteenth-century New Mexico governor.[4]

Governor Vélez Cachupín has not received the recognition he deserves for being the first New Mexico governor to recognize Genízaro property rights and the first to award Genízaros their own land grants.[5] Vélez Cachupín was an accomplished Indian fighter who personally led his troops on military expeditions, and his military campaigns were part of an overall strategy designed to achieve peace with indigenous Pueblo, Apache, Ute, Comanche, Navajo, and Genízaro peoples. He was also a skilled negotiator who was willing to meet the Plains Indians and Navajos on their own terms and smoke the sacred pipe with them after giving them large quantities of tobacco and other gifts. Earlier and later governors often simply reacted to specific crises caused by their lack of a consistent policy and by their insensitivity to the rights of Indians, Genízaros, and poor Spaniards.[6]

Tomás Vélez Cachupín was born in the seaport of Laredo to don Francisco Vélez Cachupín and doña María de la Quintana. His parents were locally well connected, partly because of their interest in the Casas Cachupinas, houses in Laredo and surrounding communities where members of the Vélez Cachupín extended family lived. The institution of the Casas Cachupinas was also a *mayorazgo*, or entailed estate, that was theoretically inherited by the eldest son in each generation of a family line under the law of primogeniture.[7] It appears that Tomás was the second of Francisco Vélez Cachupín's two sons, an accident of birth that strongly influenced Tomás for the rest of his life. The doctrine of primogeniture placed second-born sons such as Tomás in a decidedly inferior economic position, requiring them to fend for themselves without an inheritance. Like many other second sons of well-to-do families, Tomás made his career in the New World, but unlike most of them, he sought neither wealth nor noble status; rather, as he urged other family members to do in his will, he pursued distinction through great and enduring deeds that would add luster to an already famous family name.[8]

The Cachupinas of Laredo were so well known that they were immortalized in Miguel de Cervantes's *Don Quixote*. Don Quixote is asked by Vivaldo, a gentleman he meets on the road, to describe Dulcinea, the lady he serves, when Quixote says she is a princess. Vivaldo asks, with some skepticism, about Dulcinea's family and lineage, and Quixote lists several of the leading families of Spain and then says that Dulcinea is of a modern lineage: "El Toboso of La Mancha." Vivaldo replies, "Although I am descended from the Cachopines of Laredo . . . I shall not dare to compare my family with that of El Toboso of La Mancha; though, to tell you the truth, such a surname had never reached my ears till now." There appears to be no irony intended in Cervantes's reference to the "Cachopines" as a famous family, and the Cachopín family mentioned in *Don Quixote* seems to be the same as the Vélez Cachupín family.[9]

Tomás began life in the New World as a cadet in the permanent regiment of Havana in the 1740s. His service in Cuba coincided with that of Juan Francisco de Güemes y Horcasitas, the first Conde de Rivellagigedo and the future viceroy of New Spain. Güemes y Horcasitas was related to Vélez Cachupín either directly or through his wife and may have known him before coming to the Americas. The future viceroy was born in Reinosa, in the Spanish province of Santander, some forty-five miles as the crow flies from Vélez Cachupín's hometown of Laredo. Whether or not he knew Vélez Cachupín personally before coming to the New World, he probably knew he had a relative under his command in Cuba, where Güemes y Horcasitas held the post of captain general from 1734 to 1746, a period during which Vélez Cachupín was also in Havana. Upon his appointment as viceroy, the Conde de Rivellagigedo probably took Vélez Cachupín with him to Mexico City to serve in his household. Vélez Cachupín was appointed the viceroy's equerry, an official in charge of the horses in the viceregal stable, but he undoubtedly had additional responsibilities. In the viceroy's household Vélez Cachupín likely began to learn the intricacies of colonial administration. By the time he received an interim appointment as governor of New Mexico in 1749, Vélez Cachupín had absorbed a great deal of information about Spanish colonial law and practice. He may

also have had the opportunity to study books of Spanish law applicable to the
New World in the viceroy's library, such as the *Recopilación de Leyes de los
Reynos de las Indias*, which he sometimes cited almost verbatim in his decrees
as governor of New Mexico. What Vélez Cachupín lacked was experience, and
the job of governing what the Franciscans called "this miserable kingdom" of
New Mexico would soon provide an abundance of that.[10]

In 1754 Governor Vélez Cachupín conducted an extensive inspection of the
province and prepared a detailed report describing conditions in New Mexico.
The main problem he found was the threat posed to New Mexico's settlements
by the Plains Indians and the Navajo, who completely surrounded the frontier
province.[11] To solve this problem Vélez Cachupín embarked on a program to
resettle old communities that had been abandoned and establish new ones in
strategic areas. Northern New Mexico communities like Las Trampas, Truchas,
Ojo Caliente, and Abiquiu were the result. Less well known, perhaps, were the
land grants made by Vélez Cachupín and later by Governor Mendinueta in
west-central New Mexico between Albuquerque and Mount Taylor on the
Navajo frontier along the Río Puerco and the Río Grande. When Governor
Vélez Cachupín founded new communities or ordered abandoned ones resettled, he was careful to describe in detail the shape these villages should take: a
tight square of contiguous dwellings forming an enclosed, defensible plaza with
no more than two entrances that could be readily secured against attack.[12]
However, Spanish settlers often resisted this settlement pattern.[13] Urging New
Mexicans to band together in such communities in 1772, Governor Mendinueta
reported to Viceroy Bucareli that the only way for these communities to withstand repeated Indian attacks was for them to establish compact defensive villages, but this was difficult to accomplish because the pobladores were
independent types "accustomed to live apart from each other, as neither fathers
nor sons associate with each other." He asked Bucareli to order them to consolidate their scattered settlements.[14]

Both Vélez Cachupín and his successor, Pedro Fermín de Mendinueta,
repeatedly expressed this need to establish new compact defensive communities on the periphery of Spanish settlement, and their letters to their superiors
first in 1750 and later in 1770 used remarkably similar language to express this
policy and describe the resistance they had from the settlers. In 1750 Governor
Vélez Cachupín reported that Ojo Caliente, Abiquiu, and Embudo had been
abandoned,[15] while twenty years later it was Chama, Río Arriba, and Abiquiu

that Mendinueta ordered to be resettled.[16] But something had changed. Five community grants established by Vélez Cachupín in the 1750s were still alive in 1770, and three of those are still viable land grant communities today.[17]

Community grants were given to groups of settlers who would receive title to small private tracts for homesites and garden plots and who would use the remainder of the land in common for grazing and wood gathering. Private grants, in contrast, were entirely owned by one or a few individuals. In the case of some large private grazing grants, the owners would not even live on the land but could prevent neighboring communities from using the land. If water was scarce, as it usually was, livestock on a large grazing grant could monopolize available water to the detriment of neighboring communities.

Governor Vélez Cachupín used community grants to establish buffers along the Indian frontier, giving communities the resources they needed for survival. He was able to use his land grant policy to plant settlements that endured as bulwarks against Comanche, Navajo, and Ute attacks because he had a better sense of what it took to maintain those settlements. He was willing to deal directly with an often motley group of would-be settlers who would risk their lives on the Indian frontier for a chance to become landowners and vecinos. Many of this group were mestizos, some were Genízaros, and some were Indians. Vélez Cachupín found ways to encourage their land grant settlements and often took their side when they were confronted by elite stock raisers who wanted the pasture lands on their land grants. Mendinueta, on the other hand, called these settlers "churlish types . . . [whose] rough spirits will [only] be softened by contact [with other settlers]," and he often favored the elite ranchers and absentee alcaldes whose herds of sheep overran the land of the "churlish" pobladores.[18]

Like Vélez Cachupín, Governor Mendinueta was beset with Indian problems throughout his ten-year term, and like Vélez Cachupín, he personally led numerous campaigns against "los indios bárbaros," but his Indian policy was mostly a failure. By 1772 the Navajo had forced the abandonment of the Río Puerco settlements, and by mid-1774 New Mexico was the focus of an all-out Comanche attack on virtually every settlement in the province.[19] The condition of New Mexico as described by Governor Mendinueta in 1772, which had prevailed to some degree for most of his administration, was one of "incessant . . . robberies, attacks and murders."[20] Vélez Cachupín, on the other hand, was the first New Mexican governor to have some success with a policy built in part upon his recognition of Indian and Genízaro land rights. He was more sympathetic toward Spanish settlers than was Mendinueta and was responsible for numerous changes in land grant policy that were nothing short of revolutionary.[21]

Governor Vélez Cachupín made at least thirteen land grants during his term in office, five of which were community grants; Mendinueta made only two community grants. This chapter will analyze five land grants made by these governors, reassessing some of what has been written about these men and focusing on frontier problems in New Mexico in the mid-1700s. The grants we will consider are San Gabriel de las Nutrias, Carnuel, Sabinal, Los Quelites, and the San Fernando grant on the Río Puerco, also known as the Nuestra Señora de la Luz, San Fernando, y San Blas grant.[22]

An example of Vélez Cachupín's hands-on approach is reflected in the documents for the San Gabriel de las Nutrias grant south of Tomé. Early in the year 1764, twenty-one heads of families petitioned for land at a place called Las Nutrias that was claimed as part of the commons of the Belén grant but was not being used by the Belén settlers. The petitioners said that they needed land for planting, pasture, and woodlands, since land and wood were scarce where they lived at Tomé and in the Río Arriba area. Governor Vélez Cachupín ordered Alcalde Miguel Lucero to investigate the petition and learn something about the petitioners and the circumstances of their request.[23] When the Belén settlers were asked if they had any objection to the San Gabriel de las Nutrias Land grant, they said they would agree if the Belén grant could be extended southward to the confluence of the Río Puerco and the Río Grande. Alcalde Lucero recommended approval of this request and of the San Gabriel de las Nutrias grant and took a census of the pobladores (settlers). He found that they now numbered twenty-four, including three women, two Genízaros, two *coyotes*, and one Apache/Navajo Indian. Two of the women were widows with sons, and the majority of the settlers were "españoles con armas" (Spaniards with guns).[24]

Based on this report Governor Vélez Cachupín made the San Gabriel de las Nutrias land grant, but not as a permanent grant. Instead, it was a conditional license giving the settlers permission to establish a temporary settlement of up to fifty families. The petitioners had already tried to found a settlement on the grant, but it was poorly located in relation to water availability and poorly organized for purposes of defense. So Governor Vélez Cachupín told the settlers they should pick a new site on the banks of the Río Grande and construct a compact defensive settlement. When they could demonstrate to him that the new village had permanently taken root, he would make the San Gabriel de las Nutrias grant permanent and formally place the settlers in possession.[25]

The governor used the device of a temporary license to induce the settlers to fully commit themselves to staying on the Indian frontier. Earlier Vélez Cachupín settlements in the Río Arriba, such as Las Trampas (1751) and Truchas (1754), had remained firm in the face of repeated Indian raids, while others, like Abiquiu and Ojo Caliente, had been repeatedly abandoned. Since settlers acquired certain rights to their land by virtue of a formal grant, much administrative red tape had to be negotiated before they could be divested of those rights if they abandoned the grant.[26] In the case of Las Nutrias, on the other hand, no permanent rights would be acquired until the governor was satisfied that the new settlement had staying power and could survive over the long term. Vélez Cachupín knew that the pobladores would need the will and ability to fight off Indian attacks in situations where they might be greatly outnumbered. They would require a fighting spirit, firearms, and a fortress-like settlement that could be defended if it came under siege. The governor understood these requirements for frontier survival and took unusual measures to be sure that the San Gabriel de las Nutrias settlers could survive.[27]

When the San Gabriel de las Nutrias settlers requested permission to move to a site closer to the Río Grande, Governor Vélez Cachupín himself traveled to Las Nutrias in late November 1765 and asked the alcalde to bring all the heads of family to the house where he was staying. There he personally took another census that showed thirty families now living at the settlement, over half of whom were listed as mixed blood: fourteen Spaniards (*blancas*), of whom two were widows with children; nine mestizos, including one mestiza widow with children; four Indios; two mulattos; and one Indio-Genízaro. The governor listed a total of 158 persons in the settlement, counting wives and children.[28] By taking this census himself rather than having Alcalde Lucero do it, Governor Vélez Cachupín was able to evaluate the settlers face-to-face. Next, the governor went to the proposed site for the new settlement and found the location to be adequate. He measured the house lots (*solares*) himself and ordered the settlers to commence building their homes of adobe according to a plan for the settlement that would include formal streets and a plaza.[29] The next day the governor went to the place where the agricultural land was to be located and helped measure the farm tracts (*suertes*) that would be distributed to each *poblador*. The settlers agreed to set aside a bosque for gathering firewood and vigas and to limit the areas where sheep could graze.[30]

Governor Vélez Cachupín did not take long to determine that the settlement had in fact taken root after his direct participation in the land grant process. On 15 December 1765 he executed a formal grant, making permanent what had been temporary. The language of the document made it clear that property rights in the entire grant were being transferred to the settlers, including ownership of the common lands.[31] The grant was made on the condition that no one build a house outside the designated village, except for sheepherders' huts built with the permission of the town council. The governor also included three of the earliest land grant–based conservation regulations on record: existing woodlands were to be preserved, additional trees were to be planted, and no clear-cutting was to be allowed ("de ninguna manera los han de cortar por el pie"). Vélez Cachupín placed these matters in the hands of the council of citizens and their justice ("consejo de vecinos y su justicia"), who were to be appointed for the community.[32]

With such an auspicious beginning, it is surprising to find that six years later the settlers still had not moved to the grant. Governor Mendinueta discovered this fact in April 1770 while making a personal inspection at Las Nutrias. The settlers said that the soil at the new site, which Governor Vélez Cachupín had laid out with such care, was too sandy for making adobes. So the San Gabriel de las Nutrias grantees asked that they be put in possession of still another site. Governor Mendinueta ordered Alcalde Trebol Navarro to examine the new site and if he found it satisfactory, to place the settlers in possession of the land by distributing house lots to form a defensive plaza. Again, a primary condition was that no one build a house outside of the four corners of the plaza.[33] But when Trebol Navarro arrived at the site, he found the proposed settlers in a state of disarray, or so he said. They were split between those who wanted to move and those who, without any reason other than whim, wanted to stay. It was not overly sandy soil that had caused the problem, reported the alcalde, but rather the disunity of the settlers. Trebol Navarro took it upon himself to suspend the governor's order, stating that it was useless to try to establish a new settlement with so much discord among the pobladores.[34]

A year later, sixteen of the San Gabriel de las Nutrias settlers formally asked Governor Mendinueta for permission to abandon their land grant. They said that Apaches had recently killed four of their number and taken two prisoner, and all feared for their lives. But the governor was unmoved. Mendinueta denied the pobladores permission to abandon the grant because it would be seen as a sign of weakness by the Apache and other tribes who had attacked the settlement. Scolding them for their disunity and failure to obey earlier decrees, Governor Mendinueta blamed the settlers themselves for their problems, telling them that if they had built a defensive plaza as Governor Vélez Cachupín had ordered, the Apache would not dare attack them. Since the settlement now comprised thirty families, but only sixteen individuals had signed the petition, Mendinueta interpreted these numbers as a sign of factionalism. Nevertheless, he ordered Alcalde José García de Noriega to assign house lots at the new site and make the settlers build their houses of adobe.[35] When Alcalde García de Noriega informed the settlers of the will of the governor, they said that they would obey although they were very poor and suffering great hardships, having no provisions or strength to oppose the enemy."[36] Somehow the settlement of Las Nutrias survived, as can be seen on the 1779 Miera y Pacheco map, where it is shown southeast of Sabinal on the east side of the Río Grande. The San Gabriel de las Nutrias grant was never adjudicated by the surveyor general or the Court of Private Land Claims but was absorbed into the Casa Colorado grant, which was confirmed as a community grant by Congress in 1858 but later found to substantially overlap the Belén grant.[37]

But for the steady, patient, hands-on approach of Governor Vélez Cachupín at the outset, Las Nutrias may not have survived. The community continued under Mendinueta, but he was more likely to scold the settlers than support them. Governor Mendinueta usually left most of the details to alcaldes like Trebol Navarro, who seemed to polarize reluctant settlers rather than unite them. When Trebol Navarro reported to Mendinueta that the settlers were disorganized, Mendinueta took his word for it, without meeting them in person as Vélez Cachupín had done. It is apparent from several land grants and lawsuits in which Trebol Navarro was involved that he was prejudiced against the mestizo and Genízaro castes that made up sizable portions of communities like Las Nutrias. Both he and Mendinueta had narrow views as to the ability of these members of the lowest echelons of society to become good citizens who would help defend the beleaguered province. This bias was not unusual among the upper classes in New Mexico at midcentury and was shared to some extent by Vélez Cachupín. But Vélez Cachupín believed Genízaros were not inherently bad, they simply followed a different lifestyle than Spaniards due to "their love of the life of the vagabond, . . . moving from one place to another . . . causing much damage to the planted fields and livestock." This view may help explain why the settlers were reluctant to build a permanent community of adobe houses. What distinguished Vélez Cachupín from Trebol Navarro and Mendinueta, however, was the former's belief that the Genízaros were capable of reform through education.[38]

A similar situation existed on other land grants with which Vélez Cachupín, Mendinueta, and Trebol Navarro were all involved and where the settlers were primarily Genízaro/mestizo: after Vélez Cachupín helped plant and nurture a settlement it would often be abandoned because Mendinueta would accept the opinion of Trebol Navarro that the settlement was not viable.[39] A good example is the Carnuel grant made by Vélez Cachupín in 1763. The governor was quite precise about the size and configuration of the proposed settlement, as he was with the San Fernando grant, to be discussed later. He ordered that each house lot be at least fifty varas wide, that corrals be attached to each house to protect cattle against Indian raids, and that the houses be constructed of adobe. Vélez Cachupín scolded Alcalde Antonio Baca when the alcalde allotted only thirty varas to some settlers (presumably the Genízaros and coyotes) because he thought they would not work as hard as the others. Vélez Cachupín again ordered that each settler receive fifty varas.[40]

In 1771 the Carnuel settlers were forced to flee the grant due to Apache raids and asked Governor Mendinueta for permission to abandon the grant. Mendinueta again refused, instead asking Alcalde Trebol Navarro to assemble some of the Genízaros from the San Fernando grant and encourage them to resettle Carnuel with the original grantees. If they would resettle the grant, everyone would be treated equally, according to Mendinueta, but if they would not, the Genízaros would be forced to live as servants since they had no land and were not to be allowed "to wander about as vagrants."[41] When the Genízaros and the San Fernando settlers refused because of the danger, Trebol Navarro ordered the Carnuel settlers to assemble at Albuquerque and then return to Carnuel, where each settler was forced to demolish his house and all other buildings so that the settlement was left in ruins.[42] In 1774, when another group of Genízaros from the San Fernando grant offered to resettle Carnuel with thirty-five families led by Antonio Montaño, Mendinueta rejected their petition on the recommendation of Trebol Navarro, who thought that these families would also abandon the settlement in a few years, although they were generally more industrious than the first settlers. The difference between Mendinueta and Vélez Cachupín was not simply one of style but involved a fundamentally different view of community land grants on the frontier and the rights to be accorded the substantially Genízaro/mestizo population that would settle them. Vélez Cachupín realized that the defense of the province required that these settlements remain inhabited at all costs.[43]

A factional dispute among the grantees of the Belén grant southwest of Tomé provides another opportunity to examine Vélez Cachupín's land grant approach and his ways of advocating on behalf of the settlers. The argument between two Belén grant factions (the Baca faction and the Torres faction) began with a petition by twelve members of the Baca faction objecting to the establishment of a new settlement by the Torres faction at Sabinal on the southern part of the grant. The Baca faction was using the Sabinal area to pasture their horse herd and wanted to continue using the land without actually settling there. They claimed to have dug an acequia and were worried that the Torres group would enclose the woodlands, making it impossible for them to use that resource. The Baca group claimed priority over the Torres faction, telling the governor that they were the first settlers and had suffered many hardships in order to drive the enemy away, such as "eating rats, badgers, and wild plants." Whoever the first Spanish settlers were and whatever they ate, they may not have been the first to settle the Belén area, for in 1746 Genízaros led by Antonio Casados filed suit claiming that they were granted the land before any Spaniards came. This suit, to be discussed in the next chapter, was never resolved even after a lengthy trial, and the Genízaros were simply absorbed into various communities on the grant.[44]

The Torres group, represented by Felipe Tafoya, told the governor that they were the first settlers on the grant, had dug the acequia in question, and needed the grazing land at the new settlement because their cattle and sheep were being crowded out at their present location near Belén.[45] Half of the eighteen families comprising this group were Genízaro, which is probably where some of the factionalism came from, since Genízaros like Antonio Casados had been discriminated against and deprived of land and water rights on the Belén grant.[46]

Governor Vélez Cachupín ruled in favor of the Torres group, giving them "license and permission" to settle at Sabinal, on the usual condition that they build their houses in a square and that they be well armed, since they would be near the Ladrones Mountains and needed to defend themselves against the Gileno Apache, who frequented the area. Vélez Cachupín was motivated by his policy of encouraging new frontier communities, especially since San Gabriel de las Nutrias, discussed earlier, was across the Río Grande southwest of Sabinal.[47] The governor even suggested that the Sabinal settlers build a boat for communication and mutual support between the two communities. Vélez Cachupín also ordered that the Genízaro agricultural lands and houses be separate from those of the Spaniards, following the discriminatory practice of having Spaniards and Genízaros live apart; however, since all the houses were to be built in a square they would still comprise a compact settlement.[48]

The Sabinal settlement seems to have survived, for a decade later in 1776 the same factions filed another lawsuit, this time with Governor Mendinueta. The new dispute was over the temporarily abandoned settlement of San Gabriel de las Nutrias across the Río Grande from Sabinal and a continuation of the power struggle between the Belén Spaniards and the Genízaro-dominated Sabinal. The Belén settlers, led by Francisco Pablo Salazar, asked that the San Gabriel de las Nutrias land be given to them because they had initially transferred part of the Belén grant to the other group, so, they argued, it should be returned to them now that it was abandoned. The Sabinal settlers claimed *they* should get the land because they had worked harder to settle Sabinal and had to give some of their land to certain Genízaros from Tomé in order to keep the settlement alive and at full strength. The Sabinal settlers were already having problems with the Salazar group living near them and claimed that their pastures were being obstructed and their animals impounded by the Salazar faction or sent across the Río Grande to Las Nutrias. They felt that these problems would be compounded if the Salazar faction was given title to the San Gabriel de las Nutrias grant.[49] Instead of deciding the dispute, however, Governor Mendinueta referred the matter to Alcalde Diego de Borica, who ruled only that the Genízaros from Tomé could remain at Sabinal through 1776, farming and pasturing their animals, while the governor decided the case. This action was not responsive to the issue presented, and it is not clear whether the governor ever rendered a clear-cut decision about the San Gabriel de las Nutrias lands. By deferring to the local alcalde, Mendinueta missed an opportunity to follow up on Governor Vélez Cachupín's policy of encouraging new settlements and instead left the factions within the Belén grant to their own devices. In such a situation, the Spaniards who were squeezing the Genízaros within the enclave established by Vélez Cachupín usually prevailed.[50]

The Genízaros of Sabinal still felt insecure two years later, for they sent a spokesman to Durango, at the behest of Governor Anza, to petition for their own formal community rights. Father Morfi reported that more Spanish citizens from Belén had also settled at Sabinal but had built their houses "in the same disorderly and careless manner as in Belén," apparently disregarding Vélez Cachupín's 1767 order. The outcome of the Genízaros' Durango petition is unknown, but it appears that Governor Vélez Cachupín was more willing than was Mendinueta to make difficult decisions in factional disputes like this, even if the groups he supported did not always do what they promised.[51]

But Vélez Cachupín was not lenient with those he believed to be shirkers, as he demonstrated with another grant: Los Quelites.[52] Los Quelites grant on the Río Puerco was made in 1761 by Governor Francisco Antonio Marín del Valle to twenty settlers from Tomé, many of whom were Genízaros, who used the twin inducements of flattery and necessity to get this community grant. They told the governor that the settlement was needed as "a fortress against the Gila [Apache] enemy" and that if they received the grant they would name it San Francisco del Valle after the governor. Alcalde Miguel Lucero reported that the land and water there were sufficient to support thirty-five families "and as many more." He said that all but three of the proposed settlers were vagrants (with no land), that only ten had firearms, and that the rest had lances and shields. This motley group was placed in temporary possession of the land and told that they should form a settlement of up to fifty families. They were to each receive two hundred varas of land, sufficient to plant four fanegas of wheat and one-half fanega of corn.[53]

In 1765 eight grantees of Los Quelites grant who were not living there asked Vélez Cachupín for permission to withdraw from the grant because the place was not conducive to farming. This faction, led by José Gonzales, claimed that the Río Laguna and the Río Puerco had insufficient water and what water they had was so salty that it destroyed the settlers' crops. They also said that the land was fit only for raising sheep and cattle, that it was "unbearable to those of us who have nothing to breed," and that the settlement was too far from the nearest priest.[54] After an investigation that included reports from Alcalde Antonio Sedillo of Acoma-Laguna and from other settlers who were living at Los Quelites, the other side of the story emerged. Alcalde Antonio Sedillo said that water was not a problem because the settlers had other sources of water when the Río Puerco went dry, including springs and a cistern, and that their corn, cotton, and chile were thriving.[55] According to the eight settlers who remained at Los Quelites, the problem was not with the land or the water, but rather with the Gonzales faction, who simply did not want to risk their lives at a dangerous frontier settlement like Los Quelites.[56]

Governor Vélez Cachupín suggested that the water problems may have resulted from the flooding of an arroyo descending from Laguna Pueblo that tainted the water at Los Quelites with a stream of saltwater. He noted that these problems could be controlled by earthworks that would divert the water. The governor commended the tenacity and courage of the resident settlers, but for the nonresidents he had no kind words. They were cowards, according to the governor, whose problems stemmed from their failure to work hard in making the settlement a success, and they were unworthy of the grant that had been made to them. Vélez Cachupín ordered that they lose their rights to the grant and that they and their heirs be forever ineligible to receive another land grant anywhere in New Mexico.[57]

Once again, Governor Vélez Cachupín decided a dispute between two factions within a land grant about the ownership and use of land grant lands in a manner that encouraged those willing to settle in frontier communities and discouraged those who did not have the stomach for that hardscrabble life. Vélez Cachupín dealt with recalcitrant settlers differently than did other governors in that he did not simply scold them but instead found examples of the conduct he was recommending in other settlers and commended them, as he did the settlers residing at Los Quelites. While he could be scathing in his censure of shirkers, he was always specific in his criticism and specific about the conduct he was encouraging, always holding out the possibility of reform.

Another example of Governor Vélez Cachupín's pointed and practical comments is his response to a 1762 petition by forty-eight Albuquerque residents who objected to his earlier order to consolidate available horses under the control of the Albuquerque militia; they objected because horses were scarce and the settlers needed to use them in their fields. But the governor told the settlers they should be more grateful for the land grants they had received and should show more enthusiasm in defending those lands by following the example of the vecinos in the jurisdiction of Fonclara, who regularly performed their militia duty. Vélez Cachupín recommended that the horse herd be assembled without prejudice to the tending of the settlers' fields by rotating the horses to work on a different farm every eight days, when the owner was not on militia duty.[58]

Other governors' actions were not always as supportive, as illustrated by the history of the San Fernando grant, involving both Governors Vélez Cachupín and Pedro Fermín de Mendinueta. The grant, known as Nuestra Señora de la Luz, San Fernando, y San Blas, has a long and controversial history involving more than one alteration of grant documents and several altercations between the grantees and their neighbors. The history of the San Fernando grant began in the fall of 1753 with a petition by Ramón García Jurado and some families from the Villa of Albuquerque to Governor Vélez Cachupín asking for a community grant on the Río Puerco. "The Rio Puerco, named for the turbid appearance of its silt-laden currents, was the most important tributary of the Rio Grande. Rising on the slopes of the Nacimiento Mountains in the north, it meandered through a flood plain of varying width . . . with Mt. Taylor and the San Mateo/Cebolleta Mountains looming on the southwest and the slopes of the Jemez Mountains to the northeast, until joined by its tributaries, the Agua Salada and the San José it flowed into the Rio Grande." This watershed was the location of numerous land grants in the late 1760s and early 1770s. It was the last frontier of the Río Abajo area.[59]

The petitioners for the San Fernando grant said they could not support themselves on their existing lands and were forced to work for nearby Pueblo Indians, weeding their fields and hauling firewood in return for a few ears of corn. This description seems to be a bit of an exaggeration based on later statements made by the petitioners, but it must have had the desired effect of getting the governor's attention.[60] Governor Vélez Cachupín ordered Alcalde Antonio Baca to determine whether the land could be irrigated by damming the Río Puerco, whether it had sufficient timber and areas for grazing, and how many families it could support. Alcalde Baca and certain "experts in rural and farming matters" who accompanied him reported that the tract could be settled by as many as twelve families, that it contained sufficient grazing lands, and that additional lands could be irrigated by digging an acequia and constructing stock ponds (tanques).[61]

Based on this report Governor Vélez Cachupín made the San Fernando grant to the six petitioners and to six more "who are the proper ones for the purpose and who have weapons."[62] The governor again provided that the settlement should be constructed in the form of a defensive plaza with only one gate for wagons to enter and that the settlers should work together to dam the river, dig an acequia, and build their houses in a square to form the plaza. The private tracts (solares) could not be sold for four years, and the names of the six additional settlers were to be added to the act of possession by the alcalde. Governor Vélez Cachupín urged the settlers to attend Mass on holy days, teach the Indians their prayers and Christian doctrine, and preserve peace, Christian unity, and friendly social intercourse, which suggests that Navajo, Genízaro, and Spanish settlers were all living together.[63]

On 11 December 1753 Alcalde Antonio Baca went to the site of the new settlement with ten prospective settlers and Bernabe Montaño, who acted as spokesperson. Baca ordered that inquiry be made as to whether the land was public (realengas) and thus available for a grant and that adjoining landowners be notified. We do not know who, if anyone, was notified about the proposed San Fernando grant and given a chance to object, but when no objections were received the settlers were placed in possession of the grant "in equal shares of the lands, pasture, timber, water, and watering places."[64] Alcalde Baca specified the boundaries and made it clear that the entire grant was owned by the twelve grantees either as private land for planting wheat (and for house sites) or as pasturelands to be used in common by the community. The boundaries of the San Fernando grant (which were later to be the source of much confusion) were the Camino Real from Zia to Laguna on the north, the Cerrito Colorado on the south, the *ceja* of the Río Puerco on the east, and the Mesa Prieta on the west. The alcalde specified the distance from each of these landmarks to the settlement of San Fernando but did not make clear which would prevail if there was a conflict over boundaries, the landmark or the distance.[65]

In early March of 1754 Alcalde Baca distributed house lots and tracts of farmland at San Fernando, prefacing the *repartimiento de tierras* with a description of how good the land was: "quite ample, firm, and spacious, [protected] at all times from the menace of floods."[66] This gratuitous bit of hyperbole, together with the three-month gap between the *repartimiento* and the earlier act of possession, suggests the possibility that the settlers were reluctant to move to the land and needed some convincing. In a most detailed repartimiento, Alcalde Baca proceeded to name each settler, list the number of people in the household, and give each one a house lot forty varas wide and

a farm tract of three hundred by one hundred varas. He repeated the requirement that the settlers live in adjacent houses surrounding the plaza, admonished them to teach their children and servants the basics of the Catholic
religion, and told them to mark the boundaries of their farm tracts.[67]

After these precise instructions about where and how the prospective set-
tlers should live, the grantees failed to occupy the land in 1754. Five years later
Felipe Tafoya (who was mentioned earlier) filed a petition on behalf of the San
Fernando settlers before Governor Marín del Valle, who served between Vélez
Cachupín's two terms. It was probably no accident that this petition came after
Vélez Cachupín had left office, for the petition failed to mention the requirement imposed by him that the settlers build their homes and move onto the
grant within two months. Tafoya asked that the archives in Santa Fe be
searched and a copy of the grant be given to the settlers who had lost their copy
so that they could proceed with the work of settling the land and constructing
stock tanks.[68] Governor Marín del Valle realized that the San Fernando grantees had lost their right to the land by not settling there in two months, but he
agreed to regrant it if the settlers would commit themselves to form the kind
of settlement Vélez Cachupín had outlined in his earlier decree. The grantees
agreed, and Marín del Valle appointed one of their number as *teniente alcalde*
to administer justice and supervise the house building.[69] Within the next
decade the San Fernando settlement finally took root, and the settlers began
making their presence known, primarily by objecting to several grants adjacent to or overlapping their grant. Even though the boundaries of the San
Fernando grant were all natural monuments, the grant seemed elastic enough
from the settlers' point of view to extend beyond whatever neighboring grant
was proposed.[70]

In 1767 the San Fernando grantees complained to Governor Pedro Fermín
de Mendinueta that the Navajo were encroaching on their land and asked that
the Indians be ejected because they were occupying one of the few springs on
the grant, where water was extremely scarce. The settlers were probably being a
bit disingenuous, for they knew that the area around the springs had been used
by the Navajos for farming before the San Fernando grant was made and that
the Navajos had not been notified about the grant to the Spaniards. The Navajos
had planted patches of corn using drought-resistant strains of seed, often leaving the plants to fend for themselves. Since the Indians moved around and did
not carefully cultivate these patches of corn, the Spaniards sometimes assumed

that they were abandoned.[71] Besides complaining about Navajo encroachment, the San Fernando settlers expressed concern about whether a neighboring grant made to Juan Tafoya was also an encroachment upon their lands; they demanded that if the Tafoya grant was not remeasured, they would abandon their own grant. Finally, the San Fernando settlers said they planned to work on a couple of acequias that would benefit the Indians of Santa Ana, Zia, and Jemez Pueblos and asked the governor to order these Pueblo Indians, as well as other Rio Puerco Valley settlers, to help them with the work.[72]

Mendinueta sent Alcalde Bartolomé Fernández to investigate these complaints and to measure the Juan Tafoya grant again. Taking a cordel (a measuring rope one hundred varas long), Fernández measured fourteen hundred varas toward the west, stopping at some Navajo cornfields, and then measured eighty-six hundred varas to the east, giving the two leagues (ten thousand varas) from east to west called for in the Tafoya grant. Alcalde Fernández reported that he did not believe there could be any encroachment on the east because San Fernando's grant called for only a league and a half in the direction of the Tafoya grant, whereas the two grants were at least four leagues apart on the ground.[73]

When Governor Mendinueta received this report he became incensed. He accused the San Fernando settlers of violating their promise not to include false or malicious statements in their petition. The claim that the Juan Tafoya grant had not been measured was disingenuous, said Mendinueta, since the boundaries of the Tafoya grant *had* been measured and the landmarks set in the presence of some of the same San Fernando settlers who had signed the complaint. Accordingly, Governor Mendinueta fined the settlers sixty pesos de tierra (i.e., produce worth sixty pesos) and gave them a stern lecture: "If the vecinos of the Río Puerco commit such an excessive offense again they shall be punished with due severity and it will be remembered." So the San Fernando settlers, who started out complaining that they had to weed the Indians' corn to get a few ears of their own, now found themselves having to give up sixty pesos' worth of corn and other produce because they had incurred the wrath of Governor Mendinueta.[74]

The San Fernando settlers went on to file at least two more protests against neighboring land grants; apparently, Mendinueta's sixty-peso fine did not teach them any limits to the methods they could use, especially when Governor Mendinueta was involved. However, it appears that the real reason for their objection to the Juan Tafoya grant was that the San Fernando settlers did not want anyone irrigating farmland upstream from them, for they believed that if new settlers were to arrive they should live at San Fernando for better defense against Indian raids.[75]

The next grant adjacent to San Fernando's land was made in the spring of 1768 when a group of settlers from Atrisco told Governor Mendinueta they lacked sufficient pasture and woodlands, as they were hemmed in by three other land grants, and asked for land west of Atrisco in the direction of San Fernando. The Atrisqueños had tried to settle the land earlier but had been driven off by the San Fernando settlers, so in their petition they attacked the legality of the San Fernando grant, arguing that it had not been settled according to the royal laws.[76] Governor Mendinueta did not order an investigation, as Vélez Cachupín undoubtedly would have done, but simply decided that the grant requested by the Atrisqueños and the San Fernando grant did not overlap. He made the grant to the Atrisco settlers, telling Alcalde Trebol Navarro to deliver possession to the grantees after notifying the neighboring parties to appear with their documents.[77]

But true to form, the San Fernando settlers objected, and when they presented the documents for the grant made to them by Governor Vélez Cachupín, Alcalde Trebol Navarro noticed that part of the southern boundary had been scratched out. Initially it read, "on the south by the Cerrito Colorado which is about two leagues from the aforesaid settlement," but the alcalde noted that all the words after "Cerrito Colorado" had been crossed out.[78] When questioned by Trebol Navarro, one of the San Fernando settlers stated that Governor Vélez Cachupín himself had made the changes. But the alcalde had two reasons to believe this statement was not true. First, a witness stated that he had seen the original Vélez Cachupín grant document, and it was not altered. Second, and even more telling, was the argument made by Trebol Navarro based on the custom followed by officials when making changes on official documents. According to the alcalde, the proper practice was to draw a line through the erroneous portion so that the words in question were still legible and then to write the new changed language at the end of the instrument.[79]

Alcalde Trebol Navarro was correct regarding this custom, but his procedure in deciding the conflict was improper since a dispute of this seriousness should have been decided by the governor. Mendinueta had already fined the San Fernando settlers once and was in a better position to decide such a case than was the alcalde, who declared that the San Fernando settlers had forfeited any rights they might have had to the land sought by the Atrisqueños because of their alteration of the grant documents. The alcalde then set a monument at two cottonwood trees on the west bank of the Río Puerco as the boundary between the two grants and gave the Atrisco settlers possession of the land they requested. It is doubtful that the San Fernando settlers would have received more sympathy from Mendinueta, but he had more authority to decide such a case than did the alcalde.[80]

Since the San Fernando settlers were not directly punished for altering their copy of the grant documents in the Atrisco affair, they must have felt that they had nothing to lose if they tried it again. This time Mendinueta did have a chance to decide the case. In July of 1769 Luis Jaramillo, a former corporal at the Santa Fe presidio, asked Governor Mendinueta for a tract of land west of the San Fernando grant to graze his flock of one thousand sheep. He based his request on his thirty-six years of military service and the services of his father and other relatives.[81] Governor Mendinueta granted the petition much more readily than Governor Vélez Cachupín would have done when faced with a similar situation. Mendinueta simply told Alcalde Antonio Sedillo, as he had done with the Atrisco settlers, to summon the adjoining landowners to appear with their grant documents and then place Jaramillo in possession of the land if no conflict in boundaries could be found. Vélez Cachupín would certainly have ordered an investigation by the alcalde before making the grant so that *he* could rule on any objections.[82]

But the San Fernando settlers once again appeared at the Luis Jaramillo possession ceremony and asked the alcalde to suspend the proceedings so that they could again file a protest before Governor Mendinueta.[83] Their rambling protest centered around the hardships they suffered from Indian raids, lack of water, and the service they performed by protecting other settlements. It might have convinced Vélez Cachupín, but to Governor Mendinueta the question was simply one of boundaries. The San Fernando settlers argued that their boundaries were the natural landmarks called for in their grant—on the north, the road from Zia to Laguna; on the east, the ceja of the Río Puerco; on the south, the Cerro Colorado; and on the west, the Mesa Prieta—not the distances called for in their grant documents. As they stated, "Our boundaries remain without adding any [references] to leagues."[84]

Governor Mendinueta had already fined the San Fernando settlers once in connection with their protest of the Tafoya grant, so he was in no mood to countenance any more dissembling on their part. When he saw that alterations had again been made on their copy of the grant the governor exploded: "They stupidly and maliciously altered the *testimonios* of the grant and the act of possession wherever leagues were mentioned."[85] As before, it was apparent that the settlers had changed their copy of grant documents by crossing out all references to distances in leagues because no change had been made on the original. Nor were the changes on the copy made in the proper and customary manner. Accordingly, the San Fernando protest was denied, and Luis Jaramillo was put in possession of his grant. Alcalde Sedillo was directed to measure a league and a half west from the center of the San Fernando grant and to erect landmarks so that the San Fernando settlers would know once and for all where their boundary was in the direction of the Luis Jaramillo grant. If there was a gap between the two boundaries (which there was), Sedillo was to notify the governor, and the San Fernando settlers were to pay the costs of Sedillo's survey.[86]

Once again the San Fernando settlers had to pay because they aroused the ire of Governor Mendinueta. If they had exercised more discretion they may have had better success, for the position they were taking had some merit. Even today in New Mexico, surveyors faced with two types of boundary calls—one a natural landmark (like the Cerro Colorado or the Mesa Prieta) and the other a distance (as from the center of the grant to the boundary)—are required to give precedence to the natural landmark. It was not the boundary issue that primarily concerned Governor Mendinueta, however, though that was the nominal basis for his decision. When the two grants were finally surveyed there was no conflict but rather a two and one-half mile gap between them. What really swung the balance was Mendinueta's preference for a new private grazing grant over an old community grant, his close relationship with the elite stock raisers who were the recipients of the private grazing grants, and his connection with the alcaldes who placed the grantees in possession.[87]

The San Fernando grant was established by Governor Vélez Cachupín to provide a buffer settlement on the Navajo frontier but was treated differently by Governor Mendinueta when its common lands were under attack. As with the San Gabriel de las Nutrias grant, Vélez Cachupín took a particular interest in the many details of the proposed settlement, and unlike Mendinueta, he was solicitous toward the rights of the San Fernando grantees when cases came before him involving nearby land. Rather than simply chastising the San

Fernando settlers, Governor Mendinueta might have protected them by making fewer neighboring grazing grants. Instead, he privatized much of the land
in the Río Puerco watershed around the San Fernando grant for the benefit of
absentee owners, making seven private grazing grants in the area within a
two-year period after taking office.[88]

First in line a few months after Mendinueta took office in June 1767 was
Felipe Tafoya, whose grant petition had been turned down by Vélez Cachupín
the year before. Mendinueta made a grant to Tafoya in record time. The grantees who followed read like a Who's Who of New Mexican notables. There was
cartographer and Renaissance man Bernardo de Miera y Pacheco. There was
Alcalde Bartolomé Fernández, who had noticed the adjacent land when he had
placed Tafoya in possession of his grant. Tafoya wanted to acquire a grazing
grant in the San Fernando area, and Mendinueta made him a grant of almost
twenty-two thousand acres in record time, and then Bartolomé Fernández
received his own grant of more than twenty-five thousand acres.[89] Then there
was Carlos Pérez de Mirabal, who received a grant of land he learned about
when he was commissioned to place Fernández in possession. Finally there
were retired corporal Luis Jaramillo and Santiago Durán y Chávez, each with
one thousand head of sheep needing a place to graze. Jaramillo received almost
fourteen thousand acres, and Durán y Chávez received more than four thousand. Every alcalde who officiated at a ceremony of possession for one of these
grazing grants soon requested, and then received, his own grazing grant
nearby. These officials would learn about available land while performing their
official duties and then apply for a neighboring tract of land for themselves.
Governor Mendinueta made each one of these large private grants with very
little investigation and sometimes over someone else's protest, leaving it to his
alcaldes to notify adjoining landowners and the Navajo.[90] For a list of the grazing grants in the Cebolleta/Mount Taylor area on the Navajo frontier, most of
which were made by Governor Mendinueta, see appendix 3.

In 1768 thirty-seven Albuquerque residents filed a lawsuit against Alcalde
Francisco Trebol Navarro because they objected to serving under him in his
capacity as war captain, claiming that he was influenced by his father-in-law,
Antonio Baca. The petitioners claimed that both treated them unfairly, often
taking revenge on them to further their own private interests. Instead of inves-
tigating these charges, Governor Mendinueta immediately came to the defense
of Trebol Navarro, saying that as governor he had the power to appoint

whomever he felt was qualified for the post of alcalde mayor and war captain and for the petitioners to try to set conditions and limit his power was shameless and audacious.[91] The governor attacked the signers of the petition personally as insubordinate and treasonous, "not only of mixed blood, but also worthless for the king's service." He ordered them all jailed simply for filing the petition.[92] Mendinueta's harsh, sometimes vindictive approach was in sharp contrast to that of Vélez Cachupín, illustrated by the land-related lawsuits he adjudicated, to be discussed in the next chapter, and the land grants he made.

As Governor Vélez Cachupín tried to balance the interests of all landowners on the Navajo frontier, he was beset by competing forces. On the one hand, he was pressured from above to solve the "Indian problem" (of course, the Indians had a greater "Spanish problem"). Vélez Cachupín realized that to maintain the peace with the Navajo, Spanish settlers had to respect Indian land rights as long as they were at peace but be ready to fight if attacked. Pobladores willing to settle on the frontier often included a high proportion of mixed-blood settlers, Genízaros, and even some Indians.[93] If they were to remain in their settlements under the adverse conditions of the frontier, the interests of this diverse group of settlers had to be considered by the governor and protected. But Vélez Cachupín was also lobbied by elite alcaldes and large-scale ranchers who needed sizable tracts of land for their large flocks of sheep. Grazing grants to these individuals comprised the majority of the grants made by Mendinueta, yet they exacerbated the Spaniards' Indian problem, especially with the Navajo. Mendinueta's policy was all-out warfare on the Navajos and Plains Indians resulting in increased attacks on Spanish settlements.[94]

Vélez Cachupín was more successful than other governors regarding Indian affairs partly because of his policy of promoting trade with the Comanche and friendly commerce with the Navajo. When this policy was changed by Governor Marín del Valle in 1754, warfare between the Comanche and the allied Spanish-Pueblo forces resumed. When Vélez Cachupín returned to office in 1762, he soon reestablished peace with the Comanche, but it did not last. Subsequent governors' policies destroyed the carefully maintained Comanche peace as well as the fifty-year-old Navajo peace, partly through their disregard for Indian land rights. The causes can be seen in the different approaches of Governors Mendinueta and Vélez Cachupín to the land grants they made on the Navajo frontier. Both governors included language in their grants ordering the grantees not to interfere with Navajos who might be using land adjacent to or within the proposed grant. Most governors winked at these conditions, while Governor Vélez Cachupín was scrupulous in making sure that the grantees and the alcaldes honored them. When Governor Mendinueta made his grazing grants on the Navajo frontier, he seldom requested a report on whether the grant would damage third parties but went ahead with the grants even when he knew that Navajos were living on or near the land requested.[95] Although the grant documents uniformly stated that the Navajos had no objections to such grants, it was not the Navajos themselves who said this but rather the alcaldes. The true feelings of the Navajo were displayed in 1772 when they formed an alliance with the southern Apache, raided the settlements along the Río Puerco, and forced the Spanish to withdraw. By favoring elite alcaldes, Mendinueta was jeopardizing the interests of settlers in communities like Nutrias and San Fernando as well as prejudicing the property rights of the Navajos.[96] Vélez Cachupín, on the other hand, showed a much greater sensitivity to the situation on the ground with both the Navajo and the settlers living next to them.[97]

Much of the difference in the effectiveness of Governor Vélez Cachupín versus other governors such as Mendinueta sprang from their styles of governing. Mendinueta was from the old school of officials who had little understanding of the indigenous people. Because of his aloofness, Mendinueta and other governors often misinterpreted the intentions of the Indians, attacking friendly tribes and failing to support land grant settlements that were the first bulwark against hostile Indian attack. An example of this pattern occurred in 1761, when Governor Portillo y Urrisola was serving in the interim between Vélez Cachupín's two terms. Angered by an attack the previous year, Governor Portillo y Urrisola met with a group of Comanche chiefs who had been responsible for the incursion. When the negotiations broke down, the governor seized the chiefs as hostages (a violation of the code of honor normally followed) and then proceeded to slaughter more than four hundred Comanche men and capture three hundred Comanche women. When Vélez Cachupín returned to office the next year, he found the Comanche about to declare war on New Mexico. Vélez Cachupín was able to calm the situation and reestablish peace when he returned to office in 1762 by meeting personally with the Comanche chiefs, smoking the peace pipe with them, and treating them with respect.[98]

Governor Vélez Cachupín was willing to meet with land grant settlers where they lived and help them solve their problems by addressing the concrete circumstances of their lives. Unlike Mendinueta, Vélez Cachupín was willing to back the settlers when they presented evidence of wrongdoing against an alcalde. In 1763 he suspended Alcalde Antonio Baca based on a protest signed by forty-five Albuquerque vecinos that accused the alcalde of persecution, bribery, and other excesses. Vélez Cachupín appointed Miguel Lucero in Baca's place "to avoid inconveniences and disturbances both temporal and spiritual."[99]

As long as the pobladores dealt fairly with the governor he would back them up. But if they displayed cowardice, as did some of the settlers at Los Quelites, his reaction was swift and sure punishment. Vélez Cachupín showed compassion for the Spanish settlers "because of their extreme poverty," though he considered the Genízaros to be "perverse, poor, and lazy." He tried to treat them fairly, as he did the Plains and Pueblo Indians. His prescription for peace and harmony between the Indian, Spaniard, and mestizo population of New Mexico was contained in his instructions to his successor: "Be indifferent in general but in particular cases persuade each one for his best interest, . . . permit their familiarities and take part in their fun at suitable times, [and] give them the greatest consideration under the laws which protect them." [100] This is still good advice today.

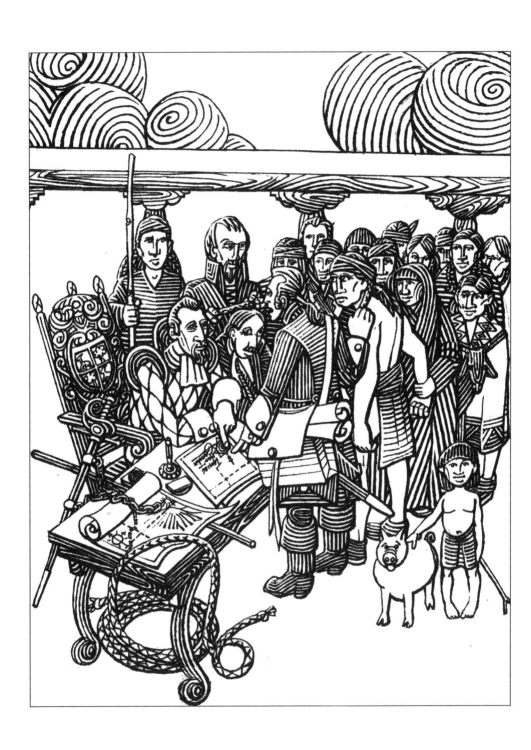

CHAPTER TEN

Tomás Vélez Cachupín and His Lawsuits

G OVERNOR TOMÁS VÉLEZ CACHUPÍN OFTEN USED HIS POSITION AS governor to protect the rights of oppressed minorities through the land-related lawsuits he decided. As a means of analyzing these cases, I will compare them with lawsuits decided by his successor, Governor Pedro Fermín de Mendinueta. The terms of the two governors spanned the period from 1749 to 1778. While Governors Vélez Cachupín and Mendinueta generally followed the same legal principles, sometimes they took different approaches and reached different results in similar cases. Vélez Cachupín was among the most legalistic and precise of all New Mexico governors in his handling of litigation, and both men generally tried to follow proper procedures. But Mendinueta was less strict, sometimes putting up with unfair procedures and siding with a corrupt alcalde without a proper hearing.[1] Vélez Cachupín tended to deal more directly with the individuals involved in the lawsuits he decided and was often personally familiar with the facts of the dispute. Instead of leaving everything to the alcalde to decide, Vélez Cachupín often based his decision on a personal inspection of the land in question, providing a detailed decision crafted in precise legal language and following it up to be sure its provisions were carried out.[2]

Land and water rights litigation in New Mexico has often turned on questions of Spanish or Mexican law, yet there has been no systematic method of determining what that law is, and the courts have sometimes ignored what accurate evidence of Hispanic law has come before them.[3] Within the past

two decades or so, a number of books and articles have been published describing Hispanic law, particularly in the frontier provinces of California and New
Mexico, and some of these publications have been cited with approval by the
courts.[4] In addition, reports rendered by expert witnesses, particularly in New
Mexico water rights adjudications, have added to our knowledge of Spanish
and Mexican law.[5] Legal historians describing Spanish and Mexican law in the
Southwest borderlands have divided between those emphasizing Spanish legal
codes as the source and test of how Hispanic legal disputes were decided[6] and
those who believe that custom, especially as defined in lawsuits and governmental communications, bears the seeds of an understanding of Hispanic law.[7]
These views are not mutually exclusive, however, for the customs and the codes
overlap substantially. Indeed, the earliest and most important codification of
Spanish law, *Las Siete Partidas*, contains several laws based on custom.[8]

It is essential to review Hispanic judicial decisions to arrive at their underlying principles, for many errors made by U.S. courts in interpreting Hispanic
law in New Mexico have arisen from a blind application of codified law or
commentaries on codified law. Often, courts have reached erroneous results
because they did not try to understand conditions in New Mexico so they
could decide an issue of Hispanic law the way a judge in New Mexico would
have done.[9] Legal decisions taken as a whole, together with official governmental communications, are the best index of what Spanish law was in New
Mexico, and the principles used by the governors as criteria for deciding these
cases provided the framework for the legal system in the province.[10] This theory applies as well to other provinces of northern New Spain like California[11]
and Texas,[12] where law books and trained lawyers were also scarce. The
approach suggested here also has a solid basis in civil jurisprudence, where
legal decisions that are generally accepted can acquire the force of precedent.
These decisions provide a richer precedent than does a statute alone because
they embody a choice between competing facts and thus fill in the gaps contained in the broad principles set forth in the statutes. The primary reasons for
reviewing these cases, however, are to understand how Governor Vélez
Cachupín applied the law in land disputes often involving oppressed members
of society and to obtain a close-up view of the social situations out of which
disputes arose.[13]

Law on the New Mexican frontier was built on concrete facts—the
nitty-gritty of who did what to whom and where—not abstract principles

conceived by Roman scholars or Spanish jurisprudents.[14] Almost no trained lawyers practiced in New Mexico prior to the American occupation of 1846, so lawsuits were generally handled by the protagonists themselves with the help of lay advocates. Sometimes a non-lawyer would represent parties to litigation, giving them advice and drafting their documents, and when Pueblo Indians were involved in a lawsuit they might be represented by the Protector de Indios, who was appointed to protect indigenous rights.[15] Before a case reached the governor, attempts at reaching a settlement were often made through informal oral proceedings before the local alcalde. If this process failed and the governor was asked to decide a dispute, the case began with a petition from the complaining party. It would then proceed with statements from each side, reports by the alcalde, and sometimes depositions from third parties. Since law books were scarce in frontier New Mexico, the final decision was almost always based upon general principles rather than on specific laws. Among all the cases reviewed, no case was found in which a specific law was cited as the basis for the decision. In the few cases where a Spanish law was cited by parties in their petitions, it was usually ignored by the judge. Thus, one needs to analyze the facts of each case, together with the historical background, to arrive at the reasons for the decision.[16]

The lawsuits decided by New Mexico's governors ran the gamut from minor criminal matters, domestic disputes, and voluminous estate proceedings to major land and water disputes, some of which were appealed all the way to the audiencia in Guadalajara or Mexico City. Generally, only when a litigant reached the audiencia level did the courts cite specific laws as the basis for their decisions.[17] When Tomás Vélez Cachupín became governor in 1749, his predecessor, Joaquín Codallos y Rabal, prepared an inventory of the criminal lawsuits and other archives turned over to the new government. Cases included disobedience of a government order, murder, kidnapping of a married woman, infliction of wounds, use of offensive or indecent language, quarreling between man and wife, insult of a woman by word of mouth, irreverence and disrespect toward a priest, gambling, being a vagrant, failing to pursue Indians who had stolen some horses, and cohabitation with a *mulata* spinster.[18] During his first five-year term Governor Vélez Cachupín was called upon to decide a similarly wide range of cases concerning theft of cows, assault and battery, a *partido* contract, debt, gambling, a dowry, witchcraft, idolatry, boundary disputes, and other land-related matters. Any one of these disputes

could lead us into another world, a world where one's reputation was as important as property rights, yet where ownership of land was often the measure of
one's worth and the basis for subsistence within a community.[19] The cases to
be discussed fall into three categories: disputes over the use of common lands,
disputes over title to land, and disputes involving Pueblo Indian land rights.[20]
These lawsuits cut across all levels of society, and the social class of the litigants often affected the outcome.[21]

Lawsuits involving the use of common lands illustrate these points, especially the protracted and bitter dispute between the residents of El Paso (then
in New Mexico) and the Suma Indians of San Lorenzo over the Indians' common woodlands (*montes*). These lands were adjacent to lands granted to the
Indians in 1764 by Governor Vélez Cachupín, who convinced the Sumas to
settle there partly on the promise of the protection they would receive from
"the pious, just [and] sovereign laws of his majesty."[22] But these common
woodlands had been used by El Paso residents for gathering firewood, *latillas*,
vigas, and willows for diversion dams, and El Pasoans still claimed the right
to gather wood and graze their animals on the lands of the Indians. In addition to grazing on the Indians' commons, Spanish shepherds followed the
sixteenth-century Castilian practice of setting fires to destroy small trees and
underbrush in order to produce better grazing lands. Although El Pasoans
had their own common lands, they preferred using those of the Indians
because they were closer and less exposed to attack from Apache raiders.[23]

Teniente Alcalde José Sobrado y Horcasitas had been granting permission
to some El Paso residents to get cartloads of wood from the Indians' land on
the condition that they bring a cartload for the alcalde, although the residents
of El Paso argued that all of them had customarily taken wood from the lands
of the Indians and did not need a permit.[24] This dispute had heated up primarily because Alcalde Horcasitas had angered both sides with his selective
permissions for wood gathering. He angered the Indians by allowing any
Spaniards in, and he angered the Spaniards he did not allow in because they
would not bribe him with free cartloads of wood. Sobrado y Horcasitas, who
had already shown his prejudice toward the Indians when he left out some of
the Indians' richest land in his measurement of the Suma's league, was
accused by the people of El Paso of trying to be the *arbitro de los montes*
(arbiter of the woods).[25]

Governor Vélez Cachupín had convinced the Suma Indians to settle at

San Lorenzo because of promised legal protection, so he could hardly do less than provide that protection when called upon. He ordered the residents of El Paso not to enter the lands of the Indians either for grazing their sheep or cutting wood and to cease building fires on their land. Instead, they were told to plant trees and willows on their own lands and to use their common lands for wood gathering even if they had to go in armed groups to protect one another from Apache raids. The governor chastised Teniente Alcalde Horcasitas for granting permission to some for wood cutting and told him not to allow it in the future. Finally, Vélez Cachupín imposed fines of up to forty pesos or two months in jail and confiscated the carts and oxen of anyone found cutting trees on the Indians' common lands. The fines were to be used to purchase agricultural tools for the Suma Indians.[26]

The governor was very pragmatic in this decision, providing specific solutions to the problems presented. He was familiar with the situation on the ground because a year earlier he had listened to the complaints of the Sumas, convinced them to settle at San Lorenzo, examined the land, and set boundary markers. Vélez Cachupín decided the case as he would any conflict between the settlers of two Spanish land grants: once the title and boundaries of the Indian lands were determined, El Paso residents were prohibited from using those lands. This situation was different from the usual case of Spanish encroachment on Indian lands contemplated in the *Recopilación* because the Suma Indians had been resettled in an existing Spanish community and given their own agricultural lands and common lands formerly used by the Spanish residents of San Lorenzo.[27]

In another case, this time involving Spanish encroachment upon the common lands of a Spanish community, the governor again decided in favor of community common lands. In 1750 seven grantees of the Alameda grant complained that José Montaño was grazing his sheep on their common lands, that he had built corrals and a log cabin about a league from the mission of Sandia, and that he had obstructed their acequia. When asked why he did not leave, Montaño responded that Father Hernández, the priest at Sandia, told him not to.[28] Governor Vélez Cachupín lost no time in ordering Montaño to depart within three days with his sheep, to pay a fine of one hundred pesos, and to destroy the corrals and other structures he had built on the Alameda grant's common lands. Failure to do any of these things would be punished by one month in jail for Montaño, and the governor ordered Father Hernández, the Sandia priest, "not to meddle, obstruct, or interrupt the course of justice."[29]

Vélez Cachupín's decision to protect the integrity of these common lands was consistent with his overall land policy. José Montaño was not living on the Alameda grant as a member of that community or taking the risks that living there entailed so he was not entitled to use the grant's common lands. Four years later, however, Montaño joined the grantees of the San Fernando grant and was given a house lot, a field one hundred by three hundred varas for planting, and the right to use their common lands. To the extent that Montaño was encouraged by the loss of his case against Alameda to obtain legitimate common-land use-rights through membership in another community grant, Vélez Cachupín's decision helped to foster frontier land grant settlements.[30] The governor could have cited in *Las Siete Partidas* the principle that a nonresident of a community owning common lands could make use of those lands only if the residents agreed,[31] but it seems that no one in New Mexico had a copy of *Las Siete Partidas*.[32] In addition, the principle was so well known and so well grounded in equity and government policy that to cite such a law was unnecessary and might cast doubt on Governor Vélez Cachupín's decision. José Montaño had to leave, even if he had the priest on his side, and an order based on a complicated law might give Montaño an opening through which to attack the governor's decision. Gaps in codified laws could become loopholes to be manipulated by a powerful litigant able to afford the expense of protracted litigation.[33]

Governor Vélez Cachupín also protected the commons of the San Fernando grant in 1766, when those grantees complained about encroachment on their common lands by flocks of sheep owned by Atrisco residents. Vélez Cachupín ordered the Atrisco settlers to stay away from the San Fernando commons, unless they had permission from that community, because those lands were for the exclusive use of the San Fernando settlers. The governor was explicit about the fine to be imposed (thirty pesos for each occurrence), the manner in which it was to be collected (the lieutenant alcalde was to seize a sufficient number of sheep to cover the fine), and how it was to be applied (the alcalde was to use the proceeds for the construction of a church at San Fernando).[34]

A decade later however, Governor Mendinueta was not as protective of the San Fernando common lands. In 1768 the Atrisco settlers again claimed land near San Fernando. This time they asked for and received a grant west of the San Fernando grant. Mendinueta also made a grazing grant to Luis Jaramillo, west of the San Fernando grant, over their strenuous objections, as discussed in chapter 9. It is not clear whether any of these grants actually encroached on their common lands, but evidently, Mendinueta made grants surrounding San Fernando that the community felt were prejudicial. The new grantees did not settle on the lands, which would have benefited San Fernando, but merely put their livestock on these unfenced tracts, to the detriment of San Fernando. Vélez Cachupín generally did not allow such grants.[35] In addition to championing the rights of community grant members to exclusive use of their common lands, Governor Vélez Cachupín almost single-handedly defined and protected Genízaro land rights on community land grants.

In 1765 Pedro Iturbieta and José Marcello Gallegos fought over a small cornfield (sixty by fifty varas) on the Belén grant, and to hear Gallegos tell it, they almost came to blows. Gallegos claimed to have purchased the land from José Quintana four years earlier but had no deed to prove it. Iturbieta alleged that the land belonged to his mother, Juana Teresa Romero, one of the original grantees of the Belén grant. Lacking deeds, each party presented affidavits from Belén settlers regarding their use of the land in order to establish their ownership. The affidavits supporting Gallegos stated that Quintana had plowed and planted the tract, which "had not been measured [allotted] on this side of the acequia madre [because] everyone [mostly Genízaros] farms land in common."[36] This lack of documentation was the nub of the problem because without measured allotments and written documents, ownership of the land depended on use, a difficult matter to prove through oral testimony. Gallegos claimed to have purchased the land for fifteen pesos to compensate Quintana for the plowing and then to have spent three years adding manure to the soil because it needed extensive reclamation before it was capable of supporting a crop. The soil was apparently too moist and/or alkaline, which caused the grass to become brown, a disease known as *chacaqüiste*.[37]

Just as Gallegos was finally plowing the land, Iturbieta appeared on the scene "with a cloth tied around his waist," together with his brother and a friend, and told Gallegos and his helper in a loud voice to stop plowing or "they would break their heads." Gallegos relented, not from cowardice he said, but out of the desire to have the matter resolved before the alcalde. Alcalde Miguel Lucero appointed Juan Francisco Baca to take statements from everyone who had any knowledge about the matter.[38] Iturbieta and the witnesses favorable to him reiterated his claim that the field belonged to Iturbieta's mother, who at one time had plowed and planted the land. It developed that Iturbieta had inherited a house near the tract in question and wanted to farm land as close as possible to where he lived. After reviewing all the affidavits, Alcalde Lucero decided in favor of Iturbieta, but the defendant's victory was short lived.[39] Gallegos appealed to Governor Vélez Cachupín, who reversed the alcalde's decision, holding that Iturbieta had not presented enough evidence to oust Gallegos from the land. Vélez Cachupín stressed the fact that none of the witnesses had contradicted Quintana's statement that he had sold the land to Gallegos, so he preferred to leave Gallegos in possession until the case was finally determined at a full hearing, and he enjoined Iturbieta not to molest Gallegos. The governor seemed convinced that the plaintiff's use of land—adding manure to cure the chacaqüiste problem—plus the one year that Quintana used the land, were sufficient to meet the possession requirement.[40]

This lawsuit tells us about the difficulties of residents of large private grants in establishing title to their land and specifically about the precarious nature of Genízaro land tenure in the mid-1700s. It also helps explain the long crusade by the Belén Genízaros for their own land grant, discussed in chapter 1.[41] Although it is not clear whether Gallegos himself was Genízaro, the land in question appears to have been unallotted land used primarily by Genízaros. The Belén grant was a private grant made in 1740 to a group of individuals from the Torres, Salazar, Trujillo, and Romero families, who comprised one large extended family through intermarriage. By 1746 Diego Torres had brought at least twenty Genízaros to the area to help populate and defend the land grant, but their settlement on the grant did not necessarily bring with it title to the land they farmed. The original Spanish settlers were allotted tracts of land on one side of the irrigation ditch, leaving the irrigable land on the other side of the acequia to be farmed in common by the Genízaros. Most residents would have had difficulty proving title since Diego Torres and his co-owners of the Belén grant claimed the entire grant themselves. They wanted the benefits of a Genízaro presence for protection against Indian raids without giving any property rights to the Genízaros in return.[42] This was similar to the initial settlement on the Ojo Caliente grant where Genízaros were not granted any property rights. Most of the other land title cases decided by Governor Vélez Cachupín involved written documents, but here Governor Vélez Cachupín recognized ownership of land based on usage and oral evidence of a sale, even though the usage was primarily in the form of soil preparation. This decision was in accordance with the general principles found in the *Recopilación* and *Las Siete Partidas*, although without some independent evidence beyond the verbal testimony of witnesses, sorting out who owned the land was a daunting task.[43]

In a 1770 case involving land in Bernalillo, Governor Mendinueta reached a similar result based on witness affidavits, again because of the lack of written documents. Cristóbal Gallegos offered Juan Roque Gallegos land on which to build a house, as well as farming land and grazing land, if Roque and his family would move to Bernalillo, help Cristóbal defend his land against Apache attack, and act as his servant. Roque accepted, selling land he owned at Cañada de Cochití and building three houses on the new land, two of sod and one of logs. After Cristóbal's death, his widow recognized Roque's right to the land through a separate deed, but Cristóbal's three children sought to set the deed aside on the ground that their father had wanted *them* to have the land.[44] Cristóbal's children told of a fight between Roque and Cristóbal in which Cristóbal was wounded in the head, leading Cristóbal to tell Roque he did not want him living there any more. But after several witnesses were examined on this point, it turned out that both Roque and Cristóbal had apologized a few days after the altercation and had settled their differences.[45] Governor Mendinueta decided in favor of Roque Gallegos based on the antiquity of his possession and on the fact that all the witnesses agreed on the essential points. Beyond this the governor was somewhat vague in his analysis, though Roque's continuous use of the land for up to thirty years seems to have carried great weight.[46] The governor's decision followed the Spanish doctrine of prescription, allowing acquisition of title to property through possession even in the absence of written documents. The period of possession varied, but if it lasted for thirty years, those in possession acquired good title no matter how they acquired the property.[47]

Both Mendinueta in this case and Vélez Cachupín in the previous case relied on evidence of possession as a major factor in their decisions. In the Bernalillo case, Mendinueta emphasized possession in recognizing an equitable right that conflicted with paper title. In the Belén case, José Marcelo Gallegos proved the four years of possession usually required for establishing title to allotments on community land grants, even though he did not have a deed. Governor Vélez Cachupín was breaking new ground by establishing settlers' rights to unalloted land, going beyond what the original grantees of the Belén grant had in mind when they invited Genízaros and others to share the grant with them.

Two important cases regarding purchases of Spanish lands by Indian pueblos were decided by Governor Vélez Cachupín, one in 1753 during his first term, the other in 1763 during his second term. In the 1753 case, San Felipe Pueblo wanted to purchase a tract of land adjoining the pueblo at a place called Angostura to prevent the land from being sold to a third party. The land in question was owned by the heirs of Cristóbal Baca, each of whom had begun to negotiate separately with the Indians based upon a supposed total value of the land of nine hundred pesos. This disorderly and potentially unfair situation was brought to Governor Vélez Cachupín's attention by Alcalde Juan Montes Vigil, who asked that appraisers be appointed to determine the value of the land for the purpose of the sale.[48] The governor agreed because the "natives of the pueblo of San Felipe . . . cannot and ought not to make purchases or sales of real property [without government approval],"[49] although they could sell personal property without approval "according to the usages of the area."[50] Vélez Cachupín appointed Miguel Montoya of Atrisco and Gerónimo Jaramillo from Los Corrales, "persons with knowledge of the law and of farming matters," as appraisers (*tasadores*) to examine the land in question and determine its value.[51]

After the appraisers had viewed the land, together with its woodlands and water availability, they were questioned separately by Alcalde Miguel Lucero. Each told the alcalde that the land was worth only six hundred pesos because it contained no woodlands ("montes muy ningunos"), and water was scarce for irrigating the farmlands.[52] The appraisals and other papers were then forwarded to Governor Vélez Cachupín, who confirmed the six-hundred-peso appraisal and ordered the heirs of Cristóbal Baca to execute a deed to the pueblo as a corporate body and to its members. The governor pointed out that San Felipe had a right to purchase the land to avoid it falling into someone else's hands and because the pueblo was increasing in size and needed to enlarge its irrigated fields. He said that it was necessary to appraise the property to prevent the kinds of frauds that other Indians had suffered in the past and that the procedure followed in this case should serve as an example for similar cases in the future.[53] To complete the sale, members of San Felipe Pueblo delivered property to the Baca heirs to make up the six-hundred-peso purchase price: 210 head of sheep, five cows with calves, one cow without a calf, one ox, one pot of lard at eight pesos, and two buckskins (*gamuzas*). The heirs, in turn, gave receipts and authorized one of their number to sign a deed to the pueblo.[54] The

Indians were placed in formal possession of the land and told to erect land-marks at their boundaries.[55]

This case illustrates the procedure followed to protect Indians who were buying or selling land. Governor Vélez Cachupín pointed out that the Indians of San Felipe, like those of other pueblos, could easily be taken advantage of because they did all their calculations on their fingers, did not know how to count above one hundred, and instead of using more precise measurements, measured and paid in heaps (*montones*). The governor justified the procedure he followed in this case as being according to the usages of the region rather than any specific law, but he was reversing the practice followed two decades earlier that had prohibited land sales by Spaniards to Indians.[56] As he did with the Sumas of San Lorenzo and the Genízaros of Belén, Vélez Cachupín was changing the rules regarding land ownership, each time in favor of a group less powerful than the Spanish elite.[57]

Ten years later Governor Vélez Cachupín was called upon to preside over a similar Spaniard-to-Indian land purchase, this time by Santa Ana Pueblo. The famous cartographer and Renaissance man Alcalde Bernardo Miera y Pacheco handled the proceedings, which involved a much larger tract 4,340 varas in length.[58] The land had been acquired by Cristóbal Martínez, known as El Cojo (the Cripple), in four separate purchases that were consolidated into one sub-stantial tract on the east side of the Río Grande.[59] Alcalde Miera y Pacheco had each of the parties appoint their own appraiser rather than appointing them himself, as Vélez Cachupín had done in the San Felipe case.[60] The appraisers arrived at the relatively high value of three thousand pesos for the tract because it consisted entirely of irrigable land.[61] Santa Ana was willing to pay this con-siderable sum, mostly in kind, because it badly needed such land. The farm-lands at the old village of Tamaya were on the Jemez River, which was largely dry in the summer months due to upstream diversions. Without more irriga-ble land the pueblo would be unable to produce enough food to survive. Santa Ana had been purchasing tracts in the Ranchito area and had purchased an *ancón* (river bend) from Antonio Baca but was not able to irrigate it due to problems encountered in digging the acequia.[62]

As mentioned previously, in 1734 Governor Cruzat y Góngora had annulled a proposed land purchase by Santa Ana,[63] and now the population had dwin-dled to about four hundred individuals.[64] That is why seventy-eight members of Santa Ana Pueblo were each willing to contribute an average of thirty-eight pesos in property to make up the three-thousand-peso purchase price. Most of the contributions were livestock: sheep and goats at two pesos each, bulls and cows without calves at twenty pesos, cows with calves and oxen at twenty-five pesos, mules from thirty to forty-five pesos, and horses from fifteen to fifty pesos.[65] It is apparent from these proceedings that individual members of the pueblo sometimes held tracts of farmland as private property,[66] for when Alcalde Miera y Pacheco put the Indians in possession of their lands, he delivered the 4,340-vara tract to the entire pueblo *and* to each individual in proportion to the amount paid by that person.[67]

In two other cases involving Pueblo Indian lands, Governor Vélez Cachupín protected the commons of both Santa Clara and San Ildefonso Pueblos. In July 1763 the governor revoked a grant to Cristóbal Tafoya and his heirs west of the Santa Clara Pueblo and upstream on the Santa Clara River because one of the conditions of the grant had been broken. The Tafoya grant had been created on the condition that it be used solely for grazing, but the grantees were farming and diverting water upriver from Santa Clara, and their cattle were damaging Indian fields. Accordingly, Vélez Cachupín revoked the Tafoya grant and made the Cañada de Santa Clara grant to the pueblo, including the land encompassed by the Spanish grant and additional land along the Santa Clara River west of the pueblo to protect Indian fields and water rights.[68]

The San Ildefonso case in 1766 involved Spanish encroachment on lands of that pueblo. Vélez Cachupín gave San Ildefonso the four square leagues it claimed and based his decision on an advisory opinion he had requested from a judge in Chihuahua. The measurement of the five thousand varas in each direction started at the cross in front of the church but was halted when it reached Spanish settlement; then, an additional amount of land was awarded to San Ildefonso in the directions where the measurement did not conflict with Spanish settlement. This compromise allowed the governor to give the pueblo the amount of land encompassed within four square leagues without having to evict any resident Spaniards. A similar compromise was made when Sandia Pueblo was resettled in 1748 amid increased Spanish settlement.[69]

The decisions of Governors Vélez Cachupín and Mendinueta show New Mexico's legal system during this period to have had a greater degree of formality in matters of procedure than in substantive law. The jurisdiction of the alcaldes and the governor to decide disputes, with occasional appeals to the audiencia, was clear. It was not always clear, however, when each one had the authority and responsibility to act. Part of the problem lay in the dual nature of the offices of governor and alcalde under the Spanish system, for these officials acted in both judicial and legislative capacities, adding to the political pressure that could be brought to bear on them. The governors had wide discretion as to whether to take a case directly or refer it to the alcalde. It should come as no surprise that policy matters often entered into the decisions of these officials, in accord with the Spanish judicial tradition where jurisprudence was the primary means of asserting royal political power. But since governmental policies were themselves sometimes contradictory, especially with regard to Indian land and water rights, it has been suggested that Spanish laws and the policies behind them were intentionally inconsistent and conflicting, giving rise to the wide gap between the law and the decisions in these lawsuits, which are essential to an understanding of Hispanic law.[70]

In Spanish legal theory all legislation sprang from the king as the permanent expression of justice. Therefore, the monarch could not lightly repeal laws, or he or she would risk being perceived as arbitrary. Instead, new laws were enacted and old contradictory ones allowed to stand. The resulting inconsistency was an attribute of the law utilized by lawyers in Spanish courts to delay the outcome of cases and confuse the issues when such confusion was in their clients' interests.[71] The formula "obedesco pero no cumplo" (I obey but do not comply) provided a certain flexibility to the administration of justice so that a local official could bend the law to meet local conditions, but he did so at his peril.[72]

The basic contradiction of Spain's land policy in New Spain was this: if colonization was to be encouraged among Spanish settlers it had to be made profitable, implying some degree of exploitation of native labor, yet the royal laws protected the Indians against such exploitation and against encroachment upon their lands. In New Mexico lawsuits, a similar conflict existed between elite Spanish owners of large private grants and mestizo residents of the grants or Pueblo Indian neighbors. These inconsistencies had to be resolved by Governors Vélez Cachupín and Mendinueta. Vélez Cachupín sometimes dealt with these seemingly irreconcilable pressures by referring the matter to a higher authority for an advisory opinion, while Mendinueta often did the opposite, referring the case down to the local alcalde and avoiding a decision altogether.[73]

With conflicting laws governing these disputes it is no wonder that specific laws were not cited by these governors in their decisions. In the few cases that were appealed to the audiencia, the appellate judges went out of their way to urge New Mexico's governors not to be too rigid in following the legal rules that did exist, but to decide cases using equitable principles applied with flexibility.[74] In New Mexico, equity, flexibility, and moderation were most often the general tests of what was fair and just. An analysis of the land-related decisions in the cases discussed in this chapter sharpens this notion of Hispanic law into more specific principles.[75] These principles are title, use or possession, government policy, need, and equity.[76]

In the case of El Paso the title of the Suma Indians to their common lands was upheld over the "custom" of El Paso residents using those lands for wood gathering. The people of El Paso had argued that the 1764 grant to the Sumas did not cover the montes (woodlands), but Vélez Cachupín had assigned these woodlands to the Indians when he marked the boundary between El Paso and San Lorenzo at the time of his 1764 visita. Governor Vélez Cachupín weighed the relative needs of the two sides and found in favor of the Indians because they depended solely on their woodlands, while El Paso citizens had their own common lands. In addition, equity and government policy favored the Suma Indians because the governor himself had promised to protect them if they would resettle at San Lorenzo south of El Paso. The residents of El Paso claimed to have enjoyed the use, custom, and easement of taking wood, timber, and willows for their dam.[77] But part of the governor's job in deciding the case was to determine whether this usage was in fact a custom entitled to protection.[78] He decided it was not.

Title prevailed over usage in the lawsuit concerning the common lands of the Alameda grant. There the offending party provided no justification for his conduct other than the fact that the Sandia priest was on his side. Title, need, and equity were all on the side of the Alameda grant. The usage of Montaño was not based on any document, and he presumably could find other places to graze his flocks, as he later did when he joined the San Fernando grant. His unauthorized usage of the Alameda grant's common lands, obstruction of the acequia, and building of corrals and other structures without permission were serious offenses that swung the balance of equity in favor of the Alameda community.[79] In the case involving the San Fernando grant, title once again prevailed over usage, this time the title of another land grant instead of an individual. The San Fernando residents had been granted title to the common lands of their land grant for pasture to be used by them only and not in common with others. The Atrisco residents had neither title nor equity on their side. They were able to obtain their own grant a few years later, however, but the owners of the two land grants continued to have disputes.[80]

The dispute between Pedro Iturbieta and José Marcello Gallegos involving land within the Belén grant illustrates a classic conflict between original grantees claiming title versus those who had helped the grantees settle the land. In this lawsuit the claimants did not have title documents, but their claims were recognized based on usage, need, and equity. Gallegos did not have a deed to the tract because it was unallotted irrigable common land used primarily by the Genízaro population of Belén. Equity dictated a decision in favor of Gallegos because he had paid for and improved the land and was trying to farm it. Government policy also favored Gallegos since he was presumably one of the settlers who were helping defend the land from attack by nomadic Indian raiding parties. Vélez Cachupín realized that if Spanish settlements were to persist in the face of Indian attack the settlers who were defending their lands had to have their property rights protected.[81]

In the second case Juan Roque Gallegos had his rights upheld by Governor Mendinueta against the claim of the heirs of Cristóbal Gallegos. Cristóbal had promised Roque a place to build his house, some farmland, and grazing rights on Cristóbal's land, but he had never given Roque a deed. When Cristóbal's children tried to renege on the deal after Cristóbal's death, the governor upheld Roque's rights based upon his long period of possession. Possession was more important than title here, but equity and government policy also played a part. The basis of Cristóbal's promise was to induce Roque to help him defend his land against Apache attack, something that Mendinueta and Vélez Cachupín before him had encouraged in their official policies.[82]

In the San Felipe and San Ildefonso cases the issues were the right of an Indian pueblo to acquire land by purchase from Spaniards and proper appraisal of the lands in question. Prior to the 1753 purchase by San Felipe Pueblo, it had been held that Pueblo Indians could not purchase land from Spaniards, though Spanish to Indian sales occurred frequently.[83] Faced with this confused situation, Governor Vélez Cachupín held that San Felipe Pueblo did have the right to purchase land from Spaniards because the pueblo badly needed irrigable land to survive. This result was reached partly because of a government policy during Velez Cachupín's administration that encouraged land acquisition by those willing to defend their homes from Apache, Comanche, and Ute attack, be those defenders Spaniards, Pueblo Indians, or Genízaros. Once the governor decided to intervene, his main concern was to establish a fair procedure for appraising the land to ensure that the pueblo would not be overcharged. Vélez Cachupín hoped that the appointment of two appraisers and other procedural safeguards would provide a model for future cases, and it did.

These lawsuits demonstrate that a set of rules did exist in New Mexico, rules that arose out of the tension between flexibility and predictability. The predictability came from the edifice of Spanish jurisprudence, built upon Roman foundations of which these governors seem to have had some awareness. The flexibility came from the prevalence of custom, which allowed governors such as Tomás Vélez Cachupín to impose the stamp of their personalities on their decisions. This dynamic counterpoint has existed throughout the history of the divergent strands of jurisprudence we call civil law and common law.[84] In New Mexico, the lack of trained lawyers and law books magnified the part played by Hispanic custom in the legal system to the point where government officials increasingly referred to "custom with the force of law" in New Mexico's Hispanic lawsuits.[85] By studying the lawsuits decided by Governor Vélez Cachupín, and to some extent those of Governor Mendinueta, we see in the facts of each case stories of the details of everyday life in mid-eighteenth-century New Mexico, stories that—when tied to the decision and analyses of the governor—tell us more about the law in New Mexico than the abstract principles found in unread legal codes.

When the issue of ownership of the common lands of a community land grant came before the U.S. Supreme Court in the Sandoval case, no attempt was made to examine this type of lawsuit for the light it might shed on the issue. If such an attempt had been made, the case of Calletano Torres of Sabinal might also have been discovered. Torres was a member of a faction attempting to settle Sabinal on the Belén grant, and he seems to have done well once he finally received his allotment there. When he died, his use-rights in the Belén grant's common lands were listed as an asset and valued in his estate. In 1780 his seven-hundred-vara tract of farmland under the main ditch was appraised at seven hundred pesos, and his "right as a settler [to use the common lands]" was appraised at two hundred pesos,[86] which indicates that the common lands were owned by members of the community, not by the government. When Governor Vélez Cachupín told the sheep owners of Atrisco that they could not graze on the common lands of the San Fernando grant without the grantees' permission, he made it clear that those common lands were owned by the land grant, not by the Spanish government, as the *Sandoval* case held.

In these decisions Governor Vélez Cachupín recognized the rights of Genízaros, Pueblo Indians, and the less powerful members of society to a degree not seen in New Mexico up to this time in the mid-1700s. As was true of his land grant policy, Tomás Vélez Cachupín was truly an advocate for the oppressed with a vision of how New Mexico's land and water could accommodate all its citizens.[87]

CHAPTER ELEVEN

THE VISION OF GOVERNOR VÉLEZ CACHUPÍN

Ever since Spaniards first settled in the southwest among the Pueblo Indians after their conquest of New Mexico, Indians and Spaniards have struggled over land and water, with each side creating its own narrative, describing the struggle from its own point of view. Since the dominant group is the one that makes the laws and writes the history, it is difficult to find a new history that reconciles and balances both narratives.[1] On a few rare occasions over the four-century span of history, since the conquest of New Mexico, these narratives have come closer together so that a precarious balance held between Spaniards, Indians, and Genízaros—their land, their water, and their beliefs. To be sure, conflict always surrounded land and water, but it was the kind of conflict that existed within a network in which Hispanos, Genízaros, and Indians were tied together in relationships involving trading and sometimes buying land among themselves. This rare but powerful situation was brought about by the advocacy of people like Bartolomé de Las Casas, Protectores de Indios like Rael de Aguilar, Governor Tomás Vélez Cachupín and his associates, and courageous priests who acted forcefully as advocates for the oppressed, and to some extent by Indian agents, modern lawyers for Pueblo Indians and Hispano farmers, but especially the parties themselves. To examine a few of these periods of relative harmony and peace is also to examine the advocates who helped make such situations possible.[2]

Diego de Vargas approached his task of restoring balance between Indian and Spanish landholdings after the reconquest by promising both groups more than he could deliver and then compromising on his somewhat extravagant promises. When he was recruiting colonists to resettle New Mexico after the Pueblo Revolt, Vargas promised those who would help him reconquer the province the land they owned before the revolt. No one knows what Spanish landholdings were prior to the Pueblo Revolt because all Spanish records were destroyed at that time, but judging from the situation around La Ciénega/ Cieneguilla discussed in chapter 5, pre-revolt Spanish residents claimed most of the land surrounding the pueblos and sometimes the pueblos themselves once they were abandoned. But when these Spaniards requested land grants of their former holdings from Governor Vargas, they received much less than they expected. Vargas realized that there would be no room for the waves of new settlers he was hoping to bring into New Mexico if all resident Spaniards were given their claimed pre-revolt holdings. So Vargas fashioned an approach that would accommodate the Pueblo Indians, the elite Spaniards who claimed much of the land, and the mostly mestizo farmers who did most of the work. Vargas proposed to use a combination of private and common lands to accomplish this balancing act.[3]

Vargas planned that the land north of La Ciénega from the confluence of the Alamo and Ciénega Creeks and the Santa Fe River all the way to the Villa of Santa Fe would be reserved for common pasture and woodlands. Grants to individuals would be limited to the areas they could plant, so someone like Francisco Anaya Almazán would receive only nine acres of irrigated planting land instead of the roughly forty-thousand-acre tract he later claimed. Vargas did provide that Anaya Almazán would have sufficient grazing land to raise two hundred head of sheep, twenty head of cattle, and one ox, but he did not indicate where that land would be. Vargas made reference to his plan for the settlement of land south of Santa Fe in a report to the viceroy, but the plan itself has not surfaced.[4] However, the plan Vargas laid out in a 1695 order to Maestre de Campo Luis Granillo for the land north of Santa Fe to present-day Española must have been similar. It was composed of a mixture of private and common lands, but unlike the area immediately south of Santa Fe, there were numerous occupied Indian pueblos north of the villa. Vargas envisioned a plan whereby he would grant lands to Spaniards "separate and distinct from those of the . . . pueblo[s] . . . and the district of the villa [so that] both being separated both may live quietly. . . . Tranquility and concord between Spaniards and Indians will follow from this, so that they may . . . become reconciled among themselves with friendship." Putting this grand vision into effect was another matter, however.[5]

Vargas could never meet the expectations of both the Spaniards, who wanted the land they thought they owned prior to the revolt, and the Indians, whose expectations of fair treatment and basic land rights were fueled by their success during the Pueblo Revolt in driving the Spaniards from New Mexico for twelve years. Vargas knew that both expectations were unrealistic, and in April of 1695, in order to make room for more colonists who would arrive the next month, he put his plan into effect.[6]

The way Vargas would deal with these conflicting expectations that were based in part on his own extravagant promises was to provide for common lands that would be used jointly by landowners previously accustomed to having their own grazing lands, common to their own families but not to other large landowners. Vargas used the concept of boundaries (normally a dividing line between two ownerships) in conflicting ways when he ordered that "the pastures of these sites [private tracts of land], and the boundaries of each hacienda are to be common and undivided, and the cattle each one will have . . . will graze [on adjacent land]." That is, the private grazing lands of the large haciendas would become common, at least to other hacienda owners.[7]

Pueblo Indians from San Cristóbal and San Lázaro did not experience the benefits of the 1695 Vargas grand design whereby Indians and Spaniards would live "separate and distinct" with "lands to sow, grass, woods, water, watering places, ejidos, and pastures." Instead, after the Vargas reconquest the two pueblos were moved to land near San Juan Pueblo and within a year were forced to move again to make way for more Spaniards. In late March of 1695, both San Cristóbal and San Lázaro petitioned Governor Vargas through their war captains, asking that they be allowed to stay on their land until harvesttime because they had already cleared their fields and cleaned their acequias and would not be able to perform that work in a new location.[8] Vargas refused the request by San Cristóbal, the larger of the two pueblos, and forced the people to move by the next (full) moon. Within weeks of the move, Vargas established the new villa of Santa Cruz de la Cañada on the very spot occupied by San Cristóbal, giving the Spaniards "lands cleared and plowed [by the San Cristóbal Indians] known for their great fertility with their ditches, acequia, and dams in working order." The members of San Cristóbal Pueblo, on the other hand, had to move to land near Chimayo of inferior quality, most of which was occupied by

Spaniards who had received grants from Vargas and previous governors. Furthermore, neither San Cristóbal nor San Lázaro were given grants of land at the new location. Vargas treated these Galisteo Basin pueblos of San Cristóbal and San Lázaro harshly partly because of their participation in the Pueblo Revolt and in part because of their apparent arrogance (from the Spanish point of view) in taking over abandoned Spanish farms on Santa Cruz Creek after the revolt "just as Spanish settlers had once taken over pueblo properties."[9] The treatment of these two pueblos by Governor Vargas reveals the flaws in his settlement plan for the Villa of Santa Fe and its surrounding area. He had given his word that the Pueblo people could stay on their lands until harvesttime, and then had changed his mind. In March of 1695 Maestre de Campo Luis Granillo inspected the area where the two pueblos were expected to settle "at the end of the Cañada they call Chimayo." It was only one-half league from "Captain Juan Luis's hacienda," and the Indians were dissatisfied with the land and soon moved to the Hopi community of Hano.[10]

During the early part of the eighteenth century, Pueblo Indians achieved greater land rights as Pueblo leaders and their advocates protested Spanish encroachment on Pueblo land and protectors of the Indians developed a land grant policy that protected both Indian and Spanish lands. These advocates measured Pueblo lands and Spanish land grants to determine if they over-lapped or had gaps in between them and gradually developed a rationale for both Hispano and Pueblo land rights. This system expanded the property rights of Pueblo Indians, though it was more honored in its breach than in its observance as encroachment on Pueblo land continued with the arrival of more Spanish settlers in New Mexico. In the mid-1780s, as the population of Spaniards approached a tipping point—a greater number of Spaniards than Indians living in New Mexico for the first time—the land distribution plan established by Vargas and expanded by Protectores de Indios such as Alfonso Rael de Aguilar was not working. Spaniards received grants of land that often overlapped Pueblo Indian land. Boundary markers were not adequate and were often moved.[11]

Several inconsistent policies regarding land seemed to exist independently as Indian property rights began to be defined. The ambiguous boundaries of common lands envisioned by Vargas in the early 1700s were not working, as Spanish cattle and sheep invaded Indian fields and competed with Indian herds and flocks, and even with the stallions of the presidial horse herd, for the same land. To make matters worse Navajo, Ute, and Comanche raids resulted in huge losses of livestock to both Spaniards and Indians. New Mexico sorely needed a broader, more consistent approach that would unite the opposing policies surrounding Spanish, Pueblo, and Genízaro land grants into a single thread that would take into account the need to protect all settlements from raiding nomadic tribes. What was needed was a governor with a broad vision of New Mexico land use and ownership.[12]

In 1749 Tomás Vélez Cachupín arrived in Santa Fe with a mandate from the viceroy of New Spain to resettle abandoned communities, plant new ones, and make peace with the Plains Indians, whose fierce raids on New Mexico's settlements had caused the abandonment of many communities. The young—aged thirty-two—recently appointed governor moved with vigor and determination on all fronts in his first term. He ordered the resettlement of Abiquiu, Ojo Caliente, and Embudo, all of them abandoned two years before he arrived in Santa Fe. He established one of the first true Hispano community grants with the 1751 Las Trampas land grant, followed in 1754 by the Truchas land grant. And he defeated a large band of Comanche warriors at the Battle of San Diego Pond in 1751 after they attacked Pecos and Galisteo in a turning point in the conflict with the Comanches. All of these accomplishments were tied together as part of an overall land grant project that by the end of his second term in 1767 had achieved the most balanced and peaceful relationship between Hispanos, Pueblo Indians, and Genízaros up to that point.[13]

Before coming to New Mexico Vélez Cachupín had worked in the court of Juan Francisco de Güemes y Horcacitas, the viceroy of New Spain, as his equerry, or master of the horse, as well as his understudy, preparing for the public office he would soon hold. Reading the reports of previous governors of New Mexico, he realized that settlers and Indians needed protection from Plains Indian raids that were causing communities like Ojo Caliente to be abandoned. He also saw the importance of providing ample common grazing lands, especially for new communities on the periphery of Spanish settlement and for the pueblos. This was in contrast with earlier times when large tracts of grazing lands were owned by one or a few individuals or not assigned to anyone but monopolized by a few large-scale stock raisers. Vélez Cachupín envisioned enough land for all, even as communities expanded, both for farming and grazing. For the first time these common lands would be delineated in land grant documents and assigned to specific communities—Pueblo Indian,

Genízaro, and Spanish—so that each community member had an interest in those lands and would be motivated to defend them from Comanche and Ute attack. While several large private individual land grants still existed, Vélez Cachupín's plan gave preference to community over private grants, and his policies and administration of justice put teeth into that preference. For example, in 1750 José Montaño, a large-scale stock raiser, was fined by the governor for grazing his sheep on the common lands of the Alameda grant, as discussed in chapter 10. Four years later, however, Montaño, with encouragement from Vélez Cachupín, became a grantee along with several others, of the San Fernando community grant, thus acquiring a legitimate interest in the common lands of that grant.[14]

By the mid-1700s Governor Vélez Cachupín had started to expand New Mexican settlements to protect the core communities around Santa Fe and Albuquerque. To the north were the community grants of Truchas (1754) and Las Trampas (1751); to the south were the communities of Carnuel and Atrisco, among others; to the northwest was the Abiquiu Genízaro community grant; and to the west were the community grants of San Fernando del Río Puerco (1753) and San Gabriel de las Nutrias (1764). Beyond these latter communities to the west was Navajo country, where Governor Vélez Cachupín made several grants, to be discussed later, in this area of west-central New Mexico, mostly in his second term.[15]

As he was encouraging Spaniards to apply for community grants, Vélez Cachupín was also helping Indian pueblos acquire land. Spanish government policy in the 1730s and 1740s had sometimes denied pueblos the right to purchase land from the Spaniards, though Santa Ana Pueblo had been buying land from Spaniards throughout most of the eighteenth century to reacquire its Ranchii'tu tract east of the Río Grande. Vélez Cachupín consistently supported Pueblo acquisition of land and protection of the land the pueblos already owned. He noted that the Pueblo Indians were naive in their dealings with Spaniards and had little understanding of the value of land because "when they buy or sell they do it by exchanging one kind [of goods] for another at the value and regulated price that they have established."[16] Often, such regulated exchanges took place at trade fairs where government officials, such as Governor Vélez Cachupín himself, were present to protect the Indians from being cheated. In 1754 Vélez Cachupín established a set of standard prices for the goods most commonly bartered by Plains Indians at trade fairs, a schedule used until the 1780s. But when it came to land, the Pueblo Indians had no idea of valuation, as they were just getting used to the idea that land could be owned and sold, let alone that a price could be attached to something that was price-less. So Vélez Cachupín introduced the requirement of an independent appraisal that would govern the price the Indians paid for land. In 1753 Vélez Cachupín oversaw the purchase by San Felipe Pueblo of a tract of land that had been offered to the pueblo at nine hundred pesos but was appraised and sold at six hundred pesos, and, as noted earlier, in 1763 Vélez Cachupín oversaw the purchase by Santa Ana Pueblo of 4,340 varas of irrigable land for three thousand pesos' worth of property. In both cases he made sure the land was properly valued, the title papers were delivered, and the Indians received a deed showing their ownership of the land.[17]

In addition to grants made to Spanish communities and Indian pueblos, Vélez Cachupín made a grant at Abiquiu in 1754 entirely to Genízaros. Abiquiu was still one of the most exposed spots in the Spanish perimeter of defense against Indian raids, though most of the Spaniards who had left the area after the devastating 1747 Ute/Comanche attack had returned. Even with a small contingent of presidio troops stationed there, Abiquiu needed a dedicated community of farmers and stock raisers who would defend their land from attack by nomadic Indian bands. Genízaros had been trying to obtain their own land grant since 1733, when twenty-five mostly Plains Indians sought a grant at the abandoned pueblo of Sandia, but Vélez Cachupín was the first New Mexico governor to see the value of a land grant to Genízaros as a bulwark in the defense of the province. He realized the value of Genízaros as fighters against other Indians when he started including Utes, Comanches, and some Apaches as part of the Pueblo Indian auxiliaries as early as 1749.[18] The Abiquiu Genízaro grant was similar in organization to a Hispano community grant like Las Trampas, with a mix of private lands for houses and gardens together with substantial common lands for stock grazing, wood, and herb gathering, all with clear boundaries setting them apart from other land grants.[19]

After a relative balance between Pueblo lands and Spanish land grants was within sight, what remained was to help Spaniards, Indians, and Genízaros defend their property rights through the New Mexico judicial system. Vélez Cachupín was an active advocate for the communities he established, not only because the viceroy had ordered the abandoned ones to be resettled but also because he realized that only a network of strong Pueblo, Hispano, and

Genízaro communities could hold New Mexico in the face of increased nomadic Indian raids. In a way, it was this threat from the outside that forced the diverse land grant communities of New Mexico to establish a viable, land-based, and interconnected group of settlements in accordance with the plan Vélez Cachupín had been working on throughout his first four-year term.[20]

At the end of his first term in 1754, Vélez Cachupín had established most of his land settlement project, achieved a tenuous peace with both the Utes and Comanches, and in the process revolutionized the land-holding system of New Mexico. But in spite of the viceroy's recommendation that Vélez Cachupín be reappointed to a second term as governor, it would be eight years before he returned for a second term in 1763. In the meantime, much of what he had accomplished fell apart when many settlements the governor had established were abandoned, Utes and Comanches renewed their raiding, and in the important Abiquiu Genízaro land grant, a witchcraft outbreak almost tore that community apart.[21]

Unfortunately, the three governors who succeeded him failed to honor the commitments made by Vélez Cachupín, while they themselves made unreasonable demands on the Plains Indian tribes and were often not willing to deal with them directly. Governor Portillo Urrisola was the worst, attacking and firing on the Comanche encampment at the Taos trade fair after refusing to negotiate a captive exchange until the Comanches had returned all the captives from the Villalpando raid; his actions caused hundreds of Comanche deaths when the Indians had come to Taos in peace to exchange captives and trade with the Spanish.[22]

When Vélez Cachupín arrived back in Santa Fe in February 1762 to begin his second term as governor, both the Comanches and the Utes were again at war with the Spanish, and the well-balanced settlement plan Vélez Cachupín had bequeathed to New Mexico at the end of his first term was in shambles. The governor moved quickly to restore the balance between Spanish and Pueblo settlements on the one hand and Plains Indians on the other. Before he could reinstate his settlement plan, however, Governor Vélez Cachupín had to renegotiate peace treaties with the Utes and Comanches. He immediately secured the release of six female Comanche captives as a goodwill gesture and when a delegation of Comanches headed by nine secondary chiefs came to Santa Fe to discuss a new peace treaty, the governor returned more Comanche captives, among whom each chief found a relative. As a result of the governor's hands-on negotiations, a new Comanche peace treaty was agreed upon that lasted throughout the governor's second term.[23]

As he turned his attention to affairs within New Mexico, Vélez Cachupín dealt with two matters regarding grazing lands for the cattle and horses of both the Spanish settlers and the Pueblo Indians. The first was making pastureland available for the horse herd of the Santa Fe presidio. The second was providing grazing land to Indian pueblos by making them land grants specifically for that purpose. One of the reasons the Comanche were such a formidable foe was their excellent horsemanship; individual warriors often owned 20 to 30 horses, elites 100 to 300 horses, and a particularly prominent leader might own as many as 1,000. Most Comanche raids on Spanish settlements were primarily for stealing horses as well as for taking captives. Horses were often scarce in Spanish settlements since they were used by both the militia and presidial troops for countering attacks by nomadic Indians as well as in the fields for plowing and other field work. Vélez Cachupín realized that assigning both pueblos and Spaniards common grazing lands either as part of their land grants or as separate grants gave them a place to graze their animals and motivation to protect their herds and their settlements.[24]

Others needing pasturelands for their horses included the citizen militias and the Santa Fe presidio. The citizen militias needed to use their horses in the fields as well, for plowing and cultivating their crops, while the alcalde commanding the militia emphasized the importance of an available horse herd "to go forth in campaigns against the enemy [nomadic Indians]." Vélez Cachupín suggested the Spanish farmers keep the horse herd together when they were not on campaigns and move from one farm to the next every eight days, pasturing the horses near where they would be performing field work. That way they would be consolidated into one herd ready to respond to an attack and could still accomplish the farm tasks.[25] In addition to providing for the horse herd of the local militia, the governor made grants that provided for common pastureland for the horses of the Santa Fe presidio. As we saw in chapter 7, in the summer of 1754 Vélez Cachupín made a grant of the lands at the abandoned pueblo of San Marcos to José Urbán Montaño with the condition that the grazing land be used for the presidial horse herd along with Montaño's cattle. This tract of grazing land was one of several set aside for the presidial horse herd following a long tradition going back to 1737, when seven areas were designated as "ancient pasturelands" (comederos antiguos) for the horse herds of the Santa Fe presidio. It is estimated that by the mid-1700s the presidial horse herd numbered from eight hundred to twelve hundred horses, and presidial cattle would also graze on commons assigned to the Santa Fe presidio.[26] Other grants discussed in this book had similar provisions allowing grazing by horses and livestock belonging to the Santa Fe presidio: the San Cristóbal grant, the Galisteo grant, and the Cieneguilla grant.[27]

In addition to the horses and livestock of the citizen militia and the Santa Fe presidio, both Spanish settlers and Pueblo Indians had large numbers of animals of their own needing a place to graze. We do not know exactly how many horses and cattle were owned by Spanish settlers, but a herd on the private grazing grant of Santiago Durán y Chávez included eight hundred mares, forty mules, one thousand sheep, and a large number of cattle.[28] The act of possession of the Galisteo grant of April 1822 limited the approximately twenty settlers to no more than one hundred head of cattle and sheep per settler. These animals, totaling as many as two thousand, would also share the grant with the presidial horse herd and the horses and livestock of the inhabitants of Santa Fe and surrounding ranches.

The Pueblo Indians also had large herds of cattle and horses and flocks of sheep for which they needed pasturelands. An approximation of the large numbers of animals raised by the pueblos can be found in the proceedings mentioned earlier over which Governor Vélez Cachupín presided in 1763, when Santa Ana Pueblo purchased 4,340 varas of land at Ranchii'tu for the huge price of three thousand pesos. Aside from some woven cotton cloth and a basket used as payment, the sale price was paid in cattle, sheep, and horses: eight horses (valued at fifteen to fifty pesos apiece), three mules (thirty to forty-five pesos), eight bulls, sixty-seven cows (twenty pesos), twenty-nine oxen (twenty-five pesos), and fifty sheep (two pesos). This substantial amount of livestock represented the purchase price of just one tract; Santa Ana bought several other tracts in the Ranchii'tu area, and these must have been purchased with horses and livestock as well, still only a fraction of the total numbers of horses, cattle, and sheep owned by Santa Ana Pueblo.[29]

The pueblo needed a place to graze these animals, so in June of 1766 Santa Ana, along with Zia and Jemez Pueblos requested a grazing grant from Governor Vélez Cachupín. As discussed in chapter 4, Felipe Tafoya was acting as the pueblos' unofficial advocate when he filed the petition alleging that the Ojo del Espíritu Santo tract had been used by the three pueblos as their common grazing land since time immemorial, and it was then being used as pasture for the stallions of the presidio's horse herd. Governor Vélez Cachupín made the grant as part of his overall plan to make Indian grazing grants adjacent to the pueblos. Also in 1766, just a few months earlier, Bartolomé Fernández submitted an almost identical petition on behalf of Cochiti Pueblo for a grant of its traditional grazing land surrounding the pueblo. The petition was granted by Governor Vélez Cachupín on the same day that he made the Ojo del Espíritu Santo grant, on 6 August 1766. For a few decades after 1766 the four pueblos of Cochiti, Zia, Santa Ana, and Jemez owned and used their own grazing land near their pueblos (see figure 2). Unlike the land use program initiated by Governor Vargas, in which common grazing lands were not clearly delineated, Vélez Cachupín was instituting a new system of communal grazing for both Spaniards and Pueblo Indians in designated areas.[30]

It was only during the last few years of Governor Vélez Cachupín's second term, in 1766 and 1767 that his balanced land grant project began to operate successfully. Vélez Cachupín set in place sanctions that penalized large-scale cattlemen whose herds encroached on the common lands of the Indians or Genízaros or against Spaniards who appropriated resources from the Indians' common lands without permission. In 1766 he notified the settlers on the San Fernando grant that no one could use the common lands of Zia, Santa Ana, and Jemez Pueblos without their permission, and anyone caught doing so would be subject to a thirty-peso fine; in the same year the governor notified Juan Pablo Martín, the owner of a large private grant adjacent to the Abiquiu Genízaro grant, not to prejudice the Abiquiu grant's common lands.[31] As mentioned earlier, in 1765 Vélez Cachupín ordered the El Pasoans who had been cutting firewood on the Suma Indians' common lands to plant more trees on their own common lands, and ordered that those caught cutting wood on the common lands of the Suma Indians be subject to a forty-peso fine, two months in jail, and confiscation of their carts and oxen.[32]

In order to maximize the amount of common lands held by Genízaros between 1765 and 1767, Vélez Cachupín made several land grants to Genízaros and upheld Genízaro land rights in a 1765 lawsuit.[33] Vélez Cachupín made the San Gabriel de las Nutrias grant in November 1765 to a group of grantees, over half of whom were mestizos or Genízaros (see appendix 4). He also made grants at Los Quelites in 1765 and Sabinal in 1767, mostly to Genízaros.[34]

Just as the Indian pueblos needed grazing land for their large herds and flocks, so did Hispano livestock owners who sought to privatize large tracts of grazing land and transfer common lands to private hands. While Cochiti Pueblo's and Jemez, Zia, and Santa Ana Pueblos' grazing grants were shared with the presidial horse herd and with each other, these Hispano grazing grants were owned by one or two individuals in their entirety. Both the Ojo del Espíritu Santo grazing grant and the Cochiti pasture grant covered land that had been used traditionally by the pueblos for grazing, which meant that the entire pueblo could use the land, not just one or two individuals. Governor Vélez Cachupín was aware of this distinction and did all he could to keep as much land in common ownership as possible, which is why the two pueblo grazing grants were so important to his overall land grant project. He realized that if this land was not owned by the Indians it would soon be privatized by nearby Spaniards.

Despite all of Vélez Cachupín's efforts, privatization is exactly what happened. Within a few years after he left New Mexico in 1767, two of his most trusted alcaldes, Bartolomé Fernández and Felipe Tafoya, would acquire private grazing grants in west-central New Mexico in the area around Cebolleta Mountain. This development took place mostly in the late 1760s after Vélez Cachupín left office. His successor, Pedro Fermín de Mendinueta, started to make more grants toward Navajo country, taking advantage of a fifty-year period of Navajo peace lasting from the 1720s to the 1770s. The Navajos did not object to grants adjacent to or overlapping their agricultural lands (if they were notified), although earlier they had refused to settle down in a mission community at Cebolleta. A mission was established there in 1749 with three priests, and Vélez Cachupín even stood as godfather to several Indian children who were baptized in 1749, but by early 1750 the Navajos had driven the priests from the new missions, marking the end of the mission program to Navajo country and the beginning of Spanish land grants in the area.[35]

Felipe Tafoya had requested a private grazing grant in Navajo country from Vélez Cachupín in 1766, along with Atrisco residents Diego Antonio Chaves and Pedro Chaves, who claimed to have been squeezed out of their traditional grazing lands on the Atrisco grant by the residents of San Fernando del Río Puerco. Because Governor Vélez Cachupín was aware of the tendency of absentee owners to privatize land on the Navajo frontier, he denied Felipe Tafoya's petition, noting that if he needed additional grazing land he and his co-petitioners could join the San Gabriel de las Nutrias grant, the San Miguel de Laredo de Carnuel grant, or, indeed, the San Fernando del Río Puerco grant. As mentioned earlier, the governor was harsh with Felipe Tafoya and the two Chaveses, telling them that the reason the three petitioners had not joined those settlements was that they "feared for their lives and they now requested this petition due to the peace currently had with the Navajos."[36]

By rejecting the petition of Felipe Tafoya and others for a large private grazing grant in 1766, Governor Vélez Cachupín was abiding by his overall land settlement project. This was the same year that the governor had made grazing grants to Cochiti Pueblo and to Zia, Santa Ana, and Jemez Pueblos, and if he allowed the land near those grants to be privatized by large-scale Hispano cattle and sheep men who were absentee owners, the stock of those Hispano ranchers would overrun and push out the animals of the pueblos, and the Navajo peace would be jeopardized. In fact, both of those things occurred.

Just a few months after Vélez Cachupín left office, Felipe Tafoya reapplied for his land grant and was readily given a private grazing grant by Governor Pedro Fermín de Mendinueta. The Tafoya grant was the first of many. Mendinueta made at least seven more grazing grants in the Cebolleta/Mount Taylor area, often disregarding the rights of the Navajos in the area. Unlike Governor Vélez Cachupín, who intentionally avoided areas planted by the Navajos by placing boundaries well short of those fields, Mendinueta made numerous grants that included areas planted by the Navajos or places where they actually lived. While Vélez Cachupín had directed Alcalde Bartolomé Fernández to avoid giving grants along the west boundary of Navajo country, Fernández told Governor Mendinueta that although "some Navajos were living at the San Miguel Spring within the grant he was requesting for himself, they could still live there and would be happy to do so because of our lawful friendship and good relations." This was the pattern of grant after grant made by Governor Mendinueta in the year or two following Governor Vélez Cachupín's departure from New Mexico. In 1768 Mendinueta made a grant to Santiago Durán y Chávez northwest of Mount Taylor that included "seven ranchos of Apache [de] Navajo . . . but they did not object . . . because they were friends and would assist them against their enemy the Ute Indians."[37]

In none of these Mendinueta grants surrounding Mount Taylor (Cebolleta Mountain), did any Navajos actually appear to speak for themselves; they were never asked whether they accepted a land grant that included land they had farmed and perhaps even lived upon. In most cases lack of objection by the Navajos was presumed, even when the evidence was to the contrary. For instance, Bartolomé Fernández reported in regard to the land that Felipe Tafoya, Diego Antonio Chaves, and Pedro Chaves requested, "I have seen . . . scattered here and there a few cornstalks, but I have never observed that the Apaches [de Navajo] lived near these small patches of corn." Of course, this method of farming was typical of the Navajo and should have alerted the alcalde that they would in fact object to a Hispano grazing grant next to or overlapping their cornfields. Most of these private grazing grant owners did not live on their grants and considered these large acreages as assets to be traded as much as grasslands to be used. For example, in 1772 Salvador Jaramillo, who owned the grant next to the one Felipe Tafoya was requesting, sold part of it to Clemente Gutiérrez, the largest sheep and cattle owner in the Albuquerque area, for fifty-six hundred pesos' worth of cattle and sheep. Jaramillo astutely noted in the deed that if the Navajos who lived on the land should want to establish a town there, Gutiérrez would lose the land, and Salvador Jaramillo would keep the purchase price. Eventually, the Navajos showed that they did object to these grants. It was not long after Mendinueta made these grazing grants that the Navajo peace ended: "A half-century of peace . . . was followed by another era of conflict [as] the settlers in the valley of Rio Puerco abandoned their [lands] and the settlements became ghost villages [and] the Navajos reasserted mastery of their territorial homeland." Just a few years after the end of Vélez Cachupín's second term as governor, his settlement plan disintegrated even further; the disregard of Navajo rights to the land they farmed and lived on had taken a heavy toll.[38]

The relatively balanced land use and ownership plan crafted by Governor Vélez Cachupín during his two terms—which reached its peak in 1766–1767— recognized and protected the land rights of all inhabitants of New Mexico: Pueblo Indians, Hispano livestock raisers, Genízaro Indians, Hispano community land-grant farmers, and even Navajos. He implemented his plan by granting a mix of private and community lands with a sophisticated array of common lands. Unlike Diego de Vargas, who had lumped all forms of common land together so that everyone's cattle and sheep "in whatever quantity would graze [on adjacent land]," Vélez Cachupín set aside at least seven different kinds of common lands: the common lands of a Hispano community land grant, the common lands of an Indian pueblo, common pastures for the presidial horse herd, the common grazing lands of an Indian pueblo, the common lands of a Genízaro pueblo granted according to the laws of the *Recopilación*, the usufructuary rights of Navajo Indians with fields and dwellings within Spanish land grants, and unappropriated common lands available for everyone's use (*tierras baldías*). By enforcing the rights created by each of these forms of common lands, Vélez Cachupín made them work as long as he was present in New Mexico.[39]

In the last years of his second term, Vélez Cachupín achieved a delicate balance in land relations between Hispanos, Pueblos, Genízaros, Navajos, and Plains Indians. He made community grants to Hispano farmers (many of whom were Genízaros) who wanted to settle on land on the periphery of Spanish settlement and defend that land from Plains Indian attack; he upheld Pueblo land rights to the four square leagues surrounding each pueblo; he facilitated the pueblos' acquisition of land through purchase from Spaniards; he made the first community grant to Genízaro Indians at Abiquiu; he granted the pueblos grazing lands that would be shared with each other and the presidial horse herd; and he minimized the privatization of vast areas of grazing land in the Cebolleta/Mount Taylor area, thereby protecting the rights of Navajo farmers who had planted fields and even established small settlements in the area. Besides restoring peace with the Utes and Comanches, Vélez Cachupín provided a more well-defined and balanced network of common land ownership and a cadre of local officials who used the judicial system to maintain the new equilibrium he had achieved. He was able to achieve all of these goals during his second term before he handed the government over to Pedro Fermín de Mendinueta in 1767.[40]

As long as Vélez Cachupín was governor he did all he could to protect the rights of the less powerful members of society. By giving them lands the governor was putting the final pieces of his land grant plan in place. Coupled with his aggressive enforcement of the land-related rights established by making these grants, Vélez Cachupín ushered in a brief period of peace, both among the different communities and with the raiding Utes, Comanches, and Navajos. However, this "Golden Age" lasted only a few years.

CHAPTER TWELVE

THE RETURN OF ZUNI PUEBLO'S
SACRED LANDS AND ARTIFACTS

T HE ADVOCACY EMPLOYED BY ZUNI PUEBLO TO OBTAIN THE RE-
turn of its important sacred lands and religious objects marked a change
in approach from the usual total reliance on lawyers; Zuni relied more on persuasion by community leaders and religious caciques than on lawyers, though
the attorneys were always ready if persuasion alone was not sufficient. In most
cases it was enough.

In the 1970s Zuni Pueblo began an intensive campaign for the return of
their sacred lands and sacred religious objects, like masks and the carved war
gods. The sacred lands included what Zunis called Kolhu/wala:wa, or Zuni
Heaven, and the Zuni Salt Lake. Zuni Pueblo's efforts in achieving the return
of Zuni Salt Lake and the sacred area known as Zuni Heaven were given a
boost by the success of Taos Pueblo in its over six-decade-long battle for the
return of the Blue Lake watershed in 1970. In an iconic moment, with Taos
Pueblo religious leaders praying together in the U.S. Senate gallery as the final
votes were cast in favor of the bill returning trust title of Blue Lake to the
pueblo, the ninety-five-year-old cacique Juan de Jesús Romero stood "joyfully
in the . . . gallery, holding aloft the tribe's three symbolic canes." Many advisers
did not believe that Congress would give Taos Pueblo title to the land, especially over the opposition of the Forest Service and powerful members of
Congress like Senator Clinton P. Anderson. After Taos Pueblo's long battle to
secure title to the Blue Lake watershed was successful, other pueblos also tried
to get their sacred lands returned using a new form of advocacy.[1]

The Zuni claims differed from the Blue Lake claim in that Zuni sought compensation for lands taken by the government, and when successful, the pueblo used some of the funds received to purchase other lost land. The advocacy methods used to get the U.S. government to return the sacred lands and to get private museums to return the Zuni war gods included some traditional legal methods along with a new form of persuasion stressing the religious significance of the land and artifacts. Those methods would form the new paradigm of advocacy for the pueblos: an emphasis on the religious importance of land once owned by the pueblo, together with a strong legal case to be used as a last resort if persuasion was not effective.[2]

Soon after the Zuni Reservation was established in 1877, Zuni Pueblo mounted a long campaign for return of its traditional lands because the reservation did not include the two most important Zuni sacred sites: Zuni Salt Lake and Zuni Heaven. After decades of lobbying Congress for return of these traditional lands, Zuni was finally successful in 1978 in getting Public Law 95–280 passed, which provided in part for the purchase by the Department of the Interior of land surrounding Zuni Salt Lake and return of that land and the lake to Zuni Pueblo. The second part of Public Law 95–280 provided an avenue for the tribe to sue for monetary compensation for loss of aboriginal lands since Zuni Pueblo had not submitted a claim before the Indian Claims Commission. In 1978 Zuni Pueblo was in a similar position to Taos Pueblo when the latter decided to seek trust title to Blue Lake. Zuni felt the same way about Kolhu/wala:wa (Zuni Heaven) as Taos did about Blue Lake, so when the Zuni lawsuit for monetary compensation was being prepared, the tribal council decided to withdraw certain religious lands from the suit and pursue trust title to these sites instead of compensation. The idea was that these lands were priceless: no amount of money would provide adequate compensation for their loss. Thus, the Zuni Heaven area was not included in the suit, nor was the area along the pilgrimage routes to Kolhu/wala:wa over which the tribe sought to obtain easements.[3]

The sacred place known to the Zuni as Kolhu/wala:wa and to non-Zunis as Zuni Heaven

> is the place where all Zunis go after death and where the supernatural
> Kokko resides under a sacred lake fed by the waters from a precious spring.
> Kolhu/wala:wa is located near where the Zuni River flows between two

mountains and then into the Little Colorado. On one of the mountains is an opening into the underworld where Zuni religious leaders . . . attempt to communicate with their ancestors and the Kokko. Near the end of the other mountain is the location where the Koyemshi or "Mudheads" were created. . . . Kolhu/wala:wa is both conceptually and geographically central to the Zuni religion. The ancient Zuni origin and migration narratives all tell of Kolhu/wala:wa and explain its place in the story of the Zunis' search for the Middle Place.

The pueblo's strategy was to purchase part of Zuni Heaven; much depended on Zuni's suit for compensation filed in the U.S. Court of Claims in 1979, which, they hoped, would provide the funds for that purchase.[4]

The trial of the Court of Claims case was held at the Utah Supreme Court in Salt Lake City in March 1982. On the first day of the trial the Zuni leaders who had come to testify after many years of preparation rose early and made cornmeal prayer offerings in a nearby spring-fed stream. It soon began raining and rained throughout the trial, which the Zunis took as a good omen. As the Zuni witnesses prepared to enter the Supreme Court chambers on the first day of trial, "three of the religious leaders went ahead of the rest, leading the way into the chambers for the first time. They were performing a War Ceremony of the Galaxy Society. No one was allowed to get ahead of them or cross their paths, and each of them was reciting the appropriate prayers as they went along." According to Zuni anthropologist Edmund J. Ladd, "There's a phrase that is used that hits the heart of the people that you are fighting against, and they used this phrase. It was used by the Zuni religious leaders to put themselves in an advantageous frame of mind, a frame of reference for what they were about to undergo. The prayers and ceremony provide stamina, perseverance, proficiency at what you're supposed to be doing, and bravery."[5]

After an extensive trial conducted by lawyer Stephen G. Boyden, which involved the testimony of numerous expert witnesses and Zuni political and religious leaders, the court ruled in 1987 that Zuni Pueblo was deprived by the United States of 14,835,892 acres of land to which the pueblo held aboriginal title. The pueblo introduced a series of maps as exhibits that showed the gradual encroachment on Zuni's traditional lands between 1876 and 1979. The court relied heavily upon these maps in reaching its decision, an excellent example of the use by Pueblo people of cartography that tells the indigenous side of the

story. The court awarded Zuni a final judgment of $25 million based on a val-
uation of $1.69/acre of the land taken. Zuni Pueblo set up a trust fund in the
net amount of about $17.5 million after payment of attorney's fees and expert
witnesses; some of these funds were used to acquire land around Kolhu/
wala:wa. During the time when this litigation was proceeding, the pueblo was
also lobbying for legislation to acquire trust title to Zuni Heaven through an
outright transfer, and in 1984 the pueblo succeeded in getting Public Law
9–408 passed, which allowed Zuni Pueblo to purchase some of the eleven
thousand acres that made up the area around Kolhu/wala:wa. Although Zuni
was successful in getting paid for lost land and obtaining trust title to Zuni
Heaven, it would soon face a major threat to the 110-mile access route to the
sacred site. It seemed that acquiring the land was just the beginning.[6]

In 1985, just one year after the pueblo obtained trust title to Kolhu/wala:wa,
a local rancher named Earl Platt threatened to stop the regular quadrennial
pilgrimage to Zuni Heaven when the pilgrims reached the part of the trail
that crossed his land. Platt, a wealthy attorney with little sympathy for the
Zunis, notified the Apache County sheriff just a few weeks before the pilgrimage was scheduled to begin that he wanted the Zuni religious leaders arrested
for trespassing when they crossed his property. This was not the first time in
its long history that the pilgrimage had been threatened. In 1880 an Anglo
homesteader with land along the sacred trail attempted to stop the Zunis,
"but they militantly enforced their rights to the pilgrimage and the sacred
trail along which they traveled." Since that time the Zunis had contacted
landowners along the pilgrimage route, including the BLM and the Arizona
Land Department, and obtained permission for the pilgrims to pass. But Earl
Platt had refused to give the tribe an easement to cross his land.[7]

After Platt's threat the Zunis obtained a temporary restraining order against
him on 12 June 1985, the same day the pilgrimage started. The pilgrimage was
concluded four days later without incident, although Platt is reported to have
said that "he had intended to disrupt the pilgrimage . . . but was unable to
locate the pilgrims as they crossed his land." To avoid such confrontations in
the future, the Zuni tribe began preparation of an extensive lawsuit against
Platt and others along the pilgrimage route, which sought a permanent pre-
scriptive easement requiring a survey and mapping of the entire 110-mile pilgrimage route. The mapping was completed in 1987, but by 21 June 1989, when
the next summer solstice pilgrimage was scheduled to begin, the easement case

had still not come to trial. Platt again threatened to disrupt the pilgrimage despite another restraining order against him. This time he was partially successful, almost causing bloodshed: "On the third day of the pilgrimage Platt drove his pickup through the line of pilgrims, reportedly hitting one of the horses and riders in the group. The Zunis on the pilgrimage [who] had taken strict vows to avoid hostility and confrontation . . . veered away from Platt" and completed the pilgrimage.[8]

After this outrageous attack the U.S. Justice Department led by attorney Hank Meshorer sued Earl Platt for contempt of court for violating the restraining order. In the ensuing trial amid a tense atmosphere in the federal courthouse in Phoenix, expert witnesses told of the long history of the pilgrimage first witnessed by Spanish conquistador Francisco Vásquez de Coronado in 1540. Attending the entire trial was a large contingent of Zunis sitting on one side of the courtroom, including members of the Bow Priests Society, who are charged with securing the safety of the pilgrimage and other Zuni religious ceremonies. On the other side of the courtroom sat Earl Platt, "several of his ranch hands, as well as his two sons, . . . [all] intent on blocking the Zunis from crossing his lands. . . . The U.S. Marshall was alerted to the possibility of open hostilities." After a tense trial during which the long history of the annual pilgrimage was presented along with evidence of Platt's overt hostility toward the Zunis, Platt was found guilty of contempt of court in September 1989 and ordered to pay Zuni Pueblo five thousand dollars. After almost a year of appeals, Pratt settled, and an easement was established that gave Zuni permanent access to its sacred Kolhu/wala:wa. Thus, the Zuni people were finally assured access to this sacred site five years after obtaining title to Zuni Heaven in 1984.[9]

Zuni War Gods

While the struggle for Zuni Heaven was proceeding, the pueblo realized the importance of the repatriation of sacred objects whose purpose is to protect sacred places. Zuni Pueblo was one of the first to start negotiating with museums for the return of such ceremonial objects. Zuni Pueblo governor Robert E. Lewis began negotiations with the Smithsonian Institution regarding an exhibit of Zuni masks in 1970, several decades before the relationship between American Indians and museums started to undergo a radical shift from

Indians as unwilling providers of objects for museum collections to Indians as planners and equal partners in deciding what objects should be part of those collections. Governor Lewis told the Smithsonian representatives that the Zuni people were disturbed by the exhibit because the masks "were sacred and associated with the Shalako, an important blessing ceremony held every winter. The masks should never be seen by uninitiated people, who could be endangered by viewing them. [Lewis] said Zuni's religious leaders had asked him to go to Washington to attempt to retrieve the masks."[10]

Many of the Shalako masks in the Smithsonian were probably collected by Matilda Coxe Stevenson, who published an article about them, while many others were taken from Zuni by Frank Hamilton Cushing. Stevenson and Cushing first came to Zuni in 1879 on an expedition sponsored by the Smithsonian Institution and led by James Stevenson, whose purpose was to gather ethnographic materials for the study of prehistoric and historic Pueblo populations. Matilda Coxe Stevenson was Stevenson's wife. When the expedition returned east, Cushing remained at Zuni and was eventually adopted into the tribe; Matilda Coxe Stevenson also stayed after her husband's death in 1888. Working independently because each one's strong personality led to personal differences, the two "amassed enormous collections of Zuni objects for the Smithsonian." Matilda Coxe Stevenson earned a reputation with the Zuni as "an intrusive and formidable woman." Like Cushing, she was often disrespectful in the name of documenting native customs before they disappeared. On one occasion, "she forced her way into a restricted area during the planting of prayer plumes in the Shalako ceremony" and refused to leave. Some of Cushing's collection activities were also unauthorized and prohibited by the pueblo. In 1880 Cushing secretly traveled to Kolhu/wala:wa, "where he looted the ancient shrines, stealing prayer sticks and other religious offerings . . . with the intention of sending much of the material to [the Smithsonian]." When the Zunis discovered Cushing's cache, they tried him in a religious court. Although Cushing was disciplined by the tribe, he was never expelled, but is still remembered as someone who had abused the trust the Zunis had placed in him. Nevertheless, "Cushing came to have problems and doubts collecting some materials for the Smithsonian . . . he apparently destroyed some of his notes on the more sacred and esoteric aspects of Zuñi religion that were not to be made public."[11]

It would take many years of negotiation to convince museum officials of the importance of the masks and that they should be returned. Some officials believed that acceding to the Zunis' request could "set the dangerous precedent of allowing groups from outside the museum to intervene in the museum's exhibits program." It would take two years for the Smithsonian just to agree to close the exhibit; it was still not willing to return the masks.[12] During this period Zuni leaders also discovered that the Denver Art Museum had a sacred Zuni war god image (Ahayu:da) on display, which led to a full-blown campaign for the return of all Ahayu:da-related and other sacred objects. The Ahayu:da, known popularly as war gods,

> are twin gods who serve primarily as protectors of the Zuni people. They also have an influence over the weather and prosperity in general and function as patrons of gaming and sports. Each year in ceremonies at the winter solstice the leaders of the Deer clan create an image of the elder brother . . . while the leaders of the Bear clan create an image of the younger brother. The two images of Ahayu:da are entrusted to the bow priests, who place them at one of a number of shrines on the mesas surrounding Zuni Pueblo. The new Ahayu:da replace an existing one that is now placed on a pile of "retired" images to remain an integral part of the shrine, gradually disintegrating and returning to the earth. The bow priest asks the Ahayu:da to protect the Zuni world from its enemies.

Once the Ahayu:da are installed at a shrine, no one has the authority to remove them. Zuni religious leaders believe that to do so unleashes their great powers, resulting in potential destruction and mayhem. "The recovery of Ahayu:da wrongfully removed from the Zuni Indian Reservation was thus of grave concern to Zuni religious leaders. To restore harmony to the world, Zuni religious leaders initiated a project to recover all stolen Ahayu:da that could be found and reinstall them at shrines on the reservation."[13]

The strategy employed utilized persuasion by religious leaders, along with possible lawsuits by tribal lawyers, and in that sense was similar to Taos Pueblo's battle for the return of Blue Lake. Over a ten-year period between 1978 and 1987, a plan was developed to effect the return of all Ahayu:da (which numbered about seventy) from museums, private collections, and art dealers. The tribe dealt first with the Denver Art Museum because that was where the first Ahayu:da was discovered. The campaign involved numerous meetings with museum officials, lawyers, and others during a period when the concept of returning artifacts to tribes on moral, ethical, and religious grounds was in its infancy. At first, the Denver Art Museum was reluctant to return the Zuni war gods to the tribe, raising arguments such as the possibility that Zuni would request the return of other items in the museum's collection. But the museum reversed its position when the tribe pointed out the Ahayu:da were stolen objects and that "the Colorado Attorney General [had] issued an opinion holding that the museum had no interest, as a public trustee, in asserting a claim to stolen objects."[14]

Zuni leaders also wanted a voluntary agreement with the Smithsonian to function as a precedent that other museums would follow. One of the early meetings with Zuni religious leaders and a few outsiders in late 1977 was "conducted almost entirely in the Zuni language. For almost two hours the only word that the non-Indians understood was 'Cushy,' a reference to Frank Hamilton Cushing. The Zuni finally decided that none of the non-Indians at the meeting were trying to be another 'Cushy.'"[15] Once trust had been established between the religious leaders and the non-Indians, the campaign developed a negotiating strategy based on Zuni's experience with the Denver Art Museum. A conciliatory approach was deemed "more appropriate to the religious nature of the matters at hand and more productive than lawsuits, which would be used only as a last resort. Underlying this approach was the Zuni ethic that in a dispute a good man goes to his adversary four times to seek resolution through reasonable negotiation before taking drastic action." The Zunis believed that if the museums understood the importance of the Ahayu:da to Zuni culture, they would agree to return the sacred images.[16]

Besides requesting the return of the Ahayu:da, the Zuni worked with the Smithsonian to prevent further theft and sale of religious objects and to secure the museum's assistance in informing the tribe when an Ahayu:da was to be offered for sale. Pursuant to this policy, the Smithsonian notified Zuni Pueblo of such a proposed sale in the fall of 1978, when an Ahayu:da from the collection of a Los Angeles doctor was scheduled to be auctioned by Sotheby's. Notified of the religious significance of the Ahayu:da, Sotheby's removed the sacred object from the sale, and the owner of the Ahayu:da decided to voluntarily return it to the tribe. On 3 January 1979 the Ahayu:da was delivered to Zuni religious leaders at a ceremony hosted by LaDonna Harris and Regis Pecos of the Americans for Indian Opportunity. Zuni leaders returned home that afternoon with the first Ahayu:da to be repatriated to the tribe. Over the next fourteen years Zuni Pueblo secured the return of sixty-seven Ahayu:da: fifty-four from museums, ten from private collections, and three from private art galleries. After the Denver Art Museum repatriated their Ahayu:da in 1980 and the Smithsonian finally followed suit in 1987, others were also repatriated so that by 1992 all Ahayu:da in the United States known to have been held outside of Zuni Pueblo had been returned. In addition to the precedent set by the Smithsonian, the passage of the Native American Graves Protection and Repatriation Act in 1990 speeded up the process.[17]

The success of the campaign for the return of the Ahayu:da stemmed in large part from the cultural and religious arguments used, which were bolstered by a powerful legal theory that would be used only as a last resort. Since the legal argument applied only to the Ahayu:da, there was little danger that it would be used to request the return of other sacred objects. According to this theory, which was so compelling that it led some collectors to return Ahayu:da before being requested to do so, the Ahayu:da were sacred artifacts whose presence at Zuni was needed for spiritual purposes; they were owned communally by the tribe and once placed at their shrine could not legally be removed. Thus, title to any Ahayu:da outside of Zuni is questionable at best: the Zuni and federal prosecutors considered them all stolen. These were the arguments that finally persuaded the Smithsonian and other collectors.[18]

Zuni Salt Lake

The lessons learned from the protection of Zuni Heaven and the return of the Zuni war gods would apply equally to the sacred Zuni Salt Lake. Reacquiring sacred lands is only the first step; protecting them is often a second, ongoing step. In the case of Zuni Salt Lake, the first step occurred in 1978, when Congress recognized Zuni's aboriginal title to those lands in the same legislation that allowed Zuni to sue the United States in the Court of Claims. Zuni Salt Lake is a volcanic cone fed by groundwater that brings salt to the lake's surface as it rises. Salt Woman, the pueblo's sacred deity, is believed to live in the lake. Zuni Pueblo allows other indigenous people, such as the Navajo (Diné), Hopi, and those of Acoma Pueblo, to obtain salt for religious purposes from Zuni Salt Lake, subject to conditions. Acoma Pueblo cannot hold certain summer dances without salt from Zuni Salt Lake, and the Navajo "use it to bless the first tear and smile of a newborn."[19] Zuni Pueblo received a deed from

the federal government conveying trust title to Zuni Salt Lake and the surrounding area in November 1985, and the pueblo held a celebration to commemorate the realization of a generations-old dream. The 762 acres of the lake
and surrounding area are now held in trust for the tribe by the United States,
and many thought that the people of Zuni would now be protected in their
regular pilgrimages to obtain salt from the lake for religious and other
purposes.[20]

A few years after the pueblo obtained title to Zuni Salt Lake, however, the
Arizona-based Salt River Project, a state-owned utility, announced plans to
open a strip mine northeast of the lake that would mine about eighty million tons of coal over the next fifty years. The project planned to build a railroad passing within three miles of Zuni Salt Lake to haul coal to a generating
station near St. Johns, Arizona, to produce electricity for Phoenix. An expert
hydrologist hired by the Bureau of Indian Affairs warned that none of the
reports about the safety of the project "establish that Zuni Salt Lake would be
safe from harm." Several pueblos in addition to Zuni filed an appeal of the
Fence Lake Coal Mine draft environmental impact statement that recommended approval of the project. Nevertheless, U.S. Interior Department secretary Gail Norton approved a permit for the mine, as Zuni Pueblo prepared to
sue the federal government for breach of its trust responsibility.[21]

When it appeared that the Salt River Project would not back down easily,
Zuni Pueblo established the Zuni Salt Lake Coalition, a group of pueblos and
environmental organizations opposing the mine. The coalition, according to
its press release, "embarked on a sustained campaign [together with twenty-two
other pueblos] to stop the Fence Lake Coal mine. It had garnered support from
hundreds of thousands of people across the country who had added their voice
to call for the protection of sacred sites." According to Zuni lawyer Pablo
Padilla, who served as tribal liaison to the coalition, "This was not a battle
between Salt River Project and the Zuni Tribe. This was a battle of values. It
just happened to play itself out between a coal mine company and a tribe. [On
one side there were] energy resources, security, those sorts of things that are
involved in producing electricity, and then [there were] the other values—having something sacred and holding onto it."[22] As a result of this campaign, the
Salt River Project announced on 4 August 2003 that it was canceling plans for
the mine and would instead purchase coal from the Powder River Basin in
Wyoming. It was an all-out victory for the pueblo. Zuni head councilman

Carlton Albert, speaking on behalf of the pueblo, summed up his feelings: "I feel relieved and it sends shivers down my back to realize how long this struggle has been and now it has come to closure. . . . If there is a lesson to be learned it is to never give up and stay focused on what you want to accomplish." At Zuni, the return of sacred lands along with sacred artifacts has helped revitalize Zuni religion.[23]

Modern Pueblo peoples have finally been successful in achieving the return of sacred lands and sacred artifacts by putting cultural and religious arguments first, as enunciated by the religious leaders, and using the courts as a last resort. While much Pueblo land has been lost, New Mexico pueblos have built on each other's successes, achieving in most cases a balance between the temporal and the spiritual relationship to the land.[24]

EPILOGUE

BEING SPOKEN FOR
OR SPEAKING FOR OURSELVES

H AVING WRITTEN ABOUT HISPANO LAND GRANTS, AND MORE RE-
cently about Pueblo Indian land grants (with Rick Hendricks and
Richard Hughes), I have attempted in this book to bring both narratives together, to reconnect them, and in some cases to resurrect lost histories. The
preceding chapters contain numerous stories about land grants made to Indian
pueblos and to Genízaros, histories devoted to pueblos that were abandoned at
varying times after the arrival of the Spaniards, and the story of a pueblo that
survived, lost its sacred lands and artifacts, and then regained them. I have
discussed Hispano land grants, sometimes in relation to neighboring Pueblo
grants and often in terms of their own history. In all cases my emphasis has
been on the advocates for those land grantees, whether they were lawyers or
the parties speaking for themselves.[1]

The Galisteo Basin pueblos of La Ciénega, Cieneguilla, San Cristóbal, San
Marcos, and Galisteo were among the eighty-one pueblos that existed in New
Mexico just before the arrival of the Spaniards under Oñate. Little is known
about the precontact history of the Galisteo Basin pueblos except what early
Spanish expeditions and maps report.[2] None of those pueblos lasted very long
after the Spanish arrival in New Mexico. La Ciénega, San Marcos, Galisteo,
and San Cristóbal Pueblos all participated in the Pueblo Revolt, but only
Galisteo Pueblo survived the return of the Spaniards under Governor Diego
de Vargas. Governor Vargas forced San Cristóbal and San Marcos to move to
lands watered by the Santa Cruz River to make room for new Spanish settlers,

and eventually some members of San Cristóbal, La Ciénega, and Cieneguilla moved to Hopi to settle at Hano. The inhabitants of San Marcos moved to Cochiti and Santo Domingo soon after the Vargas reconquest. Galisteo Pueblo lasted the longest, its inhabitants finally moving to Santo Domingo Pueblo in 1782. While we know the bare outlines of the existence and movements of these pueblos, we know very little about what happened to the Tanos who lived there. But we do know what happened to their land, and I have told that story for each of these four pueblos.[3]

Just as the Tanos of the Galisteo Basin have largely disappeared, so have some of the substantial grazing grants made to the pueblos of Zia, Santa Ana, Jemez, and Cochiti. These grazing grants have been erased from history because they were overlapped by later grants and ultimately rejected by the courts. Cochiti Pueblo received a grazing grant whose description was so complicated and whose concept was so revolutionary that it also has largely disappeared from history. Governor Vélez Cachupín achieved temporary equilibrium, signaling a fleeting and tenuous balance between Pueblo Indians and Spaniards and their land, as discussed in chapter 11. The way this balance was achieved and maintained through Spanish protectors of the Pueblo Indians and the lawsuits and land grants of Governor Vélez Cachupín is another thread that connects the land-related narratives of Spaniards and Pueblo Indians.

After Vélez Cachupín's departure, the office of the Protector of Indians was briefly reinstated from 1810 to 1821, but many of the individuals who were protectors at that time were either ineffective or corrupt. Filling the gap was an assortment of individuals acting as advocates, such as parish priests, local alcaldes, or private citizens who filed petitions on behalf of Pueblo Indians and sometimes Hispano farmers. Lay advocates in the mid-eighteenth century like Isidro Sánchez filed petitions for aggrieved Hispano complainants, but he was restrained by the governor and seen as a troublemaker. Again, it was the non-lawyers who were often the best and most effective advocates. An example of effective advocacy by a parish priest was the 1763 petition by Father Mariano Rodríguez de la Torre on behalf of Santa Clara Pueblo. Father Rodríguez requested that land upstream from the pueblo be granted outright to Santa Clara so that the pueblo would have control over its irrigation water instead of being subject to illegal upstream irrigation by Hispano grantees. Governor Vélez Cachupín agreed with the priest's recommendation and made the Cañada de Santa Clara grant to Santa Clara Pueblo in 1763. However, when the issue of the boundaries of Pueblo lands arose during the Mexican period, Indian pueblos either had no lawyers to represent them or had advocates whose representation was tepid at best, as when Felipe Sandoval acting as Protector of Indians failed to protect Pecos Pueblo from infringement on their lands in 1815.[4]

When the Americans first arrived in Santa Fe under the U.S. banners of General Stephen Watts Kearney in August 1846, Pueblo Indians sent delegations to the Palace of the Governors seeking relief from what they considered to be Spanish encroachment on their lands. Instead of going to Santa Fe to beg for their lands, though, pueblos like Santo Domingo met the Americans on their own terms, providing military displays intended to establish their sovereignty. After receiving an invitation from Santo Domingo Pueblo to visit, Kearney and an official party escorted by his mounted dragoons approached the pueblo on 3 September 1846. They were met outside the pueblo by the Pueblo governor and other officials who warned the Americans that a group of young warriors would approach them mounted and dressed for war and the dragoons should not fire on them. Kearney's cartographer, Lieutenant William Emory, reported what happened next:

> When within a few miles of the town, we saw a cloud of dust rapidly advancing, and soon the air was rent with a terrible yell. . . . The first object that caught my eye through the column of dust, was a fierce pair of buffalo horns, overlapped with long shaggy hair. As they approached, the sturdy form of a naked Indian revealed itself beneath the horns, with shield and lance, dashing at full speed, on a white horse, which, like his own body, was painted all the colors of the rainbow; and then, one by one, his followers came on. . . . As they passed us, one rank on each side, they fired a volley under our horses, which went along without pricking an ear or showing any sign of excitement. Arrived in the rear, the Indians circled round, dropped into a walk on our flanks until their horses recovered breath. . . . So they continued to pass and repass us all the way to the steep cliff which overhangs the town.

Kearney's entourage was then given a light repast of at the house of the priest, after which "the general delivered a speech to the assembled people of [Santo Domingo Pueblo] . . . which was first interpreted into Spanish, and then in

Pueblo" but which was probably understood by few members of the pueblo. The message conveyed though, by the earlier mock battle by the pueblo warriors was clear: we are here and whatever our leaders may do, you will meet us on our land on our terms as we speak for ourselves.[5]

Pueblo Indians and Hispanos were often left to their own devices, without advocates, and both looked for help wherever they could find it. One of the early advocates for the pueblos was James Calhoun, the first superintendent of Indian affairs for the territory. Soon after arriving in Santa Fe, Calhoun recommended a treaty with the Pueblo peoples to protect "these Indians in their persons and property." Like Vélez Cachupín, Calhoun believed that Pueblo Indians, as well as land-owning Hispano farmers, were entitled to representation in court. On one occasion he asked lawyer Richard Weightman to appear in court on the pueblos' behalf. Weightman represented the governor of Tesuque Pueblo in 1850, securing an acquittal on charges brought by the local alcalde. Other than this case, however, it does not appear that Weightman represented any other Pueblo Indians since the funds Calhoun requested to pay such an advocate were not forthcoming.[6]

With a lack of advocates to represent them, pueblos began to represent themselves by traveling to Washington, D.C., to meet directly with U.S. officials. In 1852 five Tesuque leaders journeyed to Washington to meet with President Millard Fillmore and petition for rights in a proposed 1850 land treaty negotiated with Governor James C. Calhoun, who initially accompanied the delegation.[7] While the Pueblo delegations to Washington did not achieve the protection of Pueblo lands they had hoped for, they did lay the foundation for future recognition of Pueblo land rights. Pueblo leaders became skilled at representing their communities and arguing their cases at the highest level of power. Although these delegations received promises from the president to investigate charges of trespass and encroachment, little specific legislation resulted from those promises. Nevertheless, the 1852 Tesuque delegation was considered a success because soon after the delegation returned, the four-square-league Pueblo grants were confirmed by the surveyor general of New Mexico, and the highly symbolic Lincoln canes were delivered to each of the pueblos.[8]

After Calhoun's death in 1852, as he was accompanying the Tesuque delegation to Washington, Pueblo Indians had few advocates for their cause. Governors like Calhoun's successor, William Carr Lane, talked about the

Pueblo Indians' equality but also believed they should be taxed. Like Lincoln, Lane did not recognize Indian sovereignty, rejecting "their autonomous rights of self government." Nevertheless, eloquent Pueblo leaders complained that taxing Pueblo Indians would deprive them of the property they had been awarded by the surveyor general and "break them up as a distinct people." [9]

One hundred years after Vélez Cachupín's vision of a balanced land ownership plan that would provide land for Pueblo Indians as well as Hispanic farmers, the only advocates the Pueblo people could look to, besides themselves, were the Indian agents and sometimes their parish priests. Many Indian agents, like Benjamin Thomas, tried to help, even appearing in court on behalf of the Pueblo Indians, but they lacked the power to formally represent the pueblos in court.[10] Beginning in 1851 Indian agents were authorized to act as liaisons between the federal government and the various Indian tribes; often, however, recommendations of Indian agents who attempted to protect Pueblo lands were ignored.[11] For example, as we saw in chapter 4, Indian Agent M. C. Williams investigated the validity of the 1766 Ojo del Espíritu Santo grant made to Zia, Santa Ana, and Jemez Pueblos and found many other grants encroaching on that one. Williams urged the commissioner of Indian affairs in Washington, D.C., to "prevent the confirmation and patenting of any more [overlapping] grants . . . until the grant to the Indians is confirmed and patented." This plea had little effect, however, as two grants overlapping the 1766 Ojo del Espíritu Santo grant were in fact confirmed.[12]

Occasionally, however, Indian agents were successful when advocating on behalf of the pueblos. In 1883 the Indian agent for Zuni Pueblo complained to the commissioner of Indian affairs that a surveying error had left two vital springs outside of the reservation boundary. Fortunately, the plight of the Zuni "got picked up by newspapers all across the nation," putting pressure on President Chester A. Arthur to rectify the matter. Some Zunis had come to Washington the year before, in 1882, on an official visit arranged by the ethnologist Frank Hamilton Cushing and had created quite a stir in Washington and beyond. So the 1883 boundary protest was big news, enough to convince President Arthur to act on the Zunis' petition. He issued an executive order redrawing the boundary lines of the Zuni Reservation to include the two springs that had been left out of the reservation initially.[13]

❧ ❧ ❧

A century later, in the mid- to late 1900s, during the adjudication of land grants by the surveyor general and the Court of Private Land Claims, lawyers, politicians, and judges presided over a system of land grant adjudication that was seriously flawed; as a result, advocates often did a disservice to their clients instead of helping them. Not only was the system defective, but the premise that zealous advocates on both sides would bring out the truth and lead to a just result was also lacking. Advocates representing their mostly Hispano clients took their fees in a portion of the land grant that was confirmed, usually one-third to one-half of the land. If a community grant was confirmed, the lawyer usually asked the court to partition the grant so that he could divide and sell his portion of the grant common lands. The court would invariably determine that the land could not be equitably divided because of the topography and because many of the parcels would be too small, so the land would be sold to the highest bidder. The lawyer would end up with the lion's share of the proceeds as his fee, and the true owners of the land would receive only a small amount of money for their share of the common lands. The only land they had left was the land where their homes and gardens were located.[14]

Hispanos learned to fill the void in effective advocacy by speaking for themselves, as did the Pueblo Indians. Numerous heirs to the Tierra Amarilla grant filed a memorial in Congress in the 1880s complaining that they were being deprived of their rights of pasturage, wood, and water on the common lands of the grant. And the heirs of the Mora grant, a part of which (like the Tierra Amarilla grant) was acquired by Thomas B. Catron, filed a similar protest regarding their common lands. In the end, the Mora and Tierra Amarilla petitions were unsuccessful, but the advocacy of the Anton Chico grant heirs brought more positive results.[15]

The Anton Chico grant was confirmed by Congress in 1860 and patented in 1883, but the patent was not received by the land grant until after 1915. Several generations of Anton Chico grant residents, which at one time comprised over 500 grant heirs, traveled to Washington to get the government to issue them the patent to the land grant. They finally had to sue government officials such as Surveyor General Henry Atkinson, who claimed the grant himself. Ultimately, the community won but had to pay their lawyer one hundred thousand acres of land to obtain the patent to the land grant, which is still operating today.[16]

Lawyers practicing before the surveyor general and the Court of Private

Land Claims had a basic conflict of interest with their clients. Their fee arrangement meant that if they were successful, their success would destroy the very thing their clients cared about—the land grant. Land grant heirs had no choice. They needed lawyers to represent them before the Court of Private Land Claims, and the fee arrangement was the only way they could pay them. To be sure it was the system that was to blame, but nineteenth-century land grant lawyers often placed their own self-interests first. It certainly would have been possible for a lawyer to collect his fee in land but have his portion of the land grant physically segregated so that the entire land grant would not have to be sold.[17]

Land grant heirs suffering the loss of their lands without an advocate to speak on their behalf sometimes turned to violence (usually against property) as a last resort. Las Gorras Blancas protested the unauthorized fencing of the common lands of the Las Vegas grant in the 1880s by cutting fences and burning barns, earning widespread sympathy and support from the general population, which led to their jury acquittal on fence-cutting charges. During the same period and into the early twentieth century, La Mano Negra in Tierra Amarilla resisted the fencing of the common lands of the Tierra Amarilla grant.[18]

Pueblo Indians and Hispano settlers on community grants used other methods besides courts and lawyers to have their voices heard. Not having anyone to speak for them, they spoke for themselves, often quite eloquently and not always with words. Santo Domingo used a mock battle to meet General Kearney on their terms. Tesuque, as well as Isleta, San Juan, and most of the other pueblos, sent delegations or petitions to Washington, as did grantees on the Tierra Amarilla, Mora, and Anton Chico grants.[19]

In recent times, advocates for both Indian pueblos and Hispanic community grants have had success both in court and in negotiations for the return of lands and sacred objects, compensation for lost land, and the exercise of use rights over traditional lands. Pueblos like Zuni and Jemez have used new methods of advocacy to regain both land and sacred artifacts. Although Zuni Pueblo used lawyers to make land claims in court, their lawyers were supported by religious leaders. When it came to recovering sacred artifacts from museums in Washington, D.C., Denver, and New York, Pueblo elders and leaders worked with lawyers to design a strategy that relied on face-to-face persuasion over a period of years to accomplish their goal. Only if that personal advocacy failed would the lawyers be brought in.[20]

One of the greatest success stories for Hispano land grant heirs is the recent case of *Lobato v. Taylor*, involving land grant claimants in southern Colorado's San Luis Valley (which was originally in New Mexico). Those heirs of settlers on the Sangre de Cristo Land grant found their rights to use what became the common lands—and particularly the mountainous tract known as La Sierra— upheld in a stunning, groundbreaking decision by the Colorado Supreme Court. This case was characterized by a long and arduous community and legal struggle culminating in victory. To date, access to La Sierra for wood gathering and livestock grazing has been provided to more than five hundred individuals who can trace their title through maps and deeds issued to their ancestors in the mid- to late 1800s. The San Luis Valley community and the legal community led by lawyer Jeff Goldstein deserve credit for their over thirty-year struggle to reclaim land rights established by their ancestors.[21]

These are the latter-day advocates for the oppressed: lawyers, religious leaders, and a land grant community or an Indian pueblo working together to achieve justice through the return of sacred objects, lost lands, or reestablishment of the right to use those lands for traditional purposes.

APPENDIX ONE

Advocates, Their Cases, and Land Grants

Date	Name of Advocate	Capacity	Lawsuit
1704	Alfonso Rael de Aguilar	Protector de Indios	Spaniards' petition for land adjacent to San Felipe Pueblo leads to request to measure San Felipe Pueblo league. SANM I: 78.
1704	Alfonso Rael de Aguilar	Protector de Indios	Measurement of the San Ildefonso Pueblo league. SANM I: 1339.
1713	Juan de Atienza	Protector de Indios	Atienza defends former Picuris governor Gerónimo Dirucaca from charges of witchcraft, cohabitation, and idolatry. SANM II: 192.
1715	Juan de Atienza	Protector de Indios	Juan de Atienza represents Pojoaque Pueblo in their claim against Miguel Tenorio de Alba for reneging on a land sale to the pueblo of land once owned by the pueblo. SANM I: 7.
1722	Alfonso Rael de Aguilar	Juez receptor (temporary magistrate)	Measurement of Santo Domingo and Cochiti Leagues and award of additional land to the pueblos. SANM I: 1343.
1733	Ventura de Esquibel	Appointed by power of attorney	Ventura de Esquibel represents Isleta Pueblo against Diego Padilla for damage to Isleta's common lands by Padilla's cattle. SANM I: 684.
1733	Anonymous advocate	Anonymous advocate	Twenty-five named Genízaros request a land grant at the abandoned Pueblo of Sandia. Governor Cruzat y Góngora denies their petition. SANM I: 1208.
1734	Baltazar Romero	Petitioner	Petition to sell Spanish lands in the Bernalillo area to Santa Ana Pueblo; Governor Cruzat y Góngora denies the request, maintaining that lands should be sold to Spaniards, not Indians. SANM I: 1345.

Date	Name of Advocate	Capacity	Lawsuit
1736	Juan Páez Hurtado	Temporary magistrate	José de Riaño asks for measurement of the lands of Santa Clara and San Ildefonso so he can see where his lands between the two pueblos are. Governor Cruzat y Góngora appoints Juan Páez Hurtado to measure the two leagues. SANM I: 1039.
1737	Juan José Moreno	Alférez of the Santa Fe presidio	At the request of Alférez Moreno, Governor Enrique de Olavide y Michelena sets aside traditional grazing areas at San Marcos, Caja del Río, Santa Cruz, La Majada de Domínguez, Las Bocas, Los Cerrillos, Maragua, and San Marcos as ancient pasturelands for the horse herds of the Santa Fe presidio. Pinart Collection, Bancroft Library, University of California–Berkeley, PE 46:1 and 46:2.
1744	Isidro Sánchez	Lay advocate	Sánchez is ordered by Governor Codallos y Rabal to stop filing petitions on behalf of poor citizens. SANM I: 183.
1745	Isidro Sánchez	Lay advocate	Petition by Albuquerque residents to sell wool. Granted. SANM II: 465 A.
1746	Francisco Córdova	Hired by Antonio Casados in Mexico City	Antonio Casados, Genízaro from Belén, obtains an order from the viceroy upholding his claim as captain of "the Genízaro Pueblo of Belen" and ejecting all Spaniards from the pueblo. Later reversed in New Mexico. SANM I: 183.
1750	Tomás Vélez Cachupín	Governor	Vélez Cachupín fines José Montaño for grazing his sheep on the common lands of the Alameda grant. SANM I: 29.
1763	Felipe Tafoya	Defender of the Indians	Tafoya oversees measurement of the San Ildefonso League and ejectment of encroaching Spaniards. SANM I: 1351.
1763	Tomás Vélez Cachupín	Governor	Governor Vélez Cachupín makes the Carnuel grant, ordering that each settler be given a house lot fifty varas wide. When Alcalde Trebol Navarro allots only thirty varas to some settlers because he thinks they will not work as hard, Vélez Cachupín overrides his decision. SANM I: 202.

Date	Name of Advocate	Capacity	Lawsuit
1765	Bartolomé Fernández	Alcalde	Vélez Cachupín ejects Miguel and Domingo Romero from Cochiti Pueblo's summer pasturelands; a year later he makes the Cochiti pasture grant. SANM I: 1352.
1765	Hermenejildo Montoya	Attorney for El Paso residents	Dispute over wood gathering between El Paso citizens and Suma Indians living on their grant near El Paso; Vélez Cachupín sides with the Suma Indians, telling the El Pasoans to plant more trees on their own common lands and use them for wood gathering. SANM I: 691.
1765	José Marcelo Gallegos	Plaintiff	José Marcelo Gallegos sues Pedro Iturbieta over a cornfield that Gallegos claims to have purchased and that he has improved. Neither party has deeds to the land because it is Genízaro land farmed in common. Vélez Cachupín decides in favor of Gallegos because he has been in possession of the land for up to four years. SANM I: 362.
1766 6 Aug.	Felipe Tafoya	Alcalde	Upon the request of Tafoya, Vélez Cachupín makes the Cochiti pasture grant to Cochiti Pueblo. PLC 172, Roll 50, fr. 220–23.
1766 6 Aug.	Felipe Tafoya	Alcalde	Tafoya asks Vélez Cachupín on behalf of Zia, Santa Ana, and Jemez Pueblos for the Ojo del Espíritu Santo grant. Vélez Cachupín makes the grant. Chapter 4.
1767 Aug.	Felipe Tafoya	Advocate	Petition to get Miguel Tenorio de Alba to sign deed to Miguel Tafoya of La Ciénega property. SANM I: 991.
1786	Carlos Fernández	Attorney for San Ildefonso and Santa Clara Pueblos	Measurement of the San Ildefonso and Santa Clara Pueblos and ejectment of encroaching Spaniards. SANM I: 1354.
1812	Felipe Sandoval	Protector de Indios	Jemez Pueblo protests unauthorized land sale by Pueblo member. Chapter 1.
1815	Felipe Sandoval	Protector de Indios	Sandoval represents Pecos Pueblo when encroaching Alexander Valle grant is made. Chapter 1.

Date	Name of Advocate	Capacity	Lawsuit
1831	Francisco Archibeque	Alcalde	Further proceedings regarding the partition of Cieneguilla lands of Pablo Montoya and family; Archibeque refuses to make partition until all agree. SANM I: 627.
1888	M. C. Williams	Indian agent	Petitions commissioner of Indian affairs seeking to protect the 1766 Ojo del Espíritu Santo grant from overlapping grants. Miscellaneous letters sent by the Pueblo Indian Agency, National Archives, Washington, D.C.
1891	George Hill Howard	Attorney for Zia, Santa Ana, and Jemez Pueblos	Seeks confirmation of the 1766 Ojo del Espíritu Santo grant for the Pueblos of Zia, Santa Ana, and Jemez. PLC 50, Roll 38, fr. 580–84.
1893	N. B. Laughlin	Attorney	Seeks confirmation of the Ojo Caliente grant for land speculator Antonio Joseph. PLC 94, Roll 43, fr. 589–99.
1894	Thomas B. Catron	Attorney for Diego Baca	Seeks rejection of the 1766 Ojo del Espíritu Santo grant and confirmation of the 1815 Ojo del Espíritu Santo grant. PLC 50, Roll 38, fr. 737.
1987	Stephen Boyden and Zuni political and religious leaders	Attorneys	Zuni Pueblo is awarded $25 million for lands lost due to U.S. occupation; Zuni uses part of the funds to reacquire sacred lands at Zuni Salt Lake and Zuni Heaven. Chapter 12.
1989	Hank Meshorer	Attorney	Zuni Pueblo establishes its rights to an easement over the 110-mile pilgrimage route to Zuni Heaven. Chapter 12.
2002	Jeffrey Goldstein and legal team, experts, and land grant community	Attorney	Successors in title of original settlers of Sangre de Cristo grant are awarded use rights for grazing and wood gathering on the La Sierra tract by Colorado Supreme Court. Lobato v. Taylor, 71 P 3d 938 (Colorado 2002).

APPENDIX TWO

Santa Fe Area Land Grants

Date	Name of Grant	Citation
1693	Lucero de Godoy, Juan	SANM I: 422
1693	Madrid, Roque de	SANM I: 476
1695	Griego, María	SANM I: 337
1695	Maese, Luis	SANM I: 478
1695	Martín, Domingo	SANM I: 477
1697	Nieto, Cristóbal—El Pino grant	PLC 81, Roll 42, fr. 454
1698	Roybal, Ignacio	
1699	Jorge, Isabel	SANM I: 411
1701	Luján, Ana	SANM I: 77
1710 (prior)	Vargas, Sebastián de	SG 137, Roll 25, fr. 1286
		PLC 6, Roll 33, fr. 745
1714	Hacienda del Álamo	PLC 155, Roll 49, fr. 494
1728	Leyba, José de	PLC 278, Roll 54, fr. 297
1731	Talaya Hill	SG 89, Roll 21, fr. 1406
		PLC 116, Roll 45, fr. 919
1732	Lucero, José Antonio	SG 147, Roll 27, fr. 345
		PLC 117, Roll 45, fr. 1097
1732 (prior)	Tenorio, Manuel	PLC 188, Roll 50, fr. 689
1733	Armenta, Luis	SG 68, Roll 20, fr. 344
1742	Archuleta, Juan Antonio, and Leonardo Gonzales	PLC 104, Roll 44, fr. 1019
1742	Archuleta, Juan Jose	PLC 124, Roll 45, fr. 1341
1742	Arias de Quirós, Diego	PLC 190, Roll 50, fr. 722
1742	Domínguez, Antonio	PLC 105, Roll 444, fr. 1054
1742	Gonzales, Salvador—Cañada Ancha	SG 82, Roll 21, fr. 378
		PLC 85, Roll 42, fr. 863
1742	Brito, Juan de León	SANM I: 85

Date	Name of Grant	Citation
1742	Maese, Catarina	PLC 119, Roll 45, fr. 1154
1742	Marquez and Padilla—Chamiso Arroyo	SG 74, Roll 20, fr. 1033
1742	Pacheco, Felipe	PLC 192, Roll 50, fr. 760
1742 (prior)	Rodríguez, Juan Felipe	PLC 120, Roll 45, fr. 1174
1742	Tafoya, Felipe	SG 99, Roll 22, fr. 1362
		PLC 67, Roll 41, fr. 194
		PLC 187, Roll 50, fr. 671
1742	Tapia, Tomás	PLC 189, Roll 50, fr. 702
1742	Valdez, Domingo	SG 141, Roll 26, fr. 480
		PLC 49, Roll 38, fr. 433
1743	Durán, Jose	PLC 12, Roll 34, fr. 937
1743	Flores, Juan Antonio	PLC 125, Roll 45, fr. 1356
1744	Rael de Aguilar, Alfonso	SG 81, Roll 21, fr. 327
		SG 104, Roll 31, fr. 479
		PLC 191, Roll 50, fr. 739
1746	Romulo de Vera, José	PLC 121, Roll 45, fr. 1198
1769	Armijo, Antonio	PLC 102, Roll 44, fr. 820
1769	Pacheco, Joseph	SG 218, Roll 29, fr. 870
		PLC 18, Roll 34, fr. 1527
1785	Cañada de los Álamos	SG 53, Roll 18, fr. 589
		PLC 53, Roll 38, fr. 987
		PLC 76, Roll 41, fr. 1024
1785	Lovato, Roque	SG 52, Roll 18, fr. 532
		PLC 180, Roll 50, fr. 486

APPENDIX THREE

Land Grants in the
Cebolleta/Mount Taylor Area on the Navajo Frontier

Date/Citation	Name of Grant	Governor	Navajo Occupation
1753 1759 (revalidated)	José Montaño, Nuestra Señora de la Luz, San Fernando, and San Blas	Vélez Cachupín	Petitioners complained they had to work for the nearest pueblos, weeding their fields and bringing firewood for a few ears of corn. Alcalde Antonio Baca would receive his own grant nine years later.
1762	Antonio Baca, Nuestra Señora de la Luz y Las Lagunitas del Río Puerco	Vélez Cachupín	Alcalde Bernardo Miera y Pacheco delivered possession and received his own grant six years later. The boundaries were "on the east, the high mountain (Cebolleta Mountain) where the Navajo Apaches cultivate." Antonio Baca was alcalde for the 1759 San Fernando grant.
1766	Diego Chaves, Antonio Chaves, and Pedro Chaves	Vélez Cachupín (rejected)	Alcalde Bartolomé Fernández reported that "I have seen . . . here and there a few corn stalks, but I have never observed that the Apaches [de Navajo] lived near these small patches of corn."
1766, 23 October	Miguel and Santiago Montoya (Bosque Grande)	Vélez Cachupín	Alcalde Bartolomé Fernández noted that "in order not to impinge upon fields that are generally planted by the Navajo Apaches to the west, he completed the remainder of 5,000 varas on the northern side."

Date/Citation	Name of Grant	Governor	Navajo Occupation
1767, 11 September	Bartolomé Fernández	Mendinueta	Alcalde Carlos José Pérez de Mirabal reported, "Having ascertained whether any of them [Navajos] lived there all answered . . . that usually when out hunting a few came to reside a short time at said spring of San Miguel." Bartolomé Fernández was alcalde for the Miguel and Santiago Montoya grant and the Diego Chaves et al. grant.
1768	Ignacio Chaves	Mendinueta	"Made under the condition that they [the grantee and family] shall not dispossess those [Navajo] Indians, nor drive them away from the land they may have in occupation."
1768, 12 February	Santiago Durán y Chávez	Mendinueta	Alcalde Bartolomé Fernández reported that the grant was without prejudice to the (Navajo) Apaches who planted at San Mateo Spring. Fernández notes that "there are seven ranchos of Apache Navajo within the grant but they did not object because they were friends and [we] would assist them against the Utes."
1768, 3 March	Bernardo Miera y Pacheco and Pedro Padilla	Mendinueta	Alcalde Francisco Trebol Navarro reported that "if the survey of the league should . . . affect the planting or pastoral lands belonging to . . . [the Navajos], it shall be reduced." Miera y Pacheco was alcalde for the 1762 Antonio Baca grant.
1768, 21 May	Carlos José Pérez de Mirabal	Mendinueta	Alcalde Bartolomé Fernández reported that several settlements of Navajos were within the grant and "most had come since I [the petitioner] have been in possession without having had any trouble." Grantee was alcalde for the 1767 Bartolomé Fernández grant.
1769	Luis Jaramillo	Mendinueta	This grant "on the slope of Navajo country to pasture 1,000 sheep and a few cows" was protested by the San Fernando settlers on the Río Puerco, who lost (see chapter 10).

APPENDIX FOUR

Census of San Gabriel de las Nutrias Settlers by Vélez Cachupín

Taken by Governor Tomás Vélez Cachupín on 28 November 1765

Name	Calidad	Number in Family
1. Tomás Montoya	con su mujer y seis hijos (with his wife and seven children)	8
2. Juan Antonio García	soltero (bachelor)	1
3. Juan Varela	con su mujer y dos hijos (with his wife and two children)	4
4. Antonio Serna	con su mujer y cuatro hijos (with his wife and four children)	6
5. Juan Miguel Chaves	con su mujer y cinco hijos (with his wife and five children)	7
6. Juan Chaves	con su mujer y cinco hijos (with his wife and five children)	7
7. José Antonio Montoya	soltero con su madre y una hermana (bachelor with his mother and one sister)	3
8. Pedro Romero	con su mujer y seis hijos (with his wife and seven children)	8
9. Antonio Montoya	soltero y para casarse (bachelor [but] getting married)	1
10. Bartolo Aragón	con su mujer y cuatro hijos (with his wife and four children)	6
11. Matías Alderete	con su mujer y siete hijos (with his wife and seven children)	9
12. Vicente Gallegos	con su mujer y cuatro hijos (with his wife and four children)	6
13. María Luisa Baca	viuda con dos hijos (widow with two children)	3
14. María Baca	viuda con seis hijos (widow with six children)	7

Todas estas catorce familias están reputadas y conocidas por blancas

(All of [the above] fourteen families are known or reputed to be whites)

Name	Calidad	Number in Family
15. Antonio Chaves	mestizo con su mujer y dos hijos (mestizo with his wife and two children)	4
16. Andrés Chaves	mestizo con su mujer y cuatro hijos (mestizo with his wife and four children)	6
17. Antonio Baca	mestizo con su mujer y un hijo (mestizo with his wife and one child)	3
18. José Antonio García	mestizo con su madre y dos hermanos (mestizo with his mother and two brothers)	4
19. José Jaramillo	mestizo, soltero (mestizo, bachelor)	1
20. Gregorio Griego	mestizo con su mujer y tres hijos (mestizo with his wife and three children)	5
21. Juan Domingo Jaramillo	mestizo con su mujer y un hijo (mestizo with his wife and one child)	3
22. José [de Salas]	mestizo con su mujer y ocho hijos (mestizo with his wife and eight children)	10
23. Francisca Salas	mestiza viuda con cinco hijos (mestiza widow with her five children)	6
24. Juan Antonio Anaya	Indio con su mujer y tres hijos (Indian with his wife and three children)	5
25. Francisco Javier Anaya	Indio con su mujer y cinco hijos (Indian with his wife and five children)	7
26. Pablo Anaya	Indio con su mujer y dos hijos (Indian with his wife and two children)	4
27. Juan Chaves	Indio con su mujer y tres hijos (Indian with his wife and three children)	5
28. Manuel Bustos	mulato con su mujer y siete hijos (mulatto with his wife and seven children)	9
29. Antonio García	mulato con su mujer y un hijo (mulatto with his wife and one child)	3
30. Sánchez	Indio genízaro con su mujer y cinco hijos (Genízaro Indian with his wife and five children)	7
total de personas (total persons)		158

NOTES

Introduction and Acknowledgments

1. David Benavides, "Lawyer-Induced Partitioning of New Mexican Land Grants: An Ethical Travesty" (Guadalupita, NM: Center for Land Grant Studies Research Paper, 2005), www.southwestbooks.org.

2. Charles R. Cutter, *The Protector de Indios in Colonial New Mexico, 1659–1821* (Albuquerque: University of New Mexico Press, 1986), 47–55. Although Spanish law provided for payment of a salary to the Protector of Indians, it is not clear how much protectors in New Mexico actually received.

3. The most corrupt of the men to hold the office of Protector de Indios was Ignacio María Sánchez Vergara, who sometimes made arguments in court that were against the interests of the pueblos he was representing and even used his position to acquire pueblo land for himself. For more on Sánchez Vergara, see Malcolm Ebright, Rick Hendricks, and Richard Hughes, *Four Square Leagues: Pueblo Indian Land in New Mexico* (Albuquerque: University of New Mexico Press, 2014), chapter 4.

4. Antonio Joseph is described by David Caffey as a secondary rather than a core participant in the Santa Fe Ring. Caffey list only fourteen members of the core group and twenty-eight secondary ring participants in his excellent study, *Chasing the Santa Fe Ring: Power and Privilege in Territorial New Mexico* (Albuquerque: University of New Mexico Press, 2014), 247.

5. James Dory-Garduño, "The 1766 Ojo del Espíritu Santo Grant: Authenticating a New Mexico Land Grant," *Colonial Latin American Historical Review* 16 (Spring 2007): 157–96; James Dory-Garduño, "The Adjudication of the Ojo del Espíritu Santo Grant of 1766 and the Recopilación," *New Mexico Historical Review* 87 (Spring 2012): 167–208; Linda Tigges, "The Pastures of the Royal Horse Herd of the Santa Fe Presidio, 1692–1740," in *All Trails Lead to Santa Fe: An Anthology Commemorating the 400th Anniversary of the Founding of Santa Fe* (Santa Fe, NM: Sunstone Press, 2010).

6. The San Cristóbal Ranch contains about 81,000 acres; in 1990 and 1991 the New Mexico Office of Archeology conducted an excavation (LA 3333) prior to the widening of U.S. 285 to accommodate the transport of nuclear waste from Los Alamos to the Waste Isolation Pilot Plant (WIPP) in Carlsbad. Christina Singleton Mednick, *San Cristóbal: Voices and Visions of the Galisteo Basin* (Santa Fe: Museum of New Mexico Press, 1996), 205, 231–33; Cordelia Thomas Snow, telephone interview, 28 May 2014.

7. Albert H. Schroeder, "Pueblos Abandoned in Historic Times," in *Handbook of North American Indians*, edited by William Sturtevant, Vol. 9, *Southwest*, edited by Alfonso Ortiz (Washington, D.C.: Smithsonian Institution, 1979), 247–48; for Lehman Spiegelberg and the Santa Fe Ring, see Caffey, *Chasing the Santa Fe Ring*, 251.

8. H. Wolcott Toll and Jessica Badner, *Galisteo Basin Archeological Sites Protection Act Site Assessment Project* (Santa Fe: Office of Archeological Studies and New Mexico Department of Cultural Affairs, 2008), 146.

9. Ebright and Hendricks, *Witches of Abiquiu*, 80–82.

10. Order of Diego de Vargas, Santa Fe, 16 March 1695, Rick Hendricks, John L. Kessell, and Meredith Dodge, eds., *Blood on the Boulders: The Journals of Don Diego de Vargas, New Mexico, 1694–97*, 2 vols. (Albuquerque: University of New Mexico Press, 1998), 1:605.

Chapter One

1. Henry Wagner, *The Life and Writings of Bartolomé de Las Casas* (Albuquerque: University of New Mexico Press, 1967), 178–82; Lewis Hanke, *The Spanish Struggle for Justice in the Conquest of America* (Boston, MA: Little, Brown, 1965); Lewis Hanke, *Aristotle and the American Indians: A Study of Race Prejudice in the Modern World* (Bloomington and London: Indiana University Press, 1959). The latter work focuses on how both Sepúlveda and Las Casas accepted Aristotle's theory of natural slavery. For a comparison of Spanish theories justifying conquest with those of other European powers, see Anthony Pagden, *Lords of All the World: Ideologies of Empire in Spain, Britain and France, c.1500–c.1800* (New Haven, CT: Yale University Press, 1995). For a recent analysis of the writings of the Spanish jurist Juan de Solórzano Pereira in this regard, see James Muldoon, *The Americas in the Spanish World Order: The Justification for Conquest in the Seventeenth Century* (Philadelphia: University of Pennsylvania Press, 1994).

2. Hanke, *Aristotle and the American Indians*, 50.

3. Ralph H. Vigil, *Alonso de Zorita: Royal Judge and Christian Humanist, 1512–1585* (Norman: University of Oklahoma Press, 1987), 37–38; Zorita even cited Aztec law as precedent for exempting the Indians of Mexico City from paying tribute.

Benjamin Keen, introduction to *Life and Labor in Ancient Mexico: The Brief and Summary Relation of the Lords of New Spain by Alonzo de Zorita* (Norman: University of Oklahoma Press, 1994), 28–30, 42–43.

4. Hanke, *Spanish Struggle for Justice*, 12–13.

5. The reform ordinances (Leyes Nuevas) of 1542 were the first laws adopted to protect Indians in New Spain. They provided for the abolition of the encomienda, of forced labor, and of tribute on the part of the Indians, who were placed under the protection of the crown. Indian slaves were set free, and advocates were to be named for them at royal expense where a Spanish owner could show no title to the Indian. Wagner, *Life and Writings of Bartolomé de Las Casas*, 114–16; Bartolomé de Las Casas, *The Devastation of the Indies: A Brief Account*, trans. Herma Briffault (Baltimore: Johns Hopkins University Press, 1992).

6. Constance Ann Carter, "Law and Society in Colonial Mexico: *Audiencia* Judges in Mexican Society from the *Tello de Sandoval Visita General*, 1543–1547" (PhD diss., Columbia University, 1971), 12–13; Susan Kellogg, *Law and the Transformation of Aztec Culture, 1500–1700* (Norman: University of Oklahoma Press, 1995), 10–15; Charles R. Cutter, *The Protector de Indios in Colonial New Mexico, 1659–1821* (Albuquerque: University of New Mexico Press, 1986), 16–17. For a discussion of lawyers in sixteenth-century Castile, see Richard L. Kagan, *Lawsuits and Litigants in Castile: 1500–1700* (Chapel Hill: University of North Carolina Press, 1981), 52–78.

7. The abuses of self-appointed *protectores* or *defensores* who took advantage of the indigenous people led to the outlawing of these positions altogether in the audiencia of Quito. Woodrow Borah, *Justice by Insurance: The General Indian Court of Colonial Mexico and the Legal Aides of the Half-Real* (Berkeley, Los Angeles, London: University of California Press, 1983), 79–91; Kellogg, *Law and the Transformation of Aztec Culture*, 13–21.

8. Cutter, *Protector de Indios*, 12–20. In Peru, Indian litigation was more often directed at the mita or requirement of forced labor, but land litigation was also prevalent. Steve J. Stern, *Peru's Indian Peoples and the Challenge of Spanish Conquest: Huamanga to 1640* (Madison: University of Wisconsin Press, 1982), 114–37.

9. Stern, *Peru's Indian Peoples*, 116.

10. Robert M. Hill II, "The Social Uses of Writing among the Colonial Cakchiquel Maya: Nativism, Resistance, and Innovation," in *Columbian Consequences: The Spanish Borderlands in Pan-American Perspective*, ed. David Hunt Thomas (Washington, D.C.: Smithsonian Institution Press, 1991), 3:294–95.

11. Charles Cutter, *The Legal Culture of Northern New Spain: 1700–1810* (Albuquerque: University of New Mexico Press, 1995), 69–102. For an evaluation of the

fairness and impartiality of several eighteenth-century New Mexican governors, see Malcolm Ebright, "Frontier Land Litigation in Colonial New Mexico: A Determinant of Spanish Custom and Law," *Western Legal History* 8 (Summer/ Fall 1995): 197–226; and Malcolm Ebright, "Breaking New Ground: A Reappraisal of Governors Vélez Cachupín and Mendinueta and Their Land Grant Policies," *Colonial Latin American Historical Review* 5 (Spring 1996): 195–233.

12. One of the worst cases on record is that of Fray Salvador de Guerra, who punished the Indian Juan Cuna so severely that he died. Cuna's only offense was mimicking the priest. Although he was reprimanded by his superiors, Guerra was back in favor by 1661, when he became notary for Fray Alonso de Posada, commissary of the Holy Office of the Inquisition. France V. Scholes, "Troublous Times in New Mexico," *New Mexico Historical Review* 12 (1937): 144–46; and Scholes, "Troublous Times," *New Mexico Historical Review* 10 (1937): 388.

13. John L. Kessell, "Spaniards and Pueblos: From Crusading Intolerance to Pragmatic Accommodation," in *Columbian Consequences: The Spanish Borderlands in Pan-American Perspective*, ed. David Hunt Thomas (Washington, D.C.: Smithsonian Institution Press, 1991), 1:127–38; Marc Simmons, "The Pueblo Revolt: Why Did It Happen," *El Palacio* 86 (Winter 1980–1981): 11–15; Carroll L. Riley, *Rio del Norte: People of the Upper Rio Grande from Earliest Times to the Pueblo Revolt* (Salt Lake City: University of Utah Press, 1995), 270.

14. For more on Diego Romero, see John Kessell, "Diego Romero, the Plains Apaches, and the Inquisition," *American West* 15 (May–June 1978): 12–16; Cutter, *Protector de Indios*, 31–33.

15. Cutter, *Protector de Indios*, 76–77, 109; Cutter, *Legal Culture*, 100–101.

16. Fray Angélico Chávez, *New Mexico Families* (Santa Fe, NM: William Gannon, 1975), 263.

17. In 1715 Rael de Aguilar II fatally stabbed Sergeant Francisco Tamarís from the Santa Fe presidio and then sought sanctuary in various mission churches. Alfonso Jr. may have been bailed out of this predicament by his father when the widow and son of Tamarís formally pardoned Alfonso Jr., after pointedly mentioning the creditors who were hounding them to pay the debts of the victim. Criminal proceedings against Alfonso Rael for death of Francisco Tamarís, Santa Fe, 14 December 1715–31 July 1716, Santa Fe, Spanish Archives of New Mexico (hereafter SANM) II: 239; a government pardon (*indulto*) was secured from Governor Felix Martínez in return for his serving in a military campaign against the Hopi, SANM II: 256a; Cutter, *Legal Culture*, 129; J. Manuel Espinosa, *Crusaders of the Rio Grande* (Chicago, IL: Institute of Jesuit History, 1942), 247.

18. Lansing B. Bloom, "A Campaign against the Moqui Pueblos," *New Mexico Historical Review* 6 (April 1931): 206, 158–226.

19. John Kessell, Rick Hendricks, Meredith D. Dodge, and Larry C. Miller, eds., *That*

Disturbances Cease: The Journals of Don Diego de Vargas, New Mexico, 1697–1700 (Albuquerque: University of New Mexico Press, 2000), 85. The fundo legal in central Mexico varied from six hundred varas measured from the outskirts (*casco*) of the Indian town to a league measured from the church in the center of the town. The Spanish claimed that the Indians would move the last building in the settlement farther from the center to increase the size of the fundo legal. It seems likely that New Mexico's Pueblo league arose from this tradition. Borah, *Justice by Insurance*, 136–137; G. Emlen Hall, *Four Leagues of Pecos: A Legal History of the Pecos Grant, 1800–1933* (Albuquerque: University of New Mexico Press, 1984), 12–13.

20. "Tienen más de lo que manda la ley," petition of Cristóbal and Juan Barela Jaramillo to Governor Vargas, Bernalillo, February 1704, SANM I: 78.

21. *Desde su fundación*, report of Rael de Aguilar, San Felipe, 23 February 1704, SANM I: 78.

22. "Tiene concedido por ley real a los pueblos de dichos naturales," Rael de Aguilar to Vargas, San Felipe, 23 February 1704, SANM I: 78. This language would seem to contradict Hall's assertion that until the mid-1700s the Pueblo league was considered as a zone of protection from Spanish encroachment rather than an area owned by the pueblos. Hall, *Four Leagues of Pecos*, 13.

23. An example of Rael de Aguilar making subtle changes in the words of others occurs when the Jaramillos ask that the lands of the Indians of San Felipe Pueblo be measured, and Rael changes that to a request that the league of the Indians be measured. Petition of Cristóbal and Juan Barela Jaramillo to Governor Vargas, Bernalillo, February 1704, SANM I: 78; report of Rael de Aguilar, San Felipe, 23 February 1704, SANM I: 78.

24. Petition of Ignacio Roybal (n.d.) and grant by Governor Vargas, Santa Fe, 4 March 1704, SANM I: 1339. This rather summary procedure was common in the early 1700s as also illustrated by the 1702 Jacona grant also made to Ignacio Roybal, but by the mid-1700s failure to notify adjoining owners became a ground for rejecting a grant under Governors Vélez Cachupín and Mendinueta. SANM I: 1352.

25. SANM I: 1339.

26. Petition of Alfonso Rael de Aquilar on behalf of San Ildefonso Pueblo to Lieutenant Governor Juan Páez Hurtado, Santa Fe, 16 September, SANM I: 1339; grant to Ignacio Roybal by Governor Vargas, witnessed by Rael de Aguilar, Santa Fe, 4 March 1704, SANM I: 1339.

27. *Recopilación de Leyes de los Reynos de las Indias* 4.12.12 and 6.3.20 (Spanish ranches not to be located near Indian communities) and 4.7.1 (Spanish communities not to be established where Indians' rights would be prejudiced).

28. When Governor Vargas reconquered the province, he promised those who

accompanied him the lands they owned prior to the revolt. Edict of Governor
Vargas published at El Paso and surrounding communities, 20 September 1693;
John L. Kessell, Rick Hendricks, and Meridith Dodge, eds., *To the Royal Crown
Restored: The Journals of Don Diego de Vargas, New Mexico, 1692–94* (Albu-
querque: University of New Mexico Press, 1995), 374–77.

29. For a list of cases in which the four-square-league standard is mentioned, see
William B. Taylor, "Colonial Land and Water Rights of New Mexico Indian
Pueblos," unpublished report on file in New Mexico v. Aamodt, No. 6639, Federal
District Court for New Mexico, 44. See also, Malcolm Ebright, Rick Hendricks,
and Richard Hughes, *Four Square Leagues: Pueblo Indian Land in New Mexico*
(Albuquerque: University of New Mexico Press, 2014), chapter 1.

30. Order of Governor Páez Hurtado, Santa Fe, September 1704, SANM I: 1339.
Governor Juan Páez Hurtado served between Governors de Vargas and Cuervo
y Valdés (1705–1707) and was a trusted lieutenant for Governor Vargas. He
supervised the settlement of Santa Cruz de la Canada in 1695 and was rewarded
with his own land grant in 1784 between Pojoaque and Nambe Pueblos.

31. "Por no [h]aber tierra de labor en que apuntar por todos vientos la legua [que es]
lo que dicen los naturales piden y no montes, lomas, ni aun de donde no se pueda
sembrar," SANM I: 1339.

32. Petition of Protector Alfonso Rael de Aguilar on behalf of San Ildefonso Pueblo,
Santa Fe, September 1704, SANM I: 1339.

33. The Spanish-speaking Pueblo governors were Cristóbal Coris of Santo Domingo,
Luis Conitzu of Jemez, Felipe Pacheco of Taos, Francisco Enecenoe of Nambe,
Antonio Cossío of Zia, and Felipe and Joseph, governors of Santa Ana and
Acoma. Certification of Alfonso Rael de Aguilar, Santa Fe, 10 January 1706,
translation in Charles W. Hackett, ed. and trans., *Historical Documents Relating
to New Mexico, Nueva Vizcaya, and Approaches Thereto, to 1773* (Washington,
D.C.: Carnegie Institution, 1923–1937), 3:366–69.

34. Rael de Aguilar certification, Santa Fe, 10 January 1706, in Hackett, *Historical
Documents*, 368.

35. On 23 April 1706, Governor Cuervo y Valdés wrote to the viceroy describing how
he had founded a new villa named after the viceroy at the location of present-day
Albuquerque. But the community did not exist: it was fabricated by Cuervo to
impress the viceroy. The thirty-five families who were supposed to have received
a community grant did not exist, the church that was supposed to have been built
there did not exist, and the orderly town did not exist. Instead, there was a collection of farms scattered along the Río Grande based on individual land grants,
many of which had belonged to these families before the Pueblo Revolt. Marc
Simmons, *Albuquerque: A Narrative History* (Albuquerque: University of New
Mexico Press, 1982), 81–92.

36. Election of Alfonso Rael de Aguilar as *alcalde ordinario* of the Santa Fe Cabildo, Santa Fe, 1 January 1707, SANM II: 130; John L. Kessell, *Kiva, Cross, and Crown* (Washington, D.C.: National Park Service, 1979), 313–14.

37. Prior to the Pueblo Revolt, Cochiti had a larger population than did Santo Domingo, but casualties during the revolt and due to epidemics and an influx of Tano-speaking Pueblo people into Santo Domingo resulted in that pueblo becoming larger than Cochiti after the revolt. Charles H. Lange, *Cochití: A New Mexico Pueblo, Past and Present* (Albuquerque: University of New Mexico Press, 1959), 11. Both pueblos gained a measure of agricultural prosperity after the revolt and became suppliers of lettuce, garlic, and chile to nearby Spanish communities. Marc Simmons, "History of Pueblo-Spanish Relations to 1821," in *Handbook of North American Indians*, ed. William Sturtevant, vol. 9, *Southwest*, ed. Alfonso Ortiz (Washington, D.C.: Smithsonian Institution, 1979), 9:190.

38. Report of Alfonso Rael de Aguilar, Santo Domingo, 8 June 1722, SANM I: 1343. As with earlier Rael de Aguilar documents, this one is entirely in his handwriting.

39. For a listing of the size of the pueblo grants, see Ebright, Hendricks, and Hughes, *Four Square Leagues*, app. 1. Other cases of land granted to pueblos beyond the Pueblo league were the Ojo de Espíritu Santo Grazing grant jointly to Zia, Santa Ana, and Jemez by Governor Vélez Cachupín in 1776, SG Report TT, Roll 7, fr. 341–90; PLC 50, Roll 01138, fr. 575–755; the Cochiti pasture grant, also made by Governor Vélez Cachupín in 1776, Juana Baca [Cochiti pasture] grant, PLC 172, Roll 50, fr. 220–23 (both discussed in chapter 4) in 1770; SG 142, Roll 26, fr. 527–708; and the Ojo de Cabra grant, where claim was made by Isleta Pueblo that the land was their common grazing land. The Departmental Assembly decided in 1845 that the land surrounding the spring was the joint commons of Isleta Pueblo and the communities of Valencia, Pajarito, and Las Padillas. A claimed grant in the area to Juan Otero was rejected. SANM I: 1381.

40. Criminal proceedings against Gerónimo Dirucaca, 8 May 1713, SANM II: 192. This case is discussed in Cutter, *Protector de Indios*, 54–55, quote on 55; and in Tracy L. Brown, *Pueblo Indians and Spanish Colonial Authority in Eighteenth Century New Mexico* (Tucson: University of Arizona Press, 2013), 46.

41. Petition of Juan de Atienza, on behalf of Pojoaque Pueblo, to Governor Juan Ignacio Flores Mogollón, Villa Nueva de Santa Cruz, May 1715, SANM I: 7; this case is discussed briefly in Cutter, *Protector de Indios*, 55–56.

42. Rodríguez Cubero was less protective of Pueblo Indians and Genízaros than had been Governor Diego de Vargas, whose two terms as governor came before (1691–1697) and after (1703–1704) Cubero's term. For example, Vargas was accused in his *residencia* of returning Indian captives (Genízaros) to the pueblos instead of giving them to the colonists as servants, but Cubero apparently reversed this

policy. Rick Hendricks, "Pedro Rodríguez Cubero: New Mexico's Reluctant Governor, 1697–1703," *New Mexico Historical Review* 68 (January 1993): 28–33; SANM I: 7.

43. Decree of Flores Mogollón appointing Rael de Aguilar as juez receptor, Santa Fe, 12 June 1715, SANM I: 7.

44. If the pueblo failed to comply with the decree, Tenorio could sell the land to someone else, as long as he returned what was paid him by the Indians. Decree of Governor Peñuela, Santa Fe, 1 April 1712, SANM I: 7.

45. Report of Alfonso Rael de Aguilar, Santo Domingo, 8 June 1722, SANM I: 7.

46. Juan de Atienza to Governor Felix Martínez, Santa Fe, April 1716, SANM I: 7.

47. "Y no haber podido venir a si quirse como debía hacerlo," Alfonso Rael de Aguilar to Governor Flores Mogollón, Santa Fe, 2 May 1716, SANM I: 7.

48. Juan Atienza Alcalá must have had good connections in Mexico City, for in 1716 his father, Joseph de Atienza Alcalá, received a license from the viceroy allowing the family to leave New Mexico. SANM II: 262.

49. Power of Attorney to Ventura de Esquibel, Pueblo of San Agustin de la Isleta, 16 May 1733, SANM I: 684.

50. SANM I: 1343.

51. Answer to Isleta Pueblo filed by Ventura Esquibel, Isleta, May 1733, SANM I: 684.

52. Declaration of Diego Padilla, Río Abajo, [18] May 1733, SANM I: 684.

53. Answer of Ventura Esquibel on behalf of Isleta Pueblo, Isleta, [19] May 1733, SANM I: 684.

54. Decrees of Governor Cruzat y Góngora, Santa Fe, 28 May 1733 and 23 June 1733, SANM I: 684; Cutter, *Legal Culture*, 90–91; SANM II: 335.

55. Ventura Esquibel surfaced again in 1734 when he petitioned for his own land grant in the Santa Cruz area. Ventura Esquibel's land grant petition was denied by Governor Cruzat y Góngora because Alcalde Juan Esteban García de Noriega reported that the land had already been granted to Diego Torres. Petition of Ventura Esquibel for the surplus lands of Diego Torres, report of Alcalde Esteban García de Noriega, and decrees of Governor Gervacio Cruzat y Góngora, 23 January through 13 March 1734, SANM I: 259.

56. Petition of los Genízaros to Governor Cruzat y Góngora, April 1733, SANM I: 1208.

57. For a good history of the Jumanos, see Nancy Parrott Hickerson, *The Jumanos: Hunters and Traders of the South Plains* (Austin: University of Texas Press, 1994).

58. Steven Michael Horvath, "The Social and Political Organization of the *Genízaros* of Plaza de Nuestra Señora de Dolores de Belén, New Mexico, 1740–1812" (PhD diss., Brown University, 1979), 130–33. For a recent summary of various definitions of Genízaros, see Oakah L. Jones Jr., "Rescue and Ransom of Spanish Captives from the *Indios Bárbaros* on the Northern Frontier of New Spain," *Colonial*

Latin American Historical Review 4 (Spring 1995): 131–33; bando of Governor Cruzat y Góngora, Santa Fe, 6 December 1732, SANM II: 378.

59. Ebright, "Frontier Land Litigation," 211–14; see also chapter 10.

60. *Que olvidados nuestros primeros pes de tanto bien y beneficio, y soltando riendas a su desordendo deseo . . . regando la [tierra] con prolijo sudor de nuestro rostro,* petition of los Genízaros to Governor Cruzat y Góngora, April 1733, SANM I: 1208.

61. Ibid.

62. Bartolomé de Las Casas, *Historia de las Indias,* book 3, chapter 102, translated in Hanke, *Spanish Struggle for Justice,* 125; Fray Angélico Chávez, "*Genízaros,*" in *Handbook of North American Indians,* ed. William Sturtevant, vol. 9, *Southwest,* ed. Alfonso Ortiz (Washington, D.C.: Smithsonian Institution, 1979), 9:198–99.

63. Proceedings in the trial of Isleta Indians for witchcraft, 11–19 February 1733, SANM II: 38. While the practices described in this lawsuit would subject a Spaniard to prosecution by the Mexican Inquisition, Indians were exempt from its jurisdiction, so this case was tried by civil authorities. Fernando Cervantes, *The Devil in the New World: The Impact of Diabolism in New Spain* (New Haven, CT: Yale University Press, 1994), 37. In the Isleta witchcraft trial, the Indian "el Cacique" had admitted being the leader of a coven of witches responsible for placing spells on the local priest and several members of the Spanish elite. According to the testimony, they made dolls that resembled their victims and then pierced them with pins. This ritual was performed by the group after donning special robes and anointing themselves with dust from a magical stone.

64. For a Genízaro witchcraft trial in which the location and destruction of power objects or idols was of paramount importance to the Spanish authorities, see *Autos sequiaos contra unos Indios Genízaros del Pueblo de Abiquiu sobre ser acusados de echiceros maleficos por su Mnro el Rdo Pe Fr, Juan Joseph Toledo y el Indio Juachinillo del mismo pueblo,* Pinart Collection, Bancroft Library, University of California–Berkeley, PE 52:5, discussed in detail in Malcolm Ebright and Rick Hendricks, *The Witches of Abiquiu: The Governor, the Priest, the Genízaro Indians and the Devil* (Albuquerque: University of New Mexico Press, 2006).

65. Order of Governor Cruzat y Góngora, Santa Fe, 21 April 1733, SANM I: 1208.

66. List of Genízaros [Alfonso Rael de Aguilar], [22] April 1733, SANM I: 1208.

67. Order of Governor Cruzat y Góngora, Santa Fe, 23 April 1733, SANM I: 1208. The abandoned Sandia Pueblo was finally settled in 1748 with a grant to 441 Tiwas who returned from the Moqui settlements.

68. Proceedings by virtue of an order of the viceroy, Count of Fuenclara, regarding the complaint of Antonio Casados and Luis Quintana for a Genízaro settlement at Belén. SANM I: 183.

69. "Contra lo dispuesto por su magad en sus leyes reales," order of Governor Cruzat y Góngora, Santa Fe, 1 March 1734, SANM I: 1345.

70. For a discussion of Santa Ana Pueblo's land purchases in the early eighteenth century, see Ebright, Hendricks, and Hughes, *Four Square Leagues*, chapter 2; Laura Bayer with Floyd Montoya and the Pueblo of Santa Ana, *Santa Ana: The People, the Pueblo, and the History of Tamaya* (Albuquerque: University of New Mexico Press, 1994), 77–79.

71. Oakah L. Jones Jr., *Pueblo Warriors and Spanish Conquest* (Norman: University of Oklahoma Press, 1966), 116–17; order of Governor Codallos y Rabal, Santa Fe, 4 February 1746, SANM II: 495. For a discussion of the Comanche-Apache war for the southern plains, see Pekka Hämäläinen, *The Comanche Empire* (New Haven: Yale University Press, 2008), 31–37.

72. Inventory of cases turned over to Governor Tomás Vélez Cachupín by his predecessor Governor Joaquín Codallos y Rabal, Santa Fe, 3 April 1749, SANM I: 1258.

73. "Es hombre cabiloso enquieto que insista a algunos pobres vecinos a que tengan pleitos haciendoles escritos y cooperando a ellos," order of Codallos y Rabal, Santa Fe, 1 March 1744, SANM I: 463. See petition of Albuquerque residents to sell wool, 16 June 1745, SANM II: 456A, cited in Cutter, *Legal Culture*, 101. Isidro Sánchez had been in trouble with the law almost a decade earlier for an alleged robbery. Pedro de Villasur, proceedings against Isidro Sánchez for robbery, Santa Fe, 25 March–April 1719, SANM II: 307.

74. Francisca Salas v. Alcalde Joseph Baca, 16 May 1744, SANM II: 453.

75. Royal orders of 1521 and 1538 prohibited officials from placing any restriction on those who "wish to write and give an account of everything that appears to them to be convenient." Hanke, *Spanish Struggle for Justice*, 9, n. 24.

76. Declaration of Antonio Casados, Santa Fe, 12 February 1746, SANM I: 183.

77. Order of Viceroy, Count of Fuenclara, Mexico City, 20 October 1745; auto of Codallos y Rabal, Santa Fe, 11 February 1746, SANM I: 183.

78. Auto of Governor Codallos y Rabal, Santa Fe, 11 February 1746, SANM I: 183.

79. The plaza of Nuestra Señora de los Dolores de los Genízaros was comprised mostly of Genízaros, and the Belén plaza, No. 2 contained a few Genízaros. Horvath, "*Genízaros* at Belén," 130–33. Of the sixty-eight family heads listed at the Genízaro plaza in 1790, twenty-seven were listed as Genízaro, and most of the Indios and several of the mestizos were designated as Genízaro in other documents. Ebright, "Frontier Land Litigation," 211–14; SANM I: 183; see also chapter 10.

80. In 1718 Cochiti Pueblo filed a complaint with the cabildo of Santa Fe against Alcalde Manuel Baca and his teniente Antonio Baca, who was his son. Governor Valverde decided in favor of the pueblo, removing Antonio Baca from office, ordering him to remove his animals from Cochiti lands, and ordering him to go

on the next two campaigns "against the enemy who invade this kingdom." Nevertheless, Antonio Baca was in office again in the 1750s and 1760s, until he, too, was removed by Governor Vélez Cachupín based on a petition signed by forty-five residents of his jurisdiction complaining of bribery, persecution, and various other offenses. In spite of this, Baca's son-in-law, Francisco Trebol Navarro, was serving as an alcalde in 1768, and again, protests were filed charging him with misconduct and of being influenced unfairly by his father-in-law, Antonio Baca. This time Trebol Navarro was upheld by Governor Mendinueta, who even appointed him acting governor at the end of his term of office. Proceedings of the Santa Fe cabildo against Manuel Baca and Antonio Baca for mistreatment of Indians, complaint of forty-five vecinos of Albuquerque against Alcalde Antonio Baca, Albuquerque, August 1763, Pinart Collection, Bancroft Library, University of California–Berkeley, PE 52:11.

81. Governor Vélez Cachupín ordered Alcalde Antonio Baca to place the settlers of Carnuel in possession of their grant, giving them house lots fifty varas square. Instead, Alcalde Baca gave some settlers lots thirty varas square and others larger lots. Vélez Cachupín shot back an order to Baca stating: "It is not within his authority to [make changes] and he shall be warned that in the future he shall not exceed his powers." Act of possession by Alcalde Antonio Baca, San Miguel de Laredo [Carnuel], 12 February 1763, Order of Governor Vélez Cachupín, 20 February 1763 and 12 February 1763, SANM I: 202.

82. Order of Governor Vélez Cachupín, Santa Fe, 3 December 1766, SANM I: 688.

83. For a discussion of the lawsuits decided by Governor Vélez Cachupín see chapter 10.

84. J. Richard Salazar, "The Felipe Tafoya Grant: A Grazing Grant in West Central New Mexico," Center for Land Grant Studies Research Paper, Guadalupita, NM, 2005, 12, www.southwestbooks.org; SANM II: 579; Chávez, *New Mexico Families*, 291. Some of the cases in which Tafoya acted as an advocate are Naranjo v. Torres's heirs, SANM I: 1348; Valerio v. Atienza, SANM I: 1050; San Felipe v. Baca, SANM I: 643; San Fernando v. Atrisco, SANM I: 111; María Romero, sale of lands by minors, SANM I: 783; SANM I: 571. As for Tafoya as alcalde of Santa Fe, see SANM I: 696.

85. Chávez, *New Mexico Families*, 291.

86. Cutter, *Legal Culture*, 87–88; Domingo Luján v. Cristóbal Jaramillo, Santa Fe, 9–24 August 1755, SANM II: 531a.

87. Tafoya alleged that San Ildefonso had suffered intrusions within their boundaries ever since the administration of Pedro Rodríguez Cubero. Petition of Felipe Tafoya, Santa Fe, February 1763, SANM I: 1351.

88. This argument was still used over two hundred years later when the Hispanic community in Taos was listing its objections to awarding trust title to Blue

Lake to the Taos Indians. Vísita of Governor Marín del Valle, *Sin admitirle el mas leve recurso*, petition of Felipe Tafoya, Santa Fe, February 1763, SANM I: 1351; measurements by Alcalde Carlos Fernández, San Ildefonso, 17–18 February 1763, SANM I: 1354. Under the Spanish doctrine of prescription, title to land could be acquired through possession alone, and if the period was at least thirty years, title could be acquired even if the property was stolen. *Las Siete Partidas*, book 3, title 29, law 21; order of Vélez Cachupín, Santa Fe, 12 November 1763, SANM I: 1351; opinion of Fernando de Torija y Leri, San Felipe del Real [de Chihuahua], 27 October 1764, SANM I: 1351.

89. "Sin abrir la puerta a muchos ejenplares que resultaran a los demas pueblos en yguales terminos," order of Vélez Cachupín, Santa Fe, 12 November 1763, SANM I: 1351; opinion of Fernando de Torija y Leri, San Felipe del Real [de Chihuahua], 27 October 1764, SANM I: 1351.

90. "La legua que el Rey Nuestro Señor . . . concede a cada pueblo," petition of Carlos Fernández to Governor Anza, Santa Fe, [May] 1786, SANM I: 1354.

91. "Un cordel encerada que contenga cien varas," order of Governor Anza, Santa Fe, 6 May 1786, SANM I: 1354.

92. Measurement proceedings by alcalde Campo Redondo, Santa Clara, 10 May 1786; referral by Governor Anza to Carlos Fernández, Santa Fe, 13 May 1786, SANM I: 1354.

93. Statement of Carlos Fernández, Santa Fe, 13 May 1786, SANM I: 1354.

94. Statement of Marcos Lucero, [18] May 1786, SANM I: 1354.

95. Order of Governor Anza, Santa Fe, 19 May 1786, SANM I: 1354.

96. "Por el enserado no da de si, y el no enserado da mucho," measurement by alcalde Campo Redondo, Santa Clara, 23 May 1786, SANM I: 1354.

97. "Un cordel compuesto de lanzos, cabrestos y coyundas," statement of Carlos Fernández, Santa Fe, [29] May 1786, SANM I: 1354.

98. Ibid.

99. Statement of Marcos Lucero, [Santa Fe], [2] June 1786, SANM I: 1354; deposition of Juan Ignacio Mestas, Santa Fe, 8 June 1786, SANM I: 1354; deposition of Cristóbal Maese, Santa Fe, 8 June 1786, SANM I: 1354.

100. Decree of Governor Anza, Santa Fe, 10 June 1786, SANM I: 1354.

101. This is evidence that a copy of the *Recopilación* existed in New Mexico at this time, for Anza says, "and having before me the royal laws." Decree of Governor Anza, Santa Fe, 10 June 1786, SANM I: 1354.

102. *Recopilación* 6.3.8; decree of Governor Anza, Santa Fe, 10 June 1786, SANM I: 1354.

103. Ibid.

104. Decree of Governor Anza, Santa Fe, 10 June 1786, SANM I: 1354.

105. Statement of Carlos Fernández, Santa Fe, [29] May 1786, SANM I: 1354.

106. Statement of Marcos Lucero, [Santa Fe], [2] June 1786, SANM I: 1354.

107. Greater recognition of Genízaro Indian property rights is evidenced by the fact that Felipe Sandoval's appointment as protector mentioned the Genízaro settlement at Abiquiu as one of his protected clients. Cutter, *Protector de Indios*, 81–83. Sandoval was raised by Vicar Santiago Roybal, from whom he would have gained additional knowledge about legal procedures as they relate to the church. Chávez, *New Mexico Families*, 283.

108. Decree of Governor Máynez, 29 March 1815; Alexander Valle grant, SG 18, Roll 14, fr. 675 et seq.

109. Felipe Sandoval is said to have been an instigator of the aborted 1805 San Miguel del Bado revolt against the central government in Santa Fe. Hall, *Four Leagues of Pecos*, 20.

110. Petition of Felipe Sandoval, Jemez Pueblo, Santa Fe, 28 August 1812, SANM I: 1355.

111. Felipe Sandoval to Governor Máynez, Santa Fe, 15 April 1815, SANM I: 1357.

112. Real Audiencia de Guadalajara, Judicial-civil 261-15-3564, "El común del Pueblo de Cochiti," f. 69; Cutter, *Protector de Indios*, 89.

113. Cutter, *Protector de Indios*, 88–92; SANM I: 1283.

114. Appointment of Sánchez Vergara as Protector de Indios, Guadalajara, 2 July 1817, SANM II: 2692; Cutter, *Protector de Indios*, 93–94.

115. Cutter, *Protector de Indios*, 94–95.

116. Petition of Sánchez Vergara to Governor Melgares, Santa Fe, 5 July 1821, SANM I: 1195.

117. Ebright, Hendricks, and Hughes, *Four Square Leagues*, chapter 4.

118. Andrés Romero, Juan José Gutiérrez, and Rafael Miera, depositions regarding land ownership in the vicinity of Sandia Pueblo, Bernalillo [Sandia], 18 May 1829, Archivo General de la Nación, Mexico City, Justicia 48:24. For a photo of the mutilated Sandia Pueblo grant, see Ebright, Hendricks, and Hughes, *Four Square Leagues*, 133.

119. Cutter, *Protector de Indios*, 95–97.

120. After the boundary litigation in 1813, the courts mandated the return to Santa Ana of land on its side of the boundary, much of which was occupied by Spaniards, many of whom claimed to have deeds from either San Felipe or Santa Ana Pueblos. Initially, Sánchez Vergara was in accord with this idea, recommending that the trespassing Spaniards be reimbursed with royal lands, without indicating where those lands were located. When lands at Santa Rosa de Cubero were suggested, San Felipe and Santo Domingo Pueblos objected, claiming that they had received the land as a grant, as indeed they had in 1770 from Governor Mendinueta. Ebright, Hendricks, and Hughes, *Four Square Leagues*, chapter 2.

121. Ignacio María Sánchez Vergara to Joaquin Montoya, 28 February 1821, Ebright, Hendricks, and Hughes, *Four Square Leagues*, 81–82.

122. Complaint by the governor and *principales* of San Felipe Pueblo against their protector, 10 May 1819, SANM II: 2738, no. 54; Cutter, *Protector de Indios*, 96–97.

123. Petition of Indians of San Juan [Chihuahua], 1 January 1822, Mexican Archives of New Mexico, Santa Fe, Roll 1, fr. 1184; Cutter, *Protector de Indios*, 102.

124. Cutter, *Protector de Indios*, 99–100.

125. Petition of six presidial soldiers for land between Santo Domingo and San Felipe Pueblos, Santa Fe, 1823, SANM I: 896.

126. Minutes of the meeting of the Territorial Deputation, Santa Fe, 12 March 1824, Mexican Archives of New Mexico, Santa Fe, Roll 42, fr. 174–75.

127. Decree of Governor Alberto Máynez, Santa Fe, 22 May 1815; approval by Ignacio María Sánchez Vergara of sale of lands to doña María Manuela Perea, Jemez, 20 February 1819, order of Francisco Trujillo, Abiquiu, 18 May 1824, SANM I: 208.

128. Surveyor General Julian decided that the Abiquiu grant was valid because the Spanish government was very lenient toward the Indians. Report of Surveyor General Julian, Santa Fe, 28 October 1885, Abiquíu grant, SG 140, Roll 26, fr. 409–40, especially 434–35.

129. SANM I: 1351.

130. White, Koch, Kelley, and McCarthy and the New Mexico State Planning Office, *Land Title Study* (Santa Fe, NM: State Planning Office, 1971), 101–4; for a description of the buried monuments or reference points in the Mora Valley Monumentation Project, see State Planning Office, *Title Study: Survey and Monumentation Project Technical Report* (Santa Fe, NM: State Planning Office, 1970), 3 and passim.

131. Herman J. Viola, *Diplomats in Buckskin: A History of Indian Delegations in Washington City* (Washington, D.C.: Smithsonian Institution Press, 1981), passim; E. Richard Hart, ed., *Zuni and the Courts: A Struggle for Sovereign Land Rights* (Lawrence: University Press of Kansas, 1995), passim; Cutter, *Legal Culture*, 99–102; Blake A. Watson, *Buying America from the Indians:* Johnson v. McIntosh *and the History of Native Land Rights* (Norman: University of Oklahoma Press, 2012), 17.

Chapter Two

1. Cordelia Thomas Snow, "A Hypothetical Configuration of the Early Santa Fe Plaza Based on the 1573 Ordinances or the Law of the Indies," in *Santa Fe Historic Plaza Study I: With Translations from Spanish Colonial Documents*, ed. Linda Tigges (Santa Fe, NM: City Planning Department, 1990), 56–57.

2. Cordelia Thomas Snow, "Dispelling Some Myths of Santa Fe, New Mexico, or Santa Fe of the Imagination," in *Current Research on the Late Prehistory and Early History of New Mexico*, ed. Bradley J. Vierra and Clara Gualtieri (Albuquerque: New Mexico Archaeological Council, 1992), 215–20.

3. In 1883 civic boosters who were more interested in tourism than accurate history staged a "Tertio Millenial Centennial" to commemorate the founding of Santa Fe in 1550, a completely fictitious date. Fray Angélico Chávez, "Santa Fe's Fake Centennial of 1883," *El Palacio* 62 (1955): 315.

4. Critics have seen the character Caliban as "an American Indian" or as "Shakespeare's sole representation of the human population of the New World." W. Gordon Zeeveld, *The Temper of Shakespeare's Thought* (New Haven, CT: Yale University Press, 1974), 250; cited in William Shakespeare, *The Tempest*, ed. Virginia Mason Vaughn and Alden T. Vaughn, 3rd ed. (Surrey: Thomas Nelson and Sons, 1999), 105.

5. The colonists from the shipwrecked *Sea Venture* eventually made their way to Jamestown and saved the colony from collapse. Lorrie Glover and Daniel Blake Smith, *The Shipwreck that Saved Jamestown: The Sea Venture Castaways and the Fate of America* (New York: Henry Holt, 2008), 1–8. Books about the shipwreck passed on to Shakespeare by his friend the Earl of Southampton were Silvester Jourdain's *A Discovery of the Barmudas, Otherwise Called the Ile of Divels* (1610) and "William Strachey's Account," now found in J. H. Lefroy's *Memorials of the Bermudas* (1877), 22–54, as cited in George F. Wilson, *Saints and Strangers* (New York: Reynal and Hitchcock, 1945), 465.

6. Miguel de Cervantes Saavedra, *The Adventures of Don Quixote* (London: Penguin, 1950). Governors Mendizábal (1659–1661) and Peñalosa (1661–1664) were said to have copies of *Don Quixote* on their bookshelves. France V. Scholes, "Civil Government and Society in New Mexico," *New Mexico Historical Review* 10 (April 1935): 103.

7. The "oldest house," with tree-ring dates of 1740–1767, may not be older than that. A structure in the approximate location of the "oldest house" is shown on the 1766 Urrutia map, but there are clearly older structures in Santa Fe. John Gaw Meem, preface to *Old Santa Fe Today* (Albuquerque: University of New Mexico Press, 1991), 74.

8. See the Santa Fe City Grant, SG 88, Roll 20, fr. 1326 et seq.; the Villa de Santa Fe Grant, PLC 19, Roll 34, fr. 1573, et seq.; and the City of Santa Fe Grant, PLC 80, Roll 42, fr. 6, et seq.

9. For an example of a "ghost grant"—a grant whose title papers were valid and which was recommended for confirmation and surveyed by the surveyor general but never submitted to the Court of Private Land Claims and thus not included on most land grant maps—see the Luis de Armenta grant in J. J. Bowden,

"Private Land Claims in the Southwest," 6 vols. (MA thesis, Southern Methodist University, 1968), 2:370–75.

10. George P. Hammond and Agapito Rey, eds., *The Rediscovery of New Mexico, 1580–1594: The Explorations of Chamuscado, Espejo, Castaño de Sosa, Morlete, and Leyva de Bonilla and Humaña* (Albuquerque: University of New Mexico Press, 1966), 36–37, 280.

11. George P. Hammond and Agapito Rey, eds. and trans., *Don Juan de Oñate: Colonizer of New Mexico, 1595–1628*, 2 vols. (Albuquerque: University of New Mexico Press, 1953), 1:17; Florence H. Ellis, Myra E. Jenkins, and Richard Ford, *When Cultures Meet: Remembering San Gabriel del Yunge Oweenge* (Santa Fe, NM: Sunstone Press, 1987).

12. In 1591 Castaño de Sosa crossed a river (probably the Santa Fe River) "which was frozen so hard that the horses were able to cross without breaking the ice." Hammond and Rey, *Rediscovery of New Mexico*, 280.

13. France V. Scholes, "Juan Martínez de Montoya, Settler and Conquistador of New Mexico," *New Mexico Historical Review* 19 (1944): 341.

14. Hammond and Rey, *Rediscovery of New Mexico*, 36–37, 280; George P. Hammond and Lansing B. Bloom, "When Was Santa Fe Founded?" *New Mexico Historical Review* 4 (1929): 188–94.

15. Hammond and Rey, *Don Juan de Oñate*, 2:1087.

16. *Kuapoge* has been translated as "bead water place" or "the place of the Olivella shells, from which they make the beads they so highly prize," among other translations. John Peabody Harrington, *The Ethnography of the Tewa Indians* (Washington, D.C.: Government Printing Office, 1916), 459–65; F. Richard Sánchez et al., eds., *White Shell Water Place: An Anthology of Native American Reflections on the 400th Anniversary of the Founding of Santa Fe, New Mexico* (Santa Fe, NM: Sunstone Press, 2010), 21.

17. Historian Lansing B. Bloom believed that by the first part of May 1610, the fields of the villa had been planted. Hammond and Bloom, "When Was Santa Fe Founded?" 194; Lansing B. Bloom and Ireneo L. Chaves, trans., "Ynstruccion a Peralta por Vi-roy," *New Mexico Historical Review* 4 (April 1929): 178–87; Governor Peralta's instructions, Hammond and Rey, *Don Juan de Oñate*, 2:1087–91; Marc Simmons, "The Naming of Santa Fe," in *Yesterday in Santa Fe: Episodes in a Turbulent History* (Santa Fe, NM: Sunstone Press, 1989), 13.

18. Bloom and Chaves, "Ynstruccion," 179–80.

19. Joseph P. Sánchez, "The Peralta-Ordóñez Affair and the Founding of Santa Fe," in *Santa Fe: History of an Ancient City*, ed. David Grant Noble (Santa Fe, NM: School of American Research Press, 1989), 28–31.

20. The date of the establishment of Analco is a subject of dispute among scholars. According to Kessell in 1610, "because certain families had already begun

constructing homes on the more suitable south side of the Santa Fe River Peralta chose to mark off the broad, rectangular plaza on the swampy north bank." "Yet by 1607 or 1608 some of [Oñate's people] . . . had begun a second settlement [after San Gabriel] they were calling the place Santa Fe." The will of Salvador Montoya refers to a tract bounded by "tierras de los Mexicanos," SANM I: 512; William Wroth, "Barrio del Analco: Its Roots in Mexico and Role in Early Colonial Santa Fe, 1610–1780," in *All Trails Lead to Santa Fe: An Anthology Commemorating the 400th Anniversary of the Founding of Santa Fe* (Santa Fe, NM: Sunstone Press, 2010), 163–78. Carroll Riley has suggested that the Mexican Indians settled Analco before the Spaniards arrived, which would place the date of Analco's founding prior to 1607. Carroll Riley, *The Kachina and the Cross: Indians and Spaniards in the Early Southwest* (Salt Lake City: University of Utah Press, 1999), 92, 103.

21. The *Recopilación* provided for three classes of municipalities in order of their size: *ciudad*, *villa*, or *pueblo*. "The classification of a municipality as *ciudad, villa* or *pueblo* . . . was more than a mere formality since these terms implied definite ranking according to prestige and importance. Also the number of municipal magistrates and councilmen allowed by law depended upon the status of the community." Marc Simmons, "Settlement Patterns and Village Plans in Colonial New Mexico," *Journal of the West* 8 (January 1969): 8–9, n. 9.

22. For the Pueblo Revolt, see Charles Wilson Hackett, ed., and Charmion Clair Shelby, trans., *Revolt of the Pueblo Indians of New Mexico and Otermín's Attempted Reconquest, 1680–1682*, 2 vols. (Albuquerque: University of New Mexico Press, 1942), passim; and Andrew Knaut, *The Pueblo Revolt of 1680: Conquest and Resistance in Seventeenth-Century New Mexico* (Norman: University of Oklahoma Press, 1995).

23. Edict by Vargas, El Paso, 20 September 1693, in Kessell, Hendricks, and Dodge, *To The Royal Crown*, 375.

24. SANM I: 8 and SANM I: 169. The case of *Arias de Quirós v. the Cabildo of Santa Fe* is discussed in Malcolm Ebright, *Land Grants and Lawsuits in Northern New Mexico* (Albuquerque: University of New Mexico Press, 1994), 91–96.

25. Gaspar Ortiz y Alarid was a land grant speculator who engaged in property transactions around Santa Fe. Petition of Santa Fe County probate judge Gaspar Ortiz y Alarid, City of Santa Fe Grant, SG 88, Roll 21, fr. 1328–35.

26. Ibid.

27. Opinion of Surveyor General Proudfit, City of Santa Fe Grant, SG 88, Roll 21, fr. 1336–38.

28. Bowden, "Private Land Claims," 2:329.

29. By the time the Court of Private Land Claims was established, a backlog of 116 grants had been approved and was awaiting congressional action. Congress

had not approved a grant since early in 1879. Ebright, *Land Grants and Lawsuits*, 45.

30. Bruce T. Ellis, "Fraud without Scandal: The Roque Lovato Grant and Gaspar Ortiz y Alarid," *New Mexico Historical Review* 57 (January 1982): 43–59.

31. Petition of the Board of County Commissioners of Santa Fe County, 14 July 1892, Villa de Santa Fe Grant, PLC 19, Roll 34, fr. 1574–78.

32. Answer and demurrer by the United States, Villa de Santa Fe Grant, PLC 19, Roll 34, fr. 1574–78. For more on Will Tipton and Henry Flipper, see Ebright, *Land Grants and Lawsuits*, 134–35.

33. Bowden, "Private Land Claims," 2:331.

34. Petition of the City of Santa Fe, 31 January 1893, John P. Victory, city attorney, John Knaebel of counsel, City of Santa Fe Grant, PLC 80, Roll 42, fr. 7–12. Knaebel was a law partner of Thomas B. Catron in the late 1880s. David L. Caffey, *Chasing the Santa Fe Ring: Power and Privilege in Territorial New Mexico* (Albuquerque: University of New Mexico Press, 2014), 94.

35. Demurrer by the United States, Santa Fe, 21 November 1893, Matthew Reynolds, U.S. attorney, City of Santa Fe Grant, PLC 80, Roll 42, fr. 15–16.

36. Bowden, "Private Land Claims," 2:332.

37. Amended petition of the City of Santa Fe, Santa Fe, 18 April 1894, City of Santa Fe Grant, PLC 80, Roll 42, fr. 37–43.

38. Answer of the United States to the amended petition, Santa Fe, 21 April 1894, City of Santa Fe Grant, PLC 80, Roll 42, fr. 153–60.

39. Answer of seventeen defendants with grants inside the Santa Fe League, Santa Fe, n.d., City of Santa Fe Grant, PLC 80, Roll 42, fr. 148–51.

40. Dissenting opinion of Justice Murray, Santa Fe, 26 May 1894, City of Santa Fe Grant, PLC 80, Roll 42, fr. 189–201. Grants rejected because they overlapped the Santa Fe League and were trumped by the Court of Private Land Claims confirmation of the Santa Fe League were Talaya Hill, Chamiso Arroyo, Juan Cayetano Lovato, Antonio Domínguez, Manuel Tenorio, Juan Antonio Flores, Juan Felipe Rodríguez, Juan Antonio Archuleta, Leonardo Gonzales grant, Antonio Armijo grant, Juan José Archuleta grant, José Romulo de Vera grant, and the Caterina Maese grant.

41. Transcription and translation of *Recopilación* 4.5.6, Santa Fe, 28 April 1894, City of Santa Fe Grant, PLC 80, Roll 42, fr. 54–57.

42. Majority opinion, Santa Fe, 26 May 1894, City of Santa Fe Grant, PLC 80, Roll 42, fr. 177–88.

43. San Francisco v. LeRoy, 138 U.S. 656 (1891); and Brownsville v. Cavazos, 100 U.S. 138 (1897).

44. For a brief discussion of empresario grants and a map of the empresario grants in Texas, see A. Ray Stephens and William M. Holmes, *Historical Atlas of Texas* (Norman: University of Oklahoma Press, 1989), 22.

45. In practice, empresario contracts in Texas in the 1820s and 1830s required the empresario to bring in at least one hundred families. Andrés Reséndez, *Changing National Identities at the Frontier: Texas and New Mexico, 1800–1850* (Cambridge: Cambridge University Press, 2004), 37–38. The settlers were each to provide "a breeding sow, twenty breeding ewes from Castille, and six hens and a cock." Translation of *Recopilación* 4.5.6, Santa Fe, 28 April 1894, City of Santa Fe Grant, PLC 80, Roll 42, fr. 54–57.

46. Dissenting opinion of Justice Murray, Santa Fe, 26 May 1894, City of Santa Fe Grant, PLC 80, Roll 42, fr. 189–202.

47. U.S. v. Santa Fe, 165 U.S. 675 (1897), 676, 691.

48. Ralph Emerson Twitchell, *Old Santa Fe: The Story of New Mexico's Ancient Capital* (Chicago, IL: Rio Grande Press: 1963), 417–18.

49. U.S. v. Santa Fe, 165 U.S. 675 (1897).

50. Ibid., 683.

51. Kermit Hall, ed., *The Oxford Companion to the Supreme Court of the United States* (New York: Oxford University Press, 1992), 927–28, 968.

52. U.S. v. Santa Fe, 165 U.S. 675 (1897), 694–700. For a discussion of the Plan of Pitic, see Michael Meyer, *Water in the Hispanic Southwest: A Social and Legal History, 1550–1850* (Tucson: University of Arizona Press), 30–37.

53. San Francisco v. LeRoy, 138 U.S. 656 (1891), 664–67.

54. Bowden, "Private Land Claims," 2:340–41.

55. U.S. v. Santa Fe, 167 U.S. 675 (1897), 676 and 691.

56. Bloom and Chaves, "Ynstruccion," 179.

57. Ibid., 187.

58. See Twitchell, *Old Santa Fe,* for example.

59. Some of the works by these scholars relating to Santa Fe include Hackett, *Historical Documents*; Hammond and Rey, *Don Juan de Oñate*; Hammond and Bloom, "When Was Santa Fe Founded?" 188–94; and Scholes, "Juan Martínez de Montoya," 340.

60. Declaration of Pedro García, 25 August 1680, translated in Hackett and Shelby, *Revolt of the Pueblo Indians*, 23–26. Two of the daughters born to Petrona Nieto were Petrona Nieto and Josefa, who kept her mother's surname of Pacheco.

61. John Demos, *The Unredeemed Captive: A Family Story from Early America* (New York: Alfred A. Knopf, 1994), passim. The title comes from the subsequent refusal of Eunice Williams (age seven at the time of her capture), to be redeemed, as she preferred instead to live among the Mohawks with her Mohawk husband. Colin G. Calloway, *The Shawnees and the War for America* (New York: Viking, 2007), xxxii–xxxiii.

62. S. C. Gwyne, *The Empire of the Summer Moon: Quanah Parker and the Rise and Fall of the Comanches, the Most Powerful Indian Tribe in American History* (New

York: Scribner, 2010), 102–18, 173–93; William T. Hagan, *Quanah Parker, Comanche Chief* (Norman: University of Oklahoma Press, 1993), 6–8.

63. "When she died in 1753, Juana Hurtado owned a rancho with three houses and managed extensive herds of cattle and flocks of sheep." Ebright and Hendricks, *Witches of Abiquiu*, 33–34. James F. Brooks, *Captives & Cousins: Slavery, Kinship, and Community in the Southwest Borderlands* (Chapel Hill: University of North Carolina Press, 2002), 99–103; J. Manuel Espinosa, trans. and ed., *The First Expedition of Vargas into New Mexico, 1692* (Albuquerque: University of New Mexico Press, 1940), 237; Rancho de Galván Grant, PLC 282, Roll 54, fr. 1095, et seq. For a discussion of this grant and Juana Galván, see Frances Leon Swadesh, "They Settled by Little Bubbling Springs," *El Palacio* 84 (Fall 1978): 19–20, 42–49.

64. Chávez, *New Mexico Families*, 83, citing Archivo General de la Nación, Mexico City, Mex. Inquisición, fr. 190; David H. Snow, "So Many Mestizos, Mulatos, and Zambohigos: Colonial New Mexico's People without History" (paper presented at the Annual Meeting of the Western History Association, Denver, CO, 11–14 October 1995).

65. Women and their children were generally well treated in captivity, in spite of the widely held belief to the contrary. Christina Snyder, *Slavery in Indian Country: The Changing Face of Captivity in Early America* (Cambridge, MA: Harvard University Press, 2010), 109, 111–13. As Rivaya-Martínez points out, there were several reasons for taking and keeping captives in addition to their economic value, including for their labor, to enhance their captor's status and influence, as child-bearers, and eventually because of the simple bonds of affection. Joaquín Rivaya-Martínez, "Becoming Comanches: Patterns of Captive Incorporation into Comanche Kinship Networks, 1820–1875," in *On the Borders of Love and Power: Families and Kinship in the Intercultural American Southwest*, ed. David Wallace Adams and Crista De Luzio (Berkeley: University of California Press, 2012), 48–50, 64–65.

66. Petrona had three daughters during her captivity, not three sons and daughters. In total, seventy-six people of all ages surrendered and were baptized at Ohkay Owingeh Pueblo (San Juan Pueblo). John L. Kessell and Rick Hendricks, eds., *By Force of Arms: The Journals of Don Diego de Vargas* (Albuquerque: University of New Mexico Press, 1992), 444.

67. Declaration of Sargento Mayor don Fernándo de Chávez, Guadalupe del Paso, 5 April 1681, in Hackett and Shelby, *Revolt of the Pueblo Indians*, 17.

68. Petrona is described as a mestiza or a Spaniard depending on the account. The other three captives were Juana de Arzate (a Tiwa Indian from Isleta), "a daughter of Nevares, [and] a soldier . . . at the presidio of Janos." Kessell and Hendricks, *By Force of Arms*, 444, 525–30.

69. Diego de Vargas, distribution of livestock and supplies, Santa Fe, 1 May 1697, in John L. Kessell, Rick Hendricks and Meredith Dodge, eds., *Blood on the Boulders: The Journals of Don Diego de Vargas, New Mexico, 1694–97*, 2 vols. (Albuquerque: University of New Mexico Press, 1998), 2:1138–40.

70. Antonio de Aguilera Isasi was alcalde ordinario of the Santa Fe cabildo in 1696, 1698, 1699, 1700, and 1702. Albert J. Gallegos and José Antonio Esquibel, "*Alcaldes and Mayors of Santa Fe, 1613–2008*," in *All Trails Lead to Santa Fe: An Anthology Commemorating the 400th Anniversary of the Founding of Santa* (Santa Fe, NM: Sunstone Press, 2010), 412–13.

71. Ted J. Warner, "The Career of Don Félix Martínez de Torre Laguna: Soldier, Presidio Commander, and Governor of New Mexico, 1693–1726" (PhD diss., University of New Mexico, 1963), 19.

72. SANM I: 638.

73. Chávez, *New Mexico Families*, 243; José Antonio Esquibel, "Notes on Cristóbal Nieto (and Others)" (unpublished manuscript in the possession of the author).

74. Simón Nieto, the legitimate son of Cristóbal Nieto, was more interested in selling land he acquired through his marriage to Francisca Maese than he was in consolidating his holdings and adding to the Cristóbal Nieto grant. Deed from Simón Nieto to Juan García de Noriega, Santa Fe, 25 September 1728, SANM I: 642. Simón Nieto also purchased two fanegas of corn-planting land in the area in 1707 from José Manuel Gilthomey, who said he received it by royal grant. The land was bounded by that of Salvador Archuleta on one side and Captain Luis Maese on the other. Deed from José Manuel Gilthomey to Simón Nieto, Santa Fe, 5 December 1707, SANM I: 639; Chávez, *New Mexico Families*, 217, 242–43.

75. Virginia Langham Olmsted, comp., *Spanish and Mexican Censuses of New Mexico, 1750 to 1830* (Albuquerque: New Mexico Genealogical Society, 1981), 9.

76. "Hija de la iglesia," diligencia matrimonia, 1711, no. 5, Fray Angélico Chávez, *Archives of the Archdiocese of Santa Fe* (Washington, D.C.: Academy of American Franciscan History, 1957); partition of land at Pueblo Quemado (Agua Fría) between Francisco Nieto and Jacinto Perea, Santa Fe, 10 July 1765, SANM I: 644.

77. Alfred B. Thomas, trans. and ed., *After Coronado: Spanish Exploration Northeast of New Mexico, 1696–1727* (Norman: University of Oklahoma Press, 1935), 227.

78. Deed from Jacinto Perea to Juan Tafoya, Puesto del Pino, Santa Fe, 1761, SANM I: 985.

79. El Pino (Cristóbal Nieto) Grant, PLC 81, Roll 42, fr. 482–83.

80. David H. Snow, "A Note on *Encomienda* Economics in Seventeenth-Century New Mexico," in *Hispanic Arts and Ethnohistory in the Southwest: New Papers Inspired by the Work of E. Boyd*, ed. Marta Weigle with Claudia Larcombe and

Samuel Larcombe (Santa Fe, NM: Ancient City Press, 1983), 347–57; Elinore Barrett, *The Spanish Colonial Settlement Landscapes of New Mexico, 1598–1680* (Albuquerque: University of New Mexico Press, 2012), 174.

81. SANM I: 644.
82. Petition by Juan Nieto for confirmation of the El Pino (Cristóbal Nieto) Grant, El Pino Grant, PLC 81, Roll 42, fr. 455–57.
83. The land shown on J. J. Bowden's map of Santa Fe grants as the Pino (Cristóbal Nieto) grant is the 1765 Nieto/Perea purchase, not the Cristóbal Nieto grant. Bowden, "Private Land Claims, 2:269.
84. Claimant's map, El Pino Grant, PLC 81, Roll 42, fr. 524–27.
85. As David Benavides has pointed out, "Fairness is ensured in our adversarial system because each party has the services of a zealous advocate." Benavides, "Lawyer-Induced Partitioning," 24.
86. Deraignment of title, El Pino Grant, PLC 81, Roll 42, fr. 529.
87. The Sebastián de Vargas grant claim was based solely on a mention of Sebastián de Vargas in the Juan de León Brito grant. As was true of at least half of the grants submitted to the Court of Private Land Claims by lawyer James Purdy, there was no grant document, only a mention of the grant or parcel of land in the description of an adjoining parcel. Another basis for assuming that there may have been a grant was statements by witnesses that Donaciano Vigil had told them that he had seen the grant papers in the archives. However, no mention is made of a grant to Sebastián de Vargas in the index prepared by Vigil of the documents in the New Mexico archives. Nor do eighteenth-century lists of documents found in the New Mexico archives mention such a grant. Sebastián de Vargas, SG 137, Roll 25, fr. 1286–1472; Sebastián de Vargas Grant, PLC 6, Roll 33, fr. 745 et seq. Only the eastern part of the Sebastián de Vargas grant was confirmed by the Court of Private Land Claims in a split decision: Justices Fuller and Stone recommended confirmation of the entire grant, Chief Justice Reed and Justice Murray recommended rejection of the entire grant, and Justice Sluss voted to confirm the eastern tract but reject the western tract. Bowden, "Private Land Claims," 2:317. The grant was surveyed to contain 13,434 acres.
88. Answer of seventeen defendants with grants inside the Santa Fe League, City of Santa Fe Grant, PLC 80, Roll 42, fr. 148–51; dissenting opinion of Justice Murray, City of Santa Fe Grant, PLC 80, Roll 42, fr. 189–202; U.S. v. Santa Fe, 165 U.S. 675 (1897).
89. Brooks, *Captives & Cousins*, 56.
90. Genízaros were mixed-blood former captives sold to Hispanos to be Christianized and perform household service or field work on a temporary basis. By 1776 they would comprise 14 percent of the population of Santa Fe. Ebright and Hendricks, *Witches of Abiquiu*, 30.

91. The Cristóbal Nieto grant in Bowden's "Private Land Claims" makes no mention of Petrona Pacheco's captivity. Wroth, "Barrio de Analco," 163–78. One scholar who is connected to Petrona Pacheco and researching Petrona's captivity period at Ohkay Owingeh Pueblo is Jodilynn Ortiz.

92. Scholes, "Juan Martínez de Montoya," 341. Scholes made a clear distinction between "some sort of post or settlement" at Santa Fe and the founding of a villa, which he says occurred in 1610. Scholes clearly did not believe the Martínez de Montoya document was evidence of a 1607 founding of Santa Fe. But the unsigned *El Palacio* article seems to discredit Scholes's opinion by stating that "he never saw the documents in London," when Scholes himself states that "the documents mentioned above were owned by Maggs Bros. of London *when I saw them*" (emphasis added). Scholes, "Juan Martínez de Montoya," 338, n. 2.

93. Beverly Becker, "Santa Fe, Est. 1610/1607," *El Palacio* 100 (Winter, 1994–1995): 14–16.

94. James Ivey, "An Uncertain Founding: Santa Fe," *Common-Place* 3 (2003): 7, www.common-place.org/vol-03/no-04/santa-fe.

95. David J. Weber, "Santa Fe," in *Jamestown, Quebec, Santa Fe: Three North American Beginnings*, ed. James C. Kelly and Barbara Clark Smith (Washington, D.C.: Smithsonian Books, 2007). In this article Weber states almost parenthetically that "Captain Juan Martínez de Montoya, *who founded Santa Fe* [in 1608] was to replace Oñate as governor" (emphasis added). Weber, "Santa Fe," 139.

96. In 1728 a small grant in the Analco area south of the Santa Fe River was revalidated by Governor Bustamante to Juan de León Brito, a Tlascalan Indian who claimed the land had been initially granted to his father by Governor Vargas. For a discussion of Tlascalans in New Mexico, see Marc Simmons, "Tlascalans in the Spanish Borderlands," *New Mexico Historical Review* 39 (April 1964): 108–10. Scholars now believe that the Analco Indians were mostly from other tribal groups, not Tlascalans. The land was adjacent to the land of Sebastián de Vargas and was again revalidated in 1742 by Governor Mendoza. Grant to Juan de León Brito, Santa Fe, 27 August 1738, SANM I: 85; José Antonio Esquibel, "Thirty-eight Adobe Houses: The Villa of Santa Fe in the Seventeenth Century, 1608–1610," in *All Trails Lead to Santa Fe: An Anthology Commemorating the 400th Anniversary of the Founding of Santa Fe* (Santa Fe, NM: Sunstone Press, 2010), 109–28.

97. Edict by Vargas, El Paso, 20 September 1693, in Kessell, Hendricks, and Dodge, *To The Royal Crown*, 375. For a discussion of the pre-revolt land distribution pattern, see Ebright, Hendricks, and Hughes, *Four Square Leagues*, 3–6.

98. For a detailed discussion of grazing land for the presidial horse herd, see Tigges, "Pastures of the Royal Horse Herd," 237–66.

99. Testimony of Hernando Martín in the lawsuit *Antonio Sisneros v. Lorenzo* over the loss of a mule, Santa Fe, 1697, SANM II: 64a.

100. Former state historian Estevan Rael-Gálvez stated: "Some are starting to say they were here as early as 1598, when Oñate came and settled in Ohkay Owingeh—they may have stopped and started building here." Marin Sandy, ed., "Where Credit Is Due," *Santa Fean: The History Issue* (February/March 2009): 28; John L. Kessell, *Spain in the Southwest: A Narrative History of Colonial New Mexico, Arizona, Texas, and California* (Norman: University of Oklahoma Press, 2002), 394, n. 3; Carroll L. Riley, personal communication, 18 December 2008. The will of Salvador Montoya refers to a tract bounded by "tierras de los Mexicanos," SANM I: 512. A deed from Andrés Montoya, *el viejo*, to Bernadino de Sena in 1729 for land south of the river is bounded by "tierras de San Miguel," SANM I: 840. Eleanor B. Adams and Fray Angélico Chávez, *The Missions of New Mexico, 1776* (Albuquerque: University of New Mexico Press, 1956).

101. Mrs. Edward E. Ayer, trans., Frederick W. Hodge, and Charles F. Lummis, *The Memorial of Fray Alonso de Benavides, 1630* (Albuquerque: Horn and Wallace, 1965), 22–23; Adams and Chávez, *Missions of New Mexico*, 37–38; George Kubler, *The Rebuilding of San Miguel at Santa Fe in 1710* (Colorado Springs, CO: Taylor Museum of the Colorado Springs Fine Arts Center, 1939), 6; France V. Scholes, "Church and State in New Mexico, 1610–1650," *New Mexico Historical Review* 11 (1936): 333; Carroll Riley, *Kachina and the Cross* (Salt Lake City: University of Utah Press, 2003), 129–30.

102. Declaration of Pedro de la Cruz, 14 September 1632, in France V. Scholes, "The First Decade of the Inquisition in New Mexico," *New Mexico Historical Review* 10 (July 1935): 240–41; D. H. Snow, "So Many Mestizos," 10; Chávez, *New Mexico Families*, 83.

103. C. T. Snow, "A Hypothetical Configuration," 56–57; C. T. Snow, "Dispelling Some Myths," 215–20.

104. C. T. Snow, "A Hypothetical Configuration," x, 127–29; Stephen S. Post et al., "Third Interim Report on the Data Recovery Program at LA 1051, El Pueblo de Santa Fe" (Santa Fe: Museum of New Mexico, Office of Archaeological Studies, submitted to the New Mexico Historic Preservation Division, NMCRIS Activity No. 90579, MNM #41), 776.

105. For lands attached to the convent, see deed from Juana de Sosa Canela of a tract "bounded on the east by lands of the convento and sown land," Santa Fe, 1713, SANM I: 162; see also deed from Cristóbal Martín and Antonia de Moraga to Diego Arias de Quirós, "bounded on the east by the Ciénega that serves as the ejido of the Villa, and on the south by lands of the convento of the Villa," Santa Fe, 1716, SANM I: 10; other deeds that refer to lands of the convento are SANM I: 744 and SANM I: 948. Another deed referring to lands and irrigation

of the Ciénega is SANM I: 331. Deeds that mention the lands planted by the governors are deeds from Alfonso Rael de Aguilar, Santa Fe, 1733, SANM I: 1228; and a revalidation of a grant to Pedro Luján in 1732, SANM I: 758. For common woodlands see the aforementioned revalidation bounded on the east by the road to El Monte; see also SANM I: 1228. For lands farmed by the Analco Indians, see deed from Andres Montoya, el viejo, bounded on the north by the lands of San Miguel, Santa Fe, 1729, SANM I: 840.

Chapter Three

1. Untitled article by Adolf Bandelier about Poseyemu, *El Palacio* 80 (2): 36–37; Richard Parmentier, "The Mythological Triangle: Poseyemu, Montezuma, and Jesus in the Pueblos," in *Handbook of North American Indians*, ed. William C. Sturtevant, vol. 9, *Southwest*, ed. Alfonso Ortiz (Washington, D.C.: Smithsonian Institution, 1979), 609.

2. Harrington, *Ethnography of the Tewa*, 163.

3. Ibid., 164; Charles H. Lange, Carroll L. Riley, and Elizabeth M. Lange, eds., *The Southwestern Journals of Adolph F. Bandelier, 1889–1892* (Albuquerque: University of New Mexico Press; Santa Fe, NM: School of American Research, 1984), 607–8, nn. 954–55.

4. On Sahagún, see Walden Brown, "When Worlds Collide: Crisis in Sahagún's *Historia Universal de las Cosas de la Nueva España*," *Colonial Latin American Historical Review* 5 (Spring 1996): 101–49.

5. David Bugé, "Preliminary Report: 1979 Excavations at Ponsipa-akeri, Ojo Caliente, New Mexico" (file no. P4369, Laboratory of Anthropology Library, Santa Fe, NM).

6. Lázaro Atienza to Alcalde Juan Esteban García de Noriega, [Santa Cruz, September 1735], SANM I: 20.

7. "Debajo de mi acequia y no eriazas como dice sino rotas por haverlas sembrado yo dos [o tres] años antes," Antonio Martín to García de Noriega, Ojo Caliente, [30 September] 1735, SANM I: 20.

8. "Vean que de manifiesto se hallarán muchas raices de palos que yo por estar corto de buyes he cortado y quemado como tambien los ceniceros se podran reconcer aunque revueltos con la buena tierra," Lázaro Atienza to García de Noriega, [Ojo Caliente], October 1735, SANM I: 20.

9. Declaration of Juan Pedro Gómez de Chávez, Santa Cruz, 11 October 1735, SANM I: 20.

10. Janet LeCompte, "The Independent Women of New Mexico, 1821–1846," *Western Historical Quarterly* 12 (January 1981): 17–35, 27; Deborah A. Rosen, "Women and Property across Colonial America: A Comparison of Legal Systems in New

Mexico and New York," *William and Mary Quarterly* 40 (April 2003): 359–61. Rosen notes that deeds of community property written by a husband would usually note that he was selling the land "with the consent of his wife." See also Ebright, Hendricks, and Hughes, *Four Square Leagues*, chapter 2.

11. The appraisers could not agree on the value of the improvements because they could not tell which improvements were made by Atienza, so the governor split the difference between the amount of the two appraisals. Decision of Governor Cruzat y Góngora, Santa Fe, 15 May 1736, SANM I: 20.

12. Ibid.

13. Petition of Juan de Abeyta, Santa Fe, 28 March 1748, SANM I: 28; decree of Governor Codallos y Rabal, Santa Fe, 30 March 1748, SANM I: 28.

14. Petition of Tomás Vélez Cachupín, [Madrid, 1761], AGI, Audiencia of Guadalajara, 300 Bancroft Library, Berkeley; Eleanor B. Adams, ed., *Bishop Tamarón's Visitation of New Mexico, 1760*, Publications in History 15 (Albuquerque: Historical Society of New Mexico, 1954), 24; Ernesto de la Torre Villar, *Instrucciones y memorias de les virreyes novohispanos*, Biblioteca Porrúa 102 (Mexico City: Editorial Porrúa, S. A., 1991), 795.

15. Opinion of Counselor General of War Altamira, Mexico City, 3 April 1750, SANM I: 1098; compliance by Governor Vélez Cachupín, El Paso, 4 September 1750, SANM I: 1098.

16. Order of Lieutenant Bustamante, Santa Fe, 15 March 1751, SANM I: 650.

17. Declaration of Pablo Francisco Villalpando, Taos, 18 March 1751, SANM I: 650.

18. Declaration signed by Blas Martín Serrano, José Martín Serrano, Diego Lucero, Manuel Dios del Castillo, and María de Herrera, n.p., April 1751, SANM I: 650.

19. Decree of Governor Bustamante, Santa Fe, 26 April 1751, SANM I: 650.

20. Report of Alcalde Juan José Lovato, Pojoaque, 18 January 1752, SANM I: 650.

21. Decree of Governor Vélez Cachupín, Santa Fe, 22 January 1752, SANM I: 650.

22. Report of Alcalde Juan José Lovato, Chama, 6 February 1752, SANM I: 650.

23. Petition of Felipe Tafoya on behalf of Francisco Durán, [Santa Fe], n.d., SANM I: 650.

24. Decree of Governor Vélez Cachupín, Santa Fe, 5 March 1752, SANM I: 650; order of Alcalde Lovato, Nuestra Señora de la Soledad del Río Arriba, 15 April 1752; relinquishment by Antonio Sandoval, Río Arriba, 22 June 1752, SANM I: 650.

25. The house of Antonio Sandoval was assigned to Diego Gómez, and Sandoval's cultivated lands were assigned to Gregorio Sandoval. Judicial Decree of Resettlement by Alcalde Lovato, Ojo Caliente, 5 May 1753, SANM I: 650.

26. Tomás Vélez Cachupín served two terms as governor of New Mexico from 1749 to 1754 and from 1762 to 1767. For an overview of the successive attempts at resettling the community of Ojo Caliente, see E. Boyd, "Troubles at Ojo Caliente, A Frontier Post," *El Palacio* (November/December 1957): 347–60.

27. "Haberse ido de poblar a otros parajes por el miedo de los enemigos . . . y haber dejado sus sitios al abrigo y de los pocos vecinos que en dicho sitio se hallan," report of Alcalde Manuel García Pareja, Soledad and Abiquiu, January 1766, SANM I: 655.

28. Statements of Santiago Lucero, Diego Martín, José Martín, José Miguel Lucero, Gerónima Pacheco (widow of Nicolás Martín), Juana de Herrera (widow of Francisco Saez), and Militia Lieutenant Pedro Martín, n.p., January 1766, SANM I: 655; order of Governor Vélez Cachupín, Santa Fe, 3 February 1766, SANM I: 655.

29. Report of teniente Francisco Durán, Ojo Caliente, 11 February 1766, SANM I: 655.

30. Order of Governor Vélez Cachupín, Santa Fe, 15 February 1766, SANM I: 655.

31. Governor Vélez Cachupín had successfully encouraged several other reluctant communities to resettle their land by 1766. See chapter 9.

32. Order of Governor Mendinueta, Santa Fe, 6 December 1767, SANM I: 655.

33. Decree of Governor Mendinueta, Santa Fe, 11 March 1768, SANM I: 655.

34. Act of possession by Alcalde Antonio José Ortiz, Ojo Caliente, 15 March 1768, SANM I: 655.

35. Decree of Governor Mendinueta, Santa Fe, 11 March 1768, SANM I: 655.

36. The Genízaro pueblo at Abiquiu was organized in a similar way with a governor, a teniente, and a war captain with two assistants. Census of 1790 of the jurisdiction of Abiquiu, Pinart Collection, Bancroft Library, University of California–Berkeley, PE 55:3, reproduced in John R. Van Ness, *Hispanos in Northern New Mexico: The Development of Corporate Community and Multicommunity* (New York: AMS Press, 1991), 152–53.

37. Act of possession by Alcalde Antonio José Ortiz, Ojo Caliente, 15 March 1768, SANM I: 655.

38. The viceroy's letter regarding resettlement is Revila Gigedo to Vélez Cachupín, Mexico City, 31 January 1751, SANM I: 1129; and Counselor General of War Altamira's opinion is Marqués of Altamira to Revillagigedo, Mexico City, 11 January 1751 and 3 April 1750, SANM I: 1098.

39. "Ocupados de un temor que han concebido los comanches debiendo las acciones pasadas tenidas con dicha nación," decree of Governor Mendinueta, Santa Fe, 31 March 1769, SANM I: 656.

40. Statement of Miguel Abeyta, José Martín, and Gregorio Sandoval, authenticated by Antonio José Ortiz, [Pojoaque], 8 April 1769, SANM I: 656.

41. "Si este es delito en todo nos sujetamos a la penas referidas hasta acabar las vidas en la cárcel llenos de prisiones," statement of Gregorio Sandoval, Diego Gómez, José Martín, Paulin Abeyta, Miguel Abeyta, Gabriel Quintana, Lucresio Muñiz, Juan Luján, Andres Mora, Juan Ignacio Alarid, Francisco Marquez, and Manuel Lucero, [Pojoaque, 8 April 1769], SANM I: 656.

42. "Si infiere que los firmantes en este escrito se hallan poseídos del miedo, pusilánimes y cobardes aún teniendo quien los defienda," order of Governor Mendinueta, Santa Fe, 10 May 1769, SANM I: 656.

43. Statement of José Martín, [Pojoaque], 14 May 1769, SANM I: 656.

44. Statement of Gregorio Sandoval, [Pojoaque], 14 May 1769, SANM I: 656.

45. Statement of Miguel Abeyta, [Pojoaque], 18 May 1769, SANM I: 656.

46. Statement of Juan Luján, [Pojoaque], 18 May 1769, SANM I: 656.

47. Statement of Andrés Mora, [Pojoaque], 20 May 1769, SANM I: 656.

48. Statement of Diego Gómez, [Pojoaque], 24 May 1769, SANM I: 656.

49. Statement of Ignacio Alarid, [Pojoaque], 27 May 1769, SANM I: 656.

50. Statement of Gabriel Quintana, [Pojoaque], 27 May 1769, SANM I: 656.

51. Statement of Francisco Márquez, [Pojoaque], 28 May 1769, SANM I: 656.

52. Order of Governor Mendinueta, Santa Fe, 20 June 1769, SANM I: 656.

53. Ibid.

54. Inspection of Alcalde Antonio José Ortiz, Ojo Caliente, 11 June 1769, SANM I: 656.

55. Ibid.

56. Herbert E. Bolton, *Pageant in the Wilderness* (Salt Lake City, UT: Spanish Historical Society, 1950), 142, 156, 159; Frances Leon Swadesh, *Los Primeros Pobladores: Hispanic Americans of the Ute Frontier* (Notre Dame, IN: University of Notre Dame Press, 1974), 42–43. The Muñis brothers apparently arranged for other Genízaros or coyotes from the Abiquiu area, including Juan Domingo and Felipe, to join the party for the purpose of trading with the Utes.

57. Apparently the priests themselves brought some trade goods, such as glass beads, to trade for food like buffalo meat. Bolton, *Pageant*, 157–59; Andrés Muñiz acted as a guide as well as an interpreter, at one point in August 1776 guiding the party "up a very high and rugged hill having so many stones that we expected to be forced to go back from halfway up.'" Muñiz had also been a part of an earlier expedition let by Lieutenant Juan Antonio María de Rivera, seeking the Ute leader Cuera de Lobo and a lost silver mine. Kessell, *Miera y Pacheco*, 83, 106. For a recent translation and discussion of the 1765 journal of the Rivera expedition, see Stephen G. Baker, *Juan Rivera's Colorado—1765: Spaniards among the Ute and Paiute Indians on the Trails to Teguayo, the Comprehensive Illustrated History with the Original Rivera Spanish Journals and English Translations*, trans. Rick Hendricks, illus. Gail Carroll Sargent (Lake City, CO: Western Reflections, 2014).

58. As was true with the Utes and the Hispanic settlers in southern Colorado in the 1850s, the only way to a peaceful settlement along the Ute frontier was through the sufferance of the Utes when they found it to be in their interest. David Merriwether, New Mexico Superintendent of Indian Affairs, to G. W.

Manypenny, Commissioner of Indian Affairs, Santa Fe, 24 November 1853, National Archives Records, Roll 547, Letters Received by the Office of Indian Affairs, 1824–81, New Mexico Superintendency, 1858–59, State Records Center and Archives, Santa Fe, NM.

59. Order of Alcalde Antonio José Ortiz and responses, Ojo Caliente, 2 July 1769, SANM I: 655.

60. Kessell, *Kiva, Cross, and Crown*, 399–405; Pekka Hämäläinen, *The Comanche Empire* (New Haven, CT: Yale University Press, 2008), 117–25.

61. Alfred B. Thomas, *Forgotten Frontiers: A Study of the Spanish Indian Policy of Don Juan Bautista de Anza, Governor of New Mexico, 1777–1787* (Norman: University of Oklahoma Press, 1932), 124.

62. Ebright, *Land Grants and Lawsuits*, 145–46.

63. Report of Governor Mendinueta to Viceroy Bucareli, Santa Fe, 26 March 1772, translated in Alfred B. Thomas, "Governor Mendinueta's Proposals for the Defense of New Mexico, 1772–1778," *New Mexico Historical Review* 6 (1931): 29–30.

64. Simmons, "Settlement Patterns," 12–19.

65. Petition of José Manuel Velarde to Governor de la Concha, Bernalillo, [September 1790], SANM I: 1062.

66. Petition of José Manuel Velarde, Bernalillo, [September] 1790, SANM I: 1062.

67. "Formen pueblo alineado y regular en el paraje que antiguamente estaba él que hoy se nombra viejo a los inmediaciones de la Cañada de los Comanches," "Tanto por la comodidad de sacar acequia para las labores que puede correr al pie de la citada población cuanto para la subsistencia y cría de ganados por todas las inmediaciones de ella," order of Governor Concha, Santa Fe, 2 September 1790, SANM I: 1062.

68. Report of Alcalde Manuel García de la Mora, Río Arriba, 16 September 1790, SANM I: 1062.

69. "No convengo de ningún modo en que se forme el pueblo en el paraje que proponen los fundadores respecto a que la experiencia tiene acreditado no poder subsistir en el en tiempo de guerra por su fatal situación," order of Governor Concha, Santa Fe, 17 September 1790, SANM I: 1062.

70. Thomas, *Forgotten Frontiers*, 124.

71. Report by Alcalde Manuel García de la Mora, Río Arriba, 20 September 1790, SANM I: 1062.

72. "Merced jurídica," petition of Antonio José Espinosa, Juan Samora, and Salvador Maese, [Ojo Caliente], September 1793, Ojo Caliente Grant, SG 77, Roll 21, fr. 9.

73. "Los abrevaderos del Río Ojo Caliente sean comunes entre ellos y el demás vecindario del partido del Río Arriba," grant by Governor Concha, Santa Fe, 11 September 1793, Ojo Caliente Grant, SG 77, Roll 21, fr. 10.

74. Act of possession by Alcalde Manuel García de la Mora, Ojo Caliente, 5 October 1793, Ojo Caliente Grant, SG 77, Roll 21, fr. 14–15. Manuel García de la Mora, born 1 January 1745, the son of Juan García de la Mora and the grandson of another Juan García de la Mora who came to New Mexico after murdering his wife in Spain because of suspected infidelity, is not to be confused with the Juan Esteban García de Noriega, an early landowner at El Rito. Chávez, *New Mexico Families*, 184, 291.

75. Grant by Governor Concha, Santa Fe, 11 September 1793, Ojo Caliente Grant, SG 77, Roll 21, fr. 10, 14–15; act of possession by Alcalde Manuel García de la Mora, Ojo Caliente, 5 October 1793, Ojo Caliente Grant, SG 77, Roll 21, fr. 10, 14–15.

76. Act of possession by Alcalde Manuel García de la Mora, Ojo Caliente, 5 October 1793, Ojo Caliente Grant, SG 77, Roll 21, fr. 14–15. Patricia Seed describes the ways in which the different European powers performed symbolic acts signifying their taking possession of their colonies in *Ceremonies of Possession in Europe's Conquest of the New World: 1492–1640* (Cambridge: Cambridge University Press, 1995). The Portuguese and the Dutch drew maps, the French performed elaborate theatrical rituals, the English used the land by building houses and especially fences on it, and the Spanish made speeches in the name of the church before they attacked and then divided the land among the conquerors by the ritual delivery of possession described previously.

77. List of "los nuevo pobladores del Ojo Caliente," Ojo Caliente Grant, SG 77, Roll 21, fr. 12–13.

78. Report of Governor Mendinueta to Viceroy Bucareli, Santa Fe, 26 March 1772, translated in Thomas, "Governor Mendinueta's Proposals," 29–30.

79. The allotments started at the Cañada de los Comanches on the north to the torreón of José Baca on the south, each settler receiving 150 varas of land along the river. If the property of the old settlers was being measured, the allotments would not all have measured exactly 150 varas but would have varied according to the terrain and the existing patterns of land use.

80. Order of Governor Mendinueta, Santa Fe, 20 June 1769, SANM I: 656.

81. Order of Governor Concha, Santa Fe, 2 September 1790, SANM I: 1062.

82. Remeasurement of Ojo Caliente lands by Alcalde Francisco Trujillo, Abiquiu, 17 September 1824, SANM I: 1189; Boyd, "Troubles at Ojo Caliente," 359–60.

83. Adams and Chávez, *Missions of New Mexico*, 78. A chasuble is an ecclesiastic garment, the outer vestment of a priest celebrating Mass.

84. Chávez, *Archives of the Archdiocese*, 53–54; Archives of the Archdiocese of Santa Fe, Loose Documents, Mission, 1680–1850, Doc. no. 2, 1796, State Records Center and Archives, Santa Fe, NM.

85. Alcalde Santiago Salazar petition in the name of the residents of Abiquiu,

Abiquiu, 8 October 1820, Archives of the Archdiocese of Santa Fe, Loose Documents, 1820, no. 15, State Records Center and Archives, Santa Fe, NM.

86. "No ser Indios de comunidad," petition of Ojo Caliente residents by Antonio García, 8 October 1820, Archives of the Archdiocese of Santa Fe, Loose Documents, no. 15, State Records Center and Archives, Santa Fe, NM.

87. Donald Jackson, ed., *The Journals of Zebulon Montgomery Pike* (Norman: University of Oklahoma Press, 1966), 387; Zebulon M. Pike, *An Account of Expeditions to the Sources of the Mississippi (1810)* (Philadelphia, PA: C. and A. Conrad, 1810), 206–7.

88. In his recommendation for confirmation of the Abiquiu grant, Surveyor General Julian noted that "the Spanish government was very lenient towards the Indians." Report of Surveyor General Julian, Santa Fe, 28 October 1885, Abiquiu Grant, PLC 52, Roll 26, fr. 434; Ebright and Hendricks, *Witches of Abiquiu*, 253–54. For a discussion of the 17,350-acre Pueblo league, see Ebright, Hendricks, and Hughes, *Four Square Leagues*, chapter 1.

89. For a discussion of the surveyor general of New Mexico, see Ebright, *Land Grants and Lawsuits*, 37–45; Bowden, "Private Land Claims," 4:1193–94.

90. Sister Ida Catherine, "Antonio Joseph" (MA thesis found in the Marion Dargan Papers, Center for Southwest Research and Special Collections, University of New Mexico, Albuquerque), 1–4.

91. Miguel A. Otero, *My Life on the Frontier*, 2 vols. (New York: Press of the Pioneers, 1935–1939), 2:239; Sister Ida Catherine, "Antonio Joseph," 4–6.

92. Bowden, "Private Land Claims," 4:1194; Myra Ellen Jenkins, "Ojo Caliente Grant—1793" (unpublished manuscript in possession of the author, 1979).

93. Sister Ida Catherine, "Antonio Joseph," 19–23.

94. Fanny Bandelier, trans., Adolf Bandelier, ed., *The Journey of Alvár Nuñez Cabeza de Vaca and His Companions from Florida to the Pacific, 1528–1536* (New York: A. S. Barnes, 1905), xx.

95. Ojo Caliente Mineral Springs, Celebrating Centuries of Healing, brochure, n.d., Ojo Caliente vertical file, Southwest Room, New Mexico State Library, Santa Fe; Sister Ida Catherine, "Antonio Joseph."

96. Rolena Adorno and Patrick Charles Pautz, *Alvar Nuñez Cabeza de Vaca: His Account, His Life, and the Expedition of Pánfilo de Narvaéz* (Lincoln: University of Nebraska Press, 1999), xxvii, contains a map of the travels of Cabeza de Vaca. The Cabeza de Vaca name was assumed by conquering Spaniards during the battles against the Muslims in southern Spain. After the Muslims had tried to take control of the mountain passes surrounding Las Navas de Tolosa, the Spanish Christians were able to penetrate their defenses and win a famous battle there on 16 July 1212, when a shepherd marked a passage through the mountains with a cow's skull, "pointing the way for safe passage of the armies

of Castile Aragón and Navarre." This account is unsubstantiated but has remained more powerful than alternate versions. Ibid., 1:298–303.

97. Cited in Sister Ida Catherine, "Antonio Joseph," 10–11.

98. Ibid., 16. For a legal history of the Cieneguilla grant, see Bowden, "Private Land Claims," 4:1015–22.

99. In 1850 construction began on what became the federal building in Santa Fe; intended as New Mexico's first state house, it later housed the Court of Private Land Claims. Twitchell, *Old Santa Fe*, 330, n. 591.

100. Petition for confirmation of the Ojo Caliente [Antonio Joseph] Grant, Ojo Caliente [Antonio Joseph] Grant, PLC 94, Roll 43, fr. 589–99; abstract of title to the Ojo Caliente Land Grant, PLC 94, Roll 43, fr. 608–13.

101. Abstract of title to the Ojo Caliente Land Grant, PLC 94, Roll 43, fr. 608–13.

102. Petition of Jesús María Olguín, Ojo Caliente Grant, PLC 88, Roll 43, fr. 7–10.

103. Opinion of Chief Justice Reed, Ojo Caliente [Antonio Joseph] Grant, PLC 94, Roll 43, fr. 602–6.

104. See *1915 New Mexico State Business Directory* (Denver, CO: Gazetteer, 1915), 524; *1919 New Mexico State Business Directory* (Denver, CO: Gazetteer), 409; Application for the State Register of Historic Sites, New Mexico Historic Preservation Division, Santa Fe.

105. Camille Flores, "Ranchers Sue Over Water Use," *Albuquerque Journal North*, 8 July 1989.

106. Jack Crellin, Forest Supervisor, Carson National Forest, to Senator Harrison Schmitt, Taos, 23 June 1980 (copy of letter in possession of the author); State Director of the Bureau of Land Management, Santa Fe, 18 July 1980 (copy of letter in possession of the author). The members of the Board of Commissioners of the Ojo Caliente grant in 1979 were Luciano Lucero, Juan B. Olguín, Filiberto García, Irene García, Alfonso Gálvez, Agustin Campos, José S. Archuleta, and Tomás García, Ojo Caliente, *La Merced de Ojo Caliente Newsletter* (unpublished manuscript in possession of the author).

107. Congressional Research Service, Library of Congress, to Manuel Luján Jr., Washington, D.C., 3 June 1981 (copy of letter in possession of the author).

Chapter Four

1. An example of the arbitrary classification is contained in Charles L. Briggs and John R. Van Ness, eds., *Land, Water, and Culture: New Perspectives on Hispanic Land Grants* (Albuquerque: University of New Mexico Press, 1987), chaps. 1 and 2; see also Pueblo of Taos, SG Report I, fr. 7, fr. 171 et seq.; Ebright, *Land Grants and Lawsuits*, 145–68; Ebright and Hendricks, *Witches of Abiquiu*, 89–105; Town of Manzano Grant, SG 23, Roll 15, fr. 649 et seq.

2. Herbert O. Brayer, *Pueblo Indian Land Grants of the "Rio Abajo" New Mexico* (Albuquerque: University of New Mexico Press, 1939). Inside the front cover Brayer shows the Ojo del Espíritu Santo grant as a non-Indian grant. See also Bowden, "Private Land Claims," 5:1252–55 (Cochiti Pasture grant) and 5:1327–33 (Zia, Jemez, and Santa Ana grant).

3. Town of San Isidro Grant, SG 24, Roll 16, fr. 9–10; the Zia, Santa Ana, and Jemez Grant, SG Report TT, Roll 7, fr. 341–90; the Zia, Santa Ana, and Jemez Grant, PLC 50, Roll 38, fr. 575–755.

4. Report by Bartolomé Fernández, [Santa Fe, April 1765], SANM I: 1352.

5. Order by Governor Vélez Cachupín, Santa Fe, 11 April 1765, SANM I: 1352.

6. Chávez, *New Mexico Families*, 236; Response of Miguel Romero, Santa Fe, [17 April 1765], SANM I: 1352.

7. Order by Governor Vélez Cachupín, Santa Fe, 18 April 1765, SANM I: 1352.

8. Response of Miguel and Domingo Romero, Santa Fe, 18 April 1765, SANM I: 1352. Vélez Cachupín also requested a response from the officers of the Santa Fe Presidio's cavalry company regarding their possible use of the area for grazing the presidio's horse herd. Tomás Madrid replied that El Capulín was not one of the areas traditionally designated as commons for the presidio of Santa Fe, although the nearby site of Pajarito was. Response of Tomás Madrid, Santa Fe, 1 October 1766, SANM I: 1352.

9. Response by Alcalde Bartolomé Fernández, Santa Fe, SANM I: 1352. This was not the end of the proceedings, however, for several more statements needed to be filed, and by that time Vélez Cachupín had left office just as Miguel Romero and his brother had hoped. On 1 March 1767, Pedro Fermín de Mendinueta took over the governorship of New Mexico from Vélez Cachupín, who remained in Santa Fe for several months to meet with Mendinueta and attempt to pass on some of his knowledge and experience to the new governor. In this instance, Mendinueta followed his predecessor's advice. On 25 April 1767, less than two months after Vélez Cachupín left office, Mendinueta made a final decision, citing Vélez Cachupín's decree of 18 April 1766 and agreeing with all of the points Fernández made, and adding that settlement by pasturing one's flocks was not sufficient settlement (Fernández did not make this argument because he had his own grazing grant). Mendinueta ordered that the land should remain open as common grazing land, without excluding the Romeros from grazing rights. Final decree by Pedro Fermín de Mendinueta, Santa Fe, 25 April 1767, SANM I: 1352.

10. Petition of Felipe Tafoya on behalf of Cochiti, [Santa Fe, July 1766], Juana Baca Grant, PLC 172, Roll 50, fr. 223 (English), fr. 220 (Spanish).

11. *Sobrantes la legua que comunmente llaman, y que este sirve para ejido de los caballos*, petition of Felipe Tafoya on behalf of Cochiti [Santa Fe, July 1766],

Juana Baca Grant, PLC 172, Roll 50, fr. 223 (English), fr. 220 (Spanish). For a
discussion of New Mexico pueblos and the Pueblo league, see Ebright, Hendricks, and Hughes, *Four Square Leagues*, chapter 1.

12. Decree by Tomás Vélez Cachupín, Santa Fe, 16 July 1766, Juana Baca Grant,
    PLC 172, Roll 50, fr. 223 (English), fr. 220 (Spanish).

13. Report by Juan María Rivera, Santa Fe, [17] July 1766, Juana Baca Grant, PLC 172,
    Roll 50, fr. 223-24 (English), fr. 220-21 (Spanish).

14. Grant by Tomás Vélez Cachupín, Santa Fe, 6 August 1766, Juana Baca Grant,
    PLC 172, Roll 50, fr. 224-25 (English), fr. 221-22 (Spanish). Governor Vélez Cach-
    upín, who made the Zia, Santa Ana, and Jemez pasture grant the same day as the
    Cochiti pasture grant, seems to have had in mind an overall land use plan for the
    area. That plan included private and community Hispanic land grants, common
    lands attached to Hispanic land grants, Indian pueblos with their four square
    leagues, and ejidos attached to Indian pueblos. *Recopilación* 6.3.8 had provided
    for ejidos attached to pueblos, and Vélez Cachupín cited that law when he made
    the Abiquiu grant. Now, the governor seemed to also have had that law in mind
    when he made the Cochiti Pueblo pasture grant. The similarity between the
    Cochiti and the soon to be discussed Zia, Santa Ana, and Jemez pasture grants
    is striking. They were made on the same day; instigated both by the pueblos
    themselves and by Felipe Tafoya, as an advocate speaking on the pueblos' behalf;
    and they provided for an absolute grant to the pueblos. The land was to be used
    by the members of the pueblos only, excluding Hispanic settlers, on the condi-
    tion that the grant also be available for the stallions of the presidial horse herd.
    In both grants the pueblos would own the grants "with legal title under a royal
    grant," and no neighboring Spaniards could use the land supposing that it was
    common pasture available to everyone (tierras baldías). Grant by Tomás Vélez
    Cachupín, Santa Fe, 6 August 1766, Juana Baca Grant, PLC 172, Roll 50, fr. 224-25
    (English), fr. 221-22 (Spanish); for the Abiquiu grant, see Ebright and Hendricks,
    Witches of Abiquiu, 89-105; *Recopilación* 6.3.8; for the distinction between ejidos
    and tierras baldías, see Daniel Tyler, "Ejido Lands in New Mexico," in *Spanish
    and Mexican Land Grants and the Law*, ed. Malcolm Ebright (Manhattan, KS:
    Sunflower University Press, 1989), 24, 28-30.

15. The boundaries of the Cochiti pasture grant were "from north to south, from
    the Rio Chiquito along the brow, center of the league, the Piñon Hill, along the
    Vallecito Road, down Peralta, up the Vallecito Road as far as the Rito de Jara,
    down along the Cañada of the Rito de Jara, up along the road from Cochiti
    towards Jemez, down the Cañada Coriz as far as the east boundary, on the west
    it passes on the other bank of the river, it goes upon the elevation of the hills on
    the little Peñasco table land as far as the Piedra Parada, as far as the old Pueblo
    of La Majada . . . the boundary continues as far as Cerro Mojino, and the Cerro

Poñil, then along the brow of the hill as far as the Rocillo slope, down the Del Norte River as far as the Rio Chiquito, the northern boundary." Grant of Tomás Vélez Cachupín, Santa Fe, 6 August 1766, Juana Baca Grant, PLC 172, Roll 50, fr. 224–25 (English), fr. 221–22 (Spanish).

16. Grant by Tomás Vélez Cachupín, Santa Fe, 6 August 1766, Juana Baca Grant, PLC 172, Roll 50, fr. 224–25, Zia Pueblo v. U.S., 168 U.S. 198.

17. Petition for confirmation of the Cochiti Pasture Grant, Santa Fe, 2 March 1893, Juana Baca Grant, PLC 172, Roll 50, fr. 219–31.

18. Zia Pueblo v. U.S., Oct. 1897, 168 U.S. 198; Bowden, "Private Land Claims," 5:1254–55.

19. Petition by Antonio Lucero, [Santa Fe, August 1728], Cañada de Cochití Grant, PLC 205, Roll 51, fr. 729 (translation), 760 (Spanish transcription).

20. Grant by Juan Domingo Bustamante, Santa Fe, 2 August 1728, Cañada de Cochití Grant, PLC 205, Roll 51, fr. 730 (translation), 760–61 (Spanish transcription).

21. Cochiti claims association with numerous ruins in what is now Bandelier National Monument, including the famous stone lions. There are actually two stone lion shrines, both important to Cochiti. The first is located on the Potrero de los Ídolos, north of the pueblo, probably on the Cañada de Cochiti grant. The second set of stone lions is "a pair of mountain lions carved into the top of two side-by-side boulders about 10 miles north of the pueblo near the ancient Pueblo of Yapashe," within Bandelier National Monument. To this day the Cochiti hunters' society venerates the stone lions, which represent a very rare instance of full-size sculpture by North American Indians. The famous nineteenth-century anthropologist Adolf Bandelier had hiked to these and other sites many times with his friend and informant José Hilario Montoya. The location of sites such as the old Cochiti Pueblo and the stone lions looms large in the legal history of Cochiti Pueblo. Their location was usually kept secret, but when the location of the old Cochiti Pueblo became a boundary call on one of the adjoining land grants, experts working for the government testified about these sites. Lange, *Cochití*, 1, 8.

22. Act of possession by Andrés Montoya, Cañada de Cochití Grant, PLC 205, Roll 51, fr. 731 (translation), 761 (Spanish transcription).

23. Chávez, *New Mexico Families*, 236; D. H. Snow, "Note on *Encomienda* Economics," 354–55.

24. Petition by Cayetano Montaño and other heirs of Antonio Lucero to Antonio Armenta, n.p., [November] 1785, Cañada de Cochití Grant, PLC 205, Roll 51, fr. 733-34 (translation), 762–63 (Spanish transcription).

25. Decision of Antonio Armenta, Pueblo of San Buenaventura, 2 November 1785, Cañada de Cochití Grant, PLC 205, Roll 51, fr. 734–35 (translation), 761–62 (Spanish transcription); Salazar, "Felipe Tafoya Grant," 3–4.

26. Fray Angélico Chávez, "Valle de Cochiti," *New Mexico Magazine* 51 (January/
    February 1973): 6–17.

27. Lange, *Cochití*, 8.

28. "Abstract of Title," Santa Fe, 12 July 1884, Cañada de Cochití Grant, PLC 205,
    Roll 51, fr. 770–81.

29. Ebright, *Land Grants and Lawsuits*, chapter 6, 127–42.

30. Decision of Henry Atkinson, Santa Fe, 25 August 1883, Cañada de Cochití Grant,
    SG 135, Roll 25, fr. 879, et. seq.; Bowden, "Private Land Claims," 5:1234–35.

31. Bowden, "Private Land Claims," 5:1235–36. "UNM Might Sell Ancestral Ground
    to Pueblo," *New Mexican*, 30 April 2000, B8.

32. Ibid.

33. Opinion of George W. Julian, Santa Fe, 27 February 1886, Cañada de Cochití
    Grant, SG 135, Roll, fr. 879; Bowden, "Private Land Claims," 5:1235.

34. Among the other petitioners was prominent Albuquerque lawyer Bernard S.
    Rodey. Rodey claimed a one-half interest in the grant. Joel Parker Whitney et al.,
    petition for confirmation of the Cañada de Cochití Grant, Santa Fe, 2 March
    1883, Cañada de Cochití Grant PLC 205, Roll 51, fr. 719–29, 757.

35. Manuel Hurtado et al., petition for confirmation of the Cañada de Cochití Grant
    and order of consolidation of the two petitions, Cañada de Cochití Grant,
    PLC 205, Roll 51, fr. 719–29.

36. Answer of the United States, Santa Fe, 11 September 1884, Cañada de Cochití
    Grant, PLC 205, Roll 51, fr. 796–803.

37. *La mesa de Cochití donde estuvieron retirados los Indios que se sublevaron*,
    petition of Antonio Lucero, [Santa Fe, August 1728], Cañada de Cochití Grant,
    PLC 205, Roll 51, fr. 729 (translation), 760 (Spanish transcription).

38. El Pino (Cristóbal Nieto) Grant, PLC 81, Roll 42, fr. 482–83.

39. Adolph Bandelier, "The Southwestern Land Court," *Nation* 52 (18 May 1891): 437;
    Will Tipton, letter to the editor, "Mr. Bandelier and the Southwestern Land
    Court," *Nation* (25 June 1891): 516–17. Tipton tried to hide his identity because of
    his friendship with Bandelier, and the letter to the editor was datelined "Denver,
    Col." and signed with the initials "P.T." See Lange, Riley, and Lange, *Bandelier
    Journals*, 575–77, n. 899, where the entire Tipton letter is reproduced. Lange,
    Riley, and Lange, *Bandelier Journals*, 575, n. 899.

40. Testimony of Will Tipton, transcript of trial, Cañada de Cochití Grant, PLC 205,
    Roll 51, fr. 841–47; Bandelier's journals mention only a few visits by Tipton (more
    in 1892), but Tipton's statement that he "was with Bandelier more than any other
    person" was surely an exaggeration. Lange, Riley, and Lange, *Bandelier Jour-
    nals*, 73.

41. Opinion of the Court of Private Land Claims, Cañada de Cochití Grant, PLC
    205, Roll 51, fr. 823–28.

42. Whitney v. U.S., 167 U.S. 529 (1897).
43. James Dory-Garduño, "The 1766 Ojo del Espíritu Santo Grant: Authenticating a New Mexico Land Grant," *Colonial Latin American Historical Review* 16, no. 2 (Spring 2007): 157–96, 183.
44. Ibid.
45. Petition of the pueblos of Zia, Santa Ana, and Jemez for the Ojo del Espíritu Santo Grant; Zia, Santa Ana, and Jemez Grant, SG TT, Roll 7, fr. 363–64 (translation).
46. Decree of Tomás Vélez Cachupín, Santa Fe, 16 June 1766, Zia, Santa Ana, and Jemez Grant, SG TT, Roll 7, fr. 374 (translation).
47. Report of Bartolomé Fernández, Santa Fe, 16 June 1766, Zia, Santa Ana, and Jemez Grant, SG TT, Roll 7, fr. 365.
48. "Lo posean con derecho legítimo mediante esta real merced," granting decree of Tomás Vélez Cachupín, Zia, Santa Ana, and Jemez Grant, SG TT, Roll 7, fr. 364.
49. Act of possession of Alcalde Bartolomé Fernández, Paraje del Ojo del Espíritu Santo, 28 September 1766, Zia, Santa Ana, and Jemez Grant, SG TT, Roll 7, fr. 367–68. The Ojo del Espíritu Santo Grant (1766) does not reach Zia Pueblo.
50. For a discussion of the neighboring grant, made to Ramón García Jurado, Antonio Montaño and five others, and its relationship with the Ojo del Espíritu Santo Grant (1766), see chapter 9, 210.
51. Brayer, *Pueblo Indian Land Grants*. Inside the front cover Brayer shows the Ojo del Espíritu Santo grant as a non-Indian grant.
52. Ojo del Espíritu Santo Grant (1815), SG 44, Roll 17, fr. 753–884.
53. Bowden, "Private Land Claims," 5:1329, 1370, 1391; Town of San Isidro Grant, SG 24, Roll 16, fr. 16–67.
54. Bowden, "Private Land Claims," 5:1329.
55. Although the authenticity of the Vélez Cachupín –certified copy of the Ojo del Espíritu Santo grant was later questioned, its genuineness had been clearly established. Dory-Garduño, "1766 Ojo del Espíritu Santo Grant," 157–96.
56. Zia, Santa Ana, and Jemez Grant, SG TT, Roll 7, fr. 386–88; Bowden, "Private Land Claims," 5:1329–30.
57. Congress did not confirm any land grants after 1879, and ten years later a backlog of 116 grants awaited congressional action. Ebright, *Land Grants and Lawsuits*, 45.
58. Petition for confirmation of the Ojo del Espíritu Santo Grant, Zia, Santa Ana, and Jemez Grant, PLC 50, Roll 38, fr. 576–84.
59. Indian Agent Williams to Commissioner of Indian Affairs, Santa Fe, 18 June 1888, Miscellaneous Letters sent by the Pueblo Indian Agency, 1874–1891, National Archives and Records Service, Microfilm Publication M941, Washington, D.C., 1973.
60. The statute providing for the first congressional appropriation for a special

attorney for the Pueblo Indians was not passed until 1898 (30 Stat 571 at 594). Although no evidence has been found of an earlier statute providing for appointment of a special attorney, Twitchell testified that the pueblos had a special attorney "before the establishment of [the 1891 Court of Private Land Claims] . . . for a long time." Hall, *Four Leagues of Pecos*, 340, n. 12. Even with a lawyer to represent them, the pueblos continued to be subject to trespass by neighboring landowners and overlapping grants.

61. Petition for confirmation of the Ojo del Espíritu Santo Grant, Zia, Santa Ana, and Jemez Grant, PLC 50, Roll 38, fr. 580–83.

62. The trial transcript is 104 pages long. Transcript of testimony, Court of Private Land Claims, Santa Fe, August 1894, Zia, Santa Ana, and Jemez Grant, PLC 50, Roll 38, fr. 586–689.

63. Ibid., fr. 737.

64. Ibid., fr. 668.

65. Testimony of Francisco Archibeque, transcript of testimony, Court of Private Land Claims, Santa Fe, August 1894, Zia, Santa Ana, and Jemez Grant, PLC 50, Roll 38, fr. 667–68.

66. Transcript of Lorenzo Lobato testimony, Court of Private Land Claims, Santa Fe, August 1894, Zia, Santa Ana, and Jemez Grant, PLC 50, Roll 38, fr. 618–19.

67. Ebright, *Land Grants and Lawsuits*, 50, lists three additional reasons under Spanish law that would justify rejection of a land grant: 1) forgery or alteration of the documents, 2) lack of proof that the grant was made, and 3) revocation of the grant by Spanish or Mexican authorities.

68. Bowden, "Private Land Claims," 5:1330–31.

69. In 1764 Governor Vélez Cachupín granted the settlers of San Gabriel de las Nutrias a temporary grant or license to establish a settlement on a grant on the banks of the Río Grande. When the settlers could demonstrate that the settlement had taken root, the governor would make the grant permanent. SANM I: 780; see also chapter 9, 198–200.

70. Henry Billings Brown served on the U.S. Supreme Court from 1890 to 1906. He authored the infamous 1896 *Plessy v. Ferguson* opinion upholding racially segregated railroad cars and providing a foundation for racially discriminatory laws until the mid-twentieth century. Hall, *Oxford Companion*, 92–93.

71. Zia Pueblo v. U.S., Oct. 1897, 168 U.S. 198, 201, 203; "Lo posean con derecho legitimo mediante esta real merced," granting decree of Governor Vélez Cachupín, Zia, Santa Ana, and Jemez Grant, SG TT, Roll 7, fr. 364.

72. In the late 1760s Alcaldes Felipe Tafoya, Bartolomé Fernández, and Carlos Pérez de Mirabal, as well as seven others, all received grazing grants in the Cebolleta/Mount Taylor area. See appendix C. One grantee named Salvador Jaramillo sold part of his grant to Clemente Gutiérrez soon after he acquired it

for five thousand pesos' worth of cows and sheep. Frank D. Reeve, "The Navaho-Spanish Peace: 1720s–1770s," *New Mexico Historical Review* 34 (January 1959): 9–40.

73. U.S. v. Sandoval, 167 U.S. Reports 278 (1897).

74. Ebright, Hendricks, and Hughes, *Four Square Leagues*, 170–78.

75. Petition of Luis María Cabeza de Baca, Peña Blanca, 23 May 1815, Ojo del Espíritu Santo Grant, SG 44, Roll 17, fr. 755 (original), fr. 761–62 (translation).

76. Grant of (1815) Ojo del Espíritu Santo Grant by Governor Alberto Máynez, 24 May 1815, Ojo del Espíritu Santo Grant, SG 44, Roll 17, fr. 755–56 (original), fr. 762 (translation).

77. Act of possession by Ignacio María Sánchez Vergara, 14 June 1815, Ojo del Espíritu Santo Grant, SG 44, Roll 17, fr. 756 (original), fr. 762–63 (translation).

78. Ebright, Hendricks, and Hughes, *Four Square Leagues*, 73–81, 129–31, 175–78.

79. Petition by lawyer John L. Watts for confirmation of the 1815 Ojo del Espíritu Santo Grant, Ojo del Espíritu Santo Grant, SG 44, Roll 17, fr. 757–60. Watts had accomplished the impossible for those same Baca heirs when he was successful in establishing their title to the same land covered by the Las Vegas Community Land grant; both grants covering the same land were recommended for confirmation by Surveyor General Pelham in 1860. Watts then waived their claim to that specific tract in exchange for an equivalent acreage to be drawn from the public domain. Bowden, "Private Land Claims," 3:793–808.

80. Opinion of Surveyor General Alexander Wilbar, Ojo del Espíritu Santo Grant, SG 44, Roll 17, fr. 785–88.

81. Bowden, "Private Land Claims," 5:1394–95.

82. GLO Commissioner S. W. Lamereaux to Surveyor General, Washington, D.C., 18 January 1895, Ojo del Espíritu Santo Grant, SG 44, Roll 17, fr. 838–40.

83. U.S. Attorney David Heahy to Surveyor General John W. March, Las Vegas, NM, 2 August 1911, Ojo del Espíritu Santo Grant, SG 44, Roll 17, fr. 849; GLO Assistant Commissioner to Surveyor General, Washington, D.C., 14 October 1916, notice re transmittal of patent, Ojo del Espíritu Santo Grant, SG 44, Roll 17, fr. 847–48.

84. Suzanne Forrest, *The Preservation of the Village: New Mexico's Hispanics and the New Deal* (Albuquerque: University of New Mexico Press, 1989), 139–40; for more on Frank Bond and especially his purchase of community land grants such as the Las Trampas and Ramón Vigil grants, see Ebright, *Land Grants and Lawsuits*, 157–64, 245.

85. Petition for the San Isidro Grant, and grant by Governor Anza, Santa Fe, 4 May 1786, Town of San Isidro Grant, SG 24, Roll 16, fr. 8–9; Bowden, "Private Land Claims," 5:1341.

86. Act of possession of the San Isidro Grant, petition for the San Isidro Grant, and

grant by Governor Anza, Santa Fe, 4 May 1786, Town of San Isidro Grant, SG 24, Roll 16, fr. 9–10; Bowden, "Private Land Claims," 5:1340.

87. Petition for confirmation of the San Isidro Grant (known as the Rancho de San Ysidro) by Francisco Sandoval et al., Town of San Isidro Grant, SG 45, Roll 16, fr. 12–14. Francisco Sandoval also petitioned the surveyor general for confirmation of the Rancho de la Santísima Trinidad grant south of the San Isidro grant.

88. Pelham report recommending approval of the San Isidro Grant, Santa Fe, 8 June 1859, Town of San Isidro Grant, SG 45, Roll 24, fr. 25.

89. Bowden, "Private Land Claims," 5:1343.

90. Ibid.

91. Strother M. Stockslager to George Julian, Washington, D.C., 17 November 1888, Town of San Isidro Grant, SG 45, Roll 16, fr. 32–43.

92. Bowden, "Private Land Claims," 5:1344.

93. For a discussion of the patenting and use of the San Isidro grant, see chapter 7 in Ebright, Hendricks, and Hughes, *Four Square Leagues*, 199–200.

94. Pelham report recommending approval of the San Isidro Grant, Santa Fe, 8 June 1859, Town of San Isidro Grant, SG 45, Roll 16, fr. 25; Bowden, "Private Land Claims," 5:1343. A comparison of the San Isidro grant with the grant to the south, known as the Rancho de la Santísima Trinidad grant, shows why the San Isidro grant confirmation was unfair. Both grants overlapped pueblos (in the case of the Santísima Trinidad, it was Zia Pueblo), and both involved questionable relationships between the petitioners and the grantees (in both cases, Francisco Sandoval was either the sole petitioner or a joint petitioner). Governor Manrique made the Santísima Trinidad grant to Ignacio Sánchez Vergara on 13 May 1809 on the condition that he farm the land and that the grant was not within the boundaries of either the San Isidro grant or Zia Pueblo. Alcalde Cleto de Miera y Pacheco investigated the request on 26 May 1809 and conferred with Zia Pueblo. Governor Manrique appeared to have made the grant according to his approval of Miera y Pacheco's act of possession, but the document was suspicious and turned out to be a forgery.

Chapter Five

1. Lange, Riley and Lange, *Southwestern Journals*, 124, 523, n. 797; Nels Christian Nelson, *Pueblo Ruins of the Galisteo Basin, New Mexico*, Anthropological Papers of the American Museum of Natural History, vol. 15, pt. 1 (New York: American Museum of National History, 1914); Toll and Badner, *Galisteo Basin Archeological Sites*, 275–304.

2. The Laboratory of Anthropology lists La Ciénega Pueblo as LA 44 and Ciene-guilla Pueblo as LA 16. Like San Cristóbal, San Marcos, and Galisteo Pueblos, when La Ciénega and Cieneguilla Pueblos were abandoned, Spaniards moved in to acquire the land, sometimes by land grant but mostly by individual deeds. In one authoritative work, Cieneguilla is located among the five Galisteo Basin pueblos that had a total population of about four thousand Indians by 1629. Elinore Barrett, *Conquest and Catastrophe: Changing Rio Grande Pueblo Settle-ment Patterns in the Sixteenth and Seventeenth Centuries* (Albuquerque: Univer-sity of New Mexico Press, 2002), 63–64.

3. D. H. Snow, "Note on *Encomienda* Economics," 354, 356.

4. Biddle Duke, "The Flow of Change: Worlds Collide in La Ciénega," *Santa Fe New Mexican*, 28 June 1992.

5. Lucy Lippard and Edward Ranney, *Down Country: The Tano of the Galisteo Basin, 1250–1782* (Santa Fe: Museum of New Mexico Press, 2010), 30.

6. Hammond and Rey, *Rediscovery of New Mexico*, 282, 288; Albert H. Schroeder and Dan Matson, *A Colony on the Move: Gaspar Castaño de Sosa's Journal, 1590–1591* (Santa Fe, NM: School of American Research, 1965), 118.

7. D. H. Snow, "Note on *Encomienda* Economics," 354–56; for a discussion of pre-revolt land holding in New Mexico, see Ebright, Hendricks, and Hughes, *Four Square Leagues*, 3–4; and Barrett, *Conquest and Catastrophe*, 63–64.

8. Kessell, *Kiva, Cross, and Crown*, 178.

9. The provincial of the Order of Saint Francis of the Province of Santo Evan-gelico concerning the matter of granting forty friars to the said province, Archivo General de Indias, Seville, 60-3-66, translation in France V. Scholes, "Documents for the History of the New Mexican Missions in the Seventeenth Century," *New Mexico Historical Review* 4 (January 1929): 48; Hacket and Shelby, *Revolt of the Pueblo Indians*, xxxviii; D. H. Snow, "Note on *Encomienda* Economics," 357.

10. "At noon on Saturday, 26 August the father commissary and I arrived at the Pueblo of Ciénega on the way to this villa the pueblo being halfway [from Santo Domingo]," declaration of Fray Gabriel de Torija, Santo Domingo, 3 June 1664; Hackett, *Historical Documents*, 249.

11. Reply of Diego de Peñalosa, Mexico, 22 October 1665; Hackett, *Historical Docu-ments*, 261.

12. López de Mendizábal died in the Inquisition jail in Mexico City before the audi-encia, or high court of Mexico, found him guilty of sixteen of the thirty-three charges against him. Cristóbal Anaya Almazán had better luck. In return for his admission of the charges against him and the renouncing of his errors, he was released. Banned from New Mexico for ten years, Cristóbal was required, on his return to the province, to "stand up during Mass on a feast day and publicly

recant his false doctrine." Kessell, *Kiva, Cross, and Crown*, 190–93, quote at 193; see also Scholes, "Troublous Times," 369–417.

13. Hackett and Shelby, *Revolt of the Pueblo Indians*, xxxviii; David J. Weber, *The Spanish Frontier in North America* (New Haven, CT: Yale University Press, 1992), 135.

14. Kessell and Hendricks, *By Force of Arms*, 386.

15. Kessell, Hendricks, and Dodge, *To the Royal Crown*, 111. There is no evidence of a grant of the Hacienda del Álamo by Vargas, but there was a landholding called the Hacienda del Álamo that was part of the estate of José de Riaño Tagle in 1744. Will of José Riaño Tagle, Santa Fe, 15 April 1743, SANM I: 963–64; Hacienda del Álamo Grant, PLC 155, Roll 49, fr. 529.

16. Kessell, Hendricks, and Dodge, *Blood on the Boulders*, 2:759. At the time of the Pueblo Revolt of 1696 some of the members of La Ciénega Pueblo had moved to Tesuque Pueblo. Kessell, Hendricks, Dodge, *Blood on the Boulders*, 1:136.

17. David H. Snow, "A Review of Spanish Colonial Archeology in Northern New Mexico," in *Current Research on the Late Prehistory and Early History of New Mexico*, ed. Bradley J. Vierra (Albuquerque: New Mexico Archeological Council, 1992), 192; Marianne L. Stoller, "A Spanish Colonial Household in 17th Century New Mexico" (paper presented at the annual meeting of the Society for Historical Archeology, Vancouver, BC, 6 January 1994).

18. Chávez, *New Mexico Families*, 87–88, 111.

19. Ibid., 54.

20. Kessell, Hendricks, and Dodge, *To the Royal Crown*, 111.

21. Los Cerrillos Grant, SG 59, Roll 19, fr. 182 et seq.

22. Olmsted, *Spanish and Mexican Censuses*, 12–13.

23. Olmsted, *Spanish and Mexican Censuses*, 12–13. The Santa Fe and Alamo census together counted 1,025 adults and 512 children.

24. Domingo de la Barreda's land bounded the Cristóbal Nieto tract discussed in chapter 2, "A City Different than We Thought," SANM I: 638. It is often said of this deed that it conveyed the old pueblo of Ciénega granted to Bernabé Jorge by Diego de Vargas. Chávez, *New Mexico Families*, 51, 145. In fact, the deed refers to two tracts, one the old pueblo of Ciénega, the other a grant from Vargas to Bernabé Jorge of a different tract. SANM I: 732.

25. Juan García de la Riva was alcalde ordinario of the Santa Fe Cabildo in 1713 and 1715–1717. Gallegos and Esquibel, "*Alcaldes* and Mayors," 414–15.

26. In addition, Juan García de la Riva was listed as owning the abandoned pueblo of San Marcos. Inventory of the archives of the cabildo of Santa Fe, 1715, SANM I: 1136. But it was the heirs of Antonio Urbán Montano who claimed the San Marcos grant based on a grant to Antonio by Governor Vélez Cachupín in 1754. The

Court of Private Land Claims confirmed the grant, surveyed at almost nineteen hundred acres, to the heirs. Bowden, "Private Land Claims," 3:437–42; see also chapter 7, "San Marcos Pueblo Grant."

27. Cordelia Thomas Snow, "In Search of Guicú: History and Land Use of the Area of La Ciénega Development, Santa Fe County, New Mexico" (unpublished manuscript in possession of the author), 14. See also, Chávez, *New Mexico Families*, 254; and John B. Colligan, *The Juan Páez Hurtado Expedition of 1695: Fraud in Recruiting Colonists for New Mexico* (Albuquerque: University of New Mexico Press, 1995), 3–4.

28. Chávez, *New Mexico Families*, 294.

29. Ibid.; will of José Terrus, SANM I: 966; Ebright, "A City Different," 406–7.

30. Chávez, *New Mexico Families*, 141–44; will of Diego Manuel Baca, Santa Fe, 1827, SANM I: 83. Juan Esteban Baca married Teodora Terrus, daughter of José Terrus (who had married Antonia, the daughter of Juan Páez Hurtado and Teodora García de la Riva, as mentioned earlier). Manuel Baca married Leonarda Fernández, then Margarita Tafoya in 1750, and finally Juana Silva in 1768. Nicolas married Teodora Fernández de la Pedrera in 1747. Chávez, *New Mexico Families*, 144, 294.

31. Deed from Manuel Baca, as executor of the estate of María de la Vega y Coca to Josefa Montoya, Santa Fe, 24 December 1751, SANM I: 539.

32. Proceedings in the partition of the lands of María de la Vega y Coca at the Cañada de Guicú, La Ciénega, Alcalde Francisco Guerrero, Santa Fe, 17 May 1764, SANM I: 109. The will of María de la Vega y Coca, which was examined by Alcalde Guerrero, was not attached to this document.

33. Power of attorney from Domingo de Luna to Miguel Tenorio de Alba on behalf of María Baca, SANM I: 991.

34. Deed from Miguel Tenorio de Alba to Miguel Tafoya, 1 March 1766, SANM I: 991.

35. Petition by Felipe Tafoya to Governor Mendinueta, Santa Fe, SANM I: 991; order of Governor Mendinueta, Santa Fe, 30 April 1767, SANM I: 991; and deed from Miguel Tenorio de Alba to Miguel Tafoya, Santa Fe, 30 April 1767, SANM I: 991.

36. *Para aplicarle en misas a dichas benditas ánimas*, deed from Miguel Tenorio de Alba as primary executor of the estate of Manuel Tenorio de Alba to Manuel Gallegos, Santa Fe, 5 April 1771, Santa Fe County Deeds, Book A-1, 25–26, State Records Center and Archives, Santa Fe, NM.

37. Deed from Miguel Tenorio de Alba to Manuel Gallegos, 5 April 1771, Santa Fe County Deeds, Book A-1, 24–25, State Records Center and Archives, Santa Fe, NM; deed from Manuel Gallegos, resident of San Clemente, jurisdiction of Albuquerque to Jaime Ortiz, Santa Fe County Deeds Book A-1, 29–30, State Records Center and Archives, Santa Fe, NM.

38. Antonio José López and Matías Tenorio v. Miguel Tenorio [de Alba], decision of Governor Mendinueta, Santa Fe, 2 March 1772, SANM I: 460. Governor Mendinueta also seemed to be saying that the right of first refusal applied only in the case of a sale, not an exchange. The basic reason for the decision was stated as follows: "It is not just to compel Tenorio [de Alba] to receive what is not acceptable to him in payment for his own property."

39. Deed from Antonio José López to Alejandro Ortega, Santa Fe, 3 August 1774, Santa Fe County Deeds, Book A-1, 23–24, State Records Center and Archives, Santa Fe, NM.

40. Deed from Alejandro Ortega to Pablo Montoya, resident of Cieneguilla, Santa Fe, 9 September 1791, Santa Fe County Deeds, Book A-1, 26–27, State Records Center and Archives, Santa Fe, NM.

41. Kessell, Hendricks, and Dodge, *To the Royal Crown*, 111; Alamo Grant, PLC 200, Roll 51, fr. 567 et seq.

42. *Geographical Description of New Mexico* written by the Reverend Preacher Fray Juan Agustín de Morfi, Reader Jubilado and son of this province of Santo Evangelico of Mexico, Year of 1782, in Thomas, *Forgotten Frontiers*, 93. The difference in Morfi's population figures and the earlier census taken by Domínguez is mostly attributable to the fact that Morfi had not made a personal inspection, as Father Domínguez had, but relied on two other works— Vélez de Escalante's *Noticias* and Martínez's *Relación*—for his census. Marc Simmons, trans. and ed., *Father Juan Agustín Morfi's Account of Disorders in New Mexico, 1778* (Santa Fe: Historical Society of New Mexico, 1977), 8–9.

43. It was later determined, when the road was reestablished, that it passed between the houses of Riaño and Alfonso Rael de Aguilar. José Riaño v. Juan Lucero de Godoy, Santa Fe, 1732, SANM I: 758.

44. Will and power of attorney of José Riaño Tagle, Santa Fe, 1 April 1743, SANM I: 963 and 964.

45. Chávez, *New Mexico Families*, 174–75. Also appearing as a witness at Teresa's marriage to Felipe Sandoval Martínez was María Francisca's husband, Juan Bautista Alarid. Teresa later married Felipe Tafoya in 1750.

46. Will of José Riaño Tagle, Santa Fe, 15 April 1743, SANM I: 963–64. Part of the improvement Riaño is referring to was the thirteen-room house at San Jose del Alamo. Riaño has been described as "one of the richest men in New Mexico in the mid-eighteenth century," which is evident from the appraisal of the property at the Alamo Ranch at over twenty-one thousand pesos. SANM I: 964; Swadesh, *Pobladores*, 34.

47. Will and power of attorney of José Riaño Tagle, Santa Fe, 15 April 1743, SANM I: 963 and 964.

48. In 1728 Antonio Sandoval married Josefa Chaves, with whom he had four

children: Vicente, José Isidro, Francisco Matías, and José Antonio. Chávez, *New Mexico Families*, 283; will and power of attorney of José Riaño Tagle, Santa Fe, 15 April 1743, SANM I: 963 and 964.

49. Proceedings in the settlement of the estate of José Riaño, Santa Fe, 17 April 1744, SANM I: 762.

50. Ibid.

51. John Walker, U.S. Deputy Surveyor, field notes of survey of Small Holding Claim No. 1234 of Miguela Bustamante, Bureau of Land Management, Santa Fe, NM.

52. Kessell, Hendricks, and Dodge, *To the Royal Crown*, 111.

53. Proceedings in settlement of the estate of José Riaño, Santa Fe, 17 April 1744, SANM I: 762.

54. Sandoval's story, including his detailed description of the country he traveled across, is found in his deposition taken by Governor Vélez Cachupín in 1750. Vélez Cachupín believed that the Mallet party should never have been allowed to leave New Mexico, and he recommended that Sandoval and his party be sent to live in Nueva Vizcaya or Sonora as settlers. In fact, Sandoval seems to have settled down in the Rancho del Álamo. Henry Morse Stephens and Herbert E. Bolton, *The Pacific Ocean in History: Papers and Addresses Presented at the Panama-Pacific Historical Society* (American Asiatic Association, 1917; repr., Toronto: University of Toronto, 2011), 389–407; Chávez, *New Mexico Families*, 283.

55. Deed from Felipe de Sandoval y Rojas to José Riaño II, Santa Fe, 3 November 1755, Book R, 478–79, Santa Fe County Deeds, County Courthouse, Santa Fe, New Mexico.

56. Documents regarding the escape of José Riaño: Pinart Colleciton, Bancroft Library, PE 52:10. Chávez, *New Mexico Families*, 265; petition of Ana María Ortiz for appointment of an administrator of the estate of José Riaño II, Santa Fe, July–August 1761, SANM II: 557. Toribio Ortiz was named administrator and presumably fulfilled his duties and transferred the property of José Riaño II to his widow, Ana María Ortiz.

57. Adams and Chávez, *Missions of New Mexico*, xv.

58. Father Domínguez describes Cieneguilla and La Ciénega as follows: "The higher settlement [Cieneguilla] is in a canyon that comes down from the San Ildefonso Springs [Arroyo de los Frijoles], and in this locality the channel of the villa's river enters it. The farms are made fertile by this water when it gets that far. A little below this settlement near the nooks between some little rock mesas, a number of springs arise (they are probably a resurgence, or outcrop, of the Santa Fe River) and run to the west in little ravines. Since this water flows downhill between rocks, they cannot change its course in order to use it for irrigation instead of the Santa Fe River. The water from these springs forms a river called Las Bocas which

takes a very winding course for about 2 leagues to the west through a valley between mesas (so broad that there is a highway through it to the missions of Río Abajo) above the mission of Our Father Santo Domingo. This settlement is called Cieneguilla.

The lower settlement [La Ciénega] lies in a kind of nook between two cañadas. None of the rivers mentioned reach it, nor does it have any water except some springs which suffice for the irrigation of the little farms, for watering the cattle, and for the use of the settlers. Here it is called Ciénega Grande, and that is just what it is, for there is a good swamp. Outlines of ancient ruins are visible at the site of this settlement, and perhaps they were pagan pueblos. These two settlements have sufficient land and water as I have explained. These lands and those of Quemado [Agua Fría] usually yield fairly good crops in accordance with what I said about the villa." Adams and Chávez, *Missions of New Mexico*, 41.

59. Eleanor B. Adams, "Fray Silvestre and the Obstinate Hopi," *New Mexico Historical Review* 38 (April 1963): 111; Adams and Chávez, *Missions of New Mexico*, xv.

60. Archives of the Archdiocese of Santa Fe, New Mexico, Santa Fe Burials, Roll 40, fr. 222–26, State Records Center and Archives, Santa Fe, NM. Ironically, José Vicente's mother was listed as "Isabel, India de Nación Cumancha (Comanche)."

61. Archives of the Archdiocese of Santa Fe, New Mexico, Santa Fe Burials, Roll 40, fr. 225–26.

62. The 1786 Spanish-Comanche Peace Treaty, in Thomas, *Forgotten Frontiers*, 329.

63. "Noticias of Juan Candelaria," *New Mexico Historical Review* 4 (1929): 282–83. The Candelaria *noticias* were considered to be sufficiently reliable to be used as evidence that the villa of Albuquerque was not founded exactly as reported in 1706 by Governor Cuervo y Valdés. Simmons, *Albuquerque*, 81–93, especially 88 and 91.

64. Diego de Vargas, edict made public in El Paso, 20 September 1693; Kessell, Hendricks, and Dodge, *To the Royal Crown*, 375.

65. Marc Simmons, *Coronado's Land: Essays on Daily Life in Colonial New Mexico* (Albuquerque: University of New Mexico Press, 1991), 147–48. While David Snow indicates that Francisco and Cristóbal Anaya Almazán held La Ciénega Pueblo instead of Cieneguilla Pueblo as encomenderos, it appears that Cieneguilla Pueblo was intended because that is the land Francisco Anaya Almazán claimed as his pre-revolt holdings and because Anaya Almazán's *escudero* (temporary trustee) was assigned to Cieneguilla Pueblo. D. H. Snow, "Note on *Encomienda* Economics," 357–58.

66. Vargas recolonizing expedition, Robledito campsite, entry of 18 October 1693, adjutant Francisco Anaya Almazán arrives with eighty mules; Kessell, Hendricks, and Dodge, *To the Royal Crown*, 387–88; grant to Francisco Anaya Almazán, Santa Fe, 2 September 1693, SANM I: 497.

67. Petition by Anaya Almazán for labor draft of Pueblo Indians and decree granting request by Governor Vargas, Puesto of El Paso del Río del Norte, 30 July 1692, SANM II: 52.

68. Grant to Francisco Anaya Almazán, Santa Fe, 2 September 1693, SANM I: 497.

69. John Kessell, "Vargas at the Gate: The Spanish Restoration of Santa Fe, 1692–1696," in *All Trails Lead to Santa Fe, An Anthology Commemorating the 400th Anniversary of the Founding of Santa Fe* (Santa Fe, NM: Sunstone Press, 2010), 225; grant to Francisco Anaya Almazán, Santa Fe, 2 September 1693, SANM I: 497.

70. Chávez, *New Mexico Families*, 24–25; France V. Scholes, Marc Simmons, José Antonio Esquibel, eds., and Eleanor B. Adams, *Juan Domínguez del Mendoza: Soldier and Frontiersman of the Spanish Southwest* (Albuquerque: University of New Mexico Press, 2012), 3–4.

71. Kessell and Hendricks, *By Force of Arms*, 249; Chávez, *New Mexico Families*, 125.

72. Petition of Felipa Rico de Rojas for revalidation of the Anaya Almazán grant and revalidation by Governor Flores Mogollón, [Santa Fe, 1714], SANM I: 497.

73. Grant to Francisco Anaya Almazán, Santa Fe, 2 September 1693, SANM I: 497.

74. Andrés Montoya had ten other children from his first marriage to Antonia Lucero de Godoy. Cristóbal had died just before he was to be married, and Manuela (married to Joaquín Sánchez), was also deceased by the time Andrés Montoya made his will. Nicolás and Diego were still bachelors. That left six Montoya children who had been assigned farmland by Andrés: daughter Josefa (married to Joseph de Santistevan) and sons Francisco, Isidro (married to Manuela Silva), Andrés the younger (married to Ana Baca), Joseph (married to Juana Quintana), and Antonio Montoya (married to Inez Baca). Will of Andrés Montoya, SANM I: 526.

75. Ibid.

76. Chávez, *New Mexico Families*, 236.

77. In September of 1775 Antonio Gurulé of Albuquerque sold a tract of land in Cieneguilla along the Santa Fe River, which was bounded on the north by property still in the name of Andrés Montoya. Gurulé inherited the land from María Montoya, apparently a descendant of Joseph Montoya, and sold it to Joseph Riaño, who had an interest in the Hacienda del Álamo grant. Riaño then sold to

Diego Romero of Cieneguilla for 235 pesos. Deed from Antonio Gurulé to José Riaño, Santa Fe, 4 September 1775, SANM I: 798.

78. Deed from Manuel Baca, as executor of the estate of María Coca, to Josefa Montoya, SANM I: 539.

79. "Quede libre para pastellos . . . con las circunstancias que unos pedazos de tierra de labor que hay en el cañón han de quedar bajo de cerca como se comprometen los que trabajan [dicha siembraban]," agreement of conciliación before Alcalde Domingo Fernández, Puesto de San Antonio de La Ciénega, 25 November 1830, Twitchell Collection, folder no. 102, State Records Center and Archives, Santa Fe, NM.

80. Agreement of conciliación before Alcalde Domingo Fernández, Puesto de San Antonio de La Ciénega, 25 November 1830, Twitchell Collection, folder no. 102, State Records Center and Archives, Santa Fe, NM.

81. Rafael Cuentas, copy of the proceedings of the audiencia of Guadalajara of 27 March 1818, Guadalajara, 14 January 1819, SANM I: 1363; Ignacio María Sánchez Vergara to Facundo Melgares, Jemez, 14 April 1819, SANM I: 1364.

82. Petition of Pablo Montoya, Santa Fe, 11 May 1831, SANM I: 627.

83. Order of Alcalde Francisco Archibeque, Santa Fe, 1 July 1831, SANM I: 627.

84. Declaration of Juan Manuel Montoya, Santa Fe, 8 July 1831, SANM I: 627.

85. Order of Alcalde Francisco Rascón, Santa Fe, 1 August 1831, SANM I: 627; opinion of Antonio Barreiro, Santa Fe, 28 July 1831, SANM I: 627. For more on Barreiro and his writings, see H. Bailey Carroll and J. Villasana Haggard, *Three New Mexico Chronicles* (Albuquerque, NM: Quivira Society, 1942), 266–318.

86. SANM I: 497; partition by Alcalde Francisco Archibeque, Cieneguilla, 21 September 1831, SANM I: 627.

87. Partition by Alcalde Francisco Archibeque, Cieneguilla, 21 September 1831, SANM I: 627.

88. Opinion of Antonio Barreiro, Santa Fe, 28 September 1831, SANM I: 627.

89. Attempted partition by Alcalde Francisco Archibeque, Cieneguilla, 12 October 1831, SANM I: 627.

90. According to the *Santa Fe New Mexican*, "Trouble between the owners of the former Taylor Ranch [predecessor of La Ciénega de Santa Fe] and La Ciénega residents began . . . after the Ortiz y Pino family sold some property in the mid-1950s to Governor John Simms." Duke, "The Flow of Change."

91. Cieneguilla Grant, SG 115, Roll 24, fr. 6 et seq. The Cieneguilla grant is sometimes called the Francisco de Anaya Almazán grant. Bowden, "Private Land Claims," 3:425–35.

92. Hacienda del Álamo Grant, PLC 155, Roll 49, fr. 494 et seq.; Bowden, "Private Land Claims" 3:435–36. The settlement of the estate of José Riaño Tagle is found in SANM I: 762.

93. Surveyor General Atkinson's reasoning was that the land requested was three miles by two miles or approximately the size of a *sitio de gañado menor*, which was the amount of land granted to pasture a herd of about three thousand sheep. Since this grant was for land sufficient to pasture two hundred sheep. Atkinson approved a grant the size of a criadero de gañado menor (1666⅔ varas square, which J. J. Bowden estimates to be 491 acres). Opinion of Surveyor General Atkinson, Santa Fe, 17 March 1879, Cieneguilla Grant, SG 115, Roll 24, fr. 59–63; Bowden, "Private Land Claims." *Sitios* were often referred to in colonial New Mexico as sites or locations, rather than a specific amount of land as was the case in central Mexico.

94. Affidavit of Juan Antonio Rodríguez, Santa Fe, 29 January 1879, Cieneguilla Grant, SG 115, Roll 24, fr. 46–50.

95. Affidavit of Tomás Rendón, Santa Fe, 20 January 1879, Cieneguilla Grant, SG 115, SG Roll 24, fr. 51–55.

96. Affidavit of Francisco Gonzales, Santa Fe, 30 August 1879, Cieneguilla Grant, SG 115, Roll 24, fr. 67.

97. Opinion of Surveyor General Henry M. Atkinson, Santa Fe, 17 March 1879, Cieneguilla Grant, SG 115, Roll 24, fr. 60–63.

98. Affidavit of P. F. Herlon, 17 March 1879, Cieneguilla Grant, SG 115, Roll 24, fr. 69–70.

99. Survey by Robert Marmon, August 1879, Bureau of Land Management, Santa Fe, NM; Bowden, "Private Land Claims," 3:432, n. 10; opinion of Surveyor General George Washington Julian, Santa Fe, 7 May 1886, Cieneguilla Grant, SG 115, Roll 24, fr. 73–85.

100. Bowden, "Private Land Claims," 3:433.

101. Survey of the Cieneguilla grant by George H. Pradt, November 1898, containing 3,202.79 acres, Bureau of Land Management, Santa Fe, NM; Bowden, "Private Land Claims," 3:433–35. Juan Antonio Rodríguez testified that about ten people lived on the grant. Affidavit of Juan Antonio Rodríguez, Santa Fe, 29 January 1879, Cieneguilla Grant, SG 115, Roll 24, fr. 46–50.

102. Toll and Badner, *Galisteo Basin Archeological Sites*, 293.

103. Barbara Ferry, "Short on Water Village Tries to Ensure Its Supply: Some Residents of La Ciénega Want County Moratorium on New Development," *New Mexican*, 20 September 1998; Julia Goldberg, "Don't Waste My Water Rights: La Ciénega Has Its Guard Up Over a Proposed Golf Course Development," *Santa Fe Reporter*, 18 December 1991; Beth Brechtel, "Activist Fears Losing Heritage: Graffiti Vandals, Souvenir Hunters and Target Shooters Threaten Rock Drawings at La Ciénega Mesa," *Albuquerque Journal North*, 22 July 1994.

104. Terry Moody, State and National Register of Historical Places coordinator, personal communication, 11 February 2013.

105. El Rancho de las Golondrinas, http://golondrinas.org/index.html.

106. Duke, "The Flow of Change"; interview with Reynaldo Romero, Santa Fe Farmer's Market, 2 August 2014.

Chapter Six

1. Frederick W. Hodge, ed., *Handbook of American Indians North of Mexico* (Totowa, NJ: Rowman & Littlefield, 1975), 2:428; Albert H. Schroeder, "Pueblos Abandoned in Historic Times," in *Handbook of North American Indians*, ed. William Sturtevant, vol. 9, *Southwest*, ed. Alfonso Ortiz (Washington, D.C.: Smithsonian Institution, 1979), 247.

2. Hackett and Shelby, *Revolt of the Pueblo Indians*, 13.

3. Hernán Cortés first met Malinche after the Battle of Tabasco, the first city he fought after reaching Mexico. Though vastly outnumbered, Cortés won the day with his cavalry and cannons. When the Tabascoan lords came to negotiate peace the next day, they brought among other gifts a woman named doña Marina, better known as Malinche. She was the daughter of an Aztec noble who had been adopted by a Tabascoan family and spoke both Mayan and Aztec. She would become extremely valuable to Cortés as a translator, but in addition, "her birth, cleverness and aplomb, and the distinction of her manner, made her far more than a mere interpreter. She became indispensable to Cortés in all delicate negotiations. Moreover, she grew very fond of him, and later on, bore him a son, don Martín. The name Malinche is a corruption of the Mexican words *ce malinalli*, one grass of penance. . . . One Grass of Penance was a name which a female born on a particular date would be given. The fortune of those born on that date would have a connection with dissension and war and the overthrow of old established things . . . she was aware of the destiny foretold for her, [Malinche] saw Cortés as the personification of the strife which would carry her to fortune. . . . In the greatest dangers she would be invulnerable. Later, when Cortés was identified with a deity fated to bring trouble, she as his attendant became semi-divine." Maurice Collis, *Cortés and Montezuma* (London: Robin Clark, 1954), 43–44.

4. Hammond and Rey, *Don Juan de Oñate*, 1:321; Schroeder and Matson, *A Colony on the Move*, 147–48.

5. Hackett and Shelby, *Revolt of the Pueblo Indians*, 13.

6. Hodge, *Handbook*, 2:428.

7. Kessell, Hendricks, and Dodge, *Blood on the Boulders*, 1:678; Frederick W. Hodge, George P. Hammond, and Agapito Rey, eds., *Fray Alonso de Benavides' Revised*

Memorial of 1634 (Albuquerque: University of New Mexico Press, 1945), 266–69; Schroeder, "Pueblos Abandoned," 247–48.

8. Edward Dozier, *Hano: A Tewa Community in Arizona* (New York: Holt, Rinehart, and Winston, 1970). Some believe that the Hopi invited Tano people from Galisteo and other Galisteo Basin pueblos to help them fight off the Utes. Mednick, *San Cristóbal*, 125. Pecos Pueblo, faced with similar population decline in 1838, moved to Jemez Pueblo. Joe S. Sando, *Nee Hemish: A History of Jemez Pueblo* (Albuquerque: University of New Mexico Press, 1982), 141–61.

9. Kessell, Hendricks, and Dodge, *Blood on the Boulders*, 1:678; Hodge, Hammond, and Rey, *Fray Alonso de Benavides*, 266–69; Schroeder, "Pueblos Abandoned," 247–48. On 20 June 1776 a Comanche raiding party attacked the community of La Ciénega, killing eleven. Father Domínguez was in Santa Fe preparing for his epic journey later that year, looking for a route to Monterey, California, with Father Silvestre Vélez de Escalante. Both priests hurried to La Ciénega, Escalante to serve as chaplain on the scouting expedition pursuing the Indians and Domínguez to officiate at the burials. Adams and Chávez, *Missions of New Mexico*, xv; Archives of the Archdiocese of Santa Fe, New Mexico, Santa Fe Burials, Roll 40, fr. 222–26, State Records Center and Archives, Santa Fe, NM.

10. Schroeder, "Pueblos Abandoned," 247–48.

11. Hall, *Four Leagues of Pecos*, 21, 162–63; Julián Josué Vigil, [The]*Vigil Index SANM I: 10*, [2] (Springer: Editorial Teleraña, 1984), www.southwestbooks.org.

12. Petition of Domingo Fernández for the San Cristóbal Grant, Santa Fe, 26 April 1822, Ethan Eaton [San Cristóbal] Grant, SG 19, Roll 14, fr. 788–89: "Al ver aquel sagrado lugar en donde tantas ocaciones se ofrecería el sacrosanto y tremendo sacrificio de la Misa y se consagraría el agustísimo sacramento según se considera ha ciento y más años que le despoblaron los naturales que le habitaban y parece que la omnipotencia divina cada dia se esmera en darnos a conocer sostiene los fundamentos de este Santísimo. lugar el que está sufriendo el ultraje de ser habitacion de Bestias, pecebre de Ovejas, y establo de Bacas y Becerros y para decirlo de una vez pozilga de Brutos." Fernández may have been suffering from advanced Parkinson's disease, which caused his handwriting to become more rigid and jittery over a twenty-year period. *Vigil Index*, 1.

13. Petition of Domingo Fernández for the San Cristóbal Grant, Santa Fe, 26 April 1822, Ethan Eaton [San Cristóbal] Grant, SG 19, Roll 14, fr. 788–89: "Por el oriente a donde comienza á esparcer el cañón para el Ojo de la Baca. El del Poniente el puertecito que asigna la donación de los de Galisteo por el norte la bajada del Pueblito. Por el sur la subida que llaman de los Comanches, cuyos linderos son los que asigno sin que quede dentro de sus huecos cosa alguna que no le comprenda ejecutando en todo las calidades prevenidas en la ley 3a y la 11, del titulo 12, libro 40 de la recopilación y soberanos decretos que hablan de la materia."

14. Ibid.; when the ayuntamiento of Abiquiu recommended that the Tierra Amarilla grant requested by Manuel Martínez be considered a community grant, Martínez objected, stating that "what is common to all is the property of no one." Malcolm Ebright, *The Tierra Amarilla Grant: A History of Chicanery* (Santa Fe, NM: Center for Land Grant Studies, 1993), 34–37.

15. Act of possession, Santissima Trinidad, in the vicinity of San Cristóbal, 15 February 1843, SANM I: 398.

16. Order by the ayuntamiento of Santa Fe, 27 June 1822; petition of Domingo Fernández for the San Cristóbal Grant, Santa Fe, 26 April 1822, Ethan Eaton [San Cristóbal] Grant, SG 19, Roll 14, fr. 788–89; order by Governor Facundo Melgares, Santa Fe, 27 April 1822, San Cristóbal Grant, 26 April 1822, Ethan Eaton [San Cristóbal] Grant, SG 19, Roll 14, fr. 788–89.

17. "La lagunita que aun con la seca presente esta llena de agua la que tapándole la compuerta es un tanque que ayuda mucho a la utilidad del riego con más otra laguna seca su extención dilatada favorable para recojer las aguas llovedizas la que no es más de tapar la compuerta y queda sirviendo en la misma forma que los naturales la tenían antes en cuya circunstancia," response by Domingo Fernández, Santa Fe, 25 June 1822, San Cristóbal [Ethan Eaton] Grant, SG 19, Roll 14, fr. 790–92.

18. Order of the ayuntamiento of Santa Fe for inspection of the San Cristóbal [Ethan Eaton] Grant, SG 19, Roll 14, fr. 791–92.

19. Report of Julián Lucero, José Miguel Baca, and Rafael Sarracino to the Santa Fe ayuntamiento, Galisteo, 8 July 1822, San Cristóbal [Ethan Eaton] Grant, SG 19, Roll 14, fr. 792–93.

20. Hall, *Four Leagues of Pecos*, 36–37.

21. Report of the ayuntamiento of Santa Fe, 14 February 1824, San Cristóbal [Ethan Eaton] Grant, Santa Fe, 27 June 1822, SG 19, Roll 14, fr. 794–96.

22. Domingo Fernández's second petition for the San Cristóbal Grant, Santa Fe, 25 June 1827, San Cristóbal [Ethan Eaton] Grant, SG 19, Roll 14, fr. 797–98.

23. Hall, *Four Leagues of Pecos*, 40–41.

24. Territorial Deputation to Santa Fe ayuntamiento, [Santa Fe], 20 June 1827, San Cristóbal [Ethan Eaton] Grant, SG 19, Roll 14, fr. 797–98; report by Santa Fe ayuntamiento, [8 August 1827], San Cristóbal [Ethan Eaton] Grant, SG 19, Roll 14, fr. 797–98.

25. Grant by Governor Manuel Armijo, Santa Fe, 9 August 1827, San Cristóbal [Ethan Eaton] Grant, SG 19, Roll 14, fr. 799–800.

26. Act of possession, San Cristóbal, 21 August 1827, San Cristóbal [Ethan Eaton] Grant, SG 19, Roll 14, fr. 801–5.

27. Hall, *Four Leagues of Pecos*, 39; act of possession, San Cristóbal, 21 August 1827, San Cristóbal [Ethan Eaton] Grant, SG 19, Roll 14, fr. 801–5.

28. Act of possession, San Cristóbal, 21 August 1827, San Cristóbal [Ethan Eaton] Grant, SG 19, Roll 14, fr. 801–5.

29. Domingo Fernández petition to Governor Chavez, Santa Fe, 2 September 1829, San Cristóbal [Ethan Eaton] Grant, SG 19, Roll 14, fr. 814–15.

30. Governor Chavez order to Alcalde Constitutional, Santa Fe, 2 September 1829, San Cristóbal [Ethan Eaton] Grant, SG 19, Roll 14, fr. 814.

31. Bowden, "Private Land Claims," 2:279–80.

32. H. R. Report no. 457, 35th Cong., 1st Sess. 314–18; Bowden, "Private Land Claims," 2:276.

33. J. J. Bowden called it the Domingo Fernández grant. Bowden, "Private Land Claims," 2:272. This is an example of a land grant named by the U.S. courts after the speculator who acquired it instead of the original grantee. Another example is the Alexander Valle grant. Originally, the grant was made to Juan de Dios Peña, Francisco Ortiz, and Juan de Aguilar in 1815 and sold to Juan Esteban Pino in 1826 before Valle purchased it in 1852. Judy Scallorn, "Alexander Valle," Box 41, Folder 3, Myra Ellen Jenkins Collection. Fort Lewis College, Durango, CO.

34. Pueblo of San Cristóbal, SG Report 11, Roll 7, fr. 391. For the Cruzate grants, see Ebright, Hendricks, and Hughes, *Four Square Leagues*, chapter 8.

35. Barbara Marriott, *Outlaw Tales of New Mexico: True Stories of New Mexico's Most Famous Robbers, Rustlers, and Bandits* (Guilford, CT: Globe Pequot Twodot Press, 2007), 69; George B. Anderson, *History of New Mexico: Its Resources and People* (Los Angeles, CA: Pacific States, 1907), 141–43; Ethan Eaton Correspondence, 1853–1892, Mauro Montoya Collection, Fray Angélico Chávez Library, Museum of New Mexico, Santa Fe.

36. Petition of Ethan Eaton for confirmation of the San Cristóbal Grant, Santa Fe, 11 October 1855, San Cristóbal [Ethan Eaton] Grant, SG 19, Roll 14, fr. 816–19.

37. Testimony of Jose María Martínez and Francisco Baca, 11 October 1855, San Cristóbal [Ethan Eaton] Grant, SG 19, Roll 14, fr. 820–22.

38. Decision of Surveyor General Pelham, Santa Fe, 18 September 1857, San Cristóbal [Ethan Eaton] Grant, SG 19, Roll 14, fr. 864–67.

39. Bowden, "Private Land Claims," 2:278.

40. Application for resurvey, Santa Fe, 11 June 1820, San Cristóbal [Ethan Eaton] Grant, SG 19, Roll 14, fr. 846–46.

41. Decision of GLO commissioner Willis Drummond, Washington, D.C., 11 November 1873, San Cristóbal [Ethan Eaton] Grant, SG 19, Roll 14, fr. 923–38.

42. Ibid.

43. Decision of Interior Secretary Delano, SG 19, Roll 14, fr. 949–52.

44. According to Mednick's *San Cristóbal*, 166: "In his younger days, Nicolás Pino was among the frustrated volunteers ordered back to Santa Fe by Governor Armijo when the Americans invaded. Pino was later arrested for conspiring to

revolt against the American government in 1847, but he opposed the Taos rebellion, however, and eventually signed an oath of allegiance to the United States."

45. Ibid. Eaton married Marcelina Chaves, daughter of Joaquín Chaves, in 1851, the same year he bought the San Cristóbal grant. Mednick, *San Cristóbal*, 157. Joaquín Chaves was one of the co-grantees whose interest in the land both Domingo Fernández and Ethan Eaton tried to terminate.

46. Ibid., 168.

47. Bowden, "Private Land Claims," 2:279–80.

48. Ebright, "The Galisteo Grant," http://newmexicohistory.org/places/galisteo-land-grant; Bowden, "Private Land Claims," 2:280.

49. Opinion of GLO commissioner James Williamson, Washington, D.C., 14 July 1879, San Cristóbal [Ethan Eaton] Grant, SG 19, Roll 14, fr. 976–1013; Bowden, "Private Land Claims," 2:280–81.

50. Mednick, *San Cristóbal*, 168–69.

51. Deposition of Thomas B. Catron [delegate to the U.S. Congress], Washington, D.C., 27 March 1896, T. B. Catron and Nicolas Pino v. Saron Laughlin, Bernalillo County District Court Cause no. 4949 (change of venue from Santa Fe County), State Records Center and Archives, Santa Fe, NM.

52. Catron v. Laughlin, 11 New Mexico Reports (January term, 1903), 615–45; Mednick, *San Cristóbal*, 169.

53. [Final] judgment and decree by Justice Benjamin Baker, [Albuquerque], 8 November 1903, deposition of Thomas B. Catron [delegate to the U.S. Congress], Washington, D.C., 27 March 1896, T. B. Catron and Nicolas Pino v. Saron Laughlin, Bernalillo County District Court Cause no. 4949 (change of venue from Santa Fe County), State Records Center and Archives, Santa Fe, NM.

54. Report of commissioners, [Santa Fe], 20 November 1903, deposition of Thomas B. Catron [delegate to the U.S. Congress], Washington, D.C., 27 March 1896, T. B. Catron and Nicolas Pino v. Saron Laughlin, Bernalillo County District Court Cause no. 4949 (change of venue from Santa Fe County), State Records Center and Archives, Santa Fe, NM.

55. Order of Justice Benjamin Baker, [Albuquerque], 17 December 1903, [final] judgment and decree by Justice Benjamin Baker, [Albuquerque], 8 November 1903, deposition of Thomas B. Catron [delegate to the U.S. Congress], Washington, D.C., 27 March 1896, T. B. Catron and Nicolas Pino v. Saron Laughlin, Bernalillo County District Court Cause no. 4949 (change of venue from Santa Fe County), State Records Center and Archives, Santa Fe, NM; Mednick, *San Cristóbal*, 169.

56. Mednick, *San Cristóbal*, 193–229.

57. Toll and Badner, *Galisteo Basin Assessment Project*, 119–43.

Chapter Seven

1. Lippard and Ranney, *Down Country*; Schroeder, "Pueblos Abandoned," 247; Harrington, *Ethnography of the Tewa*, 551–52.

2. David H. Snow, "Prehistoric Southwestern Turquoise Industry," *El Palacio* 79, no. 1 (1973): 33–51. The Cerrillos Hills contain rich deposits of turquoise, lead, copper, and silver, all of which (except silver) were mined commercially by Cerrillos Hills miners in the nineteenth and early twentieth centuries.

3. Phil C. Weigand and Acelia García de Weigand, "A Macroeconomic Study of the Relationships between the Ancient Cultures of the American Southwest and Mesoamerica," in *The Road to Aztlan: Art from a Mythic Homeland*, ed. Virginia Fields and Victor Zamudio-Taylor (Los Angeles, CA: Los Angeles County Museum of Art, 2001), 190.

4. Michael Haederle, "Saving Our Past from the Jaws of Subdivision," *Los Angeles Times*, 11 November 1996; Archaeological Conservancy, "San Marcos Pueblo" (unpublished manuscript in the author's possession); Lippard and Ranney, *Down Country*, 120–22.

5. Hammond and Rey, *Rediscovery of New Mexico*, 95–96; Marc Simmons, "Unwise Friar Met His Fate in Early New Mexico," *Santa Fe New Mexican*, 13 October 2012.

6. Archaeological Conservancy, "San Marcos Pueblo."

7. Silver ore is commonly found in lead deposits. Cordelia T. Snow, personal communication, 11 January 2013; Archaeological Conservancy, "San Marcos Pueblo."

8. Ann F. Ramenofsky, "Summary Report of the 2000 Season of Archeological Research at San Marcos Pueblo (LA 98) by the University of New Mexico" (Santa Fe: Archaeological Conservancy and New Mexico Historic Preservation Division, 2001), 50–51.

9. The other pueblo with smelting operations prior to the Pueblo Revolt was Pa'ako near present-day Cedar Crest, which had a forge and a huge copper smelting operation. Charles David Vaughn, "Taking the Measure of New Mexico's Colonial Miners, Mining and Metallurgy" (PhD diss., University of New Mexico, 2006), 187; Ann F. Ramenofsky, "Report on the Archeological Investigation of Metallurgy at San Marcos Pueblo (LA 98) Summer 2002" (Santa Fe: Archaeology Conservancy and New Mexico Historic Preservation Division, 2003), 50.

10. Cordelia Thomas Snow, "San Marcos: A Brief History of Mission San Marcos, Santa Fe County, New Mexico," http://www.newmexicohistory.org/filedetails. php?fileID=21289.

11. Kessell, Hendricks, and Dodge, *To the Royal Crown*, 409, 411, 425.

12. C. T. Snow, "San Marcos."

13. Rick Hendricks and John P. Wilson, eds. and trans., *The Navajos in 1705: Roque Madrid's Campaign Journal* (Albuquerque: University of New Mexico Press, 1996), 112.

14. Kessell, Hendricks, and Dodge, *To the Royal Crown*, 409–11.

15. The governor sent Captain Roque Madrid with twelve soldiers for lead to Madrid's mine on the Cerro de San Marcos, 3 February 1694. Kessell, Hendricks, and Dodge, *Blood on the Boulders*, 1:125.

16. The captain and soldiers came from Cerro de San Marcos, having found the mine covered up, and brought some ores. Kessell, Hendricks, and Dodge, *Blood on the Boulders*, 1:125.

17. Petition of Alferez Juan José Moreno to Governor Enrique Olavide y Michelena, Pinart Collection, Bancroft Library, University of California–Berkeley, PE 46:1; Tigges, "Pastures of the Royal Horse Herd."

18. Order of Governor Olavide y Michelena, Pinart Collection, Bancroft Library, University of California–Berkeley, PE 46:2.

19. Ebright and Hendricks, *Witches of Abiquiu*, 68–69.

20. "Por el norte, un cerrito de piedra que está en el llano; por el sur, [una] ceja que devido a arroyo de Vázquez; oriente, el camino real que va para dicho pueblo de Galisteo; y por el poniente la falda de los cerros que estan entre medio de dicho paraje y el arroyo de lo de Vázquez," petition of Antonio Urbán Montaño, San Marcos Grant, SG 102, Roll 23, fr. 15.

21. Petition of Antonio Urbán Montaño (prepared and signed by Felipe Tafoya) to Governor Vélez Cachupín, Santa Fe, early June 1754, San Marcos [Springs] Grant, SG 102, Roll 23, fr. 15 (original), fr. 20–21 (transcription), fr. 26–27 (translation).

22. Granting decree of Governor Vélez Cachupín, Santa Fe, 15 June 1754, San Marcos [Springs] Grant, SG 102, Roll 23, fr. 16–17 (original), fr. 21–22 (transcription), fr. 27–28 (translation).

23. "Norte, unas peñas coloradas, que están en el arroyo; sur, un álamo grande que está por el camino; oriente, dos sabinos; y por el poniente un cerrillo que llaman del Chachihuitl" (order of directions changed for clarity). The word *chalchihuitl* does not appear in the grant by Vélez Cachupín, nor do any of the other boundary calls. Act of possession by Alcalde Bartolomé Fernández, San Marcos, 26 July 1754, San Marcos [Springs] Grant, SG 102, Roll 23, fr. 17–18 (original, partially covered), fr. 22–23 (transcription), fr. 28–29 (translation).

24. For the Pueblo league, see Ebright, Hendricks, and Hughes, *Four Square Leagues*; Ebright, "Advocates for the Oppressed," 309–10, and passim; Ebright, *Land Grants and Lawsuits*, 65–66, 229; and Malcolm Ebright, "Hispanic Land Grants and Indian Land in New Mexico," in *Telling New Mexico: A New History*, ed. Marta Weigle (Santa Fe: Museum of New Mexico Press, 2009), 210–11.

For a case where Governor Vélez Cachupín corrected an alcalde whose act of possession failed to follow his order, see Ebright, "Breaking New Ground," 210.

25. Petition of the legal representatives of Antonio Urbán Montaño, [Santa Fe], n.d., San Marcos [Springs] Grant, SG 102, Roll 23, fr. 8–10.

26. Affidavit of Manuel Bustamante, Santa Fe, 29 February 1873, San Marcos [Springs] Grant, SG 102, Roll 23, fr. 31–34.

27. Opinion of Surveyor General Proudfit, Santa Fe, 22 December 1874, San Marcos [Springs] Grant, SG 102, Roll 23, fr. 35–36.

28. Bowden, "Private Land Claims," 3:439.

29. The claimant and his lawyer in the Cristóbal Nieto grant made no attempt to present an accurate genealogy to the court. Deraignment of title, El Pino Grant, PLC 81, Roll 42, fr. 524–27.

30. Supplemental opinion of Surveyor General George Washington Julian, Santa Fe, 23 January 1888, San Marcos [Springs] Grant, SG 102, Roll 23, fr. 41–46.

31. GLO commissioner John Wilson instructed Surveyor General Pelham "to deal with private land titles . . . precisely as Mexico would have done"; in other words, Surveyor General Julian should have followed the instructions to approve claims to the extent that they would have been approved by the Spanish and Mexican governments. There was a long history of approval of four-square-league grants in the form of a square and not a diamond shape. Ebright, Hendricks, and Hughes, *Four Square Leagues*, chapter 1.

32. An example of a grant in which the measurements in the granting decree differ from the act of possession is the Las Trampas grant, where Vélez Cachupín ordered that each settler receive a 180-vara strip perpendicular to the river. Some settlers received tracts two hundred varas wide because they were in a canyon where the length of the strip was shorter. Ebright, *Land Grants and Lawsuits*, 147–49.

33. Solomon Jacob Spiegelberg not only learned about mercantile transactions in New Mexico but also gained a good command of both Spanish and English. When Colonel Doniphan's regiment arrived in Santa Fe in the wake of General Stephen Watts Kearney's conquest of New Mexico, Solomon Spiegelberg joined him to become his sutler and "to supply his troops while they were on the march or when they were camping." Upon the regiment's return to Santa Fe, Solomon Jacob Spiegelberg was appointed sutler to Fort Marcy and at the same time established his mercantile business in Santa Fe. Floyd S. Fierman, *Guts and Ruts: The Jewish Pioneer on the Trail in the American Southwest* (New York: TAV, 1985), 8–10.

34. Henry J. Tobias, *A History of the Jews in New Mexico* (Albuquerque: University of New Mexico Press, 1990), 69. In 1882 Spiegelberg was elected Santa Fe County commissioner. Fierman, *Guts and Ruts*, 12–14, 20.

35. Tobias, *History of the Jews in New Mexico*, 69.

36. Fierman, *Guts and Ruts*, 10, citing an act to incorporate the Montezuma Copper Mining Company of Santa Fe, New Mexico.

37. Petition for confirmation of the San Marcos Pueblo Grant, Santa Fe, n.d., San Marcos Pueblo Grant, SG 102, Roll 23, fr. 8–14.

38. Opinion of Justice Joseph R. Reed, Santa Fe, 16 December 1892, San Marcos Pueblo Grant, SG 102, Roll 23, fr. 50–53.

39. Surveyor General Charles F. Easley to Justice Joseph R. Reed, Santa Fe, 28 September 1894, San Marcos Pueblo Grant, SG 102, Roll 23, fr. 57–59.

40. Stipulation between claimants Willi Spiegelberg, Lehman Spiegelberg, and Saly Raunheim by their attorney Francis Downs and Matthew Reynolds, U.S. attorney, Santa Fe, 6 October 1894, San Marcos Pueblo Grant, SG 102, Roll 23, fr. 60–61.

41. Bowden, "Private Land Claims," 3:442.

42. Hester Jones, "The Spieglebergs and Early Trade in New Mexico," *El Palacio* 38 (April 1935): 88; Fierman, *Guts and Ruts*, 17–18.

43. Jones, "Spieglebergs," 88.

44. Petition of Domingo Fernández, Santa Fe, 26 April 1822, Ethan Eaton/San Cristóbal Grant, SG 19, Roll 14, fr. 787 et seq; for the Charles Ilfeld mercantile enterprise, see William J. Parish, *The Charles Ilfeld Company: A Study of the Rise and Decline of Mercantile Capitalism in New Mexico* (Cambridge, MA: Harvard University Press, 1961).

45. David H. Snow, "Prehistoric Southwest Turquoise Industry," *El Palacio* 79 (June 1973): 40–41; Lange, *Cochiti*, 143; Stuart Northrop, *Minerals of New Mexico* (Albuquerque: University of New Mexico Press, 1959), 535; Albert Schroeder, "A History of the Area along the Eastern Line of the Santo Domingo Pueblo Aboriginal Title Area" (unpublished manuscript prepared for the U.S. Department of Justice, August 1976, Laboratory of Anthropology Library, Santa Fe, NM).

46. Lippard and Ranney, *Down Country*, 121–22, 126–27, n. 79.

47. Patrick Miller, "Pueblo Powerhouse: Centuries Ago, San Marcos Was the Hub of a Thriving Trade in Turquoise and Pottery," *Albuquerque Journal*, 28 February 2005. Lands in and around San Marcos Pueblo comprised the Calvin Ranch from the end of the nineteenth century until the 1950s, when the ranch was subdivided. The majority of San Marcos Pueblo's archaeological features are now owned by the Archaeological Conservancy, either alone or jointly with the State of New Mexico. Of the area within the site established by the Galisteo Basin Archaeological Sites Protection Act, about 60 percent is in private hands, and 40 percent is owned by the Archaeological Conservancy and the State of New Mexico. The Archaeological Conservancy has fenced and posted most of the site, which is monitored by a site steward and local volunteers. Native

Americans have unaccompanied access to the site for traditional purposes, with prior permission. Toll and Badner, *Galisteo Basin Archeological Sites*, 196–98.

48. San Marcos Pueblo was listed as number 114 on the State Register of Cultural Properties on 12 September 1969 and number 388675 on the National Register of Historic Places on 26 March 1982, SRCA. Terry Moody, State and National Register of Historic Places coordinator, personal communication, 11 February 2013.

49. Ramenofsky, "Report on the Archeological Investigation," 51–52; Lippard and Ranney, *Down Country*, 122.

Chapter Eight

1. Toll and Badner, *Galisteo Basin Archeological Sites*, 3.
2. Lippard and Ranney, *Down Country*, 107–9; Toll and Badner, *Galisteo Basin Archeological Sites*, 143–54.
3. Nelson, "Pueblo Ruins," 103–9.
4. Nelson thought the irrigation ditches were of modern origin though it is just as likely they were precontact given the evidence of precontact irrigation works at San Cristóbal (see chapter 6). Nelson, "Pueblo Ruins," 104; Adolph Bandelier, *Final Report of Investigations among the Indians of the Southwestern United States Carried on Mainly in the Years from 1880 to 1885*, 2 vols. (Cambridge: Cambridge University Press, 1892), 156.
5. Other important Galisteo Basin pueblos were San Cristóbal, San Marcos, and San Lázaro. Nelson, *Pueblo Ruins*, 5–8; Schroeder, "Pueblos Abandoned," 247–48.
6. Schroeder, "Pueblos Abandoned," 247–48; Schroeder and Matson, *A Colony on the Move*, 155.
7. Knaut, *Pueblo Revolt*, 10; Simmons, "Tlascalans," 101.
8. Hackett and Shelby, *Revolt of the Pueblo Indians*, 13.
9. Kessell, Hendricks, and Dodge, *Blood on the Boulders*, 1:69.
10. Dozier, *Hano*; David Kammer, "Galisteo Application for Registration [on the] New Mexico Register of Cultural Properties [of the] Galisteo Historic District" (New Mexico Historic Preservation Division, Santa Fe).
11. Lansing B. Bloom, ed., "Albuquerque and Galisteo: Certificate of Their Founding, 1706," *New Mexico Historical Review* 10 (1935): 48–50. In 1706 Cuervo y Valdés told the viceroy that he had established the villa of Albuquerque with all the legal requirements that such a municipality entailed, when in fact he had not. Simmons, *Albuquerque*; Kammer, "Galisteo Application," sec. 12, 14; Jim Elkus, "Galisteo: 1500–1900" (senior honors thesis, Colorado College, 1974; Southwest Room, New Mexico State Library, Santa Fe), 58–59.

12. Kessell, *Kiva, Cross, and Crown*, 357.

13. Jones, *Pueblo Warriors*, 91, 124; Bloom, "Campaign," 158–226.

14. Jones, *Pueblo Warriors*, 91, 124; Hacket, *Historical Documents*, 3:124.

15. Adams and Chávez, *Missions of New Mexico*, 214–17; Cordelia Thomas Snow, "Galisteo Mission," http://www.newmexicohistory.org/filedetails_docs.php?fileID=21292.

16. Adams and Chávez, *Missions of New Mexico*, 214–17; Kessell, *Kiva, Cross, and Crown*, 357; Kammer, "Application," sec. 12, 16; Toll and Badner, *Galisteo Basin Archeological Sites*, 85; Lippard and Ranney, *Down Country*, 112.

17. Kessell, Hendricks, and Dodge, *Blood on the Boulders*, 2:678; Hodge, Hammond, and Rey, *Fray Alonso de Benavides*, 266–69; Schroeder, "Pueblos Abandoned," 247–48.

18. Petition of Juan Cruz Aragón, act of possession of Antonio José Ortiz, grant by Governor Fernando Chacon, Santa Fe, 1 February 1799, Ojito de Galisteo Grant, PLC 164, Roll 49, fr. 851–56 (original documents, badly stained), fr. 845–47 (translation), fr. 848–50 (transcription).

19. Decree of Court of Private Land Claims, Santa Fe, n.d., Ojito de Galisteo Grant, PLC 164, Roll 49, fr. 859–61. It is presumed that Thomas B. Catron was the attorney of record because, although the attorney is signed Catron and Coors, throughout it is in Catron's handwriting.

20. Marc Simmons, *Spanish Government in New Mexico* (Albuquerque: University of New Mexico Press, 1968), 123–24, 126; Fernando de la Concha, "Advice on Governing New Mexico, 1794," *New Mexico Historical Review* 24 (1949): 236–54; Kammer, "Galisteo Application," 17–18.

21. Governor Alberto Máynez to the *alcaldes mayores*, Santa Fe, 1808, SANM II: 2114; Elkus, "Galisteo," 64–65; Kammer, "Galisteo Application," sec. 12, 17–18.

22. Petition for the Galisteo Grant, Santa Fe, [February] 1814, Galisteo Grant, SG 60, Roll 19, fr. 371–72; Schroeder, "Pueblos Abandoned," 248.

23. Decree of the Santa Fe Town Council, Santa Fe, 8 April 1822, Galisteo Grant, SG 60, Roll 19, fr. 367–518; PLC 54, Roll 38, fr. 1026 et seq.

24. Bowden, "Private Land Claims," 2:286–300; Matías Ortiz Act of Possession: Galisteo Grant, SG 60, Roll 19, fr. 1030–32.

25. Hijuela of María Nieves Mirabal, SANM I: 616; hijuela of Matías Sandoval, SANM I: 892; hijuela of José Antonio Alarid, SANM I: 58; hijuela of José Baca, SANM I: 133; hijuela of Rafael Sena, SANM I: 893; hijuela of Felipe Sandoval, SANM I: 894.

26. SANM I: 223.

27. Petition for allotments within the Galisteo Grant, Santa Fe, 3 February 1843, SANM I: 398.

28. Response of the ayuntamiento of Santa Fe, Santa Fe, 4 February 1843, SANM I: 398.

29. Approval of Diego Archuleta, Río Arriba, 7 February 1743, SANM I: 398.

30. Bowden, "Private Land Claims," 2:295.

31. Act of possession, Santissima Trinidad, in the vicinity of San Cristóbal, 15 February 1843, SANM I: 398.

32. Ibid.; Galisteo Grant, PLC 54, Roll 38, fr. 1070.

33. Kammer, "Galisteo Application," sec. 12, 19–22.

34. Affidavit of Agustín Durán, Santa Fe, 2 December 1871, Galisteo Grant, SG 60, Roll 19, fr. 383–86.

35. Affidavit of Donaciano Vigil, Santa Fe, 2 December 1871, Boundary Agreement with San Cristóbal, Galisteo Grant, SG 60, Roll 19, fr. 388–89, 393–96.

36. Bowden, "Private Land Claims," 2:289–93.

37. Petition of Luciano Chavez, Santa Fe, 20 July 1871, Galisteo Grant, SG 60, Roll 19, fr. 375–77.

38. Bowden, "Private Land Claims," 2:297–98.

39. Ibid.; Court of Private Land Claims decision, Galisteo Grant, SG 60, Roll 19, fr. 411; Ebright, *Land Grants and Lawsuits*, 111–13; U.S. v Sandoval, 167 U.S. 278 (1897).

40. Rejection of the Easley survey and resurvey, Galisteo Grant, SG 60, Roll 19, fr. 425–33; Bowden, "Private Land Claims," 2:299–300. A patent based on this acreage was issued to the heirs of the original grantees on 14 September 1927.

41. Kammer, "Galisteo Application," sec. 12, 19–22.

42. Kathryn M. Cordova, *Concha!: Concha Ortiz y Pino, Matriarch of a 300 Year Old Legacy* (Santa Fe, NM: Gran Via, 2004), 5–7.

43. The Galisteo Historic District was entered on the State Register of Cultural Properties in October 1969. Kammer "Galisteo Application," sec. 12, 19–22.

44. José Ortiz y Pino was the son of Juan Ortiz and Concepción Pino, the daughter of Nicolas Pino, who in 1883 was referred to as "the owner of the village." Richard Smith Elliot, *Notes Taken in Sixty Years* (Saint Louis, MO: R. P. Studley, 1883).

45. José Ortiz y Pino III, *Don José: The Last Patron* (Santa Fe, NM: Sunstone Press, 2007).

46. Ethelyn Nelson, "Camp Life in New Mexico," *El Palacio* 4 (1917): 19–23.

47. The sites are Las Huertas, Crestón (Comanche Gap), San Lázaro Pueblo, Manzanares Pueblo, Petroglyph Hill, Lamy Junction, Burnt Corn Pueblo, Espinoso Ridge Pueblo, La Cieneguilla Pueblo, Paa-ko Pueblo, Pueblo Blanco, Lower Arroyo Hondo Pueblo, La Ciénega Pithouse Village, Upper Arroyo Hondo Pueblo, La Ciénega Pueblo, San Marcos Pueblo, Chamisa Locita Pueblo, Galisteo Pueblo and Las Madres, San Cristóbal Pueblo, Pueblo Colorado, Pueblo Largo,

Pueblo She, La Cieneguilla Petroglyphs, Camino Real, and Rote Chert Quarry. Toll and Badner, *Galisteo Basin Archeological Sites*, 3.

48. Córdova, *Concha*, 17; Lippard and Ranney, *Down Country*, 283–84.

49. Edward H. Spicer, *Cycles of Conquest: The Impact of Spain, Mexico, and the United States on the Indians of the Southwest, 1533–1960* (Tucson: University of Arizona Press, 1962), 567.

50. For Abiquiu, see Ebright and Hendricks, *The Witches of Abiquiu*, 251–61; for Pecos, see Hall, *Four Leagues of Pecos*, 31–66.

Chapter Nine

1. Tomás Vélez Cachupín served two terms as governor of New Mexico from 1749 to 1754 and 1762 to 1767 (Francisco Antonio Marín del Valle, Mateo Antonio de Mendoza, and Manuel del Portillo y Urrisola acted as governors from 1754 through 1762). Pedro Fermín Mendinueta was governor from 1767 to 1778, holding office for two consecutive terms.

2. One example of inconsistency in early eighteenth-century land policy was the question of purchases by Pueblo Indians from the Spanish. Since the early 1700s, pueblos like Santa Ana had purchased lands from Spaniards (often purchasing their own land back). Bayer, *Santa Ana*, 76–79. Then, in 1734 Governor Gervasio Cruzat y Góngora ruled that Baltasar Romero in particular, and Spaniards in general, could *not* sell land to the Pueblo Indians. Decree of Governor Cruzat y Góngora, Santa Fe, 1 March 1734, SANM I: 1345. Reversing this policy in 1753, Governor Vélez Cachupín approved the sale to Santa Ana of the same land. Approval of sale of land from Alejandro Mora to Santa Ana Pueblo, Santa Fe, 13 May 1753, Santa Ana Pueblo Historic Documents, State Records Center and Archives, Santa Fe, New Mexico. Ebright, Hendricks, and Hughes, *Four Square Leagues*, 57. For a discussion of the procedures developed by Vélez Cachupín to protect the rights of both the Indians and the Spanish in connection with these sales, see chapter 10.

3. Reeve, "Navaho-Spanish Peace," 9–40; J. Richard Salazar, "Spanish-Indian Relations in New Mexico during the Term of Commandant General Pedro de Nava, 1790–1802," (Guadalupita, NM: Center for Land Grant Studies, 2005); Jack August, "Balance of Power Diplomacy in New Mexico: Governor Fernando de la Concha and the Indian Policy of Conciliation," *New Mexico Historical Review* 56 (April 1981): 141–60.

4. Regarding Vélez Cachupín's age, see Antonio del Valle Menéndez in collaboration with Pilar Latasa Vasallo, *Juan Francisco de Güemes y Horcasitas: Primer Conde de Revillagigedo; Virrey de México; La historia de un soldado (1681–1766)*

(Cantabria: Librería Estudios, 1998), 428–29; Ebright and Hendricks, *Witches of Abiquiu*, 65–66.

5. See chapter 10; Ebright, "Frontier Land Litigation," 211–13; decree of Governor Vélez Cachupín to Genízaros at Abiquiu, Santa Fe, 20 May 1754, PLC, Roll 38, 52, fr. 889–91.

6. Elizabeth A. H. John, *Storms Brewed in Other Men's Worlds: The Confrontation of Indians, Spanish, and French in the Southwest, 1540–1795* (College Station: Texas A & M University Press, 1975), 321–35, 465–84; Stanley Noyes, *Los Comanches: The Horse People, 1751–1845* (Albuquerque: University of New Mexico Press, 1993), 51–66; Jones, *Pueblo Warriors*, 126–39.

7. The purpose of a mayorazgo was to preserve the fame, renown, and wealth of a family by tying together its assets into an unalienable whole that was passed from first-born son to first-born son. There were several types of mayorazgo. As a rule, a regular mayorazgo passed to the first-born son, although the founder could make other stipulations. Other *mayorazgos* provided for different inheritance schemes, whereby other heirs were designated under specified circumstances. Joaquín Escriche and Juan B. Guim, ed., *Diccionario razonado de legislación y jurisprudencia* (Bogotá: Temis, 1977), 4:30–43; and Guillermo Cabanellas de las Cuevas and Eleanor C. Hoague, *Diccionario jurídico español-inglés Butterworths* (Austin, TX: Butterworth, 1991), 396.

8. In his will, Vélez Cachupín set up an annuity (*censo*) with the seven hundred thousand reales he had earned as governor of New Mexico that would go to the Casas Cachupinas estate he had been cut out of, but instead of going to the first son, Vélez Cachupín stipulated that the inheritance would go to the second son and urged the beneficiaries to always use the Vélez Cachupín surname "so that for all time the fame and glory of the family will be known and not be lost." Tomás Vélez Cachupín, last will and testament, Document P18796, Archivo Histórico de Protocolos de Madrid, Madrid, published in Malcolm Ebright, Teresa Escudero, and Rick Hendricks, "Tomás Vélez Cachupín's Last Will and Testament," *New Mexico Historical Review* 78 (Summer 2003): 285–321, 314; see also Ebright and Hendricks, *The Witches of Abiquiu*, 67–68.

9. "Aunque el mío es de los Cachopines de Laredo . . . no le osaré yo poner cón el del Toboso de la Mancha, puesto que, para decir verdad, semejante apellido hasta ahora no ha llegado a mis oídos." Miguel de Cervantes Saavedra, *El ingenioso hidalgo don Quijote de la Mancha*, ed. Luis Andrés Murillo (Madrid: Clásicos Castalis, 1978), 177, chapter 13.

10. Petition of Tomás Vélez Cachupín, [Madrid, 1761], AGI, Audiencia of Guadalajara, 300, Bancroft Library, University of California–Berkeley; Adams, *Bishop*

Tamarón's Visitation, 24; *Instrucciones y memorias de les virreyes novohispanos* (Mexico City: Editorial Porrúa, 1991), 795.

11. The sixteen-page report is neither signed nor dated, nor does it indicate to whom it was directed, but internal evidence indicates that it was written in 1754 by Vélez Cachupín or his scribe. Robert Ryal Miller, ed., "New Mexico in Mid-Eighteenth Century: A Report Based on Governor Vélez Cachupín's Inspection," *Southwestern Historical Quarterly* 79 (1975–1976): 166–81; decree of Governor Vélez Cachupín ordering resettlement of Abiquiu, Santa Fe, 21 February 1750, SANM I: 1100.

12. Such settlements were often found in other northern provinces (e.g., San Antonio, Texas, and Hermosillo, Sonora) but seldom in New Mexico.

13. Simmons, "Settlement Patterns," 7–21.

14. Governor Mendinueta to Viceroy Bucareli, 26 March 1772, in Thomas, "Governor Mendinueta's Proposals," 29. When Bucareli asked his attorney general for an opinion on the matter, Antonio Bonilla suggested that many of the settlers living in dispersed settlements may not have had titles to the lands they occupied and therefore might be induced to form new compact settlements in exchange for land titles.

15. Decree of Governor Vélez Cachupín ordering resettlement of Abiquiu, Santa Fe, 21 February 1750, SANM I: 1000.

16. Governor Mendinueta's order for resettlement of Abiquiu, Santa Fe, 2 November 1770, SANM I: 36.

17. The five Vélez Cachupín land grants are Las Trampas, Truchas, Abiquiu, San Fernando, and Las Nutrias. The first three communities are still in existence.

18. Governor Mendinueta to Viceroy Bucareli, Santa Fe, 26 March 1772, and Mendinueta to Commandante General Teodoro de Croix, translation in Thomas, "Governor Mendinueta's Proposals," 29.

19. John, *Storms Brewed*, 476–84; Hämäläinen, *Comanche Empire*, 74–86.

20. Thomas, "Governor Mendinueta's Proposals," 35.

21. The Vélez Cachupín grants are (1) Francisco Montes Vigil (SG 128, PLC 14), (2) Cañada de Santa Clara (SG 138), (3) Truchas or Nuestra Señora del Rosario, San Fernando, y Santiago del Rosario de las Truchas (PLC 28), (4) Piedra Lumbre (SG 73, PLC 30), (5) Polvadera (SG 131), (6) Abiquiu (SG 140, PLC 52), (7) Bosque Grande or Miguel and Santiago Montoya (PLC 66 and 272), (8) Nuestra Señora de la Luz de las Lagunitas or Antonio Baca (SG 101, PLC 70), (9) Nuestra Señora de la Luz, San Fernando, y San Blas, (10) Juan Gabaldón (SG 65, PLC 86 and 202, SANM I: 352), (11) Las Trampas (SG 20), (12) Nuestra Señora de los Dolores Mine (SG 162, PLC 147), and (13) Carnuel (SG 150, PLC 74).

22. The Mendinueta grants are (1) José Pacheco (SG 218, PLC 18), (2) Agua Salada or Luis Jaramillo (PLC 31, SANM I: 421), (3) Chaco Mesa or Ignacio Chávez

(SG 96, PLC 34, SANM I: 200), (4) Atrisco (SG 145, PLC 45), (5) Bartolomé Fernández (SG 78, PLC 61 and 126), (6) Felipe Tafoya (SG 99, PLC 67 and 187), (7) San Mateo Springs or Santiago Durán y Chávez (SG 134, PLC 75), (8) San Antonio de las Huertas (SG 144, PLC 90 and 269), (9) Ojo de Borrego (SG 118, PLC 95), (10) Antonio Armijo (PLC 102, SANM I: 44), (11) Juan Gabaldón (SG 65, PLC 86 and 202), (12) Paulín Montoya et al. or Ojo de San José (SG 185, PLC 182, SANM I: 584).

23. Petition of Pedro Romero, Severiano Romero, Cristóbal Baca, Juan Anto Baca, and Vicente Gallegos to Governor Vélez Cachupín, n.p., February 1764, SANM I: 780; order of Governor Vélez Cachupín to Alcalde Miguel Lucero, Santa Fe, February 7, 1764, SANM I: 780.

24. *Genízaros* were detribalized Indians living in Spanish communities. The term *coyote* was used to designate the mixed-blood children of a Genízaro. Ramon A. Gutiérrez, *When Jesus Came the Corn Mothers Went Away: Marriage, Sexuality, and Power in New Mexico, 1500–1846* (Stanford, CA: Stanford University Press, 1991), 197; Report of Alcalde Miguel Lucero, Fonclara, 14 February 1764, SANM I: 780.

25. Grant by Vélez Cachupín, 14 February 1764, SANM I: 780.

26. For example, in 1770 Abiquiu was still experiencing such severe attacks that many of its settlers had again abandoned their homes, and Governor Mendinueta ordered that they return or forfeit their lands. Decree of Governor Mendinueta, Santa Fe, 2 November 1770, SANM I: 36.

27. Vélez Cachupín praised the fighting spirit of Genízaros during the course of a lengthy witchcraft trial at Abiquiu. Opinion of Governor Vélez Cachupín, Santa Fe, 28 March 1764, Pinart Collection, Bancroft Library, University of California–Berkeley, PE 52:5; Ebright and Hendricks, *Witches of Abiquiu*, 44–45. For a description of Spanish-Indian battles on the Navajo frontier from the Spanish point of view, see Marc Simmons, *The Fighting Settlers of Seboyeta* (Cerrillos, NM: San Marcos Press, 1971), passim.

28. Census taken by Governor Vélez Cachupín, San Gabriel de las Nutrias, 28 November 1765, SANM I: 780. The predominance of mixed-blood settlers correlates with similar situations in Las Trampas, Abiquiu, Ojo Caliente, San Miguel del Bado, and Belén, where such settlers also appeared in substantial numbers. The latest work on San Miguel del Bado is Henrietta Martínez Christmas and Nancy Anderson, *The San Miguel del Bado del Rio de Pecos: The 1803 Land Grantees* (Albuquerque: New Mexico Genealogical Society, 2013), which lists at least sixteen Genízaros, Indians, or mestizos (also called *color quebrado*) among the fifty-eight grantees put in possession of the land on 12 March 1803. Christmas and Anderson, *San Miguel del Bado Grantees*, iii–vii. Sometimes the terms *mestizo* and *mulato* were used interchangeably to refer to individuals of mixed

Spanish and Indian ancestry, but here the term *mulato* probably implies mixed Spanish and black ancestry. Gutiérrez, *When Jesus Came*, 196–97; see also Adrian Bustamante, "'The Matter Was Never Resolved': The *Casta* System in Colonial New Mexico, 1693–1823," *New Mexico Historical Review* 66 (April 1991): 143–63.

29. Order of Governor Vélez Cachupín, San Gabriel de las Nutrias, 28 November 1765, SANM I: 780.

30. Order of Governor Vélez Cachupín, San Gabriel de las Nutrias, 29 November 1765, SANM I: 780.

31. "Por sí y sus herederos lo gocen y posean con total señorío . . . dejando los pastos comunes y concejiles para dicha nueva población," *auto de merced* by Governor Veléz Cachupín, Santa Fe, 15 December 1765, SANM I: 780. For a discussion of *tierras concegiles* in Spain, see David Vassberg, "The Spanish Background: Problems Concerning Ownership, Usurpations, and Defense of Common Lands in Sixteenth-Century Castile," in *Spanish and Mexican Land Grants*, ed. Malcolm Ebright (Manhattan, KS: Sunflower University Press, 1989), 12–23. Tierras concegiles (literally, "lands of the council") were common lands owned by a community land grant as distinguished from tierras baldías or *tierras realengas*, common lands owned by the king and considered public domain.

32. Auto de merced by Governor Vélez Cachupín, Santa Fe, 15 December 1765, SANM I: 780.

33. Report of Governor Mendinueta, Santa Fe, 24 April 1770, SANM I: 645.

34. Report of Alcalde Trébol Navarro, San Gabriel de las Nutrias, 28 April 1770, SANM I: 645.

35. Order of Governor Mendinueta, Santa Fe, 1 February 1771, SANM I: 791.

36. Act of possession by Alcalde García de Noriega, San Gabriel de las Nutrias, 16 February 1771, SANM I: 791.

37. Casa Colorado Grant, SG 5, Roll 12, fr. 840–89. The settlement of Las Nutrias is shown on the 1779 Miera y Pacheco map, New Mexico State Records Center and Archives, Santa Fe, and the 1842 J. C. Walker map in Malcolm Ebright, *The Tierra Amarilla Grant: A History of Chicanery* (Santa Fe, NM: Center for Land Grant Studies, 1980), 15; Bowden, "Private Land Claims," 2:207–8.

38. "Amantes de vivir vagos . . . de unos lugares a otros dispersos . . . causando muchos perjuicios en labores, y Ganados," opinion of Governor Vélez Cachupín in Abiquiu witchcraft trial, Santa Fe, 28 March 1764, Pinart Collection, Bancroft Library, University of California–Berkeley, PE 52:5.

39. Decrees of Governor Vélez Cachupín, Santa Fe, 6 February and 20 February 1763, SANM I: 202; act of possession of Trébol Navarro, San Miguel de Laredo [de Carnuel], 12 February 1763, SANM I: 202; decree of Governor Mendinueta, Santa Fe, 12 April 1771, SG Report 150, Roll 27, fr. 7–14; reports of Trébol Navarro, 16 April, 24 April, and 27 May 1771, SANM I: 46; petition of Antonio Montaño and others, report of Trébol Navarro, Santa Fe, 17 March 1774, SANM I: 46; order

of Governor Mendinueta, 23 March 1774, SANM I: 46; see also Robert Archibald, "Cañon de Carnué: Settlement of a Grant," *New Mexico Historical Review* 51 (1976): 313–28; and Frances Leon Swadesh, "Archaeology, Ethnohistory and the First Plaza of Carnuel," *Ethnohistory* 23 (Winter 1976): 31–44.

40. Decrees of Governor Vélez Cachupín, Santa Fe, 6 February and 20 February 1763, SANM I: 202; act of possession of Trébol Navarro, San Miguel de Laredo [de Carnuel], 12 February 1763, SANM I: 202.

41. Decree of Governor Mendinueta, Santa Fe, 12 April 1771, SANM 1: 202; SG Report 150, Roll 27, fr. 7–14.

42. Reports of Trébol Navarro, 16 April, 24 April, and 27 May 1771, SANM 1: 202.

43. Petition of Antonio Montaño and others, report of Trébol Navarro, Santa Fe, 17 March 1774, SANM I: 46; order of Governor Mendinueta, 23 March 1774, SANM I: 46; see also Archibald, "Cañon de Carnué," 313–28; Swadesh, "Carnuel," 31–44.

44. "Comiendo ratones, tejones, y hierbas silvestres," petitions of Domingo Baca et al. to Governor Vélez Cachupín, Belén, 6 February 1761, SANM I: 869. In a related case, Governor Joaquín Codallos y Rabal held a lengthy hearing on the petition of the Genízaro Antonio Casados and then passed the proceedings on to the viceroy, but no final decision has been found. SANM I: 183.

45. Petition of Felipe Tafoya to Governor Vélez Cachupín, Santa Fe, February 1767, SANM I: 869.

46. For a discussion of Genízaro land tenure on the Belén grant, see the lawsuit between Joséph Marcelo Gallegos and Pedro Iturbieta, Belén, May–June 1765, SANM I: 362, discussed in chapter 10.

47. Decree of Governor Vélez Cachupín, Santa Fe, 19 July 1765, SANM I: 780. Governor Vélez Cachupín used the same "licencia y permiso" language when he made the San Gabriel de las Nutrias grant in 1765.

48. Decrees of Governor Vélez Cachupín, Santa Fe, 19 July 1765 and 23 February 1767, SANM I: 869.

49. Petitions of Francisco Pablo Salazar for Belén faction and Juan Francisco Baca et al. for the Sabinal faction, Belén, 17 March 1776, SANM I: 877.

50. Governor Mendinueta to Alcalde Borica, Santa Fe, 18 March 1776, SANM I: 877; Alcalde Borica to Governor Mendinueta, Santa Fe, 31 March 1776, SANM I: 877.

51. Simmons, *Morfi's Disorders*, 35–36.

52. Quelites are edible greens like wild spinach. The most common variety is *quelites salados*, also called lamb's-quarters. These greens are cooked, as are those of the other variety: *quelites colorados*. The word *quelites* is apparently derived from the Aztec *quilitl*. L. S. M. Curtin, *Healing Herbs of the Upper Rio Grande* (Los Angeles, CA: Southwest Museum, 1965), 168–69.

53. Petition of Antonio Sedillo et al. to Governor Marín del Valle, grant by Marín del Valle, and act of possession by Alcalde Miguel Lucero, n.p., 1761, SANM I: 719.

54. Petition of José Gonzales, Simón Zamora, Antonio Fajardo, José Márquez, Gregorio Rivera, Joaquín Peralta, Juan Peralta, and Gregorio Sedillo to Governor Vélez Cachupín, n.p., n.d., SANM I: 720.

55. Report of Alcalde Antonio Sedillo, San Rafael de los Quelites, 10 July 1765, SANM I: 720.

56. Report of Antonio Sedillo, Bernardo Vallejos, Joaquín Sedillo, Juan Sedillo, Pascual García, Bartolo Olguín, Antonio Barela and Lázaro Sedillo, San Rafael de los Quelites, 10 July 1765, SANM I: 720.

57. Decision of Governor Vélez Cachupín, Santa Fe, 16 July 1765, SANM I: 720.

58. Petition to Governor Tomás Veléz Cachupín for the establishment of a guard in Albuquerque, with reply from the governor, Pinart Collection, Bancroft Library, University of California–Berkeley, PE 52:6.

59. Ramón García Jurado had been an alcalde active in Indian affairs earlier in the century, but with a mixed record. In 1703 six Tewa Indians asked that García Jurado be named to represent them in a lawsuit protesting their false imprisonment, but three decades later, in 1732, he was suspended as alcalde and banished to Zuni Pueblo for failure to pay Zia Indians for certain work he had ordered them to perform. Cutter, *Protector de Indios*, 46–47 and 78–79; Myra Ellen Jenkins, "Early Days in the Rio Puerco Valley," Myra Ellen Jenkins Papers, Center of Southwest Studies, Fort Lewis College, Durango, CO, Box 40, folder 10.

60. Petition of Ramón García Jurado, Antonio Montaño, José Montaño, Bernabé Manuel Montoya, Juan Bautista Montaño, Pedro Montaño, and Ramón García Jurado Jr. to Governor Vélez Cachupín, n.p., n.d., SANM I: 688. Another instance of Spaniards working for Indians due to a shortage of agricultural lands was reported by Governor Fernando de la Concha in 1789, and in 1773 Governor Mendinueta reported a similar land shortage that was forcing Spaniards to purchase substantial amounts of agricultural produce from the Indians. Gutiérrez, *When Jesus Came*, 304–5.

61. "Personas peritas en materia de campo y labores," order of Governor Velez Cachupín, Santa Fe, 21 October 1753, SANM I: 688; report of Antonio Baca to Governor Vélez Cachupín, Pueblo of Zia, 2 November 1753, SANM I: 688.

62. *Las más a proposito a proposito y con armamento*, grant by Governor Vélez Cachupín, Santa Fe, 25 November 1753, SANM I: 688.

63. Ibid.

64. "Por iguales partes de dichas tierras, pastos, montes, aguas, y abrevaderos," *auto de posesión*, Antonio Baca, San Fernando, 11 December 1753, SANM I: 688.

65. "Cuyos linderos se incluyen todos las doce partes mercenados de tierras de pan llevar quedando libres para pastos comunes de dicha poblazón el demás terreno," act of possession, Antonio Baca, San Fernando, 11 December 1753, SANM I: 688.

66. "Muy amplio, fíjo y capaz sin ruina que en nigún tiempo le pueda amenazar de lluvias," repartimiento de tierras, Antonio Baca, San Fernando, 11 March 1754, SANM I: 688.

67. Ibid.

68. Felipe Tafoya to Governor Vélez Cachupín, Santa Fe, n.d., SANM I: 688.

69. Order of Governor Marín del Valle, Santa Fe, 19 January 1759, SANM I: 688.

70. By 1877 the following settlements existed on the San Fernando grant, some of which involved resettlement of eighteenth-century communities that had been abandoned: La Cueva, San Francisco, Durán, and San Ignacio. Apparently, the initial settlement at San Fernando was not revived in the nineteenth century. Jerold Gwayn Widdison, "Historical Geography of the Middle Rio Puerco Valley, New Mexico," *New Mexico Historical Review* 34 (1959): 259–60. For more on the village of San Fernando, see Jenkins, "Early Days in the Rio Puerco Valley," 4–6.

71. In another example of Navajo land use, Alcalde Bartolomé Fernández mentioned fields planted by the Navajo during his act of possession for the Bosque Grande or Miguel and Santiago Montoya grant. Act of possession, Bartolomé Fernández, 29 January 1767, PLC, Roll 41, fr. 66, 90.

72. Petition of twenty vecinos of Nuestra Señora de la Luz, San Fernando, y San Blas to Governor Mendinueta, San Fernando, June 1767, SANM I: 692.

73. Report of Bartolomé Fernández, Nuestra Señora de Guadalupe, 6 July 1767, SANM I: 692.

74. "Si dichos vecinos del Río Puerco reincidiesen en semejante exceso serán castigados con severidad que corresponde, y se tendrá presente el cometido," order of Governor Mendinueta, Santa Fe, 17 July 1767, SANM I: 692.

75. Petition of San Fernando settlers to Governor Mendinueta, June 1767, SANM I: 692.

76. Petition of Atrisco settlers to Governor Mendinueta, n.p., [1768], Center for Southwest Research Collection, University of New Mexico, PC-301, Box 8, #45, folder 2; Town of Atrisco Grant, SG 145, Roll 26, fr. 1035 et seq.

77. Grant by Governor Mendinueta, Santa Fe, 8 April, 1768, SANM I: 694.

78. Apparently the Cerrito Colorado was more than two leagues from the settlements, so by crossing out the language about distance, the San Fernando settlers hoped that the landmark and not the lineal measurement could determine their southern boundary.

79. Report by Alcalde Trébol Navarro, San Fernando, 9 May 1768, SANM I: 694.

80. Ibid.

81. Luis Jaramillo to Governor Mendinueta, n.p., [July 1769], SANM I: 421.

82. Grant by Governor Mendinueta, Santa Fe, 20 July 1769, SANM I: 421, in connection with the San Gabriel de las Nutrias grant.

83. Petition of Antonio Montaño, Marcos Baca, José de Jesús Montaño, Antonio Durán, Felipe Baca, Juan Candelario, José Antonio Castelo, Tomás Gurule, Agustín Gallego, Marínano Gallego, and Juan Bautista Montaño to Antonio Sedillo, [San Fernando, July 1769], SANM I: 421.

84. "Nuestros linderos queden libres sin aditamento de leguas," petition of Antonio Montaño, Marcos Baca, Tomás Gurule, José Antonio Castelo, José de Jesús Montaño, Mariano Gallego, Felipe Baca, Antonio Candelaria, Antonio Durán, and Agustín Gallego to Governor Mendinueta, [San Fernando, July 1769], SANM I: 421.

85. "Necia y maliciosamente testaron en el testimonio de merced y posesión todos los lugares en que mencionaba leguas," decision by Governor Mendinueta, 7 August 1769, SANM I: 421.

86. Ibid. When the two grants were finally surveyed there was a two and one-half mile gap between them.

87. This rule is based on the theory that the parties are more likely to be familiar with a natural feature as a boundary than with a measured distance and therefore intend the natural feature to be the boundary. Even if marked on the ground with a landmark like a pile of stones or a cross, the measurements were never exact, and the landmark could always be moved (and often was), while a natural feature had the virtue of a degree of permanency. Curtis M. Brown, *Boundary Control and Legal Principles* (New York: John Wiley and Sons, 1957), 76–81.

88. An exception to Mendinueta's negative approach to the San Fernando settlers occurred in 1770 when the governor granted them some additional land so they could move to a location where groundwater was more plentiful. The wells they had dug in the old location were dry, though they had hired dowsers (*balisanes*) to help them locate water. Bernabé Montaño Grant, PLC, Roll 34, fr. 53–65.

89. Felipe Tafoya petition, Santa Fe, 3 December 1766, PLC, Roll 41, fr. 104–5; SANM I: 688; Salazar, "Felipe Tafoya Grant," 3–6.

90. Nuestra Señora de la Luz de las Lagunitas Grant, PLC, Roll 41, fr. 472; Felipe Tafoya Grant, made 15 June 1767, Bartolomé Fernández alcalde (SG 99, PLC 67 and 187); Bartolomé Fernández Grant, made 2 September 1767, Carlos Pérez de Mirabal alcalde (SG 78, PLC 61 and PLC 126); Ignacio Chavez Grant, made 17 February 1768, Bartolomé Fernández alcalde (SG 96, PLC 34).

91. "Con sobrada de vergonzada y audacia, poner condiciones y coarta las facultades," decree of Governor Mendinueta, Santa Fe, 28 January 1768, SANM II: 635.

92. "No sólo color quebrado, sino inútiles para el servicio del Rey," order of Governor Mendinueta, Santa Fe, 28 January 1768, SANM II: 635.

93. See appendix 4 for the census list of the settlers of the San Gabriel de las Nutrias

grant. In the census, over half are listed as either mestizo, mulato, or Indio. The terms *Indio* and *Genízaro* were used interchangeably by Alcalde Lucero in an earlier census (Fonclara, 14 February 1764) and by Governor Veléz Cachupín (San Gabriel de las Nutrias, 28 November 1765) as the three Anayas—Javier, Juan, and Pablo—are listed as Genízaro by the alcalde and as Indio by the governor. SANM I: 780. Ebright, "Breaking New Ground," 231–33.

94. According to Thomas, "The unusual relations that had obtained under Vélez were not reestablished until two decades later under Governor Anza. Mendinueta's policy was that of war which, in turn, necessitated extensive defensive measures." Alfred B. Thomas, *The Plains Indians and New Mexico, 1751–1778: A Collection of Documents Illustrative of the History of the Eastern Frontier of New Mexico* (Albuquerque: University of New Mexico Press, 1940), 38–39.

95. See, for example, the San Mateo Springs grant made to Santiago Durán y Chavez in 1768 without prejudice to the cornfields of the Navajo, SG 134, Roll 25, fr. 754 et seq.; PLC 75, Roll 41, fr. 935–36.

96. Under Spanish law, the Navajos who were not Christianized were not considered to have title to the lands they occupied, but their use rights were protected as a matter of Indian policy. As Mendinueta said, "Good treatment by the Spaniards may attract them to come under the control of the sovereign and into the pale of the church." Order of Governor Mendinueta in response to petition of San Fernando settlers, Santa Fe, 20 June 1767, SANM I: 692.

97. Frank McNitt, *Navajo Wars: Military Campaigns, Slave Raids, and Reprisals* (Albuquerque: University of New Mexico Press, 1972), 29. Although Spanish protection against Indian attacks actually declined during Mendinueta's terms, there was sufficient consistency between the Indian policy of Governors Vélez Cachupín and Mendinueta that the next governor, Juan Bautista de Anza, was able to establish prolonged permanent peace with the Comanche, allowing Spanish settlement to expand dramatically.

98. Representación del Governor D. Thomas Vélez Cachupín sobre restablecimiento de la Paz con los comanches, Archivo General de la Nación, Mexico City, Provincias Internas, tomo 161, translated in Thomas, *Plains Indians*, 148–54. Mendinueta did not always give the pobladores the same consideration, as when he jailed the petitioners who complained about the conduct of Trébol Navarro without a hearing. Ebright and Hendricks, *Witches of Abiquiu*, 80–82.

99. Order by Governor Vélez Cachupín in response to petition for removal of Alcalde Antonio Baca, Pinart Collection, Bancroft Library, University of California–Berkeley, PE 52:11.

100. Copia de la Ynstrucción que D. Thomas Vélez Cachupín . . . dexó a su successor don Franzco Marín del Valle, AGN, Mexico City, Provincias Internas, tomo 102, translated in Thomas, *Plains Indians*, 129–43, esp. 137, and 141–42.

Chapter Ten

1. Tomás Vélez Cachupín served two terms as governor of New Mexico from 1749 to 1754 and 1762 to 1767 (Francisco Antonio Marín del Valle, Mateo Antonio de Mendoza, and Manuel del Portillo y Urrisola served as governors from 1754 through 1762). Pedro Fermín de Mendinueta was governor from 1767 to 1778, holding office for two consecutive terms. SANM II: 635.

2. Ibid.

3. See Peter L. Reich, "Mission Revival Jurisprudence: State Courts and Hispanic Water Law Since 1850," *Washington Law Review* 69 (October 1994): 869, for an excellent analysis of cases in California, New Mexico, and Texas determining the water rights of Hispanic municipalities. Reich demonstrates that when these courts created the historically erroneous Pueblo Rights Doctrine, they intentionally ignored historical and legal evidence that the "doctrine" never existed.

4. Daniel Tyler, "The Spanish Colonial Legacy and the Role of Hispanic Custom in Defining New Mexico Land and Water Rights," *Colonial Latin American Historical Review* 4 (Spring 1995): 149–65; Daniel Tyler, "Underground Water in Hispanic New Mexico: A Brief Analysis of Laws, Customs, and Disputes," *New Mexico Historical Review* 66 (July 1991): 287–301; Daniel Tyler, *The Mythical Pueblo Rights Doctrine: Water Administration in Hispanic New Mexico* (El Paso: Texas Western Press, 1990); Tyler, "Ejido Lands"; Taylor, "Colonial Land and Water Rights," 189; David J. Langum, *Law and Community on the Mexican California Frontier: Anglo-American Expatriates and the Clash of Legal Traditions, 1821–1846* (Norman: University of Oklahoma Press, 1987); Michael C. Meyer, *Water in the Hispanic Southwest: A Social and Legal History from 1550–1850* (Tucson: University of Arizona Press, 1984); Ebright, *Land Grants and Lawsuits*; Charles Cutter, "Community and the Law in Northern New Spain," *Americas* 50 (April 1994): 467–80; Charles Cutter, "Judicial Punishment in Colonial New Mexico," *Western Legal History* 8 (Winter/Spring 1995): 114–29; State of New Mexico ex rel. Martínez v. City of Las Vegas, 880 P. 2d 868 (Ct. App., 1994), cites with approval; Tyler, *Mythical Pueblo Rights Doctrine*; Meyer, *Water in the Hispanic Southwest*; and Ebright, *Land Grants and Lawsuits*, among others.

5. John O. Baxter, *Spanish Irrigation in the Pojoaque and Tesuque Valleys during the Eighteenth and Early Nineteenth Centuries* (Santa Fe: New Mexico State Engineer Office, 1984); Daniel Tyler, "Land and Water Tenure in New Mexico: 1821–1846 (unpublished report on file in New Mexico v. Aamodt, No. 6639, Federal District Court for New Mexico, 1979); Michael C. Meyer and Susan M. Deeds, "Land, Water, and Equity in Spanish Colonial and Mexican Law: Historical Evidence

for the Court in the Case of the State of New Mexico vs. R. Lee Aamodt, et al."
(unpublished report on file in New Mexico v. Aamodt, No. 6639, Federal District
Court for New Mexico, 1979); Hans W. Baade, "The 'Pueblo Water Rights' of the
City of Las Vegas, New Mexico" (unpublished report prepared for Martínez v.
Las Vegas).

6. Hans W. Baade, "The Historical Background of Texas Water Law: A Tribute to
Jack Pope," *St. Mary's Law Journal* 18 (1986): 30–47; G. Emlen Hall, "Shell Games:
The Continuing Legacy of Rights to Minerals and Water on Spanish and Mexi-
can Land Grants in the Southwest," in *Thirty-Sixth Annual Rocky Mountain
Mineral Law Institute* (New York: Matthew Bender, 1991); Hall, *Four Leagues of
Pecos*, 8–14; Hall, comments at Western History Association session "Land Grant
Studies in New Mexico: New Directions," where an earlier draft of this chapter
was presented on 21 October 1994, Albuquerque, New Mexico; Joseph W.
McKnight, "Law Books on the Hispanic Frontier," in *Spanish and Mexican Land
Grants*, ed. Malcolm Ebright (Manhattan, KS: Sunflower University Press, 1989),
74–84.

7. Langum, *Law and Community*; Tyler, *Mythical Pueblo Rights Doctrine*; Tyler,
"Underground Water."

8. *Las Siete Partidas* (Madrid: Oficina de León Amarita, 1829), *partida* 1, *título* 2.
The importance of custom in the system of the *partidas* legal code is evident
from its place near the beginning, between king-made law and laws concerning
the Catholic faith. For a recent article on the history of *Las Siete Partidas* in a
volume dealing with contributions to the law (as well as to poetry, history, and
astronomy) of the Spanish monarch Alfonso el Sabio ("the Wise" or "the
Learned"), who ruled from 1252 to 1284, see Jerry R. Craddock, "The Legislative
Works of Alfonso el Sabio," in *Emperor of Culture: Alfonso X the Learned of
Castile and His Thirteenth-Century Renaissance*, ed. Robert I. Burns, S.J. (Philadelphia: University of Pennsylvania Press, 1990), 182–97. Studies of the meaning and effect of *Las Siete Partidas*, particularly its application in the Americas,
are still burgeoning. See, for example, Victor Frankl, "Hernán Cortés y la
tradición de Las Siete Partidas," *Revista de Historia de América* 53–54 (June–
December 1962): 9–74; and Anthony Pagden, trans. and ed., *Hernán Cortés:
Letters from Mexico* (New Haven and London: Yale University Press, 1986),
xvii–xx, 451, n. 9.

9. Examples of U.S. court decisions that erroneously failed to take customary law
into account are U.S. v. Sandoval, 167 U.S. 278 (1897) (rejecting the common lands
of the San Miguel del Bado Community land grant); Griego v. U.S., PLC, Roll 173,
fr. 268–70 (1898) (rejecting the Embudo Land grant because the grant document
submitted was a copy made by an alcalde); Cartwright v. Public Service Co. of
New Mexico, 66 N.M. 64 (applying the discredited Pueblo water rights doctrine

to the Las Vegas Community land grant). For a more complete discussion of
these cases and their historical background, see Ebright, *Land Grants and Law-suits*, chapters 5, 6, and 8.

10. Tyler, "Spanish Colonial Legacy," 149–65; Richard E. Greenleaf, "Land and Water
in Mexico and New Mexico: 1700–1821," *New Mexico Historical Review* 47 (April
1972): 86, "archival investigators often suspect that it was Spanish custom that
conditioned legal practice in remote areas of the empire"; Simmons, *Spanish
Government*, 176, "by and large, judgment of the *Alcaldes*. . . . conformed to the
prevailing customs of the country."

11. Langum, *Law and Community*, 30–55; David J. Langum, "The Legal System of
Spanish California," *Western Legal History* 7 (Winter/Spring 1994): 6–10.

12. For Hispanic law in Texas, see Donald E. Chipman, *Spanish Texas, 1519–1821* (Aus-tin: University of Texas Press, 1992), 250–54; Andrés Tijerina, *Tejanos and Texas
under the Mexican Flag, 1821–1836* (College Station: Texas A & M University Press,
1994), 65–78; and Cutter, *Legal Culture of Northern New Spain*, passim.

13. For a recent book that uses lawsuits and other Spanish colonial documents to
"reflect something about the everyday lives of [colonial] New Mexicans," see Linda
Tigges, ed., *Spanish Colonial Lives: Documents from the Spanish Colonial Archives
of New Mexico, 1705–1774*, trans. J. Richard Salazar (Santa Fe, NM: Sunstone Press,
2014); see also Jean-Louis Baudouin, "The Impact of the Common Law on the
Civilian Systems of Louisiana and Quebec," in *The Role of Judicial Decisions and
Doctrine in Civil Law and in Mixed Jurisdictions*, ed. Joseph Dainow (Baton Rouge:
Louisiana State University Press, 1974); Francis Deák, "The Place of the 'Case' in
the Common and Civil Law," *Tulane Law Review* 8 (1933–1934): 337–57.

14. A. N. Yiannopoulos, "Jurisprudence and Doctrine as Sources of Law in Loui-siana and in France," in *The Role of Judicial Decisions and Doctrine in Civil Law
and in Mixed Jurisdictions*, ed. Joseph Dainow (Baton Rouge: Louisiana State
University Press, 1974), 77.

15. For a discussion of the Protector de Indios, see chapter 1. For a description of
the activities of this official in New Mexico, see Cutter, *Protector de Indios*,
passim. The office of Protector de Indios was vacant from 1717 to 1810, but alcal-des like Bartolomé Fernández (SANM I: 1352), Felipe Tafoya (SANM I: 1351 and
1354), and Carlos Fernández (SANM I: 1354) sometimes acted as advocates for
the pueblos during this period. Cutter, *Protector de Indios*, 75–77, 109.

16. The absence of citations to Hispanic statutes is typical of the decisions of gover-nors of New Mexico under Spain and Mexico, though litigants themselves some-times cited law codes including *Las Siete Partidas*. Tyler, "Land and Water
Tenure," 32–36.

17. Decision of the audiencia of Guadalajara regarding sale of Santa Ana Pueblo lands to Spaniards, citing the *Recopilación*, Guadalajara, March/April 1818, SANM II: 2715.

18. Inventory of archives turned over to Governor Tomás Vélez Cachupín, SANM I: 1258.

19. Inventory of lawsuits decided by Governor Vélez Cachupín and land grants made by Governor Vélez Cachupín from April 1749 through 1754, SANM II: 525.

20. The lawsuits reviewed, some decided by Governor Mendinueta, are as follows (listed by SANM number): 29, Alameda v. José Montaño (1750); 31, Julián Rael de Aguilar v. Melchora Sandoval (1751); 51, heirs of the Alameda grant v. Pedro Barela (1778); 111, San Fernando v. Atrisco (1759); 362, Pedro Yturbieta v. Joseph Marcelo Gallegos (1765); 368, children of Cristóbal Gallegos v. Juan Roque Gallegos (1770); 460, Antonio Joseph Lopez v. Miguel Tenorio (1772); 541, Cristóbal Mestas v. Ventura Mestas (1752); 557, Antonio Baca v. Joaquín Mestas (1762); 558, Sebastian Martín v. Manuel Martín (1763); 571, Miguel Montoya v. Juan Pablo Martín (1776); 573, Juan Bautista Montaño v. Antonio Baca (1776); 592, Marcial Martín Sanjil v. Marcial Martín (1771); 643, José Antonio Naranjo v. Diego Torres (1752); 687, Juan Joseph Pacheco v. Sebastián Martín (1753); 691, San Lorenzo v. El Paso (1765); 696, José Pacheco v. Juan Alarid (1771); 783, María Romero v. María Antonia Villalpando (1766); 786, María Rosalia Romero v. Pablo Salazar (1768); 1050, Manuel Valerio v. Lazaro de Atienza (1753); 1079, Nicolas Ortiz Niño Ladrón de Guevara v. Juan Estevan García de Noriega (1751); 1122, Ventura Mestas v. Antonio Mestas (1766); 1348, San Felipe Pueblo v. Heirs of Cristóbal Baca (21 March 1753); 1349, Santa Ana Pueblo v. Quitería Contreras (1763); 1351, San Ildefonso v. Luján (1766); 1352, Cochití v. Miguel Romero (1765).

21. In one case involving the social class of the litigants, Mendinueta jailed petitioners who were complaining about an alcalde without responding to their complaint, calling some of them mixed-blood (*color quebrado*). SANM II: 635.

22. The Christianized Suma Indians had been living at Senecu, Isleta, and Socorro and totaled ninety-three individuals in twenty-seven families. The so-called heathen Sumas, living nearby on *rancherías* and numbering about forty families, also joined the settlement. Decree of Governor Vélez Cachupín, El Paso, 18 October 1764, SANM I: 1350. The ground was prepared for the grant of one league of land to the Sumas at San Lorenzo by a 1751 decree providing for grants of one league of land to other Indians in the El Paso area, which was a reversal of a 1692 decision leaving Indian lands in the hands of the Franciscans. W. H. Timmons, *El Paso: A Borderlands History* (El Paso: Texas Western Press, 1990), 36–37.

23. Declaration of Antonio Maese, Presidio del Paso del Río del Norte, 22 August 1765, SANM I: 691. For background on intentional burning of the montes in Spain, see Vassberg, "Spanish Background," 17.

24. Petition of El Paso vecinos to Alcalde Pedro de la Fuente, El Paso, August 1765, SANM I: 691. The appeal to Governor Vélez Cachupín occurred after the matter was litigated before Fuente, alcalde and captain of the presidio of El Paso. For more on Fuente during this period, see James McDaniel, trans. and ed., "Diary of Pedro José de la Fuente, Captain of the Presidio of El Paso del Norte" (January–December 1765) *Southwestern Historical Quarterly* 60 (October 1956): 260–81, and 83 (January 1980): 259–78. In his diary, Fuente refers to his lieutenant alcalde as Horcasitas, so I have followed that usage here.

25. "Árbitro de los montes," Juan Antonio García Noriega, José Manuel Telles Jiron, and Francisco García Carabajal to Alcalde Pedro de la Fuente, El Paso, August 1765, SANM I: 691. Vélez Cachupín had already had dealings with Teniente Alcalde Horcasitas when he tried to get him to organize the Indians and other residents of the area around El Paso to dig a new acequia to alleviate the problem of flooding. This was after two years of frustration with a project proposed in 1762 to construct a dam at El Paso capable of withstanding the annual floods of the Río Grande. The dam was to be funded by a tax on owners of vineyards in the area, but they refused to supply either funds or labor. Timmons, *El Paso*, 40–41; Pinart Collection, Bancroft Library, University of California–Berkeley, PE 51:1 and 51:2; Timmons, *El Paso*, 41, n. 31.

26. Decree of Governor Vélez Cachupín, Santa Fe, 30 October 1765, SANM I: 691.

27. In 1765 62 Sumas and 202 Spaniards were living at San Lorenzo. Timmons, *El Paso*, 42–43. Laws protecting Indian lands from Spanish encroachment in the *Recopilación* are 4.12.12 and 6.3.20 (Spanish ranches not to be located near Indian communities) and 4.7.1 (Spanish communities not to be established where Indian rights would be prejudiced). A royal cedula issued on 17 September 1692 also gave Indians the right of first refusal (right to meet the price of a proposed sale and purchase land adjacent to the pueblo). Taylor, "Land and Water Rights," 20–21.

28. Petition of Alejandro Gonzales, Andrés Martín, Salvador Martínez, Julián Rael, J. W. Gonzales, José Gonzales, and Juan Gaspar Gonzales to Governor Vélez Cachupín, SANM I: 29.

29. "No se entrometa a embarazar ni perturbar el curso de la justicia," decree of Governor Vélez Cachupín, Santa Fe, 23 January 1750, SANM I: 29.

30. Act of possession, Alcalde Antonio Baca, San Fernando, 11 March 1754, SANM I: 688.

31. *Las Siete Partidas* 3.28.9: "Quales son las cosas propiamente del comun de cada ciudad, o villa, de que cada uno puede usar" (What things are the common

property of every city and town, which everyone has a right to use). This law alone is explained by nine footnotes in Latin that are three times longer than the law itself. The longest note is a gloss on the part of the law that declares common property to be owned equally by rich and poor members of the community.

32. Eleanor B. Adams and France V. Scholes, "Books in New Mexico, 1598–1680," *New Mexico Historical Review* 7 (July 1942): 232; McKnight, "Law Books," 74–84.

33. Deák, "Place of the 'Case,'" 344–45.

34. Decree of Governor Vélez Cachupín, Santa Fe, 17 July 1766, SANM I: 111.

35. As noted earlier, Governor Vélez Cachupín rejected Felipe Tafoya's petition for a grant in the vicinity of San Fernando, telling Alcalde Tafoya that if he needed grazing land for his flocks of sheep he should join one of the existing settlements along the Río Puerco like San Fernando or San Gabriel de las Nutrias. Then he could use the common lands of those grants but would have to risk his life in one of those communities on the Navajo frontier. Soon after Vélez Cachupín left office, Tafoya received his own private grazing grant from Governor Mendinueta. SG Report 99, Roll 22, fr. 1362 et seq. For more on this grant, see Salazar "Felipe Tafoya Grant."

36. "No se ha echado cordel en (de) esta banda de la acequia madre sino que todos labran tierras en mancomún," statement of Juan Torres and Nicolas Torres, Belén, 31 May 1765, SANM I: 362.

37. Chacaqüiste, in New Mexico spelled *chaqüiste*, is a disease causing certain grasses to turn yellowish-brown. Rubén Cobos, *A Dictionary of New Mexico and Southern Colorado Spanish* (Santa Fe: Museum of New Mexico Press, 2003), 67. And in Mexico *chahuistle*, a disease of grasses caused by too much moisture. Francisco J. Santamaria, *Diccionario de mejicanismos* (Mexico City: Editorial Porrua, S. A., 1978), 455.

38. "Con el paño amarrado a la cintura," "nos [h]abíamos de quebrar las cabezas," petition of Joseph Marcelo Gallegos, [Belén, June 1765], SANM I: 362.

39. Prior to his inheritance, Iturbieta had farmed a field one-quarter of a league away. Petition of Joseph Marcelo Gallegos, SANM I: 362. A league is 2.63 miles, the distance traveled on horseback over flat terrain at a normal gait in an hour. Fray Angélico Chávez and Ted J. Warner, *The Domínguez-Escalante Journal* (Provo, UT: Brigham Young University Press, 1976), 4, n. 17.

40. Order of Governor Vélez Cachupín, Santa Fe, [June 1765], SANM I: 362.

41. When the Belén grant was first made in 1740 a settlement of Genízaros may already have there, as claimed by Antonio Casados in a lawsuit during the tenure of Governor Codallos y Rabal. Antonio Casados vs. Diego Torres, SANM I: 183; will of Cristóbal Torres, SANM I: 247.

42. One of the Belén leaders was Diego Torres, whose father, Cristóbal, had received a private grant north of Santa Cruz that he treated as a community grant by giving families who settled there house lots and farm tracts as well as rights to use the common lands. Cristóbal's will provided that the grant be divided among the settlers who were living there, as well as those who might settle there in the future. Diego's dissatisfaction with the communal nature of his father's land grant helps explain why he petitioned for a private grant at Belén and used Genízaros to help him settle the grant. SANM I: 247.

43. *Recopilación* 4.12.1 (four-year possession requirement for private tracts within a community grant); *Las Siete Partidas* 3.29.18 (ten-year possession requirement sufficient to acquire ownership where property acquired in good faith as by purchase).

44. Statement by Juan Roque Gallegos, Bernalillo, 30 June 1770, SANM I: 368.

45. Statements by Mariano, María Antonia, and Cristóbal Gallegos Jr., Santa Fe, 21 May 1770, SANM I: 368.

46. Decision by Governor Mendinueta, Santa Fe, 4 July 1770, SANM I: 368.

47. *Las Siete Partidas* 3.29.21 provided for the acquisition of title after thirty-year possession even if the property "had been stolen or obtained by violence or robbery." This is much broader than adverse possession in present-day New Mexico and other U.S. jurisdictions that require good faith acquisition of the property through a written document. 3 Am. Jur. 2d, 218–19.

48. Alcalde Juan Montes Vigil, petition to Governor Vélez Cachupín, March 1753, SANM I: 1348.

49. "Naturales del Pueblo de San Felipe . . . no pueden ni deben celebrar compras ni ventas de bienes raíces."

50. "Según el uso de la tierra."

51. "Personas legales y de conocimiento en materias de campo," order of Governor Vélez Cachupín, Santa Fe, 21 March 1753, SANM I: 1348.

52. Appraisal of Gerónimo Jaramillo, Los Algodones, 26 March 1753, SANM I: 1348.

53. Decree of Governor Vélez Cachupín, Santa Fe, 29 March 1753, SANM I: 1348.

54. Deed for Cristóbal Baca heirs to San Felipe Pueblo, Santa Fe, 24 April 1753, Nicolas de Ortiz, Manuel Gallegos et al., SANM I: 1348.

55. Act of possession by Alcalde Juan Vigil, 7 April 1753, SANM I: 1348.

56. In 1734 Governor Cruzat y Góngora annulled a proposed sale of lands to Santa Ana Pueblo by Baltasar Romero. SANM I: 1345.

57. Decree of Governor Vélez Cachupín, Santa Fe, 29 March 1753, SANM I: 1348.

58. For more on Bernardo Miera y Pacheco, see John L. Kessell, *Miera y Pacheco: A Renaissance Spaniard in Eighteenth-Century New Mexico* (Norman: University of Oklahoma Press, 2013); Adams and Chávez, *Missions of New Mexico*, 160–61; and Chávez and Warner, *Domínguez-Escalante Journal*, 4, n. 9.

59. For a full discussion of Santa Ana's purchase of the El Ranchito tract, see Ebright, Hendricks, and Hughes, *Four Square Leagues*, chapter 2; see also Ward Allen Minge, "The Pueblo of Santa Ana's El Ranchito Purchases, and the Adjudication of the Boundary with San Felipe" (unpublished manuscript in possession of the author).

60. Appointment of appraisers (*nombramiento de evaluadores*) by Miera y Pacheco, Santa Ana, 6 July 1763, SANM I: 1349.

61. Bernardo de Miera y Pacheco, Juan Bautista Montaño, and Francisco Pablo de Salazar, appraisal (*evaluación*), Santa Ana, 7 July 1763, SANM I: 1349.

62. Minge, "Pueblo of Santa Ana," 4–5. For a history of Santa Ana from the pueblo's point of view, see Bayer, *Santa Ana*.

63. Baltasar Romero land sale annulled by Governor Cruzate y Góngora, SANM I: 1345.

64. Santa Ana's population was counted at 404 in 1760. Simmons, "History of Pueblo-Spanish Relations," 185.

65. Miera y Pacheco acknowledgment of payment (*paga que hizieron*), 7 July 1763, SANM I: 1349.

66. G. Emlen Hall, "Land Litigation and the Idea of New Mexico Progress," in *Spanish and Mexican Land Grants*, ed. Malcolm Ebright (Manhattan, KS: Sunflower University Press, 1989), n. 12, citing *Recopilación* 6.3.20.

67. "A todo el común de esta república, según más o menos cada uno entregó de paga por ellas," report of Alcalde Miera y Pacheco, Santa Ana, 8 July 1763, SANM I: 1349.

68. The Cañada de Santa Clara grant is discussed in detail in Ebright, Hendricks, and Hughes, *Four Square Leagues*, chapter 5. The Cañada de Santa Clara grant was confirmed by the Court of Private Land Claims in 1894 but when finally surveyed in 1900 its original area was reduced to less than five hundred acres. PLC 17, Roll 34, fr. 1396–1410; Bowden, "Private Land Claims," 2:553–61.

69. SANM I: 1351. Measurement of the San Ildefonso league is discussed in Ebright, Hendricks, and Hughes, *Four Square Leagues*, chapter 1, and Sandia Pueblo is covered in chapter 4.

70. Javier Malagón-Barcelo, "The Role of the Letrado in the Colonization of America," *Americas* 18 (1961–1962): 1–17; J. H. Parry, *The Spanish Theory of Empire in the Sixteenth Century* (Cambridge: University Press, 1940), 2; Carter, "Law and Society," 9–10. In Mexico City the oidores (judges) who sat on the audiencia (the highest court in the viceroyalty of New Spain) had legislative as well as judicial functions. They advised the governor about royal policy and legislation and sometimes served as a temporary government.

71. Kagan, *Lawsuits and Litigants*, 22–32, 48.

72. "I obey but I do not execute." For a discussion of Spain's sometimes inconsistent

policies regarding the Americas, see Colin M. MacLachlan, *Spain's Empire in the New World: The Role of Ideas in Institutional and Social Change* (Berkeley: University of California Press, 1988), 13; John Leddy Phelan, "Authority and Flexibility in the Spanish Imperial Bureaucracy," *Administrative Science Quarterly* 5, no. 1 (1960): 47–65.

73. SANM I: 31 and SANM I: 1351.

74. See, for example, the opinion of Lic. Miguel de Olachea in the contested estate proceeding Julián Rael de Aguilar, et al. v. Melchora de Sandoval and Antonio de Ulibarrí, Presidio of El Paso, 1 May 1751, SANM I: 31.

75. For a similar analysis, see Cutter's *Legal Culture*, 3–11. Cutter examines six hundred civil and criminal cases from New Mexico and Texas and finds that "most magistrates heard out contending parties, sought equitable solutions, and avoided excessive legalism." Ibid., 10.

76. These principles are similar to but not identical to those found in Michael Meyer's book, *Water in the Hispanic Southwest*, which lists seven factors involved in the adjudication of water rights disputes: just title, prior use, need, injury to third party, intent, legal right, and equity and the common good. Meyer, *Water in the Hispanic Southwest*, 146–64.

77. "Uso, costumbre y servidumbre," Juan Antonio García Noriega, José Manuel Telles Jiron, and Francisco García Carabajal to Alcalde Pedro de la Fuente, El Paso, August 1765, SANM I: 691.

78. SANM I: 691; SANM I: 1350.

79. Petition of Alameda residents against José Montaño, 20 January 1750, SANM I: 29.

80. Decree of Governor Vélez Cachupín, Santa Fe, 17 July 1766, SANM I: 111.

81. Order of Governor Vélez Cachupín, Santa Fe, [June 1765], SANM I: 362.

82. Statements by Mariano, María Antonia, and Cristóbal Gallegos Jr., Santa Fe, 21 May 1770, SANM I: 368.

83. In 1734 a proposed sale of land at Bernalillo by Baltasar Romero to Santa Ana Pueblo was annulled by Governor Cruzat y Góngora because "it would prejudice the settlement [of Bernalillo] and is contrary to the royal laws which protect grants made to Spaniards." Romero was told that if he still wanted to sell he must sell to a Spaniard, not to an Indian or Indian community. Decree by Governor Cruzat y Góngora, Santa Fe, 1 March 1734, SANM I: 1345. However, Santa Ana Pueblo had been purchasing land from Spaniards as early as 1709. Ebright, Hendricks, and Hughes, *Four Square Leagues*, chapter 2.

84. Increasingly, the difference between civil and common law has narrowed so that today decision making under the two systems is often quite similar. Woodfin L. Butte, "Stare Decisis, Doctrine, and Jurisprudence in Mexico and Elsewhere," in *The Role of Judicial Decisions and Doctrine in Civil Law and in Mixed Jurisdictions*, ed. Joseph Dainow (Baton Rouge: Louisiana State University Press, 1974), 57–67.

85. See, for example, SANM I: 381 (Isleta argued that "custom with force of law" established its ownership of land at Ojo de la Cabra as common grazing land).

86. La aucion de poblador, inventory and appraisal of the estate of Calletano Torres, San Antonio de Sabinal, 25 April 1780, SANM I: 997; US v. Sandoval, 167 US 278, (1897).

87. Although not as assiduous in protecting the natives and underprivileged classes, Mendinueta generally followed the new direction set by Vélez Cach-upín, confirming earlier rulings in important cases. See, for example, the Pueblo of Cochití v. Romero, SANM I: 1352.

Chapter Eleven

1. For a more detailed discussion of contrasting beliefs about land between His-panos, Indians, and Genízaros, see Ebright, Hendricks, and Hughes, *Four Square Leagues*, introduction. This approach of finding balance and reconciliation between the dominant and indigenous narrative is similar to but different in important ways than the approach of Tracy Brown to "challenge the master nar-rative." Tracy L. Brown, *Pueblo Indians and Spanish Colonial Authority in Eighteenth-Century New Mexico* (Tucson: University of Arizona Press, 2013), 167–73.

2. Ebright and Hendricks, *Witches of Abiquiu*, 192–93.

3. Deed from Miguel García de la Rivas to Juan García de la Rivas of the "old Pueblo of La Ciénega," Santa Fe, 12 March 1704, SANM I: 441.

4. Deed from Joaquín and Juana Anaya Almazán to Andrés Montoya of the "tract called Cieneguilla," Santa Fe, 1714, SANM I: 497.

5. Order of Diego de Vargas, Santa Fe, 16 March 1695, Kessell, Hendricks, and Dodge, *Blood on the Boulders*, 1:605.

6. In April of 1695 a group of Spanish settlers in Santa Fe "were moved out of their Santa Fe dwellings . . . to make room for the [colonists brought by Juan] Páez Hurtado" in May. It was this group that had been moved from Santa Fe who forced the San Cristóbal Indians to move so the Spaniards could establish the Villa of Santa Cruz on lands cleared, plowed, and under acequias constructed by San Cristóbal Indians. John B. Colligan, *The Juan Páez Hurtado Expedition of 1695: Fraud in Recruiting Colonists for New Mexico* (Albuquerque: University of New Mexico Press, 1995), 5–6.

7. "Los pastos de sus sitios y términos de cada una de dichas haciendas sean comunes y no por indiviso y los coma el ganado que cada uno tuviere en más o menos cantidad." Spanish version translated in Kessell, Hendricks, and Dodge, *Blood on the Boulders*, 1:606 (additional phrase in brackets is mine).

8. Kessell, Hendricks, and Dodge, *Blood on the Boulders*, 1:619.

9. Lippard and Ranney, *Down Country*, 217–18. Kessell, Hendricks, and Dodge, *Blood on the Boulders*, 1:606–7.

10. Kessell, Hendricks, and Dodge, *Blood on the Boulders*, 1:610–14.

11. For a discussion of the Protector de Indios and Pueblo Indian land, see Ebright, Hendricks, and Hughes, *Four Square Leagues*, chapter 1, and chapter 1 of this book.

12. McNitt, *Navajo Wars*, 23–25.

13. For the Battle of San Diego Pond, see Ebright and Hendricks, *Witches of Abiquiu*, 74–75; for Las Trampas, see Ebright, *Land Grants and Lawsuits*, 145–68; for Truchas, see Mark Schiller, "Nuestra Señora del Rosario, San Fernando y Santiago del Rio de las Truchas Grant" (Guadalupita, NM: Center for Land Grant Studies, 2005).

14. Proceedings against José Montaño, Santa Fe, 1750, SANM I: 29; Kessell, *Miera y Pacheco*, 41; Myra Ellen Jenkins, "Early Days in the Rio Puerco Valley," 3–6, Box 40, Folder 10, Myra Ellen Jenkins Papers, Center of Southwest Studies, Fort Lewis College, Durango, CO.

15. For Atrisco, see Joseph P. Sanchez, *Between Two Rivers: The Atrisco Land Grant in Albuquerque* (Norman: University of Oklahoma Press, 2008), 3–31; and Richard E. Greenleaf, "Atrisco and Las Ciruelas, 1722–1769," *New Mexico Historical Review* 42 (January 1967): 65–25; for Carnuel, see Frances Leon Swadesh, "Archeology, Ethnohistory, and the First Plaza of Carnuel," *Ethnohistory* 23 (Winter 1976): 31–44; Robert Archibald, "Cañon de Carnué: Settlement of A Grant," *New Mexico Historical Review* 51 (October 1976): 313–28.

16. Miller, "New Mexico in Mid-Eighteenth Century," 178.

17. Sale of land by the heirs of Cristóbal Baca to San Felipe Pueblo, Governor Tomás Vélez Cachupín, Santa Fe, 21 March 1753, SANM I: 1348. In 1754 Governor Marín del Valle, who served between Governor Vélez Cachupín's first and second terms, ordered that the Vélez Cachupín price schedule remain in effect and that "settlers were not to sell defensive weapons . . . nor were they to sell stallions, mares, or mules that could be used for breeding [to the Indians]." Tigges and Salazar, *Spanish Colonial Lives*, 524–35; SANM II: 530. Ross Frank, *From Settler to Citizen: New Mexican Economic Development and the Creation of Vecino Society, 1750–1820* (Berkeley: University of California Press, 2000), 34; Thomas, *Plains Indians*, 129–43.

18. Jones, *Pueblo Warriors*, 132; For the petition to Governor Cruzat y Góngora by Los Genízaros, see Ebright and Hendricks, *Witches of Abiquiu*, 28–30. Governor Cruzat y Góngora denied that request, after which several of the petitioners acquired land at Belén, becoming part of that land grant community.

19. For the Abiquiu Genízaro land grant, see Ebright and Hendricks, *Witches of Abiquiu*, 89–94.

20. Ibid., 89–93. The grantees of the 1751 Las Trampas community grant received a private tract of irrigated farmland together with "corresponding water, pastures, and watering places" ("con sus aguas, pastos, y abrevederos"). Ebright, *Land Grants and Lawsuits*, 147–49.

21. The Abiquiu witchcraft proceedings started in 1760, two years before Vélez Cachupín's second term, and ended in 1766, one year before his second term ended. Ebright and Hendricks, *Witches of Abiquiu*, 119–233.

22. Ebright and Hendricks, *Witches of Abiquiu*, 81–82; for an in-depth account of the Portillo Urrisola action, see Rick Hendricks, "The 1761 Comanche Massacre" (paper presented at the Pike's Peak Library District's "Massacre of the Mountain West" symposium, Pike's Peak, CO, 8 June 2013). See also Hämäläinen, *Comanche Empire*, 51–52, who called the massacre "one of the worst military catastrophes in Comanche history" (51). Vélez Cachupín had achieved peace with the Comanche largely on the strength of his stunning victory over a large band of around three thousand Indians who attacked Pecos in breach of a peace treaty they had with the Spaniards. The Ute also made peace directly with Vélez Cachupín after a ruse whereby the Navajo led the Ute to believe that Vélez Cachupín would attack them like he did the Comanche, unless they negotiated a peace treaty. Vélez Cachupín met the Ute leaders at their ranchería about forty miles from Santa Fe and hammered out a peace agreement after two days of negotiating and trading. Ebright and Hendricks, *Witches of Abiquiu*, 74–79.

23. Thomas, *Plains Indians*, 152–53; Hämäläinen, *Comanche Empire*, 53–55.

24. Willard H. Rollings, *The Comanche* (New York: Chelsea House, 1989), 32–34; Hämäläinen, *Comanche Empire*, 260–61.

25. Petition of forty-eight Albuquerque residents regarding the local militia, San Felipe de Albuquerque, May 1762, Pinart Collection, Bancroft Library, University of California–Berkeley, PE 52:6.

26. The designation "comederos antiguos" came about when Alferez Juan José Moreno of the Santa Fe presidio asked Governor Enrique de Olavide y Michelena to set these areas aside as "ancient pasture lands for use by the royal horse herd [because] they have tall grasses, and abundance of water and are secure from the enemies." The other ancient pastures referred to in Governor Olavide y Michelena's order were Santa Cruz, Caja del Río, La Majada, Maragua (adjacent to Galisteo), Los Cerrillos, Las Bocas, Cieneguilla, and Galisteo. Tigges, "Pastures of the Royal Horse Herd," 248–60.

27. Galisteo Grant, SG 60, Roll 19, fr. 367 et seq.; Bowden "Private Land Claims," 2:287–88.

28. The estimate of the size of the presidial horse herd is based on the number of animals taken on campaigns (five hundred to six hundred) and the number left

at the presidio (three hundred to six hundred). Tigges, "Pastures of the Royal Horse Herd," 244; Bowden, "Private Land Claims," 2:286; Santiago Durán y Chávez grant, in Reeve, "Navaho-Spanish Peace," 34–35.

29. Bayer, *Santa Ana*, 80–81; Ebright, Hendricks, and Hughes, *Four Square Leagues*, chapter 2.

30. Dory-Garduño, "1766 Ojo del Espíritu Santo Grant," 184–86; petition of Pueblos of Zia, Santa Ana, and Jemez for the Ojo del Espíritu Santo Grant, SG TT, Roll 7, fr. 363–64 (translation).

31. Tyler, "Ejido Lands," 24, 28–30.

32. Dispute between El Paso residents and the Suma Indians of San Lorenzo del Real over wood gathering on Suma land, 16 August–30 October 1765, SANM I: 691.

33. Iturbieta v. Gallegos, SANM I: 362. This case is discussed in chapter 10.

34. San Gabriel de las Nutrias grant, SANM I: 780; Sabinal grant, SANM I: 877; and Los Quelites grant, SANM I: 720. Vélez Cachupín revoked the grant of Los Quelites in July of 1765 because some grantees were too disorganized or timid to settle in a place where they would be subject to Indian attack on a regular basis.

35. This period in the mid-1700s also marked a sharp increase in the number of Navajos in the area "due in part to pressure from the north by the Utes." Reeve, "Navaho-Spanish Peace," 17–29; Salazar, "Felipe Tafoya Grant"; J. Richard Salazar, "The Bartolomé Fernández Grant: Another Grazing Grant in Navajo Country," (Guadalupita, NM: Center for Land Grant Studies, 2005).

36. Land grants to Spaniards bordering on Navajo country were possible because of the remarkable Navajo peace, which was just about to come to an end in 1770. But in 1766 some Navajos saw it as an advantage to have Spaniards near them. Reeve, "Navaho-Spanish Peace," 36. For the use of the term *Apache de Navajo* to designate a Navajo, see Curtis F. Schaafsma, *Apaches de Navajo: Seventeenth-Century Navajos in the Chama Valley of New Mexico* (Salt Lake City: University of Utah Press, 2002); Salazar, "Felipe Tafoya Grant," 4.

37. Miguel and Santiago Montoya Grant, SG 100, Roll 22, fr. 1486 et seq.; PLC 66, Roll 41, fr. 73 et seq.; Reeve, "Navaho-Spanish Peace," 34–35.

38. Cebolleta Mountain, the highest peak of the San Mateo Mountains, which marks the south border of the Navajo universe, was renamed Mount Taylor after Zachary Taylor, the twelfth president of the United States. Pearce, *New Mexico Place Names*, 105. Felipe Tafoya Grant, SG 99, Roll 22, fr. 1362–1485; Reeve, "Navaho-Spanish Peace," 33, 38–40; Salazar, "Felipe Tafoya Grant," 4–5; Frances E. Watkins, *The Navajo* (Los Angeles, CA: Southwest Museum, n.d.), 4.

39. Kessell, Hendricks, and Dodge, *Blood on the Boulders*, 1:606. The *Recopilación*

provided that Indians should have sufficient water and woodlands and an ejido one league in length. *Recopilación* 6.3.8.

40. For the right of New Mexico pueblos to four square leagues of land, see Ebright, Hendricks, and Hughes, *Four Square Leagues*, 11–47. Vélez Cachupín met with Mendinueta in the spring of 1767 after turning over the reins of government on 1 March 1767 and passed on his recommendations for keeping the peace, most of which Mendinueta did not follow. Ebright and Hendricks, *Witches of Abiquiu*, 86.

Chapter Twelve

1. R. C. Gordon-McCutchan, *The Taos Indians and the Battle for Blue Lake* (Santa Fe, NM: Red Crane Books, 1991), 213–21; Ebright, Hendricks, and Hughes, *Four Square Leagues*, chapter 11.

2. Hart, *Zuni and the Courts*, 81–84.

3. T. J. Ferguson and E. Richard Hart, *A Zuni Atlas* (Norman: University of Oklahoma Press, 1985), 92–93; Hart, *Zuni and the Courts*, 81–84.

4. Hart, *Zuni and the Courts*, 83–84, 199; Ferguson and Hart, *Zuni Atlas*, 22–23; Frank Hamilton Cushing, *Outlines of Zuñi Creation Myths*, Thirteenth Annual Report of the Bureau of Ethnology, 1891–1892 (Washington, D.C.: Government Printing Office, 1896), 321–447, 410–12.

5. Edmund J. Ladd, "Achieving True Interpretation," in Hart, *Zuni and the Courts*, 234.

6. Among the uses to which the $17 million was put was to make a down payment on the Ellsworth Ranch in Arizona, land that the pueblo considers sacred. "Zuni Tribe's Lawsuit Nets $17 Million," *Santa Fe New Mexican*, 19 July 1991; Ferguson and Hart, *Zuni Atlas*, 88–99; Hart, *Zuni and the Courts*, 86–87.

7. "The Zuni trail is sacred, with every geologic and natural feature having special meaning." Andrew Gulliford, *Sacred Objects, Sacred Places: Preserving Tribal Traditions* (Boulder: University Press of Colorado, 2000), 76–77; Hart, *Zuni and the Courts*, 200–202; Jesse Green, ed., *Cushing at Zuni: The Correspondence and Journals of Frank Hamilton Cushing, 1879–1884* (Albuquerque: University of New Mexico Press, 1990); 375, n. 3 discusses the pilgrimage.

8. Hart, *Zuni and the Courts*, 202–3.

9. On 5 September 1990 a celebration of this court victory was held at Zuni, honoring those who had helped with this difficult litigation. Roger Anyon, "Zuni Protection of Cultural Resources and Religious Freedom," *Cultural Survival* 19 (Winter 1995), http://www.culturalsurvival.org/ourpublications/csq/article/zuni-protection-cultural-resources-and-religious-freedom; Hart, *Zuni and the Courts*, 203–6.

10. William L. Merrill, Edmund J. Ladd, and T. J. Ferguson, "The Return of the Ahayu:da: Lessons for Repatriation from Zuni Pueblo and the Smithsonian Institution," *Current Anthropology* 34 (December 1993): 528–30.

11. Zuni governor Robert E. Lewis said, "Although Mr. Cushing was usually a pretty good scholar . . . at times he elaborated on the truth or got things wrong." Anne Sutton Canfield, "Ahayu:da . . . Art or Icon?" *Native Arts/West* 1 (July 1980): 23–26. For Cushing's doubts, see Nancy J. Parezo, "Cushing as Part of the Team: The Collecting Activities of the Smithsonian Institution," *American Ethnologist* 12 (November 1985): 764–74, 762; Hart, *Zuni and the Courts*, 200. Cushing was saved from more severe punishment "by the reverence he evinced for the sacred objects." Green, *Cushing at Zuni*, 343, see also 140.

12. Matilda Coxe Stevenson, "Zuni Ancestral Gods and Masks," *American Anthropologist* 11 (February 1898): 33–40; Green, *Cushing at Zuni*, 133–35; Bowen Blair, "Indian Rights: Native Americans Versus American Museums—A Battle for Artifacts," *American Indian Law Review* 7, no. 1 (1979): 125–54.

13. Edmund J. Ladd, "An Explanation: Request for the Return of Zuni Sacred Objects Held in Museums and Private Collections," in David Grant Noble, "Zuni and El Morro," *Explorations: Annual Bulletin of the School of American Research* 1983: 32; Charles Hustitio, "Why Zuni War Gods Need to be Returned," in *Zuni History: Victories in the 1990s*, ed. E. Richard Hart and T. J. Ferguson (Seattle, WA: Institute of the North American West), sec. 2:12; Merrill, Ladd, and Ferguson, "Return of the Ahayu:da," 525, 528–30.

14. Walter A. Echo-Hawk, "Museum Rights vs. Indian Rights: Guidelines for Assessing Competing Legal Interests in Native Cultural Resources," *NYU Review of Law and Social Change* 14, no. 2 (1986): 437–53. The Ahahyu:da in the Denver Art Museum may have been removed from Zuni in the 1800s by surveyors who inadvertently left some papers with their names and addresses on them at the site in a tin can. Barton Martza, "On the Trail of the Zuni War Gods," in *Zuni History: Victories in the 1990s*, ed. E. Richard Hart and T. J. Ferguson (Seattle, WA: Institute of the North American West, 1991), sec. 2:12; Merrill, Ladd, and Ferguson, "Return of the Ahayu:da," 530, 542.

15. Merrill, Ladd, and Ferguson, "Return of the Ahayu:da," 527–28, 530–31. Stevenson's 607-page book titled *The Zuni Indians* is today often dismissed as outdated. Marc Simmons, "Ethnologist, Pioneer Documented Zuni Culture for Posterity," *Santa Fe New Mexican*, 26 May 2001.

16. According to T. J. Ferguson, "We are not talking about lawsuits, or demands or threats. Zuni is trying to build a case that is justified for moral and religious reasons to museums and traders." Canfield, "Ahayu:da," 24; Merrill, Ladd, and Ferguson, "Return of the Ahayu:da," 533.

17. Merrill, Ladd, and Ferguson, "Return of the Ahayu:da," 536. For a discussion of the Native American Graves Protection and Repatriation Act of 1990 (NAGPRA), see Kathleen Fine-Dare, *Grave Injustice: The American Indian Repatriation Movement and NAGPRA* (Lincoln: University of Nebraska Press, 2002), passim; and Andrew Gulliford, *Sacred Objects*, 13–14.

18. K. C. Compton, "Three Sacred Zuni Carvings to be Returned: Pueblo Leaders to Pick Up 'Mischievous' War Gods," *Santa Fe New Mexican*, 11 November 1987; Keith Easthouse, "The Zuni War Gods Are Going Home," *Santa Fe Reporter*, 11 November 1987; Merrill, Ladd, and Ferguson, "Return of the Ahayu:da," 536.

19. Ben Neary, "Sacred Land under Siege," *Santa Fe New Mexican*, 7 January 2001; Rebecca Schubert, "Reflections on the Sacred Salt Lake," *La Crónica de Nuevo México* 57 (August 2002).

20. Gulliford, *Sacred Objects, Sacred Places*, 76–77; Hart, *Zuni and the Courts*, 97, 201.

21. "Mining near Lake Concerns Zuni Tribe," *Santa Fe New Mexican*, 21 February 1996; Ben Neary, "Government Ready to OK Mine near Zuni Pueblo," *Santa Fe New Mexican*, 25 April 2002; Office of Surface Mining news release, 31 May 2002; Ferguson and Hart, *Zuni Atlas*, 89.

22. Hillary Rosner, "Saving a Sacred Lake: Zuni Activist Pablo Padilla," *High Country News*, 2 February 2004.

23. Ibid.; "Zuni Salt Lake and Sanctuary Zone Protected," Zuni Salt Lake Coalition press release, 7 August 2003.

24. Another pueblo (besides Taos Pueblo) that has achieved the return of sacred lands using this approach is Sandia Pueblo, with the return of the use of the slope of the Sandia Mountain in 2001. Ebright, Hendricks, and Hughes, *Four Square Leagues*, chapter 4; Compton, "Sacred Zuni Carvings"; Easthouse, "Zuni War Gods"; Merrill, Ladd, and Ferguson, "Return of the Ahayu:da," 536.

Epilogue

1. Ebright, *Land Grants and Lawsuits*; and Ebright, Hendricks, and Hughes, *Four Square Leagues*.

2. Barrett, *Conquest and Catastrophe*, 54.

3. Toll and Badner, *Galisteo Basin Archeological Sites*, n. 686; for a discussion of the Tewa/Tano Pueblo at Hopi, see Dozier, *Hano*, passim.

4. Rather than actively protect Pueblo lands, Mexican period governors sought to distance themselves from Pueblo Indian boundary disputes. Question regarding measurement of the Jemez League, Santiago Abreu decree, Santa Fe, 21 April 1833, SANM I: 1245.

5. Emory, *Notes of a Military Reconnaissance*, 64–65; Ross Calvin, *Lt. Emory Reports: A Reprint of Lieutenant W. H. Emory's Notes of a Military Reconnaissance* (Albuquerque: University of New Mexico Press, 1951), 64–65; Annie Heloise Abel, ed., *The Official Correspondence of James S. Calhoun* (Washington, D.C.: Government Printing Office, 1915), 139–42.

6. Peter Whitely, "Reconnoitering 'Pueblo' Ethnicity: The 1852 Tesuque Delegation to Washington," *Journal of the Southwest* 45 (Autumn 2003): 450; Abel, *Calhoun Correspondence*, 186–87.

7. The second Pueblo delegation to Washington was led by two Isleta leaders, Juan Andrés Abeita and Juan Reyes Lucero, in April 1868. The third Pueblo delegation in 1869, again from Isleta, received promises from President Ulysses S. Grant. The fourth delegation in 1875 was from San Juan, but the petition was signed by ten pueblos, including San Juan. Whitely, "Reconnoitering 'Pueblo' Ethnicity," 473–76.

8. Joe S. Sando, "The Silver-Crowned Canes of Pueblo Office," in *Telling New Mexico: A New History*, ed. Marta Weigle et al. (Santa Fe: Museum of New Mexico Press, 2009), 125–26. While President Lincoln readily accepted the symbolism of the Lincoln canes, he did not believe pueblos were equals in their negotiations with the United States. Rather, he "accepted the stereotype of the Indian as a heathen savage, in need of civilization and religious instruction." David Nichols, *Lincoln and the Indians: Civil War Policy and Politics* (St. Paul: Minnesota Historical Society Press, 1978), 186.

9. Whitely, "Reconnoitering 'Pueblo' Ethnicity," 474–75; U.S. v. Sandoval, 13 U.S. 28 (1913) characterized the Pueblo Indians of New Mexico as "essentially a simple, uninformed, and inferior people."

10. Denise Holladay Damico, "Benjamin Thomas," http://www.newmexicohistory. org/filedetails_docs.php?fileID=21291.

11. The Indian agents in New Mexico were part of the Federal Indian Service, which on a broader level attempted to "Americanize" the Indians by eradicating their culture to "make them into farmers [and] introduce them to Christianity." Lawrence Murphy, *Frontier Crusader: William F. M. Arny* (Tucson: University of Arizona Press, 1972), 113–14.

12. Williams pointed out that all the overlapping grants were made subsequent to the 1766 Ojo del Espíritu Santo grant. However, the 1766 Ojo del Espíritu Santo grant made to Zia, Santa Ana, and Jemez Pueblos was rejected, and the 1815 Ojo del Espíritu Santo grant of the same land was confirmed. Indian Agent Williams to Commissioner of Indian Affairs, Santa Fe, 18 June 1888, Miscellaneous Letters sent by the Pueblo Indian Agency, 1874–1891, National Archives and Records Service, Microfilm Publication M941, Washington, D.C., 1973.

13. Marc Simmons, "The Zunis Seek Justice," Trail Dust, *Santa Fe Reporter*, 3 August 1993.

14. Benavides, "Lawyer-Induced Partitioning," 4–14. For a discussion of the partition suit as applied to the Las Trampas grant, see Ebright, *Land Grants and Lawsuits*, 151–55.

15. Ebright, *Tierra Amarilla Grant*, 25.

16. Catron obtained his interest in the grant by purchasing the interest of Surveyor General Henry M. Atkinson, who had decreed that the grant was owned by Manuel Rivera after he had purchased the interests of all the heirs of Manuel Rivera. Michael J. Rock, "Anton Chico and Its Patent," *Journal of the West* 19 (July 1980): 86–91.

17. Benavides, "Lawyer-Induced Partitioning," 20–22. In one of the few cases seeking the disbarment of lawyers in the late nineteenth and early twentieth centuries, Alois B. Renehan was charged with breaching his duties of trust and full disclosure when he charged clients to collect funds to which they were already entitled and for which a fund had been established. In re Renehan, 19 N.M. 640. The other disbarment case was In re Catron 8 NM 253. In both cases the supreme court of New Mexico ruled in favor of the two lawyers and against disbarment.

18. David Correia, *Properties of Violence: Law and Land Grant Struggle in Northern New Mexico* (Athens: University of Georgia Press, 2013), 69–73; Ebright, *Land Grants and Lawsuits*, 214–16.

19. Ebright, *Tierra Amarilla Grant*," 262–64; Rock, "Anton Chico and Its Patent," 86–91.

20. Hart, *Zuni and the Courts*, 231; Merrill, Ladd, and Ferguson, "Return of the Ahayu:da," 533–37.

21. Lobato v. Taylor, 71 P. 3d 938 (Colorado, 2002), centiorari denied by the U.S. Supreme Court, Lobato v. Taylor, 540 US 1073 (2003). Lawyer Ryan Golten's article on this case discusses the long history of *Lobato v. Taylor*, both in the courts and on the ground, and analyzes its potential effect on future land grant litigation. Ryan Golten, "Lobato v. Taylor: How the Villages of the Rio Culebra, the Colorado Supreme Court, and the Restatement of Servitudes Bailed Out the Treaty of Guadalupe Hidalgo," *Natural Resources Journal* 45 (Spring 2005): 457–94.

GLOSSARY

abogado: Lawyer; in Spain, the lawyer who researched the law, wrote the briefs, and presented the legal arguments to the judge.

abrevaderos: Watering place and access thereto.

acequia: An irrigation ditch; from the Arabic *as saquiya*.

alcalde: Local governmental official with judicial, executive, and police powers.

alcaldía: The administrative area governed by an alcalde or ayuntamiento.

alférez: Ensign or standard-bearer, attached to the presidio.

asesor: Legal adviser.

audiencia: A judicial body, sometimes with legislative powers; the highest court of appeal in Mexico.

auto declarato: Explanatory decree.

ayuntamiento: Town council.

bando: Proclamation, decree.

cabildo: Municipal council; also the meeting place of such a council.

cacique: Indian religious leader.

casa consistorial: City hall; house where community meetings are held.

cédula: Order or decree, usually from the king.

comandante general: The official who administered the military political district known as the *comandancia general*.

conciliación: An arbitration proceeding.

convento: A priest's residence.

cordel: A rope for measuring land, usually fifty or one hundred varas long, usually made of yucca fiber, horse hair, or partly of leather.

Cortés: Congress of deputies in Spain.

coyote: A person of mixed Spanish and Indian blood, similar to a mestizo.

diputación: Territorial legislature.

ejido: Common land owned by a community.

encomendero: The holder of an encomienda.

encomienda: A grant of tribute—usually a cotton blanket and a bushel of corn—from each household in an Indian pueblo.

escribano: Notary, judicial assistant; an official with legal training.

estancia: Ranch, usually of medium size.

expediente: A file of papers, as of a court case or the proceedings in a land grant.

fanega: A measurement from 1.5 to 2.5 bushels, usually in the form of a basket; also used as a land measurement, i.e., a *fanega de maís* (the amount of land needed to plant a fanega of corn seed, about 8.8 acres) or a *fanega de trigo* (a fanega of wheat planting land, about 1.5 acres).

Genízaro: A term unique to New Mexico; Genízaros were Plains Indians or Navajos who were sold to Spaniards to become servants, taught Christian doctrine, and given their freedom when they reached a certain age or when they had paid off the price paid for them through their wages.

hijuela: A deed, often effecting the division of a larger tract.

jefe político: The governor.

juez comisionado: A judge specially assigned to a case.

juez de paz: Justice of the peace; successor to the alcalde during the Mexican period.

juez de primera instancia: Judge of the first instance, lower court judge.

Jusgado: General de Indios.

letrado: A lawyer; literally, "a man of letters."

licenciado: Lawyer.

merced: A grant of land or water to an individual of a community.

mestizo/a: A mixed-blood person, usually part Spanish, part Indian.

monte: Mountainous common lands used primarily for wood gathering.

oidor: Judge.

partido: A political subdivision; a sheep contract.

prefect: Governmental official during the Mexican period, subordinate to the governor, who administered a prefectura.

propios: Municipally owned property.

puesto: An outpost.

regidor: Member of an ayuntamiento.

rubric: Flourish at the end of a signature by which its authenticity is verified.

sala constitucional: The ayuntamiento's meeting place.

solar de casa: Small tract of land for a dwelling; house site.

suerte: Plot of farmland.

teniente: Assistant.

teniente alcalde: Assistant alcalde.

testimonio: A copy of land grant or other proceedings given to the parties.

tierras baldias: Public land.

tierras concegiles: Common lands of communities.

tierras de pan llevar: Irrigated land.

tierras loboriegas: Irrigated farmland.

tierras realengas: Public land of the sovereign.

vara: A unit of measurement, approximately thirty-three inches.

vecino: A landowning resident of a community entitled to vote.

villa: The largest of the Hispanic municipalities in New Mexico.

visita: A church that lacks a resident priest but is visited by a priest who conducts services occasionally.

BIBLIOGRAPHY

Abel, Annie Heloise, ed. *The Official Correspondence of James S. Calhoun*. Washington, D.C.: Government Printing Office, 1915.

Adams, Eleanor B., ed. *Bishop Tamarón's Visitation of New Mexico, 1760*. Publications in History 15. Albuquerque: Historical Society of New Mexico, 1954.

———. "Fray Silvestre and the Obstinate Hopi." *New Mexico Historical Review* 38 (April 1963): 111.

———. *Juan Domínguez del Mendoza: Soldier and Frontiersman of the Spanish Southwest*. Edited by France V. Scholes, Marc Simmons, and José Antonio Esquibel. Albuquerque: University of New Mexico Press, 2012.

———, and Fray Angelico Chávez, translators and annotators. *The Missions of New Mexico, 1776: A Description by Fray Francisco Atanasio Domínguez, with Other Contemporary Documents*. Albuquerque: University of New Mexico Press, 1956.

———, and France V. Scholes. "Books in New Mexico, 1598–1680." *New Mexico Historical Review* 7 (July 1942): 232.

Adorno, Rolena, and Patrick Charles Pautz. *Alvar Nuñez Cabeza de Vaca: His Account, His Life, and the Expedition of Pánfilo de Narvaéz*. Lincoln: University of Nebraska Press, 1999.

Anyon, Roger. "Zuni Protection of Cultural Resources and Religious Freedom." *Cultural Survival* 19 (Winter 1995), http://www.culturalsurvival.org/ourpublications /csq/article/zuni-protection-cultural-resources-and-religious-freedom.

Archibald, Robert. "Cañon de Carnué: Settlement of A Grant." *New Mexico Historical Review* 51 (October 1976): 313–28.

Arellano, Anselmo F. "Case Study: Sierra Acequias and Agriculture of the Mora Valley." Unpublished manuscript in possession of the author.

August, Jack. "Balance of Power Diplomacy in New Mexico: Governor Fernando de la Concha and the Indian Policy of Conciliation." *New Mexico Historical Review* 56 (April 1981): 141–60.

Ayer, Mrs. Edward E. *The Memorial of Fray Alonso de Benavides, 1630*. Translated by Frederick W. Hodge and Charles F. Lummis. Albuquerque, NM: Horn and Wallace, 1965.

Baker, Stephen G. *Juan Rivera's Colorado—1765: Spaniards among the Ute and Paiute Indians on the Trails to Teguayo; The Comprehensive Illustrated History with the Original Rivera Spanish Journals and English Translations.* Translated by Rick Hendricks. Illustrated by Gail Carroll Sargent. Lake City, CO: Western Reflections, 2014.

Bandelier, Adolph. *Final Report of Investigations among the Indians of the Southwestern United States Carried on Mainly in the Years from 1880 to 1885.* Cambridge, MA: John Wilson and Son, University Press, 1890; Charleston, SC: BiblioLife, 2011.

———. "The Southwestern Land Court." *Nation* 52 (18 May 1891): 437.

———. Untitled article about Poseyemu. *El Palacio* (2): 80.

Bandelier, Fanny, trans. *The Journey of Alvár Nuñez Cabeza de Vaca and His Companions from Florida to the Pacific.* Edited by Adolph Bandelier. New York: A. S. Barnes, 1905.

Barrett, Elinore. *Conquest and Catastrophe: Changing Rio Grande Pueblo Settlement Patterns in the Sixteenth and Seventeenth Centuries.* Albuquerque: University of New Mexico Press, 2002.

———. *The Spanish Colonial Settlement Landscapes of New Mexico, 1598–1680.* Albuquerque: University of New Mexico Press, 2012.

Baudouin, Jean-Louis. "The Impact of the Common Law on the Civilian Systems of Louisiana and Quebec." In *The Role of Judicial Decisions and Doctrine in Civil Law and in Mixed Jurisdictions,* edited by Joseph Dainow, 1–22. Baton Rouge: Louisiana State University Press, 1974.

Baxter, John O. *Dividing New Mexico's Waters, 1700–1912.* Albuquerque: University of New Mexico Press, 1997.

———. *Spanish Irrigation in the Pojoaque and Tesuque Valleys during the Eighteenth and Early Nineteenth Centuries.* Santa Fe: New Mexico State Engineer Office, 1984.

Bayer, Laura, with Floyd Montoya and the Pueblo of Santa Ana. *Santa Ana: The People, the Pueblo, and the History of the Tamaya.* Albuquerque: University of New Mexico Press, 1994.

Becker, Beverly. "Santa Fe, Est. 1610/1607." *El Palacio* 100 (Winter 1994–1995): 14–16.

Benavides, Alonso de. *Fray Alonso de Benavides' Revised Memorial of 1634.* Albuquerque: University of New Mexico Press, 1945.

Benavides, David. "Lawyer-Induced Partitioning of New Mexican Land Grants: An Ethical Travesty." Guadalupita, NM: Center for Land Grant Studies Research Paper, 2005. www.southwestbooks.org.

Blair, Bowen. "Indian Rights: Native Americans versus American Museums—A Battle for Artifacts." *American Indian Law Review* 7, no. 1 (1979): 125–54.

Bloom, Lansing Bartlett. "Albuquerque and Galisteo: Certificate of Their Founding, 1706." *New Mexico Historical Review* 10 (January 1935): 48–50.

———. "A Campaign against the Moqui Pueblos." *New Mexico Historical Review* 6 (April 1931): 158–226.

———. "When Was Santa Fe Founded?" *New Mexico Historical Review* 4 (1929): 188–94.

———, and Ireno L. Chaves, trans. "Ynstruccions a Peralta por Vi-Roy," with translation. *New Mexico Historical Review* 4 (April 1929): 178–87.

Bolton, Herbert E. *Pageant in the Wilderness*. Salt Lake City, UT: Spanish Historical Society, 1950.

Borah, Woodrow. *Justice by Insurance: The General Indian Court of Colonial Mexico and the Legal Aides of the Half-Real*. Berkeley, Los Angeles, London: University of California Press, 1983.

Bowden, J. J. *The Ponce de Leon Land Grant*. El Paso: Texas Western Press, 1969.

———. "Private Land Claims in the Southwest." 6 vols. MA thesis, Southern Methodist University, 1969.

———. *Spanish and Mexican Land Grants in the Chihuahuan Acquisition*. El Paso: Texas Western Press, 1971.

———. "Spanish and Mexican Land Grants in the Southwest." *Land and Water Law Review* 8 (1973): 467.

Boyd, E. "Troubles at Ojo Caliente, A Frontier Post." *El Palacio* (November/December 1957): 347–60.

Bradfute, Richard Wells. *The Court of Private Land Claims: The Adjudication of Spanish and Mexican Land Grant Titles, 1891–1904*. Albuquerque: University of New Mexico Press, 1975.

Brayer, Herbert O. "The Place of Land in Southwestern History." *Land Policy Review* 4 (December 1941): 15–20.

———. *Pueblo Indian Land Grants of the "Rio Abajo," New Mexico*. Albuquerque: University of New Mexico Press, 1939.

Brechtel, Beth. "Activist Fears Losing Heritage: Graffiti Vandals, Souvenir Hunters and Target Shooters Threaten Rock Drawings at La Ciénega Mesa." *Albuquerque Journal North*, 22 July 1994.

Briggs, Charles L. and John R. Van Ness, eds. *Land, Water, and Culture: New Perspectives on Hispanic Land Grants*. Albuquerque: University of New Mexico Press, 1987.

Brooks, James F. *Captives & Cousins: Slavery, Kinship, and Community in the Southwest Borderlands*. Chapel Hill: University of North Carolina Press, 2002.

Brown, Curtis M. *Boundary Control and Legal Principle*. New York: John Wiley and Sons, 1957.

Brown, Tracy L. *Pueblo Indians and Spanish Colonial Authority in Eighteenth-Century New Mexico.* Tucson: University of Arizona Press, 2013.

Brown, Walden. "When Worlds Collide: Crisis in Sahagún's *Historia Universal de las Cosas de la Nueva España.*" *Colonial Latin American Historical Review* 5, no. 2 (Spring 1996): 101–49.

Bugé, David. "Preliminary Report: 1979 Excavations at Paonsipa-akeri, Ojo Caliente, New Mexico." File no. P4369, Laboratory of Anthropology Library, Santa Fe, NM.

Burkholder, Mark A., and D. S. Chandler. *From Impotence to Authority: The Spanish Crown and the American Audiencias, 1687–1808.* Columbia: University of Missouri Press, 1977.

Bustamante, Adrian. "'The Matter Was Never Resolved': The *Casta* System in Colonial New Mexico, 1693–1823." *New Mexico Historical Review* 66 (April 1991): 143–63.

Butte, Woodfin L. "Stare Decisis, Doctrine, and Jurisprudence in Mexico and Elsewhere." In *Role of Judicial Decisions and Doctrine in Civil Law and in Mixed Jurisdictions,* edited by Joseph Dainow, 311–30. Baton Rouge: Louisiana State University Press, 1974.

Caffey, David. *Chasing the Santa Fe Ring: Power and Privilege in Territorial New Mexico.* Albuquerque: University of New Mexico Press, 2014.

Calloway, Colin G. *The Shawnees and the War for America.* New York: Viking, 2007.

Calvin, Ross. *Lt. Emory Reports: A Reprint of Lieutenant W. H. Emory's Notes of a Military Reconnaissance.* Albuquerque: University of New Mexico Press, 1951.

Canfield, Anne Sutton. "Ahayu:da . . . Art or Icon?" *Native Arts/West* 1 (July 1980): 23–26.

Carroll, H. Bailey, and J. Villasana Haggard, eds. and trans. *Three New Mexico Chronicles.* Albuquerque: Quivera Society, 1942.

Carter, Constance Ann. "Law and Society in Colonial Mexico: *Audiencia* Judges in Mexican Society from the *Tello de Sandoval Visita General,* 1543–1547." PhD diss., Columbia University, 1971.

Cervantes Saavedra, Miguel de. *The Adventures of Don Quixote.* London: Penguin Books, 1950.

———, and Luis Andrés Murillo, eds. *El ingenioso hildalgo don Quijote de la Mancha.* Madrid: Clásicos Castalis, 1978.

Chávez, Fray Angélico. *Archives of the Archdiocese of Santa Fe.* Washington, D.C.: Academy of American Franciscan History, 1957.

———. "*Genízaros.*" In *The Handbook of North American Indians,* edited by William C. Sturtevant. Vol. 9, *Southwest,* edited by Alfonso Ortiz, 198–200. Washington, D.C.: Smithsonian Institution, 1979.

———. *New Mexico Families.* Santa Fe, NM: William Gannon, 1975.

———. *New Mexico Roots, Ltd.* Albuquerque: University of New Mexico, General Library, 1982.

———. *Origins of New Mexico Families in the Spanish Colonial Period.* Rev. ed. Santa Fe: Museum of New Mexico Press, 1992.

———. "Santa Fe's Fake Centennial of 1883." *El Palacio* 62 (1955): 315.

———. "Valle de Cochiti." *New Mexico Magazine* 1951 (January/February 1973): 7–17.

———, and Ted J. Warner, eds. *The Domínguez-Escalante Journal.* Provo, UT: Brigham Young University Press, 1976.

Chávez, Thomas E. *Conflict and Acculturation: Manuel Alvarez's 1842 Memorial.* Santa Fe: Museum of New Mexico Press, 1989.

———. *Manuel Alvarez, 1794–1856: A Southwestern Biography.* Niwot: University Press of Colorado, 1990.

Chipman, Donald E. *Spanish Texas, 1519–1821.* Austin: University of Texas Press, 1992.

Christmas, Henrietta Martínez, and Nancy Anderson. *The San Miguel del Bado del Rio de Pecos: The 1803 Land Grantees.* Albuquerque: New Mexico Genealogical Society, 2013.

Cobos, Rubén. *A Dictionary of New Mexico and Southern Colorado Spanish.* Santa Fe: Museum of New Mexico Press, 1983.

Colligan, John B. *The Juan Páez Hurtado Expedition of 1695: Fraud in Recruiting Colonists for New Mexico.* Albuquerque: University of New Mexico Press, 1995.

Collis, Maurice. *Cortés and Montezuma.* London: Robin Clark, 1954.

Compton, K. C. "Three Sacred Zuni Carvings to Be Returned: Pueblo Leaders to Pick up 'Mischievous' War Gods." *Santa Fe New Mexican,* 11 November 1987.

Concha, Fernando de la. "Advice on Governing New Mexico, 1794." *New Mexico Historical Review* 24 (1949): 236–54.

Córdova, Gilberto Benito. *Abiquiu and Don Cacahuate: A Folk History of a New Mexico Village.* Cerrillos, NM: San Marcos Press, 1973.

Córdova, Kathryn M. *¡Concha!: Concha Ortiz y Pino, Matriarch of a 300 Year Old Legacy.* Santa Fe, NM: Gran Via, 2004.

Correia, David. *Properties of Violence: Law and Land Grant Struggle in Northern New Mexico.* Athens: University of Georgia Press, 2013.

Craddock, Jerry R. "The Legislative Works of Alfonso el Sabio." In *Emperor of Culture: Alfonso X the Learned of Castile and His Thirteenth-Century Renaissance,* edited by Robert I. Burns, 182–97. Philadelphia: University of Pennsylvania Press, 1990.

Crane, Leo. *Desert Drums: The Pueblo Indians of New Mexico, 1540–1928.* Boston, MA: Little, Brown, 1928.

Craver, Rebecca McDowell. *The Impact of Intimacy: Mexican-Anglo Intermarriage in New Mexico, 1821–1846.* El Paso: Texas Western Press, University of Texas at El Paso, 1982.

Crawford, Stanley. "Dancing for Water." *Journal of the Southwest* 32 (Autumn 1990): 265.

———. *Mayordomo: Chronicle of an Acequia in Northern New Mexico.* Albuquerque: University of New Mexico Press, 1988.

Curtin, L. S. M. *Healing Herbs of the Upper Rio Grande.* Los Angeles, CA: Southwest Museum, 1965.

Cushing, Frank Hamilton. *Outlines of Zuñi Creation Myths.* Thirteenth Annual Report of the Bureau of Ethnology to the Secretary of the Smithsonian Institution. Washington, D.C.: Government Printing Office, 1896.

Cutter, Charles R. "Community and the Law in Northern New Spain." *Americas* 50, no. 4 (April 1994): 467–80.

———. "Judicial Punishment in Colonial New Mexico." *Western Legal History* 8 (Winter/Spring 1995): 114–29.

———. *The Legal Culture of Northern New Spain, 1700–1810.* Albuquerque: University of New Mexico Press, 1995.

———. *The Protector de Indios in Colonial New Mexico, 1659–1821.* Albuquerque: University of New Mexico Press, 1986.

Cutter, Donald C. "The Legacy of the Treaty of Guadalupe Hidalgo." *New Mexico Historical Review* 53 (October 1978): 305–15.

Damico, Denise Holladay. "Arroyo Hondo Grant." http://www.newmexicohistory.org /images/uploads/pdfs/Essays_By_Denise_Holladay_Damico_reduced.pdf.

———. "Benjamin Thomas." http://www.newmexicohistory.org/filedetails_docs. php?fileID=21291.

———. "Guadalupe Miranda." http://www.newmexicohistory.org/people/ guadalupe-miranda.

Deák, Francis. "The Place of the 'Case' in the Common and Civil Law." *Tulane Law Review* 8: 337–57.

Demos, John. *The Unredeemed Captive: A Family Story from Early America.* New York: Alfred A. Knopf, 1994.

Dory-Garduño, James. "The Adjudication of the Ojo del Espíritu Santo Grant of 1766 and the Recopilacíon." *New Mexico Historical Review* 87 (Spring 2012): 167–208.

———. "The 1766 Ojo del Espíritu Santo Grant: Authenticating a New Mexico Land Grant." *Colonial Latin American Historical Review* 16, no. 2 (Spring 2007): 157–96.

Dozier, Edward. *Hano: A Tewa Community in Arizona.* New York: Holt, Rinehart, and Winston, 1970.

Duke, Biddle. "The Flow of Change: Worlds Collide in La Ciénega." *Santa Fe New Mexican,* 28 June 1992.

Dunham, Harold H. "Spanish and Mexican Land Policies in the Taos Pueblo Region." In *Pueblo Indians,* 1:151–311. 5 vols. New York: Garland, 1974.

Easthouse, Keith. "The Zuni War Gods Are Going Home." *Santa Fe Reporter*, 11 November 1987.

Ebright, Malcolm. "Advocates for the Oppressed: Indians, *Genízaros*, and Their Spanish Advocates in New Mexico, 1700–1786." *New Mexico Historical Review* 71 (October 1996): 305–39.

———. "Breaking New Ground: A Reappraisal of Governors Vélez Cachupín and Mendinueta and Their Land Grant Policies." *Colonial Latin American Historical Review* 5 (1996): 195–233.

———. "Frontier Land Litigation in Colonial New Mexico: A Determinant of Spanish Custom and Law." *Western Legal History* 8 (Summer/Fall 1995): 198–226.

———. "The Galisteo Grant." http://newmexicohistory.org/places/galisteo-land -grant.

———. "Genízaros." http://www.newmexicohistory.org/people/genizaros.

———. "Gervacio Nolan Land Grant." http://www.newmexicohistory.org/people /gervacio-nolan-land-grant.

———. "Hispanic Land Grants and Indian Land in New Mexico." In *Telling New Mexico: A New History*, edited by Marta Weigle with Francis Levine and Louise Stiver, 209–16. Santa Fe: Museum of New Mexico Press, 2009.

———. "Introduction: Spanish and Mexican Land Grants and the Law." In *Spanish and Mexican Land Grants and the Law*, edited by Malcolm Ebright, 3–11. Manhattan, KS: Sunflower University Press, 1989.

———. *Land Grants and Lawsuits in Northern New Mexico*. Albuquerque: University of New Mexico Press, 1994.

———, ed. *Spanish and Mexican Land Grants and the Law*. Manhattan, KS: Sunflower University Press, 1989.

———. *The Tierra Amarilla Grant: A History of Chicanery*. Guadalupita, NM: Center for Land Grant Studies Research Paper, 2005. www.southwestbooks.org.

———. "Whiskey Is for Drinking, Water Is for Fighting." *New Mexico Historical Review* 81 (Summer 2006): 249–98.

———, and Rick Hendricks. "Making the Best of Both Worlds: A History of Santa Ana Pueblo's Land Acquisitions, 1700–1850." Unpublished manuscript in possession of the author.

———, and Rick Hendricks. "Pueblo League and Pueblo Indian Land in New Mexico, 1692–1846." In *Ysleta del Sur Pueblo Archives*, edited by Ysleta del Sur Pueblo, 91–94. El Paso: Book Publishers of El Paso, 2001.

———, and Rick Hendricks. *The Witches of Abiquiu: The Governor, the Priest, the Genízaro Indians, and the Devil*. Albuquerque: University of New Mexico Press, 2006.

———, Rick Hendricks, and Richard Hughes. *Four Square Leagues: Pueblo Indian Land in New Mexico*. Albuquerque: University of New Mexico Press, 2014.

Echo-Hawk, Walter A. "Museum Rights vs. Indian Rights: Guidelines for Assessing Competing Legal Interests in Native Cultural Resources." *NYU Review of Law and Social Change* 14, no. 2 (1986): 437–53.

Elkus, Jim. "Galisteo: 1500–1900." Senior honors thesis, Colorado College, 1974.

Elliot, Richard Smith. *Notes Taken in Sixty Years*. Saint Louis, MO: R. P. Studley, 1883.

Ellis, Bruce. *Bishop Lamy's Santa Fe Cathedral*. Albuquerque: University of New Mexico Press, 1985.

———. "Fraud without Scandal: The Roque Lovato Grant and Gaspar Ortiz y Alarid." *New Mexico Historical Review* 57 (January 1982): 43–62.

Ellis, Florence H., Myra Jenkins, and Richard Ford. *When Cultures Meet: Remembering San Gabriel del Yunge Oweenge*. Santa Fe, NM: Sunstone Press, 1987.

Engstrand, Iris H. W. "Land Grant Problems in the Southwest: The Spanish and Mexican Heritage." *New Mexico Historical Review* 53 (October 1978): 317–36.

Escriche, Joaquín, and Juan B. Guim, eds. *Diccionario razonado de legislación y jurisprudencia*. Bogotá: Temis, 1977.

Espinosa, J. Manuel. *Crusaders of the Rio Grande*. Chicago, IL: Institute of Jesuit History, 1942.

———, trans. and ed. *The First Expedition of Vargas into New Mexico, 1692*. Albuquerque: University of New Mexico Press, 1940.

Esquibel, José Antonio. "Notes on Cristóbal Nieto and Others." Unpublished manuscript in possession of the author.

———. "Thirty-Eight Adobe Houses: The Villa of Santa Fe in the Seventeenth Century, 1608–1610." In *All Trails Lead to Santa Fe: An Anthology Commemorating the 400th Anniversary of the Founding of Santa Fe*. Santa Fe, NM: Sunstone Press, 2010.

Ferguson, T. J., and E. Richard Hart. *A Zuni Atlas*. Norman: University of Oklahoma Press, 1985.

Ferry, Barbara. "Short on Water Village Tries to Ensure Its Supply: Some Residents of La Ciénega Want County Moratorium on New Development." *Santa Fe New Mexican*, 20 September 1998.

Fierman, Floyd S. *Guts and Ruts: The Jewish Pioneer on the Trail in the American Southwest*. New York: TAV, 1985.

Fine-Dare, Kathleen. *Grave Injustice: The American Indian Repatriation Movement and NAGPRA*. Lincoln: University of Nebraska Press, 2002.

Flores, Camille. "Ranchers Sue over Water Use." *Albuquerque Journal North*, 8 July 1989.

Forrest, Suzanne. *The Preservation of the Village: New Mexico's Hispanics and the New Deal*. Albuquerque: University of New Mexico Press, 1989.

Frank, Ross. *From Settler to Citizen: New Mexican Economic Development and the Creation of Vecino Society, 1750–1820*. Berkeley: University of California Press, 2000.

Frankl, Victor. "Hernán Cortés y la tradición de Las Siete Partidas." *Revista de Historia de América* 53–54 (June–December 1962): 9–74.

Gallegos, Albert J., and José Antonio Esquibel. "*Alcaldes* and Mayors of Santa Fe, 1613–2008." In *All Trails Lead to Santa Fe: An Anthology Commemorating the 400th Anniversary of the Founding of Santa Fe.* Santa Fe, NM: Sunstone Press, 2010.

Galván Rivera, Maríano. *Ordenanzas de tierras y aguas.* Mexico City, 1849.

Gibson, Charles. *The Aztecs under Spanish Rule: A History of the Indians of the Valley of Mexico, 1519–1810.* Stanford, CA: Stanford University Press, 1964.

Glasscock, James T. "The Genízaro Outpost of San Miguel del Vado." Senior thesis, Colorado College, 1973.

Glover, Lorrie, and Daniel Blake Smith. *The Shipwreck that Saved Jamestown: The Sea Venture Castaways and the Fate of America.* New York: Henry Holt, 2008.

Goldberg, Julia. "Don't Waste My Water Rights: La Ciénega Has Its Guard up over a Proposed Golf Course Development." *Santa Fe Reporter,* 18 December 1991.

Golten, Ryan. "Lobato v. Taylor: How the Villages of the Rio Culebra, the Colorado Supreme Court, and the Restatement of Servitudes Bailed out the Treaty of Guadalupe Hidalgo." *Natural Resources Journal* 45 (Spring 2005): 457–94.

Gordon-McCutchan, R. C. *The Taos Indians and the Battle for Blue Lake.* Santa Fe, NM: Red Crane Books, 1991.

Green, Jesse, ed. *Cushing at Zuni: The Correspondence and Journals of Frank Hamilton Cushing, 1879–1884.* Albuquerque: University of New Mexico Press, 1990.

Greenleaf, Richard E. "Atrisco and Las Ciruelas, 1722–1769." *New Mexico Historical Review* 42 (January 1967): 5–25.

———. "The Founding of Albuquerque, 1706: An Historical-Legal Problem." *New Mexico Historical Review* 39 (January 1964): 1–15.

———. "Land and Water in Mexico and New Mexico, 1700–1821." *New Mexico Historical Review* 47 (April 1972): 85–112.

Gulliford, Andrew. *Sacred Objects, Sacred Places: Preserving Tribal Traditions.* Boulder: University Press of Colorado, 2000.

Gutiérrez, Ramón A. *When Jesus Came, the Corn Mothers Went Away: Marriage, Sexuality, and Power in New Mexico, 1500–1846.* Stanford, CA: Stanford University Press, 1991.

Gwyne, S. C. *The Empire of the Summer Moon: Quanah Parker and the Rise and Fall of the Comanches, the Most Powerful Indian Tribe in American History.* New York: Scribner, 2010.

Hackett, Charles Wilson, ed. and trans. *Historical Documents Relating to New Mexico, Nueva Vizcaya, and Approaches Thereto.* 3 vols. Washington, D.C.: Carnegie Institution, 1923–1937.

———, ed. *Revolt of the Pueblo Indians of New Mexico and Otermín's Attempted Reconquest 1680–1682.* 2 vols. Translated by Charmion Clair Shelby. Albuquerque: University of New Mexico Press, 1942.

Haederle, Michael. "Saving Our Past from the Jaws of Subdivision." *Los Angeles Times,* 11 November 1996.

Hagan, William T. *Quanah Parker, Comanche Chief.* Norman: University of Oklahoma Press, 1993.

Hall, Frederic. *The Laws of Mexico.* San Francisco, CA: A. L. Bancroft, 1885.

Hall, G. Emlen. *Four Leagues of Pecos: A Legal History of the Pecos Grant, 1800–1933.* Albuquerque: University of New Mexico Press, 1984.

———. "Giant before the Surveyor General: The Land Career of Donaciano Vigil." *Journal of the West* 19 (July 1980): 64–73.

———. "Juan Estevan Pino, 'se les coma': New Mexico Land Speculation in the 1820s." *New Mexico Historical Review* 57 (January 1982): 27.

———. "Land Litigation and the Idea of New Mexico Progress." In *Spanish and Mexican Land Grants and the Law,* edited by Malcolm Ebright, 48–58. Manhattan, KS: Sunflower University Press, 1989.

———. "San Miguel del Bado and the Loss of the Common Lands of New Mexico Community Land Grants." *New Mexico Historical Review* 66 (October 1991): 413.

———. "Shell Games: The Continuing Legacy of Rights to Minerals and Water on Spanish and Mexican Land Grants in the Southwest." Rocky Mountain Mineral Law Institute. New York: Matthew Bender, 1991.

Hall, Kermit. *The Oxford Companion to the Supreme Court of the United States.* New York: Oxford University Press, 1992.

Hammond, George P. *The Rediscovery of New Mexico, 1580–1594: The Explorations of Chamuscado, Espejo, Castaño de Sosa, Morlete, and Leyva de Bonilla and Humaña.* Albuquerque: University of New Mexico Press, 1966.

———, and Lansing B. Bloom. "When Was Santa Fe Founded?" *New Mexico Historical Review* 4 (1929): 188–94.

———, and Agapito Rey, eds. and trans. *Don Juan de Oñate: Colonizer of New Mexico, 1595–1628.* 2 vols. Albuquerque: University of New Mexico Press, 1953.

Hanke, Lewis. *Aristotle and the American Indians: A Study of Race Prejudice in the Modern World.* Bloomington and London: Indiana University Press, 1959.

———. *The Spanish Struggle for Justice in the Conquest of America.* Boston, MA: Little, Brown, 1965.

Haring, C. H. *The Spanish Empire in America.* New York and London: Harcourt Brace Jovanovich, 1975.

Harrington, John Peabody. *The Ethnography of the Tewa Indians.* Washington, D.C.: Government Printing Office, 1916.

Hart, E. Richard, ed. *Zuni and the Courts: A Struggle for Sovereign Land Rights.* Lawrence: University Press of Kansas, 1995.

Hendricks, Rick. "Pedro Rodrigo Cubero: New Mexico's Reluctant Governor, 1697–1703." *New Mexico Historical Review* 68 (January 1993): 28–33.

————. "The 1761 Comanche Massacre." Paper submitted for Pikes Peak Library District's symposium, "Massacres of the Mountain West," 2013.

————, John L. Kessell, and Meredith Dodge, eds. *Blood on the Boulders: The Journals of Don Diego de Vargas, New Mexico, 1694–97.* 2 vols. Albuquerque: University of New Mexico Press, 1998.

————, John L. Kessell, and Meredith Dodge, eds. *To the Royal Crown Restored: The Journals of Don Diego de Varas, New Mexico, 1692–94.* Albuquerque: University of New Mexico Press, 1995.

————, and John P. Wilson, eds. and trans. *The Navajos in 1705: Roque Madrid's Campaign Journal.* Albuquerque: University of New Mexico Press, 1996.

Hickerson, Nancy Parrott. *The Jumanos: Hunters and Traders of the South Plains.* Austin: University of Texas Press, 1994.

Hill, Robert M., II. "The Social Uses of Writing among the Colonial Cakchiquel Maya: Nativism, Resistance, and Innovation." In *Columbian Consequences.* Vol. 3, *The Spanish Borderlands in Pan-American Perspective*, edited by David Hurst Thomas, 283–99. Washington, D.C.: Smithsonian Institution Press, 1991.

Hodge, Frederick W., ed. *Handbook of American Indians North of Mexico.* Totowa, NJ: Rowman and Littlefield, 1975.

————, George P. Hammond, and Agapito Rey, eds. *Fray Alonso de Benavides' Revised Memorial of 1634.* Albuquerque: University of New Mexico Press, 1945.

Horvath, Steven M., Jr. "The Social and Political Organization of the *Genízaros* of Plaza de Nuestra Señora de los Dolores de Belén, New Mexico, 1740–1812." PhD diss., Brown University, 1979.

Hunt, Aurora. *Kirby Benedict: Frontier Federal Judge.* Glendale, CA: Arthur H. Clark, 1961.

Hustitio, Charles. "Why Zuni War Gods Need to Be Returned." In *Zuni History: Victories in the 1990s*, edited by E. Richard Hart and T. J. Ferguson, 12. Seattle, WA: Institute of the North American West, 1991.

Hutchins, Wells A. "The Community Acequia: Its Origins and Development." *Southwestern Historical Review* 31 (January 1928): 261–84.

Ivey, James. "An Uncertain Founding: Santa Fe." *Common-Place* 3 (2003): 7. www.common-place.org/vol-03/no-04/santa-fe.

Jackson, Donald, ed. *The Journals of Zebulon Montgomery Pike.* Norman: University of Oklahoma Press, 1966.

Jenkins, Myra Ellen. "The Baltasar Baca 'Grant': History of an Encroachment." *El Palacio* 68 (Spring 1961): 47–64; (Summer 1961): 87–105.

————. "Early Days in the Rio Puerco Valley." Myra Ellen Jenkins Papers, box 40, folder 10. Center of Southwest Studies, Fort Lewis College, Durango, CO.

————. "Some Eighteenth-Century New Mexico Women of Property." In *Hispanic Arts and Ethnohistory in the Southwest: New Papers Inspired by the Work of E. Boyd,* edited by Marta Weigle with Claudia Larcombe and Samuel Larcombe, 335–45. Santa Fe, NM: Ancient City Press, 1983.

———. Spanish Land Grants in the Tewa Area." *New Mexico Historical Review* 47 (April 1972): 113–34.

———. "Taos Pueblo and Its Neighbors, 1540–1847." *New Mexico Historical Review* 41 (April 1966): 85–114.

John, Elizabeth A. H. *Storms Brewed in Other Men's Worlds: The Confrontation of Indians, Spanish, and French in the Southwest, 1540–1795.* College Station: Texas A&M University Press, 1975.

Jones, Hester. "The Spieglebergs and Early Trade in New Mexico." *El Palacio* 38 (April 1935): 88.

Jones, Oakah L., Jr. *Los Paisanos: Spanish Settlers on the Northern Frontier of New Spain.* Norman: University of Oklahoma Press, 1979.

———. *Pueblo Warriors and Spanish Conquest.* Norman: University of Oklahoma Press, 1966.

———. "Rescue and Ransom of Spanish Captives From the *Indios Bárbaros* on the Northern Frontier of New Spain." *Colonial Latin American Historical Review* 4 (Spring 1995): 131–33.

Jourdain, Silvester. "A Discovery of the Bermudas, Otherwise Called the Ile of Divils" (1610). In *Saints and Strangers,* by George F. Wilson. New York: Reynal and Hitchcock, 1945.

Julian, George W. "Land Stealing in New Mexico." *North American Review* 145 (July 1887): 17–31.

Kagan, Richard L. *Lawsuits and Litigants in Castile: 1500–1700.* Chapel Hill: University of North Carolina Press, 1981.

Kammer, David. "Application for Registration [on the] New Mexico Register of Cultural Properties [of the] Galisteo Historic District." Santa Fe: New Mexico Historic Preservation Division.

Keen, Benjamin. *Life and Labor in Ancient Mexico: The Brief and Summary Relation of the Lords of New Spain by Alonzo de Zorita.* Norman: University of Oklahoma Press, 1994.

Kelly, Lawrence C. *Assault on Assimilation: John Collier and the Origins of Indian Policy Reform.* Albuquerque: University of New Mexico Press, 1983.

Kessell, John L. "Diego Romero, the Plains Apaches, and the Inquisition." *American West* 15 (May–June 1978): 12–16.

———. *Kiva, Cross, and Crown: The Pecos Indians and New Mexico, 1540–1840.* Washington, D.C.: National Park Service, 1979.

———. *Miera y Pacheco: A Renaissance Spaniard in Eighteenth-Century New Mexico.* Norman: University of Oklahoma Press, 2013.

————, ed. *Remote beyond Compare: Letters of don Diego de Vargas to His Family from New Spain and New Mexico.* Albuquerque: University of New Mexico Press, 1989.

————. *Spain in the Southwest: A Narrative History of Colonial New Mexico, Arizona, Texas, and California.* Norman: University of Oklahoma Press, 2002.

————. "Spaniards and Pueblos: From Crusading Intolerance to Pragmatic Accommodation." In *Columbian Consequences.* Vol. 1, *The Spanish Borderlands in Pan-American Perspective,* edited by David Hurst Thomas, 127–38. Washington, D.C.: Smithsonian Institution Press, 1991.

————. "Vargas at the Gate: The Spanish Restoration of Santa Fe, 1692–1696." In *All Trails Lead to Santa Fe: An Anthology Commemorating the 400th Anniversary of the Founding of Santa Fe.* Santa Fe, NM: Sunstone Press, 2010.

Knaut, Andrew. *The Pueblo Revolt of 1680: Conquest and Resistance in Seventeenth-Century New Mexico.* Norman: University of Oklahoma Press, 1995.

Knowlton, Clark S. "The Mora Land Grant: A New Mexican Tragedy." In *Spanish and Mexican Land Grants and the Law,* edited by Malcolm Ebright, 59–73. Manhattan, KS: Sunflower University Press, 1989.

————. "The Town of Las Vegas Community Land Grant: An Anglo-American Coup D'Etat." *Journal of the West* 19 (July 1980): 12–21.

Kubler, George. *The Rebuilding of San Miguel at Santa Fe in 1710.* Colorado Springs, CO: Taylor Museum of the Colorado Springs Fine Arts Center, 1939.

Ladd, Edmund J. "Achieving True Interpretation." In *Zuni and the Courts: A Struggle for Sovereign Land Rights,* edited by E. Richard Hart, 231–34. Lawrence: University Press of Kansas, 1995.

————. "An Explanation: Request for the Return of Zuni Sacred Objects Held in Museums and Private Collections." In *Zuni and El Morro,* edited by David Grant Noble and Richard Woodbury. Explorations: Annual Bulletin of the School of American Research. Santa Fe, NM: Ancient City Press, 1983.

Lamar, Howard R. *The Far Southwest, 1846–1912: A Territorial History.* New Haven, CT: Yale University Press, 1966.

————. "Land Policy in the Spanish Southwest, 1846–1891: A Study in Contrasts." *Journal of Economic History* 22 (December 1962): 498–515.

Lange, Charles H. *Cochití: A New Mexico Pueblo, Past and Present.* Albuquerque: University of New Mexico Press, 1959.

————, Carroll Riley, and Elizabeth M. Lange. *The Southwestern Journals of Adolph Bandelier, 1889–1892.* Albuquerque: University of New Mexico Press; Santa Fe, NM: School of American Research, 1984.

Langum, David J. *Law and Community of the Mexican California Frontier: Anglo-American Expatriates and the Clash of Legal Traditions, 1821–1846.* Norman: University of Oklahoma Press, 1987.

———. *Law in the West.* Manhattan, KS: Sunflower University Press, 1985.

———. "The Legal System of Spanish California." *Western Legal History* 7 (Winter/Spring 1994): 6–10.

Larson, Robert W. *New Mexico Populism: A Study of Radical Protest in a Western Territory.* Boulder: Colorado Associated University Press, 1974.

———. "The White Caps of New Mexico: A Study of Ethnic Militancy in the Southwest." *Pacific Historical Review* 44 (May 1975): 171–85.

Las Casas, Bartolomé de. *The Devastation of the Indies: A Brief Account.* Translated by Herma Briffault. Baltimore, MD: Johns Hopkins University Press, 1992.

———. "Historias de las Indias." Translated by Lewis Hanke. In *The Spanish Struggle for Justice in the Conquest of America*, by Lewis Hanke. Boston, MA: Little, Brown, 1965.

Las Cuevas, Guillermo Cabanellas de, and Eleanor C. Hoague. *Diccionario Jurídico Español-Inglés Butterworths.* Austin, TX: Butterworth Legal, 1991.

LeCompte, Janet. "The Independent Women of Hispanic New Mexico, 1821–1846." *Western Historical Quarterly* 12 (January 1981): 17–35.

Lefroy, J. H. *Memorials of the Bermudas.* London: 1877. Cited in George F. Wilson, *Saints and Strangers*, New York: Reynal and Hitchcock, 1945.

Levine, Frances. "Dividing the Water: The Impact of Water Rights Adjudication on New Mexican Communities." *Journal of the Southwest* 32 (Autumn 1990): 268.

Lippard, Lucy, and Edward Ranney. *Down Country: The Tano of the Galisteo Basin, 1250–1782.* Santa Fe: Museum of New Mexico Press, 2010.

Lipsett-Rivera, Sonya. *To Defend Our Water with the Blood of Our Veins: The Struggle for Resources in Colonial Puebla.* Albuquerque: University of New Mexico Press, 1999.

Lockhart, James. "Encomienda and Hacienda: The Evolution of the Great Estate in the Spanish Indies." *Hispanic American Historical Review* 49 (August): 413–29.

Lopez, Gregorio. *Las Siete Partidas del sabio rey don Alfonso el IX Madrid: Oficina de d. León Amarita.* Madrid: Oficina de d. Leon Amarita, 1829–1831.

López, Larry. "The Founding of San Francisco on the Rio Puerco: A Document." *New Mexico Historical Review* 55 (January 1980): 71–78.

MacLachlan, Colin M. *Criminal Justice in Eighteenth-Century Mexico.* Berkeley: University of California Press, 1974.

———. *Spain's Empire in the New World: The Role of Ideas in Institutional and Social Change.* Berkeley: University of California Press, 1988.

Malagón-Barcelo, Javier. "The Role of the Letrado in the Colonization of America." *Americas* 18 (1961–1962): 1–17.

Marriott, Barbara. *Outlaw Tales of New Mexico: True Stories of New Mexico's Most Famous Robbers, Rustlers, and Bandits.* Guilford, CT: Globe Pequot Twodot Press, 2007.

Martza, Barton. "On the Trail of the Zuni War Gods." In *Zuni History: Victories in the 1990s*, edited by E. Richard Hart and T. J. Ferguson. Seattle, WA: Institute of the North American West, 1991.

McDaniel, James, trans. and ed. "Diary of Pedro José de la Fuente, Captain of the Presidio of El Paso del Norte" (January–December 1765). *Southwestern Historical Quarterly* 60 (October 1956): 260–81, and 83 (January 1980): 259–78.

McKnight, Joseph W. "Law Books on the Hispanic Frontier." In *Spanish and Mexican Land Grants and the Law*, edited by Malcolm Ebright, 74–84. Manhattan, KS: Sunflower University Press, 1989.

McNitt, Frank. *Navajo Wars: Military Campaigns, Slave Raids, and Reprisals.* Albuquerque: University of New Mexico Press, 1972.

Mednick, Christina Singleton. *San Cristóbal: Voices and Visions of the Galisteo Basin.* Santa Fe: Museum of New Mexico Press, 1996.

Meem, John Gaw. Preface, *Old Santa Fe Today.* Albuquerque: University of New Mexico Press, 1991.

Merrill, William L., Edmund J. Ladd, and T. J. Ferguson. "The Return of the Ahayu:da: Lessons for Repatriation from Zuni Pueblo and the Smithsonian Institution." *Current Anthropology* 34 (December 1993): 528–30.

Metzgar, Joseph V. "The Atrisco Land Grant, 1692–1977." *New Mexico Historical Review* 52 (October 1977): 269–96.

Meyer, Michael C. *Water in the Hispanic Southwest: A Social and Legal History, 1550–1850.* Tucson: University of Arizona Press, 1984.

———, and Susan M. Deeds. "Land, Water, and Equity in Spanish Colonial and Mexican Law: Historical Evidence for the Court in the Case of the State of New Mexico vs. R. Lee Aamodt, et al." Unpublished report on file in New Mexico v. Aamodt, No. 6639, Federal District Court for New Mexico, 1979.

Miller, Hunter. "Treaty of Guadalupe Hidalgo." In *Treaties and Other International Acts of the United States of America*, vol. 5, doc. 129, edited by Hunter Miller, 207–428. Washington, D.C.: U.S. Government Printing Office, 1937.

———. "Treaty of Spain 1819." In *Treaties and Other International Acts of the United States of America*, vol. 2, doc. 41, edited by Hunter Miller. Washington, D.C.: U.S. Government Printing Office, 1931.

Miller, Patrick. "Pueblo Powerhouse: Centuries Ago, San Marcos Was the Hub of a Thriving Trade in Turquoise and Pottery." *Albuquerque Journal*, 28 February 2005.

Miller, Robert Ryal, ed. "New Mexico in Mid-Eighteenth Century: A Report Based on Governor Vélez Cachupín's Inspection." *Southwestern Historical Quarterly* 79 (1975–1976): 166–81.

Minge, Ward Alan. "Frontier Problems in New Mexico Preceding the Mexican War, 1840–1846." PhD diss., University of New Mexico, 1965.

———. "The Last Will and Testament of Don Severino Martínez." *New Mexico Quarterly* 33 (1963): 33.

———. "Mexican Independence Day and a Ute Tragedy in Santa Fe, 1844." *El Corral de Santa Fe Westerners* (1973): 107.

———. "The Pueblo of Santa Ana's El Ranchito Purchases, and the Adjudication of the Boundary with San Felipe." Unpublished manuscript in possession of the author.

Montoya, María. *Translating Property: The Maxwell Land Grant and the Conflict over Land in the American West, 1840–1900.* Berkeley: University of California Press, 2002.

Moorhead, Max L. *New Mexico's Royal Road.* Norman: University of Oklahoma Press, 1958.

———. *The Presidio: Bastion of the Spanish Borderlands.* Norman: University of Oklahoma Press, 1975.

———. "Rebuilding the Presidio of Santa Fe, 1789–1791." *New Mexico Historical Review* 49 (April 1974): 124.

Muldoon, James. *The Americas in the Spanish World Order: The Justification for Conquest in the Seventeenth Century.* Philadelphia: University of Pennsylvania Press, 1994.

Murphy, Lawrence R. *Frontier Crusader: William F. M. Arny.* Tucson: University of Arizona Press, 1972.

Neary, Ben. "Government Ready to OK Mine Near Zuni Pueblo." *Santa Fe New Mexican*, 25 April 2002.

———. "Sacred Land under Siege." *Santa Fe New Mexican*, 7 January 2001.

Nelson, Ethelyn. "Camp Life in New Mexico." *El Palacio* 4 (1917): 19–23.

Nelson, Nels Christian. *Pueblo Ruins of the Galisteo Basin, New Mexico.* Anthropological Papers of the American Museum of Natural History, Vol. 15, Pt. 1. New York: American Museum of National History, 1914.

New Mexico State Business Directory. *1915 New Mexico State Business Directory.* Denver, CO: Gazetteer, 1915.

———. *1919 New Mexico State Business Directory.* Denver, CO: Gazetteer, 1919.

Nichols, David. *Lincoln and the Indians: Civil War Policy and Politics.* Saint Paul: Minnesota Historical Society Press, 1978.

Nichols, Madaline W. "Las Siete Partidas." *California Law Review* 20 (1932): 260–85.

Noble, David Grant, ed. *Santa Fe: History of an Ancient City.* Santa Fe, NM: School of American Research Press, 1989.

Northrop, Stuart. *Minerals of New Mexico.* Albuquerque: University of New Mexico Press, 1959.

Nostrand, Richard. *The Hispano Homeland.* Norman and London: University of Oklahoma Press, 1992.

Noyes, Stanley. *Los Comanches: The Horse People, 1751–1845*. Albuquerque: University of New Mexico Press, 1993.

Nuttal, Zelia. "Royal Ordnances Concerning the Laying Out of New Towns." *Hispanic American Historical Review* 4 (November 1921): 743–53.

Olmsted, Virginia Langham, comp. *Spanish and Mexican Censuses of New Mexico, 1750 to 1830*. Albuquerque: New Mexico Genealogical Society, 1981.

Orozco, Wistano Luis. *Legislación y jurisprudencia sobre terreno baldíos*. Mexico City: Imp. de El Tiempo, 1985.

Ortiz, Roxanne Dunbar. *Roots of Resistance: Land Tenure in New Mexico, 1680–1980*. Los Angeles: University of California Press, 1980.

Ortiz y Pino, José, III. *Don José: The Last Patrón*. Santa Fe, NM: Sunstone Press, 2007.

Otero, Miguel A. *My Life on the Frontier*. 2 vols. New York: Press of the Pioneers, 1935–1939.

Pagden, Anthony, trans. and ed. *Hernán Cortés: Letters from Mexico*. New Haven: Yale University Press, 1986.

———. *Lords of All the World: Ideologies of Empire in Spain, Britain and France, c.1500–c.1800*. New Haven, CT: Yale University Press, 1995.

Parezo, Nancy J. "Cushing as Part of the Team: The Collecting Activities of the Smithsonian Institution." *American Ethnologist* 12, no. 4 (November 1985): 763–74.

Parmentier, Richard. "The Mythological Triangle: Poseyemu, Montezuma, and Jesus in the Pueblos." In *The Handbook of North American Indians*, edited by William C. Sturtevant. Vol. 9, *Southwest*, edited by Alfonso Ortiz, 609–22. Washington, D.C.: Smithsonian Institution, 1979.

Parrish, William J. *The Charles Ilfeld Company: A Study of the Rise and Decline of Mercantile Capitalism in New Mexico*. Cambridge, MA: Harvard University Press, 1961.

Parry, J. H. *The Audiencia of New Galicia in the Sixteenth Century: A Study in Spanish Colonial Government*. Cambridge: Cambridge University Press, 1948.

———. *The Spanish Seaborne Empire*. Berkeley, Los Angeles: University of California Press, 1966.

———. *The Spanish Theory of Empire in the Sixteenth Century*. Cambridge: Cambridge University Press, 1940.

Patrick, Elizabeth Nelson. "Land Grants during the Administration of Spanish Colonial Governor Pedro Fermín de Mendinueta." *New Mexico Historical Review* 51 (January 1976): 5–18.

Pearce, T. M., ed. *New Mexico Place Names*. Albuquerque: University of New Mexico Press, 1965.

Phelan, John Leddy. "Authority and Flexibility in the Spanish Imperial Bureaucracy." *Administrative Science Quarterly* 5, no. 1 (1960): 47–65.

Pike, Zebulon. *An Account of Expeditions to the Sources of the Mississippi (1810)*. Philadelphia, PA: C. and A. Conrad, 1810.

Poldervaart, Arie W. *Black-Robed Justice*. Santa Fe: Historical Society of New Mexico, 1948.

Post, Stephen S., Stephen C. Lentz, Mathew Barbour, Susan Moga, Nancy J. Akins, and Eric Blinman. "Third Interim Report on the Data Recovery Program at LA 1051, El Pueblo de Santa Fe." Report submitted to the New Mexico Historic Preservation Division. Santa Fe: Museum of New Mexico, Office of Archaeological Studies, 2005.

Powell, Philip Wayne. *Mexico's Miguel Caldera: The Taming of America's First Frontier, 1548–1597*. Tucson: University of Arizona Press, 1977.

———. *Soldiers, Indians, and Silver: The Northward Advance of New Spain*. Berkeley: University of California Press, 1952.

Ramenofsky, Ann F. "Report on the Archeological Investigation of Metallurgy at San Marcos Pueblo (LA 98) Summer 2002." Santa Fe: Archeology Conservancy and New Mexico Historic Preservation Division, 2003.

———. "Summary Report of the 2000 Season of Archeological Research at San Marcos Pueblo (LA 98) by the University of New Mexico." Santa Fe: Archeological Conservancy and New Mexico Historic Preservation Division, 2001.

Read, Benjamin M. *Illustrated History of New Mexico*. New York: Arno Press, 1976.

Recopilación de Leyes de los Reynos de las Indias. Madrid: Ivlian de Paredes, 1681.

Reeve, Frank D. "The Navaho-Spanish Peace: 1720s–1770s." *New Mexico Historical Review* 34 (January 1959): 9–40.

———. *Navaho Foreign Affairs, 1795-1846*. Tsaile, AZ: Navajo Community College Press, 1983.

Reich, Peter L. "Mission Revival Jurisprudence: State Courts and Hispanic Water Law since 1850." *Washington Law Review* 69 (October 1994): 869.

Reséndez, Andrés. *Changing National Identities at the Frontier: Texas and New Mexico, 1800–1850*. Cambridge: Cambridge University Press, 2004.

Reynolds, Matthew. *Spanish and Mexican Land Laws: New Spain and Mexico*. Saint Louis, MO: Buxton and Skinner Stationery, 1895.

Riley, Carroll L. *Kachina and the Cross*. Salt Lake City: University of Utah Press, 2003.

———. *Rio del Norte: People of the Upper Rio Grande from Earliest Times to the Pueblo Revolt*. Salt Lake City: University of Utah Press, 1995.

Rios-Bustamante, Antonio José. "New Mexico in the Eighteenth Century: Life, Labor and Trade in La Villa de San Felipe de Albuquerque, 1706–1790." *Aztlan* 7 (Fall 1976): 357–89.

Rivaya-Martínez, Joaquín. "Becoming Comanches: Patterns of Captive Incorporation into Comanche Kinship Networks, 1820–1875." In *On the Borders of Love and*

Power: Families and Kinship in the Intercultural American Southwest, edited by David Wallace Adams and Crista De Luzio. Berkeley: University of California Press, 2012.

Robbins, Wilfred William, John Peabody Harrington, and Barbara Freire-Marreco. *Ethnobotany of the Tewa Indians*. Bureau of American Ethnology Bulletin 55. Washington, D.C.: Government Printing Office, 1916.

Rock, Michael J. "Anton Chico and Its Patent." *Journal of the West* 19 (July 1980): 86–91.

Rock, Rosalind Z. "'Pido y Suplico': Women and the Law in Spanish New Mexico, 1697–1763." *New Mexico Historical Review* 65 (April 1990): 145–59.

Rockwell, John A. *A Compilation of Spanish and Mexican Law in Relation to Mines and Titles to Real Estate, in Force in California, Texas and New Mexico*. New York: John S. Voorhies, 1851.

Rodríguez, Sylvia. "Applied Research on Land and Water in New Mexico: A Critique." *Journal of the Southwest* 32 (Autumn 1990): 300.

Rollings, Willard H. *The Comanche*. New York: Chelsea House.

Rosen, Deborah A. "Women and Property across Colonial America: A Comparison of Legal Systems in New Mexico and New York." *William and Mary Quarterly* 40 (April 2003): 359–61.

Rosenbaum, Robert J. *Mexicano Resistance in the Southwest: "The Sacred Right of Self-Preservation."* Austin: University of Texas Press, 1981.

Rosner, Hillary. "Saving a Sacred Lake: Zuni Activist Pablo Padilla." *High Country News*, 2 February 2004.

Salazar, J. Richard. "The Bartolomé Fernández Grant: Another Grazing Grant in Navajo Country." Guadalupita, NM: Center for Land Grant Studies Research Paper, 2005. www.southwestbooks.org.

———. "The Felipe Tafoya Grant: A Grazing Grant in West Central New Mexico." Guadalupita, NM: Center for Land Grant Studies Research Paper, 2005. www.southwestbooks.org.

———. "Juan Andés Archuleta: A Brief History of His Family and of His Role during the Mexican Period." Guadalupita, NM: Center for Land Grant Studies Research Paper, 2005. www.southwestbooks.org.

———. "The Military Career of Donaciano Vigil." Guadalupita, NM: Center for Land Grant Studies Research Paper, 2005. www.southwestbooks.org.

———. "The Role of the Land Grant and Its Effect on Expansionism in Northern New Mexico, 1700–1821." Guadalupita, NM: Center for Land Grant Studies Research Paper, 2005. www.southwestbooks.org.

———. "Santa Rosa de Lima de Abiquiu." *New Mexico Architecture* 18 (September–October 1976): 13–19.

———. "Spanish-Indian Relations in New Mexico during the Term of Comandante General Pedro de Nava, 1790–1802." Guadalupita, NM: Center for Land Grant Studies Research Paper, 2005. www.southwestbooks.org.

Sánchez, F. Richard, with Stephen Wall and Ann Filemyr, eds. *White Shell Water Place: An Anthology of Native American Reflections on the 400th Anniversary of the Founding of Santa Fe, New Mexico*. Santa Fe, NM: Sunstone Press, 2010.

Sánchez, Joseph P. *Between Two Rivers: The Atrisco Land Grant in Albuquerque*. Norman: University of Oklahoma Press, 2008.

———. "The Peralta-Ordóñez Affair and the Founding of Santa Fe." In *Santa Fe: History of an Ancient City*, edited by David Grant Noble, 15–23. Santa Fe, NM: School of American Research Press, 1989.

Sando, Joe S. *Nee Hemish: A History of Jemez Pueblo*. Albuquerque: University of New Mexico Press, 1982.

———. "The Silver-Crowned Canes of Pueblo Office." In *Telling New Mexico: A New History*, edited by Marta Weigle with Francis Levine and Louise Stiver, 125–26. Santa Fe: Museum of New Mexico Press, 2009.

Sandy, Marin. "Where Credit Is Due." *Santa Fean: The History Issue* (February/March 2009): 28.

Santa Fe New Mexican. "Mining near Lake Concerns Zuni Tribe." 21 February 1996.

———. "Zuni Tribe's Lawsuit Nets $17 Million." 19 July 1991.

Santamaria, Francisco J. *Diccionario de mejicanismos*. Mexico City: Editorial Porrua, S. A., 1978.

Scallorn, Judy. "Alexander Valle," Myra Ellen Jenkins Collection, box 41, folder 3. Ft. Lewis College, Durango, CO.

Schaafsma, Curtis F. *Apaches de Navajo: Seventeenth-Century Navajos in the Chama Valley of New Mexico*. Salt Lake City: University of Utah Press, 2002.

Schiller, Mark. "Nuestra Señora del Rosario, San Fernando y Santiago del Rio de las Truchas Grant." Guadalupita, NM: Center for Land Grant Studies Research Paper, 2005. www.southwestbooks.org.

Scholes, France V. "Church and State in New Mexico, 1610–1650. *New Mexico Historical Review* 11 (1936): 333.

———. "Civil Government and Society in New Mexico in the Seventeenth Century." *New Mexico Historical Review* 10 (April 1935): 105.

———. "Documents for the History of the New Mexican Missions in the Seventeenth Century." *New Mexico Historical Review* 4 (January 1929): 48.

———. "The First Decade of the Inquisition in New Mexico." *New Mexico Historical Review* 10 (July 1935): 240–41.

———. "Juan Martínez de Montoya, Settler and Conquistador of New Mexico." *New Mexico Historical Review* 19 (1944): 340.

———. "Troublous Times in New Mexico." *New Mexico Historical Review* 10 (1937): 388.

Schroeder, Albert H. "A History of the Area along the Eastern Line of the Santo Domingo Pueblo Aboriginal Title Area." Unpublished manuscript prepared for the U.S. Department of Justice. Santa Fe, NM: Laboratory of Anthropology Library, 1976.

——. "Pueblos Abandoned in Historic Times." In *Handbook of North American Indians*, edited by William Sturtevant. Vol. 9, *Southwest*, edited by Alfonso Ortiz, 236–54. Washington, D.C.: Smithsonian Institution, 1979.

——, and Dan Matson. *A Colony on the Move, Gaspar Castaño de Sosa's Journal: 1590–1591*. Santa Fe, NM: School of American Research, 1965.

Schubert, Rebecca. "Reflections on the Sacred Salt Lake." *La Crónica de Nuevo México* 57 (August 2002).

Scott, Samuel Parsons, trans. *Las Siete Partidas*. Chicago, IL: Commerce Clearing House, 1931.

Seed, Patricia. *Ceremonies of Possession in Europe's Conquest of the New World: 1492–1640*. Cambridge: Cambridge University Press, 1995.

Shakespeare, William. *The Tempest*. Edited by Virginia Mason Vaughn and Alden T. Vaughn. 3rd ed. London: Thomas Nelson and Sons, 1999.

Shannon, Timothy. *Iroquois Diplomacy on the Early American Frontier*. London: Viking, 2008.

Shapiro, Jason S. "Before Santa Fe: Archaeology of the City Different." Santa Fe: Museum of New Mexico Press, 2008.

Simmons, Marc. *Albuquerque: A Narrative History*. Albuquerque: University of New Mexico Press, 1982.

——. *Coronado's Land: Essays on Daily Life in Colonial New Mexico*. Albuquerque: University of New Mexico Press, 1991.

——. "Ethnologist, Pioneer Documented Zuni Culture for Posterity." *Santa Fe New Mexican*, 26 May 2001.

——. *Father Juan Agustín de Morfi's Account of the Disorders in New Mexico*. Santa Fe: Historical Society of New Mexico, 1977.

——. *The Fighting Settlers of Seboyeta*. Cerrillos, NM: San Marcos Press, 1971.

——. "Governor Cuervo and the Beginnings of Albuquerque: Another Look." *New Mexico Historical Review* 55 (July 1980): 189–207.

——. "History of Pueblo-Spanish Relations to 1821." In *Handbook of North American Indians*, edited by William C. Sturtevant. Vol. 9, *Southwest*, edited by Alfonso Ortiz, 178–93. Washington, D.C.: Smithsonian Institution, 1979.

——. "The Naming of Santa Fe." In *Yesterday in Santa Fe: Episodes in a Turbulent History*. Santa Fe, NM: Sunstone Press, 1989.

——. "New Mexico's Colonial Agriculture." *El Palacio* 89 (Spring 1983): 3–10.

——. "New Mexico's Smallpox Epidemic of 1780–1781." *New Mexico Historical Review* 41 (1966): 319–26.

———. "The Pueblo Revolt: Why Did It Happen." *El Palacio* 86 (Winter 1980–1981): 11–15.

———. "Settlement Patterns and Village Plans in Colonial New Mexico." *Journal of the West* 8 (January 1969): 7–21.

———. *Spanish Government in New Mexico.* Albuquerque: University of New Mexico Press, 1968.

———. "Spanish Irrigation Practices in New Mexico." *New Mexico Historical Review* 47 (April 1972): 135–50.

———. "Tlascalans in the Spanish Borderlands." *New Mexico Historical Review* 39 (April 1964): 108–10.

———. "Unwise Friar Met His Fate in Early New Mexico." *Santa Fe New Mexican,* 13 October 2012.

———. "The Zunis Seek Justice." Trail Dust, *Santa Fe Reporter,* 3 August 1993.

Simpson, Lesley Byrd. *Exploitation of Land in Central Mexico in the Sixteenth Century.* Berkeley and Los Angeles: University of California Press, 1962.

Sister Ida Catherine. "Antonio Joseph." Master's thesis. Marion Dargan Papers. Albuquerque, NM: Center for Southwest Research, University of New Mexico.

Smith, Andrew T. "The Founding of the San Antonio de las Huertas Grant." *Social Science Journal* 13 (October 1976): 35–43.

Snow, Cordelia Thomas. "Dispelling Some Myths of Santa Fe, New Mexico, or Santa Fe of the Imagination." In *Current Research on the Late Prehistory and Early History of New Mexico,* 215–20. Albuquerque: New Mexico Archaeological Council, 1992.

———. "Galisteo Mission." http://www.newmexicohistory.org/filedetails_docs.php?fileID=21292.

———, ed. "A Hypothetical Configuration of the Early Santa Fe Plaza Based on the 1573 Ordenances or the Law of the Indies." In *Santa Fe Historic Plaza Study I: With Translations from Spanish Colonial Documents,* 56–57. Santa Fe, NM: City Planning Department, 1990.

———. "San Marcos: A Brief History of Mission San Marcos, Santa Fe County, New Mexico." http://www.newmexicohistory.org/filedetails.php?fileID=21289.

Snow, David H. "A Note on *Encomienda* Economics in Seventeenth-Century New Mexico." In *Hispanic Arts and Ethnohistory in the Southwest: New Papers Inspired by the Work of E. Boyd,* edited by Marta Weigle with Claudia Larcombe and Samuel Larcombe, 347–58. Santa Fe, NM: Ancient City Press, 1983.

———. "Prehistoric Southwestern Turquoise Industry." *El Palacio* 79, no. 1 (1973): 33–51.

———. *The Santa Fe Acequia Systems.* Santa Fe: National Park Service and New Mexico State Historic Preservation Division, 1988.

———. "So Many Mestizos, Mulattos, and Zambohigos: New Mexico's People without History." Paper presented at the annual meeting of the Western History Association, Denver, CO, 1995.

———. "A Review of Spanish Colonial Archeology in Northern New Mexico." In *Current Research on the Late Prehistory and Early History of New Mexico*, edited by Bradley J. Vierra, 185–93. Albuquerque: New Mexico Archeological Council, 1992.

Snyder, Christina. *Slavery in Indian Country: The Changing Face of Captivity in Early America*. Cambridge, MA: Harvard University Press, 2010.

Spell, Lota M. "The Grant and First Survey of the City of San Antonio." *Southwestern Bibliography Historical Quarterly* 66 (July 1962): 73–89.

Spicer, Edward H. *Cycles of Conquest: The Impact of Spain, Mexico, and the United States on the Indians of the Southwest, 1533–1960*. Tucson: University of Arizona Press, 1962.

Stampa, Manuel Carrera. "The Evolution of Weights and Measures in New Spain." *Hispanic American Historical Review* 29 (February 1949): 15.

Stephens, A. Ray, and William M. Holmes. *Historical Atlas of Texas*. Norman: University of Oklahoma Press, 1989.

Stephens, Henry Morse, and Herbert E. Bolton. *The Pacific Ocean in History: Papers and Addresses Presented at the Panama-Pacific Historical*. American Asiatic Association, 1917; Reprint, Toronto: University of Toronto, 2011.

Stern, Steve J. *Peru's Indian Peoples and the Challenge of Spanish Conquest: Huamanga to 1640*. Madison: University of Wisconsin Press, 1982.

Stevenson, Matilda Coxe. "Zuni Ancestral Gods and Masks." *American Anthropologist* 11 (February 1898): 33–40.

Stoller, Marianne L. "A Spanish Colonial Household in 17th Century New Mexico." Paper presented at the annual meeting of the Society for Historical Archeology, Vancouver, BC, 1994.

Swadesh, Frances Leon. "Archaeology, Ethnohistory, and the First Plaza of Carnuel." *Ethnohistory* 23 (Winter 1976): 31–44.

———. *Los Primeros Pobladores: Hispanic Americans of the Ute Frontier*. Notre Dame, IN: University of Notre Dame Press, 1974.

———. "They Settled by Little Bubbling Springs." *El Palacio* 84 (Fall 1978): 19–20, 42–49.

———, and David J. Snow. "Historical Archeology of the Rito Colorado Valley, New Mexico." *Journal of the West* 19 (July 1980): 40–50.

———, Julián Wilfredo Vigil, and Marina Baldonado Ochoa. "Land, Water, and Pueblo-Hispanic Relations in Northern New Mexico." *Journal of the Southwest* 32 (Autumn 1990): 288.

Taylor, William B. "Colonial Land and Water Rights of New Mexico Indian Pueblos." Unpublished report on file in New Mexico v. Aamodt, No. 6639, Federal District Court for New Mexico, 1979.

———. "Land and Water Rights in the Viceroyalty of New Spain." *New Mexico Historical Review* 50 (July 1975): 189.

———. *Landlord and Peasant in Colonial Oaxaca*. Stanford, CA: Stanford University Press, 1972.

Thomas, Alfred B., trans. and ed. *After Coronado: Spanish Exploration Northeast of New Mexico, 1696–1727*. Norman: University of Oklahoma Press, 1935.

———. *Forgotten Frontiers: A Study of the Spanish Indian Policy of Don Juan Bautista de Anza, Governor of New Mexico 1777–1787*. Norman: University of Oklahoma Press, 1932.

———, trans. "Governor Mendinueta's Proposals for the Defense of New Mexico, 1772–1778." *New Mexico Historical Review* 6 (1931): 29–30.

———. *The Plains Indians and New Mexico, 1751–1778: A Collection of Documents Illustrative of the History of the Eastern Frontier of New Mexico*. Albuquerque: University of New Mexico Press, 1940.

Tigges, Linda, ed. "The Pastures of the Royal Horse Herd of the Santa Fe Presidio, 1692–1740." In *All Trails Lead to Santa Fe: An Anthology Commemorating the 400th Anniversary of the Founding of Santa Fe*. Santa Fe, NM: Sunstone Press, 2010.

———. *Santa Fe Historic Plaza Study I: With Translations from Spanish Colonial Documents*. Santa Fe, NM: City Planning Department, 1990.

———, ed., and J. Richard Salazar, trans. *Spanish Colonial Lives: Documents from the Spanish Colonial Archives of New Mexico, 1705–1774*. Santa Fe, NM: Sunstone Press, 2014.

Tijerina, Andrés. *Tejanos and Texas under the Mexican Flag, 1821–1836*. College Station: Texas A&M University Press, 1994.

Timmons, W. H. *El Paso: A Borderlands History*. El Paso: Texas Western Press, 1990.

Tipton, Will. "Mr. Bandelier and the Southwestern Land Court." *Nation*, 25 June 1891.

Tobias, Henry J. *A History of the Jews in New Mexico*. Albuquerque: University of New Mexico Press, 1990.

Toll, H. Wolcott, and Jessica Badner. *Galisteo Basin Archeological Sites Protection Act Site Assessment Project*. Santa Fe: Office of Archeological Studies and New Mexico Department of Cultural Affairs, 2008.

Torrez, Robert J. "Crime and Punishment in Spanish Colonial New Mexico." Guadalupita, NM: Center for Land Grant Studies Research Paper, 2005. www.southwestbooks.org.

———. "'El Bornes': La Tierra Amarilla and T. D. Burns." *New Mexico Historical Review* 56 (April 1981): 161–75.

———. "The San Juan Gold Rush of 1860 and Its Effect on the Development of Northern New Mexico." *New Mexico Historical Review* 63 (July 1988): 257–72.

Twitchell, Ralph Emerson. "A Campaign against the Moqui Pueblos." *New Mexico Historical Review* 6 (1931): 158–226.

———. *The Leading Facts of New Mexico History.* Albuquerque, NM: Horn & Wallace, 1963.

———. *Old Santa Fe: The Story of New Mexico's Ancient Capitol.* 1925; Reprint, Chicago, IL: Rio Grande Press, 1963.

———. *The Spanish Archives of New Mexico.* 2 vols. 1914; Reprint, New York: Arno Press, 1976.

Tyler, Daniel. "Ejido Lands in New Mexico." In *Spanish and Mexican Land Grants and the Law*, edited by Malcolm Ebright, 24–35. Manhattan, KS: Sunflower University Press, 1989.

———. "Land and Water Tenure in New Mexico: 1821–1846." Unpublished report on file in New Mexico v. Aamodt, No. 6639, Federal District Court for New Mexico, 1979.

———. *The Mythical Pueblo Rights Doctrine: Water Administration in Hispanic New Mexico.* El Paso: Texas Western Press, 1990.

———. "The Spanish Colonial Legacy and the Role of Hispanic Custom in Defining New Mexico Land and Water Rights." *Colonial Latin American Historical Review* 4 (Spring 1995): 149–65.

———. "Underground Water in Hispanic New Mexico: A Brief Analysis of Laws, Customs, and Disputes." *New Mexico Historical Review* 66 (July 1991): 287–301.

Valle Menéndez, Antonio del, and Pilar Latasa Vasallo. *Juan Francisco de Güemes y Horcasitas: Primer Conde de Revillagigedo, Virrey de México; La historia de un soldado (1681–1766).* Cantabria: Librería Estudios, 1998.

Van Ness, John R. *Hispanos in Northern New Mexico: The Development of Corporate Community and Multicommunity.* New York: AMS Press, 1991.

———, and Christine M. Van Ness, eds. *Spanish and Mexican Land Grants in New Mexico.* Manhattan, KS: Sunflower University Press, 1980.

Vassberg, David E. *Land and Society in Golden Age Castile.* Cambridge: Cambridge University Press, 1984.

———. "The Spanish Background: Problems Concerning Ownership, Usurpations, and Defense of Common Lands in Sixteenth-Century Castile." In *Spanish and Mexican Land Grants and the Law*, edited by Malcolm Ebright, 12–23. Manhattan, KS: Sunflower University Press, 1989.

Vaughn, Charles David. "Taking the Measure of New Mexico's Colonial Miners, Mining and Metallurgy." PhD diss., University of New Mexico, 2006.

Vigil, Julián Josué. "1845 Census of Las Vegas, New Mexico." Springer: Editorial Teleraña, 1985. www.southwestbooks.org.

———. *Mexican Archives of New Mexico, 1821–1846*. Springer: Editorial Telaraña, 1984. www.southwestbooks.org.

———. *A Short Index to New Mexican Soldiers' Service Records and Enlistment Papers, 1821–1846*. Springer: Editorial Telaraña, 1984. www.southwestbooks.org.

———. *[The] Vigil Index: SANM I: 10*. Springer: Editorial Telaraña, 1984. www. southwestbooks.org.

Vigil, Ralph H. *Alonzo de Zorita: Royal Judge and Christian Humanist, 1512–1585*. Norman: University of Oklahoma Press, 1987.

Viola, Herman J. *Diplomats in Buckskin: A History of Indian Delegations in Washington City*. Washington, D.C.: Smithsonian Institution Press, 1981.

Wagner, Henry. *The Life and Writings of Bartolomé de las Casas*. Albuquerque: University of New Mexico Press, 1967.

Warner, Louis H. "Conveyance of Property, the Spanish and Mexican Way." *New Mexico Historical Review* 6 (October 1931): 334–59.

———. "Wills and Hijuelas." *New Mexico Historical Review* 7 (1932): 75–89.

Warner, Ted J. "The Career of Don Félix Martínez de Torre Laguna: Soldier, Presidio Commander, and Governor of New Mexico, 1693–1726." PhD diss., University of New Mexico, 1963.

Watkins, Frances E. *The Navajo*. Los Angeles, CA: The Southwest Museum, n.d.

Watson, Blake A. *Buying American from the Indians: Johnson v. McIntosh and the History of Native Land Rights*. Norman: University of Oklahoma Press, 2012.

Weber, David J. *Arms, Indians, and the Mismanagement of New Mexico: Donaciano Vigil, 1846*. El Paso: Texas Western Press, 1986.

———. "Land and Water Rights of the Pueblos of New Mexico under Mexican Sovereignty, 1821–1846." Unpublished report on file in New Mexico v. Aamodt, No. 6639, Federal District Court for New Mexico, 1979.

———. *The Mexican Frontier, 1821–1846: The American Southwest under Mexico*. Albuquerque: University of New Mexico Press, 1982.

———. "The New Mexico Archives in 1827." *New Mexico Historical Review* 61 (January 1986): 53–61.

———. "Santa Fe." In *Jamestown, Quebec, Santa Fe: Three North American Beginnings*, edited by James C. Kelly and Barbara Clark Smith, 135–63. Washington, D.C.: Smithsonian Books, 2007.

———. *The Spanish Frontier in North America*. New Haven, CT: Yale University Press, 1992.

———, and G. Emlen Hall. "Mexican Liberals and the Pueblo Indians, 1821–1829." *New Mexico Historical Review* 59 (January 1984): 5.

Weigand, Phil C., and Acelia García de Weigand. "A Macroeconomic Study of the Relationships between the Ancient Cultures of the American Southwest and Mesoamerica." In *The Road to Aztlan: Art from a Mythic Homeland*, edited by

Virginia Fields and Victor Zamudio-Taylor, 184–95. Los Angeles, CA: Los Angeles County Museum of Art, 2001.

Weigle, Marta, with Samuel Larcombe and Claudia Larcombe, eds. *Hispanic Arts and Ethnohistory in the Southwest: New Papers Inspired by the Work of E. Boyd*. Santa Fe, NM: Ancient City Press, 1983.

Westphall, Victor. *Mercedes Reales: Hispanic Land Grants of the Upper Rio Grande Region*. Albuquerque: University of New Mexico Press, 1983.

———. *The Public Domain in New Mexico: 1854–1891*. Albuquerque: University of New Mexico Press, 1965.

White, Koch, Kelley, and McCarthy, and the New Mexico State Planning Office. *Land Title Study*. Santa Fe, NM: State Planning Office, 1971.

Whitely, Peter. "Reconnoitering 'Pueblo' Ethnicity: The 1852 Tesuque Delegation to Washington." *Journal of the Southwest* 45 (Autumn 2003): 437–518.

Widdison, Jerold Gwayn. "Historical Geography of the Middle Rio Puerco Valley, New Mexico." *New Mexico Historical Review* 34 (1959): 259–60.

Wilson, George F. *Saints and Strangers*. New York: Reynal and Hitchcock, 1945.

Wroth, William. "Barrio del Analco: Its Roots in Mexico and Role in Early Colonial Santa Fe, 1610–1780." In *All Trails Lead to Santa Fe: An Anthology Commemorating the 400th Anniversary of the Founding of Santa Fe, New Mexico in 1610*. Santa Fe, NM: Sunstone Press, 2010.

Yiannopoulos, A. N. "Jurisprudence and Doctrine as Sources of Law in Louisiana and in France." In *The Role of Judicial Decisions and Doctrine in Civil Law and in Mixed Jurisdictions*, edited by Joseph Dainow, 69–90. Baton Rouge: Louisiana State University Press, 1974.

Zeeveld, W. Gordon. *The Temper of Shakespeare's Thought*. New Haven, CT: Yale University Press, 1974.

Zuni Salt Lake Coalition. "Zuni Salt Lake and Sanctuary Zone Protected." Press Release, 7 August 2003.

INDEX

Page numbers in italic text refer to illustrations.

buckskins, 9–10, 228
buffalo, 132, 166, 267, 310n57
Bureau of Indian Affairs, 262
Bureau of Land Management, 85, 115, 256
Bustamante, Governor Juan Domingo
  de, 8, 62, 94–95, 97, 305n96
Bustamante, Josefa, *123*
Bustamante, Manuel, 171
Bustamante, Rosa, *123*
Bustamante y Tagle, Bernardo Antonio,
  64–65, *123*
Bustos, Manuel, 282

Cabeza de Baca, Luis María, 25–27, 104,
  106, 109
Cabeza de Vaca, Álvar Núñez, 79, 81,
  313n96
cabildo, 7–8, 37, 47, 56, 122, 179, 182,
  292n80, 324n25, 373
caciques, 61, 103, 253, 291n63, 373
Caja del Río grant, 169, 274, 365n26
Calhoun, Governor James C., 268
Calvin Ranch, 340n47
Camino Real, 47, 49, *56*, 208, 344n47
Campo Redondo, José, 21–22, *123*
Campos, Agustin, 314n106
Cañada de Cochití grant, 89–90, 92, *93*,
  111, 227, 317n21; boundaries of, 94–95,
  97–99, 101; and Cochiti sacred sites,
  99–100; confirmation of, 97–101, 109,
  113; petition for, 94–97, 99, 318n34
Cañada de Cochití village, 96–97
Cañada de Guicú, 124–25
Cañada de Juana López, 126
Cañada de los Álamos, 278
Cañada de Santa Clara grant, 230, 266,
  346n21, 361n68
Candelaria, Juan, 133, 328n63
canes (Pueblo), 253, 268, 370n8
Cañón de Picurís, 9
Carnuel grant, 198, 202, 242, 249, 274,
  293n81, 346n21
Carrillo, Miguel, *56*
Carter, Jimmy (president), 85

cartography, 214, 229, 255–56, 267
Casa Colorado grant, 201
Casados, Antonio, 16–17, 203, 274,
  349n44, 359n41
Casados, Francisco, 16
Casas Cachupinas, 194, 345n8
Casas Reales (Palace of the Governors),
  36–37, 118, 154, 178–79, 267
Castaño de Sosa, Gaspar (captain), 166–
  67, 178, 298n12
Castaño de Sosa expedition, 35, 116–17,
  145–46, 166–67, 178
Castellanos, José, 116, 120
Cata, Francisco, 19
Catholic Church, 148, 209, 355n8. *See
  also* Christianity
Catron, Thomas B., 40–42, 83, 106, 110,
  158–61, 181, 270, 276, 342n19, 371n16
Cebolleta area grants, 214, 248–51, 279–
  80, 320n72
Cebolleta Mountain, 248–49, 366n38.
  See also Mount Taylor
ceremonies: of Indians, 4, 57, 96, 175,
  190; for land possession, 75, 103, 154,
  184, 212, 214, 312n76; objects for, 257–
  61, 263; shrines for, 175, 180, 190, 258–
  59, 261, 317n21; of Zuni religious
  leaders, 255, 257, 260. *See also* reli-
  gious practices
Cerrillos Hills, 165, 168, 175, 337n2
Cerros de San Marcos mines, 168,
  338nn15–16
Cervantes, Miguel de, 34, 195
chacaqüiste, 225, 359n37
Chacón, Governor Fernando, 181, 186
Chacón Medina Salasar y Villaseñor,
  Joseph (Marqués of Peñuela). *See*
  Peñuela, Governor
Chalchihuitl, Mt., 165, 170, 175, 338n2
Chama, 82, 143, 189, 196
Chamuscado, Francisco Sánchez (cap-
  tain), 166
Chamuscado-Rodríguez expedition, 35,
  145, 166, 178